Beginning XHTML

Frank Boumphrey
Cassandra Greer
Dave Raggett
Jenny Raggett
Sebastian Schnitzenbaumer
Ted Wugofski

Wrox Press Ltd. ®

Beginning XHTML

First Published April 2000
Latest Reprint August 2002

Published by Wrox Press Ltd, Arden House, 1102 Warwick Road, Acocks Green, Birmingham, B27 6BH, UK
Printed in the United States
ISBN 1-861003-43-9

Trademark Acknowledgements

Credits

Authors
Frank Boumphrey
Cassandra Greer
Dave Raggett
Jenny Raggett
Sebastian Schnitzenbaumer
Ted Wugofski

Additional Material
Paul Houle
Jon Duckett
Chris Ullman

Technical Editors/ Additional Material
Gregory Beekman
Dev Lunsford
Lums Thevathasan

Technical Reviewers
Michael Corning
Steve Danielson
Steven DeWalt
Richard Fedorich
Ryan Fischer
Paul Houle
Thomas Maxwell
Sophie McQueen
Ann Navarro
Harish Rawat
Mark Simkin
Paul Spencer
John Timney
Beverly Treadwell
Deepak Veliath

Managing Editors
Paul Cooper
Victoria Hudgson

Development Editor
Peter Morgan

Project Manager
Chandima Nethisinghe

Design/Layout
Tom Bartlett
Mark Burdett
William Fallon
Jonathan Jones
Laurent Lafon

Figures
William Fallon
Jonathan Jones

Cover
Chris Morris

Index
Alessandro Ansa

About the Authors

Frank Boumphrey

Frank currently works for Cormorant Consulting, a firm that specializes in medical and legal documentation.

He started programming in the dark ages of punch cards and machine language. One of his first projects was to help write a program that differentiated between an incoming Soviet ICBM and a flock of geese. The fact that we are reading this is evidence that it probably worked!

Burnt out by thinking in hexadecimals, he left programming and became a medical doctor, ending up as a Professor and the chief of spine surgery at a large American Midwest institution. Along the way he was involved with the introduction of MRI to the medical world.

Semi-retirement returned him to his first interest of computing and now he tries to get medical institutions to organize their medical records in a semi-rational fashion, and on the side lectures to medical personnel and healthcare executives on documentation issues. Interestingly he is most in demand by legal firms that want to rationalize their medical databases!

Frank is on the World Wide Web Consortium's (W3C's) XHTML working group, and his main objective is to help the development of XML throughout the Web.

Cassandra Greer

Cassandra was born in Glendale, California in 1966 (a very good year) but don't ask her about it because she has lived just about everywhere else but there. She claims to be from San Francisco but only because it is her favorite US city and her aunt and cousins live there. Right now she is living in Munich, Germany.

She survived both a B.A. in the German Department and M.A. (TESOL) in the Linguistics Department at Brigham Young University. At the same time she worked long hours at the BYU English Language Center, teaching English to International students, working in the Computer Lab and coming up with an occasional HyperCard stack. After graduating, she continued her teaching career in Munich and has been teaching technical English and doing translations for the past 4 years in places like BMW, Siemens, Xerox Engineering Systems, CompuNet, the Technical University Munich and the University of Munich Physics Department.

Just recently, Cassandra stumbled across the incredibly cool guys at Mozquito.com where not only her English teaching and writing skills are being put to good use, but also her experience playing with Macs and being on the Net for the past10 years.

Dave Raggett

Dave Raggett works for W3C on assignment from HP Labs. Dr. Raggett is the W3C staff contact for work on HTML, Forms, Voice Browsers and Math. He has been instrumental in initiating work on modularizing HTML to meet the needs of mobile and television; work on the next generation of Web forms, as well as work on using voice interaction for access to the Web, and work on next generation scripting languages. Educated at the University of Oxford, Dr. Raggett is married with two children, and lives near Bath in the West of England.

Jenny Raggett

Jenny Raggett is a free-lance technical writer specialising in explaining technical information at the layman level. She has recently worked with the W3C writing about the many new developments in the area of the Web for a non-technical audience. New projects now include devising Web sites for environmental groups, an activity which closely ties with her growing interest in nature conservation.

Sebastian Schnitzenbaumer

Born in 1977 in Munich, Sebastian Schnitzenbaumer spent his childhood living on an island in the Indian Ocean. After moving back to Munich as a teenager, he finished school early and started a web design consultancy. For many years, building web applications would be his main profession, from community web sites to IT-management for large companies. Over time, the demand for more interactive web applications increased: managing corporate databases over the web, editing web sites inside the browser, conducting polls and surveys, etc. The web is all about interactivity and feedback, and web forms are the major building block to enable it.

In 1998, he co-founded Mozquito.com, an internet software company initially named Stack Overflow, together with his colleague, and friend, Malte Wedel. After developing a proposal for advanced web forms in HTML, Mozquito.com joined the W3C and Sebastian became a member of the W3C HTML Working Group, participating in the development of XHTML.

Ted Wugofski

Ted Wugofski has spent his career providing technical leadership in a variety of emerging technologies: artificial intelligence, computer telephony, digital television, and mobile Internet. Ted enjoys working on products that bring the Internet to non-traditional computing devices. Ted has participated in a variety of World Wide Web Consortium working groups and led a team within the Advanced Television Systems Committee to define a markup language for digital television. When he is not traveling, Ted spends his days in Fort Worth Texas with his wife, Ana, and their three children: Sofia, Bianca, and David. You can reach him at `ted.wugofski@ieee.org`.

CSS
DOM
XHTML
JavaScript
XML

Table of Contents

Chapter 16: JavaScript 445

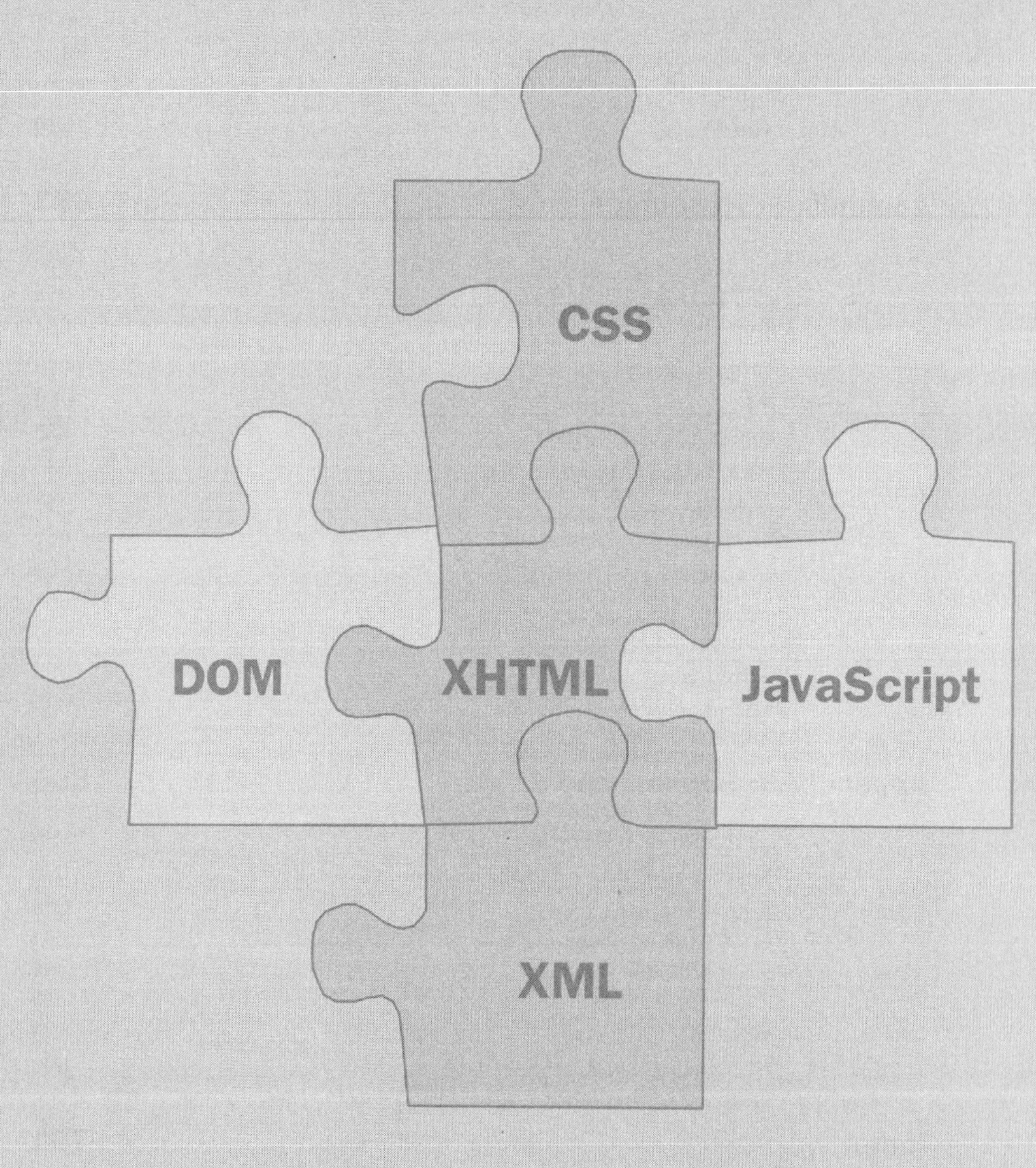
CSS
DOM
XHTML
JavaScript
XML

Introduction

This book is about XHTML – the eXtensible Hypertext Markup Language. XHTML is the next generation markup language that follows in the footsteps of HTML, the HyperText Markup Language, the language that revolutionized the Internet and connected millions of users around the world.

After using this book, you will know how to build web pages using XHTML. In the process, you will get some background on XML (the language behind XHTML), but by and large this book provides a hands-on practical approach to learning how to build web pages. It will answer the fundamental questions:

- What exactly is XHTML?
- How is XHTML different from HTML and XML?
- How do I build web pages and web sites?
- How do I make interactive web pages?

We'll answer these questions in a thorough and comprehensive way, with plenty of complete working examples. So even if you're absolutely new to Web technologies, you will gain a deep understanding of what XHTML is really about and how you can harness it to build powerful web pages.

Who Is This Book For?

This is a Wrox *Beginning...* series book, so we will try and teach you everything that you need to know from scratch, in a fast-paced turorial fashion. If you're already a seasoned web developer, this may not be the book for you.

There are two kinds of beginners for whom this is an ideal book:

- You're a beginner to programming on the Web and you have chosen XHTML as a place to start. If you're comfortable with computing and you learn fast, you'll probably be OK. However there's a lot packed into this book.
- You have had some experience of writing HTML but you wouldn't call yourself a pro, and you really don't know XML, XHTML, or the rest of that alphabet soup. You'll find some of the ground familiar, but there are a number of differences both in the details of what you write and in the way you'll need to think when creating web pages that you'll pick up along the way. You'll also be taken a little deeper into some technologies you may not have met before.

Most of all, you don't need to know anything more than the basic ins and outs of how to write text in a text editor and how to run your web browser. If you've never written a single line of any programming language, then you have nothing to fear – this is the book for you. The bottom line is that this book will teach you enough to enable you to write exciting and dynamic web pages, and open up doors to other useful technologies!

What Does This Book Cover?

This book breaks down conceptually into three parts, which cover a whole range of XHTML-related topics. Hopefully you'll find that we've done this in a logical and orderly fashion that will allow you to fully understand how XHTML works, what it can do for you and how it can be used in well designed interactive web pages.

The first part of the book teaches the basics of XHTML using plenty of hands-on working examples:

Chapters 1 and 2 explain how XHTML fits in with other Web technologies and the differences between XHTML and HTML.

Chapters 3-8 teach you the fundamentals of the XHTML language. We start with simple, practical examples in which we create web pages using XHTML. We'll add ways of linking between web pages and adding images, lists, and tables.

Chapter 9 will revisit style sheets in more detail, and show how you can separate your content from your styling ideas.

Chapter 10 teaches you some of the theory behind the XHTML language, by looking at its parent, XML.

The second part of the book looks at design issues relating to the construction of XHTML pages.

Chapters 11 and 12 cover site and page design, how to structure a site and some issues for making your pages easy to use.

Chapter 13 looks at the issues of writing for different computer-based HTML browsers and other kinds of user agent.

Chapter 14 rounds out this section with a look at including multimedia items in your pages.

The final part of the book introduces forms and scripting, teaching you how to make your web pages interactive.

Chapter 15 shows how to use forms to get input from your users.

Chapters 16-18 teach you the fundamentals of JavaScript and how to use it to spice up your web pages.

Chapter 19 explains how to use frames to write scripts that apply to many web pages.

Chapter 20 rounds off this section with an innovation in interactive forms called **Mozquito**.

Finally, the **Appendices** provide useful reference material for HTML tags, CSS properties, JavaScript objects, and other useful information.

What Do I Need To Use This Book?

Basically, you need two things:

- You will need a **text editor** in order to edit your web pages. You might have some fancy HTML editing tools, but since you are trying to learn XHTML (and since some of these tools write poor quality HTML), we'd advise sticking to writing your web pages using a simple text editor.
- You will need a **web browser** in order to view your pages. We've used Microsoft Internet Explorer 5.0 (IE5) throughout this book. While not required, it is highly recommended you use more than one web browser. This will let you see how your web page looks when run by different browsers.

Conventions

We have used a number of different styles of text and layout in the book to help differentiate between the different kinds of information. Here are examples of the styles we use and an explanation of what they mean:

Try It Outs – How Do They Work?

1. Each step has a number.

2. Follow the steps through, and get the example running.

3. Then read 'How It Works' to find out what's going on.

Advice, hints and background information comes in an indented, italicized font like this.

> **Important bits of information that you really shouldn't ignore come in boxes like this!**

Unsurprisingly, bulleted lists appear indented, with each new bullet marked as follows:

- **Important Words** are in a bold type font.
- Words that appear on the screen in menus like the File or Window menu are in a similar font to what you see on screen.
- Keys that you press on the keyboard, like *Ctrl* and *Enter,* are in italics.

HTML, XHTML, CSS, and scripting code has two font styles. If it's a word that we're talking about in the text, for example, when discussing the `<body>` tag, it's in a monospaced font. If it's a block of code that you can type in and run, or part of such a block, then it's also in a gray box:

```
<html>
  <head>
    <title>Simple Example</title>
  </head>
  <body>
    <p>Very simple HTML.</p>
  </body>
</html>
```

Sometimes you'll see code in a mixture of styles, like this:

```
<html>
  <head>
    <title>Simple Example</title>
  </head>
  <body>
    <p>Very simple HTML.</p>
  </body>
</html>
```

In this case, we want you to consider the code with the gray background, for example to modify it. The code with a white background is code we've already looked at, and that we don't wish to examine further.

Customer Support

We've tried to make this book as accurate and enjoyable as possible, but what really matters is what the book actually does for you. Please let us know your views, either by returning the reply card in the back of the book, or by contacting us via e-mail at `feedback@wrox.com`.

Downloading the Source Code

As you work through the examples in this book, you might decide that you prefer to type all the code in by hand. Many readers prefer this because it's a good way to get familiar with the coding techniques that are being used.

Whether you want to type the code in or not, we have made all the source code for this book available at our web site, at the following address:

`http://www.wrox.com`

If you're one of those readers who likes to type in the code, you can use our files to check the results you should be getting – they should be your first stop if you think you might have typed in an error. If you're one of those readers who doesn't like typing, then downloading the source code from our web site is a must!

Either way, it'll help you with updates and debugging.

Errata

We've made every effort to make sure that there are no errors in the text or the code. However, to err is human and as such we recognize the need to keep you informed of any mistakes as they're spotted and corrected. Errata sheets are available for all our books at `http://www.wrox.com`. If you find an error that hasn't already been reported, please let us know.

Our Web site acts as a focus for other information and support, including the code from all our books, sample chapters, previews of forthcoming titles, and articles and opinion on related topics.

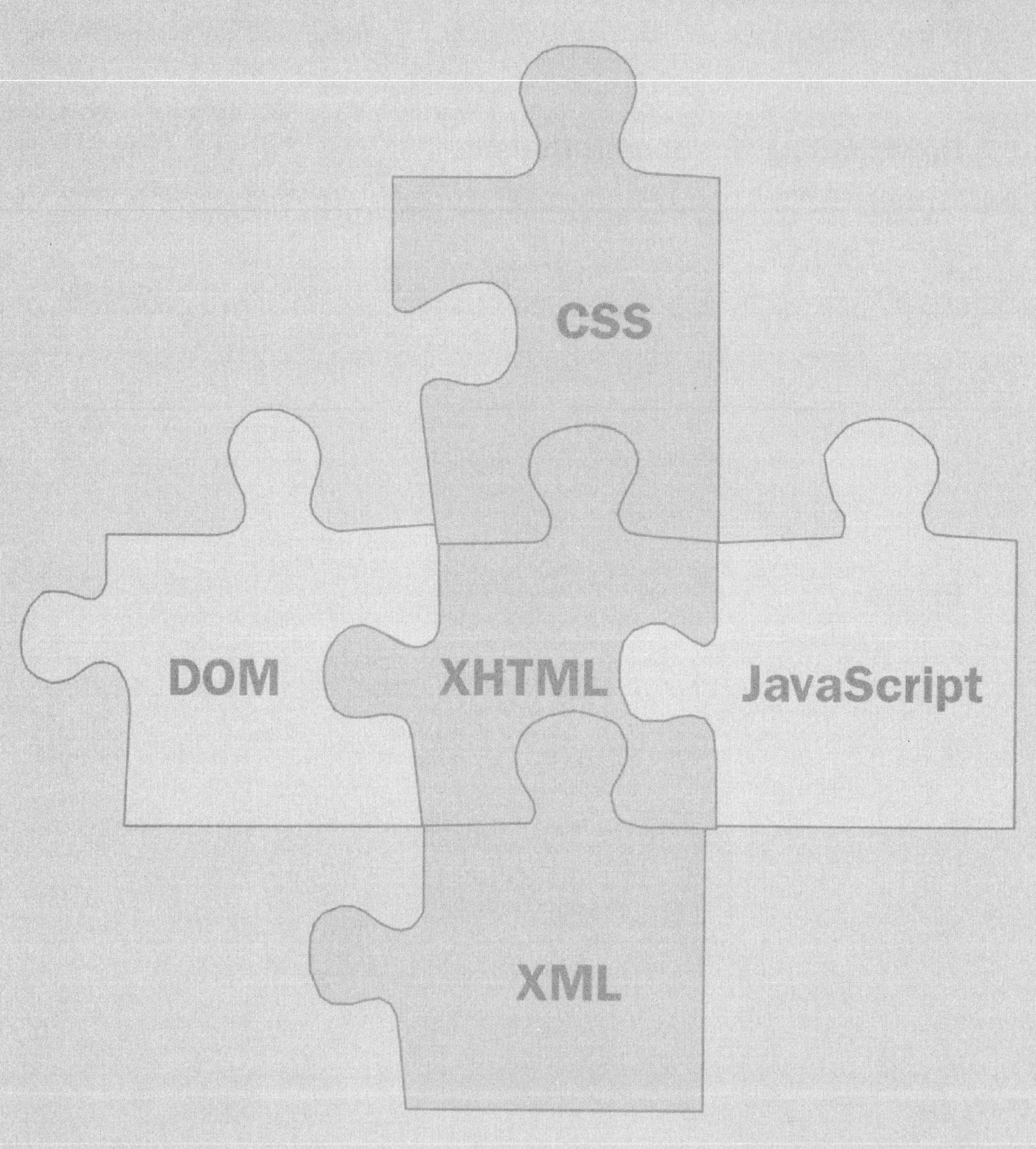
CSS
DOM
XHTML
JavaScript
XML

The Web, HTML, and Markup Languages

This book is about XHTML, the **eXtensible HyperText Markup Language**. It is based on HTML, the **HyperText Markup Language**, and conforms to the principles of XML (**eXtensible Markup Language**). There are a lot of definitions to introduce at the start of the book, especially for those fairly new to the Web. We will therefore leave discussions of XHTML and XML to Chapter 2, and instead discuss web basics and HTML in this chapter. (Those already familiar with the Web and HTML may skip this chapter, or quickly skim read it.)

In this chapter we will cover the following topics:

- what the Web is
- the different browsers and HTML editors
- the basics of the HTML language
- the mechanics of what goes on when you browse a web page
- what markup and parsing are

What Is the Web?

Web and Internet are two oft-confused terms and it's essential to get these two separate entities clear in your mind from the very start. The Internet is a network of linked nodes (computers) that started life as a Department of Defense project in the 1960s. It was in the era of nuclear paranoia and the DOD, concerned that their communications could be wiped out by a single nuclear strike, developed a computer network that would continue to function in the event of one or several of the routes through the network being damaged or destroyed.

So, the Internet is a network of interconnected nodes, in the same way that the subway system of a large city is a network of interconnected railway stations. The subway system is designed to carry *people* from one place to another; by comparison, the Internet is designed to carry *information* from one place to another.

While a subway system is built on a basis of steel (and other materials), the Internet uses a suite of networking protocols, known as **TCP/IP** (Transmission Control Protocol / Internet Protocol) to transfer information around the Internet. A **networking protocol** is simply a method of describing information packets so they can be sent down your telephone-, cable-, or T1-line from node to node, until it reaches its intended destination.

When the user tells the browser to go fetch a web page, the browser parcels up this instruction using a protocol called **TCP**. TCP is a transport protocol, which provides a reliable transmission format for the instruction. It ensures that the entire message is correctly packaged up for transmission (and also that it is correctly unpacked and put back together after it reaches its destination).

Before the parcels of data are sent out across the network, they need to be addressed, in the same way that you need to address a letter before you send it. So a second protocol called **Hypertext Transfer Protocol** (or **HTTP**) puts an address label on it. HTTP is the protocol used by the World Wide Web in the transfer of information from one machine to another – when you see a URL prefixed with `http://`, you know that the internet protocol being used is HTTP. All HTTP does is enable different computers to communicate with each other.

The World Wide Web on the other hand is the software, as such, that runs on the Internet. The architecture of the Web is based on a **client/server model**. The user's browser is the **client** and retrieves information held on a remote machine known as a **web server** that stores the different web pages and files being accessed. This web server can be located on a local network or could be found on the other side of the globe, it doesn't matter as the browser can use HTTP to find it. What was unique about the Web when it first appeared is that it provided a graphical rather than a text-based interface to the different services offered on the Internet.

History of the Web

The Web's origins can be said to stem from writing. A document or book has a structure, such as paragraphs and pages, and its text can contain references to other documents and books. An index helps to locate specific information within the work, and cross-referencing between sections allows us to follow a particular path through the book. The numbering of lines and verses further enhanced the ability of a reader to jump straight to a particular point of interest. Thus the basic document model for information on the web was set: pages of text, with links to other such pages, or to sections within those pages.

Although the Web as we know it today is very much a child of the nineties, the concept of a Web of electronically linked information is much earlier. For example Vanevar Bush in the 1940s, in an article entitled *As We May Think*, describes such a system, which he named the **memex**. Other visionaries include Douglas Englebart, who is credited with helping to develop the mouse and hypertext; and Ted Nelson, who coined the term **hypertext**.

For the modern Web, we must look to CERN, an international high energy physics research center near Geneva in Switzerland. In 1989 Tim Berners-Lee and Robert Caillau collaborated on ideas for a linked information system that would be accessible across the wide range of different computer systems in use at CERN. At that time many people were using TEX (a command-based document preparation system) and Postscript to prepare their documents; a few were using **SGML** (**Standard Generalized Markup Language**, discussed in *Chapter 2*). Tim realized that something much simpler was needed that would cope with all kinds of machines from 'dumb terminals' through to the high end graphical X Windows workstations. HTML (HyperText Markup Language) was conceived as a very simple solution, and matched with the HTTP network protocol. Both were to later evolve into something much more complex, but the initial simplicity made it very easy for other people to write their own browsers and servers (more of which later) and helped to propel the initial growth of the Web.

CERN launched the Web in 1991 along with a discussion list called `www-talk`. Other people thinking along the same lines soon joined and helped to grow the web by setting up Web sites and implementing browsers, such as, Cello, Viola, and MidasWWW. The break-through came when the National Center for Supercomputer Applications (NCSA) at Urbana-Champaign encouraged Marc Andreessen and Eric Bina to develop the Mosaic browser. It was later ported to PCs and Macs and became a run-away success story. The Web grew exponentially, eclipsing other Internet based information systems (such as WAIS, Hytelnet, Gopher, and UseNet).

Standardization efforts have either focussed on formalizing existing practices or have sought to define new features in advance of their widespread deployment. HTML 2.0 was developed in the Internet Engineering Task Force (IETF) to codify HTML as it was in mid-1994. HTML 3.2 was developed by the World Wide Web Consortium (W3C) to codify HTML as it was in early 1996. HTML 4.0, introduced in 1997, added new features for richer tables, forms and objects.

More recently, HTML 4.01 fixes a number of bugs in the HTML 4.0 specification, and provides the foundation for the XHTML specifications. The first of these is XHTML 1.0, which is the HTML 4.01 specification, but rewritten in XML. As we mentioned at the beginning of this chapter, we want to discuss XML and XHTML separately in the next chapter, so we will leave further discussion on these subjects until then. The World Wide Web Consortium is continuing work on XHTML and new specifications will be announced during 2000. You can track this work on `http://www.w3.org/MarkUp/`.

Browsers

As you can see from the history, the development of HTML standards hasn't been entirely linear. It has progressed from versions 1.0 and 2.0 of the standard straight to version 3.2 and then to 4.0, yet with no sign of a version 3.0 in between. This is down to the fast development of non-standard features in the browsers. This reached a head with version 3.0 of the standard, which was effectively obsolete before it moved out of the draft stage, and had to be amended to accommodate changes in the new version 3.0 browsers. Let's put this all into context, by giving a deeper overview of browser evolution and their changing capabilities.

A History of the Browser

We'll start with the very first web browser, which was NCSA Mosaic created by Marc Andreessen and Eric Bina. It was developed at the University of Illinois in 1993 and it changed the whole course of the Web. It allowed users for the first time to access web pages using a Graphical User Interface (GUI). Mosaic was developed for the Windows and Macintosh platforms, and it grew rapidly but was soon replaced by its follow-up Netscape Navigator. Netscape came onto the scene in 1994 with version 0.9 of their Navigator browser, when there were over 20 competing browsers already, and made a large splash. There was an HTML standard in force at the time, but Netscape forged it's popularity by creating non-standard additions to the standard, such as background images and blinking text in version 1.1 of it's browser:

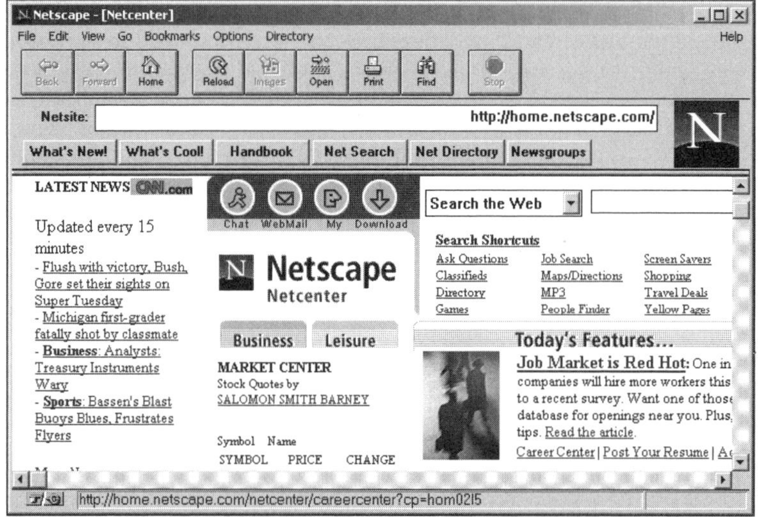

By version 2.0 it was able to support Java applets and it's very own scripting language, called JavaScript. Many additions to the Navigator browsers were incorporated into the new versions of the HTML standard, as the HTML standards struggled to keep pace with the rate of innovation. However, some of these innovations ran contrary to the spirit of the standards and indeed the purpose of HTML. It's true to say that HTML was only ever meant to govern the structure of documents on the web and suddenly found itself convoluted with all manner of presentation and style tags such as `<font>` and `<frame>`. Up until then style and structure were two very different aspects of a web page. This may seem like a sweeping statement, but consider the font of the text on a page and the color of the background. They have absolutely no influence on the underlying structure and can be kept totally separate from the actual web page. In fact we will be looking at how style and content can be divided in later chapters.

It wasn't until December 1995 that Microsoft even publicly acknowledged the importance of the Internet and announced an Internet strategy and by that point Netscape already owned 75% of the market. However while Microsoft gave Netscape a huge advantage, in March 1996 they promised to deliver a whole set of Internet technologies, and later in the year they developed version 2.0 of their prototype browser, Internet Explorer. This browser though couldn't even support HTML frames and certainly didn't boast the Java support of Netscape Navigator 2.0. It wasn't until Internet Explorer 3.0, Microsoft's first browser to offer scripting capabilities and component hosting properties in web pages that Microsoft was able to seriously challenge the dominance of Netscape Navigator.

Although Microsoft had caught up in many areas, they decided to follow a different track to Netscape by integrating their browser into their Windows operating system while continuing to give it away for free. As Netscape were charging a nominal forty dollars for the licensing of Netscape Navigator, it made it very hard to compete as their main rival was giving the competition to its flagship product away for free. Worse was to follow for Netscape.

The competition for new exciting features intensified in version 4 of both browsers, as both companies competed to become the first to create a browser that allowed the user to re-arrange the contents of the page, without having to refresh the page. This new ability was dubbed Dynamic HTML, although not strictly being enabled by HTML. While Netscape released their version of their browser first, they were stymied when Microsoft's version 4 browser and it's own version of Dynamic HTML was adopted by the standards body as the standard way of enabling dynamic content in web pages. Faced with learning two widely differing interpretations of the same feature, the public opted in droves to use the Microsoft's browser and the standard Dynamic HTML. Netscape were forced to issue a humiliating public apology for not adhering to the standards and promised that the next upgrade of the browser would fall in line with the standards. Their market share slumped to 20% (`http://browserwatch.internet.com/stats/stats.html`) and has remained there, or thereabouts, ever since.

Microsoft's dominance of the browser marketplace hasn't all been smooth running, when their integration of Internet Explorer into the Windows operating system was challenged in court by the government as being an anti-competitive practice. This court case is still ongoing (as of writing) and forms a plank of the Department of Justice's case that Microsoft is a monopoly engaged in anti-competitive practices. This hasn't stopped version 5 of Internet Explorer being built into Windows 2000. IE5 offers a wide range of Dynamic HTML and XML support. Netscape tried to compete by making the source code to Navigator freely available as Open Source and encouraged an army of volunteer developers to create a new version of the browser from scratch. They've skipped a version and are now looking to ship Navigator 6 at the end of the year.

Browsers and HTML

The reason we've discussed the history at some length is because it has a large bearing on HTML – you depend on your browser's particular interpretation of HTML to render web pages in the way it's intended. So if you have a version 2 browser, then a lot of the features of the HTML 3.2 and 4.0 standards just won't be accessible to you. You have to install the latest version of Netscape's or Microsoft's (or one of the very small rival browsers such as Opera) to be able to take advantage of the latest features in the standard.

Here's a quick summary of what version browser supports what level of features.

Version	Internet Explorer	Netscape Navigator	Opera
Version 2	Didn't support frames, Java or any script and was a pretty sparse affair.	Supports JavaScript, Java, and support for reading mail and newsgroups.	Version 2.1 was the first public release, which boasted a very small download size and multiple windows, but not much above basic HTML.

Version	Internet Explorer	Netscape Navigator	Opera
Version 3	Supports VBScript and basic style sheets and ActiveX controls. Versions 3.1, 3.2 and 3.3 were essentially bug fixes.	Short-lived version with extra abilities such as table background colors, live audio and video integration, but no style sheet support.	Added JavaScript and Netscape plug in support. Versions 3.1 and 3.2 offered bug fixes and extra security features.
Version 4	Dynamic HTML, much improved style sheets, JavaScript support (known as JScript), some HTML 4.0 features such as `<object>` tag (which allowed you to embed a multitude of components).	Limited style sheet support, Dynamic HTML supported through the non-standard `<layer>` tag, and a whole suite of mails, news, and messaging tools. Versions 4.5 and 4.65 didn't add much above better security and bug fixes. Latest version is 4.72	Version 3.5 was a new version in it's own right and added Java, style sheet, and SSL support. 3.6 is the latest version.
Version 5	Introduction of new dynamic features, behaviors and addition of XML and XSL. Most advanced browser available by some way. 5.5 is the latest release.		

Text Editors

There is a gigantic multitude of text editors on offer, some costing as much as several hundred dollars, and many given away for free. We're not going to recommend any particular page editor, but we'll list several of the most popular on offer.

Microsoft FrontPage

FrontPage 2000 comes as part of Microsoft's Office 2000 suite – it's a tool for creating and designing web pages. It offers three views of the web page. The Normal tab gives a WYSIWYG (**W**hat **Y**ou **S**ee **I**s **W**hat **Y**ou **G**et) page creation view (like the Design view in Visual InterDev), which allows you to write pages without having to code the HTML explicitly. The HTML tab allows you to write your code explicitly, and the Preview tab gives a quick view of what the page should look like in a browser:

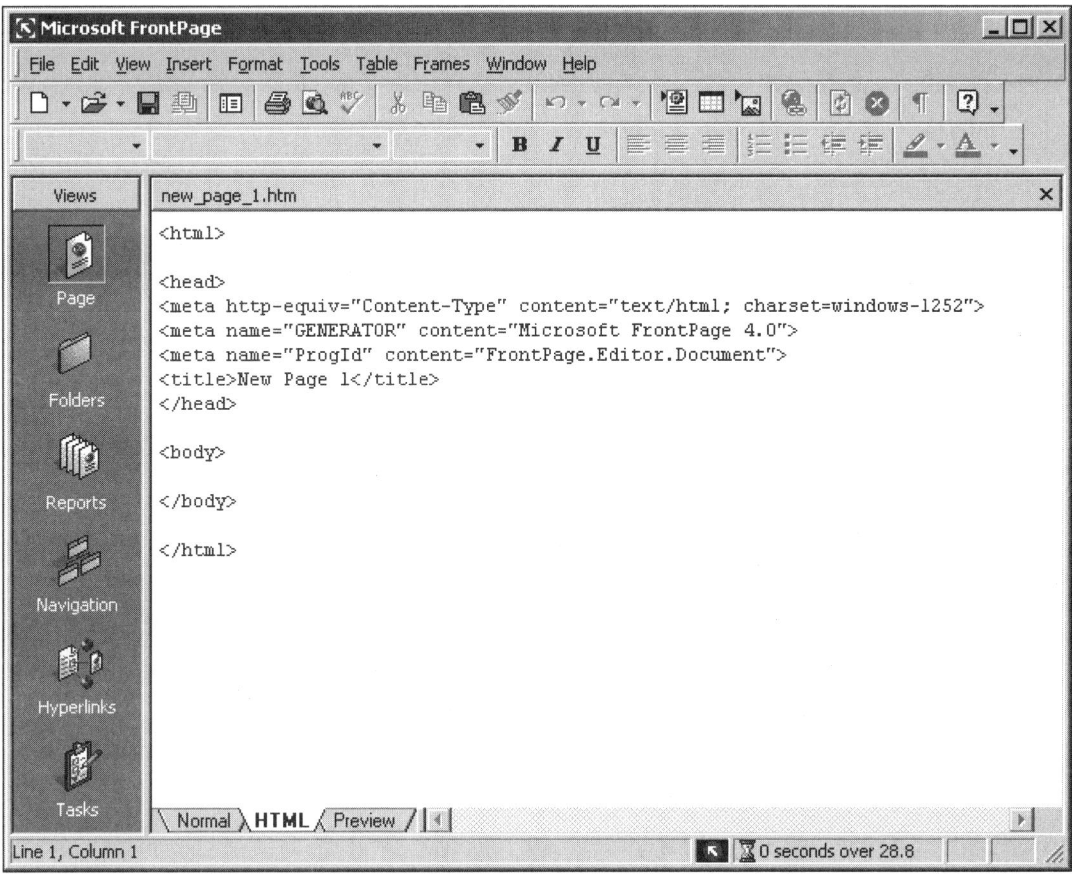

This screenshot is taken from FrontPage 2000, but you can also use Front Page 97 or 98 to edit HTML pages. The Normal and Preview tabs are able to process your HTML and give you a good idea of what your web page will look like when viewed in a browser.

One quirk of FrontPage is that it likes to 'improve' your HTML, by rearranging it. FrontPage 2000 now has a Preserve existing HTML option on the Tools | Page Options | HTML Source dialog, but older versions will still 'autoedit' your HTML for you. Beware – this window dressing can change your code and even affect the intended function of the code.

Allaire's Homesite

One of the best non-Microsoft web page editors is **Allaire's Homesite**. The evaluation copy of version 4.0.1 is currently available from their web site at `http://www.allaire.com`. The evaluation copy allows you to run the program 50 times or for 30 days –whichever elapses sooner. It features an easy-to-use interface, which allows you to keep track of your files and folders at the same time as your file contents:

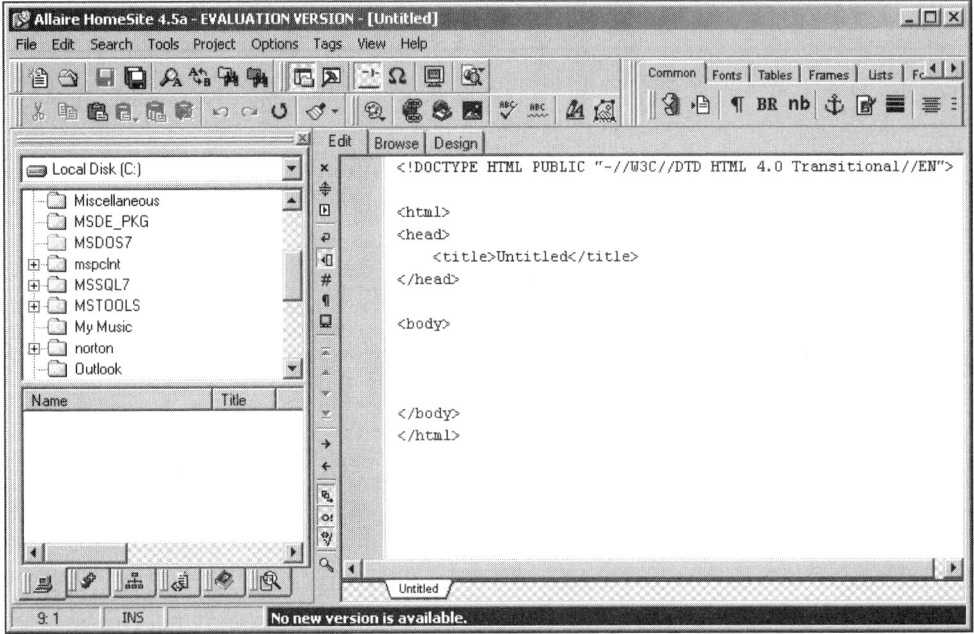

In short, Homesite is a very powerful editor, and well worth a look.

There are other editors, such as Sausage Software's HotDog (`http://www.sausage.com`), SoftQuad's HotMetal Pro (`http://www.softquad.com`), or Adobe's PageMill (`http://www.adobe.com/products/`); but if you only want a completely free editor then Arachnophilia (`http://www.arachnoid.com/arachnophilia/index.html`) is very capable. They are all useful tools with which to create web pages.

Notepad

Of course if you have Windows in any shape or form, then you already have an editor. Notepad might be a time-honored text editor, but no matter how much Microsoft promote FrontPage, there will always be people who will use Notepad as their web page editor of choice. The fact that it's been free with every incarnation of Windows certainly helps sustain its popularity.

Of course, it doesn't highlight your HTML in any way, but also it doesn't auto-generate any extra code. It doesn't feature any additional functions; but, because it's so simple, Notepad is still a very popular choice. In Windows 2000, Notepad offers a GoTo feature (under the Edit menu), which allows you to move around your documents using line numbers.

It doesn't really matter which editor you use in this book - it won't affect how you run the examples. We'll avoid any attempt to provide a tutorial on how to use any of these editorial tools – since most advanced editors have their own tutorials, and this is really beyond the scope of the book.

Now we've considered the different browsers and text editors, we'll take a look at the process involved when you start up your browser and view a web page.

What Happens When You View a Web Page

When you view a web page, you send a message from your browser to a web server, saying that you wish to view a particular page. The message passed from the browser to the web server is known as an **HTTP request**. When the web server receives this request, it checks its stores to find the appropriate page. If the web server finds the page, it parcels up the HTML contained within (using TCP), addresses these parcels to the browser (using HTTP), and sends them back across the network. If the web server cannot find the requested page, it issues a page containing an error message (in this case, the dreaded Error 404: Page Not Found) – and it parcels up and dispatches that page to the browser. The message sent from the web server to the browser is known as the **HTTP response**.

Here's an illustration of the process as we understand it so far:

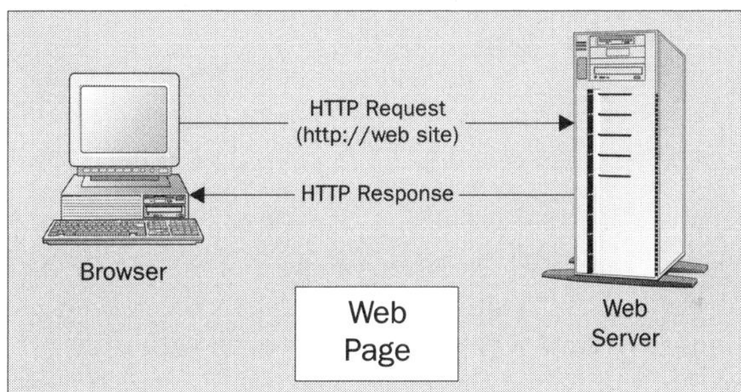

Going Deeper Into HTTP

There's still quite a lot of technical detail missing here, so let's dig further down and look more closely at exactly how HTTP works. When a request for a web page is sent to the server, this request contains more than just the desired URL. There is a lot of extra information that is sent as part of the request. This is also true of the response – the server sends extra information back to the browser. It's these different types of information that we'll look at in this section.

A lot of the information that is passed within the HTTP message is generated automatically, and the user doesn't have to deal with it directly, so you don't need to worry about transmitting such information yourself.

Every HTTP message assumes the same format (whether it's a client request or a server response). We can break this format down into three sections: the **request/response line**, the **HTTP header** and the **HTTP body**. The content of these three sections is dependent on whether the message is an HTTP request or HTTP response – so we'll take these two cases separately.

Let's illustrate our understanding of the process now:

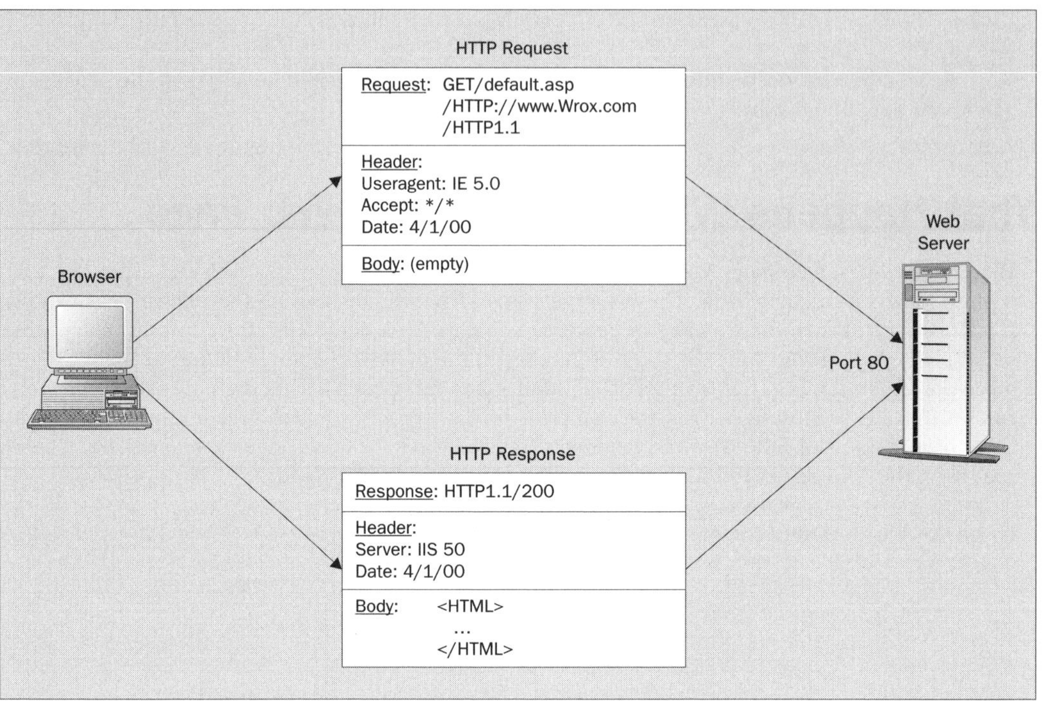

We can see that the HTTP request and HTTP response have broadly similar structures and that there is information that is common to both, which is sent as part of the HTTP header. There are other pieces of information that can only be known to either the browser or the server, and that are also sent as part of either the request or response. In this way your request for a web page is transmitted to the web server, and then in the response the web server serves information to your browser along with the HTML code needed to create the page. Your browser then uses this information and code to construct the page, which you can view. If the browser comes across a line it doesn't understand in the HTML code, it will skip it and move to the next one. This illustrates the Web as a client/server architecture at its most basic level. We're considerably simplifying what goes on here, as you don't need to know it in any more detail.

Of course, one important point is that you don't have to go out onto the Internet or your local intranet to get your web pages from a web server, you can just as easily browse pages on your own machine. For the examples on this book this is exactly what we suggest doing. For instance, I've created a folder called XHTML on my C drive and stored the web page `example.htm` in it. I can then browse it by typing the following into the browser:

So let's move on and take a look at how we'd go about creating our web page in HTML.

HTML

HTML stands for HyperText Markup Language (we will discuss markup in the next section). Let's look at the general form of an HTML document. Type the following into your text editor and save it as `simple.htm`:

```
<html>
 <head>
  <title>A basic HTML document</title>
 </head>
 <body>
  <h1>A demonstration of simple HTML</h1>
  <p>Here is a simple paragraph
  <p>Here is a second paragraph with some <b>bold text</b> and then some text in
  <i>italics</i>. This paragraph is a little bit longer than the previous one,
  so you can see what happens when the text is too long to fit on just one line
  (it just gets put onto the next line).
  <address>Frank Boumphrey frankb@wrox.com</address>
 </body>
</html>
```

We see that the document consists of the text we wish to be displayed contained between the HTML commands or **tags** that inform the browser how the text should be displayed. If you point your browser to this file, it will be displayed as follows (here we are using Microsoft's Internet Explorer 5.0, but you can use any of the recent browsers we discussed earlier):

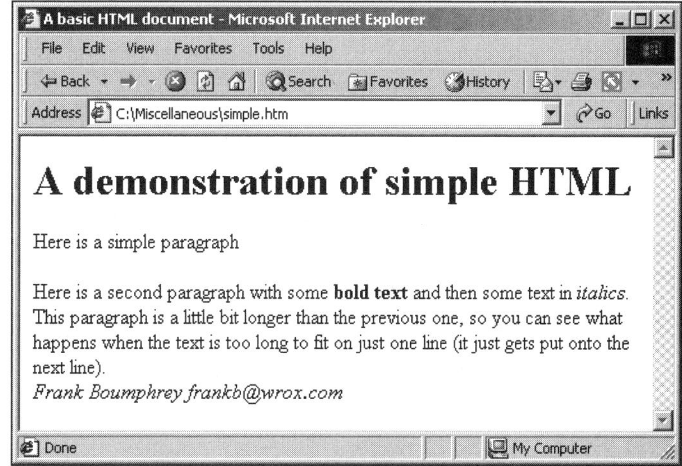

The general form of an HTML tag is:

```
<opening tag> text to be displayed </closing tag>
```

Both the opening and closing tags are enclosed within **angled brackets** (the name given to the 'less than' and 'greater than' symbols). Note that the closing tag differs from the opening tag only in that it contains a forward slash (/) before the tag name.

So, for example, if we want text to appear in **bold** we simply place that text between the HTML `<b>` and `</b>` for bold tags, as in:

```
<b>bold text</b>
```

Likewise, if we wish to place text in italics, we use the <i> and </i> for italics tags:

```
<i>italics</i>
```

As you can see, HTML is a simple language to grasp the basics of. Let's look at it in slightly more detail. Any HTML document should start with an opening <html> tag, and close with the matching </html> tag. This informs the browser that the document has been written in HTML. The HTML document contains two parts, a **head** and a **body**.

Material contained between <head> and </head> is *not* displayed on the browsers page. This section contains information about the document (meta-information), such as the title of the document. The text between <title> and </title> appears both on the title bar of the browser, and in the favorites or bookmarks list when you save the address of that particular site.

It is the material contained between <body> and </body> that is displayed on the web page. What we would normally think of as the title of the document is referred to as a **heading**, abbreviated simply to h in the HTML tags. There are a number of heading styles, the largest of which is h1. Thus the traditional 'title', or opening heading, is displayed using <h1> tags:

```
<h1>A demonstration of simple HTML</h1>
```

A paragraph of text is begun with the <p> for paragraph tag. In HTML, the closing </p> tag is optional. Thus the first paragraph in our example above is simply:

```
<p>Here is a simple paragraph
```

When HTML encounters a second <p> tag before encountering the matching and closing </p> tag for the first <p> tag, it logically assumes that we want to begin a new paragraph and thus, that the old paragraph has closed. Most HTML documents don't have a closing </p> tag, a problem discussed in terms of XHTML in Chapter 2.

Finally, we have the <address> tag. This normally contains the name and contact details of the Webmaster, the person responsible for writing/maintaining the web site.

Elements and Tags

Before we go any further, it is important that we define our terminology. Consider the following:

```
<h1>This is a level one heading</h1>
```

This entire item is called an **element**. <h1> is the **opening tag**, and </h1> is the **closing tag**. The text between these tags, This is a level one heading, is the **content** of the element. An element also has a **type**, named after its tag name, and so the example above is an h1 element type. These points are illustrated diagrammatically here:

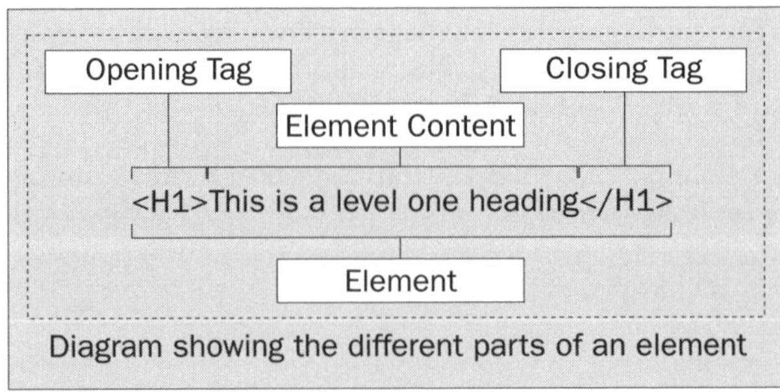

Diagram showing the different parts of an element

Tag Attributes

A tag can also possess one or more attributes, that is, additional information relating to how that element's content should be displayed. For example, the paragraph tag contains the `align` attribute, which can take one of the values `left`, `center` or `right`. Type the following into your editor and save as `attrib.htm`:

```
<html>
 <head>
  <title>Paragraph Attributes</title>
 </head>
 <body>
  <h1>The Paragraph Attribute Align</h1>

  <p align='left'> This is a paragraph with its text pushed against the left-hand
side of the page.

  <p align='center'> This is a paragraph with its text placed in the center of the
page.

  <p align='right'> This is a paragraph with its text pushed against the right-
hand side of the page.

 </body>
</html>
```

Pointing your browser to this file, you should see something similar to below:

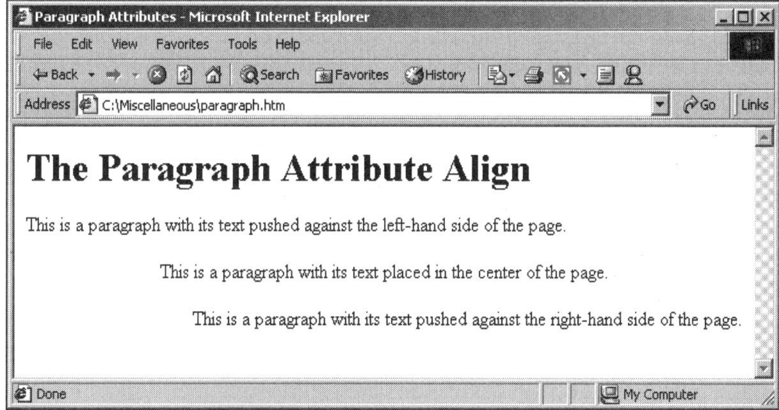

We discuss attributes in more detail in Chapter 3.

Markup and Markup Languages

HTML is a **markup language**. You might be wondering what exactly is meant by the term 'markup'. Consider this: what we do when we apply markup (add HTML tags) to a document of any kind is to give added meaning to that document. If you highlight text in a textbook you are saying "this text deserves close attention", or if you tick an entry in your checkbook you are saying, "I have balanced this item". To use a computer term we say that the markup is semantic.

Semantic Markup

Semantic and semantics are very over worked words, but the word 'semantic' is just a derivation from the Greek word for significant. The Oxford English Dictionary defines it as 'Relating to significance or meaning'. So when we say that markup is semantic we are just saying that it has meaning to the browser.

You can often make a good guess at the meaning of a particular tag in the markup just from its name, tags such as `<font>` and `<form>` are self-explanatory, but unfortunately computers are not so smart and need more help. So, if we want a computer to read and act on our markup we have to give it an additional set of instructions on what to do. Sometimes we can build these instructions into the computer software itself; else we must provide the software with a separate set of instructions.

HTML is a markup language that is designed to be readable by both computers and humans. HTML markup is markup designed to be read by a special piece of software, the browser. All browsers have a built in knowledge as to the meaning of the markup, and is able to display the content in a standard way.

HTML Markup

HTML is just one markup language of a set of many markup languages created by a meta-language (a template for creating languages) called **SGML** (Standard Generalized Markup Language). SGML creates these languages via sets of rules known as **DTD**s (Document Type Definitions). Other members of this set include a language called DocBook, TEI, and MIL-STD, all of which are used in specific but limited situations. The main elements in HTML's popularity are first its simplicity to learn, because markup languages don't have tricky programming structures to learn such as you may find in Visual Basic, Java or C++; second, HTML can be automatically generated by many third party editors so you don't need to learn any HTML to create web pages; and third, that when a browser comes across a broken line of HTML it doesn't throw out an error like most other programming languages would, it just skips the broken code and carries on to the next line. Oh, and it's also down to the phenomenal growth of the Web itself!

The concept of any SGML based language is quite simple. An SGML based language, such as HTML, is characterized by a series of tags taken from a dictionary of tags for the language. The browser contains a parser which can determine which tags form part of this dictionary. Probably the best way to explain this is to look at an example, so lets look at a simple HTML document right now.

Try It Out – A simple HTML document

1. Type the following into your text editor and call it `example.htm`:

```
<html>
<head>
<title>A simple HTML document</title>
</head>
<body>
<h1>A demonstration of simple HTML</h1>
<p>Here is a simple paragraph
<p>Here is a <b>second</b> paragraph
<address>Frank Boumphrey frankb@wrox.com</address>
</body>
</html>
```

2. You will notice that we have a series of simple sentences enclosed by tags. As we mentioned previously HTML is designed to be read by a piece of software called an HTML browser, so if I load this document into a browser, (in this case IE5) this is what I see:

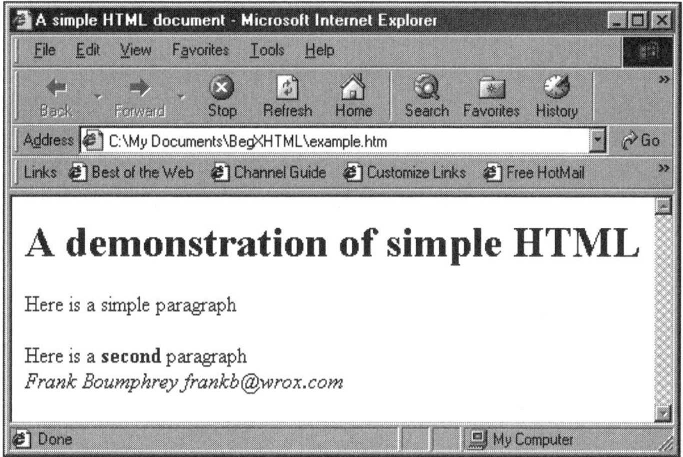

Let's have a quick look at what is going on in the 'mind' of the browser. The following description is of course somewhat simplified.

How It Works: Parsing

Here is a brief description of how a browser may process the above document in order to achieve this display. This whole process is known as **parsing**. Parsing a document is akin to applying the rules of English grammar to a sentence. Immediately you'd know that the following sentence "The rain in Spain mainly on the plain" is missing a pretty vital ingredient, namely a verb. You know to expect a verb after a noun. The process of parsing in a browser is applying the same check to the HTML language. Of course a sentence that meets the laws of grammar doesn't have to make any sense, "The plain in Spain falls mainly on the rain", is grammatically perfect but doesn't make any sense. The parsing that the browser does then is an entirely structural check on the code provided. The parsing process in a browser works as follows:

1. The browser 'reads' the document from the beginning to the end looking for tags. The tags with the format <[tagname]> are called opening tags, and the tags with the format </[tagname]> are called closing tags.

2. Every time the browser comes across a "<" it knows it is going to be reading an opening tag, and every time it comes across a "</" it knows it is going to be reading a closing tag.

3. As soon as the browser sees a "<" it looks to see where the next ">" is. The text in between these characters is the tag's content. The first word of this content is the tag name, and is also the name of the element type.

4. Once the browser has read the tag name, the browser determines if it recognizes the tag name. If the browser recognizes the tag name, the browser decides what to do with the content between the opening tag and the closing tag.

5. The browser has a dictionary of all the tags that the browser supports, and this dictionary contains the details of how to process (display) the contents of the tag. If the browser can't identify a particular tag then the browser still needs to display the contents of the tag in some kind of default manner, normally this is text which is displayed in default font without any style. Again we are going to keep things really simple at this stage, but this strategy allows for both backward compatibility of the browser when new tags are created, and also protects against programming 'typos' disastrously altering the content of the document display.

6. When it comes across `<html>` it knows that this is the beginning of an HTML document.

7. When it comes across the `<head>` tag, it knows that this information contained from this point is generic information about the header of the document, such as the title.

8. When it comes across `<title>` it goes looking for a closing tag called `</title>`. It knows that it has to display the text between the two tags in the title bar of the browser.

9. When it comes across the `</head>` tag, it knows that that is the end of the information about the document header.

10. When it sees a `<body>` tag, it knows to expect the 'meat' of the document, the text that you intend to display in the browser window.

11. When it comes across an `<h1>` tag it knows that it is dealing with a level one heading(there are six level of headings each getting progressively smaller so that six is the smallest), and that the text between the opening and the closing `</h1>` tag must be displayed in the type of heading 1, of which the default is a roughly size 24 font in bold in most browsers.

12. When it sees a `<p>` tag it knows that it has to begin a new paragraph.

13. You will notice in the second paragraph that one of the words has been put between a pair of `<b></b>` tags. This is an instruction to the browser to render the text between the tags, the elements content, in a **bold** font.

14. The text between the `<address> </address>` is the address of the webmaster. The browser displays this in italics.

15. It comes across the closing `</body>` tag which is a precursor to the end of the document.

16. Finally the browser comes across the closing `</html>` tag. It knows that it has read to the end of the document.

What we have done here is really quite simple. We have taken a document and marked up its text so that the software (an HTML browser) can display it on a computer screen.

Structural, Stylistic, and Descriptive Markup

We mentioned earlier in this chapter that HTML was only meant to define document structure but has ended up also defining document presentation as well. As a result there are three types of HTML tags. The simple example above displayed the three chief kinds of markup:

1. **Structural markup**. This is markup that lays out the structure of a document. Paragraphs (`<p>`) and headings (`<h1>`) fall in to this category.

2. **Stylistic markup**. Quite a number of the HTML (and XHTML) tags are for styling the display. The Bold tag (`<b>`) falls into this category. As we will see later, this kind of markup is not encouraged because of the problems it causes when documents are rendered in non-visual media.

3. **Descriptive (semantic) markup**. This is also known as semantic markup, but descriptive is a better term. Descriptive markup describes the nature of the content of the element. `<title>` and `<address>` are the two examples above.

Structural Markup

Structural markup is always useful, and indeed is the *raison d'être* for XHTML. Structural markup gives a document's content form and integrity.

Stylistic Markup

Stylistic markup depicts the style in which the element content should be displayed. Stylistic markup however is a double-edged sword, and is really only applicable to documents designed to be shown on the screen or to be printed. Even then the design principals for the 'postcard' shaped screen are much different to that of the 'letter' shaped page. Furthermore, the different resolutions of screen and page means that a font that looks good in one media could look terrible in another! Professional designers will want to produce two different designs for these two different media. And of course they will want a totally different design for voice browser, or a Braille reader. For this reason, the styling of a document is much better left to a style sheet. We will cover document styling in great detail later in this book.

Some stylistic markup has gone into such widespread use that it will be almost impossible to eliminate it. I know that I find myself using it without thinking. However as stated above, for reasons of accessibility and cross-media compatibility it is always better to use descriptive markup.

Descriptive Markup

The trend in web markup is to go to more and more markup of a **descriptive** nature. One of the reasons for this is that it makes searching through the myriad of documents that are on the web much easier. This is one of the main reasons that XML was introduced as a markup language.

Summary

In this chapter we have introduced the World Wide Web and Internet and made clear the difference between the two terms. We looked at how the Web works, before turning our attention to some common browsers and text editors. There are a number of companies, which offer access to this Web, and most modern computers come equipped with software that allows you to surf the Web once connected to it. To view a web page, one simply types in that pages `http` web address into your browser. Web pages, up until now, have been written in HTML, a markup language the basics of which we have covered in this chapter. However, there are problems with this, which have led to the development of a new Web language called XHTML. This is based both on HTML and XML, topics we discuss next.

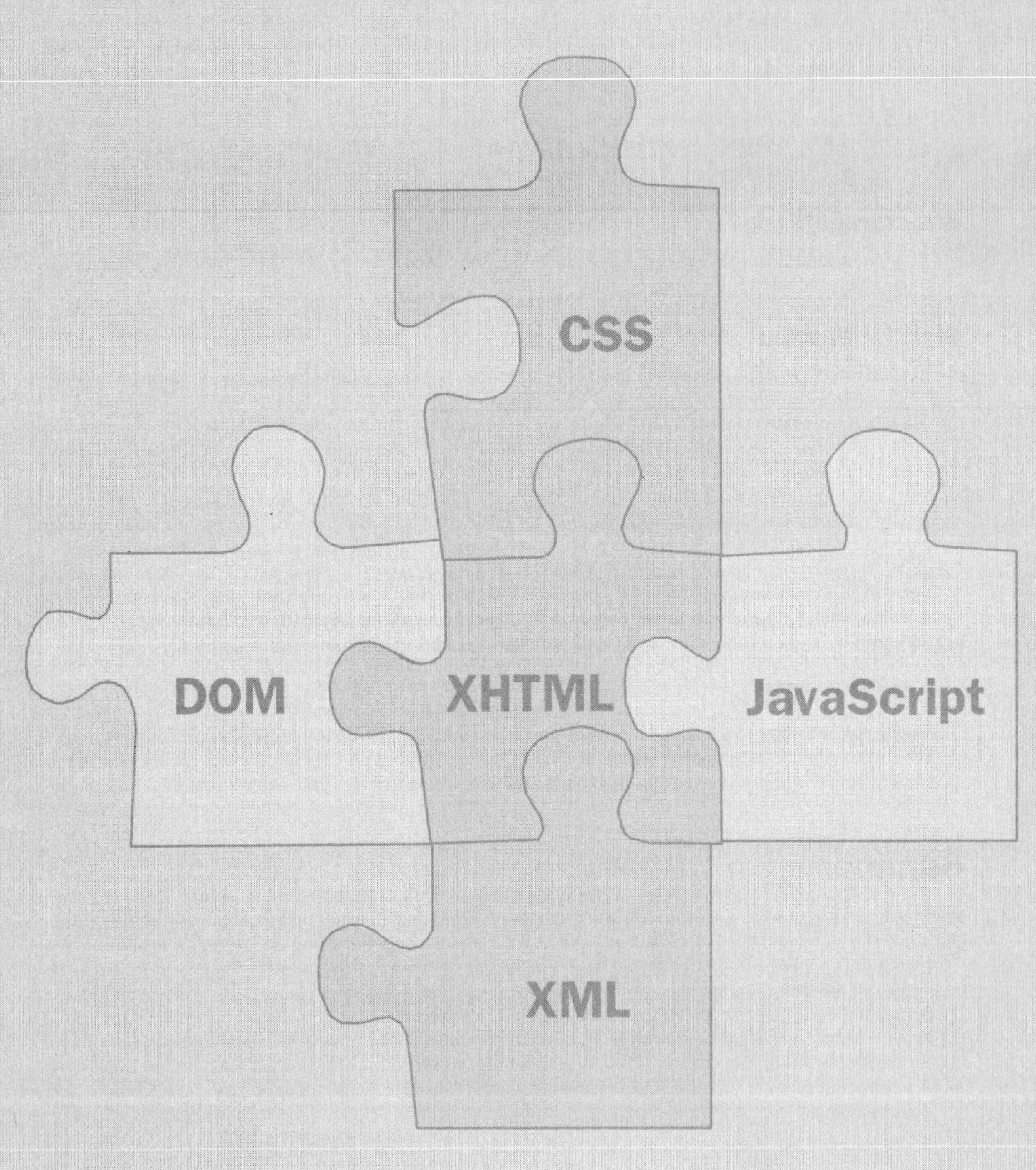
CSS
DOM
XHTML
JavaScript
XML

From HTML to XHTML

In the last chapter, we introduced you to a lot of background information about the Web and the HTML markup language. It may have been a refresher of things you're already familiar with, or it might have been mostly new to you. In this chapter, we will give you a very brief introduction to SGML and what its relation is to XHTML. We will talk about why we need XHTML. The story of why HTML is being replaced by XHTML is about the future, – the web has now become a global information utility, being used by more than just text browsers. We will be iterating some points that we've made already, but only because of their importance in producing 'well-formed' documents.

In this chapter we'll look at:

- SGML, HTML's parent
- Why HTML's days are numbered
- XML, the new language
- XML and HTML: XHTML
- XHTML and how it differs from HTML

SGML, HTML's Parent

Standard **G**eneralized **M**arkup **L**anguage (**SGML**) has been an international standard since 1986. It was originally designed for serious document work and defines nearly every known way of marking up a text. SGML is about defining what a piece of information is. For example, a heading is defined as a heading and a paragraph is defined as a paragraph. The languages utilizing SGML, for example, DocBook, TEI, and MIL-STD, were designed for quite complex and esoteric types of documents.

DocBook is designed for writing sets of books; TEI (Text Encoding Initiative) is designed for writing research orientated literary, historical, and lexicographical texts; and MIL-STD was designed for the writing of military documents.

Such an all encompassing language makes it incredibly powerful from a markup point of view. Every type of information in a text can be unambiguously defined and marked. This lets very specific pieces of information be easily found, manipulated and formatted. But from a web author's point of view, SGML's major strength is also its major drawback: This detailed markup makes it inherently complicated. To become an SGML 'guru' requires extensive study, and only a few people have fully mastered it. Therefore, for those of us who just want to design a great web site, SGML would be impractical and would amount to overkill.

Besides being impractical in general, an SGML document would need to include a very detailed **DTD (Document Type Definition)** for any browser to interpret what the SGML tags meant. In addition, any SGML-based language would also have to include a DTD. Again, this is impractical. This brings us back to HTML.

As we mentioned in Chapter 1, HTML is an example of one of those markup languages set up according to SGML. HTML uses the grammar of SGML. Using computer terms, we say that HTML is an **application** of SGML. There are several other languages that are set up according to SGML, but HTML is by far the most popular of these languages, basically because it is a lot less complex than SGML or the other languages.

The rules for each tag in HTML are spelled out in a DTD, written according to the rules of SGML. Without this DTD, a browser would have no idea how to display a page marked up in HTML. In fact, the HTML DTD is embedded in the browser - so the browser 'knows' what a `<b>` tag does. It doesn't need to go and look it up from anywhere. If you want, you can find the DTD for HTML 4.0 at `http://www.w3.org/TR/html4/sgml/dtd.html`.

We will be looking at DTDs in Chapters 8 and 9. For now, just remember that any SGML-based language requires a DTD to explain its grammar rules to whatever application is being used to read the document. We'll see why this is especially important to us shortly.

Why HTML's Days are Numbered

If HTML is simpler to use than SGML, why can't we simply continue to use HTML as it is? The problem is that the use of the Web is expanding to include user-agents (devices which have the software to connect to the Internet) other than web browsers on desktop computers. These current browsers allow a lot of leeway when it comes to inaccurate HTML markup, because a web browser can spend processing power on figuring out what the HTML is really supposed to say. This tolerance of 'bad' markup stems from the origins of HTML and browsers.

The Mosaic browser, so influential in popularizing the Web, took a very different approach to interpreting markup than traditional SGML applications. Rather than defining a type of information, tags were seen as commands to structure format. For example, Mosaic didn't consider `<p>` tags as structurally marking up paragraphs; it just saw text interspersed with commands to insert blank lines every once in a while.

Mosaic also took a very lax approach to markup syntax. For instance, if you use a start tag such as `<b>` to set the following text in bold, then any emphasis end tag will switch the emphasis off, for instance:

```
This is plain text, <b>this is in bold</i> and this is plain again.
```

The fact that Mosaic would render pretty much anything you threw at it made it very easy for people to start writing their own web pages. No need to look at a boring manual – just take a peek at someone else's markup with Mosaic's View Source menu option and experiment to your heart's content. More than likely the person whose markup you were copying had done the same thing. Very soon, large numbers of people were busily authoring in HTML without caring about what was correct. If it looked okay in Mosaic, then that was all that was needed.

New browsers came into the picture and as more people started using HTML, they came to want more and more control over the look of their documents. Browsers started introducing new tags of their own, while still retaining and enhancing their ability to render badly written HTML. Browsers have been growing larger and larger with each new version to accommodate all the different DTDs and to interpret the lax HTML syntax.

Most HTML you'll see nowadays is not 'true' HTML (in the strict sense) because it doesn't conform to HTML's rules. But since it all displays fine in a browser, nobody really minds. But now we come to the real problem: while desktop browsers have the resources needed to decipher incomplete markup, the new user-agents (cell phones, cars, palm held planners, etc.) don't have the processing power to waste on figuring out how to interpret bad markup.

Another problem relates to the sheer size and complexity of the web. You can be pretty sure that the information you want is out there somewhere, but how do you find it?

The zillions of pages on the Web are all marked up in non-descriptive tags, and the best that a search engine can do is to look at individual words in a text. This is a massive search job. It struck the people charged with bringing order to the Web, that if web pages could be marked up with descriptive (the idea behind SGML) rather than structural tags, searching would be made easier. This would mean that many more applications could harness the connectivity of the Web, simply by passing the data around. The application then decides what it wants to do with that data.

HTML is not doing the job.

So what's needed is a strict language, one that you can be sure is always marked up accurately and completely. It would also be useful if this language could be used for more than just marking up documents for display.

The solution was to write a new grammar that had most of the descriptive power of SGML but none of its complexity. This language should also be capable of interpretation without a DTD. A W3C committee was formed to find a solution. Under the leadership of Tim Bray and Jon Bosak, among many others, a solution was found that promised to be as revolutionary as the Web itself.

This solution was **XML** or the **eXtensible Markup Language**.

Enter XML

We will look at XML in some detail in Chapter 8, but let's get an idea of how it relates to what we know already, focusing on how HTML and XML combine to give the subject of this book: XHTML. In particular we will look at the simple rules for creating what is known as a **well-formed** document. The thing to bear in mind is that the rules of XML will also apply to XHTML, since XHTML is essentially written in XML.

The requirements developed by the W3C for XML are essentially that it should be easy to learn and easy to use over the Internet. A further requirement was that it should be compatible with SGML and its idea of descriptive rather than merely structural markup. XML tags aren't there to define how something should *look* - they're there to define what something *is* – the powerful idea behind SGML. From there it's up to whatever system reads the data to decide what to do with it. One might choose to display the descriptive information in a table, another might perform calculations on it, and still another might simply write the data to a database. All you have to do is mark up the data structure. XML was thus developed to be a simpler, more immediately useable version of SGML, without the inherent complexity.

Another key point about XML is that it's extensible. In other words, new tags can be created as needed and by anyone. But if just anyone can create new tags, how would the browsers be able to interpret them? Would a document need a DTD for every new set of tags? Wouldn't that inflate the already huge browsers even more?

Here's the cool thing about it all! Because XML is actually stricter than SGML, as long as you follow the rules we're about to describe for your document to be well-formed, **you don't need a DTD to interpret it**. When the document is well-formed then the user-agent (the browser or cell phone or whatever you use to connect to the Internet) will be able to parse it successfully without a DTD. When browsers are configured to recognize the specific XML rules then no separate DTD is needed to parse the document. This will greatly reduce the processing power needed by the user-agent to process a document.

> *Because it should be easily useable over the Internet, it was essential that a document should be capable of being parsed without a DTD. In SGML the user-agent always needed either built-in knowledge (like in the case of HTML browsers, where the DTD is coded into the browser) or a supplied DTD to correctly parse a document. This requirement that an XML document should be capable of standing alone accounts for most of the differences between XML and SGML.*

Well-Formed XML Documents

A well-formed XML document is one that is marked up according to the following simple rules. Don't worry, we'll be reinforcing these concepts later on, in the context of XHTML, but it's an idea to keep them in mind:

- All elements must have matching opening and closing tags
- Empty elements must be of a special form
- All elements must be nested properly
- There must be a single root element that contains all other elements

Let's take a closer look at what all this means.

There's one more important thing to mention before we go on.

> **Unlike SGML and HTML, XML is case-sensitive, so <Tag> is not the same as <TAG> or <tag>.**

This is a very big deal and it has direct implications in our upcoming discussion of XHTML.

All elements must have matching opening and closing tags

The opening and closing tags must match. The `<p>` tag in HTML is an example of where closing tags tend not to be used:

```
<p>This paragraph would be fine in an HTML browser, but would not do in an XML
context.
```

In XHTML, closing tags *must* be included:

```
<p>This is how elements like this should be marked up - always include the closing
tag.</p>
```

The implied closing tags of SGML and HTML (such as `<p>` in the first example) are not allowed.

Empty elements must be in a special form

An empty element does not consist of an opening and closing tag but of only one tag such as the `<hr>` tag in HTML, which simply draws a horizontal rule (or line) across the page. It does not enclose any content but only has only a structural effect. The correct way to signify an empty element is with a slash at the end, like this:

```
<hr/>
```

In SGML these elements just took the form of an opening tag. The user-agent would look at the DTD to see whether an element was an empty element or not. This new, more explicit form means that a user-agent can recognize an empty element without resorting to a DTD.

Empty elements can also be written as:

```
<[element name]></[element name]>
```

But it's better to get into the habit by using the first form, i.e. <hr/>.

All elements must be nested properly

All elements must nest, in other words one element must be contained within the other and they cannot overlap. The following construction is legal:

```
<firsttag><secondtag> Some text</secondtag></firsttag>
```

This construction is not:

```
<firsttag><secondtag> Some text </firsttag></secondtag>
```

There must be a single root element that contains all other elements

There must be a single element that encloses the whole body of the document. This way the parser or user-agent can tell when it has finished reading the document:

```
<rootelement>
....a whole lot of markup goes here
</rootelement>
```

Every XML document can be considered to be a tree-like structure, with one root element and several branches. Each element in the document is considered to be a **node**, a place within the tree structure where data is stored (each comment is also considered a node):

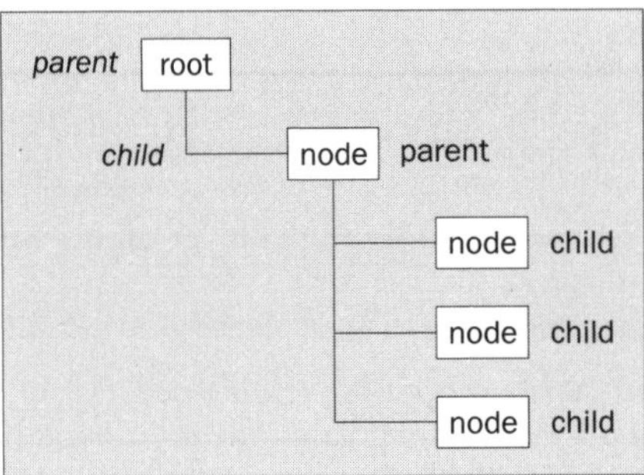

The first node is the **root element** or document node. Each node descending from it is called a **child**. Going back up the tree, the node a child is connected to is its **parent**. Each node has a parent node (except the document node), and each node can have children, which may be either text or other elements (this is discussed fully in Chapter 18).

XML Parsers

In Chapter 1 we learned about parsers and how they process a marked-up document. In order to read an XML document we need an XML parser. XML parsers come in two flavors, **validating** parsers and **non-validating** parsers. We will look at validating parsers in Chapter 8. Here we will just concentrate on non-validating parsers.

> *XML documents can have a DTD just like an SGML document. A validating parser will check that the XML document meets all the rules that are set out in the DTD. A non-validating parser just checks that the XML document is well-formed.*

An XML non-validating parser will take the XML document and check that it is well-formed. The parser can do several things with it but for our purposes we will just say it then passes the parsed document off to another piece of software (usually in the same application) to display the document in some form.

There are several XML parsers available. Throughout this book we will be using the IE5 browser as our non-validating parser. This is not to say that it is superior to other parsers, just that it is readily available.

To give you a flavor of XML, let's look at an XML document, and see what an XML parser needs do to display it.

Try It Out – Writing a Simple XML Document

1. Fire up your text editor (Notepad, or whatever you prefer) and type in the following:

```
<?xml version="1.0"?>
<!--a simple xml document-->

  <firstdoc>
    <subject>An example of an XML document</subject>
    <docinfo date="1/24/2000" id="XMLexample"/>
    <greeting>Hello XML!</greeting>
    <greeting>Hello XHTML!</greeting>
    <farewell>Goodbye SGML! </farewell>
    <footer>
       <author>Frank Boumphrey</author>
       <date>1/24/2000</date>
    </footer>
  </firstdoc>
```

2. Save it as `XMLexample.xml`. The suffix `.xml` is important, as it will tell our non-validating parser (IE5, if you have it) that we are dealing with an XML document.

3. Now open up the file in IE5 (if you have it), by right-clicking on the file and selecting Open. This is what we should see:

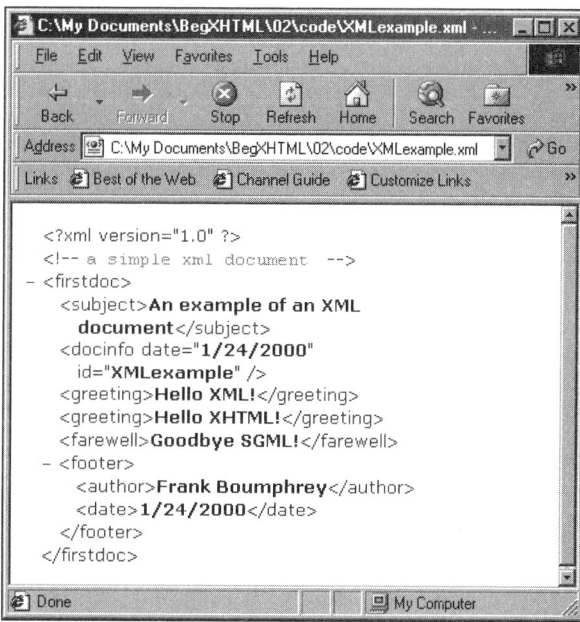

4. You will notice little minus signs against elements that have child elements, namely `firstdoc` and `footer`. If you click on these, the tree is collapsed. The minus sign then becomes a plus. See the diagram below where we have clicked on the `footer` minus sign:

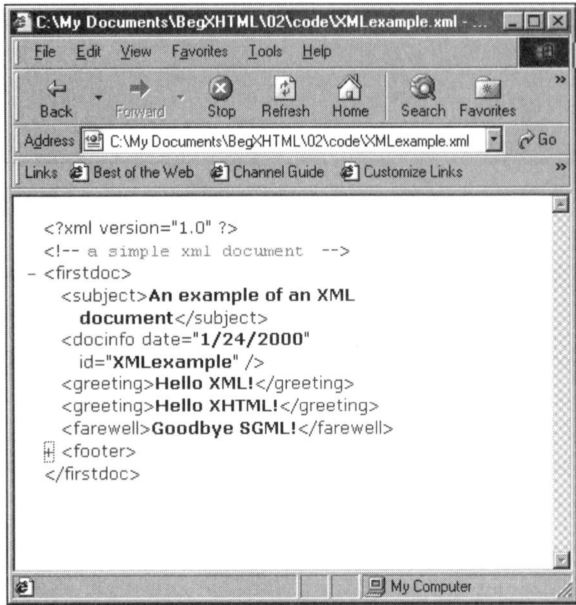

How It Works

There are several things to note here. The first is that IE5 does not attempt to style our document in any way, but just presents it as a tree structure. Let's briefly look at some aspects of our XML file - we'll leave most of it until later on in the book, when it becomes relevant, but let's pick out just a few items that illustrate what we know about XML so far.

Right at the top of our document we have put a version number:

```
<?xml version="1.0"?>
```

Don't worry about this right now – it doesn't affect our discussion of XHTML at the moment. The next line is a comment:

```
<!--a simple xml document-->
```

Comments are there to help the author of an XML page remember what they were thinking when they wrote the page, and aren't usually displayed. However, a parser considers a comment to be part of the tree structure of the document, and it will be shown if the document is displayed as a tree, as is the case here with IE5. Normally, when you display your XML data, you'll do it in such a way that comments are not shown.

Next we have our root element:

```
<firstdoc>
```

Notice how the following elements are indented to the right in the IE5 display above. This is a visual aid to help you see the hierarchy of these elements or nodes.

In our example above the `footer` node is a child of the `firstdoc` node and has two child nodes: the `author` node, which is an element node, and the `date` node, which is also an element node. These nodes have one child each, which are text nodes. The text node of `author` is the content `Frank Boumphrey`. Text nodes cannot have children.

> *If the concept of nodes is not clear to you right now, don't worry – remember, this is only supposed to be an introduction. We will be looking at this concept again in Chapter 3, and also in quite a bit of detail when we look at document object models in Chapter 18. We're just trying to understand XML enough to see how it takes us from HTML to XHTML.*

The last thing we want to see from this example is the empty `docinfo` element:

```
<docinfo date="1/24/2000" id="XMLexample"/>
```

As you can see, the element has attributes, similar to those in HTML. Attributes are properties of elements, and you'll find that you use them quite a lot in your web pages.

Now that we know a little bit about XML, let's see what happens when HTML and XML meet.

XML and HTML: XHTML

So far we have discussed SGML-based HTML, a widespread and popular language, spoken by millions of 'Netizens'. We've also discussed XML, which is extremely versatile, and capable of sophisticated display and data manipulation. The next step is to combine the advantages of these two languages to come up with a better language that we can start implementing now. This is XHTML.

XHTML is a language that uses the vocabulary of HTML and the syntax of XML. The tags and elements are (with minor exceptions) identical to those of HTML, yet because it has an XML grammar (rather than SGML), it can be displayed or interpreted by all XML user-agents. It is a language that combines the best of the XML and HTML worlds.

Let's look at some of the reasons why XHTML is such a good thing

HTML is Very Widely Used

As we have already discussed, HTML cannot meet the demands of a rapidly developing electronic world. Small mobile devices simply don't have the memory and network bandwidth needed for the high-end pages authored for desktop machines. In addition, they also often require special coding. A one-size-fits-all approach is no longer working.

But the more people speak a language, the more useful it becomes as a tool for communication. HTML is used by a whole bunch of people. There's no way you could simply convince everybody to start using 'pure' XML, no matter how much better it would be in theory. W3C's solution was to redefine HTML as a set of modular pieces that can be combined with other tag sets as appropriate. The first step was to reformulate HTML as an application of XML. That application is XHTML, compatible with both XML and HTML.

Getting the Browsers Up-to-Date

If the world switched to XML right now, all the people out there with old browsers would be left out in the cold. It takes about 2 years for 75% of the net population to update to the most current browsers. Therefore a large number of net users are without browsers that can read XML, and this is likely to remain the case for a number of years. XHTML is a language that can bridge this gap. XHTML (provided certain simple guidelines are followed) is backwards compatible and will display on browsers right down to the old version 2.0 browsers.

Getting the Different Browsers to Show the Same Thing

Portability is another benefit of XHTML. Currently HTML documents which are not well-formed are displayed differently in the different browsers, depending on the browser specific interpretation of the HTML document. This is very irritating to those searching for information or entertainment on the Web. Many web sites are turning potential visitors off by using less than optimal code, which can make it hard to view the site. With XHTML, the document will be interpreted the same way by all the browsers as well as by all the other user-agents.

Other Web-Enabled User-Agents

There are a number of new display devices coming into existence – cell phones, handheld devices, web TV, and voice browsers, to name just a few. Across the world, standards committees are hard at work to develop new ways for delivering Web content. Television broadcasters will soon be able to send WebTV content to your living room as part of the new digital television broadcasts. This will be used to offer program guides, financial, sports and other news, up to date weather reports, and all kinds of background information about the currently showing programs. Through a back channel or 'sub-carrier' to the Internet, you will be able vote for your favorites, take part in quizzes or to follow up on special offers for products and services.

Cell phone companies are releasing a new breed of mobile phones offering access to the Web. The small size of displays in cell phones presents a special challenge. The displays are typically limited to black and white, and are only capable of displaying perhaps 4 or 5 lines of 20 characters or less. This is a far cry from high-resolution full color desktop computer displays. It will be interesting to see how such phones are used. The emphasis is expected to be on timely access to information and services.

Meanwhile, other companies are working on providing access to the Web via any telephone, using voice recognition, prerecorded audio and speech synthesis. This will supersede the familiar instructions to press one for this and two for that when phoning companies on their sales and support lines. This is expected to evolve into multi-modal access where you will be able to switch between giving voice commands, and using buttons and touchpads as appropriate. Information will be presented using a mixture of speech synthesis, prerecorded audio and visual display of accompanying text, graphics and video.

These devices simply do not have the processing power to render many traditional HTML documents. They are designed for XML. XHTML allows us to reach all these devices with one set of markup.

Easy implementation for user-agents is one of the advantages of XHTML. Since XHTML has a strict grammar, the user-agent implementation (for all these devices we just described above) need not bother with non well-formed documents. That is, if your XHTML document is not well-formed then it will not be displayed. This will reduce the memory and computing requirements for these devices.

Extensibility

With XHTML you can extend the language to add your own tags by defining a new namespace. For our purposes a namespace is a set of tags unique from any other set. These namespaces are then defined in the XHTML DTD so that your user-agent will know how to interpret them. Later in Chapter 20, we will introduce you to the first new namespace of tags, the Forms Markup Language (FML). We will then walk you through how to use these new XML tags using Mozquito Technology.

It is a trivial matter to add XHTML to your own XML documents, but you will also be able to add XML to your XHTML documents. XML and XHTML enhance each other. The XML category includes function specific languages such as MathML and chemXml. XHTML can then be used in conjunction with any of these languages and future languages to take care of the structural aspects of the document.

How XHTML differs from HTML

In this section, we'll look at the differences between XHTML and HTML 4. Bear these differences in mind – there aren't that many of them, so if you are familiar with any HTML you'll be able to apply that knowledge immediately, but they may catch you out if you have already slipped into any 'bad' coding habits with HTML. You must unlearn what you have learned.

Since XHTML is a reformulation of HTML in XML, everything we learned about well-formed documents above also applies to us from now on. As opposed to HTML, XHTML requires that:

- You must provide a DTD declaration at the top of the file:

  ```
  <!DOCTYPE PUBLIC "-//W3C/DTD XHTML 1.0 Strict//EN" "">
  ```

  Before you didn't need this because the latest browsers came equipped able to decipher any type of HTML. But now with extensibility there is no way your browser can second guess new additions to XHTML.

- You must include a reference to the XML namespace in the `<html>` element:

  ```
  <html xmlns="http://www.w3.org/TR/xhtml1">
  ```

  Note that the above reads ...XHTML1, ending with a number '1' and not two letter 'L's.

- XML is case sensitive, and XHTML tag names and attribute names must be given in lower case.

- You must close tags and indicate empty elements as we've seen earlier. Tags must also nest properly, as we've seen before.
- You may not omit `<head>` and `<body>` elements, and the first element in the head *must* be the `<title>` element.
- All attribute values must be enclosed in quotation marks, and may not be 'minimized'; you must write, for example:

```
<input checked="checked">
```

instead of the old:

```
<input checked>
```

- To avoid `<` and `&` characters within `<style>` and `<script>` elements (which we'll cover in great detail later in the book) being interpreted as the beginning of markup, they must contain a CDATA line:

```
<script>
<![CDATA[
... unescaped script content ...
]]>
</script>
```

These rules make it trivially easy for browsers to determine the hierarchical structure described by the tags without knowing the exact tags beforehand. This is unlike HTML, which, in practice, demands an expert system that embodies knowledge of what elements can include which tags, and knowledge of how to deal with the real-world errors commonly found in HTML documents. XHTML makes it much easier for browsers to support combinations of XHTML and other XML tag sets, like those you may design yourself. The parser will be able to completely parse the document without any external information.

Let's see how these differences might affect us by comparing a bare-bones HTML page (full of 'bad code') and its corresponding XHTML page. Can you spot the differences between the two in relation to the list above?

First, the HTML page:

```
<TITLE>very lax<HTML>
  <HEAD>
    <TITLE>wrong</TITLE>
    <META name="description" content="Working, but really messy code, isn't it.">
    <META name="keywords" content="many, many keywords">
  </HEAD>
  <BODY>
    <CENTER>
```

```
<H1>HTML to XHTML</H1>
    <P>
      It is not that difficult to upgrade one's HTML to XHTML.<BR>
      Just follow a few rules:
    <OL>
      <LI>You need a <EM>DTD</EM> to validate against.
      <LI>refer to <EM>namespaces</EM>.
      <LI>Tags should be <EM>nested</LI>.</EM>
      <LI>Elements should be in <EM>lower case.</LI></EM>
      <LI><EM>Quote</EM> all attributes.
      <LI><EM>Unminimize</EM> attributes.
      <LI>Correctly tag <EM>empty elements</EM>.
      <LI><EM>White space</EM> handling.
      <LI>Escape or externalize <EM>script</EM> and <EM>style elements</EM>.
      <LI><EM>id</EM> instead of name.
      <LI>Tags should be <EM>closed</EM> properly.
      <LI>Handle <EM>layout</EM> with styles.
    <HR width=60% size=1>
```

This is what the messy HTML looks like on IE 5:

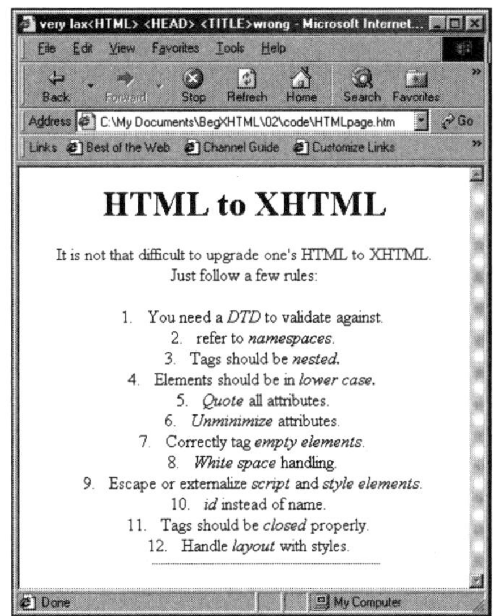

When recast into XHTML this code becomes:

```
<?xml version="1.0" encoding="UTF-8"?>
<!DOCTYPE html
     PUBLIC "-//W3C//DTD XHTML 1.0 Transitional//EN"
     "http://www.w3.org/TR/xhtml1/DTD/xhtml1-transitional.dtd">
<html xmlns="http://www.w3.org/1999/xhtml" xml:lang="en" lang="en">
<head>
    <title>Proper XHTML</title>
```

```
    <meta name="description" content="Working, but really messy code, isn't it."
    />
    <meta name="keywords" content="many, many keywords" />
</head>
<body>
  <div style="text-align:center">
    <h1>HTML to XHTML</h1>
    <p>
      It is not that difficult to upgrade one's HTML to XHTML.<br />
      Just follow a few rules:
    </p>
    <ol>
      <li>You need a <em>DTD</em> to validate against.</li>
      <li>refer to <em>namespaces</em>.</li>
      <li>Tags should be <em>nested</em>.</li>
      <li>Elements should be in <em>lower case</em>.</li>
      <li><em>Quote</em> all attributes.</li>
      <li><em>Unminimize</em> attributes.</li>
      <li>Correctly tag <em>empty elements</em>.</li>
      <li><em>White space</em> handling.</li>
      <li>Escape or externalize <em>script</em> and <em>style elements</em>.</li>
      <li><em>id</em> instead of name.</li>
      <li>Tags should be <em>closed</em> properly.</li>
      <li>Handle <em>layout</em> with styles.</li>
    </ol>
    <hr width="60%" size="1" />
  </div>
</body>
</html>
```

This is what the XHTML code looks like on IE 5:

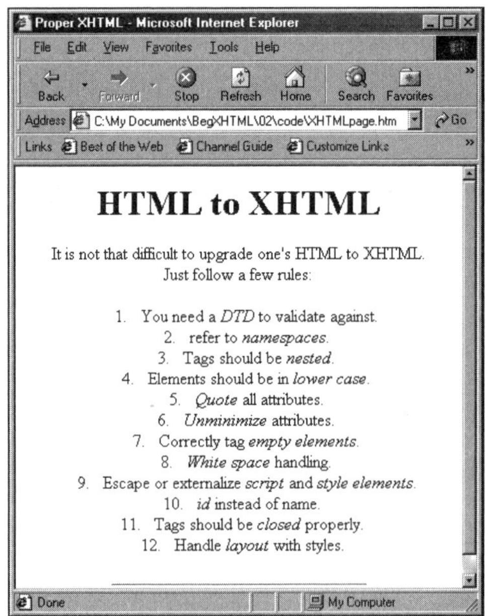

If you run both of these examples through your IE 5 browser the displayed results will look exactly the same. Why is this? To decipher the example of bad code, your IE 5 browser already contains the DTDs for all the old versions of HTML. This is one of the reasons why your browser program needs so much space on your hard drive and so many megabytes of RAM to run. Your browser does not, however, contain the DTD for XHTML, so this is why you need to include it in the above example of valid XHTML code. The tags used in both examples are the same, but the example of good code presents them according to the rules.

Backwards Compatibility Guidelines

XHTML is the future of the Web. Unfortunately, not all browsers in use are XHTML-compatible. However, by following these simple guidelines (taken from Appendix C of the W3C's XHTML 1.0 Recommendation at `http://www.w3.org/TR/xhtml1/`) all your XHTML code will display on existing HTML browsers.

Processing Instructions

These are discussed briefly in Chapter 10 and are elements that should not be displayed on the browser. However, be aware that some browsers may display them.

Empty Elements

Write empty elements like `<br/>` with a space between the tag name and the slash, as in `<br />`. This method is preferable to doing `<br></br>`. Applies also to, for example, `<img src="face.gif" />` and `<input type="text" name="clientname" />`.

Element Minimization and Empty Element Content

When using non-empty elements with no content, do not use the minimized format. For example, if (for some reason) you don't wish to specify a page's title, use `<title> </title>` and do not use `<title />`.

Embedded Style Sheets and Scripts

If either your style sheets or scripts use the characters `<` or `&` or `]]>` or `--` then you should use external style sheets and scripts instead of including a `CDATA` line. On a separate issue, note also that the current practice of including comments within style and script sections in order to 'hide' these from older versions of browsers that do not support them *may* not work in the *future.* However we see no reason to stop using them *now*, and so we use comments in the examples in this book.

Line Breaks within Attribute Values

Don't have new lines or lots of white space within attribute values because different user-agents do different things to them.

Isindex

Don't include more than one `<isindex>` element in the document head. This element has been replaced by the `<input>` element.

The 'lang' and 'xml:lang' Attributes

Use both of these when specifying the language but note that the value of `xml:lang` is used in the event of any confusion.

Fragment Identifiers

Essentially, the `name` attribute has been replaced with the `id` attribute but not all browsers currently support the latter. The simple option is just to include both, ensuring that their values are identical. For example, `<a name="sod" id="sod"> ... </a>`.

This is not the full list of recommended guidelines, but it is all that need concern us here.

The W3C

The Web is a constantly changing environment, with new technologies and standards replacing the old. It is vital that *you*, as a web author, keep yourself up to date with all the latest changes and recommendations. To that end, we recommend you become fully familiar with the W3C site and check it periodically for the latest changes.

The W3C is an international industry consortium led by Tim Berners-Lee, the inventor of the World Wide Web. Although the W3C is not an official standards body, its recommendations are viewed as the official standards for the Web.

> **The World Wide Web Consortium (or W3C) can be found at `http://www.w3.org/`**

Summary

In this chapter we looked at a number of aspects related to XHTML:

- What SGML is and how HTML originated from it
- Why HTML's weaknesses require that we find a better way of doing markup
- XML, the new language and the importance of well-formedness
- How XML and HTML join forces to create XHTML
- XHTML and how it differs from HTML

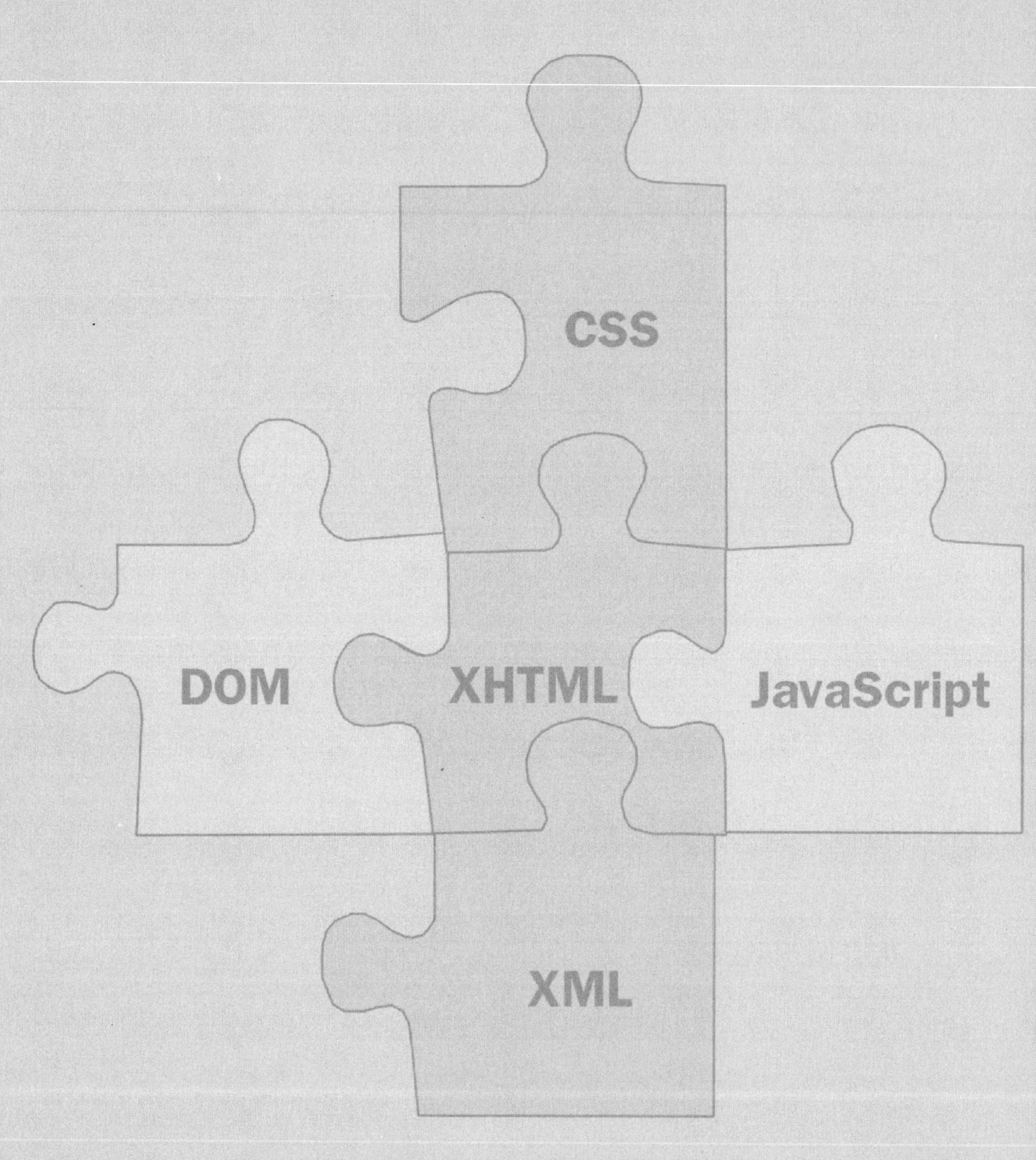
CSS
DOM
XHTML
JavaScript
XML

Getting Started

OK, now that we've looked at how and why XHTML has come about, let's take a quick look at what we can do with it. Although XHTML is, as we've already intimated, basically the HTML 4.01 specification rewritten in XML, it necessitates a different approach from the one we'd take if we just wanted to learn HTML. If you already know HTML, then in some ways you are at a slight disadvantage. We've discussed in the first chapter how style and structure have been mixed up in HTML, and XHTML goes some way to addressing this. Whereas in HTML the browser will ignore anything it doesn't understand or that doesn't parse, XHTML is a lot stricter. We introduced in Chapter 2 the idea of a well-formed document; while your browser can make an attempt with HTML to understand your code even if it isn't well formed, in XHTML it would have a rather more catastrophic effect.

In this chapter we'll be looking more closely at the idea of document structure as it assumes a greater importance in XHTML because of the division of structure and style. This will give you a good idea on what criteria an XHTML document can be assessed by the browser (or parser to be more accurate) and whether it will be accepted and displayed, or rejected with an error message. We've already considered the process of parsing an HTML document in Chapter 1, but parsing an XHTML document is more complex and requires the creation of a document tree. It's necessary to understand this before we start writing XHTML pages. Once this is understood, we can finally settle down and look at the tags that go to make the building blocks of the XHTML language. As we're separating out style though, we need to consider how we're going to display style separately, as a plain text document with no fonts, colors or margins is not what we're looking to achieve at all. The latter part of this chapter will look at style sheets, which are separate portions of code that can be stored in the header of an XHTML document, or as separate files, and contain style information such as the color, font type and weight of your text.

We will start with XHTML right from the beginning of this chapter, and at the end of the chapter you will be able to write a well formed (albeit somewhat dull) XHTML page that can be viewed in almost any HTML browser, and will parse correctly in any XML parser. We will be covering the following topics:

- The structure of documents in general
- The structure of XHTML documents
- Flow objects and Document trees
- Version Declarations
- Basic XHTML text mark up
- Style Sheets

Structuring Text Documents

Although it is traditional in books on HTML to jump right into tags and elements, as we've just mentioned, we're going to jettison this approach and begin by looking at document structure. By getting you used to looking at a document as a series of discrete 'document objects' we will hopefully avoid many of the difficulties that writers have in making the transition from the writing of simple XHTML pages, to the construction of sophisticated 'Internet applications'.

The Structure of Documents in General

Before talking about XHTML documents let's talk a little about documents in general. Documents are part of our every day life, and come in every shape and form. This book is a document, a newspaper is a document, and our bank statement is a document. The Oxford English Dictionary defines a document as:

> "Something written, inscribed that furnishes evidence or information on any subject"

The term 'document' in this book has two contexts: first it refers to the 'information' or final output that the viewer sees in the browser window (this is the displayed web page) and secondly it refers the XHTML 'document' itself containing markup and scripts (the code that goes to make up the web page). These contexts of document both broadly refer to the same item, the web page, but you need to be aware of the differences in usage.

Let us approach the concept of a document in terms of its **content**, **structure** and **style**. The content is the information contained in the document, and the structure is the way that the information that the document contains is arranged. When a document is displayed either in printed or some other form it is said to also have **style**. Let's look briefly at each of these.

Document Content

The document content is the information contained in the document, and falls into two broad categories:

- The information that the document is intended to convey, or the content proper.
- Information about the document itself, sometimes called **meta-information**.

In the case of this book, the information that the document is designed to convey consists of the text and diagrams that you are reading now. The meta- information is that material in the first few pages of the book that gives the name and address of the publisher, the ISBN number, a little blurb about the authors, etc.

Document Structure

This content is divided up into various structures, and these structures, plus their content, are the **structural objects** of the document. In the case of this book, some of the more obvious structures are the chapters, the subsections and the paragraphs. Some of the less obvious ones are the table of contents, the index, and the preface. In any case each part of the document can be considered as a discrete object that has both structure and content. So the paragraph that you are reading now has a paragraph structure, and the content is the actual text that you are reading. Together these can be considered a paragraph object.

Document Style

The **style** of a document is the way that the document is **displayed**. It could be displayed in printed form, as Braille, as a spoken document, or on a computer or television screen. Although the content and structure of the document will stay the same, the style of the document will change. In print media and screen media style will control details such as the type and size of font, the color of the print and the background, the margins and borders etc. When documents are styled a series of **flow objects** are created.

Flow Objects

Documents are usually designed to be read or heard, and as such the content of the document that is displayed **flows** from the beginning of the document to the end. In the case of a printed English document it flows from top to bottom, and from left to right. If it were an Arabic document it would flow from top to bottom and from right to left.

In order for the document to be displayed the objects of the document must be formatted and styled, and this creates a new set of objects called flow objects. A flow object is a discrete item of formatted and styled content. This paragraph that I am typing is a 'paragraph flow object' formatted in 12 point Baskerville font, and **this phrase** is a flow object of bold text. A flow object usually coincides with one of the structural objects of the document such as a paragraph or a phrase. A flow object can be as small as a single character but is usually a larger unit. However like the atom of pre-particular physics we can't create any flow object smaller than a single character! Flow objects fall into two broad groups, block flow objects, and inline flow objects.

Block Flow Objects

A block flow object is a piece of text with a line break before and after it. For example this paragraph is a block flow object, and the heading of this paragraph is another block flow object.

> "This quotation is another block flow object."

This insert is another block flow object.

Inline Flow Objects

Inline flow objects are discrete pieces of formatted text that do not have a line break before and after them. **This piece of bold text** is an inline flow object, as is *this piece of italic text.*

Style and Structure

To a large extent, style and structure overlap. For example, most paragraphs and headings will be displayed in a consistent manner. In fact most devices designed to display a document, such as an Internet browser, will have a built in default style applied to each of the structural objects of the document. Consider the `<h1>` to `<h6>` heading tags (we'll meet these later on, but they mark up headings level 1 to 6); if they were just structural then they would all look the same and all that the structure would dictate is maybe that a level two heading comes after a level one heading tag (this is not enforced in any way by the browser). However, there is also in built style information which means that each heading level displays text in a different size and weight as well:

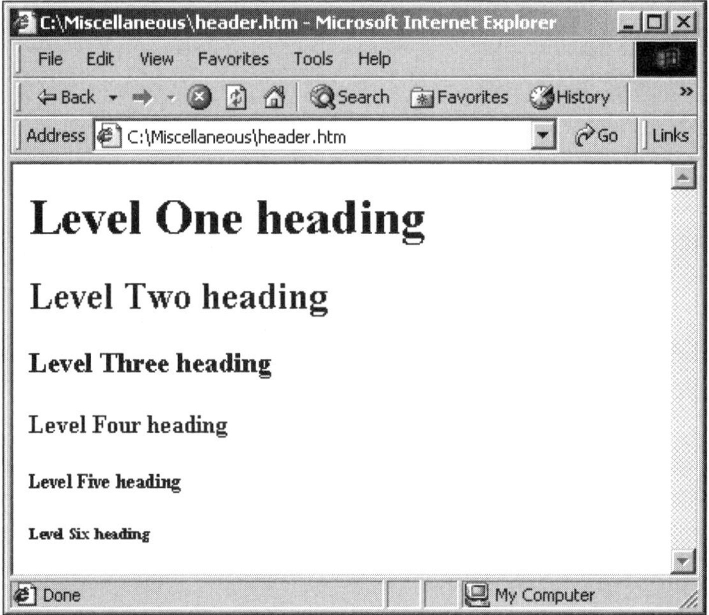

Document Trees

The relationship of one part of a document to another can be considered as a hierarchy, and this hierarchy is often expressed as a document tree. We will be looking at this in considerable detail when we learn about document object models in Chapter 18.

For now we will just look at some of the terminology we use to describe the relationships of the various parts of the document.

Nodes

Each discrete object in a document is considered a **node**, and every node has a relationship to another node. For example, this paragraph is a paragraph node. There are nodes below the paragraph node in the hierarchy. These nodes also have content, which may be other nodes, or it may be text. The text of course can be formatted in various ways, and then each piece of formatted text is considered to be a separate node with a sibling relationship (see next section) to the other text nodes.

Parents, Children and Siblings

Every node (except the document node) has a parent node, and this node might or might not have children. Text nodes do not have any children. For this reason, you will find text nodes at the bottom of the hierarchy. Text nodes are the smallest items you can find in the hierarchy, and as they can't contain anything else – think about it text can't contain anything other than text - they can't have child nodes. Nodes that share the same parent are sibling nodes.

Parsing a Document

When we break the document down into its constituent parts we are said to **parse the document**. This is what a browser or a computer will do with our XHTML document before displaying it. However as we shall see we have to give the computer clues with our markup as to where to create objects.

Let us see if we can make this clearer with a simple example.

Try It Out – Parsing a Simple Document

1. You should begin by writing this simple document out on a piece of paper (Write? Paper? What's that!):

   A simple document

   This document contains a single **heading** and two **paragraphs,** and a **footer**. This is the first paragraph.

   The second paragraph contains some *italicized* text.

   End of document

2. Now draw a box around each discrete element in the document:

A simple document

This document contains a single | **heading** | and two | **paragraphs,** | and a | **footer.** | This is the first paragraph.

The second paragraph contains some | *italicized* | text.

End of document

3. We can now express the relationships of the parts of the document by drawing a tree:

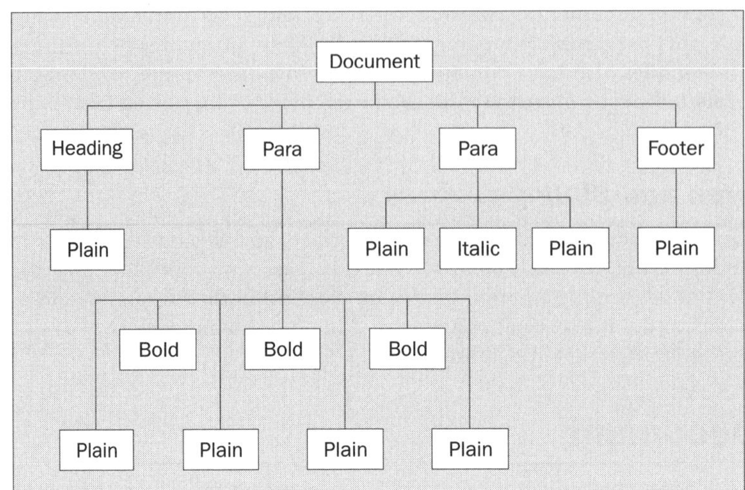

How It Works

Each of these objects will have various properties that we will look at in some detail when we consider the XHTML document model. For now just note that:

- They all have a **content** property.
- They all (except for the document node) have a **parent** property.
- They all (except for the text nodes) have a **children** property, which is a list of their children.
- They may have a **next sibling** and a **previous sibling** property.

Hopefully this brief introduction to documents and document structure will act as a good grounding on which to base your study of XHTML, which we will look at right now.

The Structure of XHTML Documents

I am sure that you are keen to get down to writing a proper XHTML document so even before we go into explanations, let us write an example of the simplest possible XHTML document.

Try It Out – A Simple XHTML document

1. Fire up your text editor and type the following:

```
<?xml version="1.0" encoding="UTF-8"?>
<!DOCTYPE html
     PUBLIC "-//W3C//DTD XHTML 1.0 Transitional//EN"
     "http://www.w3.org/TR/xhtml1/DTD/xhtml1-transitional.dtd">
<html xmlns="http://www.w3.org/1999/xhtml" xml:lang="en" lang="en">
  <head>
```

```
    <title>First XHTML document</title>
  </head>
  <body>
    <p>This is my first XHTML document.</p>
  </body>
</html>
```

2. Save this as `examp2.htm`, and then hit the Save As button, and save it as `examp2.xml`.

3. What we have here is a document that is both a well-formed XML document, and a valid and well-formed XHTML document – in fact all XHTML documents fall into this category. XHTML documents have the additional advantage that they are also capable of being shown on ordinary HTML browsers, and we will do this right now. Fire up any browser and open up `examp2.htm`. Here is what we would see in IE5.

How It Works

First, notice that we're using the Transitional DTD here and throughout the book for simplicity, because it's wider in scope than the Strict DTD. Sometimes in this book we'll use something for demonstration purposes that doesn't appear in the Strict DTD, and it's just easier to use the Transitional DTD throughout.

Notice how the part that is between the `<title></title>` tags appears in the browsers title bar, and that the only part that is displayed is the text between the `<p></p>` tags. This is a 'flow object' and the browser has automatically applied styling to it, in this case a 12 point Times New Roman font.

Now, if you have IE5, open up `examp2.xml`. This is what you will see:

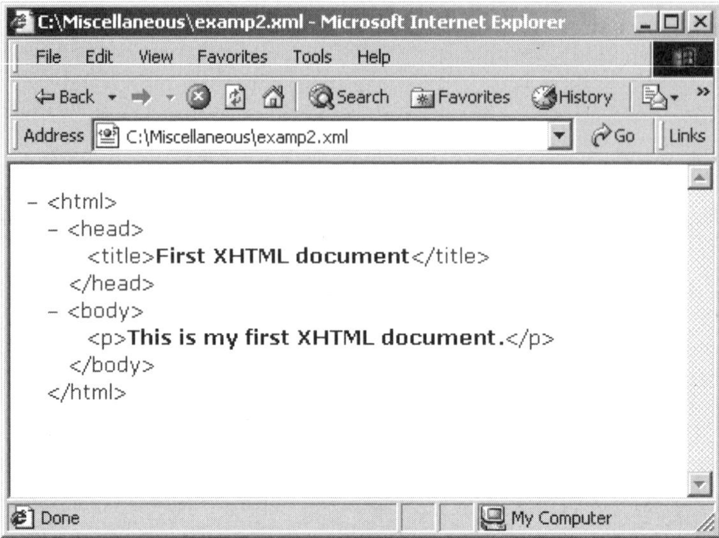

How It Works

Here, everything that we typed is displayed as a tree, although the orientation is a little different from the tree that we drew in the first part of the chapter. If you click on the little minus signs you can collapse and expand the tree to show the parent/children relationships. Here all the document objects are displayed as structural objects. There has been no attempt to apply styling to the different objects.

In this simple example we have used all the obligatory elements necessary to create an XHTML document. Although most browsers in HTML will let you get away with leaving out some of the tags and elements, this is not recommended. Here, we are learning XHTML and you must make sure to open and close every tag correctly; otherwise, it can cause errors. Part of the reason you want to use XHTML is that it will allow your document to be displayed in a very wide variety of media, and by a huge number of different user agents. To design a document just for the browser(s) that you have on your machine is not a very smart thing to do!

> *As we've seen in our history, the browser wars of the late 1990's led to the situation where sloppy markup was tolerated. Software companies felt that by providing engines that corrected sloppy and illegal markup, they would make their browsers "user-friendly" and capture a larger part of the market. This not only led to "browser bloat", but it led to other unfortunate circumstances such as the inability to properly display style sheets. In the case of Netscape the entire browser had to be redesigned from the floor up! Gecko, or Navigator 5, which at the time of writing is still undergoing development, has every promise of being an excellent HTML/XML browser.*

Before looking at the parts of an XHTML document in more detail let's remind ourselves about the difference between an element and a tag.

Elements and Tags

Let's look at the difference between an element and a tag. In the example below we have a paragraph element:

```
<p>This is my first XHTML document.</p>
```

The whole of this is a paragraph element. Each (non-empty) element consists of an opening tag, in this case <p>, a closing tag, in this case </p>, and the content of the element, in this case This is my first XHTML document.

The content plus the opening and closing tags is the element. In HTML you could get away often by omitting closing tags such as the </p> tag, but in XHTML this is not so.

The tag is called the 'p' tag. The element is correctly called the 'p' element *type*, but just about everyone will call it the 'p' element.

The Parts of the XHTML Document

As we saw in Chapter 1, HTML was designed as a language for marking up scientific documents. As such it concentrated on the structure of the document rather than any stylistic rendering of that document. XHTML of course does exactly the same.

An XHTML document has two main parts, a **Head** part, and a **Body** part. The head part contains a whole lot of information that is not intended for display, but is important in that it gives us information about the document. The body part of the document contains material that is the actual meat of the document, and is usually intended to be displayed.

A document can also have a version declaration and document type definition, both of which come before either the document head or document body. We looked at document type definitions in the last chapter, but we'll discuss the version declaration here.

Version Declaration

At the heading of each document an XML declaration is included. It isn't obligatory, but the XHMTL 1.0 standard 'strongly encourages' the use of the XML declaration in all XHTML documents. The version number refers to the number of the XML (not XHTML) standard being used, so a declaration for XML would look like this:

```
<?xml version="1.0"?>
```

This must go before the document head and body. Unlike normal tags, the version declaration boasts an extra pair of question marks within the angle brackets. The reason that its use is strongly encouraged, is that this declaration also has an encoding attribute, and if this attribute is anything other than default (UTF-4 or UTF-8), then use of this tag becomes obligatory.

DOCTYPE Declaration

See Appendix A for more details on the DOCTYPE declaration. Here we declare what DTD our document is validated against, and provide the URL so that if the browser or parser wishes to check this, it can go ahead and do so:

```
<?xml version="1.0" encoding="UTF-8"?>
<!DOCTYPE html
     PUBLIC "-//W3C//DTD XHTML 1.0 Transitional//EN"
     "http://www.w3.org/TR/xhtml1/DTD/xhtml1-transitional.dtd">
```

You can actually take a local copy of the DTD and include the URL to that instead of the W3C URL given above.

The Document Head

The head of the document is designed for important information about the document that is not part of the normal 'flow' of the document. Usually information in the head of the document will not be displayed.

Here are the elements permitted in a document head:

```
<title>          <link>       <meta>       <object>
<style>          <script>     <base>
```

According to the rules of XHTML, the `<title>` element must always be the first element, and must always be present.

As we will see, the various browsers on the market do not enforce this rule, or several other of the rules of HTML and XHTML documents. However as more and more devices start employing XHTML, it is expected that the rules will be enforced, so it is just as well to get into the habit of writing good code now! Simply stated: the document is not well formed or valid without these rules being implemented.

The head of the document contains the following information:

- A **title**: this is compulsory. All HTML and XHTML documents must have a title. There must be one, and only one title. A title is not considered to be part of the document flow, and is usually displayed in the title bar of a browser.
- **Meta** information: this is information about the content of the document. We will cover this in Chapter 8.
- **Link**ing information: the document may be associated with another document, for example the information on how to style the document may be contained in a separate document. Linking information will tell the user-agent where to find the document, and what kind of document it is.

- **Style** information: information on styling the document may be contained in the head. We will cover this briefly at the end of this chapter and in detail in Chapter 9.
- Various **objects** and **scripts**: the head of a document is also a good place to put code (covered in detail in Chapter 16) that is not designed to be part of the flow of the document.
- **Base** simply specifies the document's base URL.

The Document Body

The document body is the meat of the document. It is the part that is designed to be read. We talk about the flow of a document. Normally, an English document is designed to be read from top to bottom and from left to right. We say that a document 'flows' in this direction. If it is a Hebrew or a Chinese document it may flow in a different direction, but it still flows.

The document body then will contain a whole series of flow objects such as headings, paragraphs, lists and tables. The body can also contain comments and code.

Comments

As well as the elements, a typical XHTML document will also contain comments. These are notes that the authors of the document write to themselves and to each other. Although they will appear in the document tree, they are not designed to be displayed, or to alter the makeup or functioning of the document in any way at all, i.e. they are not part of the document flow.

Comments in XHTML, XML, SGML, and HTML documents all take the following form.

```
<!-- [comment here]-->
```

Any programmer will tell you how important comments are. They are also important in authoring documents. It is only too easy to forget why you did something in a certain manner. As a rule of thumb if the reason for something is not blindingly obvious, write a comment.

Browsers and Built-in Semantics

HTML is wildly and widely popular, and there is an expectation that when HTML type markup is used the element will be displayed in a certain manner. HTML browsers do indeed have these display semantics built into them, and, for the most part, the commercial browsers will display HTML elements in a consistent and similar manner. It's important to remember that browsers don't currently do this for XHTML, it's too new to have been incorporated into any browser on the market. So what we we're having to do is browse XHTML with an HTML browser. Also, as we've mentioned in the previous section, currently if you make a mistake in the XHTML code, the browser won't choke on it.

The expectation in the future is that just like in HTML a certain element will be displayed in a certain way, will be carried over to XHTML, and an XHTML element will indeed be displayed just like its HTML counterpart, provided they are displayed in an HTML browser. Let's have a look at these elements now.

Basic XHTML Block Elements

As we pointed out earlier, there is an overlap between structure and style. In XHTML certain elements are designed to be 'Block' flow elements, and certain elements are designed to be 'Inline' flow elements. We can have an expectation that when block elements are displayed in an HTML or an XHTML browser they will have a line break before and after them. In other words we can say that these elements have 'built in' semantics. The 'block' elements are as follows:

```
<p>   <div> <blockquote> <pre> <h1>…<h6>
```

Here are the more important of the XHTML block elements together with a note on their built-in display semantics. Note that there is no requirement for browsers to follow any particular rule of presentation, but the majority do follow the guidelines below:

Element Name	Opening and closing tag	Comments and 'built-in' semantics
Paragraph	<p></p>	This is the workhorse of the XHTML document. The majority of your text will probably be contained in paragraphs. The presentation of a paragraph depends on the browser, but there is usually a space equivalent to a blank line of text before and after the paragraph.
Division	<div></div>	This is really designed to be used with style sheets. There is usually just a line break before and after the element with no built in vertical white space.
Headings	<h1></h1> <h2></h2> <h3></h3> <h4></h4> <h5></h5> <h6></h6>	There are six levels of headings with a font size that usually ranges from 24 points down to 10. The vertical white space before and after also ranges from about 24 points down to 10 points.
Blockquote	<blockquote></blockquote>	This element actually has some descriptive semantics as well as stylistic semantics built into it, in that it was designed for the display of quotations. As well as vertical white space before and after the element, there is usually a left and a right margin indentation.
Preserve	<pre></pre>	As we will see below, Browsers usually collapse the white space in the source document into a single space. If the author uses a <pre> element though all the white space is preserved. (See example below).

Let's write examples of some of these elements and see how they display.

Try It Out – The Semantics of the Common Block Elements

1. Fire up your text editor and type the following:

```
<?xml version="1.0" encoding="UTF-8"?>
<!DOCTYPE html
     PUBLIC "-//W3C//DTD XHTML 1.0 Transitional//EN"
     "http://www.w3.org/TR/xhtml1/DTD/xhtml1-transitional.dtd">
<html xmlns="http://www.w3.org/1999/xhtml" xml:lang="en" lang="en">
  <head>
     <title> Common XHTML block elements I: p and div and blockquote</title>
  </head>
  <body>
     <p>This is a paragraph</p>
     <div>This is a div</div>
     <div>This is a div</div>
     <div>This is also a div. Note how there is no vertical whitespace between
divs.</div>
     <p>This is a paragraph</p>
    <blockquote>"This is a blockquote which has both built in style semantics as
well descriptive semantics. It is designed for quotations, so we have put quotes
around the text."</blockquote>
  </body>
</html>
```

2. Save it as `examp3.htm` and open it up in your browser:

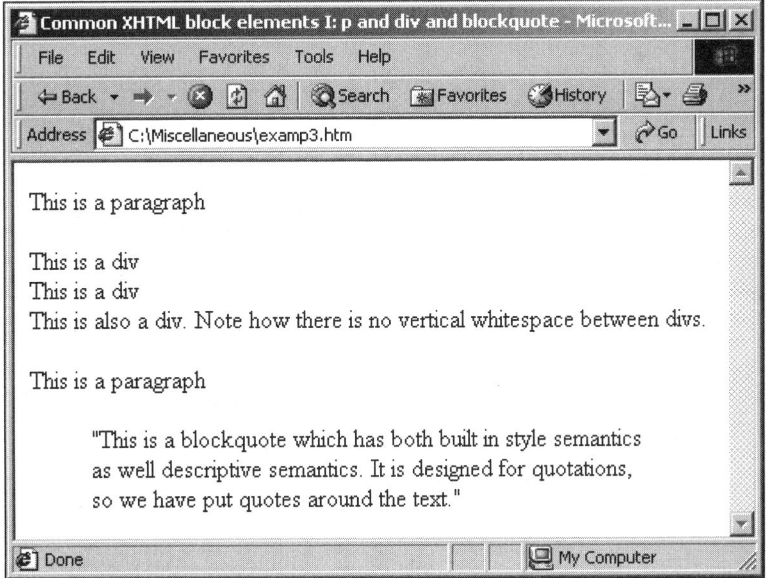

Note that there is no upper or lower margin between the adjacent 'divisions', whereas the paragraphs have an upper and lower margin equal to about the height of one line of text.

Note also that the 'blockquote' element is indented on both the left and the right margins.

Collapsing Vertical White Space

Although browsers are free to put their own interpretation on presentational semantics, it is usual to collapse the vertical white space between adjacent block flow objects. In other words when a paragraph follows a paragraph there is only one line of white space between them, and not two.

Headings

There are six levels of headings allowed in XHTML. Most HTML browsers will assign fairly consistent styling to these headings, with a font size ranging from 24 points down to 10, and a margin above and below with about the same size of the white space. Here is a simple demonstration of the headings:

```
<?xml version="1.0" encoding="UTF-8"?>
<!DOCTYPE html
     PUBLIC "-//W3C//DTD XHTML 1.0 Transitional//EN"
     "http://www.w3.org/TR/xhtml1/DTD/xhtml1-transitional.dtd">
<html xmlns="http://www.w3.org/1999/xhtml" xml:lang="en" lang="en">
  <head>
     <title> Common XHTML block elements II: Headings</title>
  </head>
  <body>

     <h1>Level One heading</h1>
     <h2>Level Two heading</h2>
     <h3>Level Three heading</h3>
     <h4>Level Four heading</h4>
     <h5>Level Five heading</h5>
     <h6>Level Six heading</h6>

  </body>
</html>
```

This is how this document would look displayed in IE5:

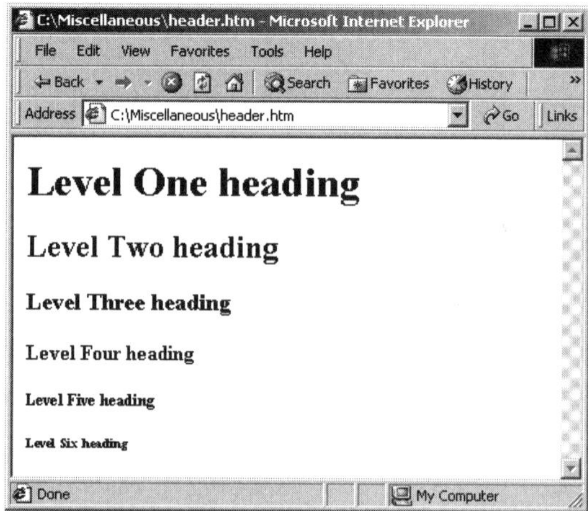

The Preserve or <pre> Element

This element is used when it is desired to maintain the formatting in the parent document.

Try It Out – The 'preserve' Element

1. Type up this example, save it as `preserve.htm`, and run it.

```
<?xml version="1.0" encoding="UTF-8"?>
<!DOCTYPE html
     PUBLIC "-//W3C//DTD XHTML 1.0 Transitional//EN"
     "http://www.w3.org/TR/xhtml1/DTD/xhtml1-transitional.dtd">
<html xmlns="http://www.w3.org/1999/xhtml" xml:lang="en" lang="en">
  <head>
    <title> Common XHTML block elements II: pre and p elements</title>
  </head>
  <body>

<p>
  The source text is identical in both these examples:

    If a is less than b then
      print "a is less than b"
    Else
      print "b is less than a"
    End if
   ' a simple VBScript example
</p>

<pre>
  The source text is identical in both these examples:

    If a is less than b then
      print "a is less than b"
    Else
      print "b is less than a"
    End if

   ' a simple pseudo VBScript example
</pre>

  </body>
</html>
```

This is what it looks like in Netscape 4.6

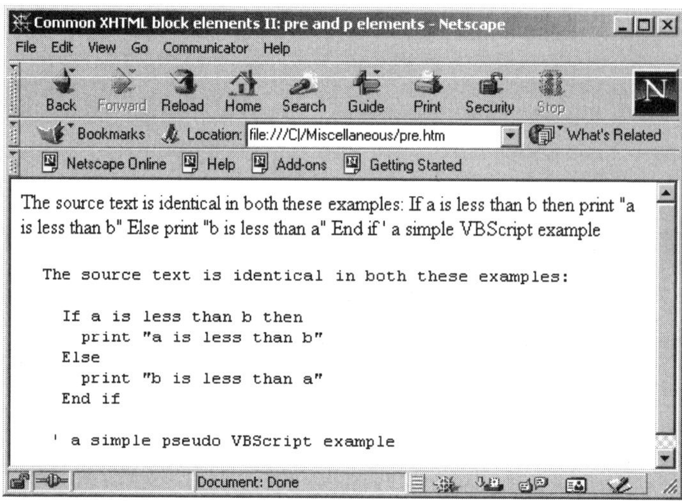

Collapsing White Space

You will have noticed in the above example that in the paragraph element all the white space is collapsed into a single space. This is the norm for all XHTML elements except the `<pre>` element. All the content of a `<pre>` element has the white space preserved. Most browsers will display the `<pre>` element in a mono-space font such as 'Courier New'.

Let's have a look at the most commonly used inline elements.

Basic XHTML Inline Descriptive Elements

These elements are used to describe their content. What we mean by this is that the name of the tag, is an indicator of the style in which the text will be displayed. So text displayed in the <q> (quotation) tag would commonly be displayed in italics. The style is implied by the name. Most browsers will display them in a distinctive manner. Style elements on the other hand, such as <i> or <b> explicitly state the style of an element, and as described in the next section, will give the same effect in screen and print media, but may be ineffectual in other media, such as speech, so descriptive elements should always be used in preference to styling elements.

Here are the inline descriptive elements:

```
<abbr>     <acronym>    <cite>     <code>     <dfn>
<em>        <q>         <samp>     <span>     <strong>    <var>
```

Some of these are associated with a certain style in existing browsers, and others are purely descriptive.

Element Name	Opening and closing tag	Comments and 'built-in' semantics
Abbreviation	`<abbr></abbr>`	This is a purely descriptive element. In most browsers it carries no stylistic or structural semantics.
Acronym	`<acronym> </acronym>`	This again is a purely descriptive element. In most browsers it carries no stylistic or structural semantics.
Cite	`<cite></cite>`	Used for citations. Most browsers will render this as **italic** text.
Code	`<code></code>`	A description element rendered as **`mono-spaced`** font in most browsers.
Definition	`<dfn></dfn>`	A description element rendered as **italic** text in most browsers.
Emphasis	`<em></em>`	A description element rendered as *italic text* in most browsers.
Quotation	`<q></q>`	This again is a purely descriptive element. In most browsers it carries no stylistic or structural semantics.
Sample	`<samp></samp>`	A description element rendered as **`mono-spaced`** font in most browsers
Span	`<span></span>`	This merely defines a span of text. In practice this is used purely as a vehicle for the style or the class attribute (see below)
Strong	`<strong></strong>`	A description element rendered as **bold text** in most browsers
Variable	`<var></var>`	A description element rendered as *italic text* in most browsers.

Try It Out – Inline Descriptive Elements

1. Let's have a look at how these elements look when displayed in a browser. Type the following code.

```
<?xml version="1.0" encoding="UTF-8"?>
<!DOCTYPE html
     PUBLIC "-//W3C//DTD XHTML 1.0 Transitional//EN"
     "http://www.w3.org/TR/xhtml1/DTD/xhtml1-transitional.dtd">
<html xmlns="http://www.w3.org/1999/xhtml" xml:lang="en" lang="en">
  <head>
     <title>First XHTML document</title>
  </head>
  <body>
     <div>This is <abbr>an abbreviation </abbr>in a division.</div>
     <div>This is <cite>a citation </cite>in a division.</div>
     <div>This is <code>some code </code>in a division.</div>
     <div>This is <em>emphasized text </em>in a division.</div>
     <div>This is <q>a quotation </q>in a division.</div>
     <div>This is <samp>a sample </samp>in a division.</div>
     <div>This is <span>a span </span>in a division.</div>
     <div>This is <strong>strong text </strong>in a division.</div>
     <div>This is <var>a variable name </var>in a division.</div>
  </body>
</html>
```

2. Here is what they look like in the Communicator 4.6 browser with large fonts:

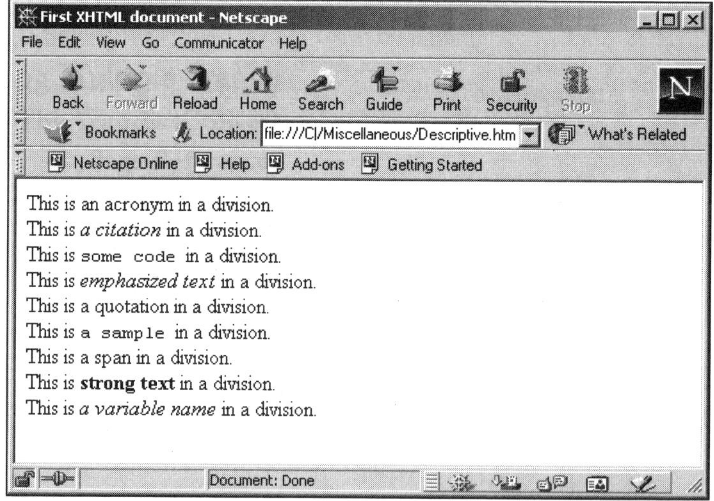

Note that there is no styling associated with `<quot>`, `<span>`, `<acronym>`, or `<abbr>`. `<code>` and `<samp>` are both displayed as a monotype fixed width font, `<emph>` and `<cite>` are italic, and `<strong>` is bold. The advantage of using these elements for markup is that in non-screen media, such as speech renderings of the page for the blind, some appropriate semantics will still be assigned to the rendering of the element. We're saying here that a vocal rendition of a web page would be able to understand tags such as `<strong>` and `<cite>` and maybe emphasize them in a way, or preface them by saying this is a quotation, whereas a page with `<i>` and `<b>` elements would be beyond such capabilities – how do you speak text in an italicized style? We look at other types of browser in Chapter 13.

Basic XHTML Inline Style Elements

XHTML also have a lot of tags with a built in styling semantic attached to them. These indicate that they should have a certain style attached to them when displayed in visual media. It is likely that non-visual user agents will also render the more common of these elements in some distinctive manner, but don't count on it! It is always better to use a descriptive element.

However that being said, italic and bold have acquired a descriptive meaning of their own quite outside their typographic use.

Element Name	Opening and closing tag	Comments and 'built-in' semantics
Big	`<big></big>`	Renders as larger text than the base text
Bold	`<b></b>`	Renders as **bold** text
Italic	`<i></i>`	Renders as *italic* text
Keyboard	`<kbd></kbd>`	Renders as **`mono-spaced`** text resembling that of an old fashioned type writer.
Underline	`<u></u>`	Renders as **underlined** text.
Small	`<small></small>`	Renders as smaller text than the base text
Strikethrough	`<strike></strike>`	Renders as ~~**strikethrough**~~ text
Sub	`<sub></sub>`	Renders as a $_{\text{subscript}}$ text
Sup	`<sup></sup>`	Renders as a ^{superscript} text
True type	`<tt></tt>`	Renders as **`mono-spaced`** text.

Try this out for yourself.

Try It Out – The Styling Elements

1. Type up the following

```
<?xml version="1.0" encoding="UTF-8"?>
<!DOCTYPE html
     PUBLIC "-//W3C//DTD XHTML 1.0 Transitional//EN"
     "http://www.w3.org/TR/xhtml1/DTD/xhtml1-transitional.dtd">
<html xmlns="http://www.w3.org/1999/xhtml" xml:lang="en" lang="en">
  <head>
     <title>First XHTML document</title>
  </head>
  <body>
     <div>This is <b>bold text </b>in a division.</div>
     <div>This is <big>big text </big>in a division.</div>
     <div>This is <i>italic text </i>in a division.</div>
     <div>This is <kbd>keyboard </kbd>in a division.</div>
     <div>This is <u>underlined text </u>in a division.</div>
     <div>This is <strike>strikethrough text </strike>in a division.</div>
     <div>This is <small>small text </small>in a division.</div>
     <div>This is <sub>sub text </sub>in a division.</div>
     <div>This is <sup>sup text </sup>in a division.</div>
     <div>This is <tt>true-type </tt>in a division.</tt>

  </body>
</html>
```

2. Save it as `style.htm`. This is how it is rendered in Communicator 4.6.

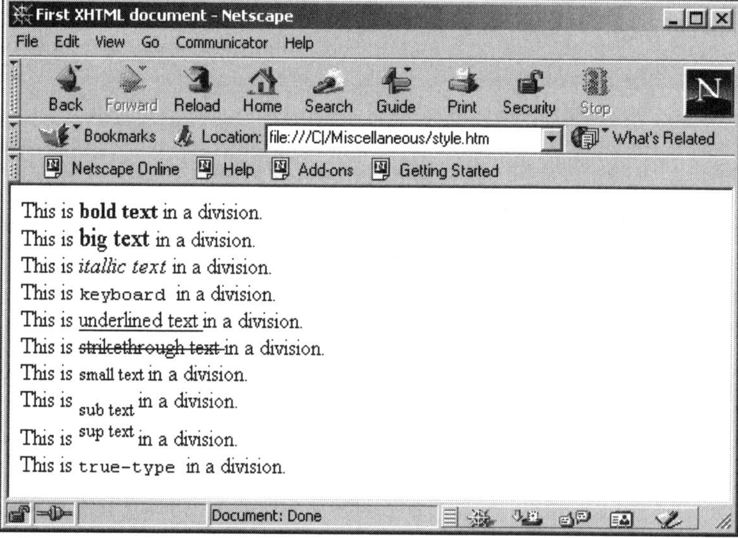

Styling Elements that Have no Style (
 and <hr />)

`<br/>` is the equivalent of a line break in XHTML. It will start a new line. `<hr/>` will produce a horizontal line across the page. Note that these elements are empty elements, and because of this must take the XML required form for empty elements. These elements will only work in visual media. They produce no effect in other media.

> **For reasons of backward compatibility it is suggested that you leave a space just before the slash in empty elements, e.g.
 and <hr />. Legacy browsers will then have no difficulty displaying the element.**

Lists

Lists are used all the time in scientific and business documents. XHTML give us an easy way to structure a list. Structurally a list is just a series of items, usually on its own line, and each usually preceded by either a bullet or some kind of number.

In XHTML when a bullet is used it is known as an **unordered** list.

When a number or letter is used to order the list it is known as an **ordered** list.

Unordered Lists

The element to create an unordered list is `<ul>`. An unordered list element can only contain list item elements. Each item in the list must be contained in a list item element `<li>`, and these list item elements are allowed to contain almost any content at all!

Try It Out – A Simple Unordered List

1. Type up the following in your favorite text editor.

```
<?xml version="1.0" encoding="UTF-8"?>
<!DOCTYPE html
     PUBLIC "-//W3C//DTD XHTML 1.0 Transitional//EN"
     "http://www.w3.org/TR/xhtml1/DTD/xhtml1-transitional.dtd">
<html xmlns="http://www.w3.org/1999/xhtml" xml:lang="en" lang="en">
<head>
<title>An unordered list</title>
</head>
<body>
  <p>Here is a simple unordered list</p>
   <ul>
    <li>First item</li>
    <li>Second Item</li>
    <li>Third item</li>
  </ul>
</body>
</html>
```

2. Save this as `unorderlist.htm`. Here is what the above code looks like when displayed in IE5:

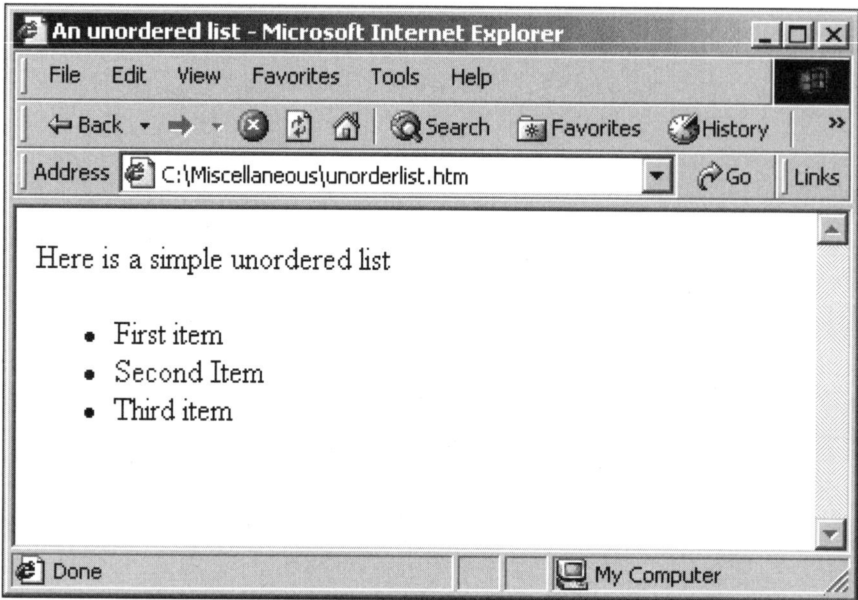

Note how each item on the list has been given a nice bullet, and how it has been indented.

Altering the Bullet Style

We can in fact change the type of bullet by using a "type" attribute. We haven't looked at attributes and styling yet, so just make the following change to your above code and run it again.

```
<body>
  <p>Here is a simple unordered list</p>
   <ul type="square">
     <li>First item</li>
```

You will notice that bullets are now square and not round!

How It Works

We will look at attributes a little later on in this chapter. For now, just note that an attribute is the way to describe or alter the property of an element. The name of the attribute here is `type`, and we have given it a value of `square`. Note especially that the value of the attribute must be in either single or double quotes.

The `type` attribute for an unordered list can take the values of `circle`, `disc` or `square`. The default is `disc`. In most browsers this will produce a solid circle, and `circle` will produce an empty circle, but the exact interpretation is left up to the individual browser.

Nested Unordered Lists

Lists can also be nested. To do this the new list must be contained within a list item (`<li>`) element. Lists cannot be nested directly inside unordered list elements without `<li>`, otherwise the browser could confuse it with the other list item elements.

> **However, most browsers will in fact allow you to get away with this incorrect interpretation, but don't do it. An XML parser will throw an error. Besides it is just as easy to write good code as it is to write poor code!**

Try It Out – Nesting a List

1. Type up the following code:

```
<?xml version="1.0" encoding="UTF-8"?>
<!DOCTYPE html
     PUBLIC "-//W3C//DTD XHTML 1.0 Transitional//EN"
     "http://www.w3.org/TR/xhtml1/DTD/xhtml1-transitional.dtd">
<html xmlns="http://www.w3.org/1999/xhtml" xml:lang="en" lang="en">
<head>
<title>An nested unordered list</title>
</head>
<body>
  <p>Here is a nested unordered list</p>
   <ul>
    <li>First item contains another list!
      <ul>
        <li>First Item in list2</li>
        <li>Second Item in list2</li>
        <li>Third item list2</li>
      </ul>
    </li>
    <li>Second Item</li>
    <li>Third item</li>
  </ul>
</body>
</html>
```

2. Here is what you will see if you save this page as `nestlist.htm` and view it in your browser:

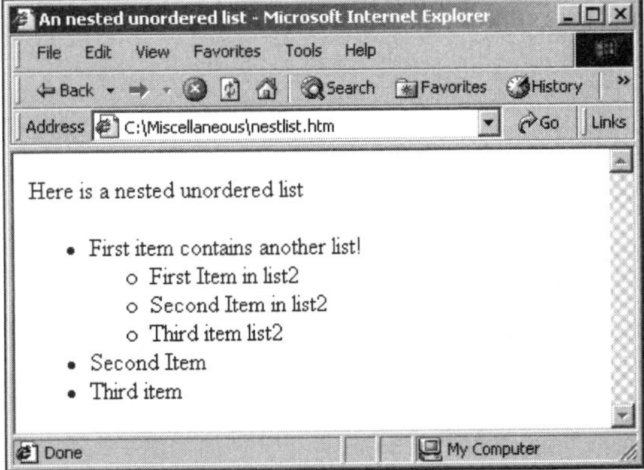

Note how the lists are neatly indented one in the other.

Ordered Lists

An ordered list is a list where the various items are numbered. The tag for an ordered list is `<ol>`. Let's change our previous nested example and change the lists from being unordered to ordered.

Try It Out – A Nested Ordered List

1. Open up `nestlist.htm` and change the lines that have been highlighted as follows:

```
<?xml version="1.0" encoding="UTF-8"?>
<!DOCTYPE html
     PUBLIC "-//W3C//DTD XHTML 1.0 Transitional//EN"
     "http://www.w3.org/TR/xhtml1/DTD/xhtml1-transitional.dtd">
<html xmlns="http://www.w3.org/1999/xhtml" xml:lang="en" lang="en">
<head>
<title>A nested ordered list</title>
</head>
<body>
  <p>Here is a nested ordered list</p>
   <ol>
    <li>First item contains another list!
      <ol>
        <li>First Item in list2</li>
        <li>Second Item in list2</li>
        <li>Third item list2</li>
      </ol>
    </li>
    <li>Second Item</li>
    <li>Third item</li>
  </ol>
</body>
</html>
```

2. Save this as `nestorder.htm` and open it up in your browser. Here is what you should see:

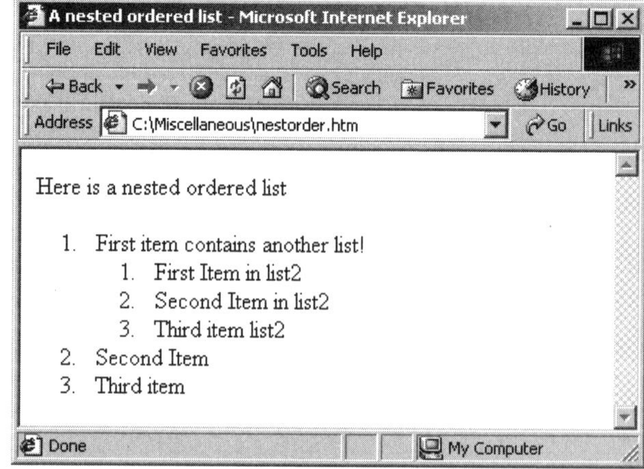

Note how the browser automatically numbers our items.

Again we can change the numbering system by using the `type` attribute and giving it a value of `"1"`, `"a"`, `"A"`, `"i"`, or `"I"`. As an exercise, substitute each of the alternate values for `type`.

Definition Lists

A definition list, `<dl>`, lists various items that need to be defined. The term to be defined is put in a definition term, `<dt>` element, and the definition itself is put in a definition description, `<dd>` element.

This type of list can be particularly useful for a long list of terms.

Try It Out – A Definition List

1. Open your favored HTML editor and type in the following:

```
<?xml version="1.0" encoding="UTF-8"?>
<!DOCTYPE html
     PUBLIC "-//W3C//DTD XHTML 1.0 Transitional//EN"
     "http://www.w3.org/TR/xhtml1/DTD/xhtml1-transitional.dtd">
<html xmlns="http://www.w3.org/1999/xhtml" xml:lang="en" lang="en">
<head>
<title>a definition list</title>
</head>
<body>
  <p>Here is a definition list</p>
   <dl>
    <dt>Element</dt>
      <dd>An element consists of the tags and the content
          of the element</dd>
    <dt>Element Attribute</dt>
      <dd>The attribute is a property of the element</dd>
    <dt>Attribute value</dt>
      <dd>The string value assigned to the element. Must
          be quoted in XHTML</dd>
   </dl>
</body>
</html>
```

2. Save it as `definition.htm`. Here is what you will see if you run this in IE5:

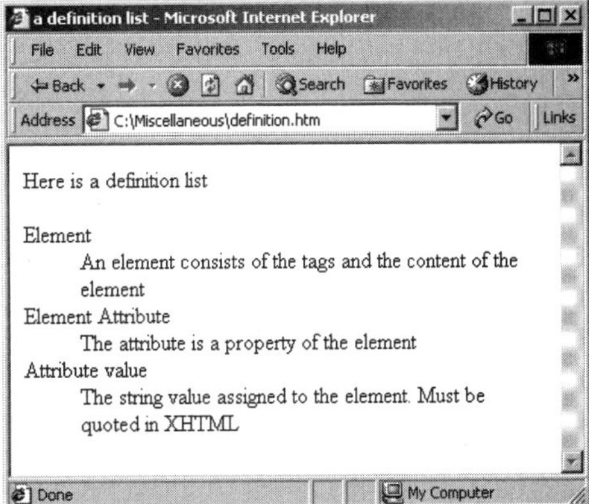

Note how the definition term uses the regular margin, and the definition description is indented.

Lists and Different Media Types

Lists are particularly useful if one is writing for numerous different types of media. They transfer well to both voice and Braille browsers. If you think your page may be displayed in these media types, consider using lists rather than tables whenever you can.

This rounds out our survey of the basic elements. All the elements allowed in XHTML can be seen in Appendix A where they are summarized.

Let's have a look now at how we can give elements a richer meaning by using attributes.

Attributes

Attributes give added meaning to an element. As XHTML is XML, XHTML attributes must follow the rules of XML. XHTML attributes are placed in the opening tag. If an attribute is present it *must* have a value, and this value *must* be quoted. By and large attributes fall into five groups.

- **Universal/Core attributes**. All presentational elements can take a set of attributes called the 'universal attributes'.
- **Language attributes**. These attributes give information about the language that the element is using.
- **Events**. These attributes apply to common user interface events. They are the basis for mouse and keyboard driven interactivity. They are used with scripts. We will be looking at these in detail in part three of this book.
- **Presentational attributes**. These attributes give information about the formatting of an element. For the most part they are deprecated and a style sheet should be used instead.
- **Specialized attributes**. These attributes are specific to certain elements. For example the 'alt' and 'src' attributes of the image element, and many of the attributes of the table element. We will enumerate these attributes as we come to each element that they apply to.

The Universal Attributes

Universal attributes are attributes that every tag shares. To be truthful though, there are no truly universal attributes that every single tag shares, but there are four attributes that most tags use and that, more importantly, are defined within the XHTML standard as being universal.

The 'id' Attribute

The `id` attribute is very important. It serves to give the element a unique identity in the document. Its value must be unique in the document otherwise the parser will throw an error.

The value of an `id` element must start with a letter or an underscore, and contain alphanumeric characters. In other words, the naming of an `id` attribute value must follow the same rules as an XML attribute or element name. `id` attributes are very important when it comes to linking to various parts of a document. This attribute has replaced **most** uses of the `name` attribute.

The 'class' Attribute

This specifies the class of an element. It is used in XHTML to associate an element with a class of display properties set out in a style sheet.

The 'style' Attribute

The `style` attribute was introduced in the HTML 4.0 standard and is one possible implementation of style in your document. Style sheets are the preferred method however (if you remember from earlier, style sheets are a declaration of display rules that are intended to be held separately from the document structure.) By adding style information within a style attribute you can attach style information to any tag that supports this property. The style attribute isn't an ideal implementation of style as it doesn't strictly separate the style from the structure, but it does allow you to incorporate various style sheet properties into your document. We will look very briefly at style sheets at the end of this chapter, before looking at it much more detail in Chapter 9. What the 'style' attribute actually does is allow us to apply style sheet properties to an individual element. The general syntax for the style element is:

```
Style=" [style sheet property]:[property value]; [style sheet
property]:[property value];...."
```

Although in the real world this attribute is hardly ever used, the use of style sheets being preferred, we will be using this attribute in quite a few of our examples in the next few chapters. For the most part the meaning of the property and its value will be intuitive.

Let's try a few examples to start us off.

Try It Out – Using the 'style' Attribute

1. Type up the following into your text editor:

```
<?xml version="1.0" encoding="UTF-8"?>
<!DOCTYPE html
     PUBLIC "-//W3C//DTD XHTML 1.0 Transitional//EN"
     "http://www.w3.org/TR/xhtml1/DTD/xhtml1-transitional.dtd">
<html xmlns="http://www.w3.org/1999/xhtml" xml:lang="en" lang="en">
<head>
<title>Using the style attribute</title>
</head>
<body style="background-color:white">

<div style="color:blue; font-size:16pt;font-family:arial,sans-serif">
This is 16 point blue,arial, type.
</div>

<div>
This is the browser default type.
</div>
```

```
<div style="background-color:blue; color:yellow;font-size:16pt;font-
family:'courier new','monospace'">
This is 16 point yellow,courier, type on a blue background.
</div>

<div style="background-color:yellow;margin:24pt;">
This is the browser default type on a yellow background with a 24pt margin all
around.
</div>
<div>
This is the browser default type again.
</div>
</body>
</html>
```

2. Save it as `style.htm`.

3. If you are running IE5 or later this is what you will see:

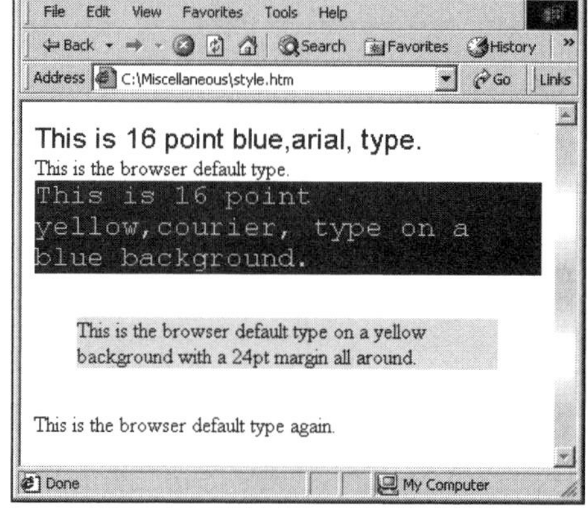

4. If you are running Netscape 4.5 onwards you would see this:

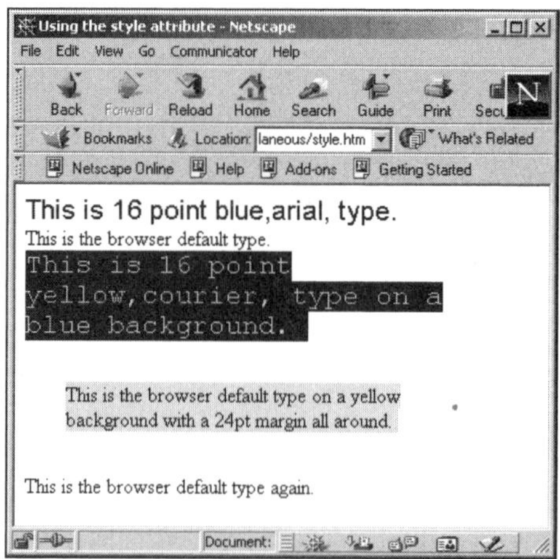

Which is just the same!

> **Note that running style sheet properties in older browsers such as IE4 or Navigator 4 when they hadn't been fully implemented will yield erratic results, or in some cases no results at all. Earlier browsers than these will choke on the style attribute.**

How It Works

In the <body> element:

```
<body style="background-color:white">
```

...we have used the style attribute to set the background color of the page to white rather than the default gray. We use the style sheet property `background-color`.

```
<div style="color:blue; font-size:16pt;font-family:arial,sans-serif">
This is 16 point blue,arial, type.
</div>
```

In this div we have used three style sheet properties, `color`, `font-size`, and `font-family`. Note how we separate each property/value with a semi-colon.

The values are fairly intuitive but note how we have included two fonts, a named font, and a 'generic' font name. (The other generic font names are `serif`, `cursive` and `fantasy`. More on this in Chapter 12.)

```
<div>
This is the browser default type.
</div>
```

The browser has its own default style for each of the XHTML elements.

```
<div style="background-color:blue; color:yellow;font-size:16pt;font-
family:'courier new','monospace'">
This is 16 point yellow,courier, type on a blue background.
</div>
```

There are two points to take notice of here. First, we have given the element its own background color, and second because courier new has a space in it we have enclosed the names in single quotes. This is not strictly necessary.

```
<div style="background-color:yellow;margin:24pt;">
This is the browser default type on a yellow background with a 24pt margin all
around.
</div>
<div>
```

Here we have used the margin property to give this element an all round margin.

The 'title' Attribute

This is an advisory title for the element. It serves to name the element. IE5 uses the title to display a 'tool tip'.

The Presentational Attributes

HTML has accumulated a large number of presentational attributes over the years. These have for the most part been deprecated in favor of style sheets. In this section we will just cover some of the more common of those that are used in conjunction with our text elements. Images and tables have their own collection of presentational attributes, and these will be covered in those chapters.

We must emphasize that for the most part these attributes are used for styling the structural element, and do not effect the structure of the element. Although we need to acquire knowledge of these attributes if we will be dealing with legacy documents or are writing for legacy browsers, we should not be using them all that much.

A well-structured document with a style sheet should be perfectly legible (if unexciting) in a legacy browser, and the style sheet will provide all the styling we need in a modern HTML browser (4+). In fact every thing in this section is deprecated, so we're not going to provide any examples on how to use these attributes and elements. They're here for your information, so you can understand them should you come across them in old HTML pages, but you should never use them!

The 'align' Attribute

The align attribute tells how an element is to align the text it contains. It can be one of three values, left right or center. The default value is left.

Presentational Attributes of the <body> Element

The body element can take several atributes that will style your page. Here is a list of them:

- **background**. The background attribute takes an URL of an image as its value. The image will be tiled across the screen.
- **bgcolor**. This takes either the name of one of the defined colors, or a hexadecimal number.
- **text**. This assigns a color to the text. Again this takes either the name of one of the defined colors, or a hexadecimal number.
- **link**. This assigns a color to a link before it has been activated. Links are discussed in the next chapter.
- **vlink**. This assigns a color to a link after it has been activated.
- **alink**. This assigns a color to a link while it is being activated.

Presentational Attributes Associated with Lists

In the section on Lists we covered the use of the type attribute to alter the bullets or numbering of lists. Just to recap, an unordered list type attribute can take the values of disc, square, or circle, and the type attribute of an ordered list can take the values 1, a, A, I, or i.

- 1 arabic numbers 1, 2, 3, ...
- a lower alpha a, b, c, ...
- A upper alpha A, B, C, ...
- i lower roman i, ii, iii, ...
- I upper roman I, II, III, ...

The style is applied to the sequence number, which by default is reset to 1 for the first list item in an ordered list.

<hr /> Attributes

Attributes on the hr element can be used to align and alter the width and length of the horizontal rule. They can also be used to define a solid or a shaded rule. Here are the attributes:

- align This can take a value of left right or center.
- noshade This takes a value of "noshade".
- size This takes a number which will express the thickness in pixels.
- width This may take either a percentage or a number. When a percentage it will give a rule width relative to the width of the window, when it is given a number value it will have an absolute width in pixels.

Presentational Elements

Along with the deprecated presentational attributes, there are two whole elements that serve presentational purposes only, and have been deprecated, `<font>` and `<basefont>`. They are of historic importance only. Although they are carried through to the XHTML 1.0 version for reasons of backward compatibility they will not be implemented in either any future versions or the modularized version.

The <font> Element

The `<font>` element is an inline element. Any content was rendered in a style that was described by its attributes.

- `size` This was an integer between 1 and 5. 3 was the default size for the element. 1 and 2 were smaller fonts, and 4 and 5 were larger fonts.
- `color` This attribute took a value of either a hexadecimal number or a string value. See Appendix C for a more detailed description.
- `face` This is a string value of a font name. Several fonts could be presented each separated by a comma.

The <basefont> Element

The `<basefont>` element allowed the setting of baseline font values. The attributes were similar to font.

Even though these elements are in the XHTML 1.0 DTD, don't use them. If you want to know more about these outdated elements consult a book on HTML.

Cascading Style Sheets

In this section we are going we are going to acquire just enough knowledge to write a basic cascading style sheet. We will see how to see how to link to a style sheet, and we will also look the basic syntax for writing a style sheet. We will go into much more detail in chapter 9.

What is a Cascading Style Sheet?

A style sheet is a declaration of display rules. It supplies information to conforming user-agents as to how to style an XHTML, HTML, or XML document. The term cascade comes from the ability of multiple style sheets to all have control over the same document. So all style sheets are in fact cascading style sheets (commonly shortened to CSS).

Cascading style sheets are governed by W3C standards. There have been two versions of the standard to date, known as CSS1 and CSS2. These standards lay out the guidelines of CSS syntax. However you are heavily dependent on what the browser supports. Only IE5 comes anywhere close to full support of even the first version of the standard. Each CSS statement details how to style either an element or a class of elements. Cascading style sheets can also contain comments.

General syntax of a CSS statement

The general syntax for a CSS statement is as follows.

```
[element or class name]{
      [1st CSS property name]:[value];
      [2nd CSS property name]:[value];
      [3rd CSS property name]:[value];
      etc....
}
```

General syntax of a CSS comment

The general syntax for a CSS comment is as follows.

```
/*[comment]*/
```

C programmers should note that although this has the appearance of a comment of the 'C' language, C++ comments where '//' comments out the rest of the line are not supported in CSS.

Here is an example of a CSS comment.

```
/*
     This is a comment.
     This comment may
     be spread over
     several lines
*/
```

By way of example let's revisit our most basic XHTML document and add a 'style element' to it.

Try It Out – Adding a Style Sheet to an XHTML Document

1. Type up the following.

```
<?xml version="1.0" encoding="UTF-8"?>
<!DOCTYPE html
     PUBLIC "-//W3C//DTD XHTML 1.0 Transitional//EN"
     "http://www.w3.org/TR/xhtml1/DTD/xhtml1-transitional.dtd">
<html xmlns="http://www.w3.org/1999/xhtml" xml:lang="en" lang="en">
  <head>
     <title>First XHTML document</title>
  <style type="text/css">  <!--
     p{
       font-size:16pt;
       font-family:'comic sans MS', 'fantasy';
       color:maroon;
     }
  -->
  </style>

  </head>
  <body>
     <p>This is my first XHTML document.</p>
  </body>
</html>
```

2. Save this as `CSS.htm`. This will display as follows in both IE5 and Navigator 4.5:

How It Works

The style sheet should always be in the head of the document, and is included as content of the `<style>` element, although as we'll see in later in this chapter that it isn't the only way to include a style sheet. Lets have a look at the elements of this style sheet. The rendition below has its lines numbered for ease of description. These numbers would of course cause an error if they appeared in our real style sheet!

```
1<style type="text/css">
2<!--
3  p{
4      font-size:16pt;
5      font-family:"comic sans MS, fantasy";
6      color:maroon;
7     }
8-->
9</style>
```

1. The `<style>` element tells our browser that we are about to feed it the contents of a style sheet. The type attribute value tells it that the style sheet is going to be a CSS style sheet.

2. This is the start of a comment which lets us hide our style sheet from browsers that don't understand such things.

3. This line tells the browser that it is about to receive information on how to style regular 'p' elements. All the style properties it is to assign to the 'p' elements are contained within the curly brackets. The opening bracket does not have to be on this line, indeed the element name, all the style properties and both curly brackets could be on the same line. How you choose to lay out your code is a matter of personal style.

4. Here is the `font-size` property. Each property follows the same pattern, the property name, a colon ':', then the property value terminated by a semicolon';'.

5. Here is the font family. Because the font name has white space in it should be quoted. Note how commas separate the different names, and how a default font name is given.

6. The last property that we define for the 'p' element is a foreground color, in this case we have used a name maroon. It is usually better to use a number value. The semicolon is optional on the last element, but it is good practice to always include it.

7. Here is the closing curly bracket. This tells the browser that it has finished reading the values for the 'p' element. For the properties we have not defined it will assign default values.

8. Here, we simply close the comment we started in line 2.

9. Finally the closing script tag tells the browser that it has come to the end of this internal style sheet.

Now when the browser reads the document proper it will assign all these properties to any 'p' element that it comes across. One thing you might also notice about the style sheet is use of the color maroon on line 5. You might assume that red and blue etc. would be understood by most browsers, but how about aqua, teal and fuchsia? And also what happens if you want your text to be dark red, crimson or scarlet and not just in one hue. We'll look at how you can change colors now.

Colors

Colors are fully discussed in Appendix C, so feel free to skip there now and have a look – it's quite a short discussion and I'll wait for you... On the basis of that discussion, you could just have easily changed line 6 in the last example to:

```
1<style type="text/css">
2<!--
3  p{
4      font-size:16pt;
5      font-family:"comic sans MS, fantasy";
6      color:#800000;
7    }
8-->
9</style>
```

And kept the nice maroon color. If you have any problems converting decimal to hexadecimal, then just call up the calculator in Windows and change the View to Scientific and any number you type will be automatically converted to hexadecimal when you click on the Hex option button.

CSS Classes

There is no need for every element in our document to adopt the same style. We can use the class attribute of an element to hang various styles on different elements of the same name.

In order to show in our style sheet that we are going to associate a style with a class, we put a period before the class name. i.e.

.[*classname*]{... *style properties here* ...}

For example:

```
.redtext {color: red}
```

Then every time we want to apply our newly created class we just set the class attribute to equal the value of our class name (minus the period).

```
<p class="redtext">Hello!</p>
```

The class remains only in force for the duration of the element. Any text coming after the closing `</p>` tag won't be in red (unless red is the default color). Let's take a look at this now:

Try It Out – Adding a 'class' to the Style Sheet

1. Open up the previous example CSS.htm and add the following code:

```
<?xml version="1.0" encoding="UTF-8"?>
<!DOCTYPE html
     PUBLIC "-//W3C//DTD XHTML 1.0 Transitional//EN"
     "http://www.w3.org/TR/xhtml1/DTD/xhtml1-transitional.dtd">
<html xmlns="http://www.w3.org/1999/xhtml" xml:lang="en" lang="en">
<head>
<title>My first XHTML page</title>
  <style type="text/css"
  <!--
     p{
       font-size:16pt;
       font-family:'comic sans MS', 'fantasy';
       color:maroon;
     }
     .bigsans{
       font-size:24pt;
       font-family:arial,sans-serif;
       color:yellow;
    }
  -->
  </style>
</head>
<body>
<p>This is my first XHTML page</p>
<p class="bigsans">This is the second paragraph of my first XHTML page</p>
</body>
</html>
```

2. Save it as CSSclass.htm and display it in your browser:

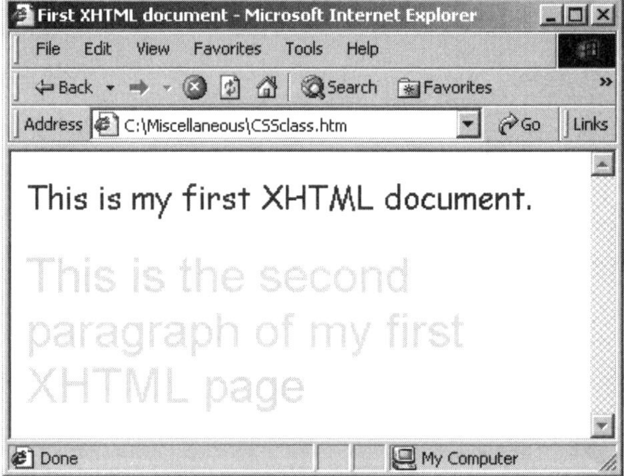

How It Works

The first paragraph is just a dumb old paragraph, and takes the default styling that we have used for all paragraphs. The second paragraph however has been given the class name of "bigsans". When the browser looks in the style sheet it sees that all elements of the class 'bigsans' should be rendered in a 24 point yellow arial font, so it does so with our second paragraph.

Linking to External Style Sheets

In the two previous examples we embedded the style sheet in the document. It is in fact preferable to have the style sheet as an external document, and to link our XHTML page to it. This is done either through an XML processing instruction or a `<link>` element. For now we will just use a link element.

Try It Out – Linking to an External Style Sheet

1. Modify our `CSSClass.htm` example as follows, cutting out and saving the lines on a clipboard that are missing here:

```
<?xml version="1.0" encoding="UTF-8"?>
<!DOCTYPE html
     PUBLIC "-//W3C//DTD XHTML 1.0 Transitional//EN"
     "http://www.w3.org/TR/xhtml1/DTD/xhtml1-transitional.dtd">
<html xmlns="http://www.w3.org/1999/xhtml" xml:lang="en" lang="en">
<head>
<title>My first XHTML page</title>
  <link rel="stylesheet" type="text/css" href="css1.css" />
</head>
<body>
<p>This is my first XHTML page</p>
<p class="bigsans">This is the second paragraph of my first XHTML page</p>
</body>
</html>
```

2. Save this page as `CSSlink.htm`.

3. Then start up Notepad (or an HTML editor that supports style sheets) and paste the following lines into the editor, remembering to remove the `<style></style>` tag lines as they are no longer needed:

```
p{
       font-size:16pt;
       font-family:'comic sans MS', 'fantasy';
       color:maroon;
     }

     .bigsans{
       font-size:24pt;
       font-family:arial,sans-serif;
       color:yellow;
    }
```

4. Save it as `css1.css` in the same folder as `CSSLink.htm` and then view `CSSLink.htm` in your browser:

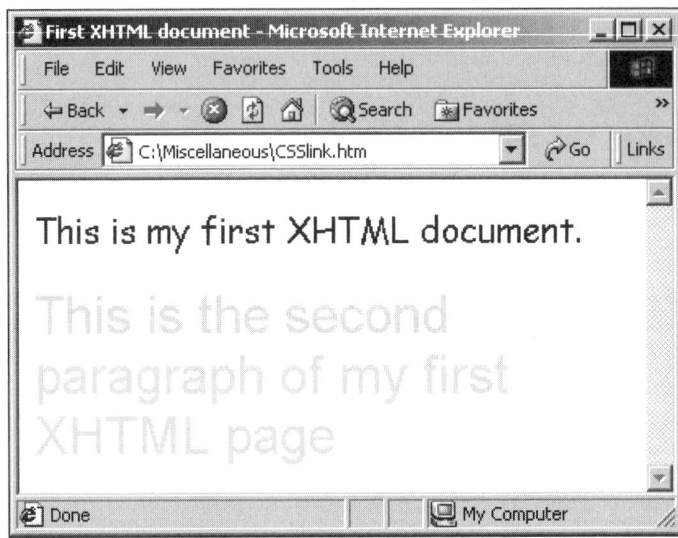

When we run this we get *exactly* the same result as with our second embedded example.

How It Works

The link element directs the browser where to find information. It contains three bits of information, and all three must be present if it is to work.

```
<link rel="stylesheet" type="text/css" href="css1.css" />
```

- The `rel` attribute tells the browser that this link is concerned with linking to a style sheet.
- The `type` attribute must be of the exact form shown here. It tells the browser that it is going to link to a CSS type of style sheet.
- And of course the `href` attribute tells the browser where to find our style sheet.
- Note that the style sheet does not contain the `<style>` tags. If these are contained in the style sheet most user-agents won't display the style information.

Cascading Style Sheets That Actually Cascade!

As previously mentioned, it is in fact possible to link a single document to multiple style sheets. This is where the ability of style sheets to 'cascade' comes in. All we have to do is provide a link element for each style sheet. If we have different style sheets, it often happens that they contain different styling instructions for the same element. Which style sheet then takes precedence? The rule is that the last style sheet shall take precedence over the others, embedded style sheets take precedence over external style sheets, and inline styling takes precedence over everything else. We will be going into this in some detail in chapter 9.

Summary

In this chapter we really sunk our teeth into the writing of an XHTML document. You now know enough to write a presentable text document. We first divided our documents according to style, structure and content. We started by examining the structure of an XHTML document, and via a simple exercise we saw how the parser will split the XHTML document up into a hierarchical tree structure. We then looked at some basic XHTML elements, and at most of their attributes, and we divided them up into descriptive elements and style elements. Then we started looking at the attributes of the basic XHTML elements and saw how those are divided up into different types of attribute, although we only looked at the universal and the now defunct presentational attributes in any detail.

Everything in XHTML is governed by the division of style and structure and a lot of the work in the XHTML standard has gone into undoing the previous mistakes of the HTML standards which considerably muddied these waters. However, while you shouldn't use the old style presentational attributes they are still supported by many browsers and we had to introduce them quickly. It is only since the introduction of style sheets (they first appeared in IE3) has it been possible to separate the style and structure. So at the end of the chapter we took a first excursion into the use of style sheets, as in the future, this is the way that everybody will be displaying style information.

We now only need to add links, images, and tables to our page, and we will have a very presentable page!

Remember that if you send an XHTML document as an XML document there will be no built in display semantics, and that you will have to supply a style sheet to tell the browser how to display the document.

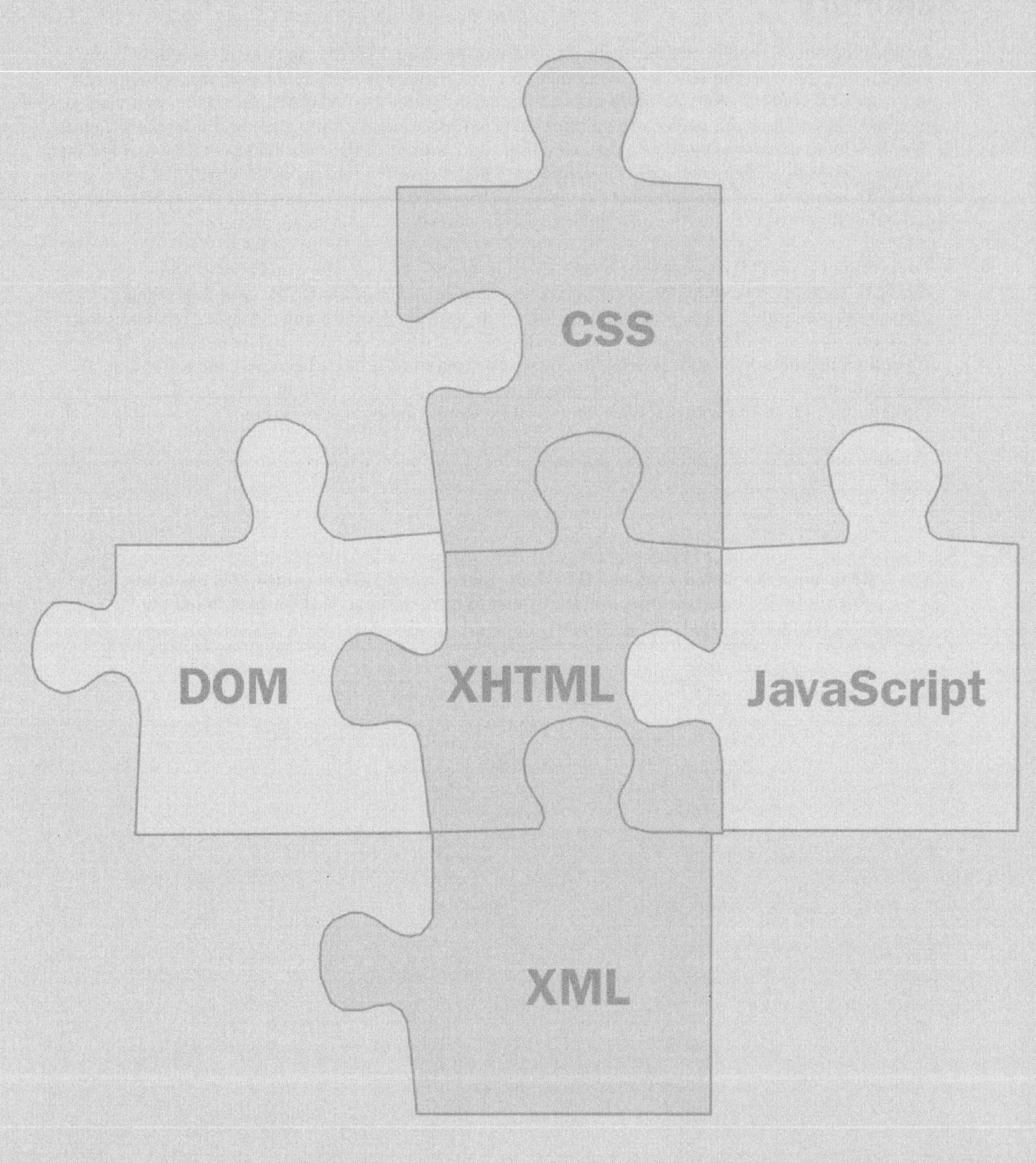
CSS
DOM
XHTML
JavaScript
XML

Links and Embedded Objects

Being able to link, or connect, one page on the Web with another is what makes the Web the great and navigable information source that it is. Not only can you 'jump' from one document to another, but you can jump from anywhere in one particular document to any position (top, middle, bottom, line 5, word 374, etc.) in any other document. To do this, of course, you must manually insert links at these places: doing so is incredibly easy, as we'll see in this chapter.

In this chapter we will cover:

- How to link one of your web pages with another of your web pages
- How to link one of your web pages with a page somewhere else on the Web
- How to link one of your web pages with any part of another page
- The different parts of a URL or **U**niform **R**esource **L**ocator (for example the `http` address)
- The `ftp` protocol and `mailto:`
- Applets and other embedded objects

Hypertext Links

I am sure that you are familiar with what a hypertext link is, either through direct experience or through our brief coverage in Chapter 1. It is a piece of text or an image that when clicked upon tells our browser to go either to a different place in a document, or to a different document altogether. This text is usually distinguished in some way from the surrounding text. The default in most browsers is a blue underlined text, but this is customizable by both the user and the web author. Once the link has been followed, the color of the link usually changes to a purple color, although again this can be changed.

Let's briefly look at some of the terminology we use when we talk about linking between pages.

When we click on a **hypertext link** (also known as a **hyperlink**, or just a **link**) we are said to **navigate** to a different **resource**. The link is what we click on. The user agent (your browser) looks for a **locator** or an **address**. The page where we click on the link and the page that we want to go to are both called **resources**. The page where the link is located is said to be the **source page**, the page that I want to **traverse** or **navigate** to is the **destination page**. Destination pages can be in various **locations**. Links can also **point** to places inside a document other than the top. When we use a link in this manner we are said to be using it as a **pointer**.

Page Locations

Destination pages can be in various different locations:

- They can be in the same folder or directory as the current page.
- They can be in different folders on the same server.
- They can be at a different address, in other words on an entirely different server.

We'll be looking at how we can use links in all of these cases, starting with the simplest – linking between files in the same directory. First, for those who may not be entirely sure about directories and folders, here's a brief refresher. If you're familiar with folders and directories, feel free to skip this section.

Computers inherit their file storage systems from the good old paper and filing cabinet days. A directory is the computer version of a filing cabinet drawer, and your sheets of paper are now called files. A filing cabinet drawer usually has cardboard folders suspended inside – in computer jargon, these are sub-directories. When a directory contains sub-directories, it is usually referred to as the main directory.

Unlike reality, though, a sub-directory can itself contain sub-directories – as can these 'sub-sub-directories', to coin a term. This is the advantage of a computer storage system. A traditional system can only have folders and pieces of paper in a filing cabinet drawer, but a computer can have as many filing cabinet drawers as it wants inside any particular drawer. Rather than refer to them all as sub-sub or sub-sub-sub, etc., we borrow more terminology from real life, namely the parent-child relationship.

Thus the main directory is called the ***parent*** *directory, and its sub-directory is referred to as a* ***child*** *directory. Obviously, these relationships can be extended to grandparent and grandchild directories, which can then all begin to get a bit confusing. The location of a particular directory on the computer is called a* ***path****. In a traditional system, this would just be the equivalent of saying "Open the drawer labeled* Employees, *suspended folder labeled* Wages, *and get me the notes on* Millennium Bonuses, *please." On a PC the computer path for this would be something like* `Employees\Wages\MillenniumBonuses.doc`*, which shows that the* `MilleniumBonuses.doc` *file is inside the* `Wages` *directory, which itself is inside the* `Employees` *directory.*

Note also that some computer systems use the term 'folders' instead of 'directories', but they are the same thing.

Let's now introduce the element XHTML uses to create links – the `<a>` element.

The <a> Element

The <a> element ('a' being short for **anchor**) is the element that XHTML uses to contain information about hypertext links. It can be used either as a link to another location or a marker for another link to point to, depending on the attributes it's given.

The <a> element accepts all the usual standard attributes, as well as the `href` attribute. This is the most important attribute when using the anchor tag as a link to another location. As for the standard attributes, we'll be looking at the use of `name` and `id` later on when we look at using the anchor tag as a destination.

The Anchor Tag as a Link Source

When you want to link from one place to another, as you've no doubt seen, you tend to have either a piece of text or an image that you click on. Around this text or image you place the <a> and </a> tags, using the `href` attribute to tell it where you want it to take you when you click on it. Like this:

```
<a href="address of web page you wish to link to">text to be clicked on</a>
```

The words text to be clicked on will appear in a different style (in IE5, the default style is underlined blue text); by clicking on this text, your browser will navigate to the web address contained in the opening anchor tag. You may not need to state the full address of the page, depending upon its location. We'll see how we navigate to pages in different locations in a moment.

Allowed Anchor Content

The anchor element can take any inline type of element as content, but cannot take a block element. So the following are all perfectly legal constructs:

```
<a href="someurl.htm">Click here</a>
<a href="someurl.htm"><b>Click here</b></a>
<a href="someurl.htm"><i>Click here</i></a>
<a href="someurl.htm"><img src="linkgif.gif" alt="Click here" /></a>
```

We will be looking at using an image as a source link later on in this chapter.

The following is *not* a legal construct:

```
<a href="someurl.htm"><h1>Click here</h1></a>
```

This should be used instead:

```
<h1><a href="someurl.htm">Click here</a></h1>
```

Note that you also cannot nest one <a> element within another.

Let's move on to look at navigating between files in various locations, also known as the issue of absolute and relative links.

Relative Links – Files in the Same Folder

There are two kinds of links we can have – **absolute** and **relative**. An absolute link is one that supplies the full specific address of the destination, rather like the address you'd put on a letter if you wanted to mail it overseas. A relative link is where you supply the information needed to get to the destination as it relates to your current position, much as you'd ask someone to drop off a note to Mrs. Roberts next door – first, you wouldn't have to put the full address on it, and secondly, if you made the same request when you were out of town, 'next door' would not mean the same house as it did when you were standing in your own kitchen at home.

Without any further ado, let's create two pages right now, place them in the same folder, and create a link between them. This will illustrate how to navigate between two files in the same folder.

Try it Out – Linking Between Pages

1. Go to your text editor of choice and type in the following:

```
<?xml version="1.0" encoding="UTF-8"?>
<!DOCTYPE html
     PUBLIC "-//W3C//DTD XHTML 1.0 Transitional//EN"
    "http://www.w3.org/TR/xhtml1/DTD/xhtml1-transitional.dtd">
<html xmlns="http://www.w3.org/1999/xhtml" xml:lang="en" lang="en">
  <head>
    <title>First hyperlink page</title>
  </head>
  <body>
    <p>This is page 1. It contains a link to <a href="page2.htm">page 2</a>.</p>
  </body>
</html>
```

2. Save this as `page1.htm`. Now use the 'save as' feature and save it as `page2.htm` in the same directory.

3. Make the following modifications to `page2.htm`:

```
<?xml version="1.0" encoding="UTF-8"?>
<!DOCTYPE html
     PUBLIC "-//W3C//DTD XHTML 1.0 Transitional //EN"
    "http://www.w3.org/TR/xhtml1/DTD/xhtml1- Transitional.dtd">
<html xmlns="http://www.w3.org/1999/xhtml" xml:lang="en" lang="en">
  <head>
    <title>Second hyperlink page</title>
  </head>
  <body>
    <p>This is page 2. It contains a link to <a href="page1.htm">page 1</a>.</p>
  </body>
</html>
```

4. Now run `page1.htm` in your browser. This is what you should see:

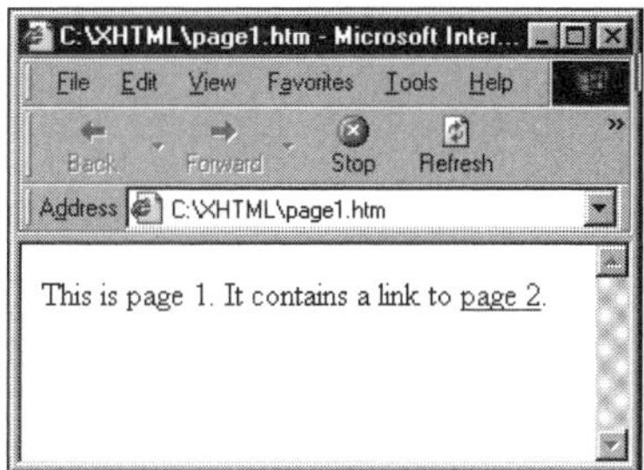

5. Click on the underlined text page2 and you will go to `page2.htm`. Click on the underlined text in that page (note that the color of the text is different, indicating that you've already been to the page it links to) and you will go back to `page1.htm` again. You can have many hours of harmless fun just going back and forth between these pages!

How It Works

As we've said, the `<a>` tag starts the anchor element. Notice how we've placed the `<a></a>` tags around the specific section of text we want to use as the link.

```
<p>This is page 1. It contains a link to <a href="page2.htm">page 2</a>.</p>
```

Most browsers display a 'fresh' link in underlined blue text, and then when the resource at the other end has been visited they change the color to a purple color – of course, this depends on whether your user has changed their preferences in their browser. You can also elect to use style sheets to make link colors and appearance match your page color scheme, and we'll see how to do that in Chapter 9.

When we click on the link the browser looks for the `href` attribute and reads its value. We've just supplied a filename, with no directory information, so the browser 'knows' that the file is in the same folder as the source page. It goes off to fetch the file, and if it finds this file, the browser loads and displays it. If the browser doesn't find the file, the browser displays an error message. I'm sure you've seen the dreaded Error 404, file not found... message several times in your browsing!

> *Note that the 404 error only occurs if you are browsing the Internet. If you are just browsing between files on your hard drive you may or may not see an error message.*

If the browser had to go out to the Internet to get the first file, then it will still have to go out to the Internet to get the second file. However it has the address of the first file stored in its memory, so all it does is work out the address of the second file from the address it has for the first file in order to retrieve it.

Let me put that another way. If I were driving to your house, you'd have to give me directions so I could get there. If it turned out that I also knew your next-door neighbor, when I wanted to visit him, I'd just go next door from your house. I wouldn't have to go home and call him to get him to tell me how to get to his house.

Relative Links – Files in Different Folders

To navigate between files in different folders we need to tell the browser how to get from the directory we're in to the directory our destination page is in. What we're going to do is create a directory structure which will let us navigate up and down between child and parent directories.

Try It Out – Navigating between Files in Different Folders

1. Somewhere on your machine, make a new directory called `examples`. It doesn't matter where you put this. In this directory, create a directory called `examp2`. Finally, in `examp2`, create `examp3`.

2. Now, type the following into your text editor of choice and name it `pagerel1.htm`. Save it in the `examples` folder.

```
<?xml version="1.0" encoding="UTF-8"?>
<!DOCTYPE html
     PUBLIC "-//W3C//DTD XHTML 1.0 Transitional //EN"
    "http://www.w3.org/TR/xhtml1/DTD/xhtml1-transitional.dtd">
<html xmlns="http://www.w3.org/1999/xhtml" xml:lang="en" lang="en">
    <title>First relative hyperlink page</title>
  </head>
  <body>
    <p>This is pagerel1.htm. It resides in the root folder.</p>
    <p> It contains a link to <a href="examp2/pagerel2.htm"> pagerel2.htm</a> in
    the examp2 folder and to <a href="examp2/examp3/pagerel3.htm">pagerel3.htm</a>
    in the examp3 folder</p>
  </body>
</html>
```

3. When you run it this is what you should see.

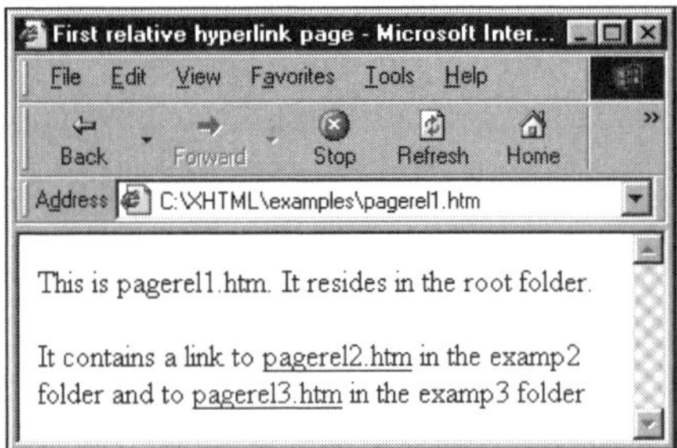

4. Now use the **Save As...** option twice. Call one of the files `pagerel2.htm` and place it in the `examp2` folder, and the other file `pagerel3.htm` and place it in the `examp3` folder.

5. Now make the following alterations to the body of `pagerel2.htm`:

```
<body>
  <p>This is pagerel2.htm. It resides in the root folder.</p>
  <p>It contains a link to <a href="../pagerel1.htm"> pagerel1.htm</a> in the
      examples folder and to <a href="examp3/pagerel3.htm">pagerel3.htm</a> in
      the examp3 folder</p>
</body>
```

6. Similarly, make alterations to the body of `pagerel3.htm`:

```
<body>
  <p>This is pagerel2.htm. It resides in the root folder.</p>
  <p> It contains a link to <a href="../../pagerel1.htm"> pagerel1.htm</a> in
  the examples folder and to <a href="../pagerel2.htm">pagerel2.htm</a> in the
      examp2 folder.</p>
</body>
```

7. Now run `pagerel1.htm` in your browser. Click on the links and you will see that your browser will navigate up and down the folders quite happily!

How It Works

Let's look first at `pagerel1.htm`. Here is the relevant line:

```
<p> It contains a link to <a href="examp2/pagerel2.htm"> pagerel2.htm</a> in
the examp2 folder and to <a href="examp2/examp3/pagerel3.htm">pagerel3.htm</a>
in the examp3 folder</p>
```

When we click on the first link, the browser goes to the anchor tag and finds the following attribute:

```
href="examp2/pagerel2.htm"
```

This tells the browser to navigate to the child folder of the current folder (the folder with `pagerel1.htm` in it), `examp2`, and find the file there called `pagerel2.htm`. Note that we must use forward slashes; not backslashes as are employed in Windows and DOS.

When we click on the second link, the browser goes to the anchor tag and finds the following:

```
href="examp2/examp3/pagerel3.htm"
```

This tells the browser to navigate to the child folder `examp2`, and then to navigate to the child folder of that folder (`examp3`) and to find there the file called `pagerel3.htm`. From this, you can hopefully see how you can go from one page to a page in a child directory. Now, let's see how to do the reverse – navigate to a page in a parent directory.

Some web servers have a setting to shut off parent folder navigation for security purposes. In such circumstances, parent (..) navigation CANNOT be used.

Let's look at `pagerel3.htm` in the `examp3` folder. Here's the relevant line:

```
<p> It contains a link to <a href="../../pagerel1.htm"> pagerel1.htm</a> in
the examples folder and to <a href="../pagerel2.htm">pagerel2.htm</a> in the
    examp2 folder.</p>
```

When we click on the second link the browser looks at the address and sees

```
href="../pagerel2.htm"
```

The two dots followed by a forward slash tell the browser that it has to go to the parent directory of the current directory and look there for the file `pagerel2.htm`.

Similarly when we click on the first link the browser sees the address:

```
href="../../pagerel1.htm"
```

This tells the browser that it has to go to the 'grandparent' folder of the current folder to find the file `pagerel1.htm`. It merely uses the address of the current file that it has stored in its memory to construct the address of the destination file.

Absolute Links – Files on Different Servers

We're now going to look at absolute links. When we want to get to a file that is on a different server (that is, a different computer) from the source file we have to give a full Internet address, like this:

```
http://www.hypermedic.com/style/index.htm
```

This address is called a URL or Uniform (sometimes Universal) Resource Locator.

The full anchor element would look like this:

```
<a href="http://www.hypermedic.com/style/index.htm">Frank Boumphrey's pages on
style</a>
```

Note also that

```
<a href="http://www.hypermedic.com/style ">Frank Boumphrey's pages on style</a>
```

will in most cases achieve the same result, as the server will supply a default page, often called `index.htm`, if no file name is given.

Case Sensitivity

If you are using a Microsoft operating system, and are testing links on your local hard drive, it doesn't matter what case you put the filename in. As far as the operating system is concerned, `Myfile.htm`, `myfile.htm`, and `MYFILE.HTM` are all the same file. This is not the case with files when they are put up on a UNIX-based server. Here, case is important. `MYFILE.HTM` is not the same as `myfile.htm`. If your link reads

```
<a href="http://www.somesite.com/myfile.htm">Click for myfile.htm</a>
```

and the file is stored on the server as `Myfile.htm` (note the uppercase M), then we will get an error message. It's best, then, to have some kind of system for naming your files, and always check your case!

URLs

Let's have a closer look at the parts that make up a full URL.

Parts of a URL

As you can see from the diagram above there are three basic parts to an URL

- The **protocol**. In this case, we're using the `http://` protocol. This is an essential part of the URL. We will look at some of the other protocols later on in this chapter.
- The **domain name**. This is the site on which the page is running. A site runs on a server, which has a unique number called an **IP address**. Most often, though, we use an alias for that number, a text name which is easier for us humans to remember, but which translates to an IP address. In my case it is `www.hypermedic.com`. I don't even know offhand what the number is, although I have it written down (somewhere...!)
- The **resource location**, or the location of the file on the server. One navigates to this in the manner we have already looked at above. Every domain has a root folder, and if you just type the domain name, e.g. `www.hypermedic.com`, you will arrive in the root folder of the site you're looking at. Usually, you'll be met with a default page.

Pointers: Using <a> as a Destination

The anchor element can act as a destination as well as a source. To do this, we employ the `name` or `id` attribute to label each individual anchor, so that we can point to a specific anchor by its label.

When we use the anchor element as a destination inside a document, we are said to **point** inside that document to that destination. The starting point (another anchor, the **source**) can either be in the same document or in another document.

Using the 'name' Attribute

On the destination anchor, we employ the `name` attribute and use the following syntax:

```
<a name="middle">Some text</a>
```

We can, if we wish, leave out the text when we are using the anchor element as a destination, so this is perfectly acceptable:

```
<a name="middle"></a>
```

Let's look at how we use the anchor element to point to this destination. When we use the anchor element to point to a place other than the top of a document we are said to be using it as a **pointer**.

Pointing to an Anchor

The general syntax for pointing to an anchor is as follows. The important thing to note here is the # sign separating the actual address from the destination anchor's name.

```
<a href="[address of document]#[name of anchor]">some text</a>
```

If we are pointing to a destination anchor in the same document we can leave out the address, so we'd use something like this:

```
Go to the<a href="#middle">middle</a> of the document.
```

This would take us to an anchor such as this:

```
<a name="middle"></a>
```

This, however, will only work in an HTML browser. It won't work in most XML-based user agents. To do this we have to use an `id` attribute as a destination.

Using the 'id' Attribute

This is actually the preferred way to point inside both HTML and XML documents. We've introduced it second because there's a little more to it – the way we've seen already is more straightforward.

As we saw in Chapter 3, an id attribute *must* have a unique value in the document. No other id attribute in the document can have the same value. The advantage of this is that in a large document our validating parser will tell us if we have a duplicate id, whereas if we have a duplicate name value, it will remain silent.

We still need to use the <a> element as our source element, but the cool thing is that we can use any element with an id attribute as our destination element. For example, using this as our source anchor:

```
The <a href="#h3_cl">church liturgy</a> in the middle ages.....
```

...we can jump to this location:

```
<h3 id="h3_cl">Church liturgy in the Middle Ages</h3>
```

Note that the id attribute is attached to the <h3> tag now, rather than using an <a> tag. This is a much cleaner way of pointing to a destination, but the problem is that older browsers do not support it. To overcome this problem we have to use a little trick. Remember that using name, we'd lose out on the support of newer user agents, and using id we lose out on older browsers. Given that we're working with XHTML, aiming for a newer audience would be the preferable way to lean if you had to choose. Anyway, here's the trick.

The source link is just the same:

```
The <a href="#h3_cl">church liturgy</a> in the middle ages.....
```

However, we now use both an id and a name in the destination.

```
<h3><a name="h3_cl" id="h3_cl">Church liturgy in the Middle Ages</a></h3>
```

You could also do this, although it is slightly harder to see what you're doing:

```
<h3 id="h3_cl"><a name="id_cl">Church liturgy in the Middle Ages</a></h3>
```

One of the most common uses of linking within a document is creating a hypertext table of contents, where you can jump from the top of a long document to specific places within that document. Let's see how we can do something like that.

Try It Out – Linking Within a Document

1. Enter the following in your text editor. Note the long paragraphs of text – I'll explain later, but this is simply to fill space and make the document large enough to scroll off the bottom of the page. Feel free to substitute any text you want in here, or you can copy and paste the text from lorem.txt (available with the downloadable code on our website).

```
<?xml version="1.0" encoding="UTF-8"?>
<!DOCTYPE html
     PUBLIC "-//W3C//DTD XHTML 1.0 Transitional//EN"
    "http://www.w3.org/TR/xhtml1/DTD/xhtml1-transitional.dtd">
<html xmlns="http://www.w3.org/1999/xhtml" xml:lang="en" lang="en">
<head>
<title></title>
</head>
<body>
<a name="index" id ="index"></a>
<h1 class="title">Church Liturgy throughout the ages</h1>

<div><a href="#cl_rom">Church Liturgy in Roman times</a></div>
<div><a href="#cl_dark">Church Liturgy in the Dark ages</a></div>
<div><a href="#cl_mid">Church Liturgy in the Middle ages</a></div>
<div><a href="#cl_ref">Church Liturgy in Age of Reformation</a></div>
<div><a href="#cl_mod">Church Liturgy in Modern times</a></div>

<h3><a id="cl_rom" name="cl_rom">Church Liturgy in Roman times</a></h3>

<p>"Lorem ipsum dolor sit amet, consectetaur adipisicing elit, sed do eiusmod
tempor incididunt ut labore et dolore magna aliqua. Ut enim ad minim veniam, quis
nostrud exercitation ullamco laboris nisi ut aliquip ex ea commodo consequat. Duis
aute irure dolor in reprehenderit in voluptate velit esse cillum dolore eu fugiat
nulla pariatur. Excepteur sint occaecat cupidatat non proident, sunt in culpa qui
officia deserunt mollit anim id est laborum Et harumd und lookum like Greek to me,
dereud facilis est er expedit distinct. Nam liber te conscient to factor tum poen
legum odioque civiuda. Et tam neque pecun modut est neque nonor et imper ned
libidig met, consectetur adipiscing elit, sed ut labore et dolore magna aliquam"
</p>
<div><a href="#index">Return to index</a></div>

<h3><a id="cl_dark" name="cl_dark">Church Liturgy in the Dark ages</a></h3>
<p>"Lorem ipsum dolor ....... dolore magna aliquam"
</p>
<div><a href="#index">Return to index</a></div>

<h3><a id="cl_mid" name="cl_mid">Church Liturgy in the Middle ages</a></h3>

<p>"Lorem ipsum dolor ....... dolore magna aliquam"
</p>
<div><a href="#index">Return to index</a></div>

<h3><a id="cl_ref" name="cl_ref">Church Liturgy in Age of Reformation</a></h3>

<p>"Lorem ipsum dolor ....... . dolore magna aliquam"
</p>
<div><a href="#index">Return to index</a></div>

<h3><a id="cl_mod" name="cl_mod">Church Liturgy in Modern times</a></h3>
<p>"Lorem ipsum dolor ....... dolore magna aliquam"
</p>
<div><a href="#index">Return to index</a></div>
</body>
</html>
```

2. Save this page as `internal.htm`. Now view the page in your browser. You should see the following:

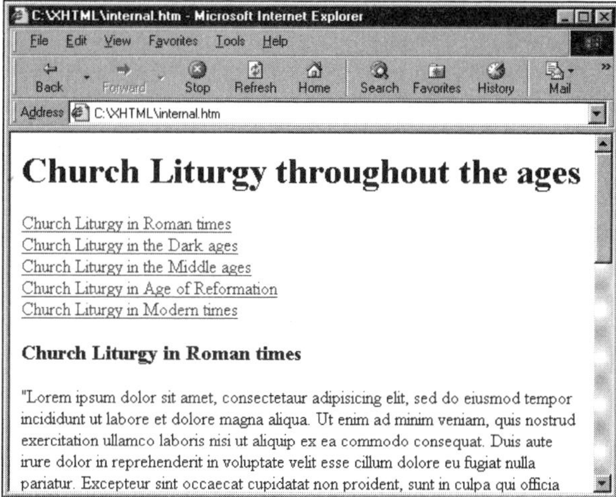

3. If you click on any of the links, you should be taken to the relevant link. Clicking on the Return to index link below each paragraph will take you back to the top.

How It Works

At the top of the document we are using the anchor element as a source. Note how we use the hash mark (#) to identify and point to the name or id of our destination.

```
<div><a href="#cl_rom">Church Liturgy in Roman times</a></div>
```

We've also used the trick we talked about earlier to make the links work in both old HTML browsers and newer XML agents:

```
<h3><a id="cl_rom" name="cl_rom">Church Liturgy in Roman times</a></h3>
```

Note how we've given each destination anchor element both an `id` and a `name` attribute of the same value.

To improve navigation within the document, at the end of each section we have provided a link back to the index. This also serves to show that pointers can work both backwards and forwards, and that a single destination can have several pointers to it.

You might be wondering now about all that Latin:

> *Lorem ipsum dolor sit amet, consectetaur adipisicing elit, sed do eiusmod tempor incididunt ut labore*

This is a piece of nonsensical Latin-like text that apparently originated in the 16th century. It was used by typographers when they wanted to get the overall appearance of a font without being distracted by the meaning. We can use it now to depict any block of text where the meaning is not important. There are several versions of lorem ipsum dolor. I got mine off a CompuServe bulletin board some years back! Every serious web designer needs a copy of this... seriously, though, it's useful to have a block of nonsense text so you can see what a page will look like without having to write the real text first.

Destinations in Other Files

We've seen how to link to other files already. You'll probably have noticed that each time, we were delivered to the top of the document in question. Now that we've seen how to point to various places inside the same document, you may be wondering if there's a way to combine these two techniques and point to the middle or bottom, say, of a separate document. You might have guessed from the syntax we showed above for linking to destination anchors that you can simply include both an address and a destination anchor name, like this:

```
<a href="[address of document]#[name of anchor]">some text</a>
```

Let's alter the above example to make our table of contents into a separate file.

Try It Out –Pointing to Locations in Another Document

1. Open up `internal.htm` and make the following changes:

```
<?xml version="1.0" encoding="UTF-8"?>
<!DOCTYPE html
     PUBLIC "-//W3C//DTD XHTML 1.0 Transitional //EN"
    "http://www.w3.org/TR/xhtml1/DTD/xhtml1-transitional.dtd">
<html xmlns="http://www.w3.org/1999/xhtml" xml:lang="en" lang="en">
<head>
<title>Church Liturgy throughout the ages </title>
</head>
<body>


<h3><a id="cl_rom" name="cl_rom">Church Liturgy in Roman times</a></h3>

<p>"Lorem ipsum dolor sit amet, consectetaur adipisicing elit, sed do eiusmod
tempor incididunt ut labore et dolore magna aliqua. Ut enim ad minim veniam, quis
nostrud exercitation ullamco laboris nisi ut aliquip ex ea commodo consequat. Duis
aute irure dolor in reprehenderit in voluptate velit esse cillum dolore eu fugiat
nulla pariatur. Excepteur sint occaecat cupidatat non proident, sunt in culpa qui
officia deserunt mollit anim id est laborum Et harumd und lookum like Greek to me,
dereud facilis est er expedit distinct. Nam liber te conscient to factor tum poen
legum odioque civiuda. Et tam neque pecun modut est neque nonor et imper ned
libidig met, consectetur adipiscing elit, sed ut labore et dolore magna aliquam"
</p>
<div><a href="index.htm#index">Return to index</a></div>
```

```
<h3><a id="cl_dark" name="cl_dark">Church Liturgy in the Dark ages</a></h3>
<p>"Lorem ipsum dolor ........ dolore magna aliquam"
</p>
<div><a href="index.htm#index">Return to index</a></div>

<h3><a id="cl_mid" name="cl_mid">Church Liturgy in the Middle ages</a></h3>

<p>"Lorem ipsum dolor ........ dolore magna aliquam"
</p>
<div><a href="index.htm#index">Return to index</a></div>

<h3><a id="cl_ref" name="cl_ref">Church Liturgy in Age of Reformation</a></h3>

<p>"Lorem ipsum dolor ....... . dolore magna aliquam"
</p>
<div><a href="index.htm#index">Return to index</a></div>

<h3><a id="cl_mod" name="cl_mod">Church Liturgy in Modern times</a></h3>
<p>"Lorem ipsum dolor ........ dolore magna aliquam"
</p>
<div><a href="index.htm#index">Return to index</a></div>
</body>
</html>
```

2. Save this page as `external.htm`. Now create a new page called `index.htm` in the same directory:

```
<?xml version="1.0" encoding="UTF-8"?>
<!DOCTYPE html
     PUBLIC "-//W3C//DTD XHTML 1.0 Transitional //EN"
    "http://www.w3.org/TR/xhtml1/DTD/xhtml1-transitional.dtd">
<html xmlns="http://www.w3.org/1999/xhtml" xml:lang="en" lang="en"><head>
<title></title>
</head>
<body>
<a name="index" id="index"></a>
<h1 class="title">Church Liturgy throughout the ages</h1>

<div><a href="external.htm#cl_rom">Church Liturgy in Roman times</a></div>
<div><a href="external.htm#cl_dark">Church Liturgy in the Dark ages</a></div>
<div><a href="external.htm#cl_mid">Church Liturgy in the Middle ages</a></div>
<div><a href="external.htm#cl_ref">Church Liturgy in Age of Reformation</a></div>
<div><a href="external.htm#cl_mod">Church Liturgy in Modern times</a></div>
</body>
</html>
```

3. Open `index.htm` in a browser. This is what you should see:

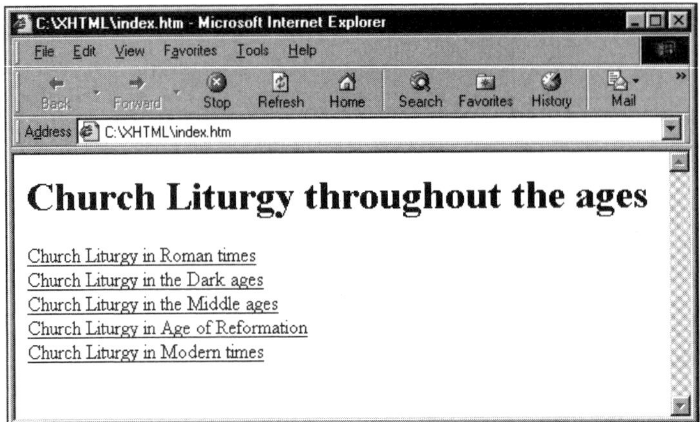

4. It should behave just as the original `internal.htm` page we wrote does, except this time we're linking to different points in a separate document. The Return to index links should take you back to the index page.

How It Works

You'll note that we've not changed our destination anchors at all, for example:

```
<h3><a id="cl_rom" name="cl_rom">Church Liturgy in Roman times</a></h3>
```

What we *have* done is to change the source anchors so that they include the filename of the page we want to link to:

```
<div><a href="external.htm#cl_rom">Church Liturgy in Roman times</a></div><br />
```

Note that we're using the relative address for our linked page, but we could also use a full absolute URL here. This brings up a good point – when should we use relative and absolute addresses?

In fact, there are pros and cons to using both approaches, and these will be discussed further in Chapter 8. We'll just introduce them briefly here, to give you a feel for what you should be doing.

Relative Addresses

If we design a site of several pages with paths relative to the document, all the addresses are said to be document-relative addresses.

There's another kind of relative address, called a root-relative address, which means that rather than expressing the address relative to the document (e.g. 'go up 2 directories, then across and down one'), we express it as relative to the root directory of the site the page is on. These addresses look like absolute addresses but don't specify the site address (e.g. `www.hypermedic.com`*).*

The advantage of a site that uses relative addresses is that if we move the complete site to a different server, all the hyperlinks are still good, since they don't include the name of the server in the address. As long as we've left the directory structure the same, relative links should work.

You should use relative links when you're linking to local pages on your own site.

Absolute Addresses

If we use absolute URLs in our local links, we have the problem that if we move our site to a different address we will have to change every single local link in our site. Even though there is software that will handle this task, it is still a pain.

With this in mind, by and large the preferred way to handle local links is to make them all relative links. You should obviously use absolute addresses for external links.

This brings us naturally to another concern of web masters every-where, and that is the subject of **link rot**.

Link Rot

When we construct our initial page we may make links to several other pages authored by people other than ourselves. Over the passage of time many of these URLs may go off the air, so our page is now left with 'bad' or 'broken' links. This process is known as link rot. To prevent link rot you can either manually test all your links on a regular basis, (and in spite of good intentions, human nature being what it is, this is unlikely to happen) or you can invest in a piece of software that does it for you!

We will examine this further in Chapter 11 when we discuss site design and maintenance.

Using Images as Source Links

As we saw above, the anchor element can take any inline element as content, and this means that we can use an image as a link. We'll be looking at images in the next chapter, but essentially all we do is place an image element inside the anchor element.

To do this we use the following general syntax:

```
<a href="[address]"><[image element] /></a>
```

As an example, here's what the code for a link to the Cormorant Internet Services pages would look like. Instead of putting text we have used a `.png` image (explained in Chapter 5) of their logo.

```
<a href="http://www.cormorant.com"><img src="images/corm4.png" /></a>
```

Here is what the image would look like in a browser window.

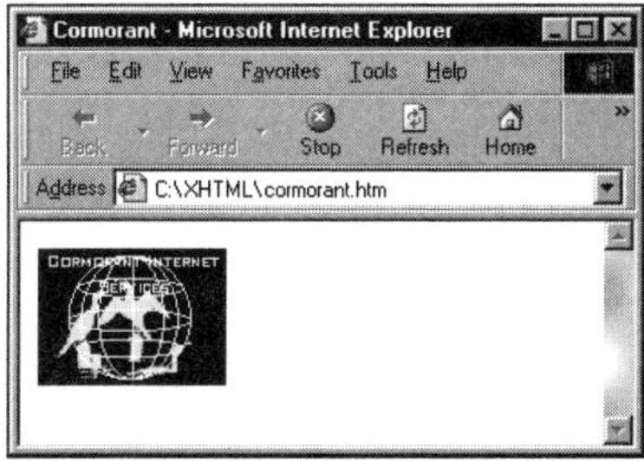

The image is surrounded by a blue border by default. We will see how to customize images that are to be used as source links in the next chapter.

Images and Logos as Links

We would insert a word of caution right now. Just because you *can* do something doesn't mean that you *should*! By and large it is probably not a good practice to use images as links unless it fits with a theme of a site. The following are legitimate uses of an image as a source link.

- The image is essential information. Thus clicking on a state or a country on a map may bring up information about that state.
- The logos are likely to be very familiar to the reader, and need no additional information to explain what is going on. Logos for IE5 or Netscape Communicator fall into this category.
- You are trying to 'brand' a logo.

Now, let's move on and look at other protocols that allow us to link to more than just web pages, specifically file downloads and e-mail.

Linking Using Different Protocols

So far we have been looking at linking using the `http` protocol. There are numerous other protocols for traversing the web (e.g. Gopher, WAIS, FTP etc.). Most of these need not concern us. However we will look at the `ftp` protocol and the `mailto` instruction in a little more detail, as we may want to incorporate both of these into our web pages.

The ftp Protocol

The File Transfer Protocol (or `ftp`), as the name suggests, is used for transferring files across the Internet. In the days before `http` this was probably the most widely used protocol after e-mail. It is still widely used. When you have finished writing your XHTML pages the chances are that you will upload them to a server using an ftp client. When you download the latest version of a browser, or the latest game from an Internet site, the chances are good that you will be using the `ftp` protocol. We can initiate the `ftp` protocol from our XHTML pages also, in which case the browser has its own ftp client.

Using ftp is simple. We use the `<a>` element just like we did to link to (X)HTML pages, but we specify an absolute address with `ftp://` as the protocol.

```
<a href="ftp://[address of folder or file]>download this</a>
```

Here is an example of a line that we would use if we wanted our page to access the `wrox.com` files.

```
Access files for download at the <a href="ftp://www.wrox.com">Wrox site.</a>
```

The mailto: Instruction

This is not a protocol, it is a way of calling up a mail client to send e-mail. A mail client is a program such as Microsoft Outlook Express that provides the interface for your user to compose and read e-mails. You may have met the `mailto:` instruction in your travels around the Web already – you click on a link labeled 'contact us' and up pops your client, with the destination e-mail address filled in for you.

Here is how we achieve this same effect:

```
<a href="mailto:frank@hypermedic.com">Mail to Frank</a>
```

Now when the reader clicks on the text Mail to Frank, on most browsers an e-mail client program will open up with the address `frank@hypermedic.com` already in the `To` bar.

Adding Additional Information to the E-Mail Form

In fact we can do much better than this! We can put in a subject line, a cc line, and even some default text. Let's try this out ourselves.

Try It Out – Filling in an E-mail Client

1. Type the following into your text editor and save it as `mailto.htm`:

```
<?xml version="1.0" encoding="UTF-8"?>
<!DOCTYPE html
     PUBLIC "-//W3C//DTD XHTML 1.0 Transitional //EN"
    "http://www.w3.org/TR/xhtml1/DTD/xhtml1-transitional.dtd">
<html xmlns="http://www.w3.org/1999/xhtml" xml:lang="en" lang="en">
  <head>
    <title>Mailto example</title>
  </head>
  <body>
    <a href="mailto:frankb@wrox.com?cc=frank@hypermedic.com&subject=a
    subject&body=enter data here">Mail to Frank</a>
  </body>
</html>
```

2. Now run it in your browser and click on the Mail to Frank text. This is what you see in IE5:

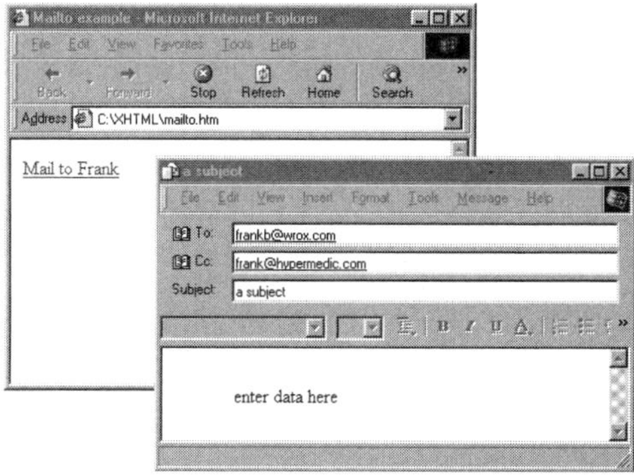

As you can see the title bar, subject bar and the cc bar have been filled in, as well as some default body text.

How It Works

The secret lies in what we put after the e-mail address:

```
<a href="mailto:frankb@wrox.com?cc=frank@hypermedic.com&subject=a subject&body=
        enter data here">Mail to Frank</a>
```

You can see that we have put a question mark, followed by a string of text. Everything after the question mark is called a query string, and is sent along to the mail client. Here is our query string.

```
cc=frank@hypermedic.com&subject=a subject&body=enter data here
```

What we have here are three **property/value pairs** separated by ampersands (&):

Property	Value
cc	frank@hypermedic.com
subject	a subject
body	enter data here

The mail client takes these values and reads them into the appropriate place in the mail form. This works for most mail clients, but there are a few that may not accept a query string.

Here is the preferred format for `mailto` links. Note that we provide the e-mail address as normal text in case the browser doesn't support `mailto`, or if the user wants to contact us another way.

```
<a href="mailto:frankb@hypermedic.com">Mail to Frank</a> at frankb@hypermedic.com
```

Other Connecting Elements

Although this chapter is about linking one web page to another, we should note that there are a variety of other items that we can link our page to:

- Using the `<link>` tag we can link to a style sheet, as we saw briefly in Chapter 3 – this will be covered more fully in Chapter 9. It can also be used for other purposes – see Chapter 11.
- The `<applet>` tag allows us to link to a Java applet from our web page. You don't have to be a Java programmer to take advantage of this facility, as many Java applets can be obtained free over the Web.
- Any object – such as a page of text, an image, a multimedia file or an ActiveX object – can be added to (or **embedded** in) your web page by use of the `<object>` element.

- JavaScript, or indeed any scripting language, may be embedded in your web page to provide some interaction between the page and the person viewing it, using the `<script>` element. We'll be introducing JavaScript properly in Chapter 16.

We have already seen the `link` tag in Chapter 3; we will look at applets and objects in this chapter.

Objects and Applets

One of the most powerful features of modern programming is that they can embed programs in other programs. This power is brought to a web page using the `<applet>` and `<object>` tag.

The `<applet>` tag allows a Java applet (kind of a mini-application) to be embedded in a web page, and the `<object>` tag can be used to embed any object in a web page, including an image, a sound file, a text file, or even another XHTML page. The `<object>` tag is only supported in IE4+ browsers.

The <applet> element

Java is a full programming language introduced by Sun Microsystems. The chief advantage of Java is that it can run on a wide range of platforms. Java applets can also be embedded in a web page by using the `<applet>` element.

We are not going to tell you how to write Java, that is a full book in its own right (if you're interested in Java, may we suggest Beginning Java 2, by Wrox Press, ISBN 1861002238), but we will look at how to embed a Java applet in our web page.

The `<applet>` element was deprecated in HTML 4.0, but it has just proven too useful, and appears untouched in XHTML 1.0. It is doubtful that it will ever be deprecated again! Applets are supported in N2+ and IE3+ browsers.

Applets can be had for free from many websites. A good place to start your search for applets is `http://java.sun.com/applets/`. We are going to have a look at the clock applet that can be downloaded from `http://java.sun.com/openstudio/applets/clock.html`.

The `<applet>` element takes a few attributes, notably `codebase`, `code`, `width`, and `height`. The `codebase` attribute contains the path to the Java **class** file containing the applet, and the `code` attribute contains the name of this file. The `height` and `width` attributes determine the size of the embedded applet on the screen.

Applets also may contain `<param>` elements which pass additional information to the applet, determining various parameters. `<param>` elements take name and value attributes, and you use a separate `<param>` element for each parameter you want to supply.

Try It Out – Running an Applet

1. Create a new directory on your machine and call it something like `applets`. Download the applets file from `http://java.sun.com/openstudio/applets/clock.html`.

2. This applet is included in a zip file with several others. Unzip the file it into the new folder you created. The unzip process should have created its own directory structure within your `applets` directory that looks something like this:

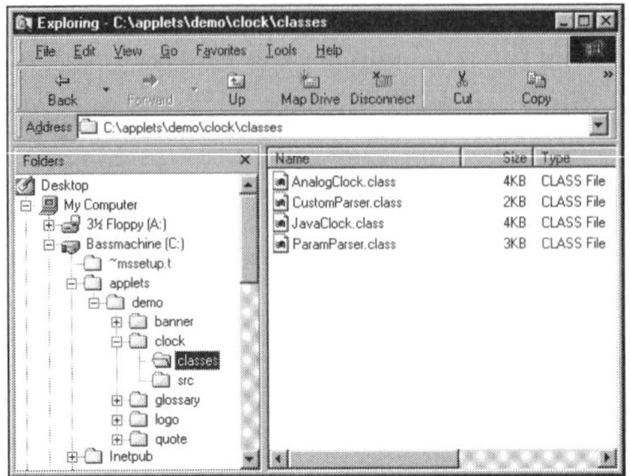

3. Type up the following file, and save it as `clockapplet.htm` in the same folder as you created to put the applet.

```
<?xml version="1.0" encoding="UTF-8"?>
<!DOCTYPE html
     PUBLIC "-//W3C//DTD XHTML 1.0 Transitional //EN"
    "http://www.w3.org/TR/xhtml1/DTD/xhtml1-transitional.dtd">
<html xmlns="http://www.w3.org/1999/xhtml" xml:lang="en" lang="en">
  <head>
    <title>Clock Applet example</title>
  </head>
  <body>
  <h3>The Clock Applet example</h3>
    <applet codebase="demo/clock/classes/" code="JavaClock.class" width="250"
    height="250">
      <param name="bgcolor" value="ff0000" />
      <param name="border" value="20" />
      <param name="ccolor" value="ffff00" />
      <param name="cfont" value="Arial|BOLD|18" />
      <param name="nradius" value="85" />
   </applet>
  </body>
</html>
```

4. This is what you should see when you view the page in a browser:

Here is an analog clock which shows the client's time! Do note that these applets may take a little time to load, and so will slow down the loading of your page to varying degrees depending on the size of the applet.

How It Works

The following line of code announces to our browser that we are dealing with an applet. The `codebase` attribute is the URL path that directs our browser to the folder where we have stored our Java applet, and the `code` attribute is the class that the browser must actually run.

```
<applet codebase="demo/clock/classes/" code="JavaClock.class" width="250"
height="250">
```

Note that the `classes` folder should contain all the Java classes that are necessary to run the applet.

Next follow a set of `<param>` elements list of parameters that we can set for the applet. If we don't set a particular parameter, the applet will use a default value. Here are the parameters this particular applet takes:

```
<param name="bgcolor" value="ff0000" />
```

This is the background color represented as a hexadecimal number.

```
<param name="border" value="20" />
```

This parameter determines the distance between the clock and the border.

```
<param name="ccolor" value="ffff00" />
```

Here we set the clock's face color, again as a hexadecimal number.

```
<param name="cfont" value="Arial|BOLD|18" />
```

This sets the details of the font to use for the clock's numbers.

```
<param name="nradius" value="85" />
```

Finally, this sets the radius of the clock in pixels. We remember to close the `<applet>` element:

```
</applet>
```

It is important to note that the parameters vary from applet to applet, and in fact the author of the applet should provide us with a list of all the allowable parameters. For more about applets visit `http://java.sun.com/applets/`.

The <object> Element

The `<object>` element was HTML's vision of a universal element whereby any object could be embedded in a page. An object could be an image, a multimedia file or even an ActiveX object. The `<object>` tag takes the `data` attribute, which specifies the file the object comes from.

Let's look at a couple of examples. First, here is an example of how to embed a text file in a page.

Try It Out – Embedding a Text File in a Page

1. Type up the following in your favorite text editor.

```
<?xml version="1.0" encoding="UTF-8"?>
<!DOCTYPE html
     PUBLIC "-//W3C//DTD XHTML 1.0 Transitional //EN"
    "http://www.w3.org/TR/xhtml1/DTD/xhtml1-transitional.dtd">
<html xmlns="http://www.w3.org/1999/xhtml" xml:lang="en" lang="en">
  <head>
    <title> Embedding a text object </title>
  </head>
  <body>
    <h2>Embedding a text object</h2>
    <object data="Lorem.txt" height="250" width="400" />
  </body>
</html>
```

2. Save this as `element_object.htm`.

3. Now put a copy of the 'lorem ipse' text in a text file called `lorem.txt` in the same directory as this file.

4. Run this in IE4 or 5. This is what you will see.

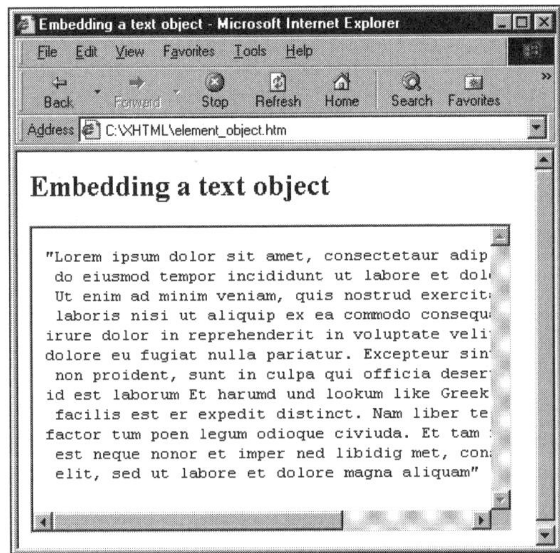

In fact, you'll probably find that instead of the text wrapping, you get one long line. OK, so we cheated a little by putting line breaks in the middle of our paragraph....

How It Works

The `<object>` tag is used to embed any object in an XHTML document. Just like the `<applet>` tag, it has `height` and `width` attributes, to define the size of the embedded object. But it uses the `data` attribute to tell it where to get the object:

```
<object data="Lorem.txt" height="250" width="400" />
```

It is important that a display area is supplied for the document. The height and width attributes lay out the dimensions of the display area. If as in this case the display area is not large enough, scroll bars are provided.

Now let's see how using the object element can be used to embed another XHTML page in our page.

Embedding Another Page

In fact what we are planning to do is embed the XHTML page from the applet example above in a new XHTML page. We can simply alter the XHTML file from the last example:

```
<?xml version="1.0" encoding="UTF-8"?>
<!DOCTYPE html
     PUBLIC "-//W3C//DTD XHTML 1.0 Transitional//EN"
    "http://www.w3.org/TR/xhtml1/DTD/xhtml1-transitional.dtd">
<html xmlns="http://www.w3.org/1999/xhtml" xml:lang="en" lang="en">
  <head>
    <title>Clock Applet example</title>
  </head>
  <body>
  <h3>The Clock Applet example page embedded!</h3>
  <object data="clockapplet.htm" type="text/html" width="350" height="350">
    Could not display clockapplet.htm
  </object>
  </body>
</html>
```

If we did this, we'd see this when we ran the page:

Note how the XHTML page `clockapplet.htm` is displayed in the space we have provided for it, and how as we have not provided quite enough vertical space, a scroll bar appears! Here we use the object tag with a `data` attribute that gives the address of the page that we wish to embed in our current page. The `type` attribute, which we also haven't seen before, gives the MIME type of the object that we want to embed.

```
<object data="clockapplet.htm" type="text/html" width="350" height="350">
```

The text between the `<object></object>` tags is in fact text that will be displayed if the page is shown in a browser that does not support the `<object>` element, which includes all current Netscape browsers.

```
      Could not display clockapplet.htm
   </object>
```

Summary

We saw in this chapter how to link one web page with another by use of the `<a>` tag, and saw the various ways of doing it depending on whether the destination page was on the same or a different server (machine) as the source page. As part of that discussion, we also looked at the various parts of a URL (Uniform Resource Locator) and at the tag attributes `name` and `id`, and how to point into any part of a document. We then looked at the advantages and disadvantages of relative and absolute addresses, and the situations where one would use one over the other. A look at the different protocols available and an introduction to embedding objects closed the discussion.

During our discussion of the `<a>` tag we briefly mentioned that we could use an image as the content, rather than text, to be clicked on to take us to another document; the next chapter discusses how to use images in your web page much more fully.

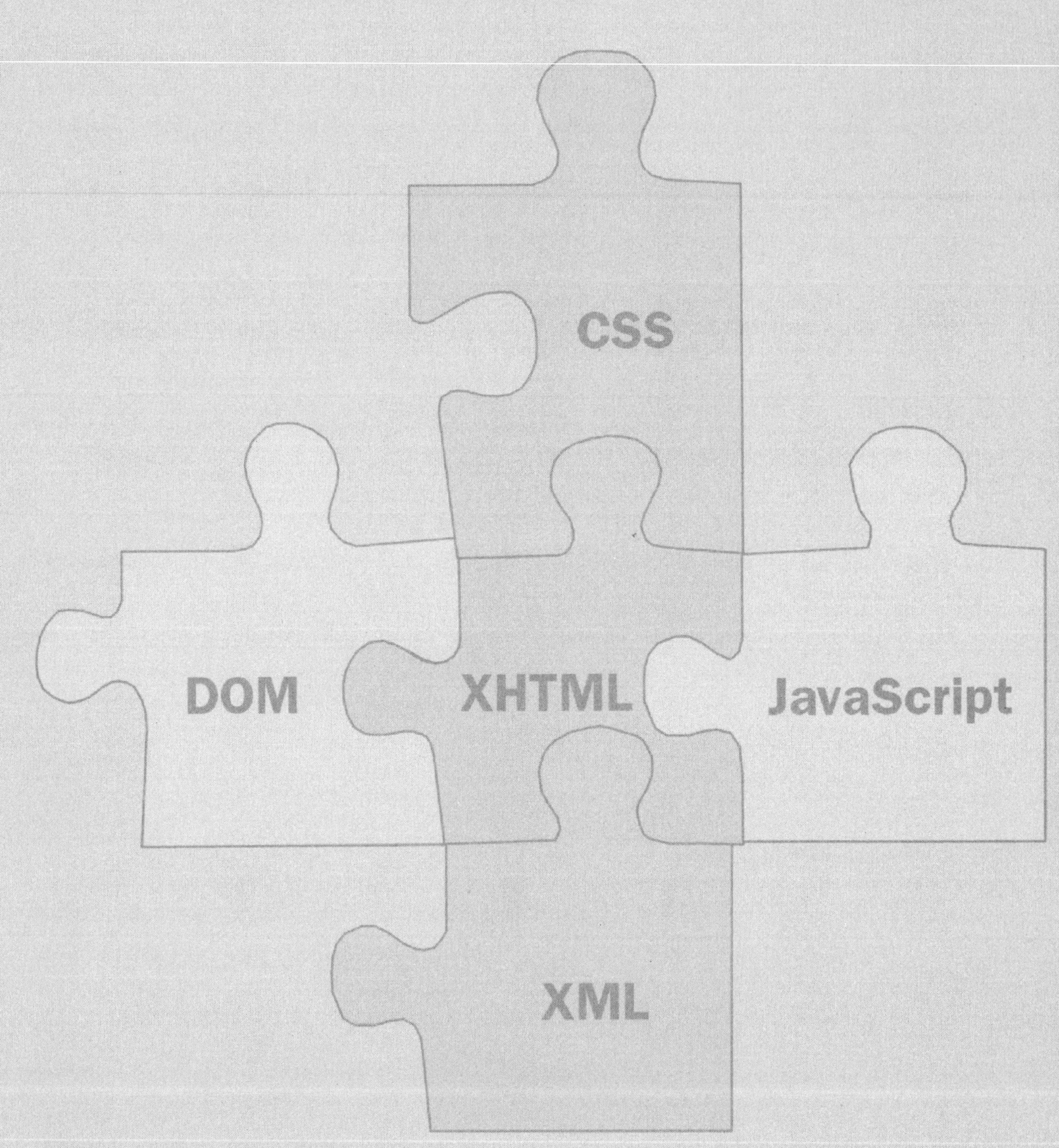
CSS
DOM
XHTML
JavaScript
XML

Images

To date we have just looked at how to add simple flow objects to a page, and how to link between various pages. If you have done any web browsing at all you will notice that a large part of web design concerns images. In this chapter we are going to look at how to embed images into our pages, and we will also look at some of the general principles behind the use of images. We will not be looking at the design aspect of images as that is beyond the scope of this book. However, at the end of this chapter, we have URLs for image manipulation packages, many of which have their own design advice and tutorials.

We will, of necessity, have to talk about styling issues and style sheets a little in this chapter, as it is almost impossible to have a discussion of images without mentioning style. We have in several places used the 'style' attribute without a full discussion of the style properties. For the most part their meaning is intuitive, where it is not the reader should refer to Chapter 9 or Appendix D.

It should be emphasized that to add images to an XHTML page we are relying on the built-in semantics of the HTML browser. If the XHTML page is delivered with the XML mime, no images will appear unless further instructions are given to the browser.

At the end of this chapter you will have a good idea as to how to add an image to your page, and how to optimize an image for fast download. We will cover:

- What an image is
- Adding images to the pages
- The different types of images used on the World Wide Web
- The difference between a bit mapped and a vector image
- Optimizing images for download speed
- Image maps
- Best practices and tips
- Further resources

It is actually simplicity itself to add an image to an XHTML page. Placing the image exactly where you want it and making it look good takes a bit more work!

Bitmap and Vector Graphics

Where "clothes make the man", images often make the web page. Images are used to make buttons, bullets, logos, and banners. Images can be simple decoration, or they can be at the heart of what you are trying to say.

When you see one of these images on a web page, what you are actually seeing is a bunch of dots, called **pixels**. Your eyes see all of these pixels and, since they are small, your brain combines them into a coherent picture. Since we need to store these images on computers and send them over the Internet, we need a file format to describe these images. An image format is the way in which these pixels are described in a computer file

There are two types of computer graphics on the web – **bitmaps** and **vectors**. The most popular web image file formats are GIF, JPEG, and PNG; all of these are bitmap graphic formats. There have been many competing web vector graphic formats, but none have been widely adopted. The forthcoming emergence of the W3C Scalable Vector Graphics (SVG) standard hopes to change this; we talk about SVG near the end of this chapter.

Bitmaps

Bitmap graphics have information about each pixel stored in the file. Take a look at the "silly head" image below.

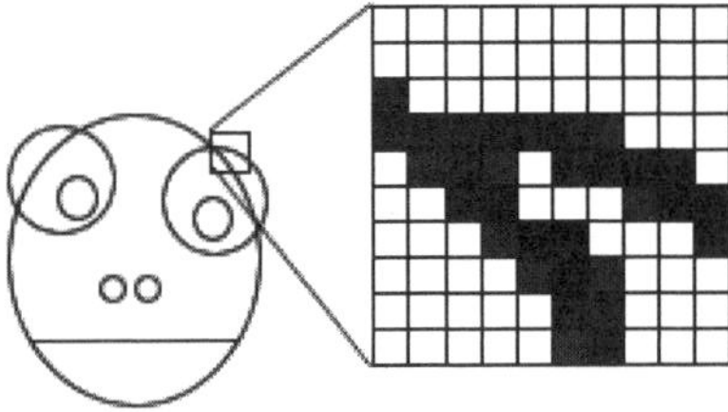

If you zoom into the square region near the right eye, you can see that the image is actually composed of five different color pixels: white, black, and three shades of gray.

A bitmap graphic might store these pixels by assigning a value to each color. For the sake of our "silly head" lets assign the value "0" for white, "4" for black, and "1", "2", and "3" for light gray, medium gray, and dark gray (respectively). This is a simplification, of course, since most bitmaps have many more colors!

The bitmap file for this image (or this portion of the image) might then be stored as:

```
0000000000
0000000000
4000000000
4444321000
0342034320
0024000144
0001420002
0000141000
0000043000
0000014000
```

One benefit to bitmaps is that they are generally easy for a browser to display. The browser simply reads each bit of data in the image file and draws a pixel accordingly. Bitmaps also tend to be very good for continuous tone images such as photographs or artwork with soft or blurry edges.

One disadvantage of bitmaps is that a large bitmap will take up more memory than a small bitmap that has the same number of colors. This also means that the large bitmap will take longer to download than the small bitmap. We will talk about downloading bitmaps later in this chapter.

Another problem with bitmaps is that if you try to scale the bitmap (make it larger or smaller) what appeared as a straight line or a smooth curve may suddenly appear jagged or have breaks. This is because the bitmap does not really know anything about "lines" or "curves", it only knows about pixels. Some smart algorithms may improve the appearance of scaled bitmaps, but, in general, line-oriented art will suffer. In many cases, you will be better off using vector graphics for this type of image.

Vector Graphics

Vector graphics do not store information about each pixel in the image. Rather, vector graphics store mathematical equations that describe how to redraw the image. In essence, vector graphic files contain a collection of lines, curves, and splines that are combined to draw the image.

If you look back at our "silly head" bitmap, you can see that the image is composed of eight shapes: six circles, one oval, and one line. Therefore, the image can be stored in the file as a sequence of these shapes:

```
oval(0, 0, 82, 75) - the face
circle(0, 3, 31)   - the outer left eye
circle(14, 17, 13) - the inner left eye
circle(44, 9, 31)  - the outer right eye
circle(53, 23, 13) - the inner right eye
circle(26, 45, 8)  - the left nostril
circle(36, 45, 8)  - the right nostril
line(7, 64, 60, 0) - the mouth
```

Vector graphics are resolution independent. This means that the image can scale larger and smaller without *significantly* impacting on the size of the file. In addition, this means that the image can scale without impacting on the quality of the image that the user sees. As mentioned before, when you try and scale a bitmap graphic, you will often see a poorer quality image.

One disadvantage of vector graphics is that they are not very good at irregular images – things that can't be easily described by a line or a circle. While vector graphics are great for line art and illustrations, they are generally inappropriate for photographs and blurry images. Bitmaps are a better solution for these types of images.

One of the key features of both bitmap and vector graphics is that their file formats attempt to reduce the amount of memory required to store and send the image on the Internet. This is accomplished through the use of compression technologies.

Lossless and Lossy Compression

It is very important that web-based graphic file formats keep the file sizes as small as possible. This is because it costs money and time to move images around the Internet. If it takes too long to load an image used on a web page, many users will simply click to another web page. It does not matter how great your web page looks if it takes so long that nobody uses it!

One of the biggest differences between image formats is in the way in which they reduce the size of their files – in other words, the type of image compression that they use. There are two main types of compression:

- **Lossless compression** means that even when the graphic file is compressed, the image will not lose any quality. In most cases, vector graphics employ lossless compression. The GIF and PNG file formats also use lossless compression.
- **Lossy compression** means that information is lost when the graphic file is compressed. In most cases, the algorithm is smart enough to remove information that is not visible to the viewer. The JPEG file format uses lossy compression.

File Formats

There is a wide variety of graphics on the web, but most of the graphics use one of three formats:

- GIF
- JPEG
- PNG

In fact, the vast majority of graphics use GIF and JPEG, but the recent emergence of PNG as a World Wide Web Consortium standard promises to make it an important graphic format.

The Graphics Interchange Format, or GIF, was developed by the CompuServe in the late 1980s to store graphics used over its network. The Joint Picture Experts Group graphic file format, or JPEG (pronounced "jay-peg"), was developed for storing photographs. The Portable Network Graphics format, or PNG (pronounced "ping"), was developed as a patent-free replacement for the GIF format.

GIF File Format

The GIF file format was designed specifically for delivery of graphics over online networks. GIF uses a compression scheme called **LZW**, named after the inventors Lempel-Ziv & Welch.

CompuServe initially released the GIF standard in 1987 as **GIF87a**. The standard was subsequently updated in 1989 and 1990 as **GIF89a**. Pretty much any web browser that supports the basic GIF format will support any of these standards. In other words, you don't need to worry about what version of GIF you are using! These file formats are native MIME (Multimedia Internet Mail Extensions) types in most browsers, including Netscape Navigator and Microsoft Internet Explorer.

The GIF file format can support 8-bit color. 8-bit color means that a GIF image can contain 2^8, or 256 colors. In contrast, a JPEG image can contain 2^{24}, or over 16 million colors – you will learn about JPEG images following this section. In order to optimize the quality of your GIF images, you will need to define what colors are in your 256 color palette (this is usually not difficult since it is often done automatically by your graphics tool).

GIF compression is lossless. As you learned earlier, lossless compression means that the GIF compression algorithm will not cause a loss in image quality when the image is compressed. Having said this, there will be a loss in image quality if you start from a 16 million color image and compress it to 256 colors!

There are three special types of GIF images:

- **Transparent** GIFs
- **Interlaced** GIFs
- **Animated** GIFs

Let's look at these three types of GIF images in more detail.

Transparent GIFs

The GIF89a specification provides you with a way to make images that are not rectangles, such as triangles, circles, and irregular shapes.

The way that you do this is to select one color to be the "transparent" color. When you draw your image, anywhere that the transparent color is drawn, the color underneath will show through. Normally, you will select the background color in your graphic to be the transparent color:

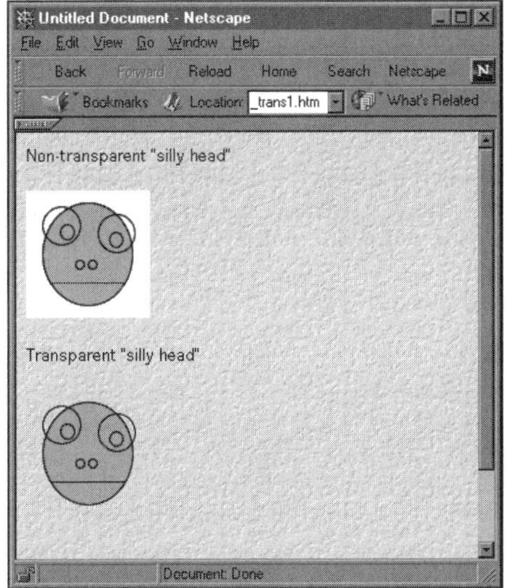

There are two principal advantages to using transparent GIFs. First, you can create images that appear to float above your web page. Second, you can create images that are not square. Both of these advantages are very important when you are designing your web page. There are so many rectangles in the web browsing experience (your browser, frames, buttons, input fields, etc.) that anything that can break away from this visual "prison" is quite useful.

We will talk about *using* transparency later in this chapter.

Animated GIFs

The GIF89a format provides you with a way to combine a collection of GIF images into a single file and then play back each image in sequence, one at a time, to create simple slide shows. If you play back the slide show quickly, the images can look like an animation.

Each image in the GIF file is called a frame. Each frame can have a custom color palette, different play back speed, transparency, and other GIF features. The animation can play back once, play back repeatedly (the animation starts over once it has ended), or repeat a specified number of times.

Here is an example of an animated GIF that has 9 frames:

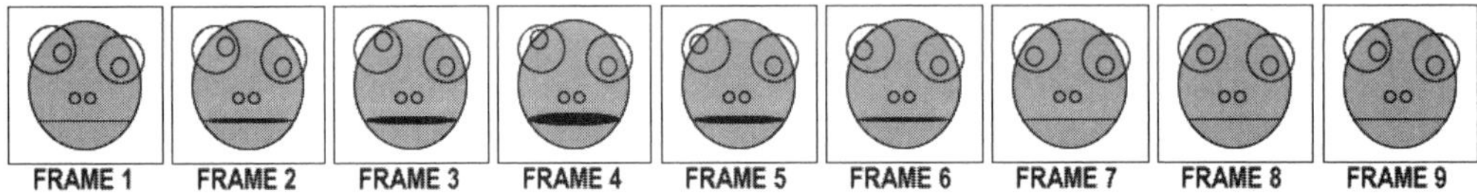

As you can probably see, our silly head's left eye rotates counter-clockwise and the mouth opens and closes.

We will talk about *using* animation later in this chapter.

Interlaced GIFs

You have probably visited web sites in which an image seems blurry and then incrementally appears less blurry until the image is finally in focus. These images are examples of interlaced GIFs.

Conventional GIF images store images one line at a time, from top to bottom. This means that as a web browser draws the image, it will draw the image one line at a time, from top-to-bottom.

With interlaced GIF images, non-adjacent lines are stored together. This means that as the image is decoded, pixels from all over the image can be drawn, rather than drawing the image one line at a time.

Interlaced GIFs provides users with a way of getting a rough sense of your image without having to wait for the entire image to be displayed. In addition, many people find the blurry-to-sharp transitions visually appealing.

Unfortunately, interlacing often makes text in an image unreadable until the entire image is rendered, making interlaced GIFs useless for small graphics or graphics that contain a lot of text (such as navigation bars and buttons). Interlacing is more appropriate for larger images (such as illustrations) and especially images that do not contain text (such as photographs).

A better file format for photographs is the JPEG file format, which we discuss next.

JPEG File Format

The Joint Picture Experts Group designed the JPEG file format specifically for storing photographs and photograph-like images. The JPEG file format stores color information using 24 bits per pixel; this means that a JPEG image can contain more than 16.7 million colors.

The JPEG compression scheme uses perceptual coding techniques. This means that the JPEG compression scheme tends to remove information in the higher color frequencies, colors that are harder for the human eye to perceive differences.

JPEG uses a lossy compression scheme, which means that some information is lost in order to reduce the size of the image file. A mathematical technique called discrete cosine transformation is used which allows you to choose how much compression you want to apply to your image. This flexibility is usually built into your graphics tool and it allows you to trade off the size of the file for the quality of the final image.

Let's look at a portion of a photograph:

Let's zoom in on the little boy's face and compare the original image with the image after it has gone through JPEG compression at 50%:

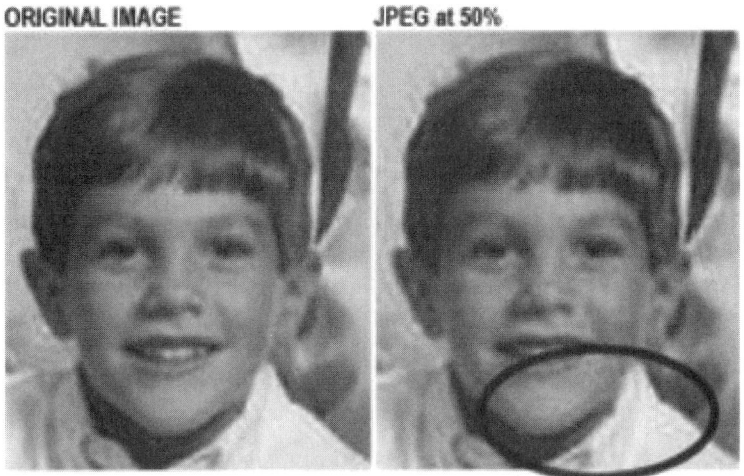

If you look carefully at the chin area of the little boy, you will see a checkerboard pattern. These are called compression artifacts and are typical of JPEG images.

Artifacts aside, JPEG is still the best mass-market compression scheme for photographs. You just need to carefully balance the size of the image with the quality of the image.

Progressive JPEG

The newer progressive JPEG, or p-JPEG file format provides you with a way of creating photographic images which start out blurry and then come progressively into focus. A p-JPEG image is stored much the same as a interlaced GIF image: the image is stored as a series of scans that together make up the entire image.

Some older web browsers do not support p-JPEG images, so you should use them with caution: make sure your users either have support for these images or that they are willing to suffer the dreaded "broken image link" icon!

While GIF and JPEG are quite established graphic file formats, a new file format called PNG has begun taking the Web by storm.

PNG File Format

The World Wide Web Consortium endorsed the PNG file format as a non-proprietary (and royalty-free) alternative to the GIF file format. As mention previously, the GIF file format was developed by CompuServe based on the LZW algorithm. The LZW algorithm is owned by the Unisys Corporation and, subsequently, Unisys charges licensing and royalty fees to any graphics tool developer that makes software that can save a file in the GIF file format.

The PNG file format was developed to replace the GIF file format and provide many of the capabilities found in some older graphic file formats. These features include:

- True color, indexed color, and grayscale image support
- Alpha channel transparency
- Gamma correction

As with the GIF file format, the PNG file format uses a lossless compression scheme. This means that no information is lost and quality does not suffer.

Unlike GIF (and JPEG, for that matter), PNG can be stored at different bit depths. As explained earlier, GIF files are stored only at 8-bit or lower bit depths and JPEG files are only stored at 24-bit bit depths. The PNG file format allows you to choose between one of three bit depths:

- 8-bit color
- 24-bit color
- 32-bit color

The higher the bit depth, the greater the color fidelity and the larger the file size.

In addition to providing flexibility with the bit depths, the PNG file format provides variable transparency. If you remember our previous discussion on transparent GIFs, with the GIF file format, you chose a single color and that color became transparent in the image. This meant that for any pixel, it was either transparent or it was not.

The PNG file format supports variable transparency through an **alpha channel**. The alpha channel is 8 bits that can be used to control up to 256 levels of partial transparency.

While the PNG file format is very powerful and flexible, its support in web browser is still patchy. While most of the newer browsers support the PNG file format, they may not support all of the PNG features. Be careful using PNG files if many of your users still have older browsers.

The <img> Element

An image is added to the page using an 'image' (`<img>`) element. This is an **empty**, **inline** element that has two required attributes, `src` and `alt`. The `src` attribute gives the address of the image to be loaded, and the `alt` takes a string value that is displayed if for any reason the graphic file cannot be displayed. Although as we noted, the HTML browsers will let us get away with leaving out the `alt` attribute, this is not recommended because not only do many people browse with graphics turned off, but it will make your pages meaningless on non-graphic user-agents, and to sight impaired individuals.

Here is the general syntax for using the `<img>` element:

```
<img src="[address or path to image]" alt="some descriptive text" />
```

The `alt` attribute is required, and although most browsers let you get away with omitting it, you never should. It is very important for the visually impaired, and for pages that are going to be shown on non-visual media; omitting it may result in navigational difficulties within the page.

Let's look right away at how to add an image to a page.

Try It Out – Adding an Image to a Page

1. We will add an image of the Mona Lisa to a page. This image can be downloaded from the Wrox site along with all the code from this book. (Remember to save the picture in the same directory as the following code, otherwise you'll have to fill in the full path to where you've saved the `img src`.) Type the following in a text editor:

```
<?xml version="1.0" encoding="UTF-8"?>
<!DOCTYPE html
     PUBLIC "-//W3C//DTD XHTML 1.0 Transitional//EN"
     "http://www.w3.org/TR/xhtml1/DTD/xhtml1-transitional.dtd">
<html xmlns="http://www.w3.org/1999/xhtml" xml:lang="en" lang="en">
<head>
  <title>Background Image</title>
</head>
<body bgcolor="#666633">
  <div style="text-align:center;"><img src="../pictures/monalisa_sm2.jpg"
alt="Mona Lisa" /></div>
</body>
</html>
```

2. Save the file as `monalisa.html` and run it in your browser. This is what you will see:

How It Works

First of all, note the line that embeds our image in the page:

```
<img src="../pictures/monalisa_sm2.jpg" alt="Mona Lisa" />
```

...which imports the image into our browser. I am using a relative path here, my 'html' file is in an '`examples`' folder, which is a sub-folder of the '`ch5`' folder, as is the '`pictures`' folder. The double-period at the beginning of the path in the `src` attribute causes the browser to begin searching the path from the '`ch5`' folder.

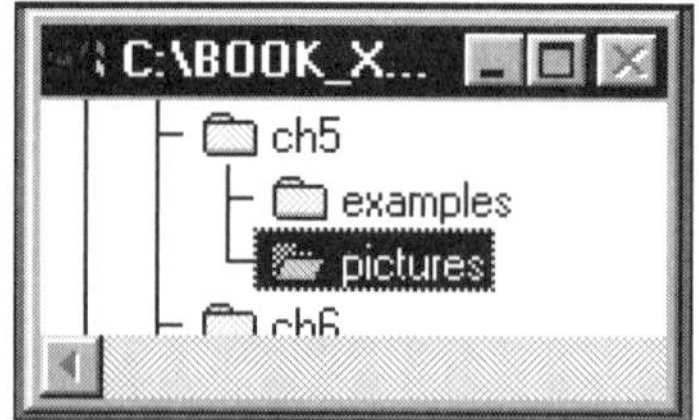

The `alt` text tells people with non-visual media that the image is 'Mona Lisa'.

I want to center the image on the page so, although there are other ways to do it, I have chosen to place the `<img>` element in a `<div>` element with the `style` attribute set to `center`.

```
<div style="text-align:center;">.......</div>
```

Lastly, when one is displaying Mona Lisa one wants to display it on a suitable background. Here we have used the `bgcolor` attribute of the body tag to paint a suitable color background. We will look at the mechanics of this right now.

The `bgcolor` attribute takes as its value a hexadecimal string, which represents a color, as do all color values in HTML. This is covered in Appendix C; feel free to skip there briefly now to see how this works.

Image Attributes

The `<image>` element can take the following attributes:

`src`	`alt`	`longdesc`	`height`	`width`	`usemap`
`ismap`	`align`	`border`	`hspace`	`vspace`	

We've already looked at the two required attributes, `src` and `alt`, so let's look at the optional ones.

The Optional Attributes

The `<img>` element takes a number of optional attributes.

The 'longdesc' Attribute

This is an attribute that is not supported in most browsers. It provides an URL to a text file that is a longer description of the picture. It is likely that the newer voice browsers will support this.

The syntax is:

```
longdesc="[URL of text file containing a description of the graphic]"
```

The 'width' and 'height' Attributes

The `width` and `height` attributes set aside spaceon the page in which to display the graphic. The syntax is:

```
width="[width in pixels]" height="[height in pixels]"
```

If the width and height do not match the size of the graphic, the graphic will be squeezed or stretched to fill the allotted space. As we will see these attributes should be routinely used as, if used correctly, it speeds up loading of your web page.

Always Include Width and Height

The width and height of images should always be included whenever practical, and should of course equal the width and height of the raw image. The reason for this is that most browsers will make a first pass through a document and print out all the text, plus a spot for the images with the `alt` text in place.

If the `width` and `height` attributes have been included the browser knows how much space to reserve for the images. If it doesn't reserve the correct amount of space the whole screen will have to be repainted every time an image is placed into its location. The following screenshot illustrates this point. It shows what a browser screen looks like after the pictures have been located on the page, but before they have been downloaded:

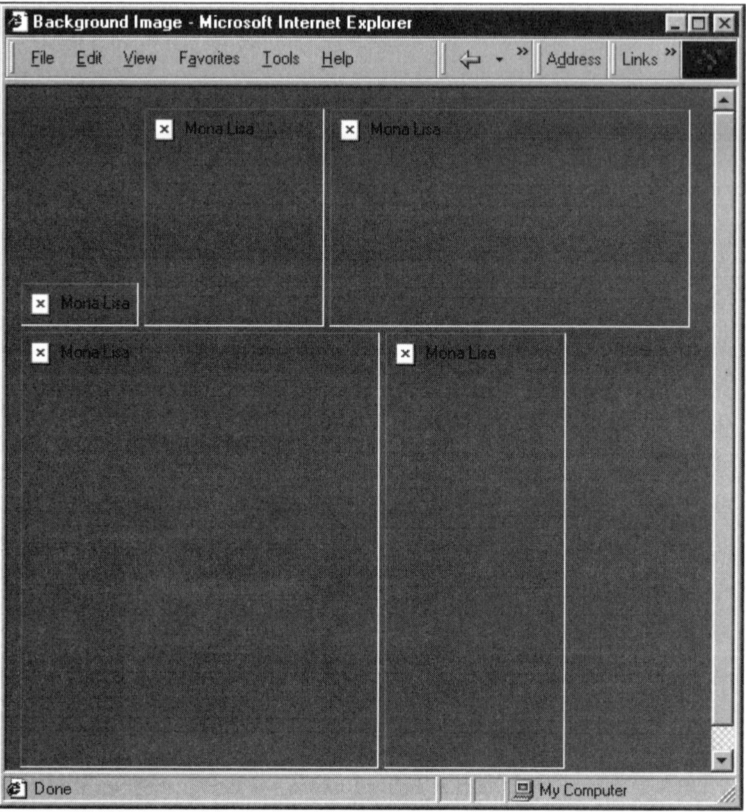

Note how all the images *except* the first one, which did not have a width and height specified, have the correct amount of space allocated. The first image has a default amount of space allocated. When the image is loaded the second and third images will be pushed to the right, or would be if they had been put in place.

The 'hspace' and 'vspace' Attributes

These are deprecated attributes that are included in the transitional DTDs but probably will not be included in the modular DTDs. The effects that you can get with these attributes can be achieved just as well with style sheets. We are reviewing them here because our examples will demonstrate the 'inline' nature of images and their relationship to the baseline.

The hspace attribute takes a numeric pixel value. This value equals the number of pixels to be used as space on either side of the image. The syntax is:

```
hspace="[numeric pixel value]"
```

The vspace attribute also takes a numeric pixel value equal to the number of pixels to be used as space above and below the image. The syntax is:

```
vspace="[numeric pixel value]"
```

Let's look at this in practice.

Try It Out – Using the 'hspace' and 'vspace' Attributes

1. This example uses leonardo.jpg and leonardo.gif to demonstrate the use of vspace and hspace. We have used the <u> tag only to graphically demonstrate the baselines – it has been deprecated, and you should not use it. Type up the following:

```
<?xml version="1.0" encoding="UTF-8"?>
<!DOCTYPE html
     PUBLIC "-//W3C//DTD XHTML 1.0 Transitional//EN"
     "http://www.w3.org/TR/xhtml1/DTD/xhtml1-transitional.dtd">
<html xmlns="http://www.w3.org/1999/xhtml" xml:lang="en" lang="en">
  <head>
    <title>Background Image</title>
  </head>
  <body bgcolor="#666633">
    <div>
    <u>aa<img src="../pictures/leonardo.jpg" alt="Leonardo Da Vinci" />aa
    aa<img src="../pictures/leonardo.gif" alt=" Leonardo Da Vinci " />aa</u><br />
    <u>bb<img src="../pictures/leonardo.jpg" alt=" Leonardo Da Vinci " hspace='25'
    />bb
    bb<img src="../pictures/leonardo.gif" alt=" Leonardo Da Vinci "/>bb</u><br />
    <u>cc<img src="../pictures/leonardo.jpg" alt=" Leonardo Da Vinci " vspace='25'
    />cc
    cc<img src="../pictures/leonardo.gif" alt=" Leonardo Da Vinci "/>cc</u><br />
    </div>
  </body>
</html>
```

2. When you run this on a browser, this is what you will see. We have included the underlined text before and after each image so that you can see where the baseline is:

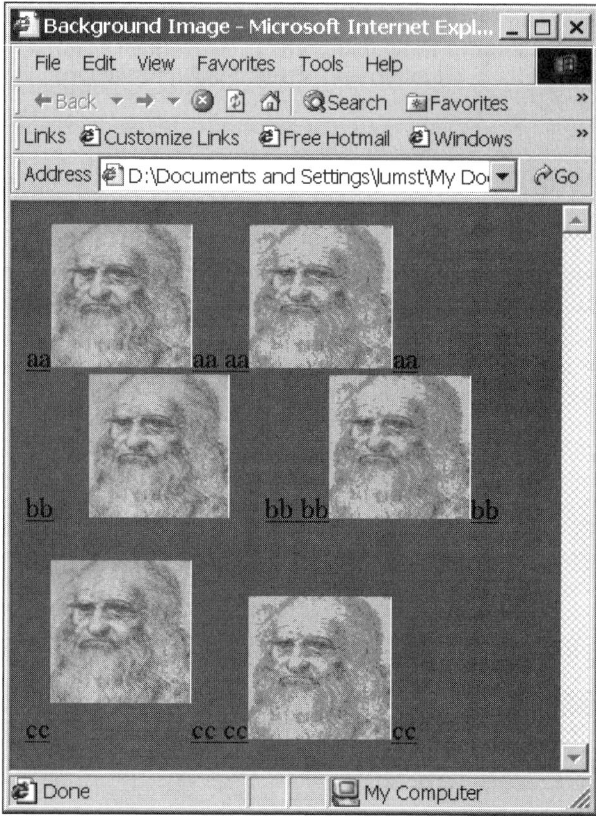

Note in passing how much better the JPG looks than the GIF with its limited palette, for this complex sketch. This is the case even though a casual glance would suggest that there are few colors in this image.

How It Works

In the first line the images have been given no horizontal or vertical spacing. They are hard up against the text before and after them. Note how the images rest on the text baseline.

In the second row, the first image has been given an 'hspace' value of 25. This will produce a left and a right margin to the image. It still rests on the baseline for that line.

In the third row the first image has been given vspace value of 25 pixels. This produces a top and a bottom margin of 25 pixels. The left and right spacing is unchanged.

These effects are much better produced by style sheets than by these deprecated attributes.

Style sheet alternative to hspace and vspace

As we will see in Chapter 9 we can use the `margin` properties of an element instead of `hspace` and `vspace`. Using the inline version would give the following code for hspace:

```
<img style="margin-left:25px;margin-right:25px;" src="...... />
```

and for vspace we would have:

```
<img style="margin-top:25px;margin-bottom:25px;" src="...... />
```

The 'align' Attribute

Like the `vspace` and `hspace` attributes this attributes is deprecated, and it is recommended that either style sheets or the style attributes be used instead.

The `align` attribute can take one of the following values:

`top | middle | bottom | left | right`

These values allow us to align text with the image, and to flow text around an image. The `<img />` element is an inline element which will rest on an existing baseline of a line of text, as we saw in the `hspace` examples above. This is the equivalent of `align="bottom"`.

`align="right"` will place the image on the right side of the block in which the image is contained and flow text around it.

`align="left"` will place the image on the left side block in which the image is contained and flow text around it.

`align="top"` will place the top of the image on the underside of a line that runs through the top of the text. The so called "text-top line".

`align="middle"` will place the middle of the image at the line that runs through the middle of the text. The so called "mid-text line".

To appreciate where an image is going to line up with text we need to appreciate the various lines associated with a line of text. The following graphic illustrates the general idea:

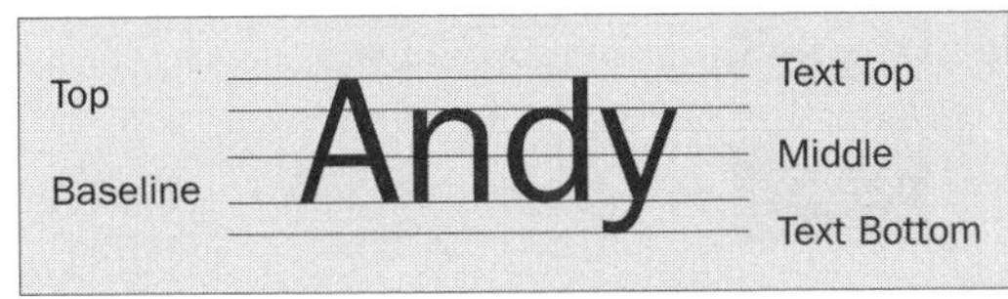

All inline objects, which include text and images take the baseline as their reference points. Let's take a quick look at how text and images are aligned. We can do it with the deprecated attribute align, or we can do it using the `style` attribute.

Let's first of all look at three attributes of the align attribute: `bottom`, `middle` and `top`.

Try It Out – Aligning Images and Text using the 'align' Attribute

1. Type up the following or download it from the Wrox web site:

```
<?xml version="1.0" encoding="UTF-8"?>
<!DOCTYPE html
    PUBLIC "-//W3C//DTD XHTML 1.0 Transitional//EN"
    "http://www.w3.org/TR/xhtml1/DTD/xhtml1-transitional.dtd">
<html xmlns="http://www.w3.org/1999/xhtml" xml:lang="en" lang="en">
  <head>
    <title>Using the align attribute to align text and images</title>
  </head>
  <body bgcolor="white">

    <div>Here is a logo
    <img src="../pictures/logo.gif" alt="logo"  />
    sitting on the baseline, the default or align="bottom".
    </div>

    <div>Here is a logo
    <img src="../pictures/logo.gif" alt="logo" align="middle" />
    with the middles lined up, align ="middle".
    </div>

    <div>Here is a logo
    <img src="../pictures/logo.gif" alt="logo" align="top" />
    with align set to "top".
    </div>
  </body>
</html>
```

2. Now run it in your browser:

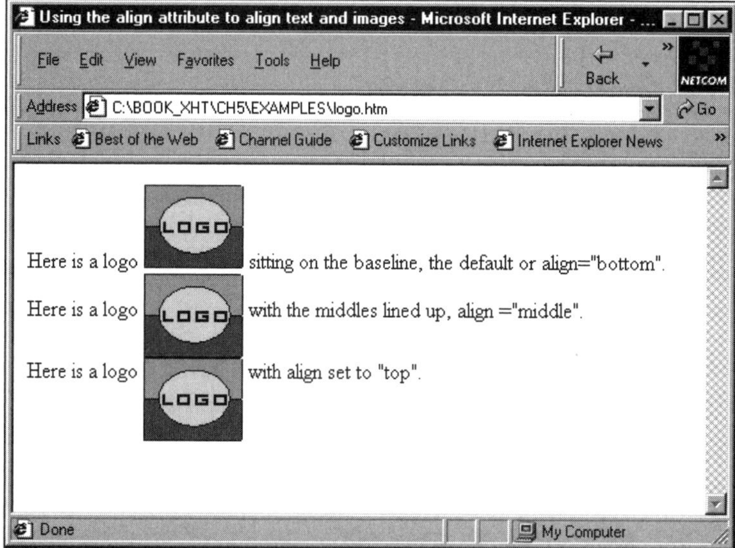

How It Works

In the first line, the bottom of the image sits on the baseline of the text.

In the second line, the middle of the image lines up with the base line of the text.

In the third, the top of the image lines up with the top of the text. The top in this case is not only the top of the ascender (the part of the letter that goes up), but that and a bit more called the 'internal leading'.

Now let's look at how to get these effects using the vertical-align property of CSS.

Try It Out – Aligning Images and Text Using the 'style' Attribute

1. Type or download the following file:

```
<?xml version="1.0" encoding="UTF-8"?>
<!DOCTYPE html
     PUBLIC "-//W3C//DTD XHTML 1.0 Transitional//EN"
     "http://www.w3.org/TR/xhtml1/DTD/xhtml1-transitional.dtd">
<html xmlns="http://www.w3.org/1999/xhtml" xml:lang="en" lang="en">
  <head>
    <title>Using CSS properties to align text to images</title>
  </head>
  <body bgcolor="white" style="font-size:16pt;">

    <div>Here the CSS property
    <img src="../pictures/logo.gif" alt="logo" style="vertical-align:baseline;" />
    has been set to baseline.
    </div>

    <div>Here the CSS property
    <img src="../pictures/logo.gif" alt="logo" style="vertical-align:middle;" />
    has been set to middle.
    </div>

    <div>Here the CSS property
    <img src="../pictures/logo.gif" alt="logo" style="vertical-align:top;" />
    has been set to top.
    </div>
    <!--
    <div>Here the CSS property
    <img src="../pictures/logo.gif" alt="logo" style="vertical-align:text-top;" />
    has been set to text-top.
    </div>
    -->
    <div>Here the CSS property
    <img src="../pictures/logo.gif" alt="logo" style="vertical-align:bottom;" />
    has been set to bottom.
    </div>
    <!--
    <div>Here the CSS property
    <img src="../pictures/logo.gif" alt="logo" style="vertical-align:text-bottom;"
    />
    has been set to text-bottom.-->
    </div>
  </body>
</html>
```

2. You will have to run this file in IE 4 or better, as Netscape 4 does not understand the `vertical-align` property. Note that we have made the font larger in order to display the subtle differences between the base line and bottom properly:

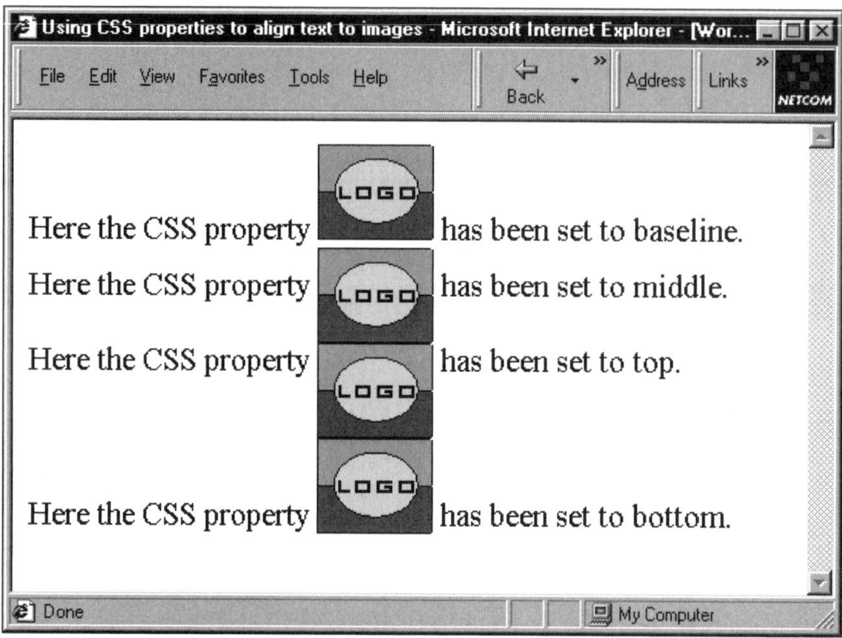

How It Works

In the first example the `vertical-align` property has been set to `baseline`. This will align the bottom of the image with the baseline.

In the second example the `vertical-align` property has been set to `middle`. This will align the middle of the image with the baseline in IE 5.

In the third example the `vertical-align` property has been set to `top`. This will align the top of the image with the top of the tallest element in the line, in this case the text.

We commented out the `text-top` property, as this would have given in this instance exactly the same result as the last example. With the vertical-align property set to text-top, the top of the image is aligned with the top of the tallest text on the line.

In the last example the `vertical-align` property has been set to `bottom`. This will align the bottom of the image with the bottom of the lowest element on the line – in this case the bottom of the font.

We commented out the `text-bottom` property as this should have given in this instance exactly the same result as the last example. With the `vertical-align` property set to `text-bottom`, the bottom of the image is aligned with the bottom of the parent element's font. In fact in IE 5 the image is (incorrectly) aligned with the base line rather than the bottom of the font.

Style Sheet Use

Here, for reference, we have included the inline CSS form as well as the `align` attribute. This should allow down level browsers to display what we want:

```
<img src="../pictures/leonardo.jpg" alt="Leonardo Da Vinci" align="right"
style="float:right;" />
```

See Chapter 9 for a full description of style sheets.

The 'border' Attribute

The `border` attribute, which is also deprecated, allows us to put a border around an image. The syntax is:

`border="[`*`border width in pixels`*`]"`

Its chief use was in removing the blue border that appeared around an image when it was made part of a link. Here is an example of using the `border` attribute.

Try It Out – Using the 'border' Attribute

1. Type up the following page and save it as `border.htm`:

```
<?xml version="1.0" encoding="UTF-8"?>
<!DOCTYPE html
     PUBLIC "-//W3C//DTD XHTML 1.0 Transitional//EN"
     "http://www.w3.org/TR/xhtml1/DTD/xhtml1-transitional.dtd">
<html xmlns="http://www.w3.org/1999/xhtml" xml:lang="en" lang="en">
<head>
<title>Borders around a Leonardo Image</title>
</head>
<body bgcolor="#666633">

<div>
<a href="leonardo.txt"><img src="../pictures/leonardo.jpg" alt="Leonardo Da Vinci"
longdesc="leonardo.txt" /></a>
<a href="leonardo.txt"><img src="../pictures/leonardo.jpg" alt="Leonardo Da Vinci"
longdesc="leonardo.txt" border="0" /></a>
</div>

<div>
<img src="../pictures/leonardo.jpg" alt="Leonardo Da Vinci"
longdesc="leonardo.txt" />
<img src="../pictures/leonardo.jpg" alt="Leonardo Da Vinci"
longdesc="leonardo.txt" border="5" />
</div>
</body>
</html>
```

2. This is what is produced:

How It Works

Both of the images in row 1 are links. The border in the second image has been removed by setting `border="0"`. The images in row two, though, are not links. In the second image, we have added a 5-pixel wide border.

Style Sheet Use

Again this attribute (`border`) has been deprecated in favor of using style sheets. For the record, here is what the equivalent inline style attribute would look like:

```
<img style="border-width:25px;" src="..." />
```

The 'ismap' and 'usemap' Attributes

These attributes are used when we want to make an image into an image map. The `usemap` attribute is used when the coding for the image map is on the client side, the `ismap` attribute when it is on the server side.

We will look at client-side mapping at the end of this chapter; server-side mapping is hardly ever used nowadays, and, therefore, we will not cover it.

Image Effects

We've seen how to include images in your pages, now let's look at how you can make the images you use look more impressive.

Using Transparency

Now that we have a basic understanding of the GIF, JPEG, and PNG file formats, we are going to go into a little bit more detail on creating transparent images.

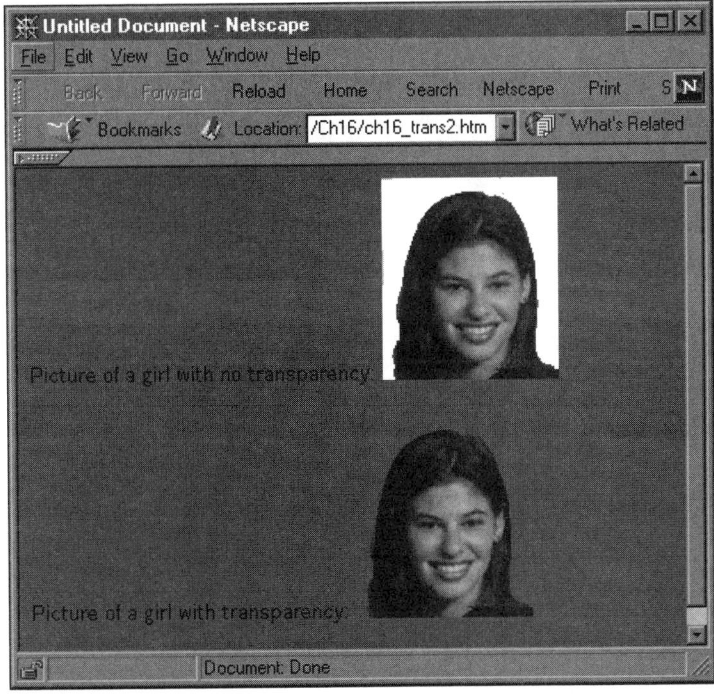

The screenshot above shows the difference between an image with transparency and an image without transparency. Quite simply, transparency provides you with a way of creating non-rectangular images.

There are two ways of making transparency: you can use a "transparency hack" that makes your image look like there is transparency, or you can use the masking facilities built into the file format.

While the transparency hack will work with GIF, PNG, and JPEG file formats, you will need to use the GIF file format or the PNG file format if you wish to use masking; the JPEG file format does not support transparency masking.

The Transparency Hack

The transparency hack is very simple to do. All you have to do is set the color of the background color of your image the same as the background color of the web page. It is possible to select one color and make this transparent. This allows us to create some quite nice effects, although they are labor intensive! Here is an example. It employs absolute positioning of our GIF with the transparent background, and use of the `clear-dot.gif` (downloadable with the support files) to move the text around. We could just have easily used the CSS `margin-left` property.

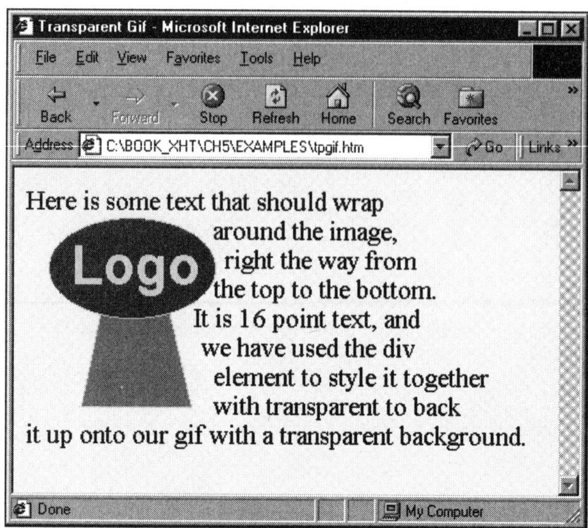

Remembering again that we need to place the image in the same directory as our `.htm` file, here is the code that we used to achieve the above screenshot:

```
<?xml version="1.0" encoding="UTF-8"?>
<!DOCTYPE html
     PUBLIC "-//W3C//DTD XHTML 1.0 Transitional//EN"
     "http://www.w3.org/TR/xhtml1/DTD/xhtml1-transitional.dtd">
<html xmlns="http://www.w3.org/1999/xhtml" xml:lang="en" lang="en">
<head>
<title>Transparent Gif</title>
</head>
<body bgcolor="#ffffcc">

<div style="position:absolute;left:.2in;top:.3in;">

<img src="../pictures/logo2.gif" alt="transparent gif"  align="left"/>
</div>
   <div style="font-size:16pt; ">Here is some text that should wrap</div>
   <div style="font-size:16pt; "><img src="../pictures/dot_cl~1.gif" hspace="72"
alt="" /> around the image, </div>
   <div style="font-size:16pt; "><img src="../pictures/dot_cl~1.gif" hspace="77"
alt="" /> right the way from </div>
   <div style="font-size:16pt; "><img src="../pictures/dot_cl~1.gif" hspace="75"
alt="" />the top to the bottom. </div>
   <div style="font-size:16pt; "><img src="../pictures/dot_cl~1.gif" hspace="67"
alt="" />It is 16 point text, and</div>
   <div style="font-size:16pt; "><img src="../pictures/dot_cl~1.gif" hspace="70"
alt="" />we have used the div </div>
   <div style="font-size:16pt; "><img src="../pictures/dot_cl~1.gif" hspace="75"
alt="" />element to style it together</div>
   <div style="font-size:16pt; "><img src="../pictures/dot_cl~1.gif" hspace="75"
alt="" />with transparent to back </div>
   <div style="font-size:16pt; "> it up onto our gif with a transparent
background.</div>
</body>
</html>
```

If you are looking for a good shareware program to experiment with these properties of GIFs, we would recommend "Gifcon32" from "Alchemy Mindworks". See them at `www.mindworkshop.com`.

The Transparency Hack is a Hack, Not a Solution!

As cool as the transparency hack may be, it does not work all of the time. There are three well-known cases in which it will fail – the first you can control, but the second two are out of your hands:

- First, the transparency hack works great when placing an image on a solid background. Problems arise when you try to place an image on a patterned background. This is because it is very hard for you to control positioning of the image with pixel-level precision. If you are off even a couple of pixels, it will look like mismatched wallpaper!
- Second, the user can override the background color of your web page. In Netscape Navigator's Edit | Preferences | Colors dialog box, the user can click on "Always use my colors, overriding document". This will cause the background color to change and your image to stick out like a sore thumb! Fortunately, very few people override the document's color, so most of the time you will be safe.
- Third, the color generated in your graphics program may not always match the color generated by the browser's `bgcolor` attribute – minute differences in color can make the "transparent" part quite visible.

On the other hand, if you have JPEG and you want to make it transparent, you have little choice but to use the transparency hack (unless you are willing to convert the JPEG to a GIF or PNG).

Transparency Masks

The GIF file format uses single-bit masking to provide transparency. What this means is that you can specify a single color to represent transparency and transparency is either "on" or "off" for a pixel.

The PNG file format is more flexible in that it uses an 8-bit alpha channel for transparency. What this means is that you can use up to 256 colors to represent different amounts of transparency: from opaque to translucent to transparent.

Using Animation

Where transparency provides you with a way of breaking out of the "square" web, animation provides you with a way of breaking out of the "static" web. With animation, you begin to add visual elements that add energy and dynamics to your web page, without the complication of scripting languages or video.

Animations are very good at drawing the attention of the user. This can be a good thing when you want them to move their eyes to a location on your web page. This can also be a bad thing if you really want the user to pay attention to something other than the animation.

When you design your web page, you need to be careful to use animations to lure the user's attention but not distract them from your message. Otherwise, your web site will be ineffective, or worse, your users will be annoyed. Keep in mind that animations significantly increase the size of your images and subsequently increase the download time.

Animated GIFs are one of the few ways of adding visual multimedia without having to resorting to plug-ins. This makes it very simple for you to build animations and, more importantly, know that they work right on most web browsers.

As you learned earlier, you can create a GIF file that consists of a collection of images, much like slides in a slide show. In animation, each "slide" is called a frame. Each frame is shown for a brief period of time and, if shown fast enough, makes it appear as if images are moving around on the screen.

Image Maps

In the last chapter we saw that an image can be used as an anchor. We also mentioned that an image could be turned into an image map by specifying the coordinates to create various shapes as 'hotspots'. When the user clicks on the image, the coordinates of the mouse click are returned and corresponding actions are then taken, such as that provided by a hypertext link. In other words we make different areas of the image into links.

This can be useful in a wide range of circumstances, from real maps, to diagrams to making custom tool bars.

In this section we will have a look at how to make an image into an image map.

Coordinates

Any point on an image can be expressed by a set of coordinates, an 'x' value, and a 'y' value. This is rather like the simple graph plotting that you learnt at school.

Just like at school the 'x' value starts at zero on the left, and increases as we go to the right. However unlike at school, the 'y' value in computer imaging starts at zero at the top and increases as we go down. The accompanying illustration shows this for a rectangular image:

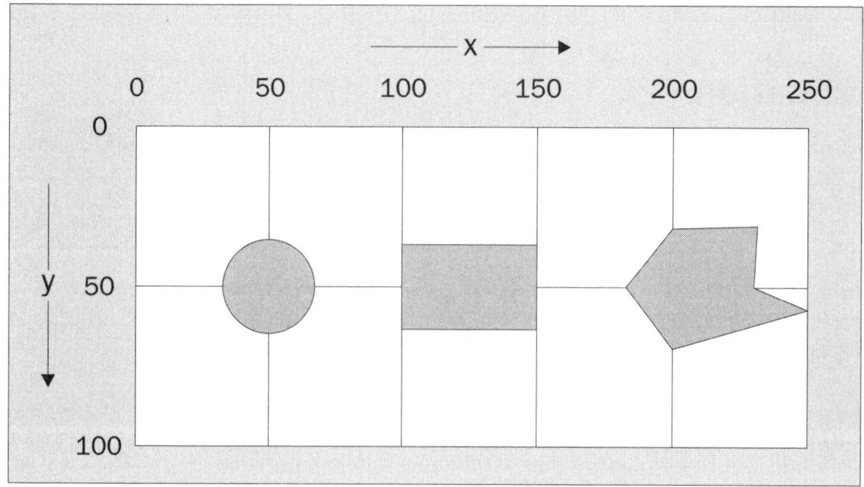

Areas, Shapes and Units

We can map out various areas on the image by using coordinates and various shapes. The shapes used in image maps are circles, rectangles and polygons. The units of measurement employed are pixels.

Circles

The coordinates of a circle are give as the (x,y) coordinate of the center of the circle, plus the radius. The general syntax for this is:

```
[x co-ordinate of circle center],[y co-ordinate of circle
center],[radius of circle]
```

Thus in the illustration above, the coordinates for the area of the circle would be expressed as 50,50,15.

Rectangles

Rectangular areas are expressed by the (x,y) coordinate of the top left corner of the rectangle followed by the (x,y) coordinate of the bottom right hand corner. The general syntax for this is:

```
[x coordinate top left],[y coordinate top left],[x coordinate bottom
right],[y coordinate bottom right]
```

Thus in the illustration above the coordinates for the area of the rectangle would be expressed as 100,35,150,65.

Polygons

The area of a polygon is expressed by a comma-separated list of the (x,y) coordinates of the various points. For example:

```
x1,y1,x2,y2,x3,y3,..etc.
```

The coordinates for the area of the polygon in the illustration above would be:

```
180,50, 200,25, 225,25, 225,50, 250,65, 200,70
```

The spaces have been put in for reasons of clarity.

Now that we have seen how to express areas, let's try it on a real map.

Mapping Out Areas

We have provided a map of Ohio for you that shows the various locations of the "Amish Wear" apparel stores. We want to make each of the locations into a 'clickable area', but first we have to map out the areas on the map. There are programs that will automatically create an image map for you, but unless you are making a lot of maps it is probably just as easy to do it by hand.

Try It Out – Defining Areas by Sets of Coordinates

1. The first thing to do is to load our image into an image editing program. In every program that I've seen, if you select the 'pointer' or 'outline' tool, you will get a readout of the (x,y) coordinates of the tools location.

2. In the illustration below we are using Corel Photo-Paint 8, but you can use any image editing program. You can see that the pointer tool has been selected. Make sure the settings are set to pixels and not some other unit.

3. For this exercise, we will define a circular area, but a rectangle of equivalent size could also be used. I place my cursor over the center of each of the locations and read off the coordinates. 12 pixels seem to me about right for the radius of the circle:

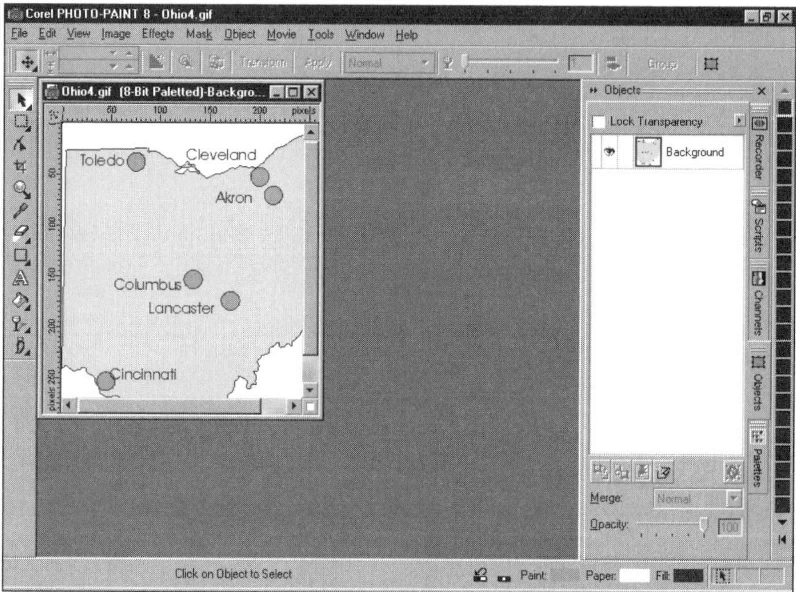

4. Now hold the mouse pointer over each town or location for which you will want to place an image map, this will be the center of the circle image map. Read the [x, y] coordinates in your graphics program and record these values. Here is a table of the coordinates and the code that will locate a 12 pixel radius circle around each location:

Location	X coordinate	Y coordinate	Area description
Cleveland	200	52	200,52,12
Akron	215	69	215,69,12
Toledo	75	37	75,37,12
Columbus	135	153	135,153,12
Lancaster	171	174	171,174,12
Cincinnati	44	255	44,255,12

Now that we have defined the areas on our map of Ohio, let's look at how to code these into 'clickable' links in our XHTML page.

Try It Out – Making a Clickable Image Map

1. First of all type the following into your text editor:

```
<?xml version="1.0" encoding="UTF-8"?>
<!DOCTYPE html
     PUBLIC "-//W3C//DTD XHTML 1.0 Transitional//EN"
     "http://www.w3.org/TR/xhtml1/DTD/xhtml1-transitional.dtd">
<html xmlns="http://www.w3.org/1999/xhtml" xml:lang="en" lang="en">
  <head>
    <title>Image maps of Ohio locations</title>
  </head>
  <body bgcolor="white">
    <h1 align="center">Amish Wear</h1>
    <h2 align="center">Find the Ohio store nearest you</h2>
    <div align="center">
    <img src="../pictures/ohio4.gif" alt="Ohio locations" />
    </div>
    <div align="center">
    <img src="../pictures/ohio3.gif" alt="Ohio locations"  />
    </div>
    <div align="center">
    <a href="cle.htm">[Cleveland]</a>
    <a href="akr.htm">[Akron]</a>
    <a href="tol.htm">[Toledo]</a>
    <a href="col.htm">[Columbus]</a>
    <a href="lan.htm">[Lancaster]</a>
    <a href="cin.htm">[Cincinatti]</a>
    </div>
  </body>
</html>
```

2. Save it as `ohio.html`. This will produce a page just like the following:

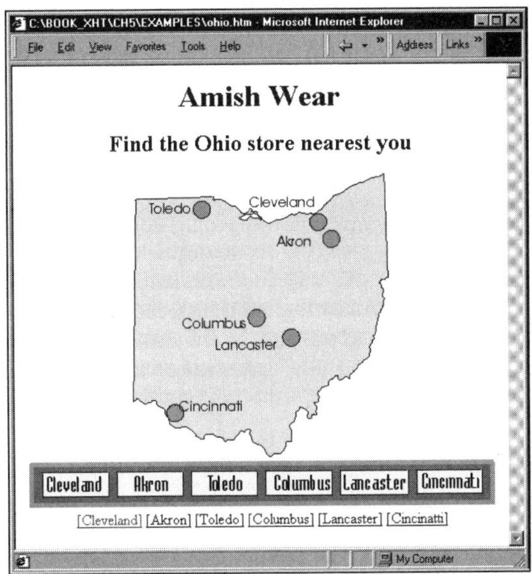

3. The links at the bottom of the page are functional, but we want our user to be able to click on either our map or our custom tool bar to get to our other pages.

4. Make the following additions to our original XHTML code

```
<?xml version="1.0" encoding="UTF-8"?>
<!DOCTYPE html
     PUBLIC "-//W3C//DTD XHTML 1.0 Transitional//EN"
     "http://www.w3.org/TR/xhtml1/DTD/xhtml1-transitional.dtd">
<html xmlns="http://www.w3.org/1999/xhtml" xml:lang="en" lang="en">
  <head>
    <title>Image maps of Ohio locations</title>
  </head>
  <body bgcolor="white">
    <h1 align="center">Amish Wear</h1>
    <h2 align="center">Find the Ohio store nearest you</h2>
    <div align="center">
    <img src="../pictures/ohio4.gif" alt="Ohio locations" usemap="#oh1" border="0"
    />
    </div>
    <div align="center">
    <img src="../pictures/ohio3.gif" alt="Ohio locations"  />
    </div>
    <div align="center">
    <a href="cle.htm">[Cleveland]</a>
    <a href="akr.htm">[Akron]</a>
    <a href="tol.htm">[Toledo]</a>
    <a href="col.htm">[Columbus]</a>
    <a href="lan.htm">[Lancaster]</a>
    <a href="cin.htm">[Cincinatti]</a>
    </div>

    <map name="oh1">
      <area shape="circle" coords="200,52,12"
        href="cle.htm" alt="Link to Cleveland store page" />

      <area shape="circle" coords="214,70,12"
        href="akr.htm." alt="Link to Akron store page" />

      <area shape="circle" coords="75,38,12"
        href="tol.htm" alt="Link to Toledo store page" />

      <area shape="circle" coords="134,153,12"
        href="col.htm" alt="Link to Columbus store page" />

      <area shape="circle" coords="171,174,12"
        href="lan.htm" alt="Link to Lancaster store page" />

      <area shape="circle" coords="46,254,12"
        href="cin.htm" alt="Link to Cincinatti store page" />
    </map>
  </body>
</html>
```

5. Now when our pointer hovers over any of the locations on the map of Ohio, a hand will appear, plus in IE 5 a small info box giving the `alt` text, and clicking on any of the locations will take us to the appropriate page. In other words we have created a simple link.

How It Works

We have added a `usemap` attribute to our image, and have given it a value of `#oh1`:

```
usemap="#oh1"
```

Note the hash mark: this tells the browser to go and look for a map element, within the same HTML document, with the name of "oh1". The names of all your maps should be unique in the document. The `<map>` element should be in the same document when using the hash symbol (#) alone. The map element can be referenced from another document if the path is given similar to a `src` attribute for the `<img>` element. The name attribute is a required attribute. For obvious reasons it must be unique!

```
<map name="oh1">
```

The map element contains several 'area' elements that give information about the link areas of the image. The 'map' element must contain at least one `<area>` element:

```
<area shape="circle" coords="200,52,12"
    href="cle.htm" alt="Link to Cleveland store page" />
```

The first attribute is shape. Here we are using the circle value. The other permitted values are `rect` and `poly`. The default is `rect`, in other words if no shape is given then `rect` is assumed.

The `alt` attribute serves the same purpose as it does in an image, and is a required attribute. In IE 5 a small info box will pop up containing this when the cursor hovers over a link area.

The `href` attribute gives the address of the link.

If you press the *Tab* key you will see that you can cycle through all the 'hotspots'. As each one becomes active it will be outlined. Pressing the *Enter* key will then connect you to the link. You can specify the order by using the `tabindex` attribute.

Other 'area' Attributes

Here is a list of all the attributes that an `<area>` element can take together with a comment on each one:

`shape`	(see above)
`coords`	(see above)
`href`	(see above)
`nohref`	Use if no link is intended. Usually some script is executed instead.
`alt`	(see above)

Table Continued on Following Page

tabindex	The order in which each of the areas is accessed with the *tab* key.
accesskey	Defines a keystroke to use instead of a click. Pressing *alt/*[keystroke] will highlight the area. Make sure that you don't select any of the common browser letters (f,e,v,a,t,h) for your keystroke choice!
onfocus	For use with scripting
onblur	For use with scripting
target	For use in displaying the destination link in another frame (see Chapter 7).

Using Images Effectively

We have already looked at how to position images on pages and how to wrap text around them. The following sections are best practices, tips, and advice on how best to manipulate the use of images within your pages.

Sizing Images

We looked at how we could stretch, squeeze, and distort our images into a given space using the width and height attributes. You may be tempted to do this to create a button or an icon from a large image, or to use a small image to fill up more space. Resist the temptation!

If you are enlarging a smaller image, the pixellation will become very obvious if the enlargement is too big, and if you want to create a small icon from an image it is better to use an image program to create a separate file. Consider the following page where we have made a 'button' from the head of Mona Lisa:

```
<?xml version="1.0" encoding="UTF-8"?>
<!DOCTYPE html
     PUBLIC "-//W3C//DTD XHTML 1.0 Transitional//EN"
     "http://www.w3.org/TR/xhtml1/DTD/xhtml1-transitional.dtd">
<html xmlns="http://www.w3.org/1999/xhtml" xml:lang="en" lang="en">
  <head>
    <title>Leonardo Image</title>
  </head>
  <body bgcolor="#ffffaa">

    <div>
    <img src="../pictures/monalisa_ico.jpg" alt="ml_icon"  width="38" height="45"
      vspace="5" hspace="10" /><br />
    <img src="../pictures/monalisa_head.jpg" alt="ml_icon"  width="38" height="45"
      vspace="5" hspace="10" /><br />
    </div>
  </body>
</html>
```

Here is what we see:

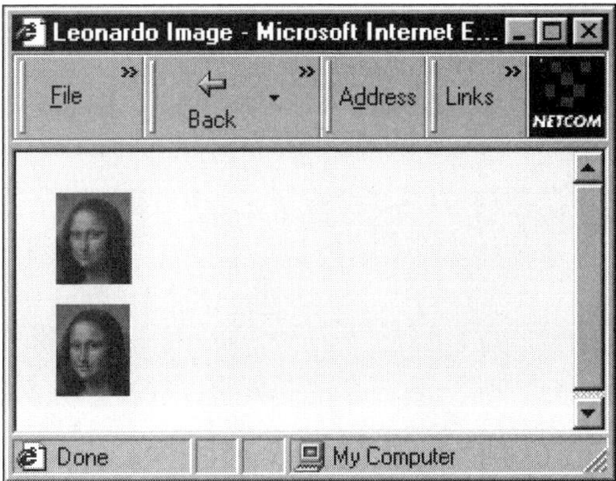

The icons are the same size on the page, but the second item has been squeezed into the space. The original size was 97 x 95 and its file size is 6K. The first icon was produced in an imaging program, and its file size is 1.2K.

Size Really Matters

Unfortunately, you can't just look at the size of a file and know how long it will take to download that file. Different users will have different download times based on the type of connection they have to the Internet. On a corporate or university T1 connection, an image may take a couple of seconds, whereas that same image may take several minutes on a residential 28.8kbps modem connection.

Know your audience – if you want to target the millions of users who are dialing into the Internet from their homes, be conservative with your images and make them small. Keep your images below 28k and your icons below 10k.

There are plenty of techniques for reducing the size of an image. Some of the more popular are described below.

Resize the image

With bitmap graphics, the larger the image the larger the file size. Consider the following images:

Full Size = 14kB

75% of Full Size = 9kB

50% of Full Size = 6kB

As you can see, we save over 57% of the file size when we reduce the picture to 50% of its original size.

Turn Off Dithering

Dithering is when different colored pixels are used within an image to simulate a color that does not exist in the image's color palette:

As can be seen in the images above, there is very little perceivable difference between the three images and yet dithering adds 15% to the file size of the normal GIF image. So, unless it is vital that you represent the color accurately, turn off dithering

Turn Off Anti-Aliasing

Aliasing is when you add pixels of different colors to smooth out jagged lines. Lets look back at our "silly head" picture both in its aliased form and its anti-aliased form:

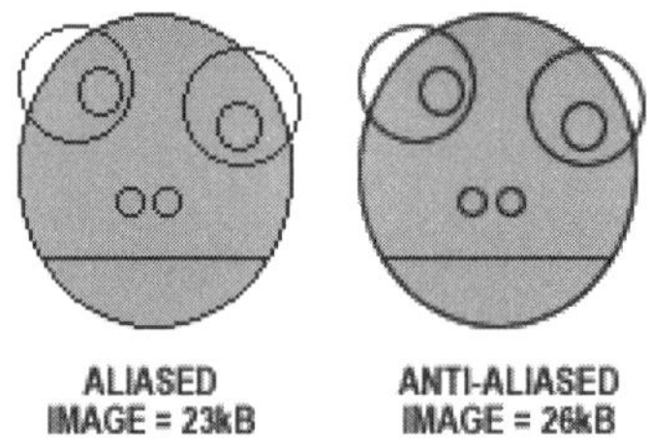

As you can see, as simple an image as this saves over 10% of the file size going from an anti-aliased image to an aliased image.

Reduce the Bit Depth

You may remember that the GIF file format supports **up to** an 8-bit color depth; this means that a GIF can have as many as 256 colors or as few as 2 colors. As you reduce the number of possible colors for each pixel, you reduce the overall size of the file.

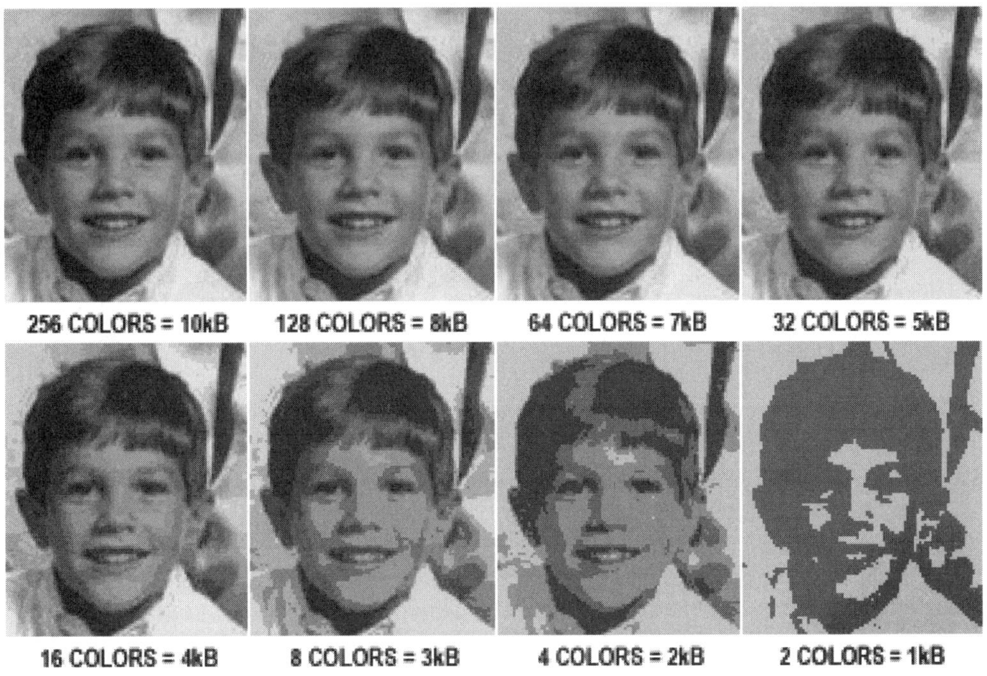

In the figure above, we start with an image that has a 256 color bit-depth. As we reduce the bit-depth to 128 colors, we have a 20% reduction in file size with little perceivable loss in quality. In fact, we can approach 32 colors at half the original file size before we see a loss in quality!

There is no rule of thumb on how small you can make the bit depth before you see a loss in quality. It all depends on how many colors are actually being used and the nature of the image.

You may also be able to reduce the bit-depth for PNG images. Recall that the PNG file format supports three different bit-depths: 8-bit, 24-bit, and 32-bit. If you start with a 32-bit or 24-bit image, you may be able to lower the bit-depth and maintain an acceptable level of quality.

Change the Artwork

A more drastic means of reducing the file size is to change the artwork. We are not talking about arbitrarily changing the images on your page (although that may work!), rather you may want to take advantage of the way in which a compression algorithm works.

For example, we mentioned earlier that the GIF file format is based on a line by line compression of the image and that the GIF file format works best at compressing large fields of color. What this means is that GIF works best when the solid colors run left-to-right. Consider the following two pictures. They are the same image rotated 90 degrees:

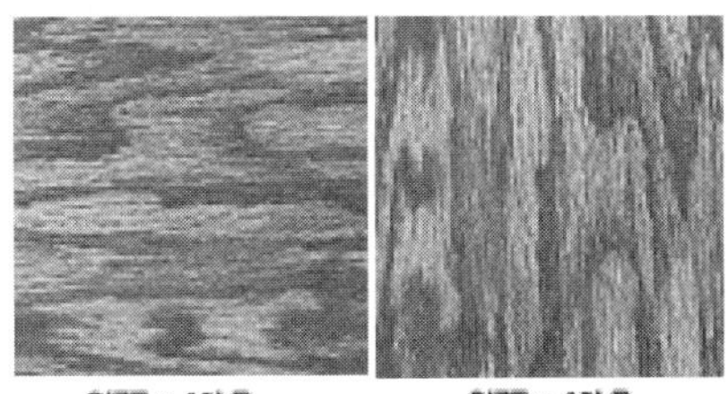

As you can see in the illustration, if we show the same pattern in a horizontal orientation, we save 23% of the file size. If the orientation has no significance to the meaning of the web page, then this is a very simple way of reducing the file size.

Likewise, we have talked quite a bit about how JPEG was designed for photographs. This is because the JPEG compression method is optimized to handle color gradients. If your GIF image has a lot of shading or blending, you might consider converting the image to the JPEG file format.

My Home Page

The "My Home Page" image, for example, had the following file sizes:

- Saved as a GIF file: 7kB
- Saved as a JPEG file: 4kB

Saving the image as a JPEG is a 42% reduction in file size!

Increase the Compression Ratio

The JPEG file format also allows you to increase the compression ratio in order to reduce the file size. As we explained in the section on JPEG above, the JPEG file format uses a lossy compression method, which means that as you increase the compression ratio you will see a loss in quality:

As you can see in the figure above, as you increase the compression there is a reduction in the quality of the image. The key is to find the "sweet spot" in which there is a significant reduction in file size and little loss in quality. I would say that occurs at 80% quality in the figure above.

Low Bandwidth Graphics

Earlier in this chapter we talked about the importance of graphics in web page design. In fact, graphics can make or break a web page in more than one way! First, if there are no graphics, the web page can be boring and identical to thousands of similar web pages. People will quickly click off to another web page. We talk about this in Chapter 12 when we look at concepts behind designing web pages.

Second, if it takes too long to load your web page because of a large number of graphics (or large graphics), people lose their patience and quickly click off to another web page. Some people claim that you lose half your audience if your page does not load in 5 seconds!

So, the challenge is to learn how to make small and speedy graphics.

Download Speeds

The old saying used to be that the three most important things about a web page were content, content, and content.

But web users are impatient souls and recent research shows that only about 20% of pages get read, 10% are never scrolled, and the majority are just scanned! With this in mind probably the most important things about a web page becomes download speed and ease and speed of navigation.

Certainly the biggest complaint about a page is that it takes forever to load. And, of course, the biggest culprit here is images.

There are several things you can do to keep your image content lean and mean. The average "pull down" rate for a 28 K modem is 2KB per second, and it can be slower. Any page with more than 50K worth of graphics needs to go on a diet! Start applying some of the following measures. Ask yourself:

- **Is this image really necessary?**

  Often a nice piece of formatted text will work just as well.

- **Does the image have to be this large?**

  Doubling the dimensions of an image quadruples the download time. By using borders and other techniques, an image's apparent size can be kept the same even while the actual size is much smaller.

- **Can I decrease the quality of the image and/or reduce its number of colors?**

  Obviously there is a tradeoff between image size and quality. With a picture like Mona Lisa the trade off should be on the side of quality. With a logo or a diagram the trade off should be on the side of smaller size.

- **Can I use thumbnails instead?**

  If you have a lot of images you may want to consider using 'clickable' thumbnails that connect to the real image. In fact you may just want to provide an index!

- **Can I leverage cached images?**

  A browser will cache –store in memory for fast retrieval– all the recent pages and images that it has visited. This means that when you revisit a page, the download speed will be considerably faster than previously. You need to be aware of this fact for two main reasons:

  - When developing pages you may think that your download speed is considerably faster than in fact it is. The reason for this is that even though you may be going out to a server, all your images are already cached on your browser.
  - Because images are downloaded to the client's machine, you can in fact speed up download time by using the same images in several different pages. Provided the address of the image is the same, the client will collect the image from its cache rather than going out onto the Internet.

  Cached images do not have to be downloaded so cache images whenever you can. If you have an introduction page or some page you anticipate the user will spend some time over. It may be a good idea to cache images into "hidden" elements for use on other pages. Also it is a good idea to reuse images whenever possible.

Where to Find Graphics

There are many places on the web where you can find graphics; many of which are royalty-free! When you download a graphic from another site, make sure that you have the right to use the graphic, that there are no royalties associated with the graphic, and whether there are requirements on how you use the image. It is quite common for some sites to say you may download an image as long as you give credit to the image's origin or publish an appropriate copyright. Some popular "galleries" include:

Microsoft's **Internet Explorer Multimedia Gallery** contains many free backgrounds, banners, and other images:
`http://msdn.microsoft.com/workshop/design/creative/mmgallry.asp`

The **Agricultural Research Service** provides an image gallery of digital photographs related to, oddly enough, agriculture:
`http://www.ars.usda.gov/is/graphics/photos/index.html`

PhotoDisc is one of the best sites for royalty-free digital photography:
`http://www.photodisc.com/am/`

MediaBuilder has large collection of free animated GIFs in categories from animals and alphabets to transportation and war:
`http://www.animfactory.com`

ArtToday claims that they have "the largest searchable, categorized set of clipart, photos, fonts, web graphics, and sounds available on the Internet":
`http://www.arttoday.com/`

FullMoon Graphics has hundreds of odd and wonderful graphic themes for web pages:
`http://www.fullmoongraphics.com/`

Useful Graphics Tools

There are a variety of tools for working with graphics. Some are free, some are online, and some... well you have to buy those. Most of these programs allow you to download a free demo so you can "ride before you buy."

Adobe Photoshop has been the market leader in image editing tools for some time. With Photoshop you can produce web graphics that support rollovers and animation:
`http://www.adobe.com/`

Macromedia Fireworks is an image editing program designed for creating web graphics. This program comes highly recommended since it supports rollover effects, GIF animation, web optimization, and image slicing:
`http://www.macromedia.com/software/fireworks/`

GIFWorks is a neat online GIF image editor. You don't need to download anything and you can manage transparencies, crop images, and convert color palettes:
`http://www.gifworks.com/`

Microsoft FrontPage now includes their Image Composer product. Image Composer is a feature rich program that makes it easy to manage non-rectangle images through extensive control of alpha channels (see the discussion on PNG transparency above). There is an extensive array of special effects and support for animation:
`http://www.microsoft.com/frontpage/imagecomposer/imagecomposer1.htm`

JASC's **Paint Shop Pro** is a popular graphics editor that provides great painting and image editing tools. There is support for many file formats and a host of deformation, effects, and filters:
`http://www.jasc.com/`

Scalable Vector Graphics (SVG)

At the beginning of this chapter we talked about the two different types of images: bitmaps and vectors. We then spent the bulk of this chapter only talking about bitmaps. This is because there has been no vector graphic standard to make an impact in the marketplace.

The World Wide Web Consortium hopes to change all that with the emerging Scalable Vector Graphics (SVG) standard. At the time that this book was written, SVG had not reached the "recommendation" phase, but it promises to make an impact on how graphics are defined on the web.

SVG is used for describing two-dimensional graphics in XML. SVG will support three types of graphic objects: vector-based shapes, bitmaps, and text. These graphic objects can be grouped, styled, transformed, and composited into previously rendered objects. SVG also supports alpha channels, filter effects, and animation.

If you want to learn more about SVG, check out the World Wide Web Consortium's home page for SVG: `http://www.w3.org/Graphics/SVG/`

Summary

In this chapter we looked at images and how to employ them in our web pages. We saw how to place an image on an HTML page, and examined the use of the various attributes of the `<img>` element. We looked at how to align text to our images, and also saw why it is important to use the `alt`, `width`, and `height` attributes.

We then took a brief look at image caches. We looked at the various image formats in common use, and discussed their pros and cons. We also saw how to make a client side image map. Our next topic for discussion is how to use tables.

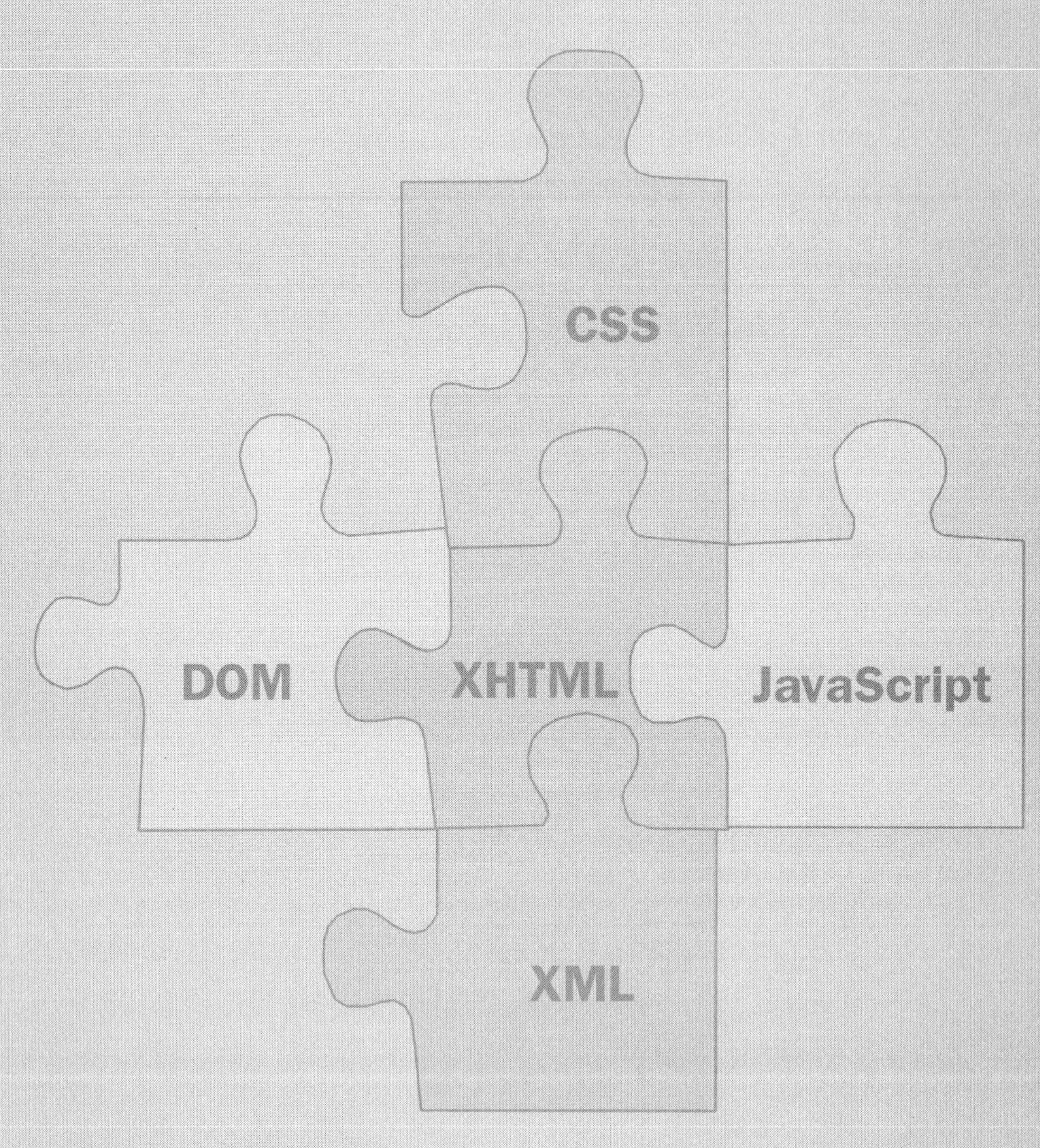
CSS
DOM
XHTML
JavaScript
XML

Tables

Tables are a very useful method of displaying data, and in this chapter we will look at a table's structure, and how it is represented in XHTML. XHTML's `<table>` element allows us to define the structure and content of a table, and allows us to add numerous refinements of presentation. Style sheets allow us to add additional style.

We will emphasize the difference between structure and style. In the first part of the chapter will look at the structural properties of tables, and in the second part we will look at the XHTML styling properties. Although we will leave a discussion of style sheets to Chapter 9, we're in the awkward position of having to demonstrate certain style sheet properties on our tables in this chapter, to show how they will be taking over from the XHTML styling attributes. The problem is that although we'd like to tell you to always use style sheets, they're not fully supported even in current browsers. What we're going to do, then, is to show the current XHTML attributes *and* the equivalent CSS properties that can substitute for them.

Lastly we will briefly look at the use of tables to lay out a page. Style sheets have superceded this use as well, but again, until browsers that support style sheets become more widespread we will still be using tables, even though it is really a bit of a hack!

In summary, then, we'll be looking at:

- Table structure
- Table presentation
- Using tables for layout

We have been stressing throughout this book the difference between the structure of a document and the way that a document is styled. In particular, we have stressed the value of XHTML for structuring a document so that it can be presented across a variety of different media types. Nowhere is this difference more important than in a table. You'll find that tables present us with more issues than most XHTML elements.

The Oxford English Dictionary describes a table as:

> *"An arrangement of numbers, words, or items of any kind in a definite and compact form, so as to exhibit some set of facts or relations in a distinct and comprehensive way, for the convenience of study, reference, or calculation. Now chiefly applied to an arrangement in columns and lines occupying a single page or sheet."*

It is really difficult to improve on that definition, except perhaps to say that tables need not be confined to pages or sheets. The important thing is that a table has a definite structure, and this is quite separate from its style. For example, take the following two tables. They have identical content and structure, but very different styles!

Basic Table

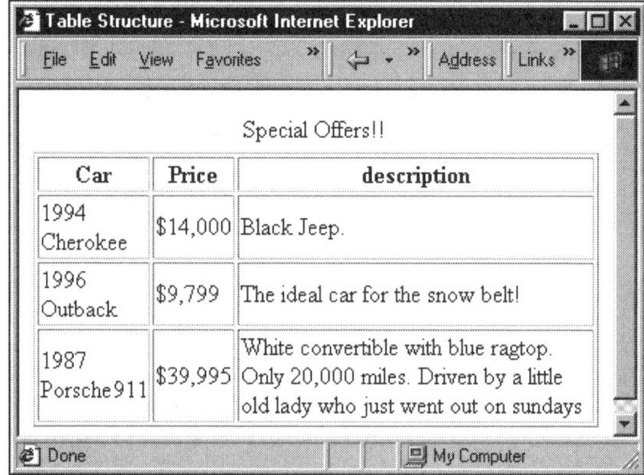

Styled Table

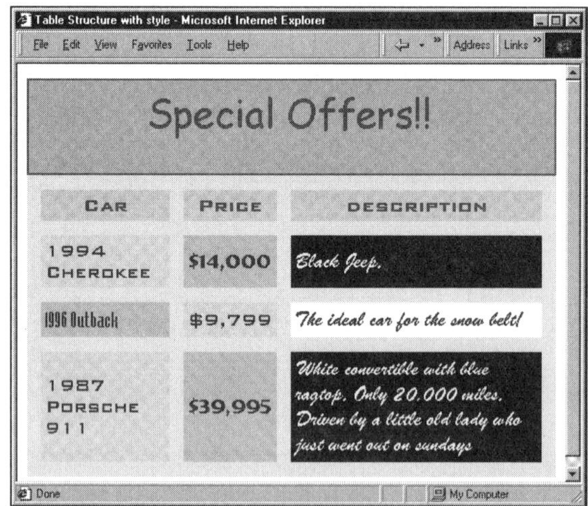

I hope I'm not overstressing the point that document (and in particular table) structure is very different from presentational style! There are millions upon millions of ways that the table structure can be styled. But the structure and content of the table will remain unchanged. On that note, let's turn our attention first to how we can set up the structure of our tables.

Table Structure

As we've seen, a table allows the arranging of information in columns and rows. Tables follow a fairly well-defined structure: nearly all tables have a caption, which is a title of some kind announcing the content and purport of the table; a heading that announces the content of each column; and many tables also have footers summarizing the contents of the column.

Headers and footers are particularly important in media types other than a scrolling screen. In paginated media, the table headers and footers will be repeated at the head and foot of each page. In screen media the table contents may scroll between the headers and footers, and in voice media the header and footer may be repeated before and after the intonation of a row's cell content. I'm speculating here, but for example, a voice browser's presentation of a table charting economic recovery in post-war Europe might go something like this:

> *"Row 3 Column 1, year '1945', column 2, coal output in Europe in thousands of metric tons '1,457'"*

It might be a little more concise than that, but I'd advise you to keep an eye (ear?) out for what browsers come out in the coming months, so you can always be best prepared for how to set out your content so that it's accessible to as wide a cross-section of users as possible. We'll look into other user agents in more depth in Chapter 13.

The body of the table essentially just contains the content in a tabulated form. The following diagram illustrates the structure of a table:

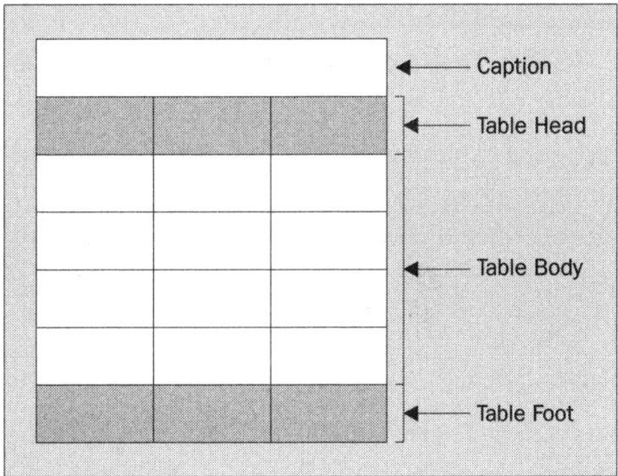

XHTML and Table Structure

All the structural parts of a table are reflected in XHTML markup.

Here are the chief structural elements of the table in XHTML:

- **table**: this element encloses the whole of the table construct. It can include all of the following elements: `<caption>`, `<thead>`, `<tfoot>`, `<tbody>`, and `<tr>`.
- **caption**: this element is optional. When it is included it must be the first element in the table.

- **thead**, **tfoot**, and **tbody**: these three elements are also optional. When they are included they must appear in the order listed here. It may seem strange that `<tfoot>` should come before `<tbody>`, but there is method in this madness! The idea is that a browser can lay out the `<thead>` and `<tfoot>` and have the contents of `<tbody>` scroll between them.
- **tr**: the `<tr>` element marks up the rows of the table. `<tr>` elements can be contained either in the table element or the `<tbody>`, `<thead>`, and `<tfoot>` elements. When any of these last three elements are present `<tr>` elements cannot be contained directly within the table, but must be in one of these table sub-sections. `<tr>` elements can only contain `<th>` and `<td>` elements.
- **th** and **td**: these elements represent the individual cells of the table, and are always contained in a `<tr>` element. `<th>` is usually used for a cell in a header, and most user agents will center the text in the cell and render it in bold type. `<td>` is the standard cell. Both `<th>` and `<td>` can contain just about every type of XHTML element as well as plain text.

Let's look at how to use these elements to build simple tables.

Building Simple Tables

Let's start off with a look at the simplest possible table. We will build a table of two rows and two columns:

Try It Out – A Simple Table

1. Type up the following and save it as `table1.htm`.

```
<?xml version="1.0" encoding="UTF-8"?>
<!DOCTYPE html
     PUBLIC "-//W3C//DTD XHTML 1.0 Strict//EN"
    "http://www.w3.org/TR/xhtml1/DTD/xhtml1-strict.dtd">
<html xmlns="http://www.w3.org/1999/xhtml" xml:lang="en" lang="en">
  <head>
    <title>A simple table</title>
  </head>
  <body bgcolor="white">
    <table border="1">
      <tr><td>Row 1-Col 1</td><td>Row 1-Col 2</td></tr>
      <tr><td>Row 2-Col 1</td><td>Row 2-Col 2</td></tr>
    </table>
  </body>
</html>
```

2. This is what it looks like in IE5:

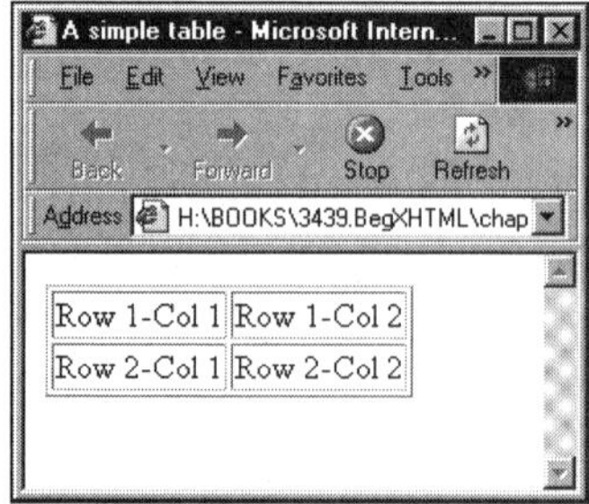

How It Works

The table is represented by a table element in XHTML. Everything that comes between the two <table> tags is either concerned with the structure of the table, or with table content.

```
<table border="1">
...
</table>
```

We have used the border attribute and given it a value of 1, just so that we can see what we're doing. Don't worry about that for now. We will be looking at this attribute in more detail later on.

Within the <table> tags come our row and cell definitions:

```
  <tr><td>Row 1-Col 1</td><td>Row 1-Col 2</td></tr>
  <tr><td>Row 2-Col 1</td><td>Row 2-Col 2</td></tr>
```

Adding a Header and a Caption

What we have just created is the simplest possible table. Nearly all tables, though, have headers at the top of each column, and most of them have a title or caption.

These items are particularly important when we are writing for non-screen media, because if they are absent there is no way for the user to be informed of the table's content.

You may be tempted to replace the caption with a heading element. Resist the temptation. Again, when we're merely dealing with screened media, no difference will be noted, but the difference may be more serious in other media types. Style sheets and CSS properties give us the ability to decorate our elements any way we want, let's make sure that first and foremost our document is structurally sound!

Try It Out – Adding a Header and a Caption

1. Change the following lines of table1.htm, and save the result as table2.htm.

```
<?xml version="1.0" encoding="UTF-8"?>
<!DOCTYPE html
     PUBLIC "-//W3C//DTD XHTML 1.0 Strict//EN"
    "http://www.w3.org/TR/xhtml1/DTD/xhtml1-strict.dtd">
<html xmlns="http://www.w3.org/1999/xhtml" xml:lang="en" lang="en">
  <head>
    <title>A simple table with headings and a caption</title>
  </head>
  <body bgcolor="white">
    <table border="1">
  <caption>A simple XHTML table</caption>
  <tr><th>header 1</th><th>header 2</th></tr>
  <tr><td>Row 1-Col 1</td><td>Row 1-Col 2</td></tr>
  <tr><td>Row 2-Col 1</td><td>Row 2-Col 2</td></tr>
    </table>
  </body>
</html>
```

2. This is what it you should see if you view the file in IE5:

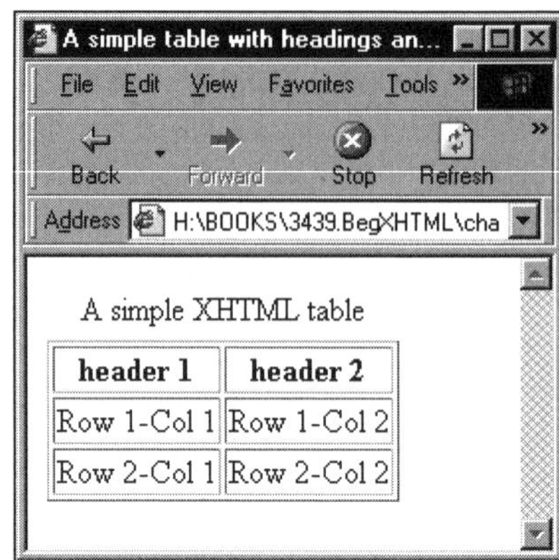

How It Works

In this file we have simply added the following lines of text:

```
<caption>A simple XHTML table</caption>
<tr><th>header 1</th><th>header 2</th></tr>
```

This produces two cells of the header type. Note that we use the `<th>` cell element instead of the `<td>` cell element for our headers, and that the resulting text is bold and centered.

Adding Further Structure to the Table

We can further divide our table into a head part, a body part, and a foot part using the `<thead>`, `<tbody>`, and `<tfoot>` elements.

We can build fairly complex tables just using the `<tr>` and the `<td>` elements, so why go to the trouble of using these further subdivisions? The simple answer is that it gives us an easy way to access the table's content using script and the document object model (we will cover this in a later section of the book), and it also allows us to more easily decorate our table with style properties.

Let's look at using these subdivisions now. First we will divide our table up, and then we will apply different styles to each part of the table.

Note that when we do subdivide our table in this manner, the `<tr>` element is not permitted to be a direct child of the `<table>` element, it must be contained in one of the subsections.

Try It Out – Adding Head, Foot, and Body Structures

1. Alter `table2.htm` as shown and save it as `tablestruc.htm`.

```
<?xml version="1.0" encoding="UTF-8"?>
<!DOCTYPE html
     PUBLIC "-//W3C//DTD XHTML 1.0 Strict//EN"
    "http://www.w3.org/TR/xhtml1/DTD/xhtml1-strict.dtd">
<html xmlns="http://www.w3.org/1999/xhtml" xml:lang="en" lang="en">
  <head>
```

```
    <title>A structured table</title>
  </head>
  <body bgcolor="white">
<table border="1" style="background-color:yellow;">
  <thead style="background-color:red;">
    <tr><th>header 1</th><th>header 2</th></tr>
  </thead>

  <tfoot style="background-color:teal;">
    <tr><td>footer 1</td><td>footer 2</td></tr>
  </tfoot>

  <tbody>
    <tr><td>Row 1-Col 1</td><td>Row 1-Col 2</td></tr>
    <tr><td>Row 2-Col 1</td><td>Row 2-Col 2</td></tr>
  </tbody>
</table>
  </body>
</html>
```

2. Here is what the table looks like:

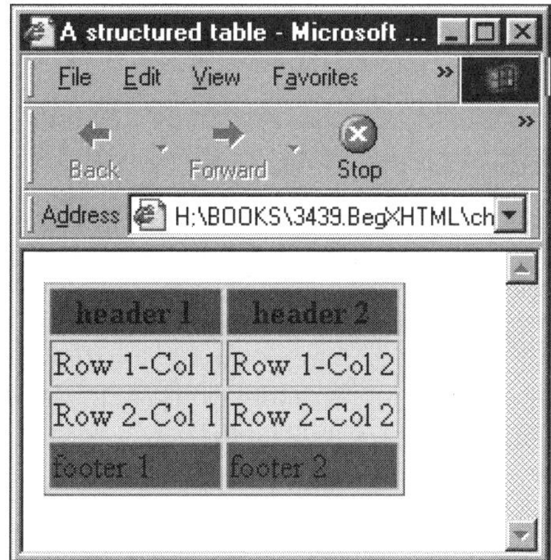

How It Works

We've altered the `<table>` element slightly by including a `style` attribute. In real life, as we've said, we would probably use a style sheet, which we'll learn how to do properly in Chapter 9.

```
<table border="1" style="background-color:yellow;">
```

We've also introduced the `<thead>` element, giving it a different background color just for variety:

```
  <thead style="background-color:red;">
    <tr><th>header 1</th><th>header 2</th></tr>
  </thead>
```

Note that we now define our header cells within the <thead> element. We now go on to define our <tfoot> element and its contents:

```
<tfoot style="background-color:teal;">
  <tr><td>footer 1</td><td>footer 2</td></tr>
</tfoot>
```

Note that within the <tfoot> element we actually use <td> elements to define the footer cells – there's no separate element like there is for headers.

Finally, we present our table's body:

```
<tbody>
  <tr><td>Row 1-Col 1</td><td>Row 1-Col 2</td></tr>
  <tr><td>Row 2-Col 1</td><td>Row 2-Col 2</td></tr>
</tbody>
```

Spanning Rows and Columns

Each individual compartment in a table is a cell, and in most cases we will want an equal number of cells in each row, and in each column. How do we handle the case where we want a cell to cover more than one row or column? In XHTML we use the colspan and rowspan attributes.

Using 'colspan' and 'rowspan'

colspan and rowspan are attributes of the <td> and <th> element. The general syntax is:

```
<td colspan="[integer]">
```

```
<td rowspan="[integer]">
```

The integer value is the number of rows or columns to be spanned. The affected cell will take the place normally occupied by this number of rows or columns, and can cause unwanted results if you forget to remove the cells whose place is supposed to be taken up!

Let's try this out now.

Try It Out – Using colspan

1. Type up the following and save it as colspan.htm:

```
<?xml version="1.0" encoding="UTF-8"?>
<!DOCTYPE html
     PUBLIC "-//W3C//DTD XHTML 1.0 Strict//EN"
    "http://www.w3.org/TR/xhtml1/DTD/xhtml1-strict.dtd">
<html xmlns="http://www.w3.org/1999/xhtml" xml:lang="en" lang="en">
  <head>
    <title>A simple table</title>
  </head>
  <body bgcolor="#ffffff">
```

```
      <table border="1">
        <tr><td colspan="2">Row 1-Col 1 & 2</td><td>Row 1-Col 3</td></tr>
        <tr><td>Row 2-Col 1</td><td>Row 2-Col 2</td><td>Row 2-Col 3</td></tr>
        <tr><td>Row 3-Col 1</td><td>Row 3-Col 2</td><td>Row 3-Col 3</td></tr>
      </table>
    </body>
  </html>
```

2. This is what you should see when you view the page in your browser:

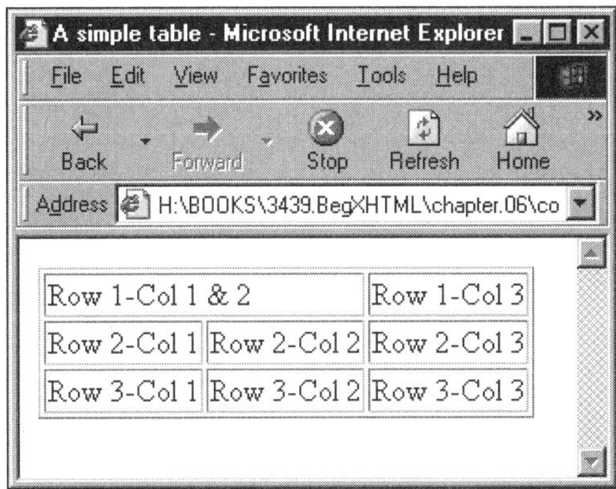

How It Works

We have made a simple table of 3 rows and three columns. The key line of XHTML here is:

```
    <tr><td colspan="2">Row 1-Col 1 & 2</td><td>Row 1-Col 3</td></tr>
```

We set the `colspan` attribute value to 2. Note how the first cell now extends into the second column.

Note also that we removed one of the `<td>` elements, so there are only two cells in this row. Here's what would happen if we didn't remove the cell:

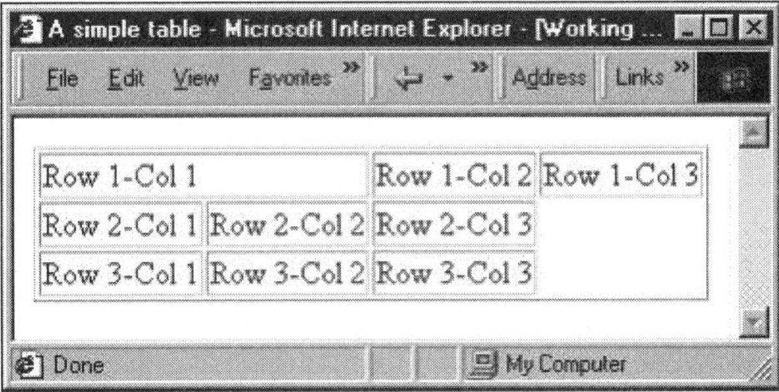

This is probably not what we intended!

Using `rowspan` is just as simple.

Try It Out – Using Rowspan

1. Alter the source for the last page as follows, and save it as `rowspan.htm`:

```
<?xml version="1.0" encoding="UTF-8"?>
<!DOCTYPE html
     PUBLIC "-//W3C//DTD XHTML 1.0 Strict//EN"
    "http://www.w3.org/TR/xhtml1/DTD/xhtml1-strict.dtd">
<html xmlns="http://www.w3.org/1999/xhtml" xml:lang="en" lang="en">
  <head>
    <title>A simple table</title>
  </head>
  <body bgcolor="#ffffff">
    <table border="1">
      <tr><td  rowspan="2">Row 1 &amp; 2-Col 1</td><td>Row 1-Col 2</td><td>Row 1-
      Col 3</td></tr>
      <tr><td>Row 2-Col 2</td><td>Row 2-Col 3</td></tr>
      <tr><td>Row 3-Col 1</td><td>Row 3-Col 2</td><td>Row 3-Col 3</td></tr>
    </table>

  </body>
</html>
```

2. This is what you will see when you view the page:

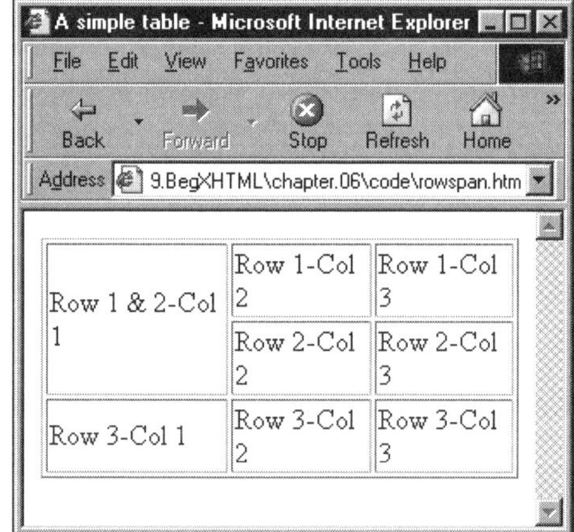

How It Works

Again the key line of code is the first line after the `<table>` tag, where we have set the `rowspan` attribute to 2:

```
<tr><td rowspan="2">Row 1 &amp; 2-Col 1</td><td>Row 1-Col 2</td><td>Row 1-
Col 3</td></tr>
```

Note once more how this time we have reduced the *second row* by a cell. Should we fail to do so, this is what we will see:

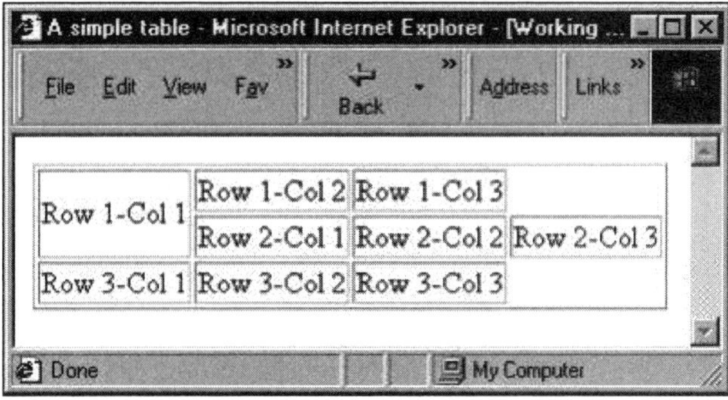

Again this is probably not what we intended!

The 'summary' Attribute

We'll only mention this briefly because it's not supported in any major browser at the present time. It is primarily designed for speech devices to give a summary of the purpose and structure of the whole table. Small devices that may not want to download the whole table could also utilize it. Although it's not currently supported, look out for it in new browsers if you intend your tabulated data to be useful to people with other types of user agent.

We now move on to discuss how tables can be styled.

Styling Tables

Tables can have styling applied to them either with a special set of attributes or with style sheets. The only implemented style sheet at present are the properties contained in the CSS1 recommendation.

In this section we are going to tell you how to apply styling to tables using both the attributes and the CSS1 properties. Remember that if you use both, the style sheet styling will override the attribute styling.

Style Sheets and XHTML Attributes

The Cascading Style Sheet specification comes in two versions – the earlier version is CSS1, and the later is CSS2. CSS2 contains all of CSS1 and also adds numerous other properties, many of them concerned with the styling and layout of tables. The problem is that none of the table styling properties of CSS2 have been implemented in any current browsers. For this reason we will not be using the more specialized of the table styling attributes for some time to come. The CSS1 properties have been implemented, so we can, and should, use these to set such things as font and color properties.

So far we have looked at the structural aspects of tables, and it is important to get these right. HTML was originally designed for the computer screen, so it is not surprising that it contains several attributes concerned with layout in that media. XHTML inherits these attributes. We will look at these in some detail, but it is important to remember that they really only apply to screen and, to a certain extent, paginated media.

Cascading style sheets also have a lot to say about laying out tables, and we will also have a brief look at the CSS properties as we go along.

Borders, Frames, and Rules

These three attributes are concerned with drawing borders around the various elements of the table. They are all attributes of the `<table>` element. The `border` attribute sets the thickness of the border; the `frames` attribute indicates what parts if any of the surrounding frame should be drawn, and the `rules` attribute proclaims where the dividing line between various cells should be drawn.

The 'border' Attribute

The `border` attribute sets the thickness of the border surrounding the whole table. It takes an integer value that is the required thickness of the border in pixels. The following screenshot illustrates the use of this attribute.

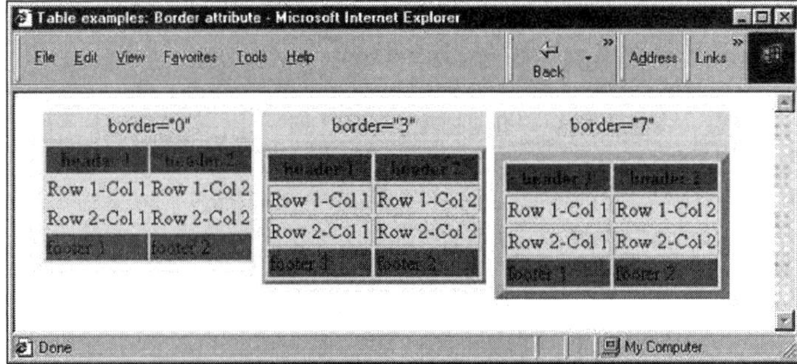

Note how the caption is not included, and the border just applies to outside of the document. However if the `border` attribute is set to `"0"` then there are no dividing lines between the individual cells.

The 'frame' Attribute

Once we have set the thickness of the frame using the `border` attribute, the `frame` attribute lets us decide where to put the frame. We don't need to have it going around the whole table. The `frame` attribute can take the following values:

`void`	Will draw no frame at all
`above`	Will produce just a top border
`below`	Will produce just a lower border

`lhs`	Will give a left-hand border only
`rhs`	Will give a right-hand border only
`hsides`	Will produce top and bottom borders
`vsides`	Will produce left and right borders
`box`	Will give a full border
`border`	Will give a full border

We leave it to you to experiment and see what these values really look like!

The 'rules' Attribute

The `rules` attribute allows us to decide how to draw dividing lines between various groups of cells. It can take the following values:

`none`	Will draw no borders around the cells
`all`	Will draw a border around every cell
`groups`	Will draw a border around tbody, thead, and tfoot
`rows`	Will draw a border between rows
`cols`	Will draw a border between individual columns

Using CSS Properties to Draw Frames and Borders

CSS has several border properties that allow us to further decorate our table should we so wish.

Here are the more commonly used ones:

- border-style
- border-width
- border-color

There are numerous variations such as `border-top`, `border-top-width`, and so on, that apply to various permutations, but we can do all we want to do with the above 3 properties.

The general syntax for these is:

```
border-*:[value1] [value2] [value3] [value4];
```

(where * is the appended qualification to border, for example `style`, `width`, `color`, etc.)

Note that one can have up to four values all separated by white space. If you set:

- one value: all four borders are set to that value
- two values: top and bottom borders are set to the first value, right and left are set to the second
- three values: top is set to the first, right and left are set to the second, bottom is set to the third
- four values: top, right, bottom and left, respectively

Try It Out – Drawing Borders and Frames

1. Type up the following in your favorite editor. Save it as `cssborder.htm`:

```
<?xml version="1.0" encoding="UTF-8"?>
<!DOCTYPE html
     PUBLIC "-//W3C//DTD XHTML 1.0 Strict//EN"
    "http://www.w3.org/TR/xhtml1/DTD/xhtml1-strict.dtd">
<html xmlns="http://www.w3.org/1999/xhtml" xml:lang="en" lang="en">
<head>
<title>A simple table with headers</title>

<style type="text/css">
  caption{
     background-color:#ccffcc;
  }
  td{
     border-style:solid;
     border-width:10pt 5pt;
     border-color:silver green blue white;
  }
</style>
</head>
<body bgcolor="white">
<table border="5" style="background-color:yellow;" rules="groups">
  <caption>Example of borders using attributes and CSS</caption>
  <thead  style="background-color:red;">
    <tr><th>header 1</th><th>header 2</th></tr>
  </thead>
  <tfoot style="background-color:teal;">
    <tr><td>footer 1</td><td>footer 2</td></tr>
  </tfoot>
  <tbody >
    <tr><td>Row 1-Col 1</td><td>Row 1-Col 2</td></tr>
    <tr><td>Row 2-Col 1</td><td>Row 2-Col 2</td></tr>
  </tbody>
</table>
</body>
</html>
```

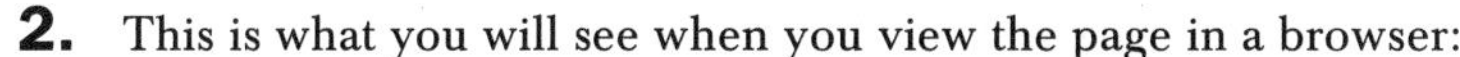

2. This is what you will see when you view the page in a browser:

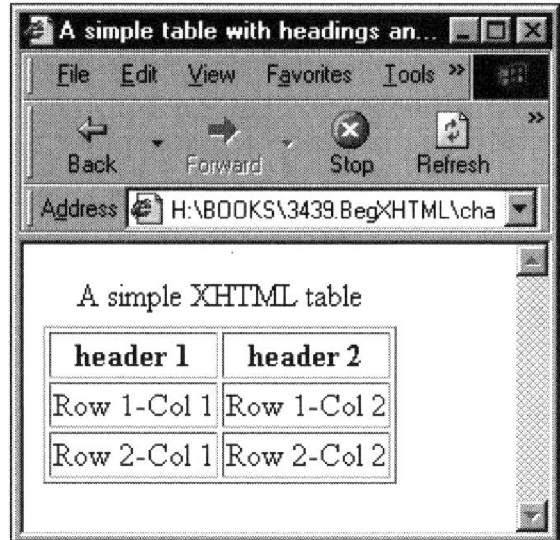

How It Works

First, note that we have included a simple embedded style sheet in our page:

```
<style type="text/css">
.......
</style>
```

We're getting a little ahead of ourselves, I guess, since we won't truly get into style sheets until Chapter 9. But we wanted to show the CSS equivalents while the issues were still fresh. Once you're more comfortable with CSS, all this will make more sense.

We have set the `background` property of the `<caption>` element to a mint green color:

```
caption{
   background-color:#ccffcc;
}
```

Next we set the `border` properties of the individual cells:

```
td{
```

All our borders will have a solid style:

```
   border-style:solid;
```

The top and bottom borders will be 10 points thick, the left and right will be 5 points:

```
   border-width:10pt 5pt;
```

We set a different color for each of the four borders (we're overdoing it a little, I wouldn't imagine that you would really want to create a table that looked like this!). Note how the different values are simply separated by spaces:

```
        border-color:silver green blue white;
    }
```

When we get on to the actual table itself, we have used an inline CSS property to set the background color. We have set the border value to 5, so we have a frame around the table 5 pixels thick:

```
<table border="5" style="background-color:yellow;" rules="groups">
```

We set the `rules` attribute to `groups`, so a border will be drawn around the `<thead>`, `<tbody>`, and `<tfoot>` group. If you look carefully you can see a border around the `<thead>` group, but the CSS border properties will override this attribute on both `<tbody>` and `<thead>`.

Cell Spacing and Cell Padding

Cell **spacing** is the space between individual cells. Cell **padding** is the space between the cell content and the border of the cell. In XHTML tables they are set by the `cellspacing` and the `cellpadding` attributes. In CSS we should be able to get even finer control using the `margin` and `padding` properties. 'Should' is used deliberately, because implementation of these properties is actually very poor in the mainstream browsers.

The 'cellspacing' Attribute

We will first take a look at `cellspacing`. This is the space between adjacent cells. The attribute is set on the `<table>` tag, and the value will apply to every cell in the table. The general syntax is:

```
cellspacing="[integer]"
```

where *`integer`* is a whole number of pixels. Note that the number of pixels is the distance between both the adjacent cells and the frame of the table. An example will make this clearer.

Try It Out – Adding Cell Spacing

1. Modify our `basic.htm` table section as follows, and save it as `cellspacing.htm`:

```
<table border="1" style="background-color:yellow;" cellspacing="20">
  <thead style="background-color:red;">
    <tr><th>header 1</th><th>header 2</th></tr>
  </thead>
  <tbody style="background-color:white;">
    <tr><td>Row 1-Col 1</td><td>Row 1-Col 2</td></tr>
    <tr><td>Row 2-Col 1</td><td>Row 2-Col 2</td></tr>
  </tbody>
  <tfoot style="background-color:teal;">
    <tr><td>footer 1</td><td>footer 2</td></tr>
  </tfoot>
</table>
```

2. This is what you will see:

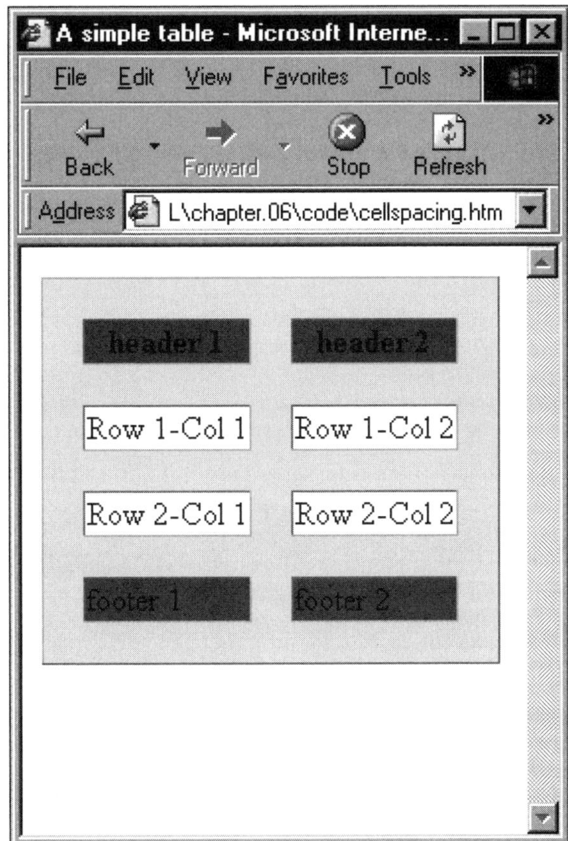

How It Works

Here is the key line of code:

```
<table border="1" style="background-color:yellow;" cellspacing="20">
```

Note that there is a 20-pixel space between each of the cells, and also between the cells and the border of the table.

cellpadding

The cell padding is the distance between the content of the cell and the border of the cell and is set with the `cellpadding` attribute on the `<table>` element. The general syntax is:

```
cellpadding="[integer]"
```

where the integer is the value in pixels. Again this will apply to all cells in the table. Here is an example.

Try It Out – Adding Cellpadding

1. Modify the file from the last example so the area between the `<table>` tags reads as follows:

```
<table border="1" style="background-color:yellow;" cellpadding="20">

  <thead style="background-color:red;">
    <tr><th>header 1</th><th>header 2</th></tr>
  </thead>
  <tbody style="background-color:white;">
    <tr><td>Row 1-Col 1</td><td>Row 1-Col 2</td></tr>
    <tr><td>Row 2-Col 1</td><td>Row 2-Col 2</td></tr>
  </tbody>
  <tfoot  style="background-color:teal;">
    <tr><td>footer 1</td><td>footer 2</td></tr>
  </tfoot>
</table>
```

2. Save it as `cellpadding.htm`. Here is the result of viewing this page in IE5:

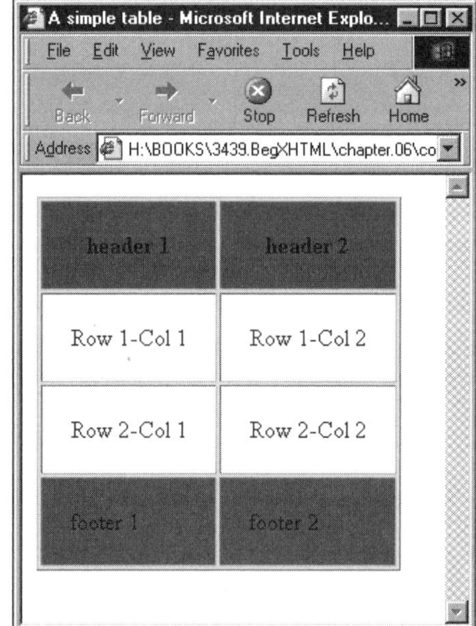

How It Works

Here's the important line:

```
<table border="1" style="background-color:yellow;" cellpadding="20">
```

Note there is a 20-pixel layer of 'padding', or blank space, around the content of each cell.

CSS Padding Properties

CSS margin properties are not implemented for the individual cells of tables. However we can get much finer control over the padding by using the CSS padding properties. With these we can decree the specific padding to the top, right, bottom, and left sides of the content.

Here are the CSS padding properties; they should actually be self-explanatory:

- `padding-left`
- `padding-top`
- `padding-right`
- `padding-bottom`

We can also use `padding` on its own, with value parameters, to set padding on all four margins; it can take up to four values separated by white space

```
padding:[value1] [value2] [value3] [value4];
```

The arrangement of the values is exactly the same as we saw in the `border` property above:

- one value: padding on all four sides are set to that value
- two values: top and bottom padding are set to the first value, right and left are set to the second
- three values: top is set to the first, right and left are set to the second, bottom is set to the third
- four values: represents padding values for top, right, bottom and left, respectively

Try It Out – Setting CSS Padding Properties

1. Here we will use the `style` attribute to set the padding values on individual cells. Modify `cellpadding.htm`:

```
<body bgcolor="white">
<table border="1" style="background-color:yellow;" >
  <thead style="background-color:red;">
    <tr><th>header 1</th><th>header 2</th></tr>
  </thead>
  <tbody style="background-color:white;">
    <tr><td style="padding-left:10pt;">padding left is set to 10 points.</td><td
style="padding:0pt 10pt;">left and right set to 10 points</td></tr>
    <tr><td style="padding:10pt 0pt;">Top and bottom set to 10 points.</td><td
style="padding:10pt;">10 points all round.</td></tr>
    <tr><td style="padding-top:10pt;">Top set to 10 points.</td><td
style="padding-bottom:10pt;">Bottom set to 10 points.</td></tr>
  </tbody>
  <tfoot style="background-color:teal;">
    <tr><td>footer 1</td><td>footer 2</td></tr>
  </tfoot>
</table>
</body>
</html>
```

2. Save it as `csspadding.htm`. Here is what we will see:

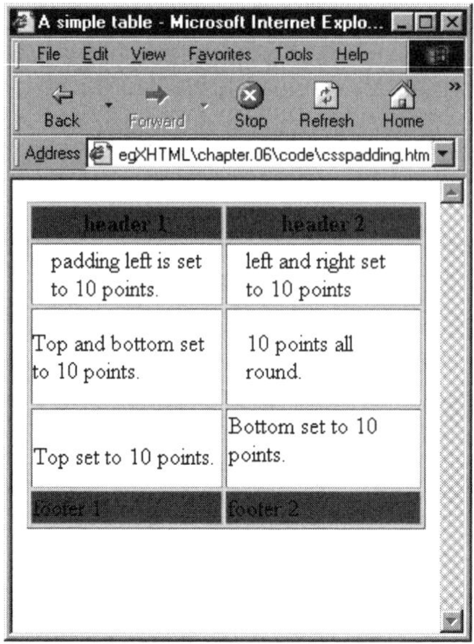

How It Works

Here we have used the `padding-left` property. It takes a single value:

```
<td style="padding-left:10pt;">padding left is set to 10 points.</td>
```

In the next cell we supply two values: the first value (which represents top and bottom) is set to 0 points, and the second value (which represents both left and right padding) is set to 10 points:

```
<td style="padding:0pt 10pt;">left and right set to 10 points</td>
```

We have reversed the situation in the third cell. The first value, which represents top and bottom, is set to 10 points, and the second to 0:

```
<td style="padding:10pt 0pt;">Top and bottom set to 10 points.</td>
```

Next, we set the value to 10 points all round by using a single value:

```
<td style="padding:10pt;">10 points all round.</td></tr>
```

In the last two cells we use the more specific properties, first `padding-top`:

```
<td style="padding-top:10pt;">Top set to 10 points.</td>
```

And here `padding-bottom`:

```
<td style="padding-bottom:10pt;">Bottom set to 10 points.</td></tr>
```

Background Color

The best way to set a background color is to use the CSS properties. However for backward compatibility with older browsers, the `bgcolor` attribute is available:

The 'bgcolor' Attribute

The `<table>`, `<tr>` and `<td>` elements can all set color using the `bgcolor` attribute. Here is the syntax:

```
bgcolor ="[color name] OR [hexadecimal color code]"
```

The 16 commonly used color names are listed in Appendix C, and the hexadecimal color codes are discussed in Chapter 9.

The CSS background-color Property

A much better way to set the background color of individual cells and sections of a table is to use the CSS `background-color` property. In fact, as you have noticed, we have been using this all along in our examples.

The general syntax for this is:

```
background-color: [color name] OR [color code];
```

Again, the color name is one of the 16 named colors, but color code can take numerous different types of code including the hexadecimal version. These are covered in Chapter 9.

Height and Width

In the now-familiar pattern we can set the width of a table with either an attribute, or by using CSS. As usual an attribute will give us backward compatibility, and CSS gives us greater flexibility. Once more if we use both, the CSS properties will override the attribute values.

Setting Widths of Tables, Columns, and Cells using Attributes

The `width` attribute can be used to set the width of both the table and the individual cells. It can take a relative value, a percentage, or an absolute value in pixels.

It is best to set the width of the columns on the first row of cells. Although they can be set on succeeding rows, the user agent, which is reading from top to bottom, will have to reflow the whole table when it comes to a new value. If there are conflicting values then various user agents use different algorithms to decide how to size the table. You can be sure that you will get a display of some kind, but it may not be the one you wanted.

> **It's much better to just place the values on the first row, and know what display you are going to get.**

In the screenshot below the first table has been set in relative values, and the second table has been set in absolute values. We'll see in a moment how to use the attributes to do this, but first we'll see how to do it in CSS and then use both methods in a single example.

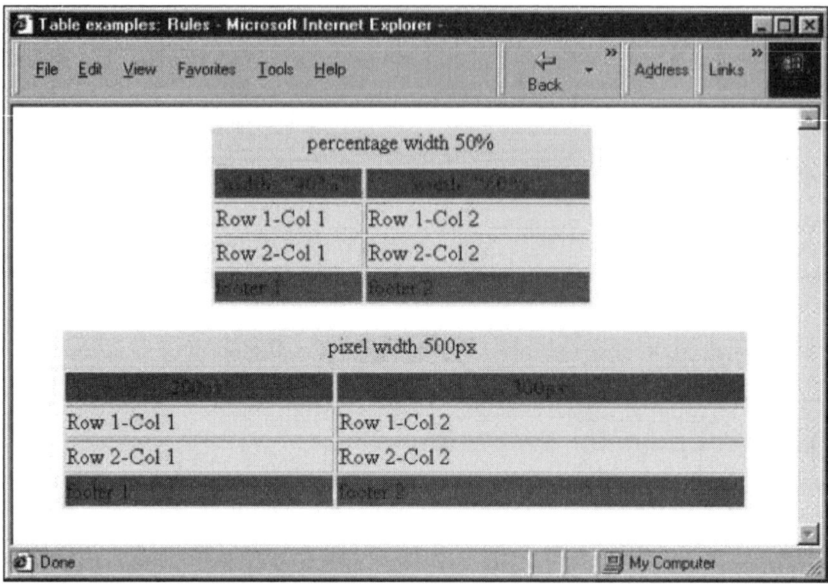

Let's look at setting widths using a style sheet.

Setting Height and Width Using CSS

A style sheet will override all values set by the `width` attribute, but in many browsers CSS values are not well supported, so it is always advisable to set both CSS values and width attributes.

It is also possible to set values for the height of cells, something that is not possible to do just using attributes. Here is an example:

Try It Out – Setting Height and Width Properties

1. Type up the following and save it as `heightwidth.htm`:

```
<?xml version="1.0" encoding="UTF-8"?>
<!DOCTYPE html
     PUBLIC "-//W3C//DTD XHTML 1.0 Strict//EN"
    "http://www.w3.org/TR/xhtml1/DTD/xhtml1-strict.dtd">
<html xmlns="http://www.w3.org/1999/xhtml" xml:lang="en" lang="en">
<head>
<title>Table examples: Width</title>
<style>
  caption{
    background-color:#aaffaa;
  }
  tr{
    height:36pt;
  }
  td{
    height:48pt;
    width:50%;
  }
```

```
</style>
</head>
<body bgcolor="white">

<table border="3" style="background-color:yellow;"  frame="void" align="center"
width="90%">
<caption>percentage width 90%</caption>
  <thead  style="background-color:red;">
    <tr><th width="40%">width="40%"</th><th width="60%">width="60%"</th></tr>
  </thead>
  <tbody >
    <tr><td>Row 1-Col 1</td><td>Row 1-Col 2</td></tr>
    <tr><td>Row 2-Col 1</td><td>Row 2-Col 2</td></tr>
  </tbody>
  <tfoot  style="background-color:teal;">
    <tr><td>footer 1</td><td>footer 2</td></tr>
  </tfoot>
</table>
<br />
</body>
</html>
```

2. Run it in your favorite browser. If that happens to be IE 5 then you will see the following:

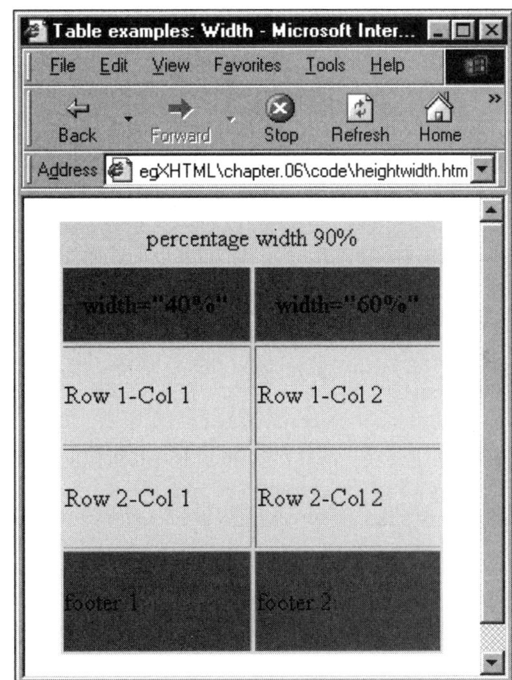

How It Works

Although we have set the `width` attributes:

```
<tr><th width="40%">width="40%"</th><th width="60%">width="60%"</th></tr>
```

they are overridden by the values that we set on the style sheet, assuming your browser of choice supports style sheets:

```
tr{
    height:36pt;
  }
  td{
    height:48pt;
    width:50%;
```

Note how the row containing the headings is 36 points high, but that this setting is overridden by the <td> setting in the other rows.

General Problems with Cell Width Settings

In the absence of either a style sheet or an attribute the width of the cells is set by a rather long and complicated algorithm. One of the things this algorithm tries to do is not break a word in the middle. Unfortunately, we can get some very long 'words' when we look at URIs and the user-agent is not smart enough to recognize them as a URI. Consider these lines from two tables. The first:

```
<tr>
<td width="200">My page</td><td width="200">Jan1</td> <td width="200">This is a
very long url</td> <td
width="200">www.someorg.com/afolder/andhereisanotherfolder/resultingin/oneofthose/
rediculouslylongurls.htm</td>
</tr>
```

And the second:

```
<tr>
<td width="200">My page</td><td width="200">Jan1</td> <td width="200">This is a
short url</td><td width="200">www.shorturl.com</td>
</tr>
```

Here is how IE5 renders this. Actually, adding a style sheet will not make a difference, so all we can do is be aware of the situation.

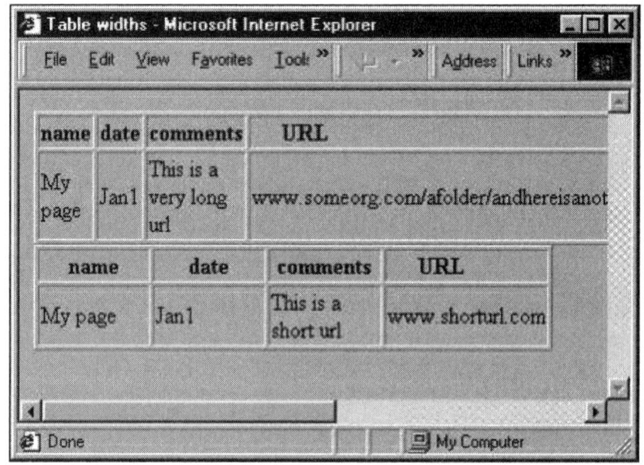

Aligning the Table Relative to the Document

The default place for a table to appear is to the left of our document, and the default place for the text to start is right after our table. If, however we use the table's `align` attribute, we can center the table and/or place it to the left or right. With the `align="left"` or `align="right"` values set, the text will flow around the table. Let's look at an example of this right now.

Try It Out – Using the 'align' Attribute

1. Type this page into your editor and save it as `align1.htm`. As before, the long block of text can be anything you want – we've pasted it from our `lorem.txt` file that is included in the code download for the book.

```
<?xml version="1.0" encoding="UTF-8"?>
<!DOCTYPE html
     PUBLIC "-//W3C//DTD XHTML 1.0 Strict//EN"
    "http://www.w3.org/TR/xhtml1/DTD/xhtml1-strict.dtd">
<html xmlns="http://www.w3.org/1999/xhtml" xml:lang="en" lang="en">
<head>
<title>A simple table with headers</title>
</head>
<body bgcolor="white">

<table border="1" style="background-color:yellow;" align="right">
  <thead  style="background-color:red;">
    <tr><th>header 1</th><th>header 2</th></tr>
  </thead>
  <tbody >
    <tr><td>Row 1-Col 1</td><td>Row 1-Col 2</td></tr>
    <tr><td>Row 2-Col 1</td><td>Row 2-Col 2</td></tr>
  </tbody>
  <tfoot  style="background-color:teal;">
    <tr><td>footer 1</td><td>footer 2</td></tr>
  </tfoot>
</table>
<div>"Lorem ipsum dolor sit amet, consectetaur adipisicing elit,
sed do eiusmod tempor incididunt ut labore et dolore magna aliqua.
Ut enim ad minim veniam, quis nostrud exercitation ullamco laboris
nisi ut aliquip ex ea commodo consequat. Duis aute irure dolor in
reprehenderit in voluptate velit esse cillum dolore eu fugiat
nulla pariatur. Excepteur sint occaecat cupidatat non proident,
sunt in culpa qui officia deserunt mollit anim id est laborum Et
harumd und lookum like Greek to me, dereud facilis est er expedit
distinct. Nam liber te conscient to factor tum poen legum odioque
civiuda. Et tam neque pecun modut est neque nonor et imper ned
libidig met, consectetur adipiscing elit, sed ut labore et dolore
magna aliquam"
</div>
</body>
</html>
```

2. Now view the page in a browser. Note how the text flows around the table.

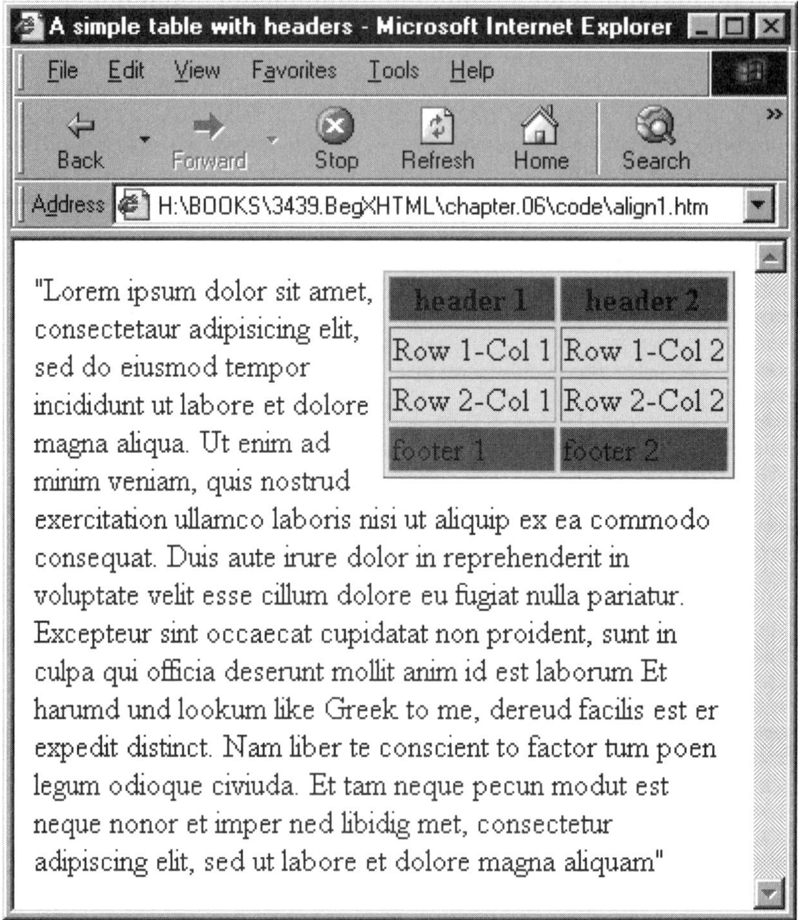

If you want to place the table to the right and have text start after the table then you must use the `clear` attribute of the `<br/>` element right after the table.

```
<br clear="right" />
```

Using CSS to Align our Table

We do the same in CSS by using the `float` property. All you'd need to do is to add the following style sheet into the `<head>` element of the above example:

```
<style>
table{
  float:left;
}
</style>
```

If you were to run it now, you'd get this:

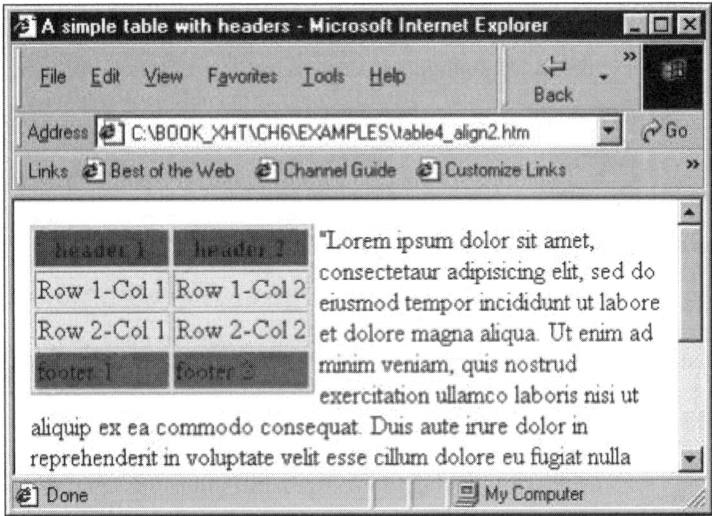

The style sheet has overridden the `align ="right"` attribute.

Aligning Tables With Other Tables

We can also align tables with respect to other tables using the `align` attribute or CSS. The default behavior is for the table to act as a block element, and for one table to follow beneath the other. However if we set the `align` attribute to `"left"` or `"right"` the table will act like an inline object and not only will text flow around it, but other tables will line up side by side. We can best illustrate this by examples.

In this screen shot we have set the `align` attribute on Table 1 to `"left"`:

```
<table border="3" style="background-color:yellow;" align="left" >
```

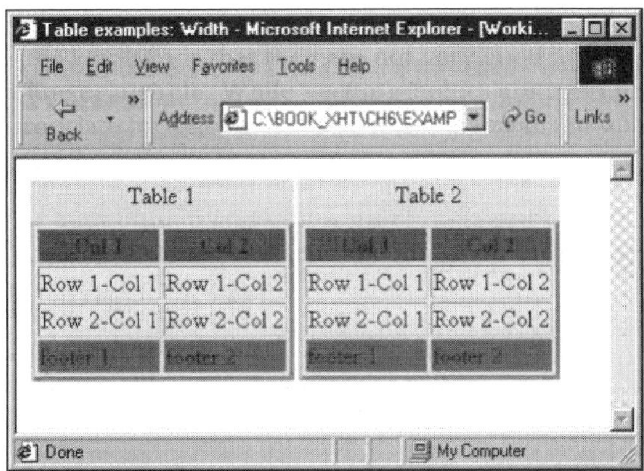

Note that the result would be the same if we set the align attribute on the second table to "left".

In the following example we have set the align attribute on both Table 1 and Table 2 to "right":

```
<table border="3" style="background-color:yellow;" align="right" >
```

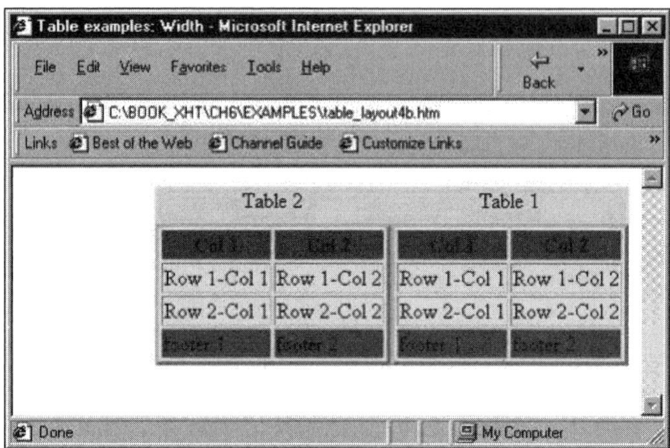

Note in particular how the order of the tables has changed. Table 2 now precedes Table 1.

Using CSS Properties

We can get the same result in CSS by using the float property. The following style sheet would produce exactly the same result as the second example above in conforming browsers:

```
table{
   float:right;
}
```

Nesting Tables

A <td> element can contain any other presentational element, including another table! This allows us to use tables to display and layout our tables. Note that this is a presentational device, and should only be used when we are expecting our pages to be displayed in large screen visual media.

Nesting tables in this manner allows us to create quite complicated displays and layouts, but like anything else it should not be overdone. It is very expensive in terms of computing power to lay out multiple tables, and multiple tables are almost impossible to render in non-visual browsers.

Aligning Text Within the Table

To align text within the cell of a table we use the valign and/or the align attribute. The valign attribute controls the vertical alignment of the text within the cell, and the align attribute controls the horizontal alignment of text in the table. Note that although the align attribute shares the same name as the align attribute used for the <table> element, the align attribute when applied to <tr> or <td> or <th> elements can take extra values.

The 'valign' Attribute

The `valign` attribute governs vertical alignment within the cell. There is no equivalent CSS1 property, although there is an equivalent CSS2 property. The general syntax is:

```
valign="[value]"
```

The possible values `valign` can take are:

- `top`
- `middle`
- `bottom`
- `baseline`

These values are best illustrated by an example.

Try It Out – The 'valign' Attribute

1. Type in the following code and save it as `valign.htm`:

```
<?xml version="1.0" encoding="UTF-8"?>
<!DOCTYPE html
     PUBLIC "-//W3C//DTD XHTML 1.0 Strict//EN"
    "http://www.w3.org/TR/xhtml1/DTD/xhtml1-strict.dtd">
<html xmlns="http://www.w3.org/1999/xhtml" xml:lang="en" lang="en">
<head>
<title>Table examples</title>
</head>
<body bgcolor="white">
<table width="100%" border="1">
  <tr><th>valign=
</th><th>"top"</th><th>"middle"</th><th>"bottom"</th><th>"baseline"</th></tr>
  <tr>
  <td width="20%">Lorem ipsum dolor sit amet, consectetaur adipisicing elit sed
    do eiusmod tempor incididunt ut labore et dolore magna aliqua</td>
  <td width="20%" valign="top">Lorem ipsum dolor sit amet, consectetaur
adipisicing elit</td>
  <td width="20%" valign="middle">Lorem ipsum dolor sit amet, consectetaur
adipisicing elit</td>
  <td width="20%" valign="bottom">Lorem ipsum dolor sit amet, consectetaur
adipisicing elit</td>
  <td width="20%" valign="baseline">Lorem ipsum dolor sit amet, consectetaur
adipisicing elit</td>
  </tr>
</table>
</body>
</html>
```

2. Here's what you'll see when you view it:

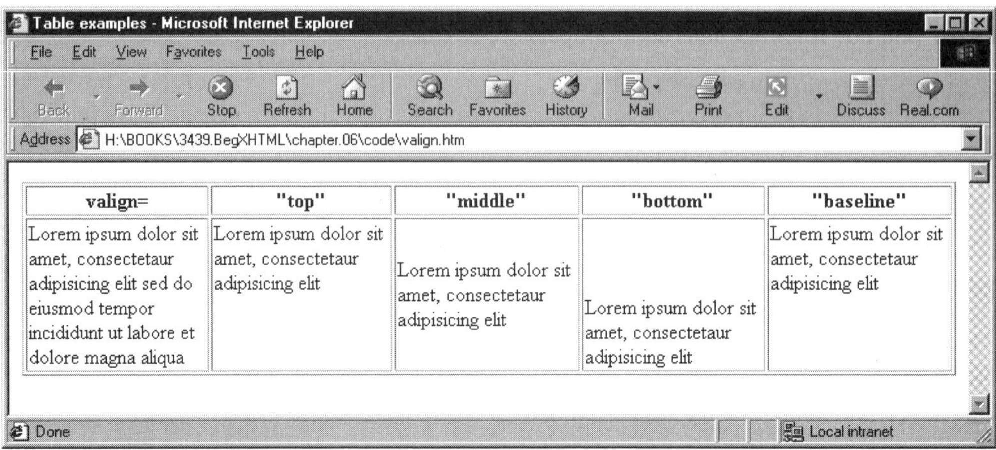

How It Works

In the first cell, we've placed more text than in the other cells, so that the cells become bigger than they need to be. That lets us see the effect of each of these values. As you can see, `top`, `middle`, and `bottom` are true to their names, whereas `baseline` gives a similar value to `top`.

The 'align' Attribute

The `align` attribute aligns text within a cell. Its possible values are:

left right center justify

We will illustrate this with a quick example. The following table contains columns for each of the first four values, and for the CSS equivalent of the `justify` attribute.

Try It Out – The 'align' Attribute

1. Type in the following code and save it as `align2.htm`:

```
<?xml version="1.0" encoding="UTF-8"?>
<!DOCTYPE html
     PUBLIC "-//W3C//DTD XHTML 1.0 Strict//EN"
    "http://www.w3.org/TR/xhtml1/DTD/xhtml1-strict.dtd">
<html xmlns="http://www.w3.org/1999/xhtml" xml:lang="en" lang="en">
<head>
  <title>Table examples</title>
</head>
<body bgcolor="white">
 <table width="100%" border="1">
  <caption>Demonstrating the align attribute</caption>
  <tr><th>"left"</th><th>"center"</th><th>"right"</th><th>"justify"</th><th>css
justify</th></tr>
```

```
  <tr>
  <td width="20%" align="left">Lorem ipsum dolor sit amet, consectetaur
adipisicing elitsed
  do eiusmod tempor incididunt ut labore et dolore magna aliqua</td>
  <td width="20%" align="center">Lorem ipsum dolor sit amet, consectetaur
adipisicing elit</td>
  <td width="20%" align="right">Lorem ipsum dolor sit amet, consectetaur
adipisicing elit</td>
  <td width="20%" align="justify">Lorem ipsum dolor sit amet, consectetaur
adipisicing elit</td>
  <td width="20%" style="text-align:justify;">Lorem ipsum dolor sit amet,
consectetaur adipisicing elit</td>
  </tr>
</table>
</body>
</html>
```

2. Here's what you'll see when you view it:

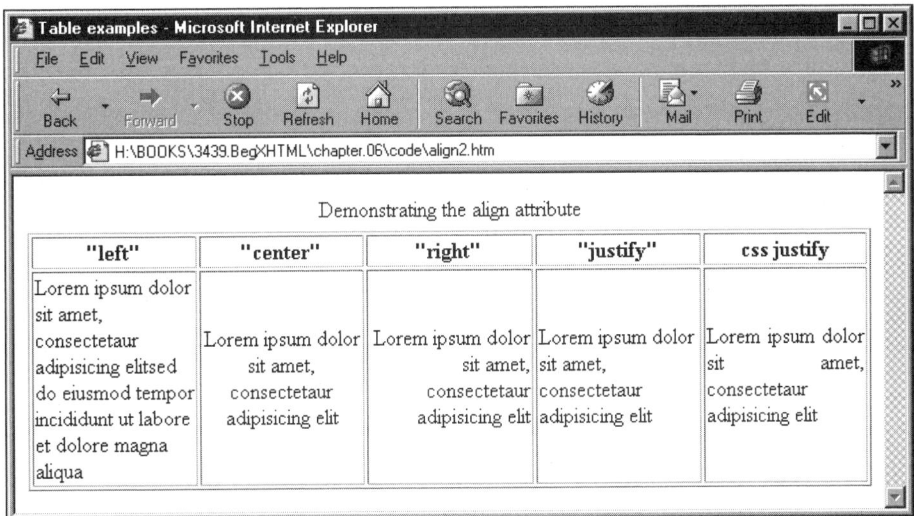

The results are fairly self-explanatory. As you can see, the CSS justification behaves slightly differently from the attribute's treatment.

Using Tables for Layout

Look at almost any commercial page on the Internet and you will see tables used to lay out content, rather than being used simply to present tabular data. The reason for this is that the commercial pages need to reach the largest audience, and so they use techniques that are supported in the largest possible number of browsers. No one can claim the credit for pioneering the use of tables to format screen layouts (although many have tried!); it is just such an obvious use of tables that the use was arrived at spontaneously by several innovators.

Until CSS layout support becomes much more common, tables will tend to be used for this purpose. We will just look at three different – but popular – layout styles.

Header and Navigation Strips

This is probably the most common of the layouts, and a representation is shown below. It consists of a table of two rows and two columns, with the first row being expanded into a single column.

```
...
<table border="0" width="98%">
<tr><td colspan="2" style="background-color:#ccffcc"><h1 align="center">Tables for
layout</h1></td></tr>
<tr>
  <td width="20%"  style="background-color:#ffffcc" valign="top" style="margin-
left:10pt;">
  <div style="margin-left:10pt;"><b>link</b
...etc.....
</div>

  </td>
  <td width="80%"  style="background-color:#ccffff">"Lorem ipsum...magna aliquam"
</td>
</tr>
</table>
...
```

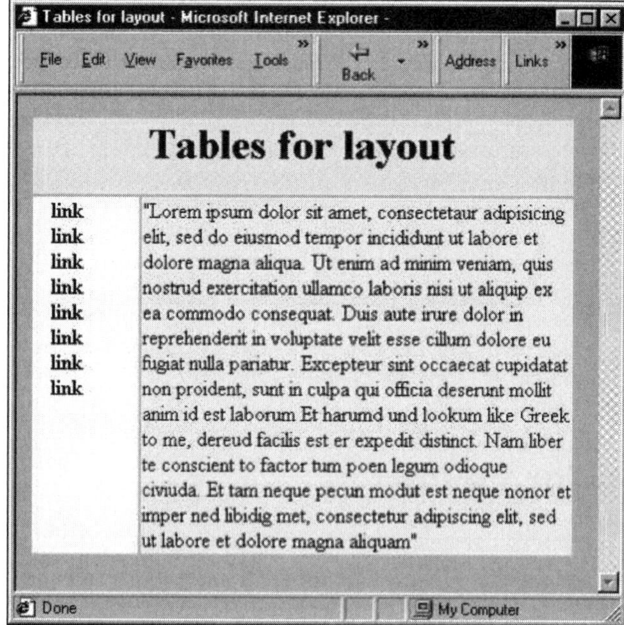

It is usual to put the title and/or a banner ad in the first row, and to place the links in the first column of the second row.

Adding a Bullet Bar

This layout is particularly popular with online magazines. A third column is added on the right-hand side, and in this column various bullets, or links to associated stories are added.

The left column contains the "inhouse" navigation links.

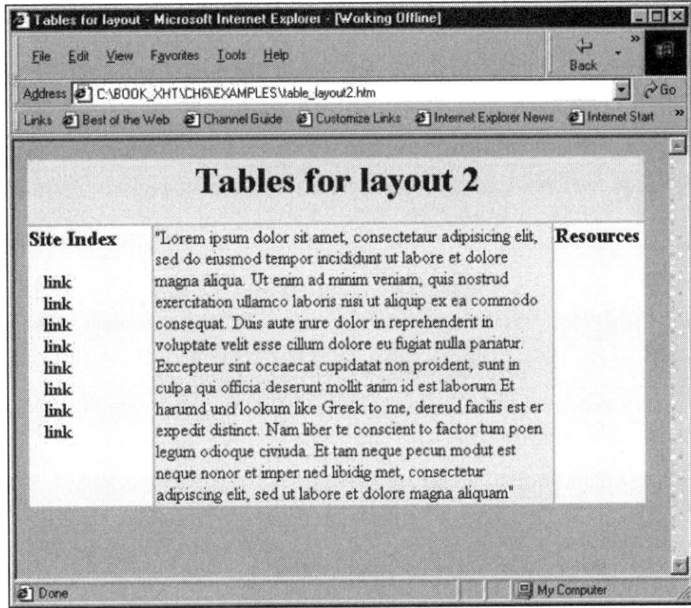

Using Tables for Margins

Written text without a margin can not only look pretty awful, but can be difficult to read. The eye has difficulty picking up a new line when it returns to the left side of the page! The following screen shot shows how tables can be used to give a pleasing layout to a simple piece of text.

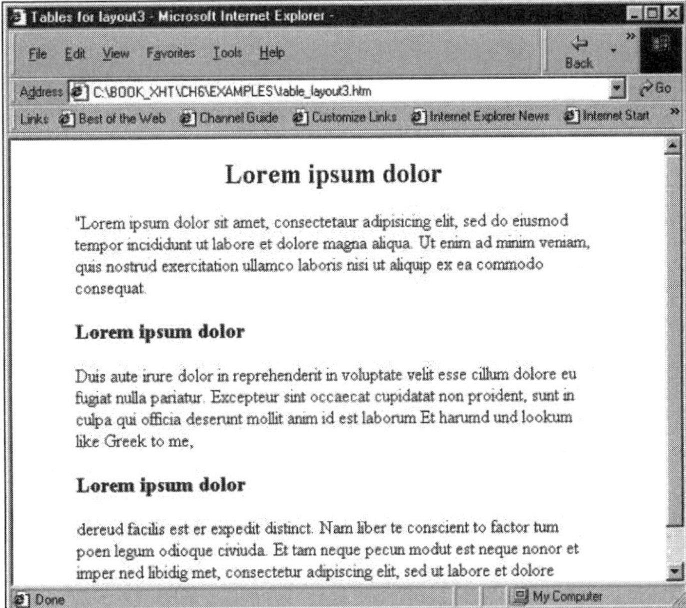

Remember these techniques described above are all only of value for visual media – they are of no use whatsoever in non-visual media, and that is what we will look at now.

Tables in Non-Visual and Non-Scrolling Media

A fuller discussion of other media is contained in Chapter 15. The discussion as it relates to tables is important enough to cover here, though, since the usefulness of tables relates mostly to large, visual media.

By visual media we mean media capable of giving a visual display. These include:

- **Scrolled** media. Typically the monitor of a computer with a full ability to scroll.
- **Paginated** media. These are usually the printed page, but can also be screen readers, or a slide show.
- **TV**. Do we need to tell you what a TV is?
- **Small device** displays. Something like a hand held computer, or the display area of a cell phone.

By non-visual media we mean:

- **Voice Browsers**. A cell phone, or a browser for use in a car, or by the visually impaired.
- **Braille** or **tactile** devices. Braille is a system whereby characters are represented by a grid of six upraised dots. These are then read by the fingertips of the visually impaired.

Using tables in other than the purely structural sense may cause problems for every type of media device except scrolled media. Let's look at the limitations of each of these in turn, and then look at some guidelines for making our tables truly accessible to every media type.

Paginated Media

Here a large table may not easily fit onto a page or a screen reader. A 'smart' user agent will break up the tables into manageable chunks, and present each chunk between the header and the footer. If a table is being used for layout the user agent will treat the content as if it was tabulated media, and will use whatever algorithm it employs to display the content as tabulated material. This may lead to some very peculiar results.

Nested tables are particularly difficult to display in paginated media, indeed the results are likely to be totally unpredictable. As a rule of thumb never use nested tables unless you are sure that your material will only be displayed on scrolled media.

TV

All the same arguments apply to tables being displayed on TV as to those being displayed on paginated media. However in some TV displays it may be possible to scroll using the remote control directional buttons.

Small device displays

Small display devices will range from 'miniature' computer screens to simple grid displays with a limited output. Most of them will not be able to display fancy styling, and some of them will not be able to support tables at all.

Most of them will have some kind of algorithm for dealing with tables, or will download material from a proxy server that has such an algorithm. One possible algorithm would be to break up the table into individual cells with each cell having a header, a footer, and a row number.

Nearly all of them will have limited computing resources.

In any case it is a safe bet to say that none (well almost none) of them will be able to deal with nested tables, and that if you use tables for presentation then the display is going to be less than optimal.

Voice Browsers

As of yet there is no standard algorithm for the interpretation of tables by voice browsers. It is almost certain, however, that they will convert the table into some kind of list. Whether the list is read by row, or by column, or whether the user has any control over which part of the table is to be read is up to the individual agent or its proxy server.

In any case it is certain that using tables for styling purposes is not recommended, and that nested tables will create a particular headache.

In fact if you think that your data is going to have heavy use on voice browsers (for example, stock market tips designed to be heard on a car browser), then consider using lists instead of tables.

Braille Readers

Tables *can* be handled on Braille readers; however, the typical Braille reader will only be able to read one row at a time! The limitations of Braille are therefore the same as for paginated media with the additional limitation that the page is reduced to a single line. For sighted people to get an idea of what it is like to read Braille from a Braille reader, consider getting all your information from a single line of text scrolling across your monitor.

Again do not use nested tables or tables for layout.

Guidelines for Accessibility

The following are a few guidelines to follow in order to make your tables fully accessible. Remember even though some elements and attributes are not supported in scrolling browsers, the chances are they will be in the proxy servers that will be converting your table for use in their non-scrolling clients:

- Do not use any style feature to differentiate different parts of the table. For example, do not use say a green and a red background color to distinguish between safe and dangerous practices.
- If a table is used for layout, make sure that the content makes sense if it is linearized. If it doesn't make sure that you provide a linearized version of your table content.

- If the table is used for layout do not use the presentation features of a table (for example, `<th>` elements are usually centered and emboldened) for styling.
- Make sure that your table is adequately structurally partitioned. Make full use of the `<caption>`, `<thead>`, `<tfoot>`, and `<tbody>` divisions.
- Do not use nested tables!

Summary

In this chapter we looked at one of the most commonly used features of XHTML, the table. We stressed the difference between the structural makeup of a table and its style, and showed you the importance of building your tables correctly.

We then had a look at how tables could be styled using both attributes and CSS.

We then looked briefly at a very common usage of tables, namely their use in laying out a page on the screen, but we also saw how although this is an extremely useful trick for scrolled media, it can present problems in non-scrolled media, especially non-visual media.

We ended the chapter with a summary of the problems encountered with using tables in different media types, and looked at some simple accessibility guidelines that would ensure that our tables would transfer well across all these different types.

In the next chapter, we'll tackle another contentious subject – frames.

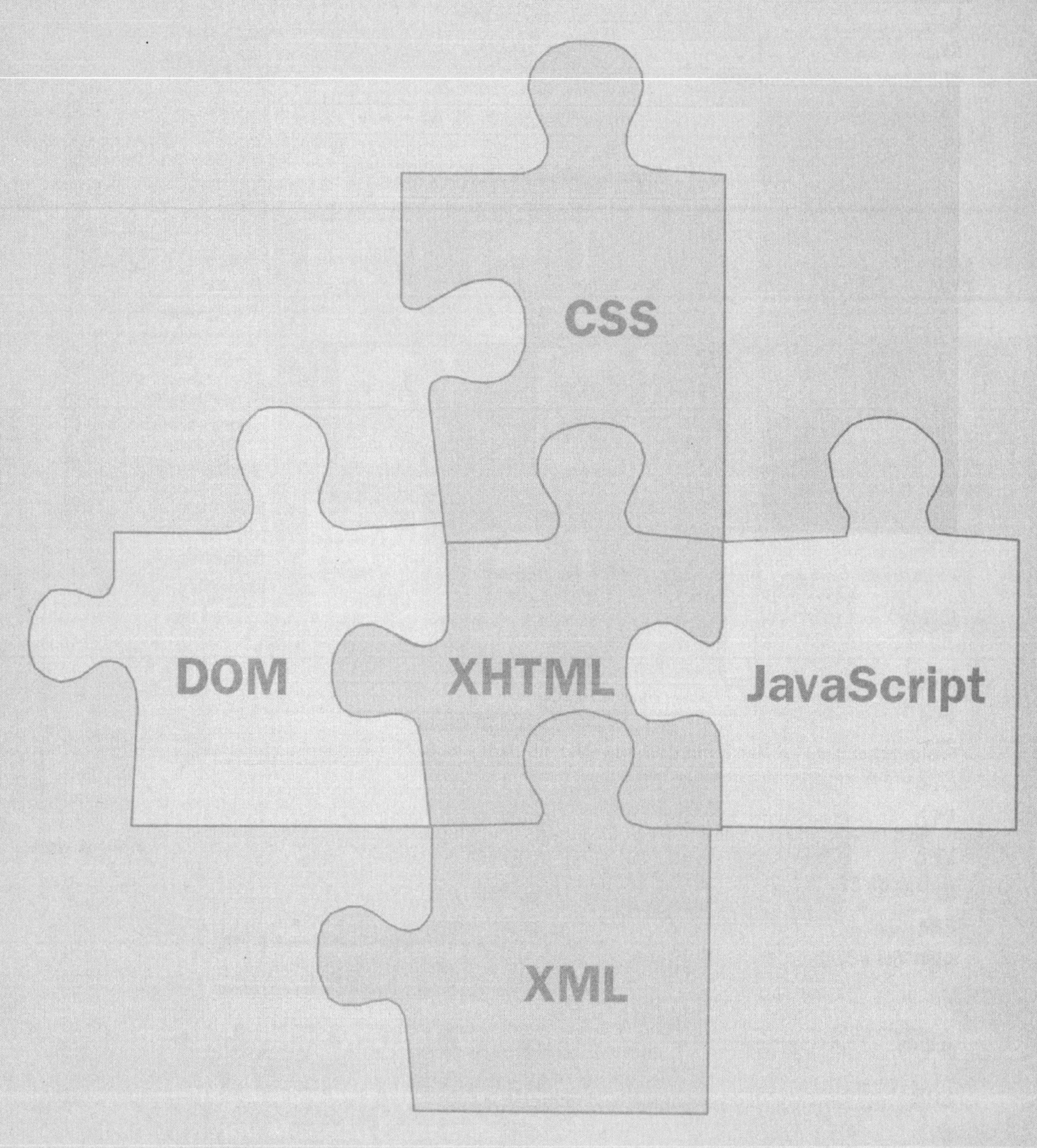
CSS
DOM
XHTML
JavaScript
XML

Frames

Frames did not become a W3C recommendation until HTML 4. It was a feature that was pioneered by Netscape during the browser wars in Navigator version 2; IE followed suit in version 3. In XHTML, frames are formally deprecated and are only included as part of the Frameset DTD (and not the Strict).

Frames allow us to display several pages within one single window. Judicious use of frames can enhance a web page, but many authors get carried away and use a multitude of frames. Partly because of this, frames have acquired a terrible reputation over the years, in some ways justified and in others not. Certainly as a presentational and browsing mechanism frames can create several problems, and can be especially difficult for small screen devices, but if used wisely they can be extremely useful.

In this chapter we will cover the following:

- how to create a set of frames
- how to use the `<frameset>` and `<frame>` elements
- how to nest frames
- the `target` attribute and its use with frames
- inline frames

Laying Out a Set of Frames

The basic concept behind frames is very simple. All we do is divide the browser (or other user-agent) window into separate sections. Each section is referred to as a **frame**. We use the `<frameset>` element to define how many separate sections or frames we require. A separate `<frame>` element is then used in each section to define what material is displayed in that section.

It is useful to decompose the word 'frameset' into 'set of frames' because doing so provides a clearer meaning to the terminology. A useful analogy is that of a stained glass window: all the separate divisions are controlled by the `<frameset>` element (decisions such as what size a particular piece of glass should be) while the content (decisions such as what color a particular piece of glass should be) is controlled by the `<frame>` element. Of course, the analogy is not exact but that is the nature of analogies.

An example illustrates this much more clearly, so let's begin one.

Frame Sets: Dividing Up the Window

The overall window is known as a **set of frames** or a **frame set**. The overall behavior of a set of frames is governed by two XHTML elements, the `<frameset>`, and the `<frame>` element.

- The `<frameset>` element is the container element, replacing the `<body>` element, and describes the layout of the frames. It does this by using a `cols` and `rows` attributes, as we'll see in a moment.
- The `<frame>` element is the element that defines the individual frames and their content.

Let's start off at the most basic level and see how to create a set of four frames in a window.

Try It Out – Creating a Frameset

1. First we need to create our frameset document. Enter the following into your text editor (or use the code downloadable from the Wrox web site at `http://www.wrox.com`) and save it as `basic.htm`:

```
<?xml version="1.0" encoding="UTF-8"?>
<!DOCTYPE html
     PUBLIC "-//W3C//DTD XHTML 1.0 Frameset//EN"
     "http://www.w3.org/TR/xhtml1/DTD/xhtml1-frameset.dtd">
<html xmlns="http://www.w3.org/1999/xhtml" xml:lang="en" lang="en">
<head>
<title>Basic frames</title>
</head>
<frameset cols="*,*" rows="*,*">
  <frame src="text1.htm" />   <!-- The first frame in the list-->
  <frame src="text2.htm" />   <!-- The second frame in the list-->
  <frame src="text3.htm" />   <!-- The third frame in the list-->
  <frame src="text4.htm" />   <!-- The fourth frame in the list-->
</frameset>
</html>
```

2. Now we need to create and save our four content files, which we'll call `text1.htm`, `text2.htm`, and so on. First, `text1.htm`:

```
<?xml version="1.0" encoding="UTF-8"?>
<!DOCTYPE html
     PUBLIC "-//W3C//DTD XHTML 1.0 Transitional//EN"
     "http://www.w3.org/TR/xhtml1/DTD/xhtml1-transitional.dtd">
<html xmlns="http://www.w3.org/1999/xhtml" xml:lang="en" lang="en">
<head>
<title>Text1</title>
</head>
<body>
  <p>1-1-1 This is a frame 1-1-1</p>
</body>
</html>
```

To make the other files, simply change the numbers in the text between the `<title>` and `<p>` tags, and re-save under the new file name. Save all of them in the same folder as `basic.htm`.

3. Run `basic.htm` in your browser (we use IE5 here), and you should see something similar to below:

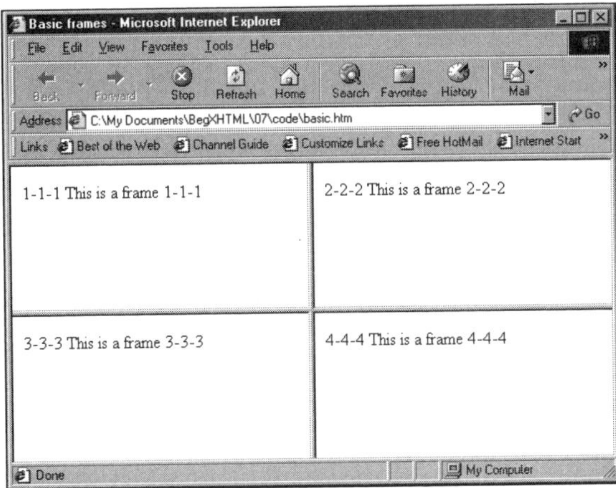

How It Works

The first important line for us is the opening tag of the `<frameset>` element (note that it replaces the `<body>` tag, which *does not* appear in the file). It is this tag (and its `rows` and `cols` attributes) that sets the overall layout of the set of frames:

```
<frameset cols="*,*" rows="*,*">
```

As is probably obvious, the `cols` attribute defines the number of columns in the set of frames and the `rows` attribute defines the number of rows in the set. Thus, specifying these two attributes defines the number of individual frames required in our set. Since we have two asterisks (*) as the value of the `cols` attribute, this means we wish to have two columns; similarly, we specify two rows. As I'm sure you know, two columns split into two rows makes four separate sections, that is, frames (think of cutting a square pizza into four).

What is not obvious is that these attributes also control the *size* of the individual frames. We'll see how we can specify dimensions in these attributes in a moment – all we need to know for now is that using the asterisk means that we'd like that row or column to take up whatever space is available (or remains if we have already specified a frame beforehand). If there's more than one frame, the browser will divide the space up between them equally. As you can see, the way we've defined it, we've said we want to divide the window up into four equal quadrants – two identical columns by two identical rows.

The `<frame>` element takes a `src` (short for 'source') attribute, which defines the source of the frames contents. Each source represents the URL of a file that will be loaded into the frame. For example:

```
<frame src="text1.htm" />   <!-- The first frame in the list-->
```

This tells the browser to display the contents of the file `text1.htm` in the first frame. This is because this line is the first to appear in the list of frames within the `<frameset>` element. The second file in the list will be displayed in the second frame, and so on. As you can see from the screenshot, frames are numbered from left to right, continuing onto the next row when the end of a row is reached. Within the XHTML file, the frames are simply numbered from top to bottom, as already indicated. If you have a lot of frames, it is a good idea to include a comment stating which frame it is (such as `<!--The first frame in the list-->`) otherwise you will just confuse yourself.

Now we've seen our basic frames example, let's backtrack a little and look at the `<frameset>` element in more detail.

The <frameset> Element

As the previous example demonstrated, the `<frameset>` element takes two specialized attributes, `cols` and `rows`, plus of course the standard attributes of `name`, `id`, `class` and `style`. (The `<frameset>` element also takes two event attributes, the `onload` and `onunload` attributes, but we will not be discussing these further.)

The 'cols' and 'rows' Attributes

The `rows` and `cols` attributes, as we have just seen, lay out the overall structure of the frameset you're creating. Their values consist of comma-delimited values, with each value quantifying the width of a column, or the height of a row. Now we've already seen them in an example, their general syntax is the following:

```
rows="height of 1st row, height of 2nd row, etc..."
 cols="width of 1st col, width of 2nd col, etc..."
```

The values can be expressed in a number of ways. We saw the asterisk being used earlier as a 'wildcard' value (that is, it can take on *any* value, a terminology stolen from a certain card game), but you can also specify the dimensions as fixed pixel values, or as percentages or ratios:

- **Pixels** – If an integer is supplied, then the integer represents the absolute width/height of the frame in pixels. This is usually mixed with a wildcard value (*) for the width/height of a second column/row, and the wildcard value will then take up the rest of the width/height available to it.

- **Ratios** – To produce a ratio we use integers followed by asterisks, like this:

```
<frameset rows="1*, 3*, 1*">
```

- **Percentages** – Another way to get a relative value for the width or height of our rows and columns is to use the percentage sign (%), like this:

```
<frameset rows="20%, 60%, 20%">
```

- **Wildcards** – We have already seen the wildcard operator (*) in action. Essentially a wild card will fill up any space that remains. If there is more than one wildcard operator present then they will divide up the remaining space equally between them. It's most commonly used in conjunction with another set of units. For example, if you wanted your left column to be 75 pixels wide, and the right column to take up whatever space remained, you'd use this:

```
frameset cols="75, *">
```

Let's see some examples of using various units to define our framesets. We'll also identify a couple of situations where the browser may interpret your frameset declaration a little differently from what you'd expect.

Try It Out – Sizing Rows and Columns

1. Let's start simply, by declaring our set of frames dimensions in pixels. Type up this XHTML page and save it as `units.htm` in the same directory as before:

```
<?xml version="1.0" encoding="UTF-8"?>
<!DOCTYPE html
     PUBLIC "-//W3C//DTD XHTML 1.0 Frameset//EN"
     "http://www.w3.org/TR/xhtml1/DTD/xhtml1-frameset.dtd">
<html xmlns="http://www.w3.org/1999/xhtml" xml:lang="en" lang="en">
<head>
<title>Basic frames</title>
</head>
  <frameset cols="75,150,*" >
    <frame src="text1.htm" id="index_frame" name="index_frame" style="background-
color:red" />
    <frame src="text2.htm" id="main_view" name="main_view" />
    <frame src="text3.htm" id="main_view2" name="main_view2" />

  </frameset>
</html>
```

2. View it in your browser. In IE5, you should see this:

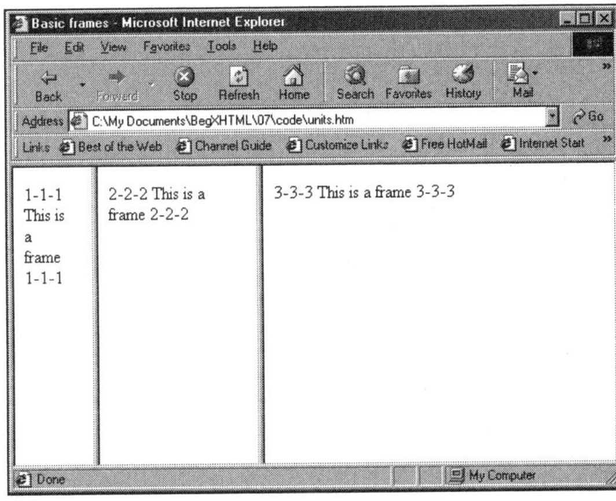

3. Now change the frameset declaration line to read as follows, and save as `units2.htm`:

```
<frameset cols="75,150,75" >
```

4. If you view the page now, you should notice that the widths we've defined are no longer being interpreted as absolute:

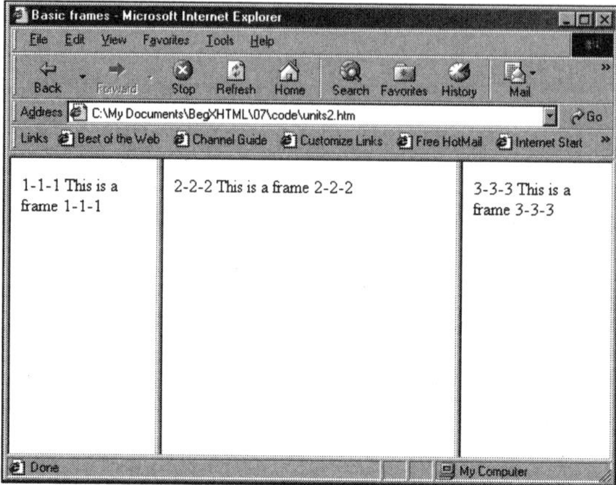

The values are actually being interpreted as ratios, even though we haven't included asterisks in the values. Let's do that now, but we'll also change the values themselves so it's obvious that something's changed.

5. Change the frameset declaration again to read as below, and save as `units3.htm`:

```
<frameset cols="1*,2*,3*" >
```

This time, you should see the following result:

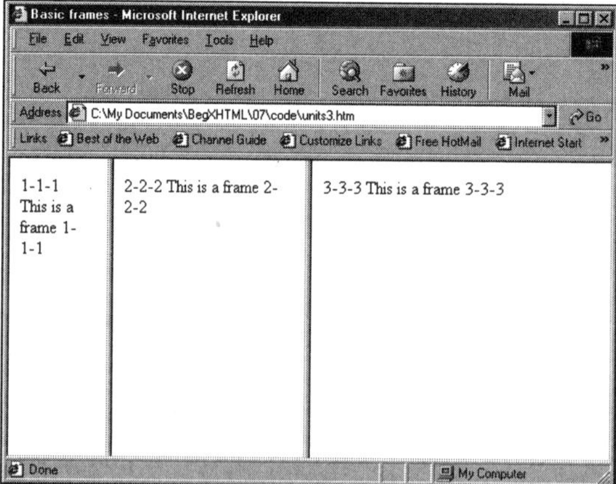

6. There's just one more to do now, percentages. Change the line one last time to read as below, and save as `units4.htm`:

```
<frameset cols="30%,55%,15%" >
```

This is what we should see:

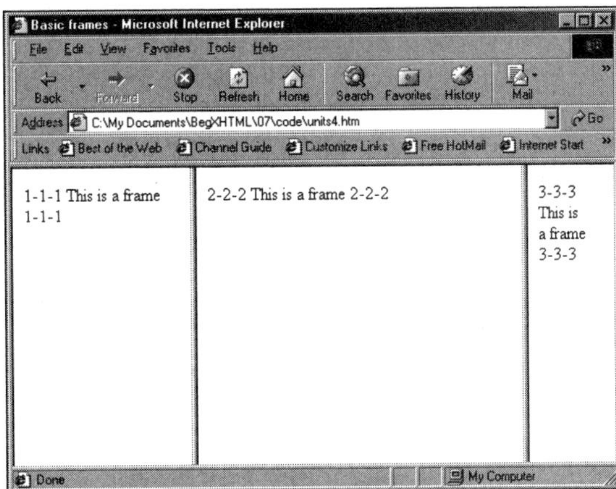

7. The columns are divided accorded to the percentage ratios. If we broaden the window the ratios will remain unchanged (so the frames will grow and shrink to keep the ratios as we set them). Try this yourself, making the browser window both smaller and larger.

How It Works

We've simply looked at the various units we can use to define our set of frames. The first time, we used this definition:

```
<frameset cols="75,150,*" >
```

Here, we used integers and a wildcard value. The first frame is 75 pixels wide, the second frame is 150 pixels wide, and the third frame, being a wildcard, takes up the remainder of the space available to it. We then changed this line so that the wildcard also became an integer:

```
<frameset cols="75,150,75" >
```

We may have thought that this would give us three precisely defined frames of 75, 150, and 75 pixels each. That's not the case, though. The browser interprets this as a set of ratios instead. Now, although this 'overloading' of the attribute (a term used to mean that depending on the values supplied, the attribute varies its behavior or interpretation of the values) will produce a fairly consistent result, we should really use the correct syntax if we want to produce a ratio.

We then proceeded to do just that. It was fairly straightforward, I think you'll agree. Finally, we looked at percentages. That, too, was fairly simple. One thing we didn't look at, and you can try out yourself simply by altering that same line in the code we've been working with, was what happens if our percentages don't add up to 100%? Well, if we enter percentages that do not add up to 100%, they will be treated as ratios. Again although the result is fairly consistent it is recommended that the correct syntax be used for ratios.

One odd situation we haven't looked at yet is when we have a wildcard operator, and all the space is already taken up. For example, if we had the following `<frameset>` declaration:

```
<frameset cols="55%,55%,*" >
```

The third frame does not show. The frame does in fact exist, and the document is in fact loaded into the third frame, but it is invisible. Other techniques can be used to show this, but it is beyond the scope of this chapter to discuss hidden frames further.

Mixing Units

It is actually possible to mix units. For example, we could have a four-column unit as follows:

```
<frameset cols="100,50%,2*,1*" >
```

This would produce a frame set with the first column 100 pixels wide, the next filling up 50% of the remaining space, and the last two columns dividing up the remaining space in the ratio 2 to 1.

However mixing units in this way is not recommended – it is liable to lead to confusion.

The <frame> Element

There should be one `<frame>` element (or a `<frameset>` element; see the section on nesting, below) for every 'cell' declared by a `cols` and a `rows` attribute in the `<frameset>`. This is what we did in our very first example, where we split the browser window into four separate sections (or frames), and used one (and only one) `<frame>` element per section to display that sections content. If a frame is omitted then the user-agent usually just leaves a blank space.

Attributes of the <frame> Element

The `<frame>` element takes the following attributes. The most important of these attributes are `src` and `id`.

src	**id**	**noresize**	**longdesc**
scrolling	**frameborder**	**marginheight**	**marginwidth**

- **src** – This attribute gives the source (i.e. the URL) of the document that is to be the content of that frame. It can be any type of file that the particular user agent supports; a text file, an XML file, an XHTML file, an image file, and so on.

- **id –** If a frame is named, it should be given a unique name. The `id` attribute is important in that it allows pages to be loaded into the named frame by an anchor element in another frame. To do this the anchor element employs its target attribute. The syntax for this is:

  ```
  target="name of target frame"
  ```

  Note that this method can only be used if the frame has been named. This is discussed in the section 'targeting frames' below. For backwards compatibility, as we've seen in other cases, we can also include the `name` attribute which is formally deprecated in XHTML 1.0 for this and certain other elements.

- **scrolling** – This takes a value of `yes` or `no`. The default is `yes`. This means that if a page is too large to fit in a frame then scroll bars will be automatically supplied. If we don't want this to happen, we put `scrolling` to `no`.

- **frameborder** – This attribute dictates whether the frame is to have a border or not with every adjoining frame (so this attribute doesn't make much sense if there is only one frame in the window). The default value is '1'. Setting the `frameborder` to '0' does away with the border for the `<frame>` element in question, as long as adjoining frames have complimentary values for shared borders.

- **noresize** – Use `noresize="noresize"` if you do not want the user to be able to resize a frame. You should be very careful about using this attribute as you may make some of your material inaccessible to the user if they have a low-resolution monitor, or on small devices such as mobile phones.

- **marginheight** and **marginwidth** – These take pixel values and define the amount of space to leave between the top and bottom (`marginheight`) or the sides (`marginwidth`) of a frames content and the border of a frame. Default values for these attributes depends on the browsers implementation. It is probably better to use CSS (see Chapter 9) margin properties on the document itself rather than use this property.

- **longdesc** – This is like the `<image>` element's attribute of the same name. It is a link to a URL that allows a description of the frame for use by non-visual browsers. Unfortunately, like its image counterpart, it is unsupported.

Nesting Frames

In our discussion of the `<frame>` element, we stressed that each section (or window division) should only use one `<frame>` element to display its content. However, it is possible for one frame to use more than one `<frame>` element to display content. This is done by using another `<frameset>` element inside the first `<frameset>` element, and specifying any number of `<frame>` elements within this second `<frameset>` element. That is, we can take one window division and divide it into further sections, leaving the other window divisions untouched. This is known as **nesting**. Harking back to our pizza analogy, we first cut the pizza into six parts (say) and then take one of those pieces and cut that into (for example) three parts. Obviously, we can divide the original pizza into any number of pieces we chose (some large, some small); likewise, we can further divide any number of those pieces into any number of smaller pieces. However, nesting frames should be done with extreme caution. It is only too easy to end up with a confusing conglomeration of frames; confusing not only to the viewer, but also to the author. The download speed is also reduced severely.

Having said that there are one or two frame-layout styles where nesting is required, particularly when we want an asymmetric layout of rows and columns. We will have a look at one of these when we look at using frames for display.

There are essentially two ways to nest frames:

- Nest `<frameset>` elements
- Import a set of frames into a `<frame>` element.

Let's look at examples of both of these.

Nesting <frameset> Elements

To nest a `<frameset>` element one simply replaces one (or as many as you wish) of the `<frame>` elements with another `<frameset>` element.

Try It Out – Nesting <frameset> Elements

1. Enter this XHTML file into your text editor and save it as `nest1.htm`:

```
<?xml version="1.0" encoding="UTF-8"?>
<!DOCTYPE html
     PUBLIC "-//W3C//DTD XHTML 1.0 Frameset//EN"
     "http://www.w3.org/TR/xhtml1/DTD/xhtml1-frameset.dtd">
<html xmlns="http://www.w3.org/1999/xhtml" xml:lang="en" lang="en">
<head>
<title>Basic frames</title>
</head>
<frameset rows="15%,70%,15%" >
  <frame src="text1.htm" id="index_frame" name="index_frame" />
  <frameset cols="25%,50%,25%" >
    <frame src="text1.htm" id="index_frame" name="index_frame" />
    <frame src="text2.htm" id="main_view" name="main_view" />
    <frame src="text3.htm" id="main_view2" name="main_view2" />
  </frameset>

  <frame src="text3.htm" id="main_view3" name="main_view3" />
</frameset>
</html>
```

2. As you can see we have replaced one of the `<frame>` elements with a `<frameset>` element. Here is what we will see in a browser:

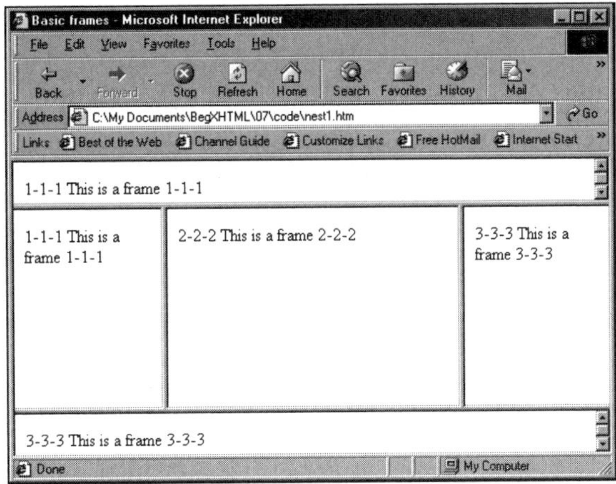

How It Works

With our first `<frameset>` element we announce that we are going to form a set of frames of three rows (but with no columns this time):

```
<frameset rows="15%,70%,15%">
```

The first row is a simple frame that we have seen before:

```
  <frame src="text1.htm" id="index_frame" name="index_frame" />
```

What should have been the second row/frame, however, is another set of frames. This we define as containing three columns but with no rows. These columns are displayed in the second row area:

```
  <frameset cols="25%,50%,25%" >
  <frame src="text1.htm" id="index_frame" name="index_frame" />
  <frame src="text2.htm" id="main_view" name="main_view" />
  <frame src="text3.htm" id="main_view2" name="main_view2" />
  </frameset>
```

Lastly we have another column, and then we close the first `<frameset>` element:

```
    <frame src="text3.htm" id="main_view2" name="main_view2" />
  </frameset>
```

This is the usual way to nest frames, and the one we recommend for most purposes. We can, however, nest frames by importing a file containing a frameset.

Importing <frameset> Files

Here is how we nest frames by importing a <frameset> file.

Try It Out – Importing FrameSets

1. Open up our original example, basic.htm. Alter it as follows:

```
<frameset cols="*,*" rows="*,*">
  <frame src="basic.htm" />
  <frame src="text2.htm" />
  <frame src="text3.htm" />
  <frame src="text4.htm" />
</frameset>
```

2. Now save it as basic1.htm (note there is now a '1' in the name). If you view it in your browser, you should see this:

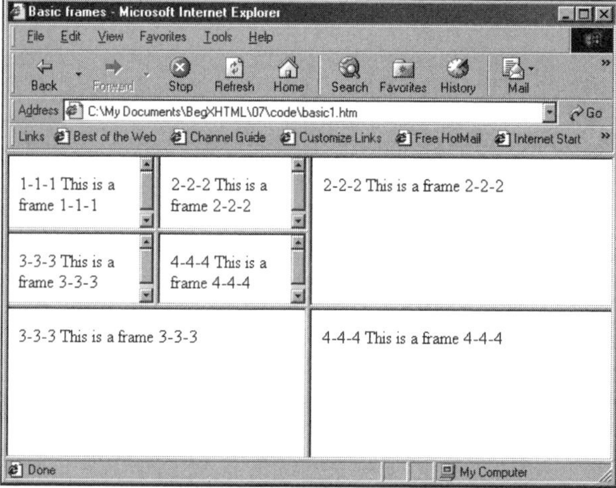

How It Works

This is easy enough to understand since, for the most part, it is jut a repeat of our first example where the browser window is split into four equal parts, or frames. The difference arises when we import or 'load in' a file to be used as the first frames content. Instead of using a simple XHTML file for the first frame, we use our original basic.htm frames file. This file contains a <frameset> element which tells the browser to divide the available area into four equal parts. The 'available area' here is not the entire browser window, but just the window of frame one. It is the same with the other three frames. When an XHTML file is loaded into frame two, for example, this tells the browser to display the contents of the file inside the 'available area'. Again, the 'available area' is just the area of the frame. Thus, one may think of each frame as a 'miniature' browser window.

Recursion

We have to be very careful not to import `basic1.htm` into `basic1.htm`, otherwise we would get endlessly loading frames. Note we did not make a mistake in specifying `basic1.htm` twice. The programming term where a file is loaded into itself is called **recursion**. This may sound a bit strange but it is a valid programming technique used in languages such as C++ and Java, and can be particularly difficult for new programmers to understand. However, this should *never* be used in XHTML. If `basic1.htm` loaded `basic1.htm` into itself, what would happen is that the browser would open up the second copy of `basic1.htm` and see that it also asks for `basic1.htm` to be loaded in, so it would load in a third copy of `basic1.htm`, open that and see that it asks for `basic1.htm` to be loaded in again, so it loads in a fourth copy, and so on, for ever and ever and ever. We would then get an endless loop of one set of frames being loaded into another set of frames being loaded into another set of frames and so on. This would never end, unless you switched off your computer or it 'crashed' before you got the chance. With such a recursion, the computer would soon run out of resources. If you really do believe that your computer has a personality and you want to pay it back for the hours of frustration it has caused you, then this is a great way to give it the equivalent of a migraine headache!

Targeting Frames

When we click on a hypertext link, the default behavior is for the new page to be loaded into the window containing the hyperlink. The `target` attribute, however, allows the new page to be loaded into a different frame of window, rather than having it being loaded into the original frame that contained the hyperlink. It will only work if the window or frame that we want to 'target' has been named.

The following elements can all take the `target` attribute:

<a>	**<area>**	**<base>**	**<form>**	**<link>**

All these elements will target a named frame or window with an URL. The syntax is:

```
target="[named frame or window]"
```

The `target` attribute can also use certain keywords to target individual frames within a set of frames. Note that the following keywords all begin with the underscore character and are case-sensitive (so `_top` is not the same as `_TOP`, for example):

_self	**_blank**	**_parent**	**_top**

The syntax employed is:

```
target="keyword"
```

A brief description of each is given below:

_self

If the anchor (or other) element uses this keyword then the new page is loaded into the frame containing the anchor element (that is, it is loaded into its self, hence the name). This is the default behavior in most user-agents.

_blank

As can be guessed, a completely new window will be created, and the new page will be loaded into this new window.

_parent

This is used with nested frames. For a set of frames like that in our first example (`basic.htm`), the parent window is simply the browser. In a nested set of frames (like `basic1.htm`), the parent window is the 'main' frame window, that is, the frame that was further sub-divided. The new page is loaded into the parent frame.

_top

This loads the new page into the main browser window directly, replacing any frames that are already there. When we are linking to external URLs, it is important that they be targeted to the '`_top`' window. If we fail to do this the external URL will be loaded into one of the frames which can produce some strange effects.

The best way to illustrate the use of the `target` attribute is by way of an example.

Try It Out – Targeting Different Frames

1. We will use a similar setup as we used for `nest1.htm` above, but we will make sure that each frame has a unique name; we will call this page `target1.htm`. We will place an index page containing `<a>` elements in the first column; we will call this page `target_index.htm`.

2. Here is `target1.htm`:

```
<?xml version="1.0" encoding="UTF-8"?>
<!DOCTYPE html
     PUBLIC "-//W3C//DTD XHTML 1.0 Frameset//EN"
     "http://www.w3.org/TR/xhtml1/DTD/xhtml1-frameset.dtd">
<html xmlns="http://www.w3.org/1999/xhtml" xml:lang="en" lang="en">
<head>
<title>Basic frames</title>
</head>

  <frameset rows="15%,70%,15%" >
    <frame src="text1.htm" name="heading_frame" />

    <frameset cols="25%,50%,25%" >
      <frame src="target_index.htm" id="index_frame" name="index_frame" />
      <frame src="text2.htm" id="main_view" name="main_view" />
      <frame src="text3.htm" id="main_view2" name="main_view2" />
    </frameset>
```

```
    <frame src="text3.htm" id="footer_frame" name="footer_frame" />
  </frameset>
</html>
```

3. And here is `target_index.htm`:

```
<?xml version="1.0" encoding="UTF-8"?>
<!DOCTYPE html
     PUBLIC "-//W3C//DTD XHTML 1.0 Transitional//EN"
     "http://www.w3.org/TR/xhtml1/DTD/xhtml1-transitional.dtd">
<html xmlns="http://www.w3.org/1999/xhtml" xml:lang="en" lang="en">
<head>
<title>Basic frames. Target_Index.htm</title>
</head>
<body>
  <div><a href="areyou.htm" target="heading_frame">Are you (header
frame)</a></div>
  <div><a href="goingto.htm" target="main_view">Going to (mid frame)</a></div>
  <div><a href="sfair.htm" target="_blank">Scarborough Fair? (new
window)</a></div>
  <div><a href="parsley.htm" target="footer_frame">Parsley (footer
frame)</a></div>
  <div><a href="sage.htm" target="_parent">Sage (parent window)</a></div>
  <div><a href="rosemary.htm" target="_top">Rosemary (top window)</a></div>
  <div><a href="thyme.htm" target="_self">and Thyme. (this window)</a></div>
  <div><a href="sandg.htm" target="main_view2">Simon and Garfunkel. (side
frame)</a></div>
</body>
</html>
```

4. Now create some simple XHTML files for the links given above. Just take the lyrics (from the old English ballad by an anonymous poet and made famous by Simon & Garfunkel) from each line as the text of the documents, with the file name as the value of the `href` attributes. For example, the first line in the body references `areyou.htm`, so create a file called `areyou.htm` with the following content:

```
<?xml version="1.0" encoding="UTF-8"?>
<!DOCTYPE html
     PUBLIC "-//W3C//DTD XHTML 1.0 Transitional//EN"
    "http://www.w3.org/TR/xhtml1/DTD/xhtml1-transitional.dtd">
<html xmlns="http://www.w3.org/1999/xhtml" xml:lang="en" lang="en">
<head>
  <title>Scarborough Fair</title>
</head>
<body>
  <p>Are you</p>
</body>
</html>
```

5. And then simply change the text between the <p> and </p> tags and re-save under the next links name for the other links.

6. Here is what the `target1.htm` page looks like in IE5 when we first run it:

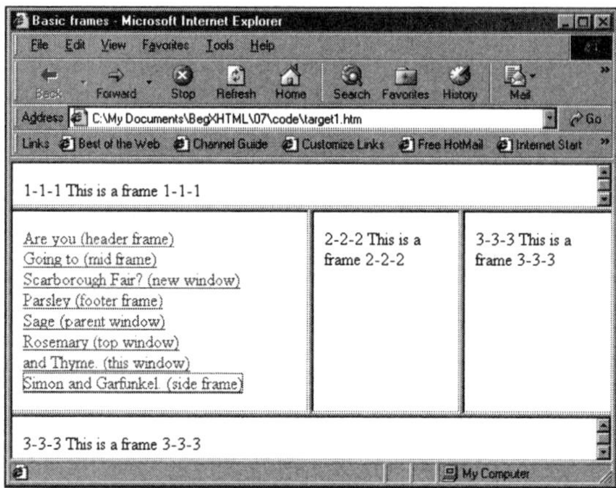

7. And after we have clicked on a few links, we see:

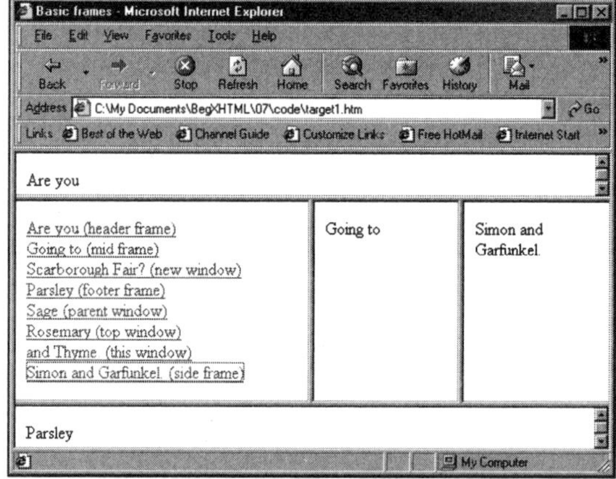

How It Works

First of all, note that all the frames in the set of frames created by `target1.htm` have been given unique names. In our index file we have targeted those names. Thus, for example, when we click on the link to Parsley in the index frame:

```
<div><a href="parsley.htm" target="footer_frame">Parsley (footer frame)</a></div>
```

it appears in the bottom (or footer) frame because we have given this link the target 'footer_frame' and this was the name we gave to our very last frame in `target1.htm`:

```
<frame src="text3.htm" id=="footer_frame" name="footer_frame" />
```

Thus, there is a simply 'pairing' (or **mapping**) of each link to one particular frame. However, there is no requirement to have this one-to-one mapping. For example, you could change all the target attributes to the value footer_frame, and then each link when clicked on would be displayed in the bottom frame.

Note, however, that there is one error in this system. When we click on the Sage link, this should appear in the middle row as one single frame, that is, the three columns in the middle row should disappear and be replaced by one frame only. What happens is that *all the frames disappear* and the link is displayed as a new frame-less page in the main browser window. That is, the browser interprets the `_parent` value of the `target` attribute as being the same as the `_top` value. Both Netscape Navigator and Internet Explorer have this fault. Unfortunately, as we have seen, this 'loose interpretation' is only too common with the mainstream HTML browsers; hopefully the XHTML browsers will be more accurate.

Inline Frames

We can, in fact, include a frame in our regular XHTML page by using an `<iframe>` element. Here is how we do this:

Try It Out – Inline Frames

1. Enter the following into your text editor and save as `inline.htm`:

```
<?xml version="1.0" encoding="UTF-8"?>
<!DOCTYPE html
     PUBLIC "-//W3C//DTD XHTML 1.0 Frameset//EN"
     "http://www.w3.org/TR/xhtml1/DTD/xhtml1-frameset.dtd">
<html xmlns="http://www.w3.org/1999/xhtml" xml:lang="en" lang="en">
<head>
<title>Basic frames</title>
</head>
<body>
<p>Here is some regular text in a paragraph.</p>
 <iframe src="text1.htm">
You will see this text if your browser does not support iframe
</iframe>
</body>
</html>
```

2. Run this in your browser – here is what we see in IE5:

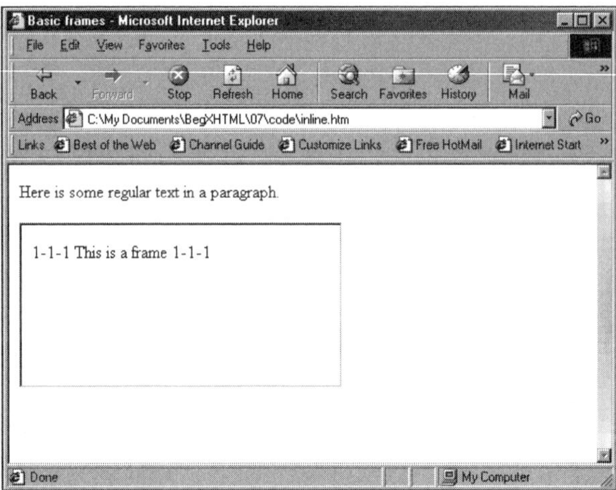

IE5 supports `<iframe>` so we see the inline frame; however, Netscape Navigator does not support this feature. There's not really a whole lot to say about iframes, so we'll move on, but it takes most of the same attributes as the `<frame>` element, with some slight differences (like not having to be part of a frameset document).

CSS and Frames

Style sheets can be applied to any of the pages that the frames contain. However applying styling to a frame has no effect what so ever to the pages it contains! In other words, styling is not inherited from the `<frame>` element. The only rudimentary styling that we can employ when using frames is the by using the `marginheight` and `marginwidth` attributes, which we discussed earlier. More on the Cascading Style Sheet (CSS) language can be found in Chapter 9.

The <noframes> Element

Should a browser not support frames then we can still get some kind of display by using the `<noframes>` element. As many devices such as voice readers and small screen devices will not support frames, we should provide an alternative display if we want our pages to reach this audience.

Here is an example of how to do this.

Try It Out – Using the <noframes> Element

1. Add the following into `basic.htm` (our first example) and save it as `noframes.htm`:

```
<?xml version="1.0" encoding="UTF-8"?>
<!DOCTYPE html
```

```
     PUBLIC "-//W3C//DTD XHTML 1.0 Frameset//EN"
     "http://www.w3.org/TR/xhtml1/DTD/xhtml1-frameset.dtd">
<html xmlns="http://www.w3.org/1999/xhtml" xml:lang="en" lang="en">
<head>
<title>Basic frames</title>
</head>
<frameset cols="*,*" rows="*,*">
  <frame src="text1.htm" />   <!-- The first frame in the list-->
  <frame src="text2.htm" />   <!-- The second frame in the list-->
  <frame src="text3.htm" />   <!-- The third frame in the list-->
  <frame src="text4.htm" />   <!-- The fourth frame in the list-->
<noframes>
  <h3>Announcement</h3>
  <p>This browser does not support frames</p>
</noframes>
</frameset>
</html>
```

2. Running it in your browser, you should see the same screen as we saw in our very first example. This is because your browser supports frames. However, here is how the above looks in Mosaic 2, which does not support frames:

Using Frames for Display

Many sites use frames to great effect, Microsoft for example. Browsing the web will provide other examples. However, we thought that we would just end with an example of one of the more typical layouts. Type this into your editor and call it `typical.htm`:

```
<?xml version="1.0" encoding="UTF-8"?>
<!DOCTYPE html
     PUBLIC "-//W3C//DTD XHTML 1.0 Frameset//EN"
     "http://www.w3.org/TR/xhtml1/DTD/xhtml1-frameset.dtd">
<html xmlns="http://www.w3.org/1999/xhtml" xml:lang="en" lang="en">
<head>
<title>Basic frames</title>
</head>
<frameset rows="80,*,60" >
  <frame src="top1.htm" id="top_frame" name="top_frame" scrolling="no" />
  <frameset cols="20%,*" >
```

```
        <frame src="index1.htm" id="index_view" name="index_view" frameborder="no" />
        <frame src="start_text.htm" id="main_view" name="main_view" frameborder="no"
    />
      </frameset>
      <frame src="bottom1.htm" id="bottom_frame" name="bottom_frame" frameborder="1"
    scrolling="no" />
    </frameset>
    </html>
```

This example has a permanent header and footer. The left column frame consists of an index, and the right column frame provides a place to show the pages referred to in the index. The screenshot below provides an example of a typical layout:

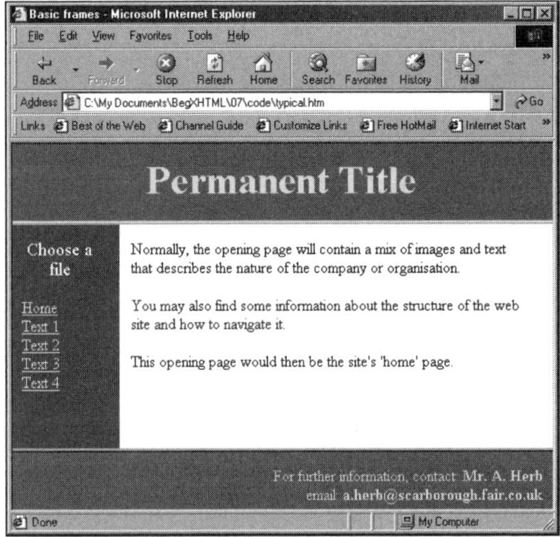

The individual pages in the frames are styled using CSS, which we don't cover until Chapter 9. If you want the code for these pages, they are all available on the Wrox web site for this chapter; obviously, the names of the files are the values of the `src` attributes in the above code. However, you will be able to make files like these for yourself after you have read Chapter 9.

For a real-life example of a frames layout check out `http://www.ceram.co.uk/`.

Summary

In this chapter we had a look at using frames as a display device to show multiple pages on the same screen. We demonstrated how to do this using the `<frameset>` and `<frame>` element. Note that if you are using frames then you must use the Frameset DTD, and that the `<frameset>` element replaces the `<body>` element. We then looked at how to nest frames, and how to send a document to a particular frame using the `target` attribute. Inline frames were also looked at, and we finished with an example of a fairly typical frame layout design.

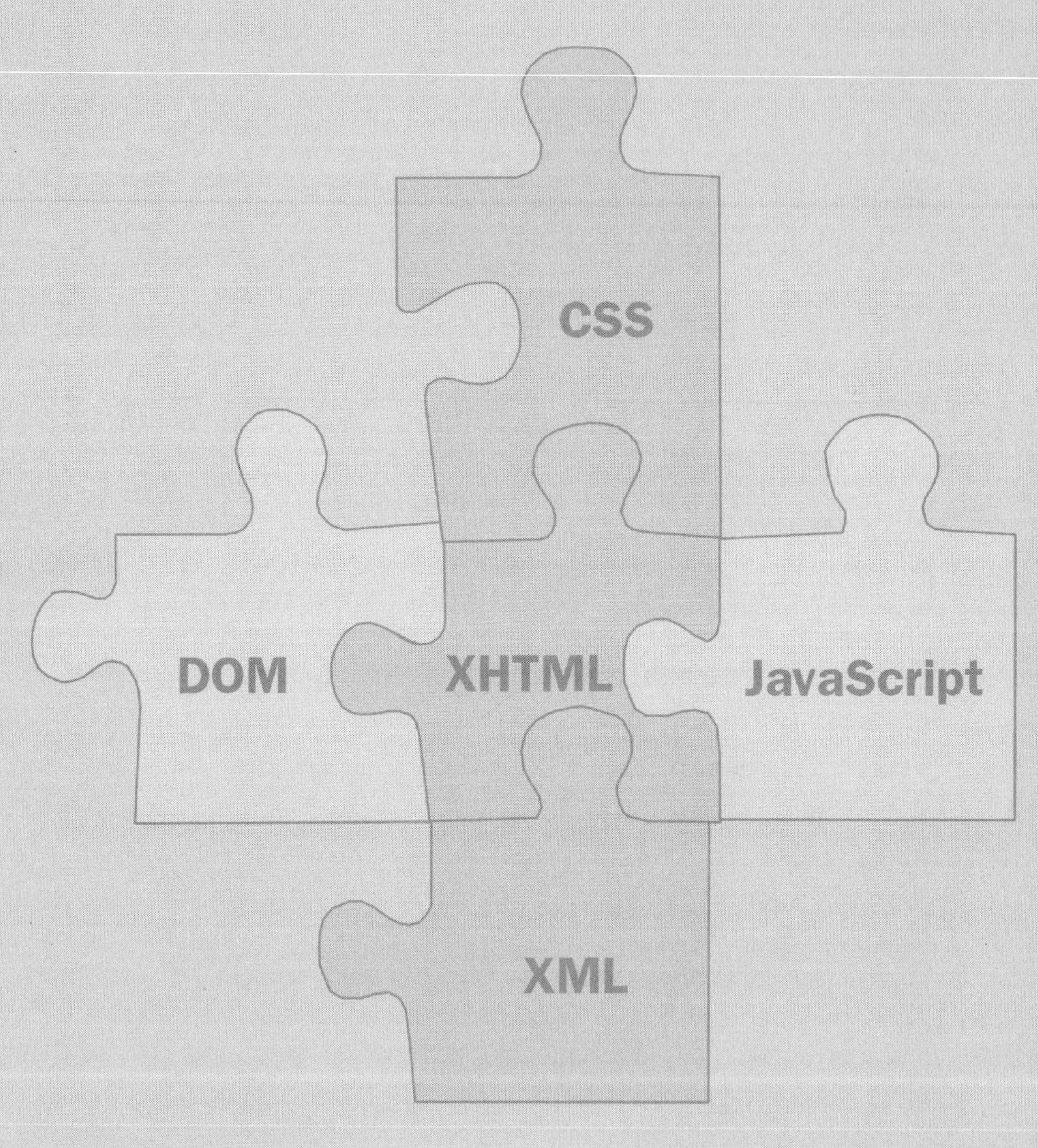
CSS
DOM
XHTML
JavaScript
XML

Meta-Data

A document exists to convey information. A web document does this not just through text, but also via any pictures and media files embedded within it, and in the links it has to other resources. A document also contains a second kind of information, and that is information about itself (for example, a table of contents). This is known as meta-information, and is the focus of this chapter.

The meta-information of a web document is information such as what kind (XHTML, HTML, XML, etc.) of a document it is, it's namespace, the name or title of the document, a summary of the content of the document, the relationship it holds to other documents, its style, and so on. All information of this type is contained within the `<head>` of the document, and is conveyed by a special set of element types.

In this chapter we will cover the following:

- Search engines and how information is found on the Web
- The `<meta>` and `<title>` elements
- The `<link>` and `<base>` elements
- Namespaces
- Mime types

Meta-Data

First of all, let's look at the reasons why we should generate meta-data to describe our documents. We need to describe:

- The content and topics covered by our documents so that 'netiziens' looking for those particular topics can find them. Describing content also allows search engines to classify our documents.
- Our document's relationship with other documents so that an intelligent user agent can place it in relation to other documents on our site.
- The document type in order that browsers – and other user agents that are going to display or otherwise manipulate our document – can find out what kind of document they are dealing with.

Finding Information on the Web

For those who have already tried a search engine, it will come as no surprise that searching the Web for information is a very imprecise art! Fire up most search engines and type in a keyword and a whole series of pages will be returned, and most of them will be quite irrelevant to our needs. However, this problem could be solved if everyone included meta-information in all of their documents placed on the Web.

Search Engines

Search engines fall into a few general types:

- Those that search a human generated database.
- Those that search a database generated by a 'spider' or 'robot'.
- Those that do a limited search of web pages and try and classify a document based on that search.
- Those that do a full text search.

Human-Generated Database.

The first kind of engine is a search engine such as Yahoo's. To be included on a Yahoo page, someone somewhere has had to have submitted the name of the page to be cataloged, and the subject areas that it should be cataloged under. The page is then theoretically visited by a human who rates the relevance of the page to the subject, and places this information in a database. With the explosion of pages on the web this is no longer completely feasible, and even Yahoo has had to resort to 'robots' to crawl pages and look for data.

Yahoo is the Web's most popular search engine and can be found at `http://www.yahoo.com/`. If you wish to register your site with Yahoo, scroll to the bottom of their page and check out the link How to Suggest a Site which contains all the necessary information for doing this.

Spiders and 'Bots'

The second kind of search engine employs a 'robot' of some kind to 'crawl' the web. A robot, in the web-sense, is a computer program that automatically searches the Web, retrieving documents and any documents that are linked to it. This 'bot', known also as a 'spider', is programmed to look for certain kinds of information and automatically transfer it to a database. Many of these engines will only look at the first few lines of a document, while others will only look at the information contained in the `<meta>` and `<title>` tags. A few will search the whole document.

To fine out lots more about web robots, check out 'The Web Robots Pages' at `http://info.webcrawler.com/mak/projects/robots/robots.html`.

Partial Text Searches

These engines will just scan the first few lines of a document, and will probably look particularly hard at the `<title>` and `<meta>` tags, and possibly the `profile` attribute of the `<head>` element.

Full Text Searches

This kind of search engine is typically found on a large site such as Microsoft. It will typically do a search of the full text content of a site.

Other Search Engines

Check out the following popular search engines:

- `http://www.altavista.com/` AltaVista, one of the largest engines on the Web.
- `http://www.excite.com/` Excite, one of the Webs most popular search engines.
- `http://www.google.com/` Google, one of the best search engines on the Web.
- `http://www.lycos.com/` Lycos, another highly popular search engine.
- `http://37.com` '37.com' is so named because it uses 37 different search engines.

For an absolute wealth of information about search engines, submission tips, listings of search engines, comparisons and details on how differing engines work, check out the excellent 'Search Engine Watch' web site at `http://www.searchenginewatch.com/`.

Automated search engines, however, rely to a large extent on the document to contain information about itself and its contents. Let's look at how to use the elements found in the head of the document to do this.

Document Information

Most of the information about a document and its contents will be found in the head of the document and in the document prolog. Servers will also add an HTTP header to the document when it sends it. This will contain further, server-generated information about the document. We will look at the information contained in the document prolog and the header a little later in this chapter. First we will look at the `<head>` element and it's content.

The <head> Element

In XHTML, the `<head>` element is mandatory and *must* contain a `<title>` element; the `<head>` element may also optionally contain a *single* `<base>` element.

The `<head>` element can contain zero or more of the following elements: `<script>`, `<style>`, `<meta>`, `<link>` or `<object>`.

In addition, the `<head>` element also takes an attribute which is useful for the description of meta-data, the `profile` attribute. This attribute takes a single URI as its value, and this URI should contain a file with details about the document. There is at present no agreed upon manner for laying out a file referred to by the profile attribute, but it may very well in the future contain an RDF file (see later).

The <title> Element

All XHTML documents must contain a `<title>` element. The `<title>` is not usually displayed as a flow object in most user agents, but rather it will appear in the title bar at the top of the page.

The `<title>` element is the single most useful piece of meta-data that a document can contain, so be sure to make a title that is both descriptive and accurate. Many 'bots' will do a scan of the title, so if there is one particular keyword you want to emphasize, make sure it is in the title.

For example, avoid 'cute' titles such as 'Getting Extensible' (it is even questionable whether this is appropriate as your first heading, but that is a matter of taste) and instead use a more informative title such as 'Converting HTML to XHTML'.

The <meta> Element

The `<meta>` element is specifically designed to convey information about the `<meta>` content of a document. It is an empty element that takes the following attributes: `name`, `http-equiv`, `content` and `scheme` (as well as the universal `dir`, `lang` and `title` attributes).

The `<meta>` element *must* contain a `content` attribute. It must also contain either a `name` or an `http-equiv` attribute, and can in fact contain both; the `scheme` attribute is optional.

The 'name' Attribute

The `name` attribute is used if the `content` attribute is primarily intended to be interpreted by the browser or some other user agent such as a robot. We can infact use any name we wish, but certain names have a well-defined meaning, and we would be advised to use these. For example:

- `name="keywords"`: - this informs the user agent that the `content` attribute is going to contain a comma separated list of keywords
- `name="description"`: - this informs the user agent that we are going to give a narrative description of the page
- `name="summary"`: - this informs the user agent that we are going to give a brief summary of the page

The 'content' Attribute

The `content` attribute contains all the meta-information that we wish to register. Again this can take any form although there is a general agreement that certain forms are best. For example if we have given the `<meta>` element the name of "keyword" the `content` attribute should be a list of comma separated keywords, and if we have given the element the name of "description" the `content` attribute should in fact contain a short description.

Let's look at a simple example of using a `<meta>` element.

Example of the <meta> Element with a 'name' Attribute

Here is a `<meta>` element used to provide a list of keywords and a description of a page for a search engine. This particular page is from an article on a sports medicine site that provides articles for medical professionals:

```
<head>
<title>Sports medicine: Surgery of the anterior cruciate ligament (ACL).</title>

<meta name="keywords" content="surgery, orthopedic surgery, sports medicine, knee,
ligament, anterior cruciate, ant. cruciate, ACL" />

<meta name="description" content="Surgical procedures for the repair of the
Anterior cruciate ligament of the knee. Indications, techniques, and
rehabilitation." />
</head>
```

The first thing to note is that we can use as many `<meta>` elements as we want within the `<head>` section of a document.. Note also how the three elements complement each other. An archivist, whether human or robotic, that visits this page would be able to give a succinct and informative title and description. Note how the keywords have been listed in order of increasing detail. This again helps the archivist categorize the page.

Some page writers feel compelled to add keywords that will attract a lot of general traffic to their site, such as adding 'pornography' and other more graphic terms to the list of keywords. Resist this temptation. Not only is it anti-social, but it is also counter productive. First, the customers you would attract are not likely to be interested in your products (and may even try to hack your site in revenge!). Secondly, if they are interested in your products they will probably take this as an example of your business ethics and go to a competitor.

The 'http-equiv' Attribute

The `<meta>` element is also designed to complement information about the document that is contained in an HTTP header. We will look at HTTP headers under a section of that name later on in this chapter.

When the `http-equiv` attribute is used, information contained in the `content` attribute is interpreted as if it was contained in the HTTP header, and this allows us to employ it for a couple of rather nice tricks.

Tricks with 'http-equiv'

http-equiv= "refresh"

We can use the `<meta>` tag to automatically refresh our page. Most browsers support this method. To refresh a page, the `<meta>` element must take the following general form:

```
<meta http-equiv= "refresh" content="[time];URL='[URL]'" />
```

Where [time] is an integer which represents the time in seconds after which we wish our page to be 'refreshed', and [URL] is the address of the page we want to replace it with. Note how the URL value is contained in single quotes as the attribute value is in double quotes.

Try It Out – Refreshing a Page

1. Type-up the following page into your text editor and call it Refresh1.htm:

```
<?xml version="1.0" encoding="UTF-8"?>
<!DOCTYPE html
     PUBLIC "-//W3C//DTD XHTML 1.0 Transitional//EN"
     "http://www.w3.org/TR/xhtml1/DTD/xhtml1-transitional.dtd">
<html xmlns="http://www.w3.org/1999/xhtml" xml:lang="en" lang="en">
<head>
  <title>Refresh Demo</title>
  <meta http-equiv="refresh" content="5;URL='Refresh2.htm'" />
</head>
<body>
  <p>This is page A</p>
</body>
</html>
```

2. Refresh2.htm can be any valid page but here we have used:

```
<?xml version="1.0" encoding="UTF-8"?>
<!DOCTYPE html
     PUBLIC "-//W3C//DTD XHTML 1.0 Transitional//EN"
     "http://www.w3.org/TR/xhtml1/DTD/xhtml1-transitional.dtd">
<html xmlns="http://www.w3.org/1999/xhtml" xml:lang="en" lang="en">
<head>
  <title>Refresh Demo II</title>
</head>
<body>
  <p>Like magic, it changes into page B!</p>
</body>
</html>
```

Now load up page Refresh1.htm. After 5 seconds it will be replaced by page Refresh2.htm.

How It Works

When a browser downloads a page it will have appended to it an HTTP header that is generated by the server. This header can include a whole host of information. A conforming browser (and most browsers are) will look to see if there are any <meta> tags with the http-equiv attribute.

Finding one, the browser will now read the content of this <meta> element as if it had been contained in the HTTP header. The browser will now refresh the page in exactly the same way it would have had we had included refresh information in the original HTTP header.

This method can be very useful if we ever move pages about our site. We can leave a solitary page behind that will direct the client to the new pages location.

Here's another use of the `http-equiv` attribute.

http-equiv= "expires"

When pages are downloaded from the server, they are cached (i.e. saved) on the client machine (although this can be turned off). The next time your browser makes a request for the page, instead of going off to the server your browser will load the cached copy. This works fine in most cases and saves considerable Internet bandwidth. However, if our page contains dated material, say it is a news magazine, we will want to make sure that the browser downloads a fresh page as soon as it is published.

Here is an example:

```
<meta http-equiv="expires" content="Mon, 22 Nov 1999 09:27:00 EST" />
```

Note that the date must be in a recognized format; we have used the full date format here.

This means that if the browser retrieves a page from it's cache, and the page is after the expiry date, it will automatically download a fresh version.

PICS-Rating

In this example we use the `<meta>` element to display a standard PICS-rating (see PICS section below).

We have used a content label for a site that was generated for us by visiting RSACi (`http://www.rsac.org`) and filling out a questionnaire. Here, the 'PICS-Label' is written according to the syntax of RSACi (**R**ecreational **S**oftware **A**dvisory **C**ouncil on the **I**nternet):

```
<meta http-equiv="PICS-Label"
content='(PICS-1.1 "http://www.rsac.org/ratingsv01.html" l gen true comment "RSACi
North America Server" by "foo@bar.com" for "http://www.somesite.com" on
"1995.01.16T08:15-0500" r (n 0 s 0 v 0 l 0))' />
```

This is an example tag - to get an actual tag, go to `http://www.rsac.org`. The RSACi software generates the entire rating string, and we just need to paste it into the `content` attribute. Note how we have to use single quotes for the `content` value because the generated string contains double quotes.

The 'scheme' attribute

This attribute was new to the HTML 4.0 standard and was meant to be used to describe some scheme that should be employed in interpreting the document. It's meaning is rather unclear, and it is not supported, but it could be useful in proprietary software.

The <link> Element

The `<link>` element has many uses, primarily to describe a link to an external resource. The only required attribute is the `type` attribute, which describes the media type. Although this element has a lot of potential, it is in practice rarely used outside of site management. In fact the only real use it finds is in linking to a style sheet. The following line would be contained within the head section of your document:

```
<link rel="stylesheet" type="text/css" href="mystyle.css" />
```

It links to an external style sheet called `mystyle.css` in which various styles would have been declared (such as setting the font size to 12pt within the body section, and so on). This is discussed in much more detail in Chapter 13 (Different Media Types).

In the management of large sites the `<link>` element can be extremely useful for the automatic generation of tables of contents, and of link management. However, these tasks require specialized (and often proprietary) software that is beyond the scope of this book.

Here is a brief description of each attribute and the content it should contain.

- `href` – this, of course, is the address of the link.
- `charset` – this describes the character set that the document referred to by the link employs.
- `hreflang` – the language code, as per RFC1766 (Request for Comments 1766 'Tags for the Identification of Languages', a document with a list of recommended language abbreviations).
- `type` – this is the mime type of the document, such as `text/html`, `text/css`, etc.
- `rel` – the relationship of the document in the link to the current document. We will se how to use this attribute in Chapter 11 when we look at site design.
- `rev` – basically, how the document described in the link looks at this document. This is rarely used.
- `media` – a description of the media type (such as screen, printer, etc.).

The <base> Element

This element takes a single `href` attribute which describes the base URL of the document.

For example, say a document had an address:

```
http://www.somesite.com/site/thatpage.htm
```

Then the base `href` could be:

```
http://www.somesite.com/site/
```

The importance of this element becomes evident if we move the document to another address. Say we have a link in our document to `thatpage.htm`, then there are two ways we could reference that document, either with the full URL:

```
<a href="http://www.somesite.com/site/thatpage.htm">Another page</a>
```

or with a relative link:

```
<a href ="thatpage.htm">Another page</a>
```

If we move the page to another area on our site, then normally we would have to change any relative links in our document. However, if we had set a base `href` value, then the browser would use this address for any relative links. That is, relative links are turned into absolute links by combining them with the base URL of the document.

PICS

PICS is an acronym for **P**latform for **I**nternet **C**ontent **S**election. It was originally designed to help parents and teachers control what children accessed on the Internet, but has since expanded as a labeling system for general content.

The label, once generated, can be sent (if your server allows it) as part of an HTTP header. The label can be included under both the 'protocol' or the PICS-label header. To find out how to do this you would need to talk to your Internet service provider. A full discussion of the details is beyond the scope of this book.

We can however easily include our PICS label in the `<meta>` element, and we looked at an example of how to that above. Generating a PICS compatible label is no easy task, and again the details of how to do it is beyond the scope of this book. However, it is a fairly easy matter to get someone to generate one for us for free! Visit `http://www.rsac.org` for one place that does this. Certainly, if your site contains any questionable material you should generate a PICS label for it and include it in a `<meta>` element. If you are writing a site directed mainly towards children you should also include a label, as some parents configure their software to block any site that does not have a PICS rating.

You can read all about PICS at `http://www.w3.org/PICS/`. This site will also give leads to more information for those who want it.

RDF

The **RDF** (or **R**esource **D**escription **F**ramework) is an XML based syntax developed by a working group of the W3C that can be used to describe content of various pages. It is quite an involved syntax, and a full discussion of it is beyond the scope of this chapter. Those interested in more details should visit `http://www.w3.org/RDF/`. All we need to note is that we can in fact use an RDF vocabulary to build up a profile of our page and all its connections. Special RDF enabled software can then catalog our page very accurately, and place it in a hierarchy of other pages.

RDF enables groups and interested parties to describe their own language; in other words, RDF is a meta-language. One such language is the Dublin Core language that describes the content of books. This language was developed by a consortium of libraries and has become the *de facto* language for describing book content. More information on the Dublin Core language can be obtained from `http://purl.org/DC/documents/rec-dces-19990702.htm`.

We can in fact use RDF in our documents without really having a full understanding of the syntax. All we have to do is add a few lines of markup in the `<head>` of our document. The best way to illustrate this is by means of an example.

Here is an example using the Dublin Core language:

```
<rdf:RDF
   xmlns:rdf="http://www.w3.org/1999/02/22-rdf-syntax-ns#"
   xmlns:dc="http://purl.org/dc/elements/1.0/">
  <rdf:Description
        rdf:about="http://www.hypermedic.com/style/index.htm"
        dc:creator="Frank Boumphrey"
        dc:title="Styling XML"
        dc:description="An index page to a site devoted to using and styling XML"
        dc:date="1999-09-10" />
</rdf:RDF>
```

We will go into details of the content below but just note that this XML document can be include in the `<head>` element of your document, and RDF enabled soft ware can read it. The `<rdf:RDF>` element will be ignored by any browser that does not understand it, and that's all of them! However, not to worry, because this information is not put there for your browser but for any RDF aware robot that visits your page.

How It Works

The first thing to notice is that the element name contains a colon. This tells an XML parser that the element belongs to another namespace (see below):

```
<rdf:RDF
```

In fact in this element we are going to use two namespaces, the RDF namespace:

```
   xmlns:rdf="http://www.w3.org/1999/02/22-rdf-syntax-ns#"
```

And the Dublin Core namespace:

```
   xmlns:dc="http://purl.org/dc/elements/1.0/">
```

Next, we have a `Description` element with an `about` attribute from the RDF namespace:

```
  <rdf:Description
        rdf:about="http://www.hypermedic.com/style/index.htm"
```

And then some attributes from the Dublin Core namespace:

```
            dc:creator="Frank Boumphrey"
            dc:title="Styling XML"
            dc:description="An index page to a site devoted to using and
              styling XML"
            dc:date="1999-09-10" />
```

A robot visiting this page that understands the Dublin Core language will know exactly what this means. We get a pretty good idea our selves – for example, we see that this references a document called 'Styling XML' that was written by Frank Boumphrey and available from the 'hypermedic' site (the value of the `rdf:about` attribute).

And, finally, there is the closing tag of the RDF element from the RDF namespace:

```
    </rdf:RDF>
```

RDF can get pretty complex, but by using the "Monkey see, monkey do" approach above we can start using it now with only a minimal grasp of the languages involved. For example, we can use the above code snippet and simply change the URL to your own web page, and then change the creator and title attributes etc. accordingly.

Namespaces

Every element and attribute in an XML document belongs to a namespace. In fact a namespace of a document is simply the name given to the list of all the elements in a document.

The concept of namespaces is simplicity itself, and to use them is almost as simple. We have in fact already made use of it in the last section. Namespaces are a means by which we can use an element from one document type and embed it in another document type.

All the elements in XHTML have names, and collectively these names are said to belong to the XHTML namespace. If we give this collection of names a unique name itself, then we can identify any element belonging to the namespace with a special syntax. This means that no matter where the element so identified is found, we can be sure that it belongs to the namespace. The general syntax we employ to identify an element or attribute as belonging to a namespace is as follows.

```
    [unique namespace name]:[element or attribute name]
```

In XHTML, the namespace is declared with the `xmlns` attribute of the `<html>` tag:

```
    <html xmlns="http://www.w3.org/1999/xhtml" xml:lang="en" lang="en">
```

Here, we see that the name of the XHTML namespace is `http://www.w3.org/1999/xhtml`. This leads us nicely into the necessary requirement of having a unique name for the name of the namespace.

URI's as Unique Names

One name that is designed to be unique is a URI, and so a URI is usually used for the namespace name. For example I have a domain under my control called `www.hypermedic.com`. If I wrote an XML document, I could put all the element names in a namespace and call it `www.hypermedic.com/myxmlnamespace`, and be quite sure that no one could legally use that name. It should be made very clear that we are not using this as an address, there should be no expectation that any thing will be found at this address; we are merely using it as a unique name.

We have already seen the name of the RDF namespace, it is:

```
http://www.w3.org/1999/02/22-rdf-syntax-ns#
```

To identify the XML element `Description` as belonging to the RDF namespace we could put:

```
http://www.w3.org/1999/02/22-rdf-syntax-ns#:Description
```

And if I now put this element into my XHTML page, a conforming browser would understand that the `Description` element is not an XHTML element but is rather an RDF element.

However, dotting my document with elements like this would be very cumbersome and, undoubtedly, the colon in the name (`http://` etc.) would confuse any software that was trying to read the namespace. We therefore provide an alias for the namespace name. It's rather like the A. A. Milne poem:

> "James James Morrison Morrison Wetherby George Dupree,
> Commonly known as 'Jim' "

If I provide an alias for the RDF namespace, I could call it anything I wanted, Fred, George, or even rdf!. The last seems to be the most suitable alias, so I inform the browser that I want `rdf` to stand for `http://www.w3.org/1999/02/22-rdf-syntax-ns#` by putting `rdf` after the `xmlns` attribute:

```
xmlns:rdf="http://www.w3.org/1999/02/22-rdf-syntax-ns#"
```

We can now rewrite the `Description` element much more conveniently as:

```
rdf:Description
```

We let our user agent know both the namespace we are using and the alias we are giving it, in a namespace declaration.

Namespace Declarations

A namespace must be declared before it is used. The general syntax for declaring a namespace and assigning an alias to it is:

```
xmlns:[alias]= "[namespace name]"
```

A namespace should be declared in either the element that is going to use them or in an ancestor element. For example in the RDF example we have two namespace declarations

```
<rdf:RDF
   xmlns:rdf="http://www.w3.org/1999/02/22-rdf-syntax-ns#"
   xmlns:dc="http://purl.org/dc/elements/1.0/">
```

Now whenever the user-agent sees an element or attribute beginning with `rdf:` it knows it belongs to the `http://www.w3.org/1999/02/22-rdf-syntax-ns#` namespace, and when it sees an element or attribute starting with `dc:` it knows it belongs to the `http://purl.org/dc/elements/1.0/` namespace.

Namespace Defaulting

There is another way to declare a namespace and that is simply to declare it without an alias. For example:

```
<html xmlns="http://www.w3.org/1999/xhtml">
<head>
  <title>Basic XHTML Document with namespace declaration<title>
</head>
<body>
  <p>All these elements are in the xhtml namespace</p>
</body>
```

Because all the elements are descendants of the `<html>` element where the namespace is declared, they are assumed to be in the XHTML namespace.

Note that we could have put our RDF and Dublin Core namespaces in the root element of our document and this would be quite legal:

```
<html xmlns="http://www.w3.org/1999/xhtml"
   xmlns:rdf="http://www.w3.org/1999/02/22-rdf-syntax-ns#"
   xmlns:dc="http://purl.org/dc/elements/1.0/">

<head>
<title>Basic XHTML Document with namespace declaration<title>
<rdf:RDF>
<rdf:Description
        rdf:about="http://www.hypermedic.com/style/index.htm"
        dc:creator="Frank Boumphrey"
        dc:title="Styling XML"
```

```
        dc:description="An index page to a site devoted to using and styling XML"
        dc:date="1999-09-10" />
</rdf:RDF>
</head>
<body>
<p>All the unprefixed elements are in the xhtml namespace, the prefixed elements
belong to the namespaces declared in the document root element.</p>
</body>
```

HTTP Headers

When your browser, or other client, requests a page from a server using the HTTP (**H**yper **T**ext **T**ransfer **P**rotocol) protocol, there are, in its simplest form, four separate parts to the transaction:

- The client opens a connection
- The client makes a request
- The server sends a response
- The server closes the connection

Let's look at each of these.

When the client (i.e. browser) opens a connection it will connect to the server at the address in the URL. The client then makes a request to the server, and this is contained in an HTTP request header. This header will contain a whole lot of information about the file and the client. The easiest way to show what goes on is with a simple example.

Client-Request HTTP Header.

Suppose I request a page with the URL `http://www.hypermedic.com/style/index.htm` by clicking on a link in a Netscape 2.0 browser. Here is what may actually be sent to the server.

```
GET /style/index.htm HTTP 1.0
Accept: text/plain
Accept: text/html
Accept: text/xml
Accept: text/*
Accept: image/jpeg
Accept: image/gif
Accept: image/*
Accept: */*
If-Modified-Since: Wed, 24 Nov 199919:35:24
User-Agent: Mozilla/2.00
```

How It Works

First of all, the URL contains information about which protocol is to be used; in this case it is the http protocol:

```
http://www.hypermedic.com/style/index.htm
```

Next, it contacts the server at this address:

```
http://www.hypermedic.com/style/index.htm
```

And if contact is made it sends the header above.

The first line

```
GET /style/index.htm HTTP 1.0
```

gives the location of the document in the servers content directory. The first word indicates that the GET protocol is being used; the last words indicate that HTTP 1.0 is the version of the HTTP protocol being used.

The next few lines give the mime types that the browser is willing to accept.

```
Accept: text/plain
Accept: text/html
Accept: text/xml
Accept: text/*
Accept: image/jpeg
Accept: image/gif
Accept: image/*
Accept: */*
```

The last one, `*/*`, in effect means "failing all else just send me what you have there"!

The next line

```
If-Modified-Since: Wed, 24 Nov 199919:35:24
```

is generated by some clients. It looks to see if a page of the URL is cached, and if it is then it looks at the date it was cached. It then asks the server if there have been any modifications to the file since that date. If there has been no modification the server simply sends back a message to that effect and the client uses the cached page.

As we saw above, we can over-ride this mechanism using the `http-equiv="expires"` and a date.

The next line

```
User-Agent: Mozilla/2.00
```

provides the server with information about the client; this allows the server to send different pages to different clients.

The last line:

```

```

is simply a blank line. This tells the server that it has come to the end of the header.

If the server finds the page requested, it will send back that page with an HTTP header attached to it. This information then becomes part of the file that is cached on the client. This will include information such as the date, mime type of the document, and the size of the document.

Here is what the server response header may look like:

```
HTTP/1.0 200 OK
Date: Wed, 24 Nov 1999 19:35:24
Server: Apache/1.1
MIME-version: 1.0
Content-type:text/html
Last-Modified: Wed, 24 Nov 1999 12:31:54
Content-length: 1342

<?xml version="1.0" encoding="UTF-8"?>
<!DOCTYPE html
     PUBLIC "-//W3C//DTD XHTML 1.0 Transitional//EN"
     "DTD/xhtml1-transitional.dtd">
<html xmlns="http://www.w3.org/1999/xhtml" xml:lang="en" lang="en">
...
```

How It Works

Again the information is all on separate lines. The first consists of three parts:

```
HTTP/1.0 200 OK
```

- The HTTP version number.
- A Status code. This is a number between 200 and 599. Here, 200 means every thing is fine. You are probably familiar with number 404, an error code meaning 'File not found'.
- An explanation. These are server specific.

The next three lines are more self-explanatory, comprising the date and server name, and the mime protocol version number being employed:

```
Date: Wed, 24 Nov 1999 19:35:24
Server: Apache/1.1
MIME-version: 1.0
```

The next line is generated by the server, and the server decides what the mime type is by looking at the files 'dot extension'. However, the decision the server makes is configurable. If you need a new mapping between an extension and a mime type, it can be added to the server.

```
Content-type:text/html
```

The last few lines need little explanation:

```
Last-Modified: Wed, 24 Nov 1999 12:31:54
Content-length: 1342

<?xml version="1.0" encoding="UTF-8"?>
```

Content length is the length of the file in bytes, the blank line tells the browser that it has come to the end of the header information, and then the file proper begins.

It should be emphasized that the whole file, including the header, is cached by the client.

Mime Types

Mime types are very important meta-information as they let the user-agent know what kind of document it is about to receive, and thus allow the user agent to display it in the correct format.

There are numerous types of mime (**M**ultipart **I**nternet **M**ail **E**xtensions) types and these predate the Web. Indeed, as the name suggests, they were originally designed as an extension to the original mail protocol used to describe the document being sent.

> *We are using document in the broadest terms here to include images and movie clips etc.*

We have already had a look at some of the mime types in our examples. A full listing can be obtained via the `ftp` protocol from:

```
ftp://ftp.isi.edu/in-notes/iana/assignments/media-types/
```

A mime type consists of two parts:

```
[type]/[subtype]
```

The major types include text, image, audio, video, and application.

Some of the subtypes of the text type that we will use in this book include plain, html, xml, css, sgml, and rtf.

The mime type is very important in client/server relationships as it is the mime type that tells a client what kind of document it is receiving. It is in fact left entirely up to the server to generate the mime type, and most do this on the 'dot extension' of the document. So `somefile.htm` and `somefile.html` would be sent as the mime type of `text/html`, and `somefile.xml` would be sent as the mime type `text/xml`. If the server does not recognize the extension it will usually send the file as `text/plain`.

If the browser loads the document from a local folder, it will go through the same kind of process; in other words it will use the extension to try and figure out the type of file being offered to it.

Try It Out – Mime Types

1. Type the following document into your text editor:

```
<?xml version="1.0" encoding="UTF-8"?>
<!DOCTYPE html
     PUBLIC "-//W3C//DTD XHTML 1.0 Transitional//EN"
     "http://www.w3.org/TR/xhtml1/DTD/xhtml1-transitional.dtd">
<html xmlns="http://www.w3.org/1999/xhtml" xml:lang="en" lang="en">
<head>
  <title>Basic Doc</title>
</head>
<body>
  <p>A simple document</p>
</body>
</html>
```

2. And save it as the following

- `mime1.htm`
- `mime1.xml`
- `mime1.txt`
- `mime1.jnk`

3. Now open your browser and view each document in turn. Here is what you will see if you open the files in IE5. If you use other browsers the display may vary. A brief explanation follows each picture.

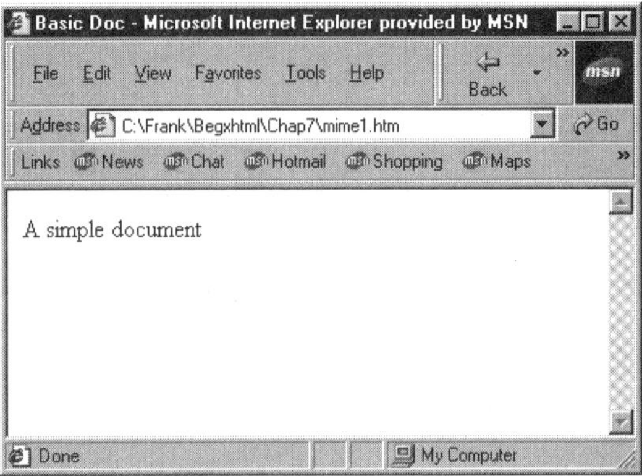

4. Here the document is treated as an HTML file, and is displayed as such.

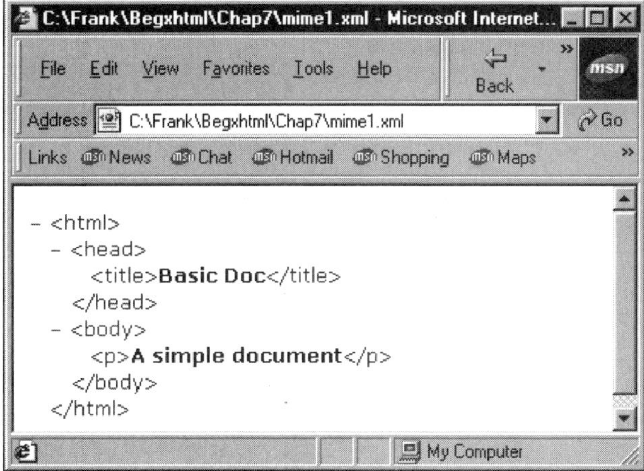

5. Here we see the typical IE5 display of an XML document.

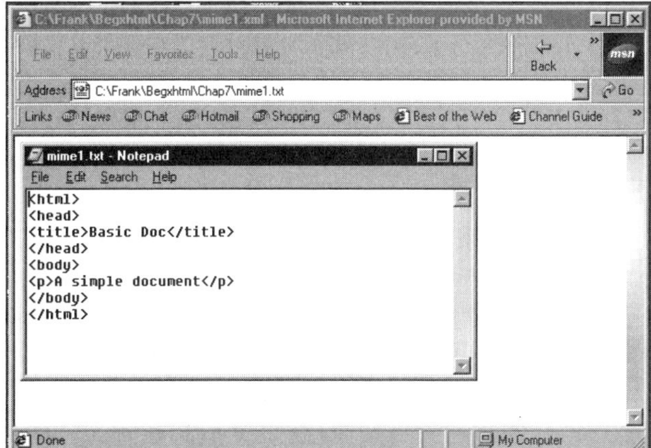

6. The default behavior here is to open the text file in my default text reader (which happens to be Notepad in my case) and not in the browser.

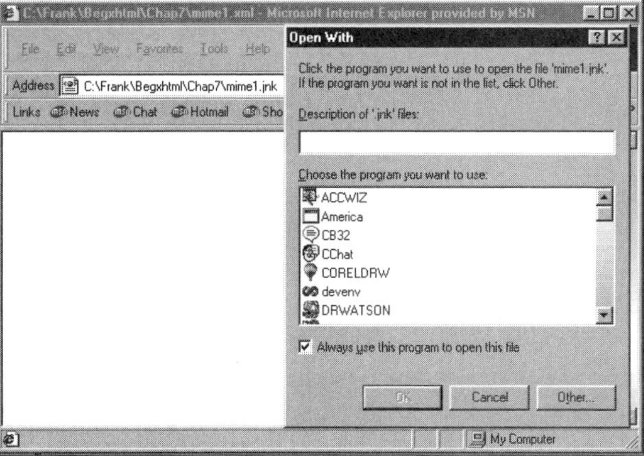

7. Here the browser does not recognize the mime type, and so asks me what application I would like to view it in.

8. What happens though if I send the junk file over a server? The answer to that depends on the server. Using Microsoft's Personal Web Server here is what we see when we send the junk file `mime1.jnk` to our client:

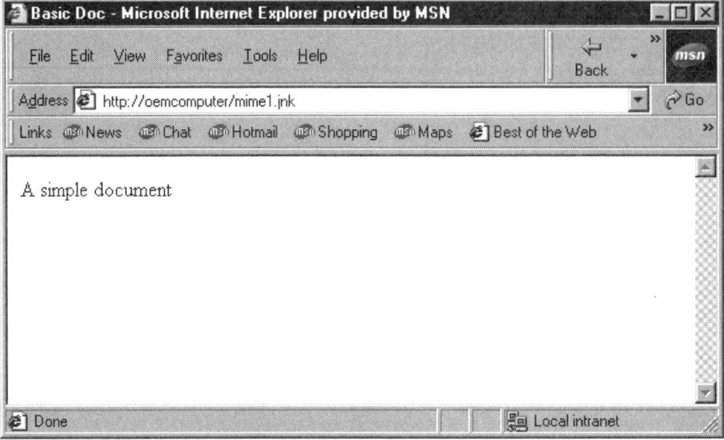

9. The PWS server is clever: it peeks inside the file, sees the root element is `<html>` and delivers the document as `text/html`.

To see the default mechanism in operation we can use the following file:

```
<greeting>Hi there!</greeting>
```

and save it as `mime2.sgml` (or `mime2.jnk`). Now when the server sends it to our client, we see the following:

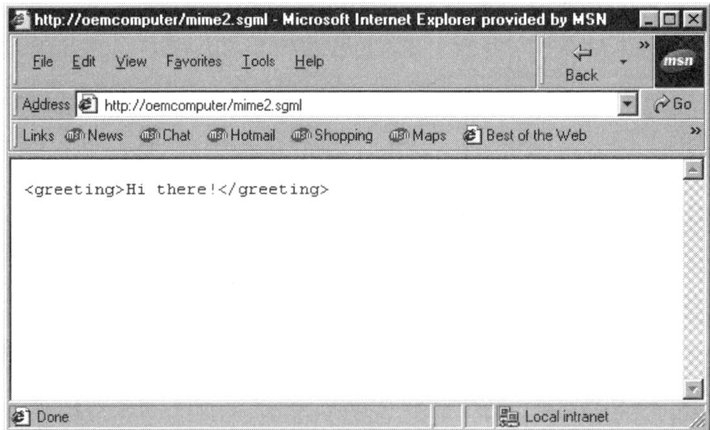

This is the expected behavior: PWS did not recognize the suffix `.sgml`, and so delivered the file as a `text/plain` mime type.

You can find out more about mime types at `http://www.irvine.com/~mime/`.

Summary

In this chapter we looked at the data that describes the document and its contents. This is known as meta-data.

We looked at how to use the `<meta>` and `<title>` tags to define a documents content, and also had a brief look at how this could be done by using the emerging RDF syntax. These can be used by 'spiders', programs that automatically 'crawl the web' to compile search engine data (such as that from Google).

The `<link>` and `<base>` tags are used in linking to other documents, such as an external style sheet; the `<base>` tag is used to turn relative links into absolute ones.

We then showed that a namespace is simply the name given to the list of all the elements in a document, and showed how a namespace declaration is used in an XHTML document. The use of other namespaces (such as Dublin Core) was also shown.

We then closed the chapter with a discussion of HTTP headers and mime types.

CSS
DOM
XHTML
JavaScript
XML

Style Sheets for the Web

If you have used a computer for any kind of desktop publishing no doubt you will have come across the idea of a style sheet or document template. In its simplest form, a document template consists of a number of styles such as Normal, Heading1, Heading2, and so on. As you type you can apply one of the available styles to the text so that headings assume the correct font size and weight, paragraphs take on the correct margins, and images have the appropriate white space around them.

Style sheets for XHTML work on similar – but not identical – principles. In this chapter we will learn how to compose a simple style sheet for an XHTML document in a language called CSS (Cascading Style Sheets). Using this, we can control the size and colour of text on the screen, define the preferred font for the different components of a document, set their background color or image and control the amount of 'white space' inserted around an element.

In this chapter, we will cover the following:

- The advantages of using a style sheet for your XHTML document
- The CSS style sheet language
- Control of text color (including the text of hypertext links)
- Specifying the background color for the whole or just part of a document
- Specifying the font for a given paragraph, heading or other part of a document
- The control of 'white space' through style sheets
- How to apply a named style with the `class` attribute

Bringing Style to the Web

Before Style Sheets

In the beginning, HTML offered no control over style at all but was merely for marking up the components of a document in terms of their *function* in the sense of the role they played in the document: heading, list, paragraph, and so on. The way that HTML concentrated on functional aspects of a document of HTML was to its advantage, as it enabled documents to be viewed on all kinds of platforms, from Unix and dumb terminals to PCs and Macintoshes. The idea was that the software at the receiving end – in other the words the **browser** – could use the HTML markup to see which part of the document performed which function. It could then use its own mechanisms to render the text on the screen as it saw fit. The same document could thus be viewed on all kinds of machines on the 'Net, an idea which brought about the success of the Web.

But people have a natural interest in the look of their documents and, before long, new HTML tags were being added to control aspects of style. During the mid-nineties the Mosaic browser, and later Netscape Navigator, added some simple HTML tags and attributes to control this aspect of web documents, departing from the idea that mark-up was simply about control of document structure. These new tags were instantly popular with everyone apart from the academic purists, who saw them as contaminating the language. "After all," they claimed, "HTML is all about structured documents, and style has nothing to do with structure." They certainly had a point. However, the more popular the Web became, the more the designers wanted control over presentation. Before long all kinds of tricks were in use to make HTML documents behave as they wanted. A classic of its time was the small transparent GIF image, which could be used as a 'spacer' to push text aside, create artificial margins, or to vertically space lines.

The `<table>` element was even more amenable when it came to assisting with the layout of web pages, with the table cells used to position images and text to give the effect of a multi-column layout. Meanwhile, when it came to headings, designers could hardly be content with the idea that the browser would choose the font for them, and so began to use images for these rather than HTML's `<h1>` - `<h6>` elements. The end result of all these tricks was to greatly complicate the markup, with a page's structure and styling becoming intertwined such that one couldn't be separated from the other.

Style Sheets to the Rescue

In late 1995 there was a meeting of the World Wide Web Consortium and other interested parties to discuss a solution to all these problems: style sheets for the Web. Using a special language, it was advocated that soon everyone would be using style sheets as a separate 'layer' to specify presentational aspects of documents. The rogue HTML tags and tricks employed by web designers would finally be redundant. Although it has taken longer than expected, the web style sheets are finally with us and are widely implemented on all major browsers.

The Advantages of Using Style Sheets

- **You can change the whole look and feel of your document with a few easy edits**. This aspect relates to the process of separating the functional part of the document (the XHTML) from the presentational aspects (the style sheet). When you use Word or another desktop publishing package you use a style sheet or template to present the text properly on the page. If you do this efficiently and in an organized manner then you can attach a new template and re-style the document without fuss. The same principle lies behind the efficient use of a web style sheet. If you structure a document with XHTML and then superimpose a style sheet to specify the presentation then you can easily re-style the whole text by editing the style sheet or swapping it for another one. On the other hand if you sprinkle the text liberally with `<font>` tags, `<br />` (line-break) tags and non-breaking spaces to create the layout, then changing the overall style will be much more tricky and time consuming.

- **The same style sheet can apply to several documents**. You can re-use the style sheet to get the same 'look and feel' for a group of documents; this is extremely useful.

- **The markup is neater and the content is more maintainable**. Nowadays, web pages are often very complex, so much so that if you look at their source it's almost impossible to understand. Instead of looking like a document with tags to structure its components, the page looks more like part of a computer program. This was not the intention of the original designers of the Web. Style sheets free the markup from the tremendous amount of clutter in the form of `<font>` tags, `<br />` tags, GIF images for headings, and other tags controlling presentation. This makes the document easier to mark up, read and maintain.

- **Style sheets make it possible to gear the text to a range of devices rather than just desktops**. With CSS you can make stylistic control a separate process. This approach of keeping structure and presentation apart has tremendous benefits when it comes to fine-tuning web content for different devices such as mobile phones, television, palm-top computers, and so on (this is discussed fully in Chapter 13). For display on a color computer screen, for example, a style sheet might concentrate on color and layout. The style sheet for rendering the very same document into speech (useful if you are accessing via a car phone, for example) would instead focus on the pitch of the voice, the volume, and so on:

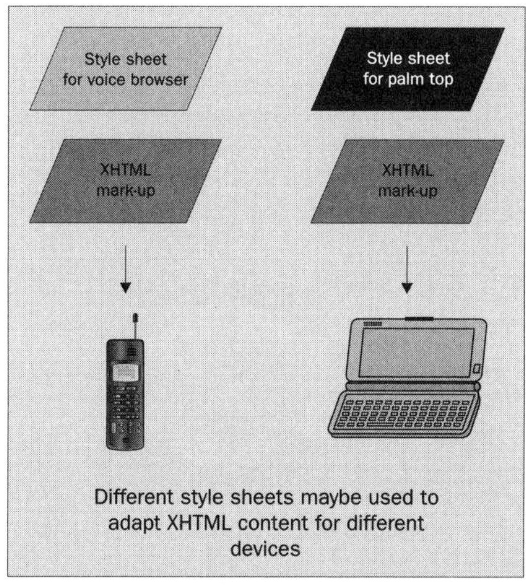

Different style sheets maybe used to adapt XHTML content for different devices

- **Documents are faster to download** with style sheets. Lots of people use GIF images for headings and other text which they want to appear large on the screen. These images take some time to download, particularly on slow connections to the Internet. A style sheet gives you a much simpler and faster way of generating headings in a variety of fonts. That said, you do not have quite the same control over the exact look of the headings as you might were you to use a GIF, especially if you want to use an unusual font.

The Cascading Style Sheet (CSS) Language

The most popular language for writing style sheets for XHTML documents is called **CSS** – the Cascading Style Sheet language. This language was invented by Bert Bos and Håkon Lie at the World Wide Web Consortium with contributions from Chris Lilley, Dave Raggett and many others. The idea was to design a style sheet language which would give authors great flexibility when it came to controlling layout and yet, at the same time, would be easy enough to write that even non-programmers could design their own style sheets for the Web. The idea was that either CSS could be incorporated in the HTML itself – by using special elements and attributes for the purpose – or it could be the content of a completely separate file. This latter arrangement involves linking the style sheet to the document, the style sheet file taking on a different file extension.

Future Directions

CSS has now been through a number of stages of development. The initial specification, CSS1, released in 1996, was primarily concerned with relatively simple style sheet functions such as color, font, background image, and so on. Following on from this, CSS2 (1998) included further and more sophisticated features. These included features associated with page-based layout (for printing), support for downloadable fonts, and the definition of rectangular regions for displaying different parts of documents, giving freedom to lay out documents without resorting to using HTML tables as a means to position items on the screen.

Work on CSS3 has now begun and should be completed during the year 2000. The new version will bring with it many new features organised as modules; some examples of *possible* modules are listed below:

- Values and units
- Aural style sheets
- Columns
- Text flow and related topics
- Paged media
- Vertical text and Ruby
- Color
- Numbering and lists
- Backgrounds
- Text and fonts

CSS3 will, in effect, have all of the features that users expect from a desktop publishing environment, as well as a range of features especially suited to the context of an international and multimedia web.

The XSL Language

This chapter covers the use of the CSS language for styling XHTML documents because this is the most common way to date, and a method suitable for the non-programmer to understand. An alternative style sheet language for programmers for styling XML documents currently being developed is the eXtensible Stylesheet Language or XSL language. Aimed, by and large, at complex documentation projects, XSL has many uses associated with the automatic generation of tables of contents, indexes, reports and other more complex publishing tasks, especially printing.

Support for CSS

For a browser to understand what to do when it finds a CSS style sheet attached to a document it needs not only to understand the syntax of the language itself, but also to know how to render the text and images in the appropriate way on the screen. Support for CSS is now reliable for a number of features but for other features it is far from perfect. The best place to find out which features are supported and which are not is `http://webreview.com/pub/guides/style/style.html`.

The WebReview site is highly recommended. It includes three up-to-date and very useful lists to which all authors should refer. These are as follows:

The Master List
This is the mother of all CSS charts, listing every aspect of the CSS specification and identifying how well it is supported by Netscape 4, Internet Explorer 3 and Internet Explorer 4 for both Mac and Windows 95.

The Safe List
This is the list you'll refer to again and again – every CSS property that is completely or partially supported by all browsers.

The Danger List
This is the list of properties to stay away from – the ones for which support is nonexistent, buggy or quirky.

Why Hasn't Support for CSS Been Better?

When Microsoft's Internet Explorer 3 was released, implementation of CSS was at best experimental. Indeed IE 3 went out with a certain amount of support for CSS even before the specification for CSS1 was finished. Needless to say, the resulting implementation did not tie in with the specification.

Netscape responded by adding a way of setting style properties via JavaScript. However, this was neither thorough nor consistent in its handling of stylistic features. Microsoft then greatly improved their support for style sheets in Internet Explorer 4 although still failed to do a lot of the basics. Netscape grudgingly added some support for CSS syntax to Navigator 4. There were, however, many bugs which meant that a number of properties simply couldn't be used. Microsoft, upon seeing how little real work had been done by Netscape, did not bother in its IE 5 release to patch up or even implement CSS1 properly, let alone CSS 2.

Better Times to Come

All in all, then, support for style sheets in the past has been rather disappointing. However, all is changing. Enter now a new company in Norway called OperaSoft who have been diligently working away producing a lightweight browser that fully implements the CSS1 specification (see `http://www.opera.com/index.html`). This has taken them a long time and we hope that by the time this book goes to press that you will be able to benefit from their excellent work. Meanwhile Netscape has gone open source with the Mozilla project and we can expect a very much more thorough implementation of CSS in the next release of Navigator (`http://www.netscape.com`). Furthermore, you can expect to see good support for CSS from other newcomers into the browser market, such as Hewlett Packard's ChaiFarer XML web browser (`http://www.internetsolutions.enterprise.hp.com/chai/chai_farer.html`).

How CSS Style Sheets Work

When an XHTML document is displayed by a browser, ordinarily the browser defaults to using its own ideas about how the text and images should be laid out on the screen. So, for example, one browser might choose Times Roman to display the text for paragraph elements, while another might instead default to a sans serif font such as Arial. What a style sheet does is to tell the browser more specifically how to render the document whether on screen, on paper, or even to voice.

Formatting Objects

The diagram below shows a very simple document in terms of its component parts with heading elements, list elements, paragraph elements and, within these, images and hypertext links. A paragraph, a heading, or a list: these are all examples of **formatting objects**. These are 'objects' from the perspective of the software that displays the document. Text is said to **flow** within a formatting object.

Why 'Cascading' Style Sheets?

The name 'Cascading Style Sheets' implies that more than one style sheet can interact together (or merge) together to produce the final look of the document: individual style sheets from different sources can be combined. CSS allows you to write a short style sheet to override a few properties in the browser's built-in style sheet.

Inheritance of Style Sheet Properties

One of the most important aspects of CSS is the way that properties are inherited from one element to another. For instance, suppose you have a paragraph which has been given CSS properties which say that it should be displayed as blue text and in italic. Any elements contained within that paragraph – its **child** elements – will inherit these properties from their parent paragraph. Bold text within the paragraph will still be blue and italic and, of course, bold. Similarly, any text within the paragraph which has been marked up as `<strong>` will still be blue.

Navigator 4's support for inheritance is not entirely reliable. In particular, it doesn't work well for tables or for elements appearing after a table. Workarounds include using style rules to specify the font family for `<p>` and other tags.

How to Write CSS

Here is a simple example of a stylistic 'rule' written in CSS:

```
h1 {font-size: 12pt; font-weight: bold; color: red;}
```

This example simply states that Heading 1 elements should be 12-point bold red text. We look more at the use of CSS to make text a particular color in more detail during the course of this chapter.

You can see that the syntax for the stylistic rule is relatively straightforward. The element to which the style applies is given first and a **property list** specifying the style then follows afterwards. The diagram below illustrates this with another example:

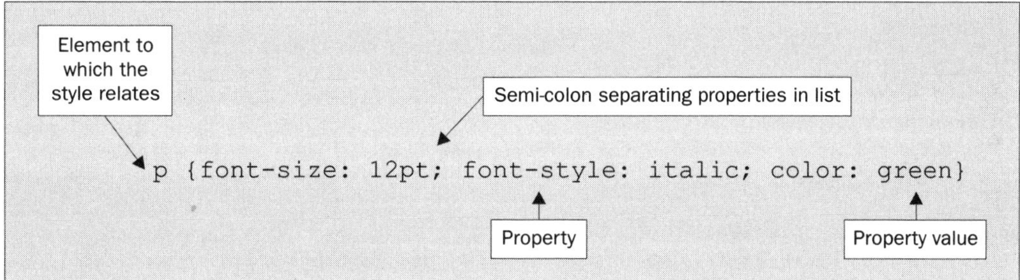

The property list is enclosed in curly brackets and successive properties are separated by a semi-colon. The properties themselves consist of a **property name** and a **value**, separated by a colon.

It doesn't matter how you space out the rules or where you place new lines. Also, CSS rules are case-insensitive. That means that the following rules have exactly the same effect as each other:

```
p {
  font-size: 120%;
  font-style: italic;
}

p {font-size: 120%; font-style: italic;}

p {FONT-SIZE: 120%; font-style: ITALIC;}

p {font-size:120%;  font-style:italic;}
```

A complete style sheet consists of one or more stylistic rules contained in the `<style>` element, which itself is part of the document head. You can see the `<style>` element in use in the example below.

If you want to give the same style to a whole lot of tags you can do this:

```
h2, h3, h4 {color:green;}
```

The effect will be that <h2>, <h3> and <h4> elements will be colored green. This shortcut saves having to write out three rules, one for each tag.

Try It Out – Writing a Simple Style Sheet

Here is a simple style sheet to try out.

1. Take this simple XHTML document and save as `first-attempt.htm`:

```
<?xml version="1.0" encoding="UTF-8"?>
<!DOCTYPE html
     PUBLIC "-//W3C//DTD XHTML 1.0 Transitional//EN"
     "http://www.w3.org/TR/xhtml1/DTD/xhtml1-transitional.dtd">
<html xmlns="http://www.w3.org/1999/xhtml" xml:lang="en" lang="en">
<html xmlns="http://www.w3.org/1999/xhtml" xml:lang="en" lang="en">
  <head>
    <title>Trying out a style sheet</title>
    <style type="text/css">
    <!--
      p {font-size:120%;}
      h1 {color:green; }
      h2 {color:green; font-size: 90%;}
      b { color:red; }
    -->
    </style>
  </head>
  <body>
    <h1>The first attempt<br />
       <b>at a style sheet</b></h1>

    <h2>I am a second-level heading</h2>

    <p>I am a paragraph which should be displayed in a larger font than
normal.</p>

    <p>The same style will be applied to all paragraphs in the document.</p>
  </body>
</html>
```

2. Try out the document on your browser. The style sheet should affect the way the text is displayed and you should see the following or similar:

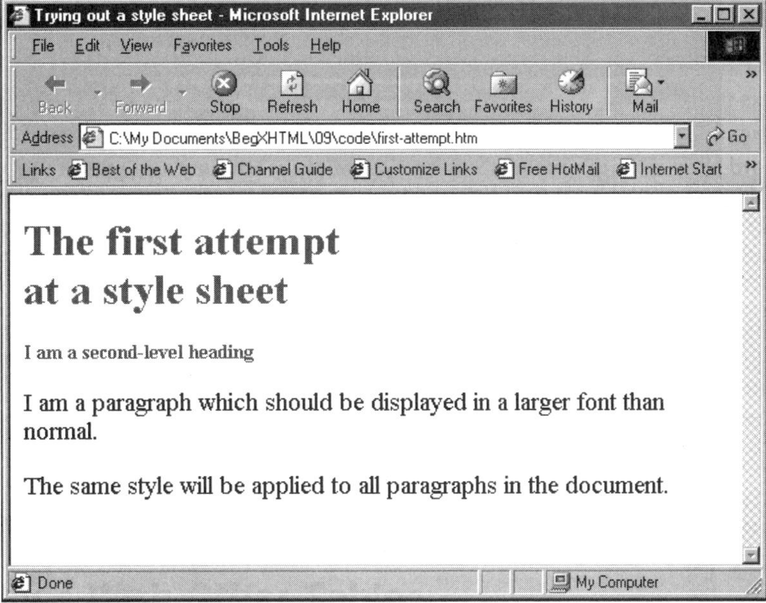

How It Works

The style sheet inserted in the document has had the effect of making the Heading 1 element green and the size of the Heading 2 element reduced slightly. Meanwhile, because the `<b>` element was given the color red, it changed the color of the main Heading 1 halfway through the text.

Note that we've enclosed the CSS in comments to hide it from older browsers which may try to render the contents to the screen as text if they don't understand style sheets.

Example of a Linked Style Sheet

Rather than include the style sheet inside the XHTML document, we can create a separate style sheet file and link our XHTML document to it. A separate style sheet file normally has the '.css' file extension. We then use the `<link>` element to attach that style sheet to our XHTML file. In the example above, we can separate the style sheet from the document quite easily.

Try It Out – Example of a Linked Style Sheet

1. Cut and paste the style sheet from the above XHTML document into a new text file, add the comment line to the top, and save the file as `first-link.css` (note that we do not need the `<style>` tags in an external style sheet):

```
/* This is the style sheet to be linked */
p {font-size:120%;}
h1 {color:green; }
h2 {color:green; font-size: 90%;}
b { color:red; }
```

2. Now delete the `<style>` elements from the XHTML document and add in the `<link>` statement, so that the document now looks just like the following:

```
<?xml version="1.0" encoding="UTF-8"?>
<!DOCTYPE html
     PUBLIC "-//W3C//DTD XHTML 1.0 Transitional//EN"
     "http://www.w3.org/TR/xhtml1/DTD/xhtml1-transitional.dtd">
<html xmlns="http://www.w3.org/1999/xhtml" xml:lang="en" lang="en">
  <head>
    <title>Trying out a style sheet</title>
    <link rel="stylesheet" href="first-link.css" />
  </head>
  <body>
    <h1>The first attempt<br />
    <b>at a style sheet</b></h1>

    <h2>I am a second-level heading</h2>

    <p>I am a paragraph which should be displayed in a larger font than
normal.</p>

    <p>The same style will be applied to all paragraphs in the document.</p>
  </body>
</html>
```

3. Save as `linking.htm` and display the file in your browser – you should see exactly the same screen as before.

How It Works

The critical line is:

```
<link rel="stylesheet" href="first-link.css" />
```

This simply informs the browser to style the document with the style information contained within the file given as the value of the `href` attribute. One advantage of this method is when, say, one department in a company makes various 'approved' styles which all company documents must follow. The author of the document then simply needs to include one line (the `<link>` statement) to turn their document from a plain XHTML document into one that has a company 'look and feel' to it.

Note that the style sheet does not have to be in the same folder as the XHTML document. For example, in such a company, a manager in one department could author an information document for new recruits and then link it to a style sheet stored in the Human Resources departmental folder as so:

```
<link rel="stylesheet" href="HRdept/new_staff.css" />
```

The path to the file can be as long as necessary. For example, the 'new staff' style information may be stored in a general information folder within the employees folder:

```
<link rel="stylesheet" href="HRdept/employees/gen_info/new_staff.css" />
```

However, you may wish to link to a style sheet stored on a totally different machine, or even one in a totally different country. For example, if you are in the USA but are writing a document for the UK-based branch of the company, you simply give the full URL of the location of the style file as the value of the `href` attribute:

```
<link rel="stylesheet" href="http://www.somecompany.com/UK.css" />
```

Note that this is similar to typing in the address (i.e. the full URL of the location) of an XHTML document into your browser, except that it is for a CSS document this time. For the rest of this chapter, though, we shall just stick to including the style information within the XHTML document for ease of readability.

Common Mistakes in Writing CSS

Here are some of the simple things to get wrong. Remember that writing CSS is a bit like programming in the sense that even a small error can throw the whole thing out and produce surprising results:

- Check that you have put semicolons (';') between the properties in the list. This is very easily forgotten.
- Check that you have not forgotten the `</style>` end tag.
- Browsers are very sensitive to markup problems. This applies particularly to tables. The solution is to check that you have indeed written valid XHTML or use the HTMLTidy (Appendix B) program to tidy the markup.
- If you have specified a color by name, make sure that it really is one of the 16 color names allowed by CSS (these are shown later). If it isn't, then the text may be shown in black.
- If you have specified a font, again check the spelling. Browsers are not in the slightest bit tolerant of spelling mistakes! Also, remember that font names of more than one word should be quoted and that quotes are not allowed anywhere else.

- On that note, check that you have spelt 'color' in the US-English way (not 'colour' with a 'u', which is the UK-English way).
- Is the problem with your browser rather than with you? Although in our examples we try to use CSS properties that work properly across platforms, it is quite possible that the property you are using does not work properly on your browser. This applies to those using Netscape Navigator 4 and Internet Explorer 3 or 4 – even IE 5 is far from perfect.

Local Styles with the 'style' Attribute

Sometimes you may not want to write a complete style sheet for a document, but you do need to change the style for a small number of elements on a 'one-off' basis. For example, perhaps there is a particular paragraph that you want displayed in a larger italic font. Or maybe a number of words within a paragraph need to be displayed in a different color to draw attention to them. Rather than write a complete style sheet for the document, this kind of styling can be accomplished by using a special attribute designed for the purpose, This is the `style` attribute. Do not make the common mistake of confusing the style *element* (for embedding a style sheet) with the style *attribute* (for defining a local style); the two are quite different.

Try It Out – Using Local Styles

1. Enter the following XHTML document into your text editor:

```
<?xml version="1.0" encoding="UTF-8"?>
<!DOCTYPE html
     PUBLIC "-//W3C//DTD XHTML 1.0 Transitional//EN"
     "http://www.w3.org/TR/xhtml1/DTD/xhtml1-transitional.dtd">
<html xmlns="http://www.w3.org/1999/xhtml" xml:lang="en" lang="en">
  <head>
    <title>Trying out a local style</title>
  </head>
  <body>
    <h1>Using local styles</h1>

    <p style="font-size: 150%">I am a paragraph which should be displayed in a
larger font than normal.</p>

    <p style="color: green">A paragraph in a different color but normal font
size.</p>
  </body>
</html>
```

2. Save the file as `local.htm` and then look at it in your browser. The result should be similar to the following:

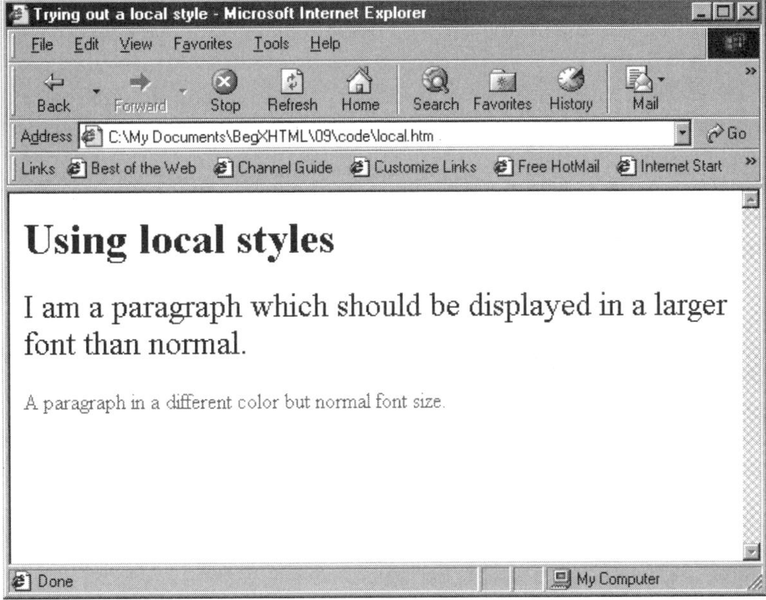

How It Works

The `style` attribute has applied a CSS style to the paragraphs in question. In the first paragraph the style attribute was used to apply the `font-size` property and in the second paragraph it was used to apply the `color` property which changed the color of the text to green.

Using the 'style' Attribute with the <span> Element

The `style` attribute can be used with many XHTML elements and you can apply local styles to headings, lists, block-quote elements, and so on. Very useful in this context is the `<span>` element to indicate a phrase to receive a particular style. Look at the following:

```
<p>This text <span style="color: green">is positively green</span> with <span
style="color: green; font-size: 140%">green</span>
```

The `<span>` element with the `style` attribute says in effect "start using this style here". Then when the end tag is encountered the style is switched off again. Even if the color for the text has been set by the browser default already, this will be overwritten by setting the color property on the `<span>` element. You can set multiple properties in this way, for instance, like this:

```
<span style="color: green; font-size: 140%">green</span>
```

Using the 'style' Attribute with the <div> Element

The `style` attribute also comes into its own with the `<div>` element. Suppose you want to give three paragraphs in succession a particular style as well as perhaps set the font to red text of a smaller size. The `<div>` element can be used with the `style` attribute like this to mark where the text style should change:

```
<div style="color:red; font-weight:80%">
```

and a closing `</div>` tag marks where the changed style should end.

Note About the 'style' Attribute

You may have worked out for yourself that the use of the `style` attribute removes most of the benefits of style sheets, namely that you can separate style from your document. It's useful for trying things out, because you can simply add the attribute in to most elements and see what effect it'll have. We'll see later how to use named styles to apply more specific styles using classes, and then you can apply those techniques to the `<span>` and `<div>` elements just like you would the `style` attribute. The difference is that the actual definition of the style remains in the style sheet, and you can thus alter it separately from your content.

How CSS Properties Inherit

As explained earlier in this chapter, CSS properties are passed down from one element to another. This example shows this idea in practice.

Try It Out – Showing Inheritance

1. Enter this simple XHTML document into your text editor and save as `second-attempt.htm`:

```
<?xml version="1.0" encoding="UTF-8"?>
<!DOCTYPE html
     PUBLIC "-//W3C//DTD XHTML 1.0 Transitional//EN"
     "http://www.w3.org/TR/xhtml1/DTD/xhtml1-transitional.dtd">
<html xmlns="http://www.w3.org/1999/xhtml" xml:lang="en" lang="en">
  <head>
    <title>Trying out a style sheet</title>
    <style type="text/css">
    <!--
      body {font-style: italic}
      p {font-size:120%}
      h1 {color:green; font-size:200%;}
      h2 {color:green; font-size:120%;}
      b {font-size: 150%}
    -->
    </style>
  </head>
```

```
  <body>
    <h1>The second attempt<br />
    <b>at a style sheet</b></h1>
    <h2>I am a second-level heading</h2>
    <p>I am a paragraph which should be displayed in a larger font than
   normal.</p>
    <p>The same style will be applied to <b>all</b> paragraphs in the
   document.</p>
  </body>
</html>
```

2. Now view the XHTML document containing the style sheet in your browser. The result should be similar to the effect shown below:

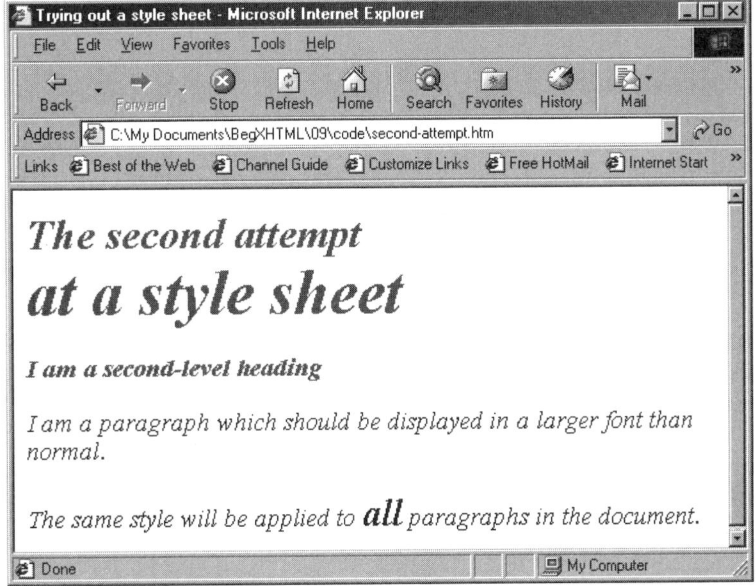

How It Works

The inclusion of a style requirement on the `<body>` element has the effect of changing all the text in its descendants; in this case its children headings and paragraphs. If the body is given an italic font style, as in the example above, then all the text is shown italic.

You can also see the result of setting `<b>` (bold text) to 150%. The word 'all' is emboldened and is displayed as such. However it has also inherited the larger font size from its parent element `<p>`. The result? Very large text indeed!

Setting the Color of the Font

You will have seen in the preceding examples how CSS can be used to set the color of the text. This section looks at the use of the `color` property in more detail. The `color` property is very useful and can be applied to almost any element. This means that you can use it not only to set the text color for documents, but individual paragraphs, words and phrases can be given a color of their own.

The easiest way to specify a color is to use one of the standard key color names. These are the 16 colors taken from the Windows VGA palette and are:

aqua	black	blue	fuchsia
grey	green	lime	maroon
navy	olive	purple	red
teal	silver	white	yellow

If you want to specify a color not on this list then you need to use either an RGB value or hexadecimal value. The way this is done is explained in Appendix C. An alternative is to use coded values for colors, giving very precise control. These are used in later examples in this chapter.

Here are some simple examples of the use of the `color` property to set the color of XHTML elements:

```
body {color: maroon}
  h1 {color: teal}
  h2 {color: olive}
```

Try It Out – Setting the Font Color

1. Type this simple XHTML document into your text editor:

```
<<?xml version="1.0" encoding="UTF-8"?>
<!DOCTYPE html
     PUBLIC "-//W3C//DTD XHTML 1.0 Strict//EN"
    "http://www.w3.org/TR/xhtml1/DTD/xhtml1-strict.dtd">
<html xmlns="http://www.w3.org/1999/xhtml" xml:lang="en" lang="en">
  <head>
    <title>Example of font color</title>
    <style type="text/css">    <!--
      body {font-size: 120%; color: blue;}
      p {color:red}
    -->
    </style>
  </head>
  <body>
    <h1>The Redwing</h1>
    <h2>A winter bird</h2>

    <p>The <strong>redwing</strong> is a winter bird which may occasionally be
seen in suburbs. A flock of 50 or more were briefly attracted
to Bracknell in Berkshire, UK during the winter of 1995.</p>
  </body>
</html>
```

2. Save as `redwing.htm`, run the document through your browser and have a look at the results. The whole of the body text is set to blue text in a larger font. The paragraphs are then separately specified in red:

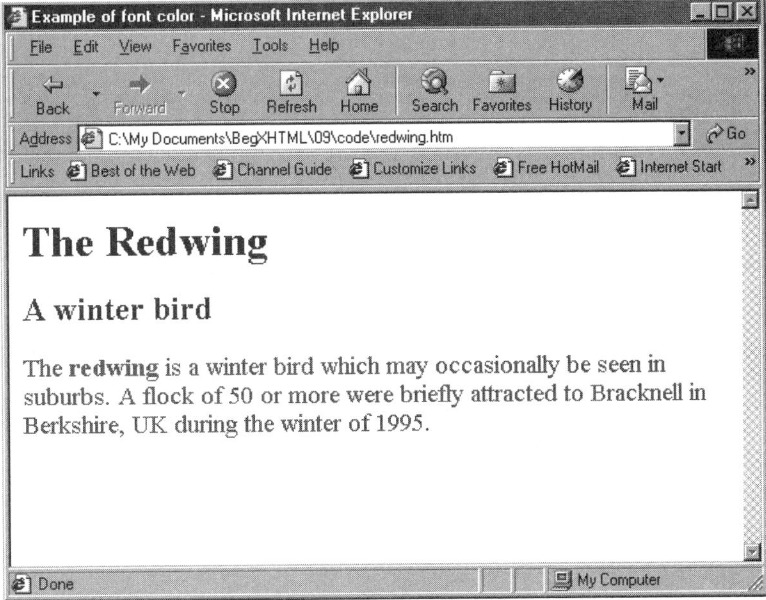

How It Works

The `font-size` property (which you will come across later) sets the body to 120% larger than normal so all text should be slightly larger than normal. The `color` property is used to set the body of the document to blue which means that all the text might come out in this color. This would be the case were it not for the color property being used to set paragraph elements specifically to red.

Try It Out – Another Example of Font Color

1. Add the following line to the style section of the above document:

```
<style type="text/css">
<!--
   body { font-size: 120%; color: blue;}
   p {color:red}
   strong {color:black; font-style: italic;}
  -->
  </style>
```

2. Save as `redwing2.htm` and display it in your browser. You should see the following:

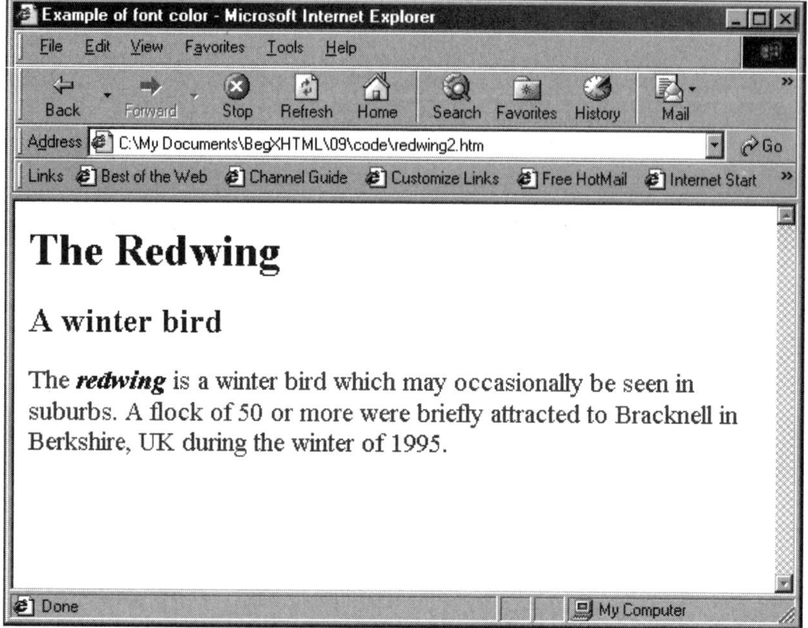

How It Works

CSS properties can be applied to character-level elements (like <b>, <strong> and <span>) as well as block elements (such as <p>, <h1> and <blockquote>). In this example, the <strong> element is set to black italic text and locally overrides the red text specified for paragraph elements.

Using 'Hex' Numbers to Specify the Color of Text Precisely

In Appendix C we explain that a common way of specifying color is to use a hexadecimal (or 'hex' for short) code. With CSS, this provides a way to be more precise about the color you want: you are no longer limited to the 16 named colors described earlier. When we specify the color as a hexadecimal value in CSS, we must prefix it with a # as in the example below.

Try It Out – Using a Hex Code to Specify Color

1. Enter the following into your text editor:

```
<?xml version="1.0" encoding="UTF-8"?>
<!DOCTYPE html
     PUBLIC "-//W3C//DTD XHTML 1.0 Strict//EN"
    "http://www.w3.org/TR/xhtml1/DTD/xhtml1-strict.dtd">
<html xmlns="http://www.w3.org/1999/xhtml" xml:lang="en" lang="en">
  <head>
    <title>Example of font color</title>
    <style type="text/css">
```

```
    <!--
      body {
        margin-left: 10%;
        margin-right: 5%;
        font-family: Trebuchet, Arial, sans-serif
           }
      h1 { margin-left: -8% }
      h2 { margin-left: -4% }
      h2 { color: #006699 }
      em { font-style: italic; font-size:120%;}
      pre { font-style:italic; font-size:150%;}
      b { color:#006699 }
      pre { font-family: Trebuchet, Arial, sans-serif; color:#006699;}
    -->
    </style>
  </head>
  <body>
    <h1>Canterbury Tales</h1>
    <h2>The Prologue</h2>
    <pre>Whan that Aprille with his shoure sote
    The droghte of Marche hath perced to the rote
    And bathed every veyne in swich licour
    Of which vertu engendered is the flour</pre>

    <p><b>shoures</b> showers. </p>

    <p><b>sote</b> sweet. It is disyllabic.</p>

    <p><b>droghte</b> dryness. Pronounced <em>druuht</em> </p>

    <p><b>rote </b>root.</p>

    <p><b>And bathed every veyne in swich licour</b>: And bathed every vein (of
tree or herb) in such moisture....</p>

    <p><b>flour</b> flower.</p>

  </body>
</html>
```

2. Save the file as `ctales.htm` and then run it through your browser. You should see something similar to the screenshot on the following page:

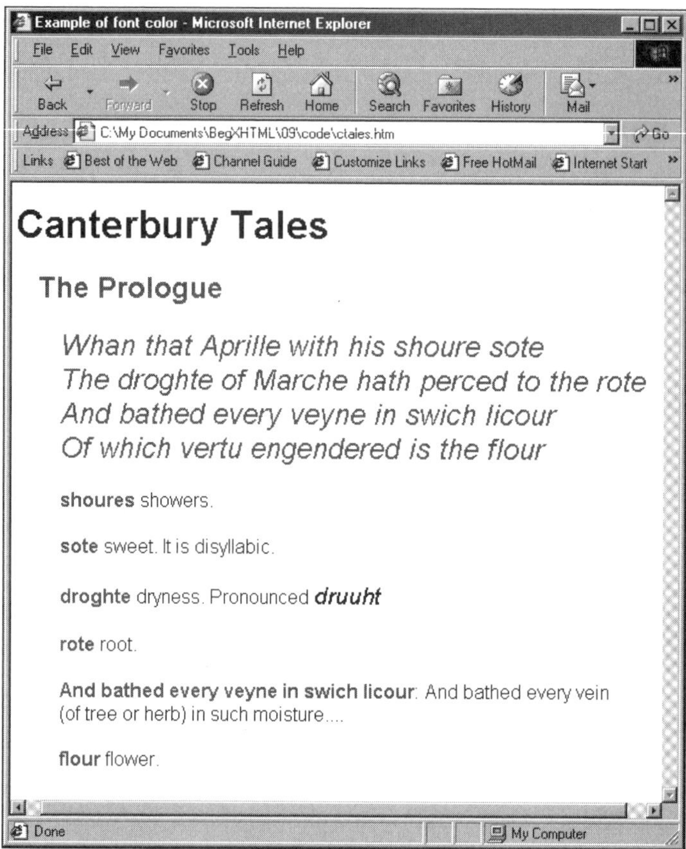

How It Works

Heading 2 elements have been set to turquoise by giving them the color coded as #006699. The same color has been used for the bold type. Meanwhile emphasized text has been made larger than normal italic. The text of the poem itself is actually preformatted text but the font is specified as Arial (it would normally be Courier) and the size 150%. The `<pre>` element has also been set to italic by using the `<font-style>` property.

Setting the Color of Hypertext Links

We now move onto the subject of setting the color of hypertext links. A short discussion of hypertext links in terms of page layout and design is given in Chapter 12. You have the option of setting the color of unvisited, visited and active links. An active link is simply a link which you have selected with the cursor. All anchor elements with an `href` attribute will be put into one (and only one)of these three groups and displayed in the appropriate way, as dictated by the style sheet.

Try It Out – Setting the Color of Hypertext Links

1. Type this simple XHTML document into your text editor:

```
<?xml version="1.0" encoding="UTF-8"?>
<!DOCTYPE html
     PUBLIC "-//W3C//DTD XHTML 1.0 Strict//EN"
    "http://www.w3.org/TR/xhtml1/DTD/xhtml1-strict.dtd">
<html xmlns="http://www.w3.org/1999/xhtml" xml:lang="en" lang="en">
  <head>
    <title>Example of font color</title>
    <style type="text/css">
    <!--
      h1 { margin-left: -4% }
      h2 { color: #990066 }
      h3 { color: black }
      h4 { color:#990066;}
      pre { color: #990066}
      em { color: #FF6633 }
      A:link { color: black }
      A:visited { color: blue }
      A:active { color: lime }
    -->
    </style>
  </head>
  <body>
    <h1>Canterbury Tales</h1>
    <h2>The Prologue</h2>
    <pre>Whan that Aprille with his <a href=xxx">shoure</a> sote
    The <a href="xxx">droghte</a> of Marche hath perced to the rote
    And bathed every veyne in <a href=yyy>swich licour</a>
    Of which vertu engendered is the flour</pre>
  </body>
</html>
```

2. Save as `ctales2.htm` and run in your browser. This is the result we obtained:

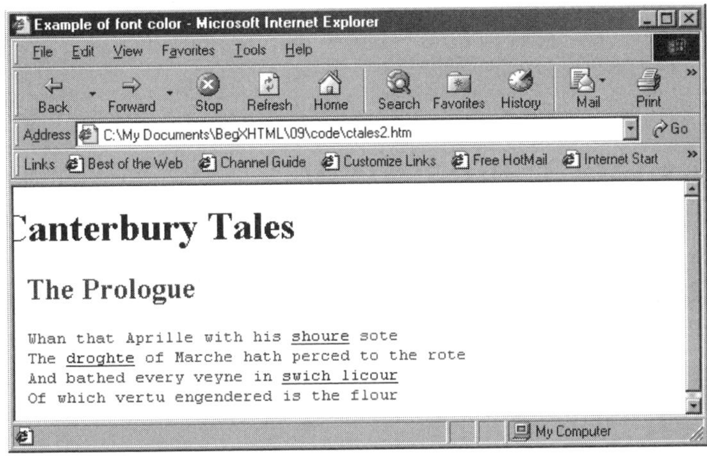

3. Try clicking on a link. As you press down with the cursor the link should go green. After you have used the link (visited it) it should be shown as blue. Of course, none of the links actually point to anything.

How It Works

The CSS `color` property has been associated with a particular kind of hypertext link. These are the critical lines to do the job:

```
A:link { color: black }
```

sets the color of unvisited links to black:

```
A:visited { color: blue }
```

sets the color of visited links to blue:

```
A:active { color: lime }
```

sets the color of active links to lime.

You can of course go further and make hypertext links look completely different from their default style. For example, some people like to remove the underline:

```
A:link {text-decoration: none}
```

Or you can add a background to the hypertext link:

```
A:link {background-color: black; color:yellow}
```

An Alternative Method

You can also set the color of hypertext links using the `<body>` tag attributes. For example:

```
<body bgcolor="white" background="texture.jpg" text="black"
 link="navy" vlink="maroon" alink="red">
```

Setting the Background Color

The useful thing about CSS is that it allows you to set the background color for individual parts of the document. Thus you can bring out a certain paragraph by setting the background color to a pastel shade, for example or give a heading special treatment by reversing out the text on a black background. You can also set the background color for the whole document. For example:

```
body { color: black; background: white; }
```

In this example, there are two properties in use: `color` which sets the color of the text, and `background` which sets the color of the page background. Although it is optional, we recommend always adding the semicolon after the last property.

Giving Paragraphs and Headings a Background Color

To give paragraphs, headings, lists and other XHTML elements a background color, simply apply the `background` property to the element in question. For example:

```
p { color: red; background: yellow; }
h2 { color: blue; background: lime; }
```

You can also use the `padding` property to extend the color outside the limits of the text area, as explained later in this chapter.

Setting a Background Texture

Background textures are accomplished by one of two methods. Either you can use attributes belonging to the XHTML <body> element, or you can use CSS. The latter method gives you more control, especially over the position of the background. Using the CSS method you can also decide to only give specific parts of the document a background, for example just a single paragraph or heading.

It is of course possible to create your own, but why not first try downloading a selection of background textures from the Web to play with. Go on-line, load your favorite browser and then search on the words 'backgrounds for Web pages'. A number of references to sites supplying (often free) background textures should come up. For example, Netscape provides a variety of free background images at `http://www.netscape.com/assist/net_sites/bg/ backgrounds.html`. In general it seems to be best to choose either a very light image and then overlay black or some other dark-colored text over it, or to choose a dark background and lay white or other very light text over it. Highly decorative, almost psychedelic backgrounds can make it very hard to read the text.

Try It Out – Inserting a Background Texture for Your Page Within XHTML

1. Type the following 'surreal' XHTML document into your text editor and save it as `haggis.htm`:

```
<?xml version="1.0" encoding="UTF-8"?>
<!DOCTYPE html
     PUBLIC "-//W3C//DTD XHTML 1.0 Transitional//EN"
     "http://www.w3.org/TR/xhtml1/DTD/xhtml1-transitional.dtd">
<html xmlns="http://www.w3.org/1999/xhtml" xml:lang="en" lang="en">
<head>
<title>Example of a textured background</title>
</head>
<body bgcolor="yellow" background="yellow_fabric.gif">
<h1>Episode 7: Trip to Another Dimension</h1>
<p> The mighty Captain Haggis shrugged off his attackers with his
famous ground-black-pepper sneeze. As the evil Cutlery Clan fell to the
floor coughing and sneezing and rubbing at their tearing eyes, Captain
Haggis quickly ate his Dimensional Neaps 'n' Tatties and plunged headlong
into the dreaded Mustard Dimension. </p>
```

```
<p> Does Captain Haggis know no fear? Will he be able to withstand the
scorching mustard heat? And will he be able to rescue the sacred
Three-Legged Haggis in time to save all of Haggisdom from the evil machinations of
the ruthless Cutlery Clan?...</p>

<p> Tune in to next weeks thrilling episode: "A Mustard Been Here Before".</p>
</body>
</html>
```

2. The result is a file with the yellow texture repeated across the background:

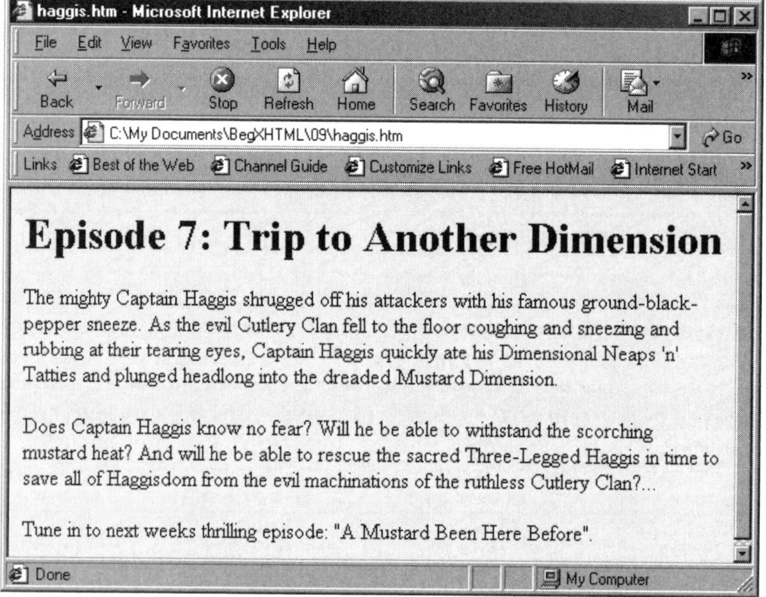

How It Works

The `background` attribute specifies the file containing the image to repeat across the background. We have also specified a background color too (using the `bgcolor` attribute) just in case the browser is unable to render the image. If the image you use is very long it will look as though it is merely repeated downwards. If you use a long thin image with a pattern on one side only, the effect is that a border is created down the page.

Using CSS to Position a Background Image

CSS can be used to set the background not only for the whole document, but for specific elements. For example, you can use CSS to set the background image for a heading element. In the next example, CSS is used to allocate a background image to a `<pre>` (preformatted text) element. A single image is used and the browser is told explicitly not to repeat this by using the `background-repeat` property. You can use any light image to demonstrate this for your self; we use the image from the previous example.

Try It Out – Using CSS to Insert and Position a Background Image

1. Take the following XHTML file:

```
<?xml version="1.0" encoding="UTF-8"?>
<!DOCTYPE html
    PUBLIC "-//W3C//DTD XHTML 1.0 Strict//EN"
   "http://www.w3.org/TR/xhtml1/DTD/xhtml1-strict.dtd">
<html xmlns="http://www.w3.org/1999/xhtml" xml:lang="en" lang="en">
<head>
<title>background color</title>
<style type="text/css">
<!--
pre {
       background-color: white;
       background-attachment: fixed;
       background-image: url(yellow_fabric.gif);
       background-position: top left;
       background-repeat: no-repeat;
       padding:2em
      }
  h1 { margin-left: 10% }
  h2 { color: #990066 }
pre { color:black; font-size: 150%; font-family:arial}
-->
</style>

</head>
<body>
<h1>The naming of cats</h1>

<pre>The naming of cats is a difficult matter,
It isn't just one of your holiday games
You may think at first I'm as mad as a hatter
When I tell you a cat must have three different names</pre>
</body>
</html>
```

2. Save the document as background.htm and look at it with your browser. What should happen is that the image associated with the <pre> element is inserted as a background texture, for example as follows:

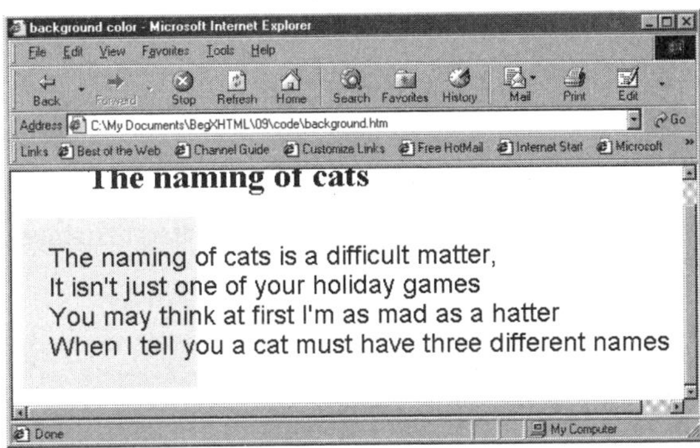

How It Works

CSS has been used to associate a number of background properties with the `<pre>` element. Although the simplest option is to use the `background` property to set a background image, here more subtle properties (`background-color`, `background-image`, `background-repeat`, `background-attachment` and `background-position`) are used. Using these individual properties you can use CSS to position a background image and to control whether it 'tiles' the background or only appears once. Note that you have to choose an image with a size that can contain the text you wish to be displayed; we deliberately choose a small image here to illustrate that fact.

In our next example the image is repeated (or 'tiled') across the background, so we do not have to worry about the image size.

Try It Out – a Background Texture Repeated Behind Text

1. Change the style sheet of the previous document to:

```
<title>background color</title>
<style type="text/css">
<!--
pre {
       background-color: white;
       background-attachment: fixed;
       background-image: url(yellow_fabric.gif);
       background-position: top left;

       padding:2em
      }
  h1 { margin-left: 3% }
  h2 { color: #990066 }
pre { color:black; font-size: 150%; font-family:arial; font-style:bold}
-->
</style>
```

2. Save the document as `background2.htm` and look at it with your browser. What should happen is that the image associated with the `<pre>` element is inserted as a background texture, for example as follows:

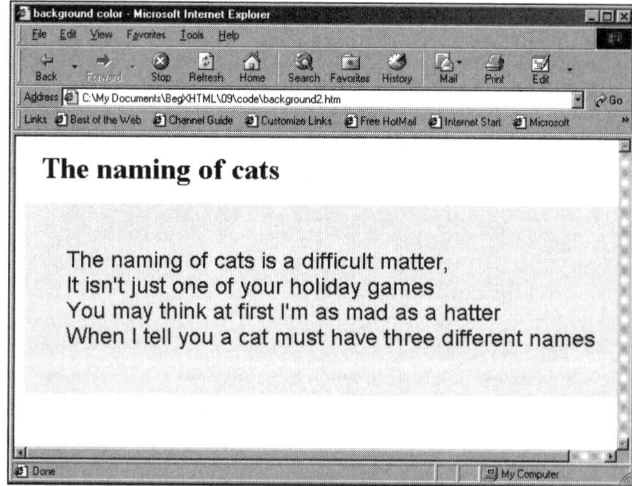

How It Works

In this example, the background consists of a repeated `.jpg` file which serves as a background texture to a single element in the document. Whereas in the previous example the property `background-repeat` was used to specifically say that the background should not be repeated again and again, in this case this is exactly the effect we want. The small `.jpg` file (`pastels.jpg`) has been tessellated (or 'tiled') across the background. Notice that the text is set to bold by the use of the `font-style` property, and that the `padding` property has been used to make the background cover an area outside the normal boundaries of the text. We talk about this later on.

The fixed background attachment means that the background doesn't scroll and stays in place. Notice the use of `background-color` to set the background to white should the texture not be shown. The `margin-left` property, used to push the heading in, is explained in the following section.

The Background Color for Table Cells

It's easy to set the color for table cells. All you do is to give the table cell elements a style in the style sheet. For example:

```
td { background: #FFCCFF }
th { background: #FF99FF }
```

This sets the color of all table cells that are table data or table header cells to the hexadecimal colors specified.

Borders, Margins and White Space

Having discussed color and backgrounds we now move on to look at the related subject of improving the look and feel of documents by adding 'white space' and borders around elements. CSS uses the idea of the 'box model' to specify the position of borders, padding, margins and content as shown below. The content box contains the text or image itself, for example a paragraph of text, a list, a heading or a `<blockquote>` element. Surrounding this is an area called the *padding* into which an image or background color behind the content can spread. If you have some text and you want to extend the color background beyond the border of the text, then you need to set the padding. The border goes between the padding and the margins and this can be set separately. The margins are transparent and reveal the background of the body 'through' them:

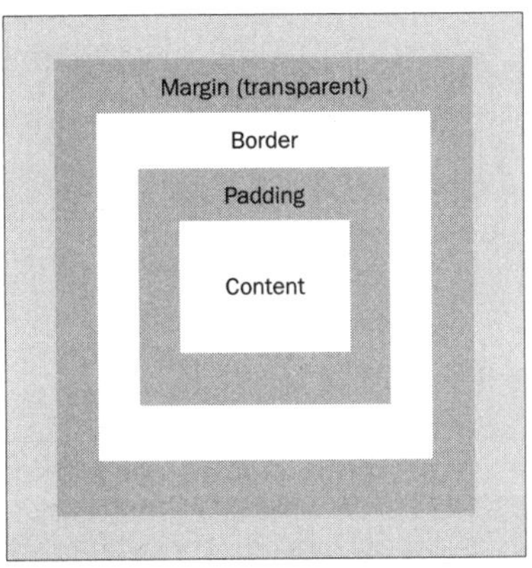

Setting the Page Margins

Another way to add white space to a web page is to go for larger margins. You can set the left and right margins with the `margin-left` and `margin-right` properties.

Try It Out – Altering the Page Margins

1. Enter the following XHTML document into your text editor, save the file as `margins.htm` and run it in your browser:

```
<?xml version="1.0" encoding="UTF-8"?>
<!DOCTYPE html
     PUBLIC "-//W3C//DTD XHTML 1.0 Transitional//EN"
     "http://www.w3.org/TR/xhtml1/DTD/xhtml1-transitional.dtd">
<html xmlns="http://www.w3.org/1999/xhtml" xml:lang="en" lang="en"><head>
<title>Trying out page margins</title>
</head>
<body>
<h1>Twelfth Century </h1>
<p>When William the Conqueror defeated Harod at Senlac in 1066, it meant much more
for England than the winning, or losing, of the battle of Hastings.</p>
</body>
</html>
```

2. Now add a style sheet into the head section as so:

```
<head>
<title>Trying out page margins</title>
<style type="text/css">
<!--
body { margin-left: 10%; margin-right: 10%; }
-->
</style>
```

3. Save the file as `margins.htm` again and look at it with your browser. You should see that the margins of the whole document have been made larger. For example:

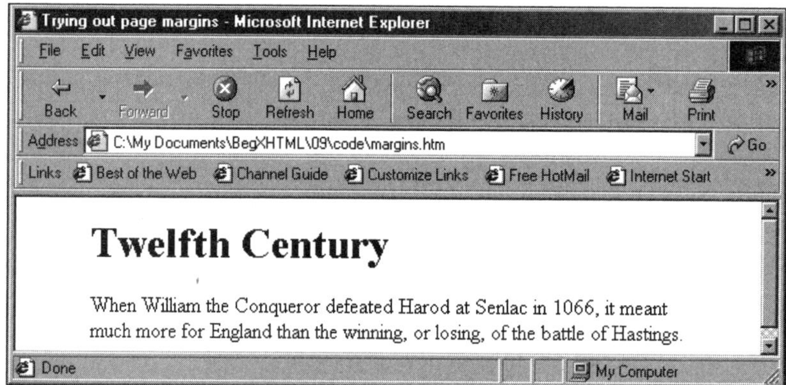

How It Works

The style sheet sets both margins to 10% of the window width, and the margins will scale when you resize the browser window. You can experiment with the style sheet by changing the margin value to 15%, to –5% (negative value) and so on. If you construct a style for paragraphs for example like this:

```
p { margin-left: 3%}
```

then all paragraphs will be indented with regards to the document as a whole.

To make headings a little more distinctive, you can make them start *within* the margin set for the <body> element, for example:

```
body { margin-left: 10%; margin-right: 10%; }
  h1 { margin-left: -8%;}
  h2,h3,h4,h5,h6 { margin-left: -4%; }
```

The margins for the headings are additive to the margins for the body. Negative values are used to move the start of the headings to the left of the margin set for the body.

Controlling the White Space Above and Below a Heading

The `margin-top` property specifies the space above and the `margin-below` specifies the space below.

Try It Out – More Space Between a Heading and Text

1. Using the XHTML file from the previous example, add extra space between the heading and the text below it by inserting the following additional style into your style sheet.

```
<style type="text/css">
<!--
body { margin-left: 10%; margin-right: 10%; }
h1 { margin-top: 10%; margin-bottom: 5%; }
-->
</style>
```

2. Save the file as `margins2.htm`. You should see something similar to the following when displayed in the browser:

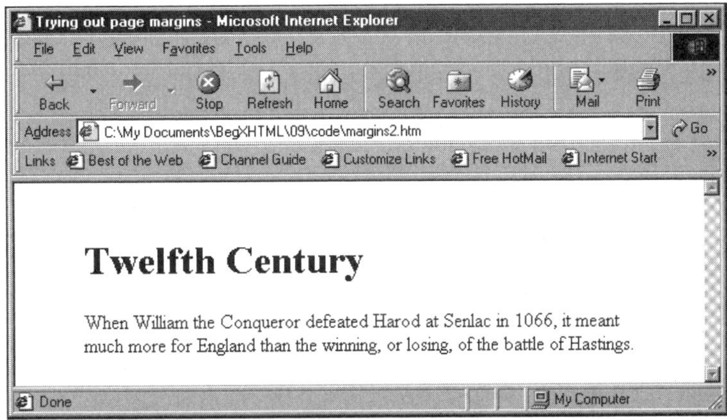

The space between the heading 'Twelfth Century' and the paragraph below it is larger, as is the space above the heading (compare it with the previous screenshot).

Space Before or After a Specific Heading

To specify the space above a particular heading, you should create a named style for the heading. This idea is covered later in the chapter, but because the mechanism is useful in our current context, we will explain briefly what is involved.

What you do is to use the `class` attribute in the markup, for example:

```
<h2 class="subsection">Getting started</h2>
```

The style rule is then written as:

```
h2.subsection { margin-top: 8em; margin-bottom: 3em; }
```

The rule starts with the tag name, a dot and then the value of the `class` attribute. Be careful to avoid placing a space before or after the dot. If you, do the rule won't work. There are other ways to set the styles for a particular element but the `class` attribute is the most flexible.

When a heading is followed by a paragraph, the value of `margin-bottom` for the heading isn't added to the value of `margin-top` for the paragraph. Instead, the maximum of the two values is used for the spacing between the heading and paragraph. This subtlety applies to `margin-top` and `margin-bottom` regardless of which tags are involved.

First-Line Indent

Sometimes you may want to indent the first line of each paragraph. The following style rule emulates the traditional way paragraphs are rendered in novels.

Try It Out – First-Line Indent

1. Enter the following XHTML document into your text editor:

```
<?xml version="1.0" encoding="UTF-8"?>
<!DOCTYPE html
     PUBLIC "-//W3C//DTD XHTML 1.0 Transitional//EN"
     "http://www.w3.org/TR/xhtml1/DTD/xhtml1-transitional.dtd">
<html xmlns="http://www.w3.org/1999/xhtml" xml:lang="en" lang="en">
<head>
<title>Trying out page margins</title>
<style type="text/css">
<!--
body { margin-left: 10%; margin-right: 10%; }
     p { text-indent:5%}
-->
</style>
</head>
<body>
```

```
<h1>Twelfth Century </h1>

<p>When William the Conqueror defeated Harold at Senlac in 1066, it meant much
more for England than the winning, or losing, of the battle of
Hastings.</p>

<p>It was responsible for the introduction into the country of an entirely
different model of life and a new set of ideas.

</body>
</html>
```

2. Save as margins3.htm. You should see the following or similar when you view the file in your browser. The first line of each paragraph is indented:

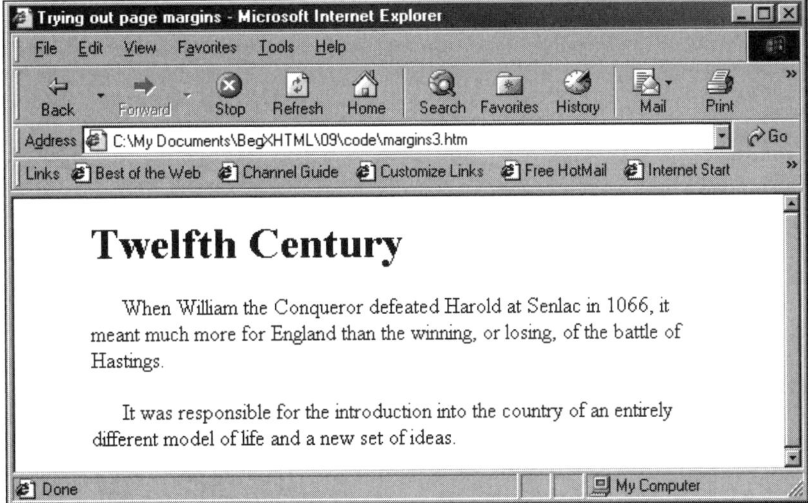

Borders

You can easily add a border around a heading, list, paragraph or a group of these enclosed with a <div> element. For instance:

```
div.box { border: solid; border-width: thin; padding: 0.2em; }
```

which can be used with markup such as:

```
<div class="box"> Some text, paragraphs, or whatever </div>
```

The content within this <div> element will be enclosed in a box with a thin line around it. Although borders are potentially useful, be careful not to use them where they would add to the clutter of the page, and distract from the text.

There is a limited choice of border types:

```
dotted    dashed    solid    double
groove    ridge     inset    outset
```

The `border-width` property sets the width. Its values include **thin**, **medium** and **thick** as well as a **specified width** e.g. 0.1em. The `border-color` property allows you to set the color.

CSS Properties Used to Control Fonts

Having introduced the topic of fonts we can now go on to a discussion about how to specify the font for your XHTML document. There are a number of CSS properties for this very purpose. Here, we will look at a selection of these, concentrating on the simplest ways to achieve effects. For those who would prefer a much more detailed appreciation of the subject, there are a number of pointers from the W3C site (at `http://www.w3.org`), under 'CSS'. The properties we use here are reliably implemented by the major browser vendors. Use these properties rather than the old-fashioned `<font>` tag which not only clutters your markup but also makes it very difficult to make simple font changes across a whole document in an easily managed way.

The CSS font properties that we cover are:

- `font-size`
- `font-style`
- `font-weight`
- `line-height`
- `font-family`

Setting the Font Size

You can control the font size with the `font-size` property. The simplest way to specify the font size is with percentage values, which is the method we use in this chapter. These are interpreted by the browser as being relative to the size of the parent element of the element you're describing. So, for example, if you specify the font size of bold text as 120% within a 10-point paragraph, then the bold text will be 12-point (because 120% of 10 is 12).

If you are accustomed to an ordinary desktop publishing environment then you will be more familiar with using point size to define the size of the text on a page. You may be surprised to learn, then, that specifying the font size in terms of points is not a reliable method with style sheets for Web documents. With CSS of course you can specify point sizes like this:

```
h1 {font-size: 20pt}
h2 {font-size: 18pt}
h3 {font-size: 14pt}
```

The trouble is that when it comes to displaying the document, *different browsers will show the text in different sizes.* For example, 7-point Verdana may look like 6-point on some computer screens with the result that the font is actually too small to read.

> **In general, a font size will appear smaller on Netscape Navigator than on Microsoft's Internet Explorer.**

Try It Out – Specifying the Font-Size

1. Enter the following XHTML document into your text editor:

```
<?xml version="1.0" encoding="UTF-8"?>
<!DOCTYPE html
     PUBLIC "-//W3C//DTD XHTML 1.0 Transitional//EN"
     "http://www.w3.org/TR/xhtml1/DTD/xhtml1-transitional.dtd">
<html xmlns="http://www.w3.org/1999/xhtml" xml:lang="en" lang="en">  <head>
    <title>Example of setting the font size</title>
    <style type="text.css">
    <!--
      body {font-size: 140%}
    -->
    </style>
  </head>
  <body>
    <h1>The Redwing</h1>
    <h2>A winter bird</h2>

    <p>The redwing is a winter bird which may occasionally be seen in
suburbs. A flock of 50 or more were briefly attracted to Bracknell
in Berkshire, UK during the winter of 1995.</p>
  </body>
</html>
```

2. Save the file as `font-size1.htm` and have a look at it on your browser:

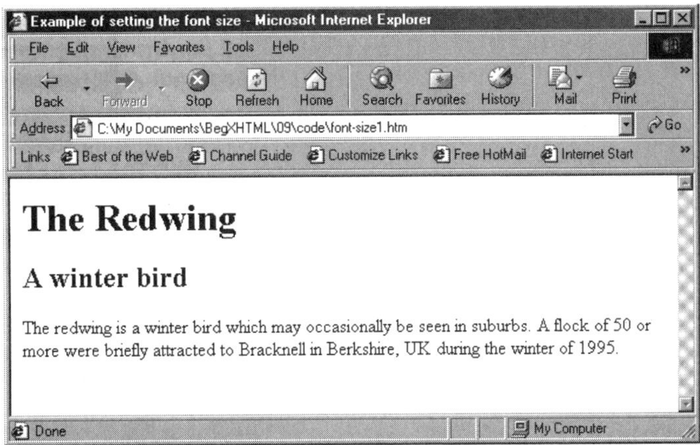

How It Works

The `font-size` property has set the body of the document to a larger font size. Setting the body text means that you affect all the elements in the body, including paragraphs and headings. You can experiment decreasing the font size to see how small the font size gets before the text becomes hard to read. Try setting it to 70%, for example. You may also like to try using points instead of percentage to specify the font. For example, change the style of the `<body>` tag from `body {font-size: 140%}` to `body {font-size:16pt}`.

Setting the Font Size for a Specific XHTML Element

You can also set the font so that it's different for all headings, paragraphs, block-quote elements, bold text, unordered list, and so on. This example shows how different heading elements can be given different font sizes.

Try It Out – Setting the Font Size for Heading Elements

1. Enter the following XHTML document into your text editor:

```
<?xml version="1.0" encoding="UTF-8"?>
<!DOCTYPE html
     PUBLIC "-//W3C//DTD XHTML 1.0 Transitional//EN"
     "http://www.w3.org/TR/xhtml1/DTD/xhtml1-transitional.dtd">
<html xmlns="http://www.w3.org/1999/xhtml" xml:lang="en" lang="en">
  <head>
    <title>Example of setting the font size</title>
    <style type="text/css">
    <!--
      p {font-size:90%}
      h1 {font-size:380% }
      h2 {font-size: 200%}
      h3 {font-size: 150%}
      blockquote {font-size: 70%}
      b {font-size:70%}
    -->
    </style>
  </head>
<body>
  <h1>A demonstration of relative font sizes</h1>
  <h2>I am a reasonably sized heading2 element</h2>
  <h3>I am a slightly smaller heading3 element</h3>
  <p>I am a little paragraph</p>

  <blockquote>I am a blockquote element displayed in a much much
smaller font than normal and you can <b>hardly see me at all
in fact</b></blockquote>
  </body>
</html>
```

2. Save the file as `font-size2.htm` and have a look at it on your browser. The result of our own experiment is shown opposite:

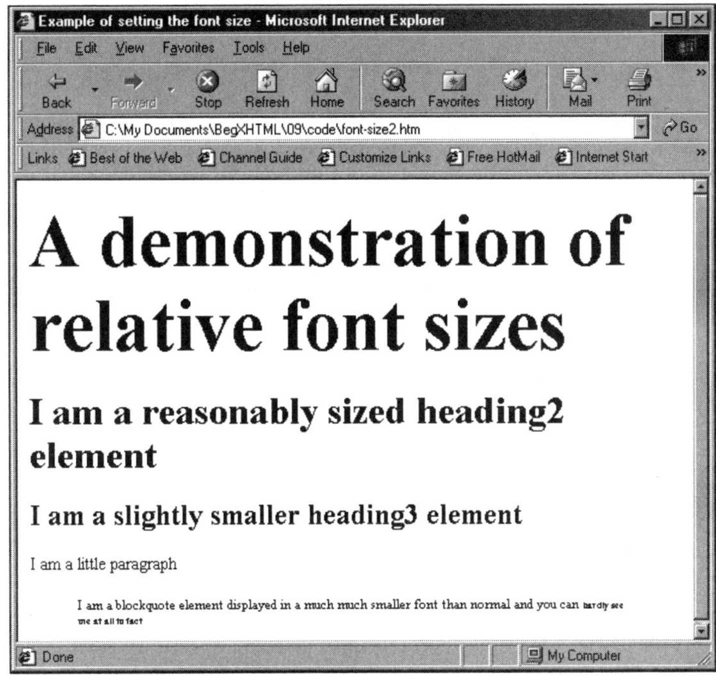

How It Works

The heading elements have been displayed larger or smaller depending on the percentage value they were given in the `font-size` property. The font size – certainly when expressed as a percentage – is taken relative to the enclosing element. So, for example, the size of the `<strong>` element is taken as relative to the `<p>` element that encloses it. The size of a `<p>` element is meanwhile taken relative to the enclosing `<body>` element.

Font Weight

You can set the weight of the font with the `font-weight` property. This instructs the browser to use a lighter or bolder font, as you feel appropriate. One way of specifying the weight is to use a number to indicate how dark the font should be. Choose from 100 (light) through 200, 300, 400 and so on, up to 900, which is dark. The use of numbers to indicate font weight is now supported by IE4, IE5 and by Netscape Navigator 4. Another method involves using the keywords **bold**, **bolder**, **lighter**, and **normal**.

Here are some simple examples:

```
h1 {font-weight: bolder}
h2 {font-weight: 300}
h3 {font-weight: lighter}
h4 {font-weight: 900}
```

Font Style

The font style relates to whether the text is italic, oblique or normal. The first two options are actually the same thing: some typographers use the word 'italic' whereas others prefer 'oblique'.

Most browsers render the `<em>` (emphasis) element in italic and the `<strong>` element in bold.

Try It Out – Changing the Font Style

1. Type this simple XHTML document into your text editor:

```
<?xml version="1.0" encoding="UTF-8"?>
<!DOCTYPE html
     PUBLIC "-//W3C//DTD XHTML 1.0 Transitional//EN"
     "http://www.w3.org/TR/xhtml1/DTD/xhtml1-transitional.dtd">
<html xmlns="http://www.w3.org/1999/xhtml" xml:lang="en" lang="en">
  <head>
    <title>Example of setting the font size</title>
    <style type="text/css">
    <!--
      p { font-style: normal }
      em { font-style: italic; font-weight: bold; }
      strong { text-transform: uppercase; font-weight: bold; }
    -->
    </style>
  </head>
  <body>
    <h1>September 1993</h1>
    <h2>Mac Mosaic and Win Mosaic are released</h2>
    <p>The release of the Mosiac browser makes the Web available to a much wider
audience. All kinds of people devise their own home pages as it becomes
fashionable to <em>"put yourself on the Web"</em> and devise your own "home page".
Even quiet and retiring software engineers place all kinds of personal information
and photographs on the <strong>Internet</strong>.</p>
  </body>
</html>
```

2. Save the file as `font-size3.htm` and have a look at it on your browser:

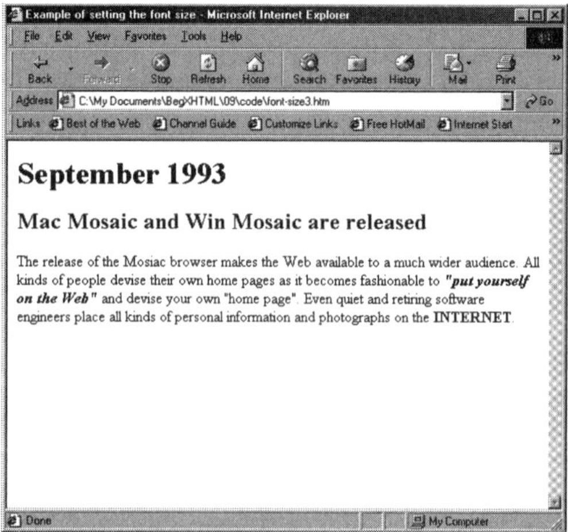

Forcing the Text to be Lower or Upper Case

The CSS `text-transform` property can be used to force the text to be all in uppercase or all in lowercase (for example, `text-transform: lowercase`). It is sometimes useful to transform the first word or so in a paragraph into uppercase at a slightly reduced point size.

Try It Out: Making the First Words of a Paragraph Upper Case

1. Enter the following XHTML document into your text editor:

```
<?xml version="1.0" encoding="UTF-8"?>
<!DOCTYPE html
     PUBLIC "-//W3C//DTD XHTML 1.0 Transitional//EN"
     "http://www.w3.org/TR/xhtml1/DTD/xhtml1-transitional.dtd">
<html xmlns="http://www.w3.org/1999/xhtml" xml:lang="en" lang="en">
  <head>
    <title>Approximating the small-caps style</title>
    <style type="text/css">
    <!--
      span {text-transform: uppercase; font-size: 90%}
    -->
    </style>
  </head>
  <body>
    <h2>Approximating the small-caps style</h2>

    <p><span>Once upon a time</span> in a land far away, there lived a wood cutter
and his daughter. Life was hard and they often went hungry. One day, ...</p>
  </body>
</html>
```

2. Save the file as `small-caps.htm` and look at it on your browser. You should see something similar to the following:

How It Works

The <span> element is used to single out a group of words to receive the upper case style. The style for this element says that the text should be transformed to upper case and be 90% of the usual size. This has the effect of making the text look like 'small caps'.

Line-Height

The line-height property specifies how far apart the lines in a paragraph or other element should be displayed. A line height of 200% effectively doubles the distance between lines. The line height is generally equivalent to the point size of the text so that 12-point type has a line height of 12pt. If you increase the line height of a paragraph consisting of 10pt Times by say, 120%, the result will be an increase of line height to 12 pts; if you up the line height to 200% then the result is a 20pt line height, and so on.

Try It Out – Adjusting the Line Height

1. Take the same document as above, and alter it as follows:

```
<style type="text/css">
<!--
  span {text-transform: uppercase; font-size: 90%}
  p { line-height: 200%}
-->
</style>
```

2. Save the file and look at it on your browser. You should see that the text enclosed in <p> elements is now double spaced.

Setting the Font Name

Many browsers are running on machines with lots of fonts already installed. You can take advantage of this to make your text look distinctive. CSS allows you to name the font you want to use. Let's assume you want to make a wedding invitation on the Web, and want to use the font called 'Nuptial BT'. You can use the following CSS rule:

```
body { font-family: "Nuptial BT" }
```

Try It Out – Specifying the Font Name

1. Enter the following XHTML document and accompanying style sheet into your text editor:

```
<?xml version="1.0" encoding="UTF-8"?>
<!DOCTYPE html
     PUBLIC "-//W3C//DTD XHTML 1.0 Transitional//EN"
     "http://www.w3.org/TR/xhtml1/DTD/xhtml1-transitional.dtd">
<html xmlns="http://www.w3.org/1999/xhtml" xml:lang="en" lang="en">
  <head>
    <title>Example of font color</title>
    <style type="text/css">
```

```
    <!--
      body { font-family: "Nuptial BT";
      font-size: 300%; text-align: center }
    -->
    </style>
  </head>
  <body>
    <p>You are cordially invited to the wedding of<br />
Daphne Johnston and Marcus Llewelyn-Smith, ....</p>
  </body>
</html>
```

2. Save the file as `wedding.htm` and look at it on your browser. You should see a result similar to the following:

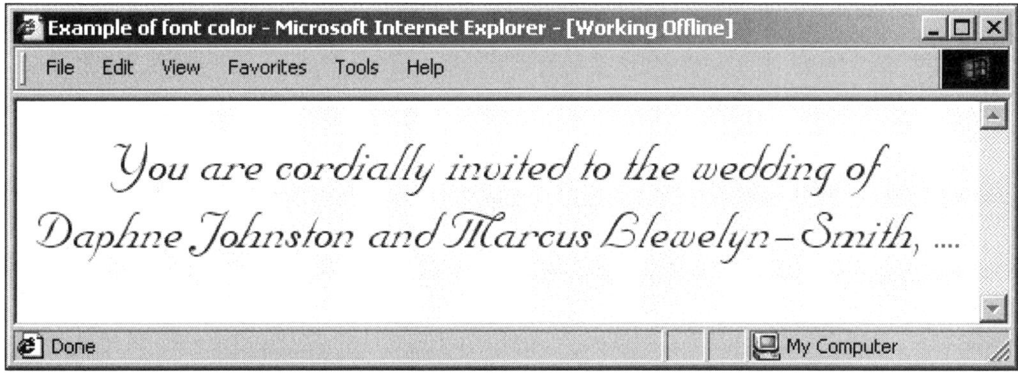

How It Works

The `font-family` property specified the font to use. Should this not be available on the computer viewing the document, a browser default font will be used instead.

Specifying Alternative Fonts for the Browser to Use

Suppose you want to use Garamond as the font for the entire document. This is the critical line you might insert into your style sheet:

```
body {font-family: Garamond, "Times New Roman", serif}
```

However, suppose Garamond is not a type available on the computer displaying the document? Without an alternative the browser will simply use a default font and the document may look less pleasing as a result. In CSS you can, in fact, specify no end of alternative font families in order of preference. The browser will start with the first one in the list (Garamond in this example) and if that is not available, the browser will try the next one along (Times New Roman here), and so on. If none of the fonts in the list are available, the browser will stick with the current font.

Try It Out – Specifying a List of Alternative Fonts

1. Enter the following XHTML document into your text editor:

```
<?xml version="1.0" encoding="UTF-8"?>
<!DOCTYPE html
     PUBLIC "-//W3C//DTD XHTML 1.0 Transitional//EN"
     "http://www.w3.org/TR/xhtml1/DTD/xhtml1-transitional.dtd">
<html xmlns="http://www.w3.org/1999/xhtml" xml:lang="en" lang="en">
  <head>
    <title>Style Sheet History</title>
    <style type="text/css">
    <!--
      h1{ font-family: Georgia, "Times New Roman", Garamond, Times, serif }
      p { font-family: Verdana, Arial, Helvetica, sans-serif }
    -->
    </style>
  </head>
  <body>
    <h1>November 1995</h1>
    <p>Style sheets for HTML documents begin to take shape Bert Boss, Håkon Lie,
Dave Raggett, Chris Lilley and others from the
World Wide Web consortium convene in Versailles near Paris to discuss the
deployment of Cascading Style Sheets (the name infers that more than one style
sheet can interact to produce the final look of the document). Using a special
language, the CSS group advocated that everyone would soon be able to write simple
styles for HTML. The SGML community suggest an alternative a LISP-like
language called DSSSL.</p>
  </body>
</html>
```

2. Save the file as `fonts.htm` and look at it on your browser. What you see will depend on which fonts you have on your machine.

How It Works

The fact is that many browsers may not have access to your preferred font. To cope with this, CSS allows you to specify a list of fonts in order of preference. CSS also provides three generic font family names you can use: *serif, sans-serif,* and *monospace.* These are valuable as a means of last resort for selecting the font. The 'serif' is a very general category, included as the ultimate fallback.

If the font name contains a space, such as `"Times New Roman"` we recommend you enclose the name in quotation marks as shown above. Note that font names are case insensitive, but it is good practice to use the correct case.

Inventing your Own Named Styles

This topic has been left until late in the chapter as the idea of named styles comes into its own only once you have experimented with CSS, and feel fluent in the use of at least a range of properties.

In many word processing packages you select a named style from a list and apply it to a paragraph or other text. For example, in Word, you have styles such as Heading 1, Body Text, and Footer, and you can also define your own. In CSS you can similarly invent a style and then name it for subsequent use in a document. The trick is accomplished by using a special kind of CSS notation of which here are three simple examples:

```
p.special { color: red; background: yellow }
p.small { font-size:90%}
p.large{ font-size:200%}
```

The first 'rule' says that all paragraphs named 'special' should be red text on a yellow background. The second says that all those named 'small' should be in a font 90% smaller than usual. Meanwhile paragraphs named 'large' should be in a font twice as large as normal size.

But how, once you have invented a named style, do you apply it to a particular piece of text? You apply a named style by means of the `class` attribute, which can be used with all XHTML elements. Here is a paragraph marked up in such a way that it will take on the style defined as 'special'.

```
<p class="special">This paragraph will be displayed with red text on a yellow
background </p>
```

The class attribute is so called because it is used to identify a given **class** of elements, in this case all paragraphs of type 'special'.

You can devise named styles for elements other than paragraphs. For example you might choose to devise a named style for Heading 2 elements, for block-quote elements, and so on. This idea is demonstrated in the example that follows.

Try It Out – Inventing and Applying your own Named Styles

In this example, a number of named styles are devised called 'color', 'small' and 'normal'. These in effect consist of three styles for three different kinds of paragraphs. Having invented the styles and placed them in the style sheet they are applied with the `class` attribute as need be by the paragraphs in the document.

1. Enter the following style sheet consisting of three named styles for paragraphs and insert it into a document between the `<style>` and `</style>` tags in the usual way. The document you choose can be any simple XHTML document with a selection of paragraph elements. If you prefer you can use the document that we use below.

```
<?xml version="1.0" encoding="UTF-8"?>
<!DOCTYPE html
     PUBLIC "-//W3C//DTD XHTML 1.0 Transitional//EN"
     "http://www.w3.org/TR/xhtml1/DTD/xhtml1-transitional.dtd">
<html xmlns="http://www.w3.org/1999/xhtml" xml:lang="en" lang="en">
  <head>
    <title>Example of named styles</title>
    <style type="text/css">
    <!--
      p.color {
        background: yellow;
        padding: 1.5em;
        border: none;
        margin-left:0.5%;
        width:100%
      }
      p.small {
        font-size:small;
        margin-left: 30%}
      p.normal {
        font-weight: bold;
        font-size: larger;
        color: black;
        margin-left: 30%
    -->
    </style>
  </head>
  <body text="black" link="blue">

    <h1>The Redwing</h1>
    <h2>A winter bird</h2>

    <p><img src="bird.gif" alt="bird" /></p>

    <p class="color">The redwing is a winter bird which may occasionally be seen
in suburbs. A flock of 50 or more were seen in Bracknell in Berkshire, UK
during the winter of 1995.</p>

    <p class="normal">The redwing is easily identified by the white eye-stripe
over its eye and by the red under its wings which can be seen only when
in flight. </p>

    <p class="normal"> The bird is most often seen in flocks sometimes mixed in
with fieldfares and even greenfinches. </p>

    <p class="small">The best time to see Redwings is in late November when
they feast on berries in gardens. Another favorite haunt is the village
football pitch. </p>
  </body>
</html>
```

2. Save the file as `redwing3.htm` and have a look at it on your browser. The screen on the left below shows the result of this example on our browser; the screen on the right shows almost the same code but with very slight adjustments to the CSS properties specified.

The advantage of constructing a template is that only a minor tweak affects the look and feel of several components of the document. You edit the style and all the elements of that class change accordingly. This is very much like desk top publishing where if you alter a style in your template, the repercussions are seen right through the document:

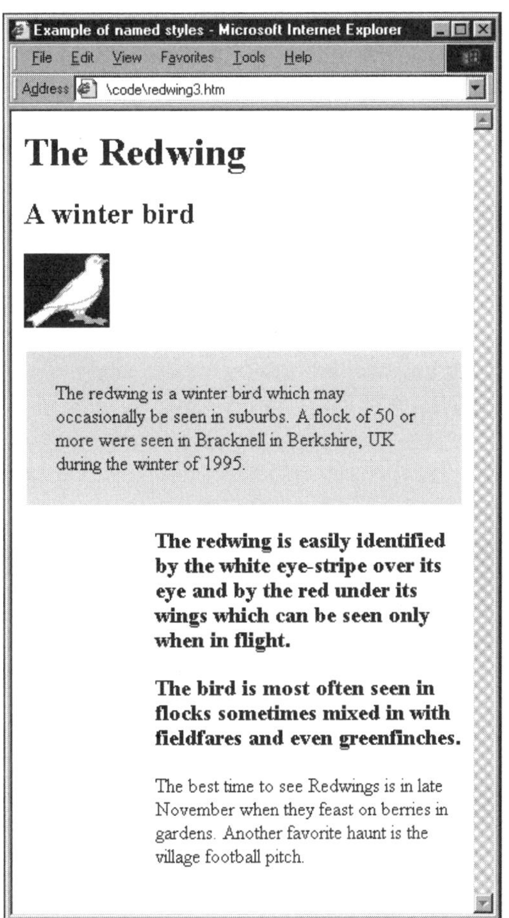

Summary

In this chapter we have looked at how to style our web documents by using style sheets, rather than by adding style (such as bold or italic) to the text or element we wish styled. This is the preferred way, and allows a great deal of flexibility when we come to modify the 'look and feel' of our documents.

We looked at how to color our text, how to space it out, how to use margins, how to change the font size, how to add images either in a single occurrence or as a 'tiled' background, and how to make our own named styles using the Cascading Style Sheet (or CSS) language.

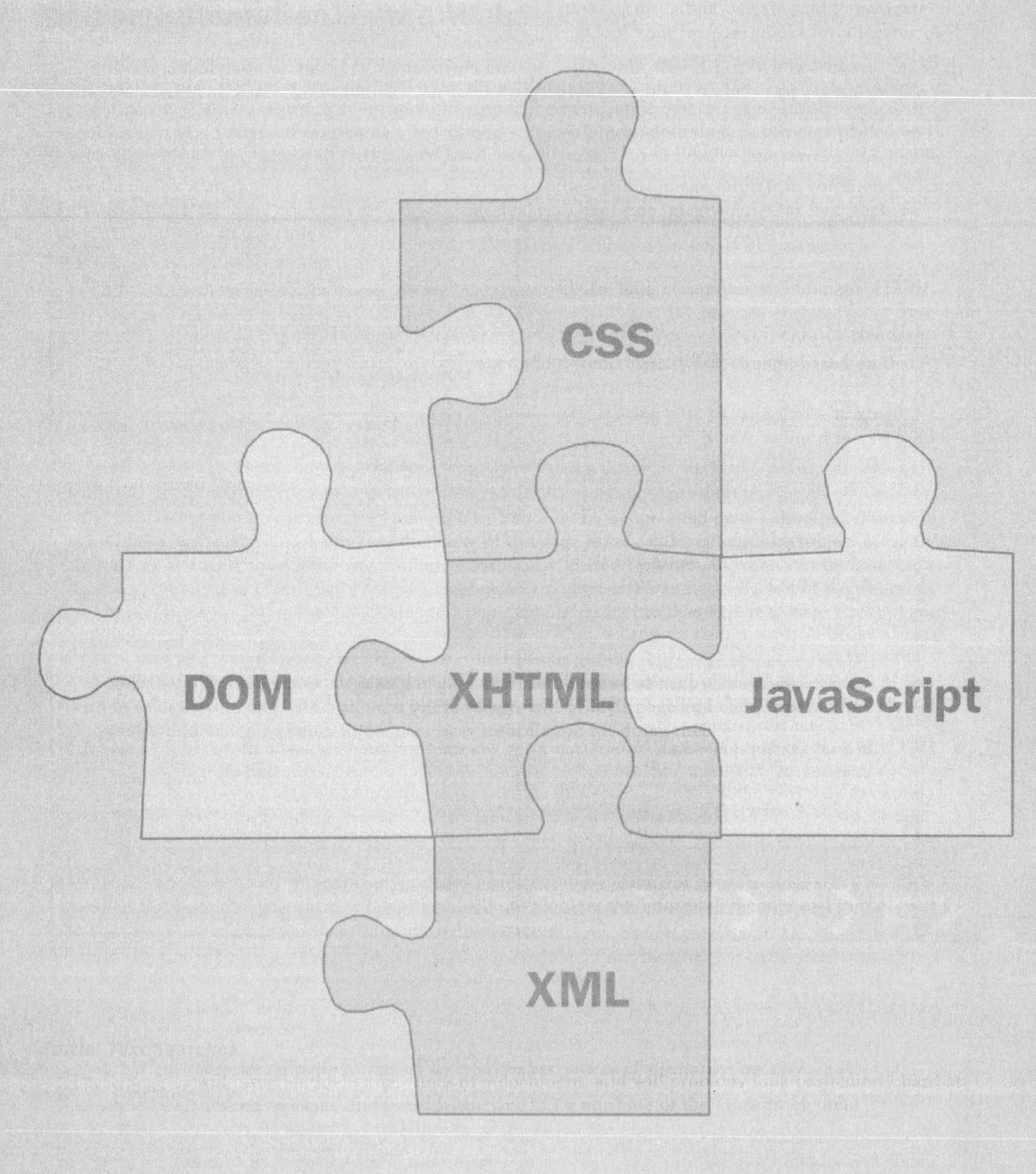
CSS
DOM
XHTML
JavaScript
XML

An Introduction to XML

We've already been introduced to XML briefly in Chapter 2, where we saw how it relates to our favorite topic, XHTML. In this chapter, we'll be looking at it on its own, as XML in its own right. Some of it will be familiar to you, as it applies equally to the XHTML we've already learned. It should help to throw a different angle on XHTML, and maybe you'll see a little about why putting HTML into XML syntax is such a good idea, even if you don't yet know enough to make use of it yourself.

So in this chapter we will see:

- Some background to help us understand the importance of XML
- What XML is and how to write an XML document
- Some of the associated specifications surrounding XML
- How to style XML for display in a browser

What is XML?

XML got the name **Extensible Markup Language** because it is not a fixed format like HTML. While HTML has a fixed set of tags that the author can use, XML users can create their own tags (or use those created by others, if applicable) so that they actually describe the content of the element. So, let's dive straight in and look at an example.

At its simplest level XML is just a way of marking up data so that it is self-describing. What do we mean by this? Well, as a publisher Wrox makes details about their books available in HTML over the Web. For example, in XHTML we might display details about this book like so:

```
<?xml version="1.0" encoding="UTF-8"?>
<!DOCTYPE html
     PUBLIC "-//W3C//DTD XHTML 1.0 Transitional//EN"
     "http://www.w3.org/TR/xhtml1/DTD/xhtml1-transitional.dtd">
<html xmlns="http://www.w3.org/1999/xhtml" xml:lang="en" lang="en">
<head>
   <title>Beginning XHTML</title>
</head>
```

```
<body>
<h1>Beginning XHTML</h1>
   <h3>ISBN 1-861003-43-9</h3>

<h4>Authors</h4>Frank Boumphrey, Ted Wugofski, Sebastian Schnitzenbaumer, Jenny
Raggett, Dave Raggett<br />

<p>US $39.99</p><br />

<p> XHTML is a powerful technology for creating web site content. Learn how to
create exciting pages using a technology that combines the benefits of XML with
the existing wide coverage of HTML.</p>

</body>
</html>
```

As you know, that's all you need to do if you want put information about a book on a web page. It will look something like this:

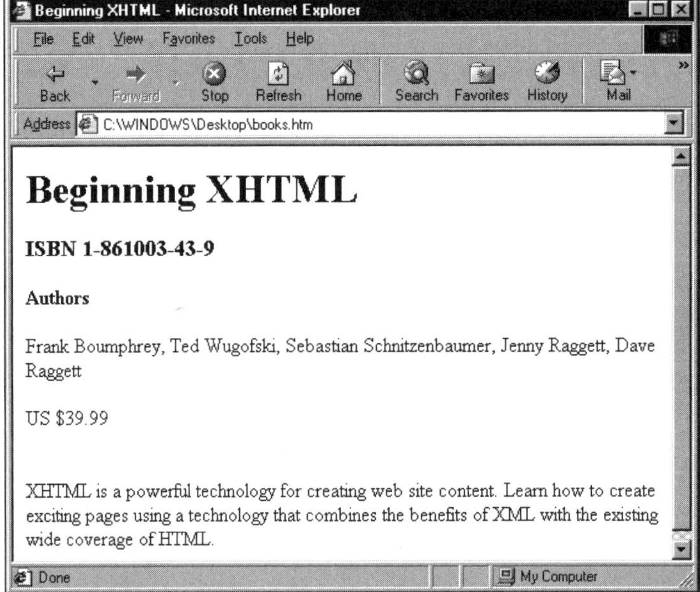

So, when we are building our web pages we have a lot of this data in XHTML. But the markup doesn't give you any information about what you are displaying. There is no way that you can tell, from just the tags, that you are displaying information about a book. With XML, however, you can create your own tags; they can actually **describe** whatever content you are marking up: hence the term **self-describing data**.

So, how could we mark up the information in a more logical way, using XML, so that we know what we have in the file? In the following Try It Out, we will create our first XML document (OK, if you don't count our many XHTML documents which are also XML!) that mimics the data held in the above XHTML example.

Try It Out – My First XML Document

1. Fire up your text editor and type in the following, which we will call `books.xml`. Make sure you type it in exactly as shown, since XML is case sensitive and spaces must be in the correct positions:

```
<?xml version="1.0"?>
<books>
<book>
   <title>Beginning XHTML</title>
   <ISBN>1-861003-43-9</ISBN>
   <authors>
      <author_name>Frank Boumphrey </author_name>
      <author_name>Ted Wugofski </author_name>
      <author_name>Sebastian Schnitzenbaumer </author_name>
      <author_name>Jenny Raggett </author_name>
      <author_name>Dave Raggett </author_name>
   </authors>
   <description> XHTML is a powerful technology for creating web site content.
Learn how to create exciting pages using a technology that combines the benefits
of XML with the existing wide coverage of HTML.</description>
   <price US="$39.99"/>
</book>
</books>
```

2. Save the file as `books.xml` to any folder you want on your hard drive. Now, open the XML file in Internet Explorer just as you would open an HTML file. Here is how our XML version of the book details is displayed when we open it in IE5:

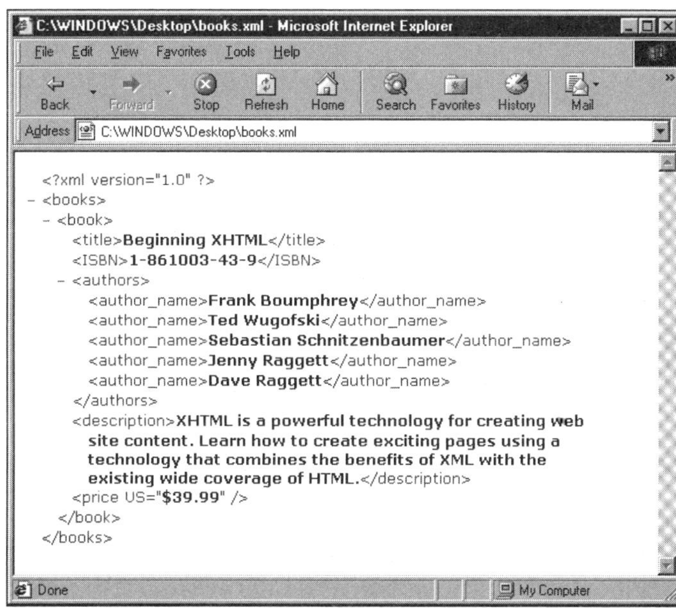

How It Works

Let's go through our code step-by-step and take a look at exactly what is happening:

```
<?xml version="1.0"?>
```

This is the **XML prolog**. It tells the receiving application that they are getting an XML document compatible with version one of the XML specification. Note that the `xml` is in lowercase and that there are no white spaces between the question mark and the opening `xml`.

All XML documents must have a unique opening and closing tag; `<books>` is ours, as we have a file containing data about books:

```
<books>
  ...
</books>
```

This is known as the **root** element. Nearly all XML tags MUST have a corresponding closing tag; unlike HTML you cannot miss out end tags and expect your application to accept it. The only exception to this is called an **empty** element, in which there is no element content. An example of this in HTML would be an `<img>` tag. In XML, if you have an empty element you must add a slash before the closing delimiter, such as `<tag attribute="value" />`:

> **Note that XML, like XHTML, is case sensitive, so `<BOOK>`, `<Book>` and `<book>` would be treated as three different tags.**

Within this we are describing data about a specific book, so we use an opening tag that explains what will be contained by the tag. Here we are using `<book>`:

```
<books>
<book>
  ...
</book>
</books>
```

In the same way that we made sensible opening and closing tags for the document using the `<books>` element, we use similarly descriptive tags to mark up some more details, this time the title of the book and its ISBN number (the one that is just above the bar code on the back of the book). These go inside the opening and closing `<book>` tags:

```
    <title>Beginning XHTML</title>
    <ISBN>1-861003-43-9</ISBN>
```

As there are several authors on this book we put the list of authors in **nested** elements. We start with an opening <authors> tag and then nest inside this an <author_name> tag for each author. Again these go between the opening and closing <book> tags. In this example we put them under the ISBN:

```
    <authors>
       <author_name>Frank Boumphrey </author_name>
       <author_name>Ted Wugofski </author_name>
       <author_name>Sebastian Schnitzenbaumer </author_name>
       <author_name>Jenny Raggett </author_name>
       <author_name>Dave Raggett </author_name>
    </authors>
```

This is a very important aspect of XML as data, because it allows us to create **hierarchical** data records. This structure would not fit easily into the row and table model of relational databases (without the use of linked tables), whereas it fits fine in our text file.

Next, we added the description of the book. Here we are using an element called <description>, although it could equally be something like <precis>, <details> or <synopsis>.

```
    <description> XHTML is a powerful technology for creating web site content.
 Learn how to create exciting pages using a technology that combines the benefits
 of XML with the existing wide coverage of HTML.</description>
```

We then added the price of the book to the document. Here you can see that we are using an empty element tag, with the closing slash in the tag. The currency and amount are actually held within the `US` attribute:

```
    <price US="$39.99"/>
 </book>
```

> **Note that, in XML (as in XHTML), all attribute values must be contained in quotes.**

And that's all there is to it. You have just created your first XML document. It is plain text, its tags describe their content, and it is easily human-readable.

From this alone, you can tell that we are now talking about a book. The tags that meant little in our XHTML version, such as <h3> and <p>, are gone. In our XHTML example, the ISBN number of the book was held in <h3> tags. When we mark up the data about a book using XML, the ISBN number is in tags that are called <ISBN>. Now, this seems a lot more logical and it is simple to see what we are talking about.

But what about how it looks in a web browser? Browsers understand tags such as <h3>, referring to a category 3 heading, but we cannot expect a browser to understand tags that we are making up ourselves! As XML is such a new technology, browsers are only just starting to support it; Internet Explorer 5 was the first browser to offer support for the XML specification. It is, of course, the one we will use for the examples in this chapter.

As it is, our XML version is not as attractive to look at as the HTML version but, as we said, HTML is language specifically for displaying data on the web. XML is just a way of marking up your data. It is still possible to make our XML documents more attractive using a style sheet, which we'll see how to do shortly.

The Data Revolution

As computers have found their way into more areas of our work and home life, we are storing ever-increasing amounts of information electronically. The tendency is to think of our business data mainly residing in relational databases, such as SQL Server, Oracle or DB2. The reality, however, is that we probably have more data in other formats:

- Quotes and reports in word processor formats, such as Word or Word Perfect
- Web pages in HTML
- Presentations in PowerPoint
- Mail and memos in mail servers such as Exchange and Notes

Some of this data is replicated and some of it is as good as lost, because not everyone knows how to access it. In addition, the ubiquity of the Internet has meant that we are trying to share more and more data with people in other physical places.

But what has all this got to do with XML? Going back to our book example, Wrox uses the type of book information we have just seen for many purposes: for web pages, trade catalogs, public catalogs, information for retail purchasers (bookshops) and so on. Many of these require the information in different formats so we need to be able to use the information in different ways.

The great news is that if we can mark up our book details just once in XML, and then we can re-purpose it. So, if we were to create an XML file containing all of our book catalog we would *not* need to put it in HTML for the Web, and then individually mail the retailers with new book details, and so on. As we will see later in the chapter, we can just re-format the one XML source to suit each purpose.

Furthermore, if people want to find out about specific books, they could just collect information about those that they are interested in, rather than wasting bandwidth having to download a large file with a lot of irrelevant data. This is because we can easily offer a search facility that goes through `<title>` elements looking for the title they want.

Breaking Beyond Data Display

Up to now, it may seem as though we have been concentrating on how XML can be an alternative to HTML. Let's quickly expand this view a little and see the other effects of marking up our data as XML. We will then take a look at some of the associated specifications and techniques that you need to learn.

As XML is just stored and transferred as plain text it has strong advantages over most other data formats. For example, because it is pure text it is not a proprietary format that can only be used on certain platforms or with limited applications – **any** application could be written to accept pure text. Also, the data is easy to validate. You may recall that we said SGML uses a DTD to define the rules of any markup language written in SGML. Well, so does XML. This means that applications can verify the structure and content of an XML file.

This universality is one of the main reasons why XML is an ideal subject for applications, as well as displaying data on the Web. It can transcend different operating systems and is ideal for distributed computing environments.

So, not only are we seeing XML being used as a way of presenting data that is marked up as HTML, it is also being used for many other purposes, including:

- **Data transfer**: from the book details we could send details of orders and financial transactions, in XML, that will be able to be understood by any platform
- **Re-usable data storage** in plain text files rather than pre-purposed formats, such as HTML and proprietary word processor files
- **Interface descriptors** for components

Of course, we cannot cover all of the reasons in this book. But what we will do is show you enough to give you a feel for the breadth of XML. From this point you will hopefully be able to see how it can help you in certain situations.

A Closer Look at Creating XML Documents

The XML 1.0 specification lays out two types of XML document, either **well-formed** or **valid**. The distinction between the two is simple:

- Well-formed documents comply with the rules of XML syntax. For example, all elements must have a corresponding end tag, or else have a closing slash in the empty elements; every document must have a unique opening and closing tag, etc.
- Valid documents are not only well-formed, they also comply with a DTD.

Well-Formed Documents

The XML 1.0 specification defines the syntax for XML. If you understand the specification properly, you can construct a program that will be able to 'look' at a document that is supposed to be XML. If the document conforms to the specification for XML, then the program can do further processing on it. The idea underlying the XML specification is, therefore, that XML documents should be intelligible as such, either to humans or processing applications.

Being well-formed is the minimum set of requirements (defined in the specification) that a document needs to satisfy in order for it to be considered an XML document. Here, requirements are a mixture of ensuring that the correct language terms are employed and that the document is logically coherent in the manner defined by the specification (in other words that the terms of the language are used in the right way). You can see the XML specification at `http://www.w3.org/tr/xml/`. There is also a helpful annotated version of the specification available at `http://www.xml.com/axml/testaxml.htm`.

So, what are these rules? You'll be pleased to hear that nearly everything we need to know about well-formed documents can be summed up in three rules:

- The document must contain one or more elements.
- It must contain a uniquely named element, no part of which appears in the content of any other element. This is known as the root element.
- All other elements must be kept within the root element and must be nested correctly.

So, let's look at how we construct a well-formed document.

The XML Declaration

This is actually optional, although you are strongly advised to use it so that the receiving application knows that it is an XML document and also the version used (at the time of writing this was the only version):

```
<?xml version="1.0"?>
```

Note that the `xml` should be in lowercase. Note also that the XML declaration, when present, must not be preceded by any other characters (not even white space). As we saw previously, this declaration is also referred to as the XML prolog.

In this declaration, you can also define the language in which you have written your XML data. This is particularly important if your data contains characters that aren't part of the English ASCII character set. You can specify the language encoding using the optional `encoding` attribute:

```
<?xml version="1.0" encoding="iso-8859-1" ?>
```

The most common ones are shown in the following table:

Language	Character set
Unicode (8 bit)	UTF-8
Latin 1 (Western Europe, Latin America)	ISO-8859-1
Latin 2 (Central/Eastern Europe)	ISO-8859-2
Latin 3 (SE Europe)	ISO-8859-3
Latin 4 (Scandinavia/Baltic)	ISO-8859-4
Latin/Cyrillic	ISO-8859-5
Latin/Arabic	ISO-8859-6
Latin/Greek	ISO-8859-7
Latin/Hebrew	ISO-8859-8
Latin/Turkish	ISO-8859-9
Latin/Lappish/Nordic/Eskimo	ISO-8859-10
Japanese	EUC-JP or Shift_JIS

If you want to read more about internationalization, check out the W3Cs page on this topic at `http://www.w3.org/International/`.

Elements

As we have already seen, the XML document essentially consists of data marked up using tags. Each start tag/end tag pair, with the data that lies between them, is an element:

```
<mytag>Here we have some data</mytag>
```

The start and end tags must be exactly the same, except for the closing slash in the end tag. Remember that they must be in the same case: `<mytag>` and `<MyTag>` would be considered as different tags.

The section between the tags that says, "`Here we have some data`", is called **character data**, while the tags either side are the **markup**. The character data can consist of any sequence of legal characters (conforming to the Unicode standard), except the start element character <. This is not allowed in case a processing application treats it as the start of a new tag. If you do need to include them you can represent them using `<` for < and `>` for >.

The tags can start with a letter, an underscore `(_)`, or a colon character `(:)`, followed by any combination of letter, digits, hyphens, underscores, colons, or periods. The only exception is that you cannot start a tag with the letters `XML` in any combination of upper or lowercase letters. You are also advised not to start a tag with a colon, in case it gets treated as a namespace (something we shall meet later on).

Here is another example, marking up some details for a hardware store:

```
<inventory>
   <buckets>
      <bucket>
         <make>Addis</make>
         <capacity>3 litres</capacity>
      </bucket>
      <bucket>
         <make>Metro</make>
         <capacity>2.5 litres</capacity>
      </bucket>
   </buckets>
</inventory>
```

If you remember back to the three rules at the beginning of this section, you will be able to work out that this is a well-formed XML document. We have more than our one required element. We have a unique opening and closing tag: `<inventory>`, which is the root element. The elements are nested properly inside the root element.

Let's have a look at some more examples to help us get the idea how a well-formed XML document should be constructed.

At the simplest level we could have either:

```
<my_document></my_document>
```

or even:

```
<my_document/>
```

To make sure that tags nest properly, there must be no overlap. So this is correct:

```
<parent>
   <child>Some character data</child>
</parent>
```

while this would be incorrect:

```
<bad_parent>
      <naughty_child>
            Some character data
</bad_parent>
      </naughty child>
```

This is because the closing `</naughty_child>` element is after the closing `</bad_parent>` element.

Attributes

Elements can have attributes. These are values that are passed to the application, but do not constitute part of the content of the element. Attributes are included as part of the element's opening tag, as in HTML. In XML all attributes must be enclosed in quote marks. For example:

```
<food healthy="yes">spinach</food>
```

Elements can have as many attributes as you want. So you could have:

```
<food healthy="no" tasty="yes" high_in_cholesterol="yes">fries</food>
```

For well-formedness, however, you cannot repeat the attribute within an instance of the element. So you could not have:

```
<food tasty="yes" tasty="no">spinach</food>
```

Also, the string values between the quote marks can not contain the characters `<`, `&`, `'` or `"`.

Other Features

There are also a number of other features of the XML specification that you need to learn if you progress to using XML frequently. Unfortunately there is not space to cover them all here. We will, however, briefly describe a few of them.

Entities

There are two categories of entity: **general entities** and **parameter entities**. Entities are usually used within a document as a way of avoiding having to type out long pieces of text several times within that document. They provide a way of associating a name with the long piece of text so that wherever you need to mention the text you just mention the name instead. As a result, if you have to modify the text, you only have to do it once.

CDATA Sections

CDATA sections can be used wherever character data can appear within a document. They are used to escape (or delimit) blocks of text that would otherwise be considered as markup. So if we wanted to include the whole of the following line, including the tags:

```
<to_be_seen>Always wear light clothing when walking in the dark</to_be_seen>
```

We could use a CDATA section like so:

```
<element>
<! [CDATA[ <to_be_seen>Always wear light clothing when walking in the
dark</to_be_seen> ]]>
</element>
```

And the whole line, including the opening and closing `<to_be_seen>` tags, would not be processed or treated as tags by the receiving application.

As we've seen, it's actually part of the XHTML recommendation to wrap your scripts and embedded style sheets in CDATA sections, however in our experience existing browsers fall over when they meet this in a `.html` document.

Comments

It is always good programming practice to comment your code – it's so much easier to read if it is commented in a manner that helps explain, reminds you about, or simply points out salient sections of code. It is surprising how code that seemed perfectly clear when you wrote it can soon become a jumble when you come back to it. While the descriptive XML tags often help you understand your own markup, there are times when the tags alone are not enough.

Comments in XML use exactly the same syntax as those in XHTML (well, obviously, since XHTML is written in XML):

```
<!--I really should add a comment here to remind me about xxxxx -->
```

In order to avoid confusing the receiving application, you should not include either the "-" character in your comment text.

Processing Instructions

These allow documents to contain instructions for applications using the XML data. They take the form:

```
<?NameOfTargetApplication    Instructions for Application?>
```

The target name cannot contain the letters `xml` in any combination of upper or lower case. Otherwise, you can create your own to work with the processing application (unless there are any predefined by the application at which you are targeting your XML).

Valid Documents

As we mentioned earlier, valid documents are well-formed documents that conform to a DTD. When we read a book, manual or magazine article we rarely notice its structure; if it is well written then the structure will be transparent. Yet, without structure there would be no communication. We may notice headings and paragraphs, but many other aspects pass us by. For one thing this structuring makes the information in the document intelligible, either by us or to an application using it. Furthermore, it means that when a document is parsed, by an application for example, it can be checked for the presence of required portions.

There are many programs, known as **parsers**, available for XML. Some of these parsers are able to validate a document against its DTD, in which case they are known as **validating parsers**. If the document does not follow the structure of the DTD the parser will raise an error.

Assuming that, in the first instance, we have an appropriate and well-planned structure for a type of document, then the resulting document instances should be logically complete with respect to its predefined structure. So, in our book example earlier we had:

- The unique opening and closing tags of `<books>`
- A `<book>` element, which encapsulates all information on a specific book
- Followed by a title, in a `<title>` element
- Then the ISBN in the `<ISBN>` tags
- Followed by the author, description, and price elements

If we had to exchange a lot of information about books, in this format, with different people, then there would be many advantages to writing a DTD (or document type definition). Such a book DTD would lay out the structure of how we expect books following the book DTD to be marked up. While we do not need one to write an XML document, it would mean that anyone following the DTD would be able to write an XML file about books that would be valid according to our DTD. In this manner, we could guarantee that any application using the book information, marked up according to our DTD, could understand the document; it could even check that the document followed the DTD in order to prevent the application showing errors if we passed in the wrong data.

So, if we had written any applications to process an XML file, created according to our book DTD then, in fact, we would be able to process *any* files that were valid according to the book DTD. In which case, if Wrox had different members of staff all writing XML documents about the books they could all follow the DTD to make sure that they were valid. Then, should other publishers adopt the same DTD, the bookstores who might make use of our XML files would be able to use the same applications to process the files sent from several different publishers.

Writing DTDs

Document Type Definitions are part of the original core XML 1.0 specification. In order to learn about DTDs we will develop one for our sample `books.xml` file. They are written in a language called **Extended Backus-Naur Form**, or EBNF for short. The DTD needs to declare the rules of the markup language, which we said at the beginning of this chapter:

- Declare what exactly constitutes markup
- Declare exactly what our markup means

Practically speaking, this means that we have to give details of each of the elements, their order, and say what attributes (and other types of markup) they can take.

> *They are an example of what is known as a **schema**, but this should not be confused with XML Schemas, which offer similar extended functionality above DTDs but are written in XML syntax.*

The DTD can be declared internally (actually in the XML document) within a **Document Type Declaration** (note that, to avoid total confusion, we **do not** shorten this term to DTD!). Nevertheless, this *is* where the terminology starts to get confusing! The document type declaration is used in the XML file, which is written according to a document type definition, so that a processing application knows that the XML file has been written according to a document type definition. The DTD can, alternatively, be an external file. In this case, a document type declaration within the XML document will 'point' to this external DTD.

Referencing a DTD From an XML Document

In order that many XML documents can be written according to a single DTD, the DTD for our books example would be external. So, we need to add a document type declaration to the `books.xml` example, so that a processing application knows that it has been written according to the books document type definition:

```
<!DOCTYPE books SYSTEM "books.dtd">
```

Here, `books` is the name of the root element and the name of the document type definition. In this case we have followed it with the keyword `SYSTEM` and the URI of the DTD, a value that a processing application could use to validate the document against the DTD. This, of course, means that there must be an instance of it available from that location.

As we are just trying this out as a test we could just keep the DTD in the same folder as the XML document. However, if we were to make it available to all we would have to give a location for it that would be available to any application. So we might choose:

```
<!DOCTYPE books SYSTEM "http://www.wrox.com/DTDlibrary/books.dtd">
```

As we discussed earlier, it is possible to include the DTD within the document type declaration (in the XML document). In other words, the rules in the DTD could be placed within this declaration, rather than in a separate file. However, in most cases you will want to reference an external file, so we will only look at this. After all, there is no point copying the DTD into several files, if you can just have it in one place.

To do this we also add the `standalone` attribute to the XML declaration of the XML document (which comes directly before the document type declaration – remember that nothing is allowed to come before the XML declaration, not even white space):

```
<?xml version="1.0" standalone="no" ?>
<!DOCTYPE books SYSTEM "books.dtd">
```

If the value of the `standalone` attribute is `no`, this indicates that there may be an external DTD (or internally declared external parameter entities - but do not worry about this second option until you get more involved in creating complex XML documents). If the value is `yes`, then there are no other dependencies and the file can truly stand on its own.

It is very easy to get confused between Document Type Definitions and Document Type Declarations. To clarify, just remember that a document type declaration either refers to an external document type definition, as in the example we are about to see, or else it actually contains one in the form of markup declarations.

Writing a DTD for the Books Example

Creating your own markup language using a DTD need not be excessively complicated. Here is the external DTD for our books example. As you can see, it is very simple:

```
<!DOCTYPE books [
<!ELEMENT books (book+)
<!ELEMENT book (title, ISBN, authors, description?, price+)>
<!ELEMENT title (#PCDATA)>
<!ELEMENT authors (author+)>
<!ELEMENT author (#PCDATA)>
<!ELEMENT description (#PCDATA)>
<!ELEMENT price EMPTY>
<!ATTLIST price
          US       CDATA      #REQUIRED
>
]>
```

You can write it in a simple text editor, just as we did with the XML document. Alternatively, there are pieces of software that will help you to create them (for more details on these check out `http://www.schema.net/`). Let's take a closer look at this. Here is the opening line:

```
<!DOCTYPE books [
```

This gives the same name as the root element of the document. `<!ELEMENT` is used to declare elements, in the format:

```
<!ELEMENT name (contents)>
```

Where `name` gives the name of the element, and `contents` describes what type of data can be included and which elements can be nested inside that element. The `books` element must include the element `<book>` at least once, denoted by the use of the + symbol (which indicates one or more instances):

```
<!ELEMENT books (book+)>
```

The `<book>` element, declared in this line:

```
<!ELEMENT book (title, ISBN, authors, description?, price+)>
```

must include exactly one instance of each of the `title`, `ISBN` and `authors` elements, and at least one `price` element, in that particular order. The question mark after the `description` element means that this element is optional. We then have to define each of these elements individually. Here is a brief summary of the operators we can use to describe element content:

Symbol	Usage
,	Strict ordering
|	Selection, in any order (can be used in conjunction with +, * and ?).
+	Repetition (minimum of 1)
*	Repetition
?	Optional
()	Grouping

Next we see the line:

```
<!ELEMENT title (#PCDATA)>
```

This indicates that the title element can contain **character data**, indicated by `#PCDATA`. The # symbol prevents PCDATA from being interpreted as an element name. While the `authors` element can contain one or more `author` elements:

```
<!ELEMENT authors (author+)>
```

The `author` elements contain character data, as does the `description` element.

When we came to the `price` element in our `books.xml` file, there were no closing tags; the element was an **empty** element. It did, however, have an attribute to indicate its currency. This was how it looked in our `books.xml` example:

```
<price US="$39.99"/>
```

So we need to declare the element as being empty, and also declare the attribute that it can take. First we will use this line:

```
<!ELEMENT price EMPTY>
```

to indicate that the elements name is price, but that it is an empty element. Then we have to declare the attribute using the `<!ATTLIST`... instruction, the data types or possible values and the default values for the attributes:

```
<!ATTLIST price
          US       CDATA       #REQUIRED
>
```

Each attribute has three components: a name (e.g. `US`), the type of information to be passed (in this case character data, `CDATA`), and the default value (in this case there is not one, but we are required to provide a value).

Then we just have to close the opening `DOCTYPE` declaration:

```
]>
```

That covers the example book DTD, `books.dtd`, for the `books.xml` example. You will find it with the rest of the code for this chapter at `http://www.wrox.com/`. If you want to create one yourself, you can simply use a text editor, such as Notepad, just save the file (which will have the same name as your root element) as `"books.dtd"`.

Obviously, if you have a well-formed instance of an element in a document, but do not declare it in the DTD, then it cannot be validated. An element is only valid if:

- There is a declaration for the element type in the DTD which has a name matching that of the element itself
- There are declarations for all of the element types, attributes and their value types in the DTD
- The data type of the content matches that of the content schema defined in the declaration (e.g. `PCDATA`)

Styling XML

So far we have created our first application of XML, a language for exchanging data about books, and we have created an XML document in our `books.xml` file. This is great for defining data, as our tags clearly explain their content and it is written in plain text, which is easy to transfer. However, if we are putting things up on the Web we want our pages to look good. As our earlier example showed, even in an XML-aware browser, such as IE5, a plain XML file did not look that impressive:

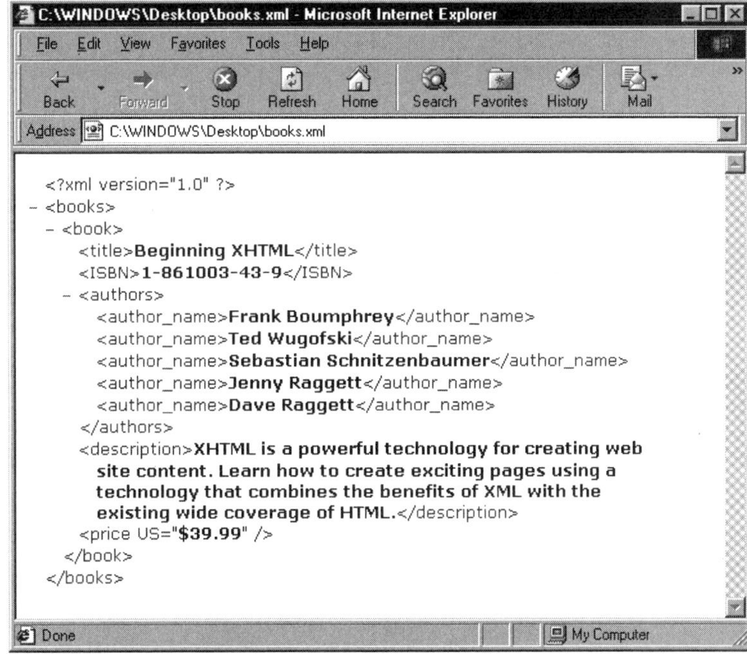

This is because the tags that we have proposed for our book example don't say anything about how the tags should appear on the page, whereas XHTML tells the browser how the data should look. So, to make it look attractive we must supply another file, a style sheet.

Cascading Style Sheets

CSS is a rule-based language comprising of two sections:

- A **pattern matching** section, which expresses the association between an element and some action
- An **action section**, which specifies the action to be taken upon the specified section

For XML, this means that we have to specify an element and then specify how it has to be displayed. So, if we were to develop a cascading style sheet for our `books.xml` file, we would have to specify a style for each of the elements that contain markup that we want to display.

It is important to decide whether the values are to be displayed in-line or as a block. The difference being that, if they are in-line the next element will be displayed as if it were on the same line as the previous one, whereas if it is displayed as a block, each will be treated separately. We need to make this decision for each object in CSS.

Let's try it out and write a style sheet for our books.xml file.

Try it Out – Displaying XML with CSS

1. We start by opening up our favorite text editor again we will be saving this file as books.css. Type in the following code:

```
title {
     display:block;
     font-family: Arial, Helvetica;
     font-wieght: bold;
     font-size: 20pt;
     color: #9370db;
     text-align: center;
     }
ISBN {
     display:block;
     font-family: Arial, Helvetica;
     font-weight: bold;
     font-size: 12pt;
     color: #c71585;
     text-align: left;
     }

authors {
     display:inline;
     font-family: Arial, Helvetica;
     font-style: italic;
     font-size: 10pt;
     color: #9370db;
     text-align: left;
     }

description {
     display:block;
     font-family: Arial, Helvetica;
     font-size: 12pt;
     color: #ff1010;
     text-align: left;
     }
```

2. Save the file as books.css. We have now finished creating our first style sheet for XML. The only problem is that our books.xml file has no way of telling how it should be associated with this style sheet. So we will have to add a link to this style sheet into our original XML file.

3. To add the link to the style sheet, open up your books.xml file again, and add the following line between the XML prolog and the opening <books> element:

```
<?xml version="1.0"?>
<?xml:stylesheet href="books.css" type="text/css" ?>
<books>
```

4. Open books.xml in your browser and you should see something like this:

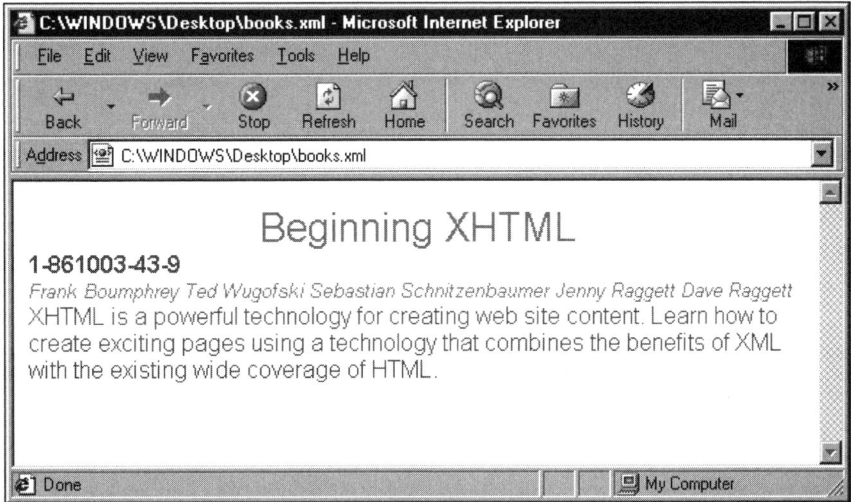

How It Works

CSS files do not need a special header, so we went straight on and declared which elements we needed to display. In this case we are just adding styling for the <title>, <ISBN>, <authors>, and <description> elements. So we can add them to the file like so:

```
title {

      }
ISBN  {

      }

authors {

      }

description {

      }
```

This specifies the pattern matching section.

Having declared the elements that we want to display, we must associate some action with it. So, let's see how to display the content of the `<title>` element. We want it to be displayed as a block, so within the curly brackets { } we add the directive to display the element as a block:

```
title {
     display:block;
     }
```

This simply specifies that we want to make the title a block level element. We still need to specify the style the title should be displayed in.

> **All properties are specified with a colon delimiting the attribute and values and have a semi-colon after them.**

So, we added a font to display the content of the `<title>` element. In the screen shot you have just seen the browser is using the Arial font. However, in case the machine using the file does not have Arial, we have allowed it to use Helvetica instead. In addition, we want it to appear in the center of the screen, in a size 20pt, bold font, and in a lilac color. So, we add some more action rules, or style elements. As you can see, these are very similar to those used for HTML.

```
title {
     display:block;
     font-family: Arial, Helvetica;
     font-wieght: bold;
     font-size: 20pt;
     color: #9370db;
     text-align: center;
     }
```

We can then add some similar rules for the other element content we want to display, for example:

```
authors {
     display:inline;
     font-family: Arial, Helvetica;
     font-style: italic;
     font-size: 10pt;
     color: #9370db;
     text-align: left;
     }
```

You can see from the screen shot that the authors, despite being in separate elements in the `books.xml` file are displayed on the same line.

Finally, we included an extra line in our `books.xml` file to tell it to use the correct CSS file:

```
<?xml version="1.0"?>
<?xml:stylesheet href="books.css" type="text/css" ?>
<books>
```

The `href` attribute acts just like it would in HTML, while the `type` attribute specifies the type of style sheet that is being attached. This is an example of a processing instruction, which you may remember us talking about them earlier in the chapter when we were discussing XML syntax.

> **Remember that, because the style sheet link is still in the XML file, the values of the attributes still need to be kept in quotation marks for the XML to be well-formed.**

Obviously, there is a lot more to CSS than we can describe here, such as all of the appropriate styling tags. To find our more, check out the specification at `http://www.w3.org/style/css/` or pick up a copy of a dedicated book, such as *Professional Style Sheets for HTML and XML* published by Wrox Press (ISBN 1-861001-65-7) – although the XSL section of this book is somewhat out-of-date.

XSL

Having seen how easy it is to create a style sheet for our XML using CSS, we should briefly introduce the **eXtensible Stylesheet Language**, or **XSL**. XSL is far more powerful than CSS, *but*, if you are only interested in displaying the XML *as it is* for display on the Web, then CSS is a far simpler option.

There are two key parts to XSL. The first covers its transformation abilities: it can actually be used to transform XML into HTML, or a number of other languages. At the time of writing, this section, known as **XSLT**, was still a working draft although it was near completion. It is ideal for transforming data into another form for use on the Web.

In addition, there is another area in development to specify formatting semantics. This is particularly useful for creating print versions of documents, such as `PDF` or `TeX` documents.

Undoubtedly one of the prime uses of XSLT at the moment is to transform XML into HTML for display in browsers that do not support XML, and to transform one XML vocabulary into another. XSLT is far too big a subject to go into in depth in this book. We just wanted to bring its existence to your attention!

If you want more information you might try `http://www.w3.org/tr/xslt`.

Summary

This brief XML overview was included so you could get a basic idea of what XML is outside the context of XHTML. We can't get much into pure XML in this book really, but we wanted to step back briefly and look at a slightly bigger picture. It's true that most of the benefits of XML are not really directly available to a beginning web developer but if you intend to take your skills further you'd do well to keep an eye on what you can do with XML, because a lot of the things you can do to XML you can also do with XHTML, for instance transforming it with XSL might come in useful for other user agents because you could then apply the relevant transformation for whichever user agent you wanted to display on.

In the next chapter, we'll be looking at some aspects of site design.

CSS
DOM
XHTML
JavaScript
XML

Site Design Concepts

Up until now we have been mainly looking at designing individual pages. However, a page is merely part of a web site, and although good web site design starts with good page design, planning a web site is probably the most important part of a web developer's job.

Poor site design leads to sites that are difficult to use, difficult to maintain, and expensive. Too often, however, site design gets very little attention until these problems manifest themselves, and then they are almost impossible to fix without re-building the site from the ground up. Luckily, it is just as easy to put together a well-designed site as it is to put together a poorly-designed site: all that is required is common sense and a few basic principles.

There is a saying that the three most important things to remember when designing a **web page** are:

- Speed of download
- Speed of download
- Speed of download!

Similarly the three most important things to remember when designing a **web site** are:

- Ease of navigation
- Ease of navigation
- Ease of navigation!

Admittedly, there are other factors too, but a well-designed web site is easily navigated, and vice versa.

In this chapter, we will cover the following:

- General concepts of site design
- Site planning
- Linking policies
- Building linking and meta-information into our sites
- Site structure and modularization
- Site branding
- Site management

General Concepts

The general concepts of site design are easy enough, indeed they are just an extension of common sense. Although we will cover all of the topics listed below in more detail throughout this chapter, it is helpful to have an overall view of the concepts involved.

- **Know the site's purpose and intended audience** – This is probably the largest factor in deciding the structure and overall tone of your site. Is it a humble home page? A site to provide password-protected information to business clients? A site to advertise goods? And so on. A clear idea of the purpose of your site is essential to its planning. For example, a site intended for Hard Rock fans, say, will be quite different from a site intended to show fluctuations in share prices on a stock market.
- **Keep your audience orientated** – This cannot be stressed enough: once the site's purpose has been agreed upon, ease of navigation becomes the number one priority. People hate being lost, and this applies just as much to cyberspace as it does to the real world. A well-planned and well-structured site should orientate its users at all points within that site.
- **Site branding** – It is important to keep a consistent look and 'feel' to all of your pages. There is nothing more annoying to a user than navigating a site where the page layout keeps on changing (just think how you feel when your favorite magazine re-designs and re-launches itself).
- **Scalability** – If we are planning a site for a large corporation, then we will know from the very beginning that it is going to be an extensive site, and we will take time to design it accordingly. However, if we are only building a small site we may be tempted just to 'throw a few pages together' and place them in a single folder. Small sites, whether business or personal, do have a tendency to grow, and any site should be planned with growth in mind.
- **Separate functions** – This really goes along with scalability. Plan to keep the design, content creation, and network management aspects of the site separate, even if the same person is responsible for all three roles to start with. This allows different people to perform the different tasks, whether it be taking on a new employee or a more artistic friend with a great idea for a new design for your personal site.

This chapter will cover all of these topics in more detail, but it's good to keep the basic concepts in your mind as we go through it.

Planning

Although you may think it is much more fun to write the pages for a site than it is to plan the actual site, building a great site really does start with its planning. If you don't take the time to plan your site then you are likely to be left with a series of great looking pages that do not fit into a single whole, are difficult to navigate and give the impression of a disjointed, rather amateurish site.

Market Analysis

Before we do anything, some basic market research is required. First of all, we need a clear idea of what we want to actually *do* with our site.

Site Purpose

Defining the purpose of our site is an essential first step. This applies equally to the planning of a large corporate site as it does to the planning of a personal web site. It is always a good idea to write down the mission or aim of our planned site. Once we have done this, we then need to decide who our audience will be.

Site Audience

Ask yourself these questions:

- Who will be the primary audience for this site?
- Will this site be solely for this audience, or will it appeal to other audiences?
- What kind of graphics and style will appeal to this audience?
- Will I just be conveying information, or will I also be selling products to this audience?
- What is the best way to convey information to this audience?
- What is the attention span of this audience?

The last point is particularly important and frequently over looked. A site selling products to a teenager must be of a very different overall feel and design to a site conveying information to particle physicists. Once these questions have been answered, though, we are in a good position to design our site and the pages for it.

Story Boards

Now that we have decided what our site is going to do, and the potential audience of it, we can start planning its design. It is always a good idea to start off with a piece of paper, or a set of `2 x 4` cards, and draw out a rough sketch of the site. Decide what groups of pages you are going to need, then move them about and organize them in various ways (bearing in mind the principles expounded in this chapter) to see which structure suits your sites needs best.

This paper or card 'story board' structure of your site that you create does not have to be complex. Indeed, it should really be very simple because if it is not, the chances are that any site based on it will confuse your audience as they try to navigate their way through its various pages.

Scalability

Many very large sites originally started out as very small sites (for example, `http://www.ccf.org`) and, unless we plan for success, we may be faced with the prospect of completely redesigning our site to make it manageable right at the peak of our success. Not only that, but badly organized sites are difficult to manage, prone to error, and expensive to run.

Luckily, it is just as easy to build a site that scales well as it is to build a site that does not. All it takes is a little foresight. We'll look at exactly how this is done later on. As a bonus, a scaleable site makes link management very easy – which brings us nicely to the next section.

Linking Policies

The layout of the links on a site is the single most important reason for the success or failure of a site. There are certain well known rules that should be followed.

- **The three click rule** – Web surfers are an impatient bunch: if they cannot find the information they need in three clicks of a mouse button then they are likely to go elsewhere. The only possible exception to this rule is in an academic site where users are likely to be conditioned to making arduous searches. However, even here one should try and follow the three click rule. Note that the physical impact of this rule is that it limits the number of layers we can have in a hierarchical site structure. Thus, the three click rule is about more than just 'clicking', and can be the foundation stone of your sites architecture.
- **The seven link rule** – Research (Jacobsen) has shown that the most new links that a surfer can cope with without getting confused, is seven per page. In practice it is a good idea to keep it below this number. Five would seem to be ideal. Of course, if we have a home and an index link on every page then these do not count as new links.
- **Keep the viewer orientated** – The user should always have a way of getting back to a known point in your site. This means in most cases providing a link to the home page and the parent page on all your pages. If the page is a reference page, a 'back button' (see later) should be provided.

Linking Paradigms

There are certain well-known linking paradigms that the user has come to expect. Using one of these paradigms will help to orient the user. The two most common linking paradigms are to have top and bottom links, or to have side links.

Top and bottom links

You can either have a row of plain word links near the top/bottom of your page, or you can create more fanciful 'navigation bars' where the links are placed within a differently colored area or bar from the background, or are composed of images, and so on.

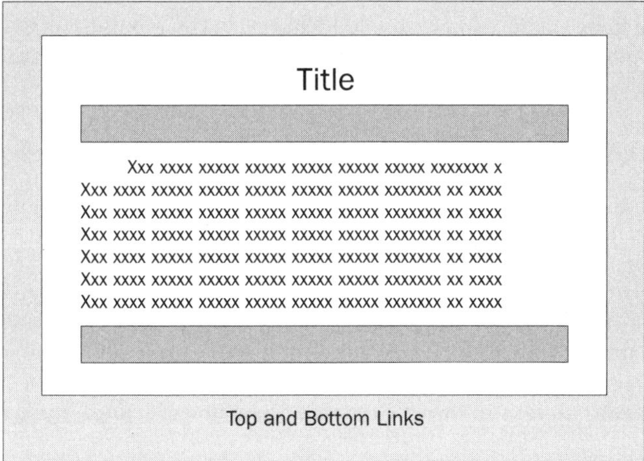

Top and Bottom Links

Side links

The same applies here as for above: either have a list of plain word links without any special formatting, or create side bars to contain your links. Note that when side links are employed, it is usual to have them on the left-hand side of the page. In some cases – for example, many of the news pages – local links are kept on the left-hand side of the page, and the off-site links are kept to the right-hand side of the page. This helps to orientate the user, as they know when a link will take them off your site.

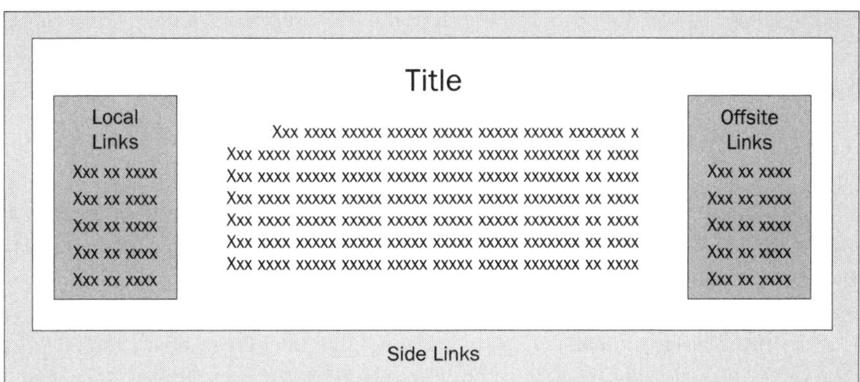

Side Links

Many pages, of course, use both top and side links. Often in this case the top links are used for all the general site links – such as the home page, an index, or a search engine, and so on – while the side links are used for all the more specific or detailed site links that correspond to the particular page being viewed.

Make links accessible

Make sure that the links are accessible to someone without a mouse or other pointing device. This usually means avoiding the use of image bars or providing a text alternative if you do.

Keep 'em busy!

The general idea is to keep people on our site (why else would we build one?). There are two ways we can do this: either avoid any external links, or provide the user with lots of tantalizing links that they will just want to click through.

The former is rather anti-social, but there is certainly no reason why we should put external links in the first two levels of click through. Putting an external link on your home page is just asking for the user to leave your site! So let the reader first go through some of the information you want to put across, before advertising other sites that they can visit.

It is also a good idea to let the user know when a link is to an external site. We can do this by putting our external links in a single page, perhaps called 'Other Resources', or we can provide a small logo that will tell the reader that they are leaving your site. See the Microsoft site for examples of using this trick.

Incidentally putting external links in one spot makes the management of 'Link Rot' (discussed later) much easier.

Linking Don'ts

There are several linking don'ts which you should be aware of. These apply to the 'formal' links that are part of your overall design, not the ones scattered throughout your text. We'll talk about those in a minute.

- **Don't just use frames** – Remember that a site that keeps all it's links in a separate frame may be completely inaccessible to a browser that does not support frames. If you must use frames always be sure to provide a no frames version of your site.
- **Don't pull the welcome mat** – Many sites leave their users floundering as soon as they leave the home page. Make sure that all your pages have a link that is of potential interest to the viewer.
- **Don't forget the exit** – Although we don't want to encourage our viewer to leave our site too soon, we should always allow them an exit other than pressing the browser's Back button. A well-kept list of other resources satisfies the old sales adage of always giving a customer satisfaction. A viewer is likely to bookmark, or mark as a favorite, any site that is a portal to all the information that they want.
- **Don't let them leave too soon** – Having just said 'give the viewer a way out', don't let them leave too soon! Let them wander about your site for a bit. An experienced car salesman will always let the customer browse for a bit before asking them if they want any help. The bottom line is, don't put external links in your opening material!
- **Don't forget to include text links** – Omitting these makes your site inaccessible to those without image viewing ability.
- **Don't create orphan pages** – An orphan page is a page with no links to it. A rapidly growing site is bound to accumulate some of these. Run a software check from time to time to make sure all your pages are linked.

Inline Links

When we discussed linking policies in the last section, we were referring to the links that were formally laid out in all our pages (such as top and side links). We will also have another series of links in most pages, those that reside within the text of the page. These are the so-called **inline links**. There are some rules that should be followed when using inline links.

- **Keep the inline links to a minimum** – There is nothing worse than trying to read a page that is scattered with inline links. Every time the reader comes to one, they have to make the decision whether or not to click on it.
- **Avoid opening links** – Especially avoid inline links in the opening paragraph or statement. This is the last place that we want to distract our user, or to suggest that the site will swamp them with too much information. At the first hint of 'information overload', users will exit the site and try and find something less complex, and more easily digested, elsewhere on the Web.
- **Keep the reader orientated** – When a user clicks on a link, do not take them to the middle of another page; instead, take them to a definite section. Whenever feasible take them to the start of a logical structure (see later) in your site.
- **Keep the reader on site** – If possible, do not take your reader off site with an inline link. Take them to an area on-site that is set aside for off-site links. If you must take them off site, it is always a good idea to insert a small inline logo (with a text alternative) that lets the user know this. This is all part of the policy of keeping the user orientated.

Linking and Meta-Information

In the previous sections we looked at how to use links to bind our site together into a coherent whole, and how to use them to ease navigation around our site. We can also use links, and the `<link>` element, to provide meta-information about our site.

As our site grows the chances are that we will want to automate many of the tasks in site maintenance, such as building a table of contents, or providing an index to our site.

The <link> Element

We looked briefly at the `<link>` element in Chapter 4. The `<link>` element is used as a vehicle to contain the address of another page in the form of a URL. One of the best uses of the `<link>` element is that it can be used to describe the position of any page on our site. It has two attributes, `rel` and `rev`, that can be used to do this.

The 'rel' and 'rev' Attributes

The rel attribute is used to describe the position of the page it points to in relation to the page that contains the <link> element. For example

```
<link rel="parent" type="text/html" href="http://mysite.com" />
```

The rev attribute is used to describe how the named page considers the page containing it – it's essentially the rel attribute but in reverse. For example if we used rev instead of rel in the above <link> element we would have:

```
<link rev="child" type="text/html" href="http://mysite.com" />
```

If we set up all our pages with these elements it now becomes an easy matter for software to divine the layout of our pages.

Let's see how we would use the <link> element to index the following minimal site, where our pages are called home.htm, pageA.htm, pageB.htm, page1.htm and page2.htm:

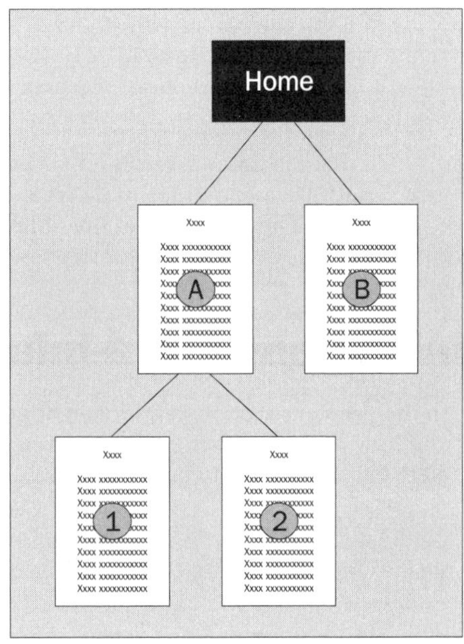

If we set up our linking policy correctly, our home page would contain the following link elements:

```
<link rel="child" type="text/html" href="pageA.htm" />
<link rel="child" type="text/html" href="pageB.htm" />
```

This specifies that both page A and B are child pages of our home page. Likewise, page A would contain the following <link> elements:

```
<link rel="child" type="text/html" href="page1.htm" />
<link rel="child" type="text/html" href="page2.htm" />
```

This specifies that both page 1 and 2 are child pages of page A.

Now it is easy to write software to perform a whole host of functions such as producing a table of contents for our site. The `<link>`elements can also be used to check that any other relative links in the page are also correct.

As part of the general policy of scalability, it is good to get into the habit of using `<link>` elements on even small sites. A friend of mine (ahem!) did not include `<link>` elements on some sites "because they were too small" and has bitterly regretted this lack of foresight!

Labeling Links

We can also use the `class` attribute to label our individual links. Even labeling every link with a classification as simple as "external" or "internal" can give a lot of information to software and will make large sites much easier to manage.

Here are a few of the labels you might consider using:

- **Internal:** pages that are on site, for example:

```
<a href="../../locallink.html" class="internal">...</a>
```

- **External:** pages that are off site:

```
<a href="http://www.bigdaddy.com/index.htm" class="external">...</a>
```

- **Reference:** a page intended as reference material that is not included in the normal hierarchy of our site
- **MasterPage:** a page that defines a section or module of our site
- **ChildPage:** a page other than a master page that resides in a section or a module of our site
- **FragId:** a link to a particular part of a page – use as e.g. Reference/FragId
- **Image:** a link to an image

The above are just suggestions. We can, of course, use any classification we want, but the important thing is that we decide on a consistent labeling policy early on and use it before our site gets too large.

Meta-Information

We covered the `<meta>` element in Chapter 8. Here, I want to encourage you to put a meaningful `meta` element on every page, with a list of keywords and a description of the page. This makes it easy for external software to automatically index our pages. We may want to use the `scheme` attribute as a flag to indexing software that this `<meta>` tag is intended for indexing.

Now that we have seen how to prepare our pages, and the links of our pages for scalability and growth, let's look at how to structure our site.

Site Structuring

However we plan to lay out our site, we will almost certainly be using just a few basic structures. If we think of these structures as modules then their integration into the site becomes much easier.

Linear Structure

A **linear structure** is a sequence of pages that all follow on from each other in a logical order. There is no choice about which page to go to next: there is only the next one in line. Usually, all these pages will reside in the same folder.

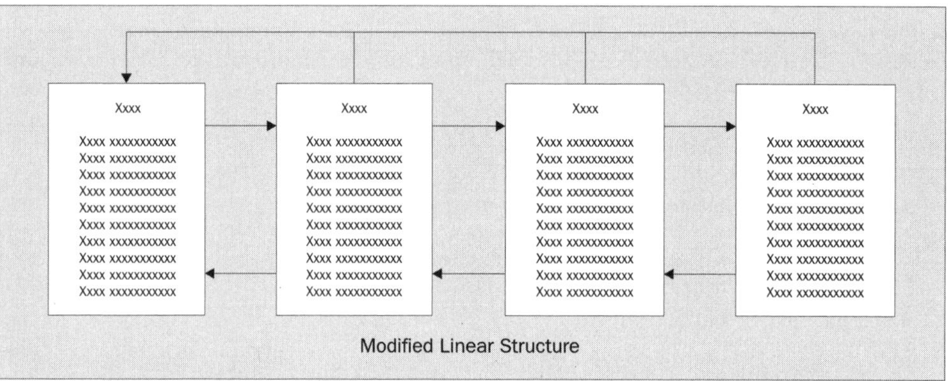

Modified Linear Structure

Thus, page 1 will be followed by page 2, which will then be followed by page 3, and so on until the last page is reached. Typically, there is also a link in each page back to the beginning of the structure.

Such structures are normally found in slide shows (see, for example, the XHTML slide show at `http://www.w3.org/Talks/1999/12/XHTML-XML99/slide1.html`), or in the checkout area of an e-commerce site where they want to lead the buyer through a logical series of steps. Whenever we shop on the web, we are invariably led through such a series of pages.

Hierarchical Structure

A **hierarchical structure** is more complex than a linear structure, and such a sequence of pages is normally thought of as having a 'pyramid' structure. There is a master page at the top of the pyramid, and this leads down into pages that deal with the topic in greater detail. A user thus has a choice about which page to view next. Usually, all the pages in such a structure are about a single topic. The following figure illustrates a three-tier pyramid structure – any number of layers are possible, but we prefer to stick to the physical limitations imposed by the 'three click' rule, as this aids a user's navigation of the site:

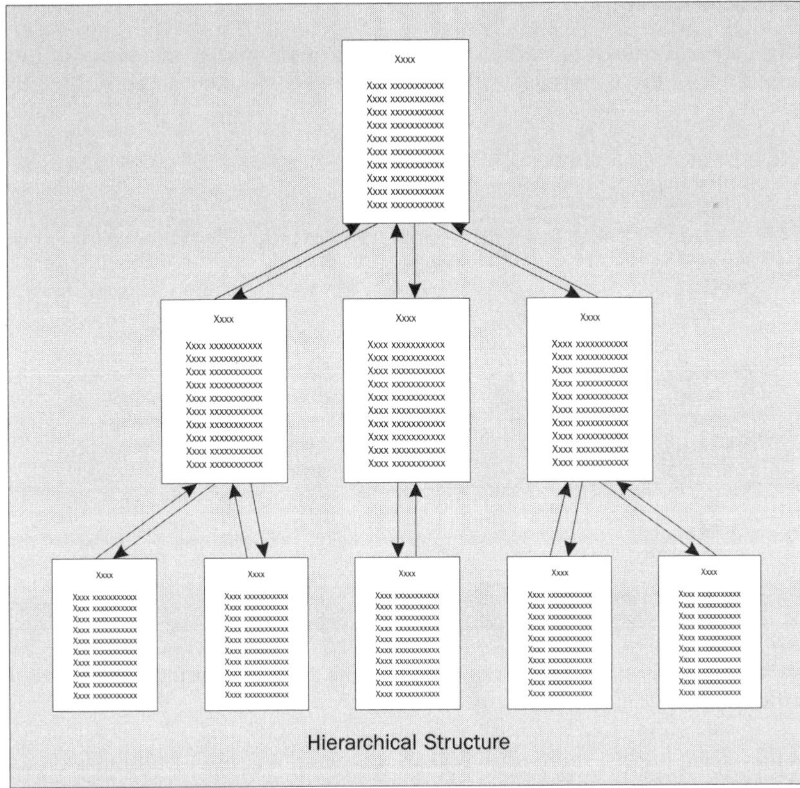

Hierarchical Structure

Typically, each of the tiers of pages will reside in its own folder. Each page will have links to its child pages and to the master page of the module; it goes without saying that each page will also link back to the home page, and to any other relevant orientation pages.

The 'three click' rule limits most hierarchical structures to three layers, and the 'seven link' rule limits each layer to seven pages. If a hierarchy gets larger than this, it is time to start thinking about dividing it into two separate modules. How you do this depends on the site and its information content. There is no requirement to have both of the new modules equal in size, or to have both of them in the same structure. For example, a sub-topic could be moved from the hierarchical structure and placed in an adjacent linear structure.

Combined Structure

As indicated above, in many cases there will be a combination of linear and hierarchical structures. Typically many child pages will contain links to sibling pages. Do not over do this though as a plethora of links can disorientate the viewer. The viewer should always have a good idea of where they are in your site. Although I'm repeating myself, I can't stress enough that people don't like being lost!

Modular Site Design

In fact, any large site will consist of a whole series of modules built up of a series of hierarchical or linear structures. Each of these modules will share graphics, style sheets, and scripts. Here is a typical small site:

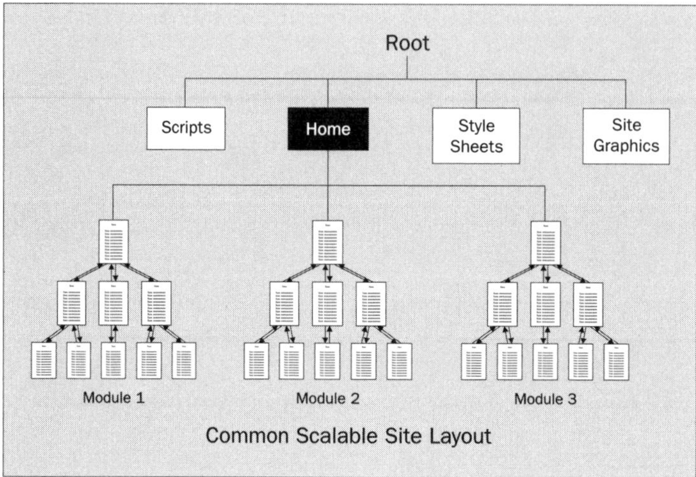

The modules are branched off the home page, and all the ancillary folders containing our scripts, style-sheets and graphics are on the root element.

Although this may seem logical, there is no reason why we can't put our modules on the root itself. The following shows the structure of a large site. Only a few of the modules are shown, but they are all on the root element:

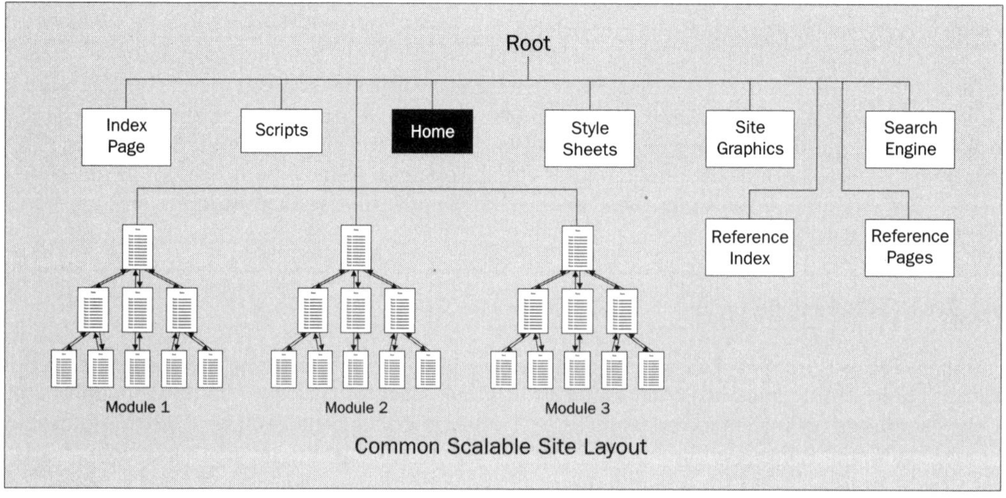

This site has also expanded to include a table of contents or site map, an index page and a search engine. All these make navigation through a large site much easier.

> **Search engines are a tremendous boon for users of sites. There are several that can be had for free. Visit `http://www.webmonkey.com` or search the Web with Yahoo to find out how to get such an engine for your site.**

If we have the foresight to label all our pages with meaningful `<meta>` and `<link>` elements we can build a new index and table of contents using simple software. As by this time all our modules are under the control of separate teams, we just run this software once a day, and can always be assured of an up-to-date index and site map. Showing how you'd go about writing this software is unfortunately beyond the scope of this book.

The site also includes a lot of reference material. This is material that does not easily fall into a single module or which needs to be shared among several modules. It is always a good idea to put material that might fall into this category into a separate folder right at the beginning of the site building; otherwise, we will be faced with the prospect of moving files from one module to another, or of linking from one module to another. This can disorientate the user. Furthermore, all reference files can (and should) be provided with a 'back' link (see below).

Advantages of Modular Design

The advantages of modular design should now be quite apparent, but it is useful to have them explicitly listed:

- **Scalability**: a modular site can grow to any size without overwhelming the resources
- **Orientation**: users hate the feeling of being lost in cyberspace; a modular site keeps the user orientated, and keeps them coming back
- **Coherent Links**: a modular site allows ease of navigation
- **Ease of Maintenance**: a modular site is easy to maintain
- **Division of Labor**: this goes with ease of maintenance. Different teams can be responsible for each module, and the roles of content provider, designer, network administrator, and Internet engineer can all be separated. Each can then concentrate on what they do best.

Internet Applications

Many sites will contain a group of pages that can only be described as an 'internet application'. This is a group of pages that are designed to act and function as a coherent whole, in much the same way as an application (like a spreadsheet package, for example) on our desktop. Such a group of pages may be used to (say) search for and purchase an airline ticket, or to plan a trip, or to purchase a car, and so on. These pages may be bound to together using cookies, frames, and/or client and server side script.

A full description of an internet application is beyond the scope of this book, although it is discussed in more depth in Chapter 19. Typically, Internet applications are said to consist of three tiers, a data layer, a business layer, and a presentation layer.

The data layer will contain all the data that the application uses as raw material; the business layer consists of the logic need to manipulate this data; and the presentation layer is the interface that receives user input and displays the results. The following figure illustrates this concept:

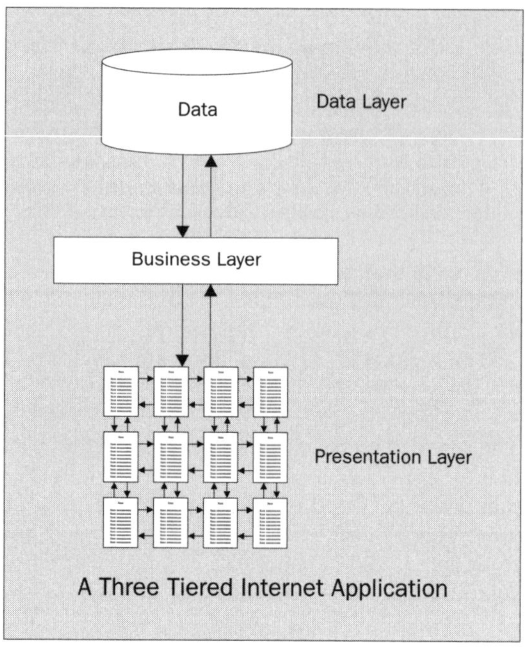

The data layer is usually a database residing on a server, although increasingly the data is being stored as a structured XML file. The business layer will usually reside on the server, although a lot of the primary manipulation of data will also be carried out using script on our XHTML pages; and the presentational layer is, of course, our set of web pages.

In reality, if we plan to set up any e-commerce site we will be including an Internet application in our site. If we intend to sell from our site, then the position of the application should be sketched in our original story board: Internet applications should be organized as separate modules.

Branding

Any marketing guru will tell us that branding is the single most important thing we can do to push our product. Customers should be able to associate a name, a logo, an icon, or even a particular font or color scheme with our site.

If we are building a site for a particular company then most of these decisions will have already been made for us. If, however, we are starting from scratch, we need to give some thought to these issues.

Trademarks and Logos

Spend a little time thinking about a logo. If you are not a professional designer, you may even want to employ a designer to create a logo for you. A good logo has the following characteristics:

- It is simple
- It is memorable
- It is unique
- It is adaptable

This is not a book on design, but look around you at various logos and see how they conform to these rules.

Once you have a logo, place it discreetly on every page and at every reasonable opportunity, but without going overboard...

Color Schemes

Give some thought to the color scheme that you are going to employ, and then use it on *every* page of your site. This gives a global feel to your site. Again color schemes should not be obtrusive, and should be designed to show off the content of your site, as discussed in the next chapter.

Company Style

Although some style elements are out of our control, such as which font a user might have on their platform, a lot are not. Use a style sheet to enforce a 'company style'. Make sure that margins are consistent from page to page, that headings are the same size and color, and that all your pages of a certain type use the same linking paradigm.

Remember that images, style sheets and client side scripts are cached, so once loaded on a user's machine they take no time at all to load on to our page.

Page Design

The concepts of page design are fully discussed in the next chapter; here we will just look at a few of the concepts that relate to site design as a whole.

The Inverse Pyramid

In school and college we were taught to develop an argument from basic principles. In other words all our essays had a pyramidal structure facts-thesis-conclusion. In marketing we want to present our conclusions *first*!

Research shows that people do not read web pages, they just scan them looking for information. If they find the information they're looking for, they may then start to read, but only 5% of page look-ups result in the page being scrolled (Jacobsen)! This makes it imperative that we put all the information in an eye-catching heading. The tabloids are masters of this. Who can resist headlines like these?

> **"Titanic survivor found alive on iceberg"**
> **"Elvis alive and arrested for indecent exposure in Des Moines"**

This is not to suggest that your content should follow this trend, but at least make sure that your page template is set up in such a way that you get your message across at the top of the page. For example, "New molecule found in gas cloud in deep space" is far more informative than "Space story: chemistry". Be aware of what your audience will want or looks for from your site, and title your sections specifically for them.

Linking Paradigms

The following page is the HTML Writers Guild page at `http://www.hwg.org`. It demonstrates good usage of the side links (or 'two column') linking paradigm. The links on the left of the page take us to the standard departments, and the links on the right of the page take us to recent or temporary links.

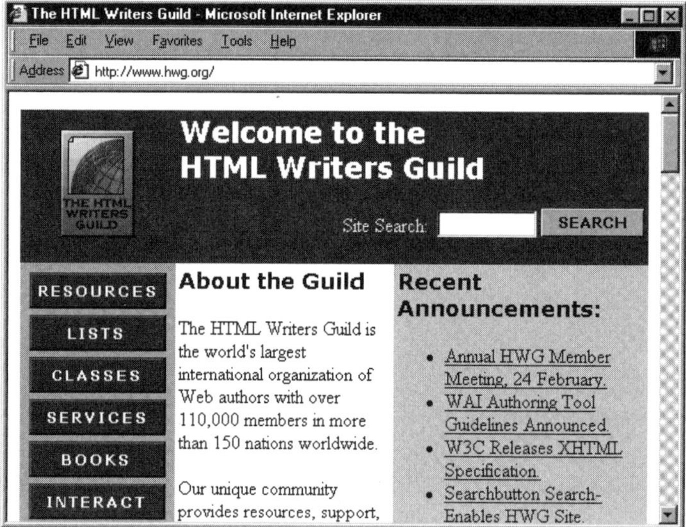

Validation

All your web pages should validate against the XHTML Document Type Definition (or DTD). This will allow the use not only of XML tools to manage your site, but will also allow us to use all the XHTML tools that will shortly appear on the market.

Personalization

Personalization is where a visitor views your web page on their browser, and the page will contain their own name. So, for example, if Angus McFool views your web site, then you may have some text that says "Welcome back to my web site, Angus!". Similarly, if Hamish McBrilliant viewed your pages at the same time, he would see the text "Welcome back to my web site, Hamish!". Obviously, this is done through some automatic programming, where the person's name is inserted into the web page. This can be done through the use of cookies or it can be done on the server side. Server side personalization is much more powerful and will not be covered in this book, but we will look a little at using cookies in Chapter 17.

If you are operating a store, personalization of your site is a must. Even if you are not operating a store, if you expect repeat visitors, or if your site is password accessed, then personalization is a very nice added touch.

Site Management

We will just end this chapter with a few words on site management. If the site has been set up correctly this should not be a time-consuming chore. In fact, most of the work of the site should be just updating the site with fresh content, and removing old!

Content Management

New content is the lifeblood of any site, and is what keeps visitors coming back. If you are producing a large number of fresh pages, consider stashing them in a data store, and using a CGI or ASP program to incorporate them into a page template. The exact way to do this is beyond the scope of this book. Essentially, though, the content is composed as a fragment of XHTML which can be imported into our template page by scripts operating on the sever. One advantage of doing this is that if a decision is made to change the 'house style' then only the template pages need to be changed.

Moving Pages

If a page becomes obsolete we may need to move it to a different area of our site. However people may still have links to this page, so we need to leave behind a flag to let people know where the page has been moved to.

Here is a typical page that we leave behind:

```
<html>
  <head>
    <title>Moved Page</title>
  <meta http-equiv="refresh" content="5;'../strict.htm'" />
  </head>
  <body>
    <h3>Page moved</h3>
    <p>This page has been moved to
    <a href="../strict.htm">www.mysite/strict[2].htm</a>.
    Please update your bookmarks or favorites list.</p>
  </body>
</html>
```

Obviously, the new page must exist at the specified location.

Organize Labor

When sites get large several people will become involved in its organization. However, it is always a good idea to have only one or two people with posting privileges (that is, with the 'right' to modify the content of the web site). If too many people have posting privileges, the lines of responsibility become blurred.

However, with good site design teams can be assigned various areas and functions in the site and there will be no duplication of effort. In fact, much of the routine maintenance can be done using software. Most of the 'out of the box' HTML authoring packages have some kind of software associated with them. If you want customized software for your site, you'll probably need to write your own, and that is definitely out of scope for this book!

Links and Link Rot

However well managed a site is there are going to be links, both internal and external, that do not work. Luckily, there are now programs (although there are no free ones available) that will run through all of the links on your site, and check that each link is still valid. We would suggest doing this at least once a month. On a really large site, sections of the site can be tested on a rotating basis.

Once a bad link is found, the page that contains the link must be manually reviewed to see if removing the link leaves the sense of the page unchanged. Usually, all that has to be done is to remove the link or put in a replacement link.

Summary

In this chapter we looked at some of the factors involved in designing a site. We stressed the importance of having a coherent link policy to bind our pages together, and learned that there was a great deal of truth in the adage that the three most important things in site design were "ease of navigation, ease of navigation, ease of navigation!"

A modular structure of site design was proposed as being the most scalable, and one that led to the most easily managed sites.

We also looked at the importance of building meta data and data about link relationships into our pages so that this can be used by automated tools in site management.

Branding was discussed as an important marketing tool, and the value of having a consistent 'house style' was stressed.

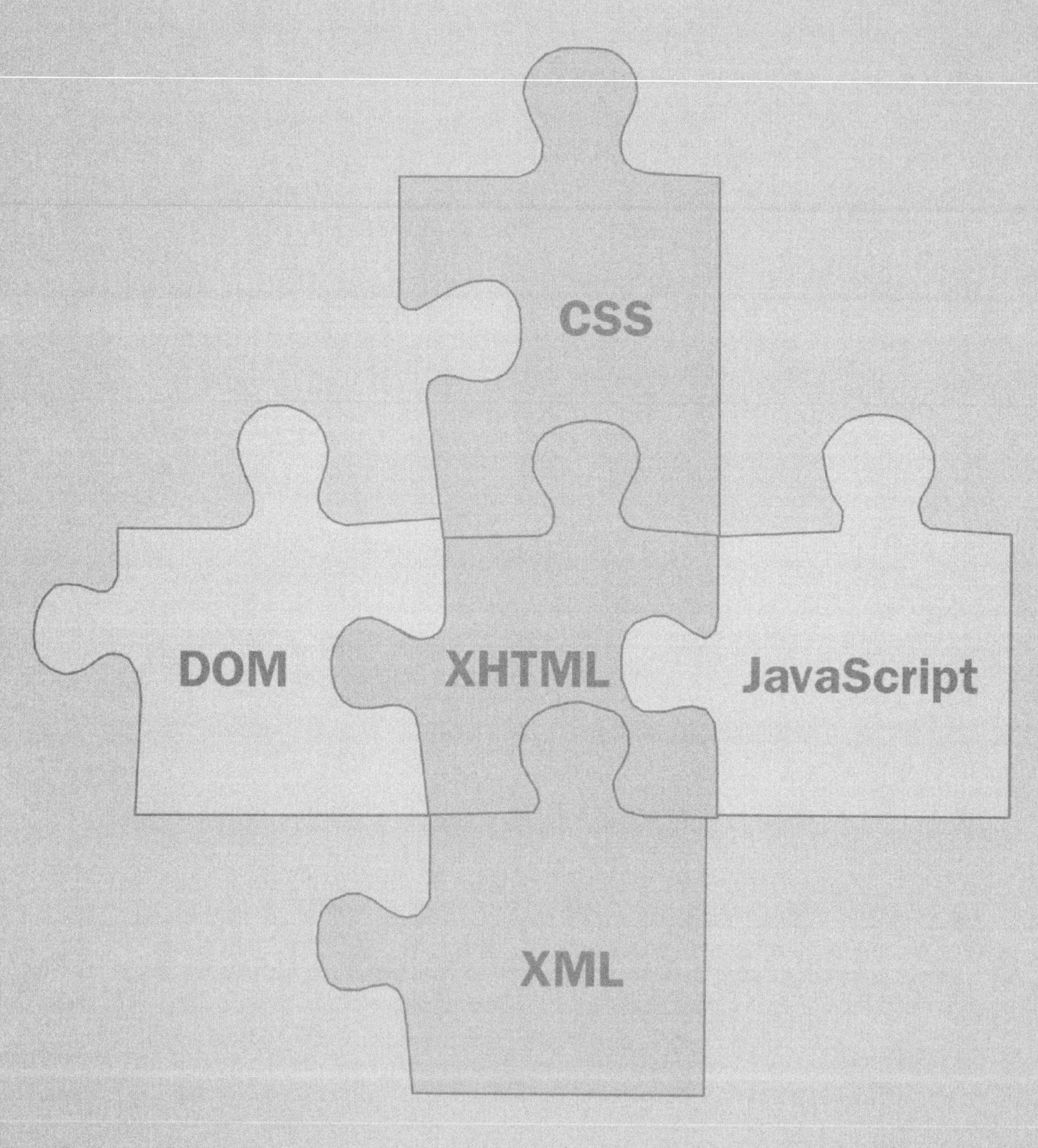
CSS
DOM
XHTML
JavaScript
XML

Page Design

This chapter looks at how you can improve your page design in terms of color, font and positioning of content on the page. We'll be talking about design rather than the details of how to implement the design elements using XHTML and CSS, which you will have learnt from other chapters. Since we're covering a wide range of subjects in a relatively short space, the treatment of each topic is naturally not that deep, but we hope it's useful nonetheless.

In this chapter we will cover:

- Something about the use of color in layout, including how to specify the color you want and which colors go together.
- Hypertext links and page layout, including the number of links on the page and their color.
- A little about the use of background images for web pages, in terms of what works and what does not.
- Something about the use of fonts, which ones to choose and which sizes and combinations are useful for Web pages
- The use of CSS to improve layout, with a few examples of what can be done

The Use of Color on Web Pages

We begin with a brief discussion of color. There are a number of ways of setting the color of XHTML elements and Chapter 9 gives many examples and explains their use. Appendix C talks about how colors are defined and the browser-safe palette, so if you haven't read about that yet you should take a brief look now. This section gives some hints on how to choose a color scheme for your Web pages.

The Background Color

Which color should you use for the background? This is really a matter of personal taste but we have found that most people do not object to pastels. The following shades, taken from the browser-safe palette, are examples of colors that have been used with success.

Color	Hex value	RGB value
light peach	FFCC99	255, 204,153
light yellow	FF9999	255, 255, 153
light cream	FFFFCC	255, 255, 204
light beige	CCCC99	204, 204,153
light pink	FFCCFF	255, 204, 255
light green	CCFFCC	204, 255, 204
pale turquoise	CCFFFF	204, 255, 255

Remember that you can set the background color for either the whole document or for specific paragraphs, headings, lists and so on. This is covered in Chapter 9, especially the CSS `background` property.

The Color of the Text

You can set the color of the text using a numerical value, just as you can the color of the background. The CSS `color` property does the trick. You can choose to color the text for a given paragraph or a given heading, or make all heading 1 elements one color and all heading 2 elements another color. How to do this is covered in Chapter 9. When it comes to the choice of color for text, remember that you must have sufficient contrast between the background and text colors, and that it is best to specify both rather than to leave the choice to the browser default. This avoids the possibility that someone who's modified their browser to provide, say, white text on a black background, would have their background overridden to white by your page, but their text would remain black.

The larger the font, the more leeway you have in your choice of color, in that light colored heavy fonts can be read even though smaller sized text would be almost illegible.

It is worth noting that when documents are printed, the background color is usually left white. This means that text set to white against a dark background might look fine on the screen, but on paper nothing shows up!

Color Combinations on your Web Page

Many Web authors stick to a simple color scheme based on only three or four colors. Shades of the same color can be used successfully. Rather nice is to take a pastel shade as the background and then find a much darker shade of the same color for the text. For example:

- Dark forest green text on a pastel green base
- Maroon text on a fairy pink background
- Deep blue text on a sky blue background

Another idea is to limit your colors to black, white and two other contrasting colors, one of which is light and the other dark. For example:

- black, dark gray, sand, and white.
- black, dark blue, light blue, and white
- black, olive green, orange, and white

The 216-color Webmaster's Palette is available from `www.visibone.com` which is well worth a visit. Colors are shown in terms of brightness, vividness and hue and also more subtle attributes such as whether they are hard, dull, weak or faded.

Hypertext Links

Some people (software engineers are particularly prone) go overboard with hypertext links. The idea that everything can be interconnected fascinates them. They imagine that, by linking everything together (in however unstructured a way), information somehow magically blossoms and gains in depth and utility.

In extreme cases, programmers proudly arrange for hypertext links to be inserted automatically from a keyword each time it is encountered. So, for example, each instance of a given word in a manual becomes hypertext and is linked to a designated page elsewhere in the document. If the word in question appears five times in a paragraph, then so be it: five identical hypertext links will manifest themselves in close proximity on the page, much to the amazement of the reader!

Here are some simple rules of thumb for the beginner using hypertext links

- **Think about them in the context of an overall site map and design**. Design the site as a whole before you start to insert hypertext links into your pages. This sounds like common sense but few people do it! The trouble is that once you have got the hang of the anchor element, hypertext links become irresistible and the temptation to insert them ad-hoc is strong.
- **Don't use hypertext links in very large numbers**. Hypertext links can be distracting in large numbers. If you are designing Web pages for the general public, keep the number of hypertext links down to a few important and useful ones. A large number of links may the spoil the design of the page and make it harder to read the text.
- **Make sure that your links are well organized for maintenance purposes**. Each time you reorganize your files or update the information, you need to be sure that all the links still work. The more links the more likely it is that broken links will occur! The more disorganized your site the less likely it is that sooner or later the links will go wrong.

- **Avoid a dazzling array of links in distracting bright colors**. Occasionally you see that the author has chosen to insert bright red links which are not underlined. First of all the reader is confused because the links don't actually *look* like links. Also the bright red may mislead some readers who think that red text actually means important pieces of information, rather than a hyperlink. Bright colors look particularly odd where the author has opted such a large number of hypertext links rather than a few carefully chosen ones. If the author has been judicious in his use of links and kept them to a modest number, then brightly colored links may work, especially if they are part of a carefully thought-out overall page design.
- **Don't choose a color for your links that is hard to distinguish from the general text**. The other extreme is to choose a color almost indistinguishable from the general color of the text. The author has seen dark green and dark brown hypertext links used on occasion. If you choose to switch the underlining of hypertext links off then it is particularly hard to distinguish links from the text.
- **Look out for combinations of color which would be hard for a color blind person to see**. Some readers are color-blind. Confusion between orange, brown and olive green is common so hypertext links which are not underlined may well not be seen as links.

Background Images

Background images for web pages remain extremely popular although nowadays there are less of the busy background images dominating Web page text. There are many fun (and free) backgrounds available on the Web. To find them, search on "free backgrounds". There are also many tools available for converting your own image into a tile that will look nice as a background. It is best to use a graphic with only a very narrow range of colors, which will fade into the background rather than stand out and take over the screen. Make sure also that you keep the graphic small for download time. The image needs to be either a GIF or a JPEG.

Here are simple rules of thumb to follow with regards to the background to use:

- **Don't use tiled background images which dominate the text**. Tiled images are the simplest background image. This is where a small graphic is specified and the browser automatically tiles it across the background of your document. It all depends on your taste. The bottom line, though, must surely be that any text is easily readable against the background.
- **Try using a side panel and leave the text on a plain background**. Side panels are a kind of tiled image. However, they are constructed so that they run down the side of the page only, so as not to interfere with the text. The idea is that the browser repeats them in the usual way, but because they are so long and thin, effectively they are only repeated downwards. You can either make your own images for the purpose, or download one of the many "borders" available on the Web. The advantage of the side panel is that you shift the text away from covering the image down the side of the screen so that the words show up properly on a simple plain color, as in the example below.
- **Photographs** can be used as backdrop images. You need to make them load fast. If you are going to show content over the top, you need to blur the photo and reduce the contrast dramatically. As a JPEG image the photo will not only compress well but will not interfere with the text.

We'll now turn our discussion to the use of fonts.

Considerations in Using Fonts

A **font** is a set of characters that all share the same visual characteristics. Characters of a particular font are all in the same type family, are all of the same size and all have the same attributes such as italic, bold, underlined etc. So, strictly speaking, Helvetica 14pt bold is one font and Helvetica 12pt italic is another.

Times Roman, Helvetica, and Arial are all examples of **types**. The main categories of type include Sans Serif, Serif, Script, Monospaced, and Decorative, and examples of each of these are given below.

Serif Fonts

10pt Times New Roman *Times New Roman italic* **Times New Roman bold**

10pt Garamond *Garamond italic* **Garamond bold** ***Garamond bold italic***

Sans-serif Fonts

10pt Arial *Arial italic* **Arial bold** ***Arial bold italic***

10pt Arial Narrow – this is more compact than the regular Arial type face

10pt Arial Black – a bolder version of Arial

8pt Verdana – this is very readable at smaller point sizes – this is set in Verdana 6pt

Monospace Fonts

10pt Courier New

Script/Cursive Fonts

10pt Lucida Calligraphy - an example of a cursive typeface

12pt Bradley Hand ITC

Decorative Fonts

14 pt Impact

14pt Amelia BT

14pt Bauhaus Md BT

Bitmapped and Outline Fonts

You will have heard talk of **bitmapped** fonts and **truetype** fonts. Many beginners are confused as to the difference between these. We will explain a little to clarify the situation.

A bitmap is stored by the computer as a series of "1"s and "0"s. Each 1 or 0 corresponds to a point in a rectangular array. The character is described in terms of a pattern composed of pixels illuminated according to the pattern of 0s and 1s in the array. The trouble with bitmapped fonts is that they take up a large amount of storage space. A bitmapped font containing 256 characters, each drawn in a grid of 24 by 16 pixels would need about 12 Kbytes of storage on disk. Imagine now that you need 12 different point sizes each in normal, bold, italic, and bold italic. This amounts to 48 different fonts occupying a rather large amount of disk space. Now that people expect to have certainly dozens of fonts available on their machine, bitmapped fonts have become impractical.

The alternative to the bitmapped font is the **outline font**. An outline font contains a mathematical description of the outline of each character. These descriptions – which take up very little space on disc – can be used by the computer to draw letters, numbers and other characters on the screen as required. To draw a character, an interpreter takes the mathematical description, scales the character to the size required, and then decides which pixels on the screen to illuminate. The outlines are therefore used to generate bitmaps for the fonts as and when they are needed.

Truetype fonts are outline fonts which use a specialised programming language for **hinting** – the adjustments of the outline to match the size of the pixels – some 200 hundred instructions are included in the language but good hinting is very hard to do. Windows and the Mac all come with inbuilt support for truetype fonts, which are the most widely used fonts. Because truetype fonts (often labelled "TT") fonts use clever hinting and because they are scalable outline fonts, they are highly recommended for web page design. There are tools which allow you to define your own fonts, but they don't use hinting. For large decorative headings this is not such a problem.

Using Fonts on Your Web Pages: Simple Guidelines

Having introduced a little discussion on the subjects of fonts in the context of computing, we now go on to include some simple guidelines on how to use fonts in practice.

- **You are best using the common truetype fonts which you know are likely to be on most peoples' machines**. Arial, Times Roman, Courier, Verdana, and even Century Gothic are common. If you use an unusual font, always remember to specify alternatives for browser which haven't got the font you specified. This is easily done in CSS with the `font-family` property which can be used to specify a default of "serif" or "sans serif" for the text. Browsers can choose the best match they have to these categories and your pages should look fine.
- **Decorative fonts are best left for headings**. Even then, try to specify a default font using the CSS `font-family` property, as above.
- **Don't go overboard on fonts and use too many different ones on the same page**. Normally using two will suffice: one for headings and one for the text. Certain combinations of font don't usually work. For example, don't use a script and italic font on the same page, don't use more than one decorative font on the same page.
- **Try using different weights of the same type to make the page look more interesting**. If you have a rather boring page with no graphics, try setting key phrases to a strong bold (CSS provides the `font-weight` property) and these will pull the reader to the page. Not only does the use of contrasting weights make the page more attractive, it is one of the most effective ways of organizing information.

- **Never put two sans serif typefaces on the same page** unless you are absolutely sure that you know what you are doing. If you want to use two typefaces on the same page, you should take them from two different categories of type.
- **Be careful using small size type**. If the lower case letters of a font are small in relation to the size of the capitals, the font will not be legible at small font sizes. In particular if you use cursive (handwriting) fonts for emphasis you will find you need to increase their size to match the legibility of neighboring text. Fonts like Verdana are especially designed for screens including small font sizes and are therefore recommended for paragraph text. Times New Roman is also fairly legible at small sizes.
- **In general a font size will appear smaller on Netscape Navigator than on Microsoft's Internet Explorer**. If you make the text just comfortably visible on Microsoft IE, it will be illegible on Netscape Navigator! This is a great nuisance to designers. Point size is stated to be 1/72 of an inch, but a screen inch is not a 'physical' inch. It might be so on paper but not on a screen. Why does this happen? The problem arises because the point size has to be mapped to a specific number of screen pixels. If the ratio of pixels to point size were identical for each browser, all would be fine and style sheet authors could relax. Unfortunately, the ratio varies so you cannot guarantee that a given point size will be translated into a given number of pixels (and therefore a given size of glyph) when shown on the screen.

Below is an example web page showing just some of the types and fonts available. Notice the confusion caused by so many fonts!

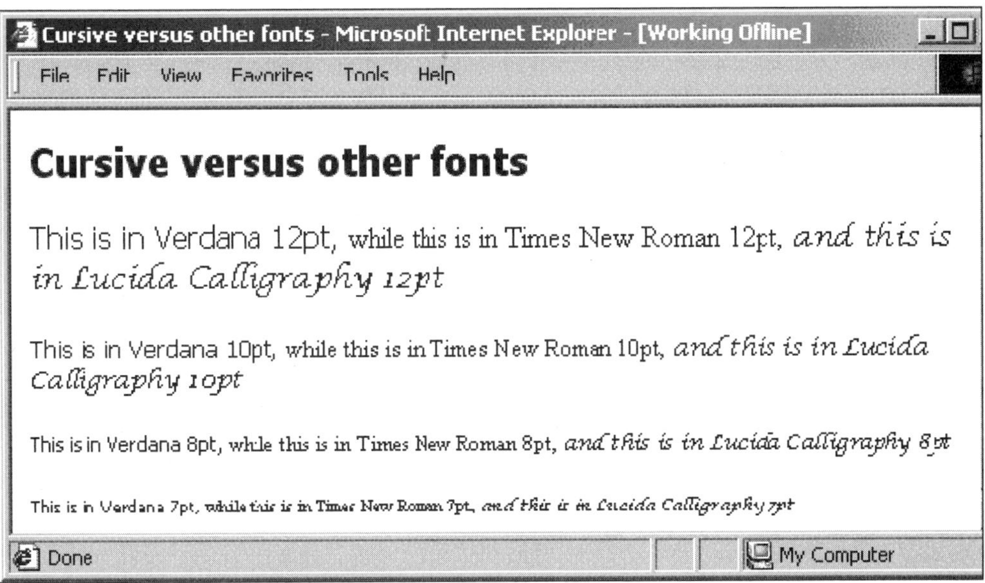

We'll now have a look at some text layout issues.

The Layout of Text

Here are some ideas for laying out text on your pages. The idea here is to get you thinking about design issues rather than implementation in XHTML. On the other hand, where a simple CSS property is useful, we indicate this briefly in the text.

- **Repetition: repeat some aspect of the page design throughout the entire site**. The repetitive element might be a certain kind of font, a particularly bold font used for headings (use the CSS `font-family` property), a specific margin setting for the page, the use of rules across the page of a particular thickness, and so on. Of course color is very useful as a repetitive element: try giving all the headings a certain color (the CSS `color` property does the trick) or using a subtle background behind headings (which you can do with the CSS `background` property)
- **Contrast keeps the attention of the reader**. Make your pages more interesting by using contrast to grab peoples' attention. For example, you can make the headings "reversed out" on black and use a large bold sans-serif font. This could contrast text in a straightforward font such as Times. Another idea is to use a background color behind text in certain paragraphs (the CSS `background` and `padding` properties are useful).
- **Space out the text and introduce margins and other "white space" for easier reading and a nicer layout**. CSS provides the `padding` and `margin` properties for these purposes. There is also a property called `line-height` which pushes the lines of text further apart.
- **Keep things simple.** Avoid using a technology or new trick just for the sake of it, and keep distracting ads to a minimum. Don't expect people to download plugins – they won't! Instead, they will tend to go elsewhere. Concentrate on delivering the information rather than making the page look so super-amazing that the message disappears in a haze of animated graphics, blinking text and other gimmicks.
- **Avoid the need for scrolling except where possible**. Users generally look at the content area of the page and ignore the navigation menu bars and ads when they scan a new page. If a page doesn't look relevant to the user's needs, the Back button will invariably be clicked after two to three seconds.
- **Don't use blinking text!** Except under very rare circumstances, blinking text simply annoys people. The same goes for animated text: use it very sparingly if at all.
- **Try and use the layout of the text to help navigation**. Many large sites today have grown complex interfaces to match. How can these be simplified? Sometimes such a site has 60 or 70 hypertext links on its home page, and these lead to a wealth of diverse material on perhaps hundreds of pages. Although people who know the pages well may be able to find what they want without too much difficulty, for the newcomer or occasional visitor, the number of links may be confusing.

  The W3C home page (below) is an example of a site that has evolved over a number of years into a deep web of complexity in its own right! The site is very large and very much text-based with practically no graphics. Finding your way around can be a challenge unless you are a technical "insider".

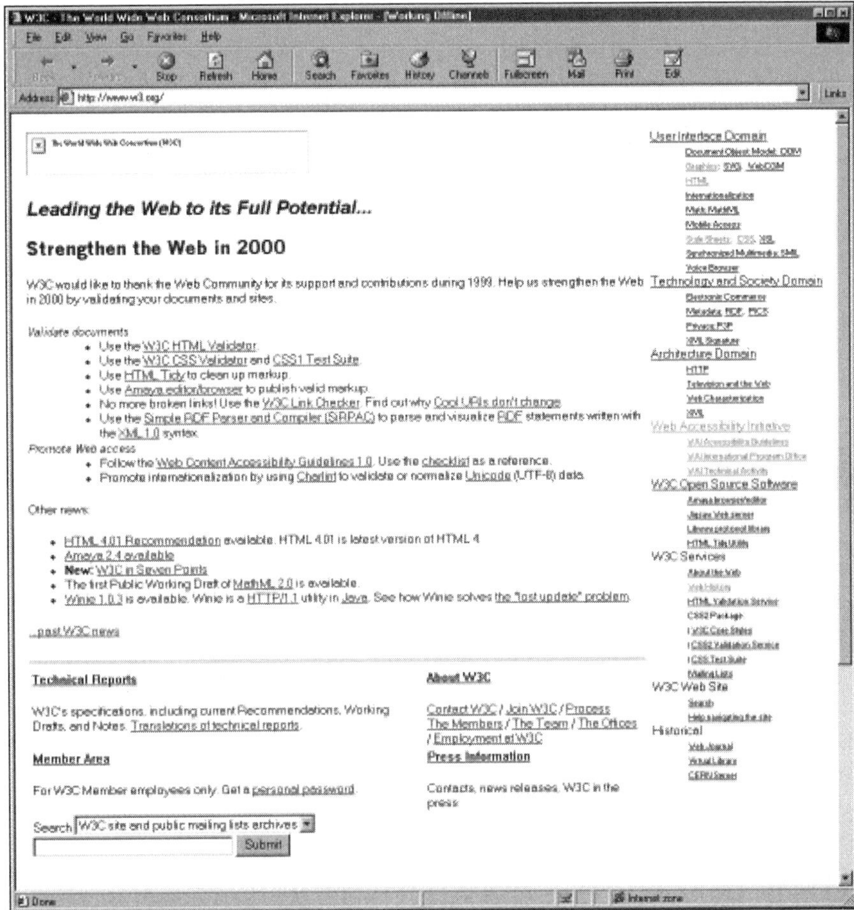

Here's one way we could make the same information more accessible by introducing a different layout. The difference is that headings have been chosen to organize the text, and color used to help separate the categories.

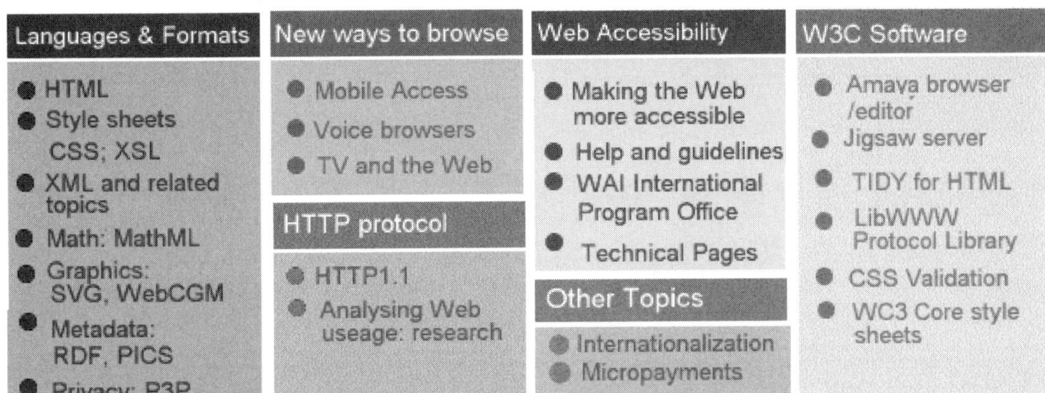

- **Keep in mind the audience for the site**. What sort of people will visit it? Why will they visit it, and what kind of prior knowledge will they have? The page design and layout will need to reflect the different needs of these kinds of groups. Although it is easier to hope that all these groups can share the same interface, in practice this is impossible because each group will have its own way of perceiving the area, its own model and expectations of the domain, and its own terminology.
- **Use the page layout to make obvious the headings people will be looking for.** Once you have understood the needs of the various sets of user, you can go onto the next stage and attempt to establish the headings that each group of visitors to the site would most anticipate. In other words, give them the headings that they would hope to find on a page designed just for them, and use the page layout to help those headings stand out. You may need to ask users directly which headings they think are useful, and which ones are missing from initial rough designs for pages. Guessing is always risky!

Links to Information on Page and Site Design

You might like to have a look at the following:

- `http://www.useit.com/` – Jakob Nielsen's masterful essays on good and bad design. Nielsen writes specifically about user interface, not about design in the graphical sense of the word.
- `http://www.webpagesthatsuck.com/` – Vincent Flanders invites you to learn good design by studying examples of bad design.
- `http://www.webreference.com/` – provides links to articles, tutorials and design resources.

Using CSS for Page Layout: Some Examples

CSS provides an easy-to-use way of making the layout of web pages more interesting. If you want to see what CSS can do, why not have a look on the World Wide Web Consortium CSS page at `http://www.w3.org/style/css`. The page has a link to Core Style Sheets and here you can experiment with a number of specially-designed style sheets for web pages. Meanwhile to whet your appetite, here are three contrasting ways of presenting the same document (the CSS1 specification itself) using style sheets. If you want to see how it's done, go to the W3C site and have a look at the source code for generating these examples and more.

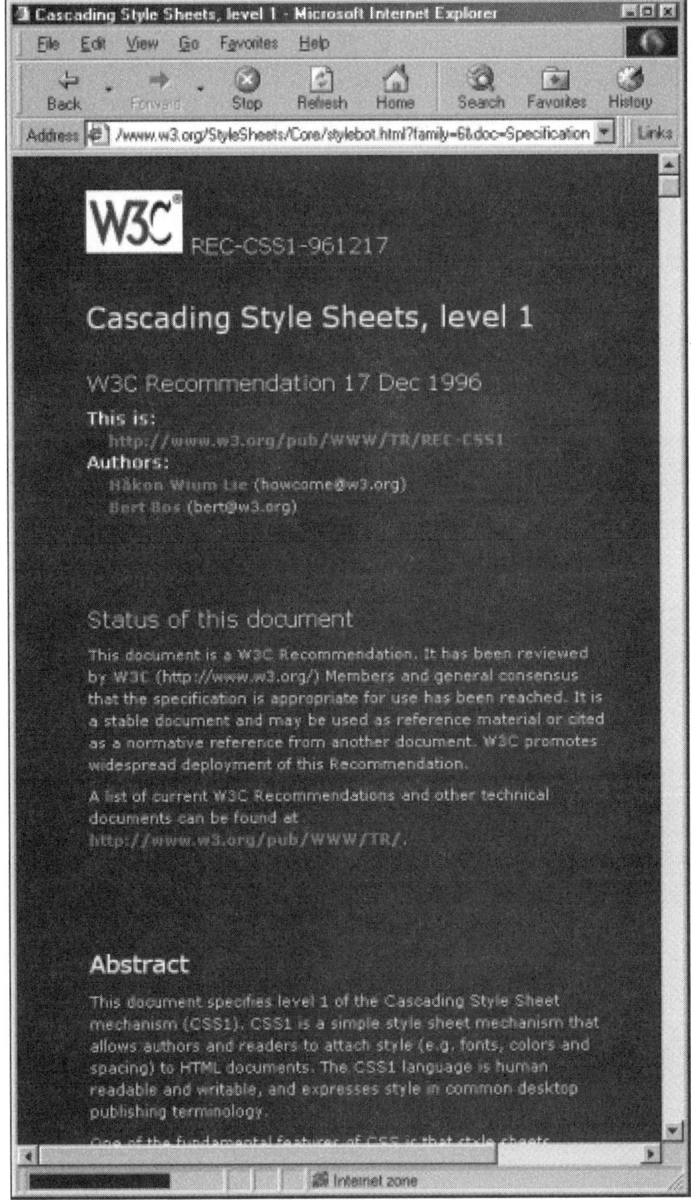

Features

Hypertext links have been set (using CSS) to a different color from the browser default.

The color and font of text is controlled. Use `font-family` and `color` properties to do this. Notice effective use of black background with the `color` property to set the font color for different elements.

The relative weighting of headings has been changed from the browser default by using `font-weight` properties. Space has been inserted before headings to make it easier to read the text. This can be done with `margin` and `padding` properties.

This page would *not* be useful if printed as the white text would not show up if the background color was not also printed out.

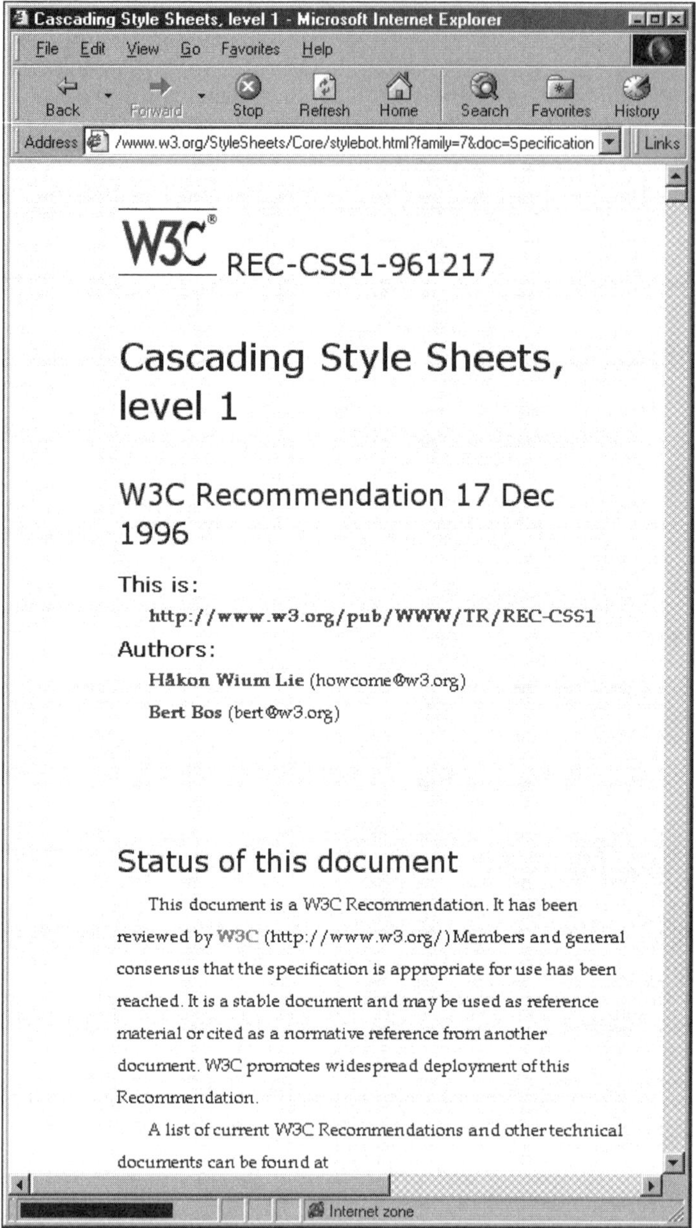

Features
White background with black sans-serif text; hypertext links highlighted red against yellow (trust me!).

The font-family property has been used to carefully control the font for the document including the size of the headings.

The font for the headings is set up to be different from the main body of the text.
A large left-hand margin has been used to indent the text. Meanwhile the headings have been set up with less of a margin; this is especially the case with the top level heading.

The lines of text have been spaced out by using the line-height property which makes the text easier to read.

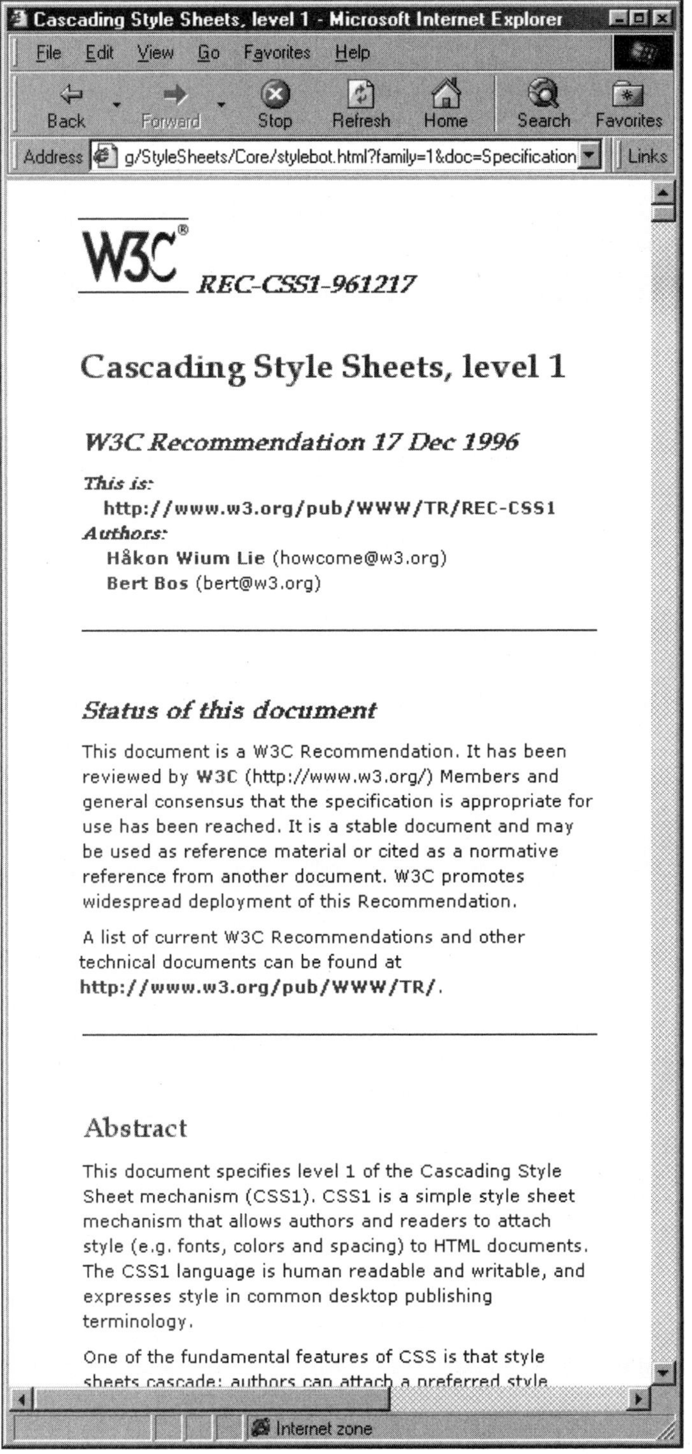

Features
Heading specified as Georgia, Minion Web, Palatino.

The font-weight property has been used to carefully control the look and feel of headings.

The line-height property has been used extensively to space text lines apart.

Margins top and bottom used to insert more "white space" into the layout.

Use of rules across the page to add cohesion to the design.

Worrying About Browsers

We'll now look at how to worry about different browsers when writing your XHTML pages. To do that, we'll just take a brief recap on how a browser works

HTML Browsers

HTML processors, better known as HTML browsers are simply SGML processors that have been built to handle one specific kind of document type. They have built-in knowledge of the HTML DTDs, and they also have a default built in style sheet.

This figure illustrates how an HTML browser works.

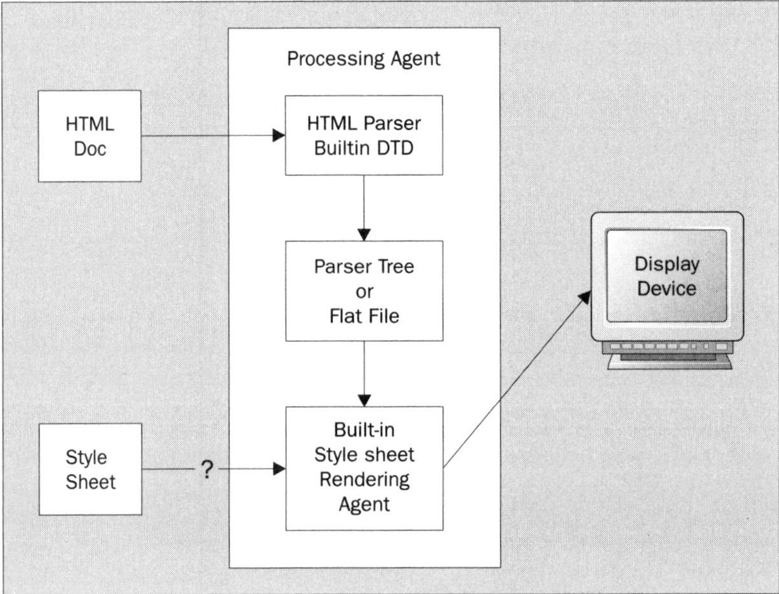

You will notice that a browser will not read an external DTD, it has the HTML DTD 'hard-wired' into it. Similarly, although the version 4 and up browsers handle style sheets, HTML browsers have a default style sheet 'hard-wired' into them, and an external style sheet is strictly optional.

The problem with most browsers is that they don't strictly conform to an official HTML DTD. They not only allow all kinds of bad markup but they also allow markup that is proprietary. That would not be so bad, but also sadly most of the browsers choke on some perfectly valid markup. Particularly badly handled is CSS. What this means is that a content author (you!) cannot be sure that their perfectly valid markup will display the way that it should!

There is absolutely nothing wrong with a browser manufacturer putting in experimental markup, but they should also support the standards! Authors, however, should only rely on experimental markup for authoring pages when they know that their audience is going to have the correct software to view it.

These problems arose because of the so-called 'browser wars', which we touched upon at the beginning of the book.

The Browser Wars

HTML started off as an academic format for the exchange of academic papers. It became mainstream when NCSA produced the first Mosaic browser that was capable of displaying Images. Many of the Mosaic team left NCSA and went to found a new company called Netscape. They soon started adding new functions and elements to their browser. About this time Microsoft realized that they had missed the boat, and in an effort to catch up produced their first IE browser and gave it away for free!

Netscape and IE were soon involved in a war to see who could add the coolest feature to their browser. This led to several great innovations such as JavaScript (produced by Netscape) and Java Applets, but it also gave us such elements as 'blink' and 'marquee'. Problems arose for the author because while the browser makers always supported their own legacy features (however bad) they did not give support to their rival's features, however good! Obviously something had to be done.

HTML was being standardized by the IETF standards body, but this body could not move nearly fast enough to keep up with events. What happened was that an industrial consortium was formed, the W3C, to issue recommendations for web interoperability. The director of the consortium was fittingly Tim Berners-Lee, the father of HTML, and both Netscape and Microsoft became members.

Both of these giants now at least pay lip service to the idea of standards, although they both still have a tendency to go off in their own direction. Most of the non-compliance with official recommendations are now small, but they are there nonetheless. As a web author it is our job to try and author a page that is viewable by anyone. This means that not only should we author a page that is in compliance to the official recommendation, but that we should also test the page on as many browsers as possible to ensure that there are at least no glaring problems.

Browser Usage

At the time of writing, Navigator 4.7 was the latest Netscape release, with the release of Gecko imminent, and IE5.0 is the latest Microsoft version. Bear in mind that it takes about 2 years for 85% of users to convert to the latest version.

Monitoring Your Clients

Although there are general figures available, all serious authors should monitor the viewers visiting their own site. This does not mean that we have to write complex scripts, all we have to do is sign up with a service that will do this for us. Typically they will ask you to install a small logo image on your page, and every time a user downloads their image the statistics will be recorded. We can then look at the statistics for our page anytime we want. There are several free services for doing this. Webtracker at `http://www.fxweb.com` is one such service.

Note, though, that the type of page you have can impact the type of browser that visits it. Cutting edge computer users, like programmers or gamers, tend to have higher end browsers, while home users may still be using older browsers, especially if they use AOL, where IE2 is the standard browser.

Differences Between Netscape and IE

We'll just summarize the areas in which Netscape and Internet Explorer differ.

- **Fonts** – The `<font>` tag was introduced in Netscape 2.0 and supported in all 2+ browsers. It has been deprecated in HTML 4.0, and will not be seen in the XHTML 2.0 specs.

  The CSS `font` property is supported in the 4+ browsers. Remember, though, that for a particular font to be displayed it must be on the clients platform. There are various technologies available for downloading fonts for particular pages. However both Microsoft and Netscape are pushing different technologies, so if you are going to use these technologies you will have to write different pages for different browsers.

- **Forms** – Forms are universal to all browsers and will be discussed in Chapter 15. The main problem that an author will encounter with forms is that the different browsers use a different Document Object Model to access the elements of the forms with scripting!

- **Layers** – `<layers>` is a proprietary Netscape element. Although you can do a lot of neat things with layers (and indeed if you are going to use animation in Netscape you will be forced to use them), our advice is not to use layers. They are not part of the official W3C recommendations, and CSS positioning allows you to do everything that you can do with layers. However, CSS positioning is not well supported by Netscape, although the word is that it will be by Gecko.

- **Frames** – Frames are supported in the main stream browsers after version 2. There are minor ways that Netscape and Microsoft differ if you are using script to access the frames (they use slightly different document models to handle the script), and you would be advised to test your pages in both browsers if you are using scripting.

- **Scripting** – Although some version of JavaScript will work in all browsers, some people will turn off the scripting engines in their browsers. This means that you should always let a viewer know if your page relies heavily on script. You can use a `<noscript>` element to show material on browsers that do not support scripts. Browsers that do support scripting will ignore the content of this element.

  The biggest difference between the two browsers is that Netscape browsers do not support VBScript, and interestingly neither do IE5 browsers running on Macs!

- **Style Sheets** – The first support for style sheets was found in IE3, but quite frankly this was so off base that it is not really worth using style sheets with this version! Luckily there are very few versions of IE3 remaining out there.

  Both IE4+ and NN 4+ give support for CSS1. IE5 is now compliant with about 97% of the spec. and includes good support for the positioning properties of CSS2. The major problem with IE5 is that it does not support the `white-space` property, which makes viewing of code and such difficult if our XHTML pages are sent as XML. The support in Gecko for CSS1 looks as if it will be close to 100%.

  It is especially important to test your pages if you are using style sheets.

- **DOM handling** – Unfortunately the Document Object Models of Netscape and Microsoft are very different, which makes it almost impossible to script a single set of pages for both browsers. Both do, however, handle a small subset known as the JavaScript DOM, and if we are aiming to use the DOM for general use we would be well advised to confine ourselves to this subset.

  IE5 has almost full support for both the W3C level 1 HTML and XML DOMs. Gecko has good support for both. Netscape 4 gives no support for either of these. DOMs are discussed in Chapter 18.

Dealing with Different Browsers

Faced with the fact that different pages will be rendered in different ways by different browsers, how do we, as authors, deal with this? Theoretically we can do any of the following:

- Write to the lowest common denominator
- Write pages that degrade gracefully to different browsers
- Write for just one browser
- Write different pages for different browsers
- Write one page and dynamically alter it on the server

Which option we elect to follow will depend chiefly on our intended audience, and the kind of page we are writing.

Our Audience

It is almost impossible to predict our audience, however our pages will probably be directed towards one of the following general categories.

Captive Audience

If we are writing pages for an Intranet , in other words an internal company network, we can have a fairly clear idea of our audience, and more importantly of the kind of browser they will be using. This means that we can just go ahead and write one kind of page, and be sure that it will meet the needs of our audience.

General Audience

Most pages will be written with a general audience in mind. Note that if we are writing a page for a government or other public site we will need to make sure that our page is fully accessible. In fact it is good practice to follow the accessibility guidelines (see later on in this chapter) in every page we build! If we do this we can be sure that our page can be viewed by anyone.

If the page is purely informational we will probably not be too worried about minor differences in presentation between different browsers and platforms as long as our content is easily viewable and understandable.

Artistic Pages

If we are writing for an artistic audience, or if we are particularly artistic ourselves, we will want to have complete control of how our page is laid out. We will want it to look exactly the same on different browsers. We will probably use a lot of graphics, and will even use 'invisible graphic' tricks to position our page elements in exactly the place we want them.

A major advocate of this philosophy is David Siegel. To learn more on how to render pages that are 'artistically correct' visit `http://www.dsiegel.com`

Commercial Pages

These are pages that buy and sell, or carry out other commercial activities. If you want to see an example of a great set of commercial pages visit `www.amazon.com`. In a commercial page our prime consideration is clarity and ease of use.

Now let's look at the options we have for dealing with cross-browser issues, always remembering our audience to help us decide on the best course of action.

Degrading gracefully

This is the basic concept behind style sheets. By 'degrading' we mean that if your browser does not support style sheets, it 'degrades' to a simple presentation. A style sheet can layout your page almost any way you want and can make your page as attractive and as fancy as you wish. However, if the browser viewing the page does not support style sheets your page should still be perfectly presentable and readable.

If you follow this approach do the following.

- Write a page that conforms to the lowest common denominator, e.g Netscape 2.0.
- Now fancy it up with your style sheet using the CSS1 specification. You can also add positioning from CSS2 if you wish.
- View your page on whatever browsers you have available (and if you are a commercial operation this may mean a lot of browsers).
- You will find that some browsers (the Netscape browsers) do not support positioning correctly, so if you use positioning make sure that you page degrades to these browsers.
- Be aware that IE3 misinterprets a lot of style sheet properties. You may even want to 'browser-sniff' (see below) and not send a style sheet to IE3 pages.

Write for Just One Browser

We might just take the view that we will only be bothered about writing our page for one particular browser. If we take this approach we will certainly save our selves a lot of heartache and trouble when writing our pages. However, we must accept the fact that some of our audience will not see the page at all.

Actually this is a very good approach to take if we are writing for a captive audience, such as for an Intranet as we mentioned above. You can be sure that everyone will have the same browser because in the intranet situation you can have control over that fact, something you can't do with a general web audience.

Write Different Pages for Different Browsers

Another solution is to write different pages for each browser type we want to cater for. If we are going to write different pages for different browsers, we're going to need a way to find out what kind of browser we are dealing with. This process is generally known as **browser sniffing**. We can sniff for a browser either on the server side, or on the client side.

Server Browser Sniffing

As we saw in Chapter 7, when our browser asks for a page using the HTTP protocol it sends an HTTP header, and one of these headers is entitled User-Agent. Programs on the server, such as ASP or a CGI program, can be written to interpret the information in this header and send the correct page back to the client. The actual details of how this are done are out of scope for this book, but see *Beginning ASP 3.0* (ISBN 1861003382, also by Wrox Press) to see how to do this and many other things using ASP.

Client Browser Sniffing

Using JavaScript, which we'll be learning later on in the book, we can sniff for browsers on the client side, and react accordingly. We'll see how we can do this in Chapter 17.

How Many Pages should We Write?

It is of course possible to get carried away, and write a different page for every browser out there! However, if you have a really fancy page it is probably sufficient to just write special pages for IE4+, NN4 and a basic page for other browsers. Send Opera the IE4 page, unless you are using some of the special features of IE5 such as XML Islands (sorry, another topic we won't be able to cover in this book!).

Use Proxy Servers

The last method to be discussed is the method of dynamically altering our page on the server. This is where XHTML really shines!

Because XHTML is well-formed XML, we can use all the XML tools available for transforming one XML document type to another XML document type, and deliver a page suitable for almost any client. It is not in the scope of this book to go into the details of how this is done, but it is in fact very easy to do.

What happens when a device that employs a proxy server orders a file, is that the request is not sent to the server that hosts the file, but is sent to the proxy server. This proxy server will request the file from the other server, and run it through a scripting engine that will create an HTML stream that is more easily read by the small device in question. The process is illustrated graphically below.

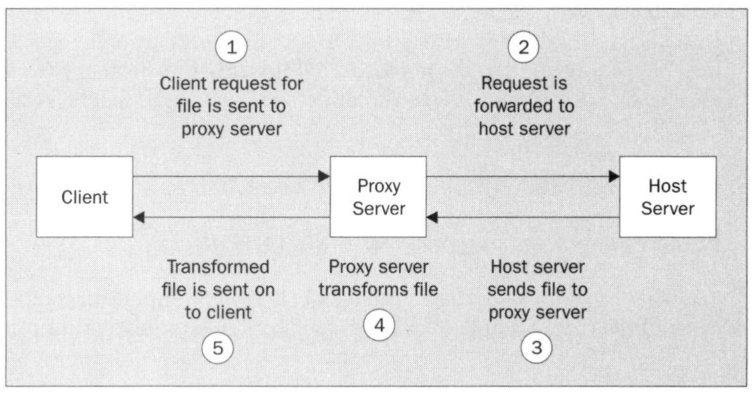

Building Pages 'on the fly'

A proxy server is strictly speaking a server that "belongs" to the client. It is likely that special clients like mobile phones or WebTV will route their page requests through their own server.

However we can use our own server to transform a page. I'm sure at some point you'll have clicked on a link whose URL was something like this (even if you didn't know it at the time) clicked on an URL such as the following link from ZDNet

```
http://cgi.zdnet.com/slink?/adeska/adt1123ba/4141:774436
```

And when the page has been delivered we have seen something like this in the title bar:

```
http://www.zdnet.com/anchordesk/story/story_4141.html
```

What has happened is that `cgi.zdnet.com/slink` is the address of a CGI program that uses the information after the query (?), namely `/adeska/adt1123ba/4141:774436` to build a page on the fly.

Wrox Press uses ASP to do exactly the same thing. If you navigate to

```
http://www.wrox.com/Consumer/Store/Details.asp?ISBN=1861001657
```

...you will get the details of the book with the ISBN number following the query. The ASP program contained in the page

```
http://www.wrox.com/Consumer/Store/Details.asp
```

has sent off for information about the book that is contained in a data store, constructed a table to contain it, and then has placed it in a standard template!

Accessibility Guidelines

Web accessibility guidelines are guidelines that are designed to make web pages accessible to people with various disabilities. However if these guidelines are followed, not only will our pages be accessible, but they will be tend to be in a form that is easily transformable to all the different media types. We can also be sure if we follow these guidelines that our pages will be readable in all the different makes and brands of browsers out there!

A whole W3C working group has been devoted to this issue, and their recommendation can be found at

```
http://www.w3c.org/TR/WAI-WEBCONTENT
```

We will just summarize their findings here. For a complete account visit the above-mentioned website. Most of the recommendations are in fact just an extension of common sense.

The 14 Guidelines

Here are the 14 guidelines provided by WAI (Web Accessibility Initiative)

Provide Equivalent Alternatives to Auditory and Visual Content

Visually impaired users cannot see images and deaf readers can't hear sound files. It is imperative that a meaningful `alt` attribute is employed in every image. Although the `longdesc` attribute is not supported in most browsers, it probably will be by proxy servers that service auditory clients, so make use of it.

Don't Rely on Color Alone

Color blindness is actually very common, so don't rely on color alone to give meaning. For example red/green colorblind people cannot tell the difference between these two colors so relying on just these colors to indicate danger or safety, bad or good practice, and so on is a no-no!

Use Correct Markup and Style

Correct markup facilitates transformations by proxy servers. Also don't use structural markup to provide styling. For example, use an `h1` element to indicate a heading, not to produce a large font! If you are using styling elements and attributes always provide an equivalent style sheet, as style sheets are easier to handle for proxy servers. Wherever it is avoidable, do not use tables for layout.

Clarify Natural Language

Use the `lang` attribute if you are using a foreign language, particularly if you are embedding it in your page. This ensures that voice synthesizers do not get confused.

Create Tables that Degrade Gracefully

We looked at this issue in more depth in Chapter 6. To summarize, don't use tables for layout, avoid nested tables, and make sure that your tables can degrade into a linear version. Adding as much structure as you can to a table simplifies the task of proxy servers that are converting your table to some other form.

Ensure that Pages Featuring New Technologies Transform Gracefully

If you are using new technology and markup, make sure that the content can degrade to an alternative form for browsers and agents that don't support it.

Ensure User Control of Time-Sensitive Content Changes

This means that if you use blinking, scrolling text or otherwise animated text make sure that it can be turned off! Blinking GIFs are a particular offender here. Persons with cognitive disabilities may not be able to handle moving text, and nor will certain specialized user agents.

All in all, blinking is to be avoided. Even those who have no difficulty reading it find it intensely annoying, and it is NOT the way to sell your product or make your visitors happy!

Embedded User Interfaces

If you embed an applet or an object in your page, make sure that this too follows the accessibility guidelines.

Design for Device Independence

Not all users will have a mouse! Make sure that your page is accessible to the keyboard. Input buttons and image maps are a case in point. Make sure that your user can navigate to an input button on a form, and always provide an text alternative to an image map. If necessary provide a separate navigation page.

Small devices have particular difficulty with the use of a frame to provide a navigation page. Always provide a 'noframes' alternative.

Interim Solutions

Just because a new technology is just round the corner that will solve all our accessibility problems doesn't mean that we shouldn't provide 'hack' solutions now. For example, the `@media` property of CSS will solve a lot of accessibility problems (see the next chapter), but unfortunately it is not well supported in the majority of user-agents on the market. Use the `@media` property by all means, but also provide an interim solution.

Use W3C Technologies

W3C has a lot of critics, but all their technologies and recommendations are designed to increase accessibility and universality. Use of their technologies will ensure accessibility.

Context and Orientation Information

Something that is quite clear on a large page may be unfathomable when the page is broken into smaller sections. Therefore whenever possible try and design your structure so that it still makes sense when broken down into small pieces. This is particularly important with tables.

Provide Clear Navigation Mechanisms

Always allow someone to leave your page! Use of image maps and frames are particular offenders in this regard.

Ensure that Documents are Clear and Simple

Do we have to explain the importance of this? The simpler your document, the easier it will be to make it accessible.

Summary

Hopefully this brief overview of page design considerations will help you to build sites that grab and hold user attention, rather than disappearing into obscurity along with a multitude of badly designed sites. We looked at the use of colors, hypertext links and background images, before moving on to discuss fonts and text layout. The next chapter will look at a few of the cross-browser issues that you may need to address when writing your XHTML pages.

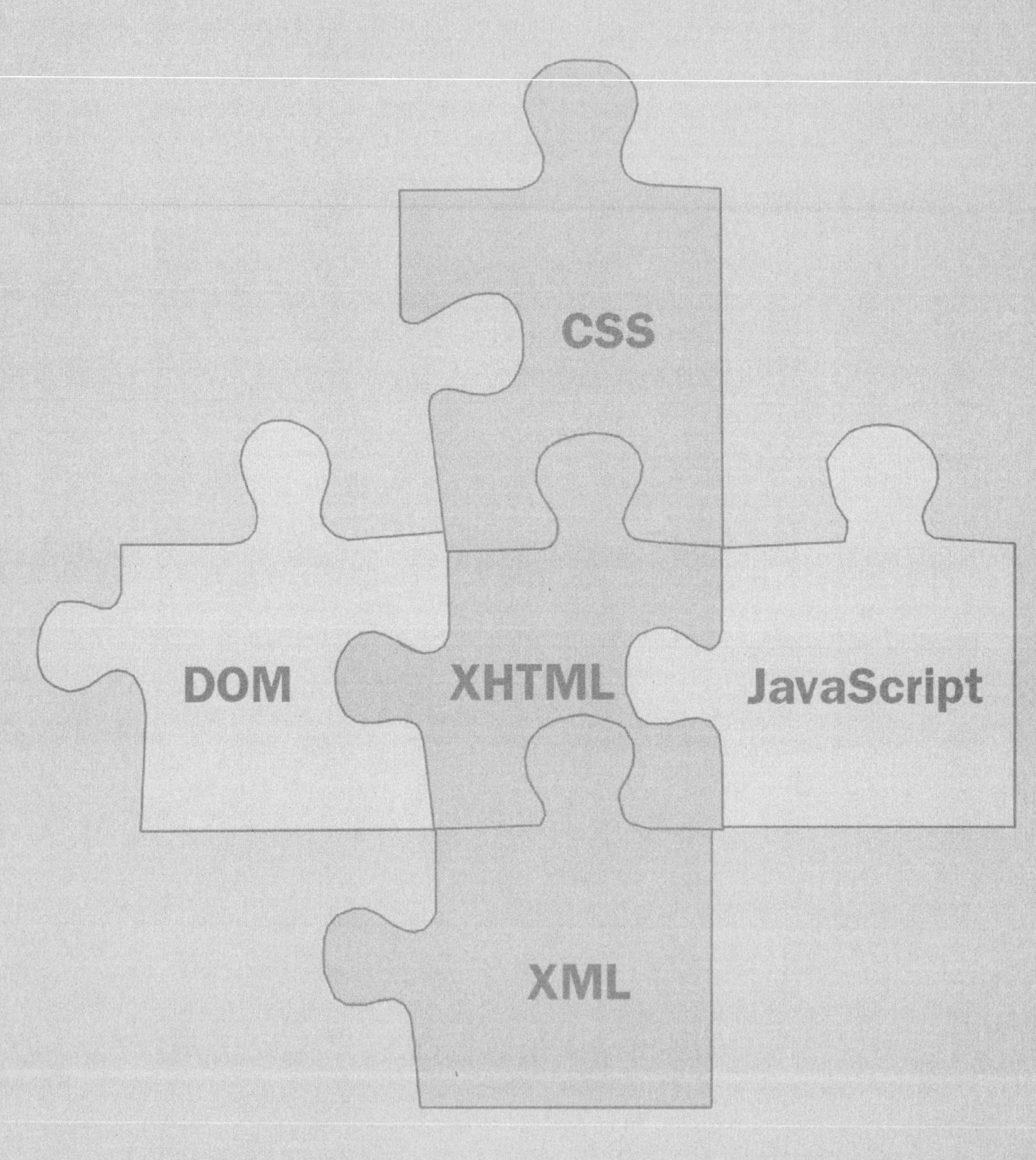
CSS
DOM
XHTML
JavaScript
XML

13

Different Media Types

The World Wide Web is a wonderful thing: computers all over the world – connected together – sharing documents and multimedia. In recent years, the World Wide Web has begun to grow beyond this comfy computer-based family of devices. The Web is now accessible on mobile phones, handheld digital assistants, and televisions.

This phenomenon has placed a considerable burden on content authors. No longer can they write their documents with expectations on how that content will be displayed. Each of these new devices represents a quite different medium from the computer: the physical characteristics of the devices are different, the relationship between the device and the user is different, and the cost of using the device is different.

Until recently, authors had little choice but to author or re-author their content with each device in mind. With the advent of Cascading Style Sheets (CSS) and something called 'media types', this began to change.

In this chapter, we will learn how to use CSS and media types to tailor our documents to different devices.

In this chapter we will cover the following:

- What media types are and why we need them
- What the role of Cascading Style Sheets is in supporting media types
- How to associate style sheets with different media types
- How to use `@media` rules and `@import` rules
- The differences between media types and strategies for handling them
- The future of style sheets in XML

First, we will define media types and try to understand why they are important.

What Are Media Types?

One of the most exciting things about writing XHTML is that whatever you write can be viewed anywhere in the world, regardless of the type of computer being used to view the content. This means that whatever content you write, you had better be prepared for it to be viewed on any number of computers, television set-top boxes, game consoles, handheld digital assistants, and mobile phones.

This would be quite a chore had HTML continued its evolutionary path of including presentational elements like `<b>` for bold and `<center>` for alignment. Fortunately, as we saw earlier in the book, the World Wide Web Consortium were aware of this and invented Cascading Style Sheets to separate presentation (how the web page looks) from content (the stuff in the web page). This means that you can now have different styles of presentations for different devices, without affecting the content of your web page.

Each of these devices is categorized as belonging to a certain media type. Media types include things like 'screen', for computer monitors, 'print' for printed paper, and 'aural' for speech synthesizers.

Known Media Types and Media Type Descriptors

So far, we have used two media types: screen and print. The Cascading Style Sheets Level 2 specification identifies a handful of other media types and qualifies this list as not being considered definitive. With the explosions of Internet appliances, there are certain to be an increasing number of new media types.

Media Type Descriptor	Description
all	The style is suitable for all devices.
aural	The style is intended for speech synthesizers. In CSS-2, there are a handful of properties related to aural style sheets.
braille	The style is intended for braille tactile feedback devices.
embossed	The style is intended for paginated braille printers.
handheld	The style is intended for handheld devices.
print	The style is intended for paginated media (like the printed page) or when representing the printed page on a screen (such as a print preview mode).
projection	The style is intended for projectors and printing to film slides and transparencies.
screen	The style is intended for color computer screens.
tty	The style is intended for devices using a fixed-pitch character grid, such as teletypes.
tv	The style is intended for television-type devices.

As shown in the table above, Cascading Style Sheets Level 2 has ten media types that represent target devices for XHTML content. The names of these media types are called 'media type descriptors'. The media type descriptors are used as values for several case-sensitive attributes described below and must be in lower case.

Style Sheet Properties Appropriate to a Media Type

Not every style sheet property is appropriate for every target device. The `volume` property, for example, refers to what's known as the median volume of a waveform. This property is clearly related to aural media types (i.e. sound) and not to visually-oriented media types.

In fact, it turns out that there are relationships between the different media types. These relationships are called media groups, and the World Wide Web Consortium identifies four of these media groups:

- Continuous or paginated media
- Visual, aural, or tactile media
- Grid or bitmap media
- Interactive or static media

Each media type is a member of one or more of these media groups. For example, the screen media type is a member of the continuous, visual, bitmap, interactive, and static media groups.

Continuous or paginated media refers to the surface on which content is rendered. If the surface can always extend to hold all of the content, the media is considered continuous. If the surface has a limited size and additional surfaces must be created to hold all of the content, the media is said to be paginated. Computer screens are continuous and printed pages are paginated. We will talk about paginated media later in this chapter.

Visual, aural, or tactile media refers to how the information is presented to the user:

- If the user must use their *eyes* to consume the content, then the media is said to be **visual**.
- If the user must use their *ears* to consume the content, then the media is said to be **aural**.
- If the user must use *touch* to consume the content, then the media is said to be **tactile**.

Computer screens are visual, aural browsers are aural, and Braille printers are tactile.

Grid or bitmap media refers to how the visual or tactile information is rendered. If the information is rendered in a predefined grid layout (every 'character' has the same amount of space), then the media is said to be grid-based. If the information is rendered pixel by pixel (every 'character' uses whatever space it needs), then the media is said to be bitmap-based. Teletypes are grid-based and computer screens are bitmap-based.

Interactive or static media refers to whether the user can interact with the content. As would be expected, when the user can interact with the content, the media is said to be interactive. When the user cannot interact with the content, the media is said to be static. Computer screens are said to be interactive and printed pages are said to be static.

The table below summarizes the relationships between media types and media groups.

Media Types	Media Groups			
	Continuous or Paginated	**Visual, Aural, or Tactile**	**Grid or Bitmap**	**Interactive or Static**
aural	continuous	aural	neither	both
braille	continuous	tactile	grid	both
embossed	paginated	tactile	grid	both
handheld	both	visual	both	both
print	paginated	visual	bitmap	static
projection	paginated	visual	bitmap	static
screen	continuous	visual	bitmap	both
tty	continuous	visual	grid	both
tv	both	visual, aural	bitmap	both

Each Cascading Style Sheet property is only valid for one or more media groups. When you are tailoring a presentation to a particular media type, you need to identify the appropriate media group and determine whether you can control the desired property for that media group.

Associating Style Sheets with Media Types

In a previous chapter, you learned how to embed and link style sheets to documents. This same mechanism may be used to associate style sheets with different devices and media types. In summary, there are four different mechanisms for specifying dependencies between style sheets and media types:

- the `style` element for embedding CSS
- the `link` element for external CSS
- `@media` rules
- `@import` rules

The following sections describe each of these mechanisms and some strategies for selecting an appropriate mechanism (in other words, which mechanism should we use?).

Using the <style> Element

The first mechanism for associating style sheets with media types is to use the `style` element's `media` attribute.

The `<style>` element's `media` attribute specifies the intended destination media for the enclosed style information. This means that the style will only be applied if the device matches the style's media type, and ignored otherwise. For example, if you write:

```
<head>
  <style type="text/css" media="print">
  <!--
    h1 { font-size: 10; text-align: center }
  -->
  </style>
</head>
```

you are indicating that when the document is printed, the content of a first level header should be rendered using a 10-point font and center-aligned.

The value of the `media` attribute can be any one of the media type descriptors previously defined (all, aural, braille, etc.). If you want to apply a style sheet to more than one media type, you can separate the media type descriptors using a comma:

```
<head>
  <style type="text/css" media="print, screen">
  <!--
    h1 { font-size: 10; text-align: center }
  -->
  </style>
</head>
```

In this example, the `media` attribute is set to `print` and `screen`. Therefore, the first level header will appear the same on the printer as on the screen.

Likewise, you can have different style sheets associated with different devices as you will see in the next exercise.

Try It Out – Using the <style> Element to Handle Different Media Types

In this exercise, you will create a simple document that will appear differently on the screen than on the printed page.

1. Type the following into your text editor:

```
<?xml version="1.0" encoding="UTF-8"?>
<!DOCTYPE html
     PUBLIC "-//W3C//DTD XHTML 1.0 Transitional//EN"
     "http://www.w3.org/TR/xhtml1/DTD/xhtml1-transitional.dtd">
```

```
<html xmlns="http://www.w3.org/1999/xhtml" xml:lang="en" lang="en">
<head>
  <title>Tempest in Style</title>
  <style type="text/css" media="screen">
  <!--
    body { font-size: 18pt }
    span.speaker {font-size: 18pt; background-color: yellow}
    span.stage {font-size: 18pt; font-style: italic}
    p.stage {font-size: 18pt; font-style: italic; text-align: center}
  -->
  </style>
</head>
<body>
  <p class="stage">Enter certain Reapers, properly habited:<br />
   they join with the Nymphs in a graceful dance; towards<br />
   the end whereof Prospero starts suddenly, and speaks; after<br />
   which, to a strange hollow, and confused<br />
   noise, they heavily vanish</p>
  <p><span class="speaker">Prospero.</span>
   <span class="stage">(Aside)</span>
   I had forgot that foul conspiracy<br />
   Of the beast Caliban, and his confederates<br />
   Against my life: the minute of their plot<br />
   Is almost come. - <span class="stage">(To the Spirits)</span>
   Well done! Avoid; no<br />
   more!</p>
</body>
</html>
```

2. Save the file as `style1.htm` and run it in your browser (we're using Microsoft Internet Explorer here). You should see something like this:

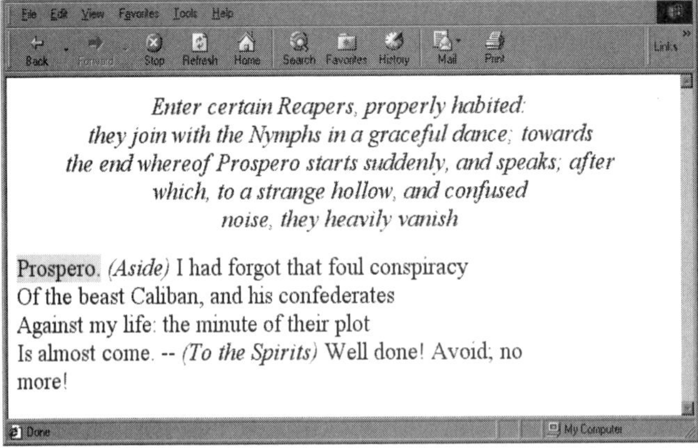

3. While running Microsoft Internet Explorer, select the File | Print menu item. After your document is printed, the print-out should look something like this:

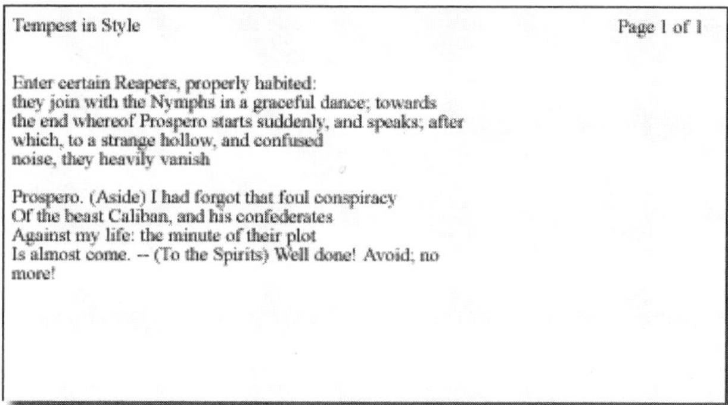

Tempest in Style Page 1 of 1

Enter certain Reapers, properly habited:
they join with the Nymphs in a graceful dance; towards
the end whereof Prospero starts suddenly, and speaks; after
which, to a strange hollow, and confused
noise, they heavily vanish

Prospero. (Aside) I had forgot that foul conspiracy
Of the beast Caliban, and his confederates
Against my life: the minute of their plot
Is almost come. -- (To the Spirits) Well done! Avoid; no
more!

4. Compare the screen version of the document with the printed version of the document. Notice the lack of text alignment, italics and so on in the printed version.
5. Edit the file style1.htm and make the following change to the <head> section:

```
<head>
  <title>Tempest in Style</title>
  <style type="text/css" media="screen, print">
  <!--
   body { font-size: 18pt }
   span.speaker {font-size: 18pt; background-color: yellow}
   span.stage {font-size: 18pt; font-style: italic}
   p.stage {font-size: 18pt; font-style: italic; text-align: center}
  -->
  </style>
</head>
```

6. Save the file as style2.htm and run it in your browser. You should see the same screen as before.
7. From within your browser, select the File | Print menu item. The printed document should now look something like this:

Tempest in Style Page 1 of 1

Enter certain Reapers, properly habited:
they join with the Nymphs in a graceful dance; towards
the end whereof Prospero starts suddenly, and speaks; after
which, to a strange hollow, and confused
noise, they heavily vanish

Prospero. *(Aside)* I had forgot that foul conspiracy
Against my life: the minute of their plot
Is almost come. -- *(To the Spirits)* Well done! Avoid; no
more!

8. Notice that the text in the printed document is now properly aligned and italicized. In addition, the font-size has been increased to 18 point!
9. Edit the file `style1.htm` (the original file) and make the following changes in the `<head>` section:

```
<head>
  <title>Tempest in Style</title>
  <style type="text/css" media="screen">
  <!--
   body { font-size: 18pt }
   span.speaker {font-size: 18pt; background-color: yellow}
   span.stage {font-size: 18pt; font-style: italic}
   p.stage {font-size: 18pt; font-style: italic; text-align: center}
  -->
  </style>
  <style type="text/css" media="print">
  <!--
   body { font-size: 10pt }
   span.speaker {font-size: 10pt; font-weight: bold}
   span.stage {font-size: 10pt; font-style: italic}
   p.stage {font-size: 10pt; font-style: italic; text-align: center}
  -->
  </style>
</head>
```

10. Save the file as `style3.htm` and run it in your browser. You should see the same screen as before.
11. From within your browser, select the File | Print menu item. The printed document should look something like this:

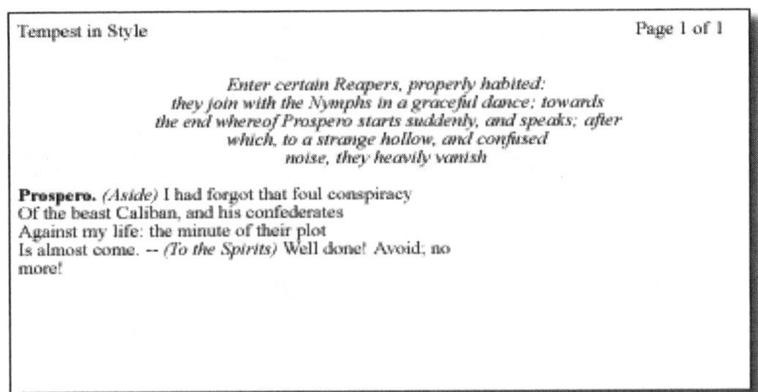

12. Notice that the text in the printed document is now a 'normal' size and that the speaker's name is in bold.

How it Works

In Step 1, you created an internal style sheet when you defined a `style` element inside the head of the document:

```
<head>
  <title>Tempest in Style</title>
  <style type="text/css" media="screen">
  <!--
   body { font-size: 18pt }
   span.speaker {font-size: 18pt; background-color: yellow}
   span.stage {font-size: 18pt; font-style: italic}
   p.stage {font-size: 18pt; font-style: italic; text-align: center}
  -->
  </style>
</head>
```

Since you assigned the value `screen` to the style element's `media` attribute, this style sheet pertains only to screen media devices. Within this style sheet, we defined four basic styles:

- the `<body>` element
- the `<span>` element in the 'speaker' class (where the `class` attribute is set to `speaker`)
- the `<span>` element in the 'stage' class
- the `<p>` element in the 'stage' class

Text within the `<body>` element has an 18-point font size; text within the 'speaker' `<span>` element has a yellow background; text within the 'stage' (for stage direction) `<span>` element is italicized; and text within the 'stage' `<p>` element is italicized and center-aligned.

Looking now at the body of the document, you will see how we applied these four styles to various text elements:

```
<body>
  <p class="stage">Enter certain Reapers, properly habited:<br />
   they join with the Nymphs in a graceful dance; towards<br />
   the end whereof Prospero starts suddenly, and speaks; after<br />
   which, to a strange hollow, and confused<br />
   noise, they heavily vanish</p>
  <p><span class="speaker">Prospero.</span>
   <span class="stage">(Aside)</span>
   I had forgot that foul conspiracy<br />
   Of the beast Caliban, and his confederates<br />
   Against my life: the minute of their plot<br />
   Is almost come. - <span class="stage">(To the Spirits)</span>
   Well done! Avoid; no<br />
   more!</p>
</body>
```

The first paragraph:

```
<p class="stage">Enter certain Reapers,… …they heavily vanish</p>
```

was assigned to the 'stage' class.

The second paragraph was not assigned to any class and so it defaults to the style of its parent element: the `<body>` element. This second paragraph includes three `<span>` elements. The first:

```
<span class="speaker">Prospero.</span>
```

was assigned to the 'speaker' class. The second:

```
<span class="stage">(Aside)</span>
```

was assigned to the 'stage' class. The third:

```
<span class="stage">(To the Spirits)</span>
```

was also assigned to the 'stage' class.

When this document is presented to the computer display device in Step 2, the style sheet associated with the screen media type is selected and its contents applied to the various elements in the document. In our case, the font-size is set to 18-point, the speaker's background color is set to yellow, and the stage directions are italicized.

At the time that this book was written, only Microsoft Internet Explorer came close to supporting all of the CSS-1 and CSS-2 style sheet properties. Unfortunately, Netscape Navigator's support is spotty, at best. We will continue to user Microsoft Internet Explorer for the remaining examples in this chapter.

In Step 3, you send the document to the printer, which is a print media device. Since there is no style sheet associated with the print media type, your web browser uses its own default style sheet; the style sheet associated with the screen media type is ignored.

In Step 5, we add the print media type to the style element:

```
<style type="text/css" media="screen, print">
```

This means that the web browser will use the same style sheet that was used for displaying the document on the screen for the printing of the document on the page.

In Steps 6 and 7, we compare the printed version of the document with the displayed version of the document. Note that the text is properly italicized and aligned.

In Step 9, you add a second `<style>` element, setting its `media` attribute to `print`:

```
<style type="text/css" media="print">
<!--
 body { font-size: 10pt }
 span.speaker {font-size: 10pt; font-weight: bold}
 span.stage {font-size: 10pt; font-style: italic}
 p.stage {font-size: 10pt; font-style: italic; text-align: center}
-->
</style>
```

Having two different internal style sheets means that you can have two entirely different presentations for the screen and the printed page. In Step 9, you changed the font-size from 18-point to 10-point and used a bold font for printing rather than the colored background used on the screen.

While using media-dependent internal style sheets is very simple, there are some inefficiencies that become more apparent as you add support for more and more devices. Quite simply, the files will get large – one way around this problem is to use external style sheets.

Using the <link> Element

The second mechanism for associating style sheets with media types is to use the `<link>` elements `media` attribute, which specifies the intended destination media for the external style information. This allows user agents to load and apply external style sheets based on the characteristics of the media where the document is being rendered.

For example, if you write:

```
<head>
  <link rel="stylesheet" type="text/css" media="print" href="myprint.css"/>
  <link rel="stylesheet" type="text/css" media="screen" href="myscrn.css"/>
</head>
```

you are indicating that the `myprint.css` style sheet should be used when printing the document, and that the `myscrn.css` style sheet should be used when displaying the document.

> **At the time that this book was written, only Microsoft Internet Explorer properly supported the `<link>` element with media types. With Netscape Navigator, if you specify anything other than the screen media type, Navigator will ignore the entire element, and therefore ignore the entire external style sheet!**

Try It Out – Using the <link> Element to Handle Different Media Types

In this exercise, we will use two external style sheets to control the display and printing.

1. Type the following into your text editor:

```
body { font-size: 18pt }
span.speaker { background-color: yellow }
.stage { font-style: italic }
p.stage { text-align: center }
```

2. Save the file as `linkscrn.css`

3. Create a new document in your text editor and type the following:

```
body { font-size: 10pt }
span.speaker { font-weight: bold }
.stage { font-style: italic }
p.stage { text-align: center }
```

4. Save this file as `linkprnt.css`

5. Edit the file `style1.htm` and make the following changes to the `<head>` section:

```
<head>
  <title>Tempest Links</title>
  <link rel="stylesheet" type="text/css" media="print" href="linkprnt.css"/>
  <link rel="stylesheet" type="text/css" media="screen" href="linkscrn.css"/>
</head>
```

6. Save the file as `link.htm` and run it in Microsoft Internet Explorer. You should see something like:

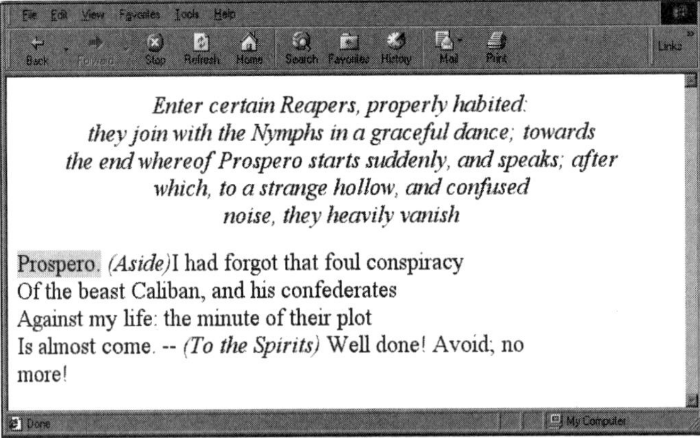

7. From within your browser, select the File | Print menu item. You should see something like:

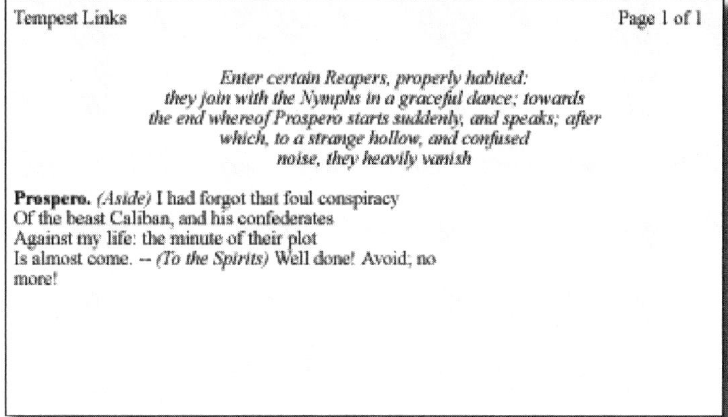
Tempest Links Page 1 of 1

Enter certain Reapers, properly habited: they join with the Nymphs in a graceful dance; towards the end whereof Prospero starts suddenly, and speaks; after which, to a strange hollow, and confused noise, they heavily vanish

Prospero. *(Aside)* I had forgot that foul conspiracy
Of the beast Caliban, and his confederates
Against my life: the minute of their plot
Is almost come. -- *(To the Spirits)* Well done! Avoid; no more!

How It Works

We simply took our two style sheets out of the document and put them into separate documents of their own. Note that the content of the style sheets wasn't changed in any way, so that what is seen on the browser and the printed page are identical to those of the last example. In the `<head>` of the document, we simply associate these external style sheets with the document content like so:

```
<head>
  <title>Tempest</title>
  <link rel="stylesheet" type="text/css" media="print" href="linkprnt.css"/>
  <link rel="stylesheet" type="text/css" media="screen" href="linkscrn.css"/>
</head>
```

We can see that there are two `<link>` elements. The first identifies the style sheet to use for the print media type and the second identifies the style sheet to use for the screen media type. The files were the style information is contained is given as the value of the `href` attribute.

When we looked at our document in the web browser, the style sheet corresponding to the screen media type was opened and used. When we sent our document to the printer, the style sheet corresponding to the print media type was opened and used instead.

Using the '@media' Rules

The third mechanism for associating style sheets with media types is to use the `@media` rules. This specifies the target media types for a set of style sheet rules. For example, if you write:

```
@media screen {
 h1 { font-size: 18pt }
}

@media print {
```

```
  h1 { font-size: 10pt }
}

@media screen, print {
  h1 { text-align: center }
}
```

...you are indicating that first level header has an 18-point font when displayed on the screen, a 10-point font when printed, and center-aligned on both media types. The third of the `@media` rules above points out that `@media` rules may apply to more than one media type. In this case, media types are separated by a comma.

Note that `@media` rules are applied in the order in which they are processed. In other words, if two applicable `@media` rules define different styles for the same element or selector, the latter `@media` rule will apply. For example, if we wrote:

```
@media print {
  h1 { font-size: 10pt }
}

@media screen, print {
  h1 { font-size: 18pt; text-align: center }
}
```

an 18pt font will be used when displaying on the screen and when printing. With `@media` rules, you can specify media-dependencies within an internal style sheet or with an external style sheet.

Using '@media' Rules Within an XHTML Document

In order to specify media dependencies within an internal style sheet, you simply include the above information within your document by use of the `<style>` element:

```
<head>
  ...
  <style type="text/css">
  <!--
   @media screen {
    h1 { font-size: 18pt }
   }
   @media print {
    h1 { font-size: 10pt }
   }
   @media screen, print {
    h1 { text-align: center }
   }
  -->
  </style>
 ...
</head>
```

In this example, the `<style>` element's content is three `@media` rules. The first `@media` rule applies to the screen media type, the second to the print media type, and the third to both screen and print media types. The benefit of this approach is that common styles (such as center-alignment in the example above) can be collected under one `@media` rule to reduce redundancy and improve maintainability of the style information. The greatest benefit, however, of using `@media` rules is when they are used in external style sheets.

Using '@media' Rules Within External Style Sheets

In order to specify media-dependencies within an external style sheet is quite straightforward. Simply write your rules in a separate file:

```
/* mystyle.css */

@media screen {         /* style rules for screen devices */
h1 { font-size: 18 }
}

@media print {          /* style rules for print devices */
h1 { font-size: 10 }
}

@media screen, print {   /* style rules shared by screen and print devices */
h1 { text-align: center }
}
```

and save as, for example, `mystyle.css`. Then, as we've done before, simply use the `href` attribute of the `<link>` element to reference the style sheet from within the XHTML document:

```
<link rel="stylesheet" type="text/css" href="mystyle.css" />
```

Make sure, though, that you do not use the `<link>` elements `media` attribute in addition to the `@media` rules within the external style sheet – the web browser might not download your style sheet!

Try It Out – Using the '@media' Rules to Create Media-Dependent Style Sheets

In this exercise, you will use `@media` rules to create a single style sheet that handles multiple media types. This is very similar to the previous examples, so we shall not show you any screen shots or go through the stages of showing you non-styled printouts etc. By this stage, you know that we need different styles for different media. However, here's our trusty example again only done this time with `@media` rules:

1. Type the following into your text editor and save as `atmedia.css`:

```
@media screen {
 body { font-size: 18pt }
 span.speaker { background-color: yellow }
 .stage { font-style: italic }
 p.stage { text-align: center }
```

```
}
@media print {
 body { font-size: 10pt }
 span.speaker { font-weight: bold }
.stage { font-style: italic }
 p.stage { text-align: center }
}
```

2. Now edit the file `link.htm`, change the `<head>` section to the following, and save as `atmedia.htm`:

```
<head>
  <title>Tempest @media</title>
  <link rel="stylesheet" type="text/css" href="atmedia.css"/>
</head>
```

3. Running this in your browser, and printing the page, you will see that both are properly formatted according to the styles contained in the `atmedia.css` file, and will look identical to those shown in Steps 6 and 7 of the previous example using the `<link>` element.

How It Works

As before, we created an external style sheet but this time with two @media rules, one for the screen and one for the printed page, and then referenced it using the `<link>` element. Unlike the previous exercise, we do not set the `<link>` element's `media` attribute. This is because we want to use the external style sheet for all media types.

Using the '@import' Rules

The fourth mechanism for associating style sheets with media types is to use the `@import` rules. These provide a way to automatically merge style rules from one style sheet into the style section of your XHTML document:

```
<style type="text/css">
<!--
  @import url("mystyle.css");
  /* rest of style section */
-->
</style>
```

If you want the import to be media-dependent, you simply add the media type after the url:

```
<style type="text/css">
<!--
  @import url ("mystyle.css") screen;
  /* rest of style section */
-->
</style>
```

Unfortunately, at the time that this book was written, the major browsers did not support the *media-dependent* `@import` rules (Microsoft's Internet Explorer does support the general `@import` rule, though).

The imported file need not be local; for example, the following is valid:

```
@import url("http://www.madeupdomain.com/reallygoodstyle.css");
```

This informs the browser to load the style sheet from the server at `www.madeupdomain.com` and use this to display the document. Styles within this imported sheet may be overridden by specifying styles within the XHTML document using those tags previously described. The advantage of importing a style sheet is that it allows us to create a basic template for all our web pages, from which individual documents may 'diverge' with overridden styles.

Printing and Paginated Media

Earlier in this chapter, we talked about media groups. One of these media groups dealt with presentation to continuous and paginated media.

As we said before, paginated media is different from continuous media in that the document content is split into discrete 'pages' when it is rendered. Continuous media, as its name implies, does not split the document content, keeping it as one continuous entity when it is rendered.

In summary, there are three ways of handling printed media:

- print media type
- page breaking properties
- `@page` rule

You can use any or all of these methods when creating a document.

The **print media type** allows us to change the presentation of the document: things like whether to use a serif or a sans-serif font, which the font-size, background-colors, etc. We talked about the print media type and other media types earlier in this chapter.

The **page breaking properties** allow us to relate how content is displayed on the pages defined by the `@page` rule: things like avoiding page breaks before certain elements and forcing an image to appear on a right-hand page, etc.

The **@page rule** allows you to define the context for printing – in essence, it allows you to describe the paper: things like the size of the paper, its margins, and so on.

We will learn about the `@page` rule and the page breaking properties in the following sections.

Page Breaking Properties

Page breaking properties provide a way for us to control where page breaks (i.e. where one page ends and the next one begins) occur when our document is printed. New sections and chapters often begin on new pages and you may wish to control page breaks around images (perhaps forcing a page break before an image or preventing a page break following an image).

For example, if we want to make a paragraph start on a new page, we would write:

```
<p style="page-break-before: always">
  This is the first paragraph of text on a new page.
</p>
```

In this example, we set the `page-break`-before property to `always`, which means that a page break will always occur before this paragraph.

You can also use style sheets, as in this example:

```
h1 { page-break-before: always }
```

This means that every level-one header will start on a new printed page.

There are several page breaking properties:

- `page-break-before`
- `page-break-after`
- `page-break-inside`
- `orphans`
- `widows`

Each of these properties can have different values that affect whether the page break occurs all of the time or under special conditions.

The 'page-break-before' and 'page-break-after' Properties

As you can guess, the `page-break-before` property controls whether a page break occurs *before* an element. Likewise, the `page-break-after` property controls whether a page break occurs *after* an element. Both of these properties can have one of the following values and meanings:

Value	`page-break-before`	`page-break-after`
"auto"	A page break should not be forced or forbidden before the element.	A page break should not be forced or forbidden after the element.
"always"	A page break should be forced (always occur) before the element.	A page break should be forced (always occur) after the element.

Value	`page-break-before`	`page-break-after`
"avoid"	A page break should be avoided before the element.	A page break should be avoided after the element.
"left"	One or more page breaks should be forced so that the element appears on the left hand page.	One or more page breaks should be forced so that the content appearing after the element appears on the left hand page.
"right"	One or more page breaks should be forced so that the element appears on the right hand page.	One or more page breaks should be forced so that the content appearing after the element appears on the right hand page.

Try It Out – Using the 'page-break-before' Property

In this example, you will get some experience using the `page-break-before` property, and see some dialogue from more than just *Prospero.*

1. Type the following into your text editor:

```
@media screen, print {
  body { font-size: 18pt }
  h1 { font-size: 24pt; text-transform: uppercase; text-align: center }
  .stage { font-style: italic }
  p.stage { text-align: center }
}

@media screen {
  body { font-family: sans-serif }
  span.speaker { background-color: yellow }
}

@media print {
  body { font-family: serif }
  span.speaker { font-weight: bold }
}
```

2. Save the file as `pb-none.css` (the 'pb' represent 'page break', so you may guess that the 'none' refers to the fact that this style sheet does not contain any forced page breaks).

3. Now open your text editor and type in the following (remember, all the code for this book is available from the Wrox web site):

```
<?xml version="1.0" encoding="UTF-8"?>
<!DOCTYPE html
     PUBLIC "-//W3C//DTD XHTML 1.0 Transitional//EN"
     "http://www.w3.org/TR/xhtml1/DTD/xhtml1-transitional.dtd">
<html xmlns="http://www.w3.org/1999/xhtml" xml:lang="en" lang="en">
<head>
  <title>Page Break Example</title>
  <link rel="stylesheet" type="text/css" href="pb-none.css" />
</head>
<body>
  <p><span class="speaker">Ferdinand.</span>
   So they are:<br />
   My spirits, as in a dream, are all bound up.<br />
   My father"s loss, the weakness which I feel,<br />
   The wrack of all my friends, or this man's threats,<br />
   To whom I am subdued, are but light to me,<br />
   Might I but through my prison once a day<br />
   Behold this maid: all corners else o' th' earth<br />
   Let liberty make use of; space enough<br />
   Have I in such a prison.</p>

  <p><span class="speaker">Prospero.</span>
   <span class="stage">(Aside)</span>
   It works.--
   <span class="stage">(To Ferdinand)</span>
   Come on.--<br />
   Thou hast done well, fine Ariel!--
   <span class="stage">(To Ferdinand)</span>
   Fol-<br />
   low me.--<br />
   <span class="stage">(To Ariel)</span>
   Hark, what thou else shalt do me.</p>
  <p><span class="speaker">Miranda.</span>
   Be of comfort;<br />
   My father's of a better nature, sir<br />
   Than he appears by speech: this is unwonted,<br />
   Which now came from him.</p>
  <p><span class="speaker">Ariel.</span>
   To the syllable.</p>
  <p><span class="speaker">Prospero.</span>
   <span class="stage">(To Ferdinand)</span>
   Come, follow. - Speak not for<br />
   him. <span class="stage">Exeunt</span></p>
  <h1>Act Two Scene One</h1>
  <p class="stage">Another Part of the Island</p>
  <p class="stage">Enter Alonso, Sebastian, Antonio, Gonzalo, Adrian,
   Franciso, and others</p>
  <p><span class="speaker">Gonzalo.</span>
   Beseech you sir, be merry: you have cause,<br />
   So have we all, of joy; for our escape<br />
   Is much beyond our loss. Our hint of woe<br />
   Is common: every day some sailor's wife,<br />
   The masters of some merchant and the merchant,<br />
```

```
    Have just our theme of woe; but for the miracle,<br />
    I mean our preservation, few in millions<br />
    Can speak like us: then wisely, good sir, weight<br />
    Our sorrow with our comfort.</p>
</body>
</html>
```

4. Save the file as `pb-none.htm` and load it into your browser (we are using Microsoft Internet Explorer). You should see something like this:

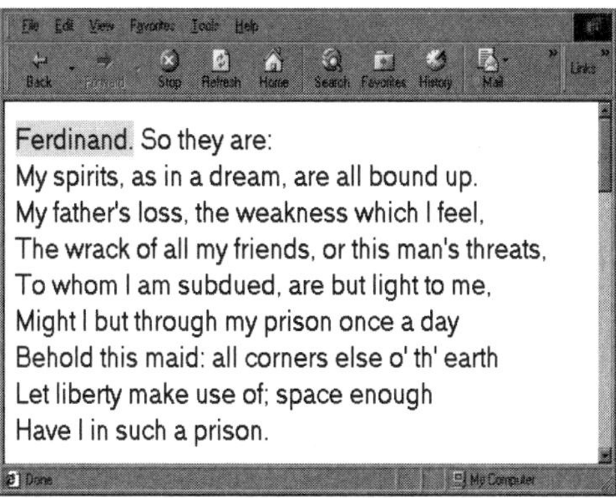

5. From within the browser, use File | Print to print the document. Two pages that look something like this should print:

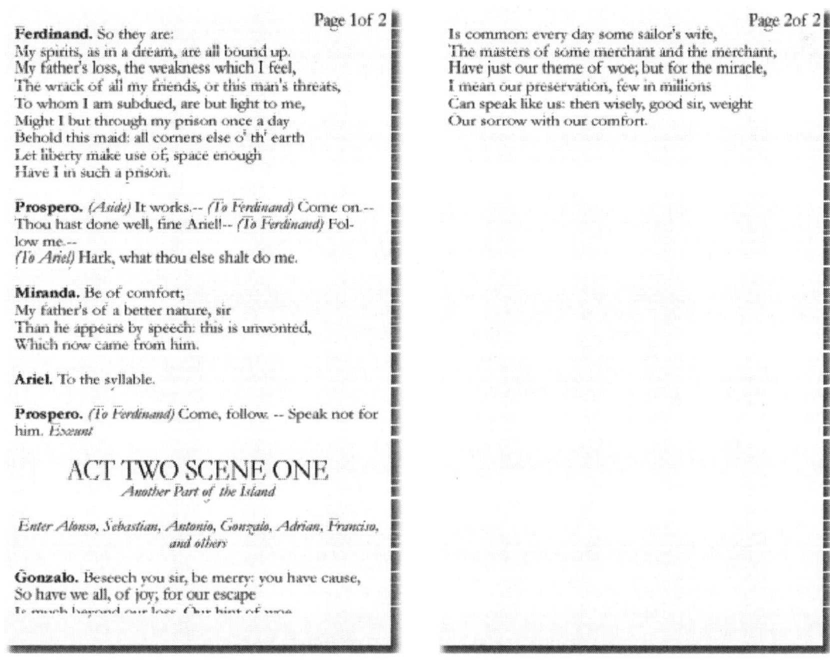

Depending on your printer set-up, the document may not print on more than one page or the 'Act Two Scene One' may appear at the top of a second page.

If the document prints such that 'Act Two Scene One' appears at the top of the second page, remove the first paragraph from the document so that 'Act Two Scene One' appears somewhere on the first page.

6. Load the file `pb-none.css` into your text editor and add the following text:

```
@media screen, print {
   body { font-size: 18pt }
   h1 { font-size: 24pt; text-transform: uppercase; text-align: center }
   .stage { font-style: italic }
   p.stage { text-align: center }
}

@media screen {
   body { font-family: sans-serif }
   span.speaker { background-color: yellow }
}

@media print {
   body { font-family: serif }
   h1 { page-break-before: always }
   span.speaker { font-weight: bold }
}
```

7. Save the file as `pb-before.css` (i.e. we are adding a page break to this style sheet).

8. Load the file `pb-none.htm` into your text editor and make the following changes to the `<head>` section:

```
<head>
  <title>Page Break Before Example</title>
  <link rel="stylesheet" type="text/css" href="pb-before.css" />
</head>
```

9. Save the file as `pb-before.htm` and run it in your browser. You should see something like this:

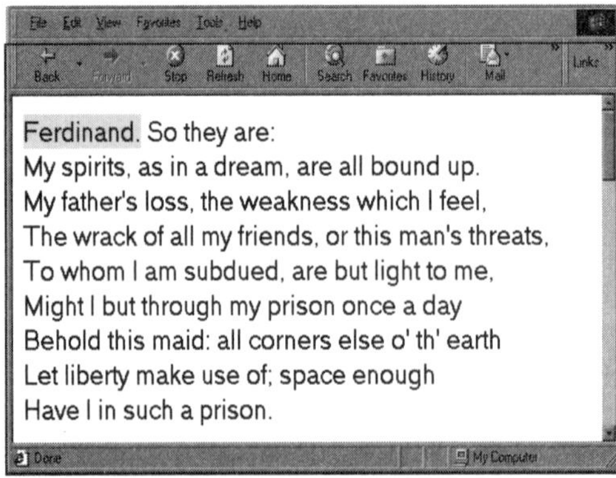

10. Print the document as before; it should now look something like this:

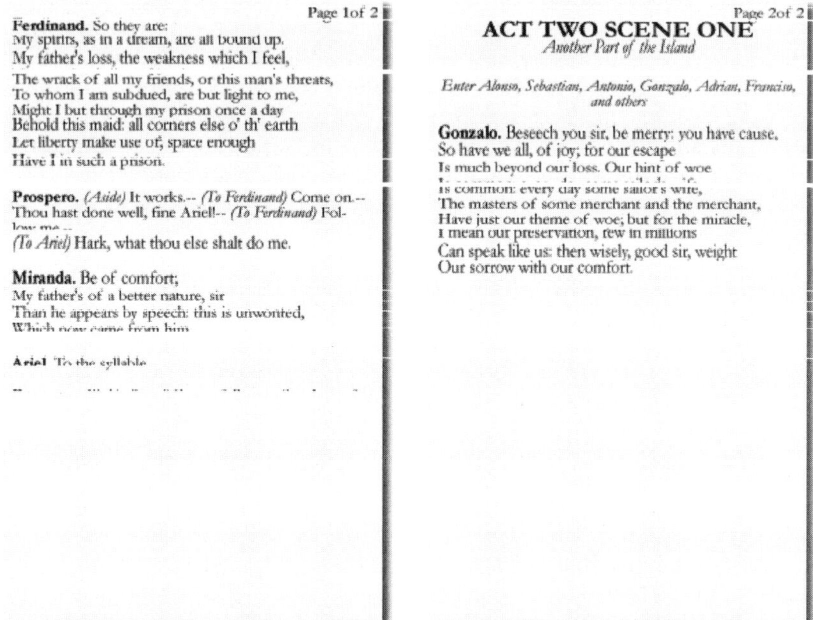

Page 1of 2

Ferdinand. So they are:
My spirits, as in a dream, are all bound up.
My father's loss, the weakness which I feel,
The wrack of all my friends, or this man's threats,
To whom I am subdued, are but light to me,
Might I but through my prison once a day
Behold this maid: all corners else o' th' earth
Let liberty make use of; space enough
Have I in such a prison.

Prospero. *(Aside)* It works.-- *(To Ferdinand)* Come on.--
Thou hast done well, fine Ariel!-- *(To Ferdinand)* Fol-
low me --
(To Ariel) Hark, what thou else shalt do me.

Miranda. Be of comfort;
My father's of a better nature, sir
Than he appears by speech: this is unwonted,
Which now came from him

Ariel. To the syllable

Page 2of 2

ACT TWO SCENE ONE

Another Part of the Island

Enter Alonso, Sebastian, Antonio, Gonzalo, Adrian, Francisco, and others

Gonzalo. Beseech you sir, be merry: you have cause,
So have we all, of joy; for our escape
Is much beyond our loss. Our hint of woe
Is common: every day some sailor's wife,
The masters of some merchant and the merchant,
Have just our theme of woe; but for the miracle,
I mean our preservation, few in millions
Can speak like us: then wisely, good sir, weight
Our sorrow with our comfort.

How it Works

In Step 1, you typed in the style sheet for your document. The style sheet consists of three sections that use the `@media` rule you learned about earlier in this chapter, and need only a brief mention here. The first section defines the style sheet properties that are shared when you view the document on the screen and when you print it; the second relates just to the screen, and the third just to the printing.

By comparing the `@media screen` style sheet properties with the `@media print` style sheet properties, we see the differences between displaying on the screen and printing on paper are:

- the document is displayed using a sans-serif font (like Helvetica or Arial) and is printed using a serif font (like Times Roman or Times New Roman)
- the `speaker` sections are displayed with a yellow background and are printed using bold text

In Step 3, we associate the style sheet with the document in the same way as we have done numerous times now:

```
<link rel="stylesheet" type="text/css" href="pb-none.css" />
```

In Steps 4 and 5 we run the document in Microsoft Internet Explorer and print the document on paper. The screen shot of the printed page should be close to what you print.

In Step 6, we add the following line to our style sheet:

```
h1 { page-break-before: always }
```

This line tells the web browser to *always* insert a page break before the `<h1>` element. This forces a new page for each section of our document. Thus, a page break is inserted before the heading 'Act Two Scene One', the only level-one heading our document contains. If you have lots of paper to spare, add `<h1>` to the beginning and `</h1>` to the end of each line in Gonzalo's speech (the last speech in the document) and print it out: you will see that each line is printed on a separate page.

The 'page-break-inside' Property

The `page-break-inside` property controls whether a page can break within an element. The `page-break-inside` property can have one of the following values:

- `auto`
- `avoid`

The value `auto` means that a page break should not be forced or forbidden within the element. The value `avoid` means that a page break should be avoided within the element.

> **Unfortunately, at the time that this book was written, neither Microsoft Internet Explorer or Netscape Navigator support the `page-break-inside` property.**

The 'orphans' Property

The `orphans` property specifies the minimum number of lines of a paragraph that must be left at the bottom of the page when the page breaks. If less than this number of lines can be printed at the bottom of the page, the page breaks before the paragraph.

For example, if you wanted to make sure that at least 5 lines of text appear at the bottom of the page, you would write the following in your style sheet:

```
p { orphans: 5 }
```

> **Unfortunately, at the time that this book was written, neither Microsoft Internet Explorer or Netscape Navigator support the `orphans` property.**

The 'widows' Property

The `widows` property specifies the minimum number of lines of a paragraph that can be printed at the top of the page when the page breaks in the middle of a paragraph. If less than this number of lines can be printed at the top of the page, the page breaks before the paragraph.

For example, if you wanted to make sure that at least 5 lines of text appear at the top of the page, you would write the following in your style sheet:

```
p { widows: 5 }
```

> **Unfortunately, at the time that this book was written, neither Microsoft Internet Explorer or Netscape Navigator support the `widows` property.**

The '@page' Rule

The `@page` rule allows you to describe the page (or paper, in the case of printing): things like its size and margins.

The `@page` rules generally take a form similar to other style sheet rules:

```
@page {
   /* properties */
}
```

For example, if you wanted to set the left margin for all pages to be 4 centimeters, you would write:

```
@page {
   margin-left: 4cm;
}
```

The `@page` rules can also be customized for left side pages and right side pages. If, for example, you wanted to set the left margin for all *left* (`@page :left`) side pages to 3 centimeters, and the left margin for all *right* (`@page :right`) side pages to 4 centimeters, you would write:

```
@page :left {
   margin-left: 3cm;
}

@page :right {
   margin-left: 4cm;
}
```

In addition, you can name your page rules, but we will talk about that later. First, we will learn about some of the `@page` rule properties: `size`, `margin`, and `marks`.

> **Unfortunately, at the time that this book was written, neither Microsoft Internet Explorer nor Netscape Navigator support any of the `@page` rule features. It is still a good idea to be familiar with these features since, given the rate of change within the Internet, we may see these features implemented soon!**

The 'size' Property

The `size` property specifies the size and orientation of the printed page. The size of a page can be either a fixed size or scalable.

Absolute

When you want the size of a page to be absolute (a fixed size), you specify the width and height using one of the following units:

- `in` (for inches)
- `cm` (for centimeters)
- `mm` (for millimeters)

Thus, if we want to specify that the page size is 8 ½ inches by 11 inches, we write:

```
@page { size: 8.5in 11in }
```

and if we wanted to specify A4 page dimensions in centimeters, we write:

```
@page { size: 21cm 29.7cm }
```

Relative

When we want the size of a page to be relative (scalable), we specify one of three values:

- `auto` – used when we want the page size to be set to the size and orientation of the target pages (the paper, for example)
- `landscape` – used when we want to override the target page's orientation and make the longer sides horizontal
- `portrait` – used when you want to override the target page's orientation and make the longer sides vertical

Thus, if we want to say that the page should be printed in landscape mode, we write:

```
@page { size: landscape }
```

As mentioned previously, at the time that this book was written, none of the major browsers supported this feature.

The Margin-Related Properties

The margin-related properties are used to set the left, right, top, and bottom margins of the page.

Property	Definition
`margin-left`	Sets the margin for the left side of the printed page.
`margin-right`	Sets the margin for the right side of the printed page.
`margin-top`	Sets the margin for the top of the printed page.
`margin-bottom`	Sets the margin for the bottom of the printed page.

For example, if we wanted a 4 cm margin on the left side of the printed page, we write:

```
@page { margin-left: 4cm }
```

If we wanted a 5 cm margin on the top of the printed page, we write:

```
@page { margin-top: 5cm }
```

The `margin` property is a short-cut for setting margins; it lets us set all of the margins using one property. For example, we could combine the following set of properties:

```
@page { margin-left: 4cm; margin-right: 3cm; margin-top: 5cm; margin-bottom: 2cm }
```

into the single property:

```
@page { margin: 5cm 3cm 2cm 4cm } /* top right bottom left */
```

Note that the order for the margin properties values is top, right, bottom, left (you can imagine the order as moving clockwise around the page, starting from the top).

The `margin` property does not require you to type in four values. In fact, you can type in anywhere from one to four values. If you write:

```
@page { margin: 5cm }
```

you will set the top, right, bottom, and left margins to 5 centimeters. If you write:

```
@page { margin: 5cm 3cm }
```

you will set the top and bottom margins to 5 centimeters and the right and left margins to 3 centimeters. If you write:

```
@page { margin: 5cm 3cm 2cm }
```

you will set the top margin to 5 centimeters, the right and left margins to 3 centimeters, and the bottom margin to 2 centimeters.

This may sound rather confusing, but it stems from the fact that most documents either have all of their margins set to the same size, or the top and bottom margins set to the same size and the left and right margins set to another size, or the left and right margins set to the same size but the top and bottom margins differ. The following table should help, where we have used the abbreviations 't' for top, 'l' for left, 'b' for bottom and 'r' for right:

Number of values in margin property	Description
1	t+l+b+r=same
2	t+b=same, l+r=same
3	t, l+r=same, b

While our examples above are all done using centimeters, the margins can be specified as a percentage, a length, or as the `auto` value.

Percentage

If you specify a percentage value, the margin is calculated as a percentage of the width or height of the page (the *width* of the page is used for the `margin-left` and `margin-right` properties, and the *height* of the page is used for the `margin-top` and `margin-bottom` properties).

Length

If you specify a length value, the margin is set to an absolute value. As with the `size` property, only the `in`, `cm`, and `mm` units may be used. Font units cannot be used because a piece of paper has no notion of font metrics.

Auto

If you specify this keyword, you are telling the web browser to use a computer value for the margins. In most cases, this means that there will be no margins (other than those specified within the content of the document).

Currently, none of the major browsers support the margin properties, but you can get a similar behavior for the left and right margins by applying the `margin-left` and `margin-right` properties to the `body` element.

Try It Out – Applying Margins to the Body Element

In this exercise, we will apply the margin property to the body element. We would like to be showing you how to apply margins to the `@page` rules, but since they don't currently work in the major browsers, this is the next best approach.

1. Load the file `pb-none.css` into your text editor and make the following changes:

```
@media screen, print {
   body { font-size: 18pt }
   h1 { font-size: 24pt; text-transform: uppercase; text-align: center }
   .stage { font-style: italic }
   p.stage { text-align: center }
}

@media screen {
   body { font-family: sans-serif }
   span.speaker { background-color: yellow }
}

@media print {
   body { font-family: serif; margin-left: 3cm; margin-right: 3cm }
   span.speaker { font-weight: bold }
}
```

2. Save the file as `pb-margins.css`

3. Load the file `pb-none.htm` into your text editor and make the following changes:

```
<head>
  <title>Page Margin Example</title>
  <link rel="stylesheet" type="text/css" href="pb-margins.css" />
</head>
```

4. Save the file as `pb-margins.htm` and run it in your browser. You will see the same screen shot as before because we have not changed the screen style sheet properties, so we will not show that shot here.

5. However, you should see a difference when the document is printed:

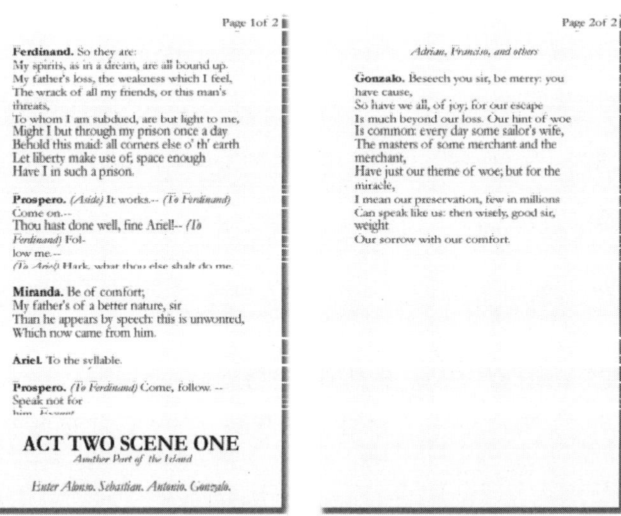

Page 1of 2

Ferdinand. So they are:
My spirits, as in a dream, are all bound up.
My father's loss, the weakness which I feel,
The wrack of all my friends, or this man's threats,
To whom I am subdued, are but light to me,
Might I but through my prison once a day
Behold this maid: all corners else o' th' earth
Let liberty make use of; space enough
Have I in such a prison.

Prospero. *(Aside)* It works.-- *(To Ferdinand)* Come on.--
Thou hast done well, fine Ariel!-- *(To Ferdinand)* Fol-
low me.--
(To Ariel) Hark, what thou else shalt do me.

Miranda. Be of comfort;
My father's of a better nature, sir
Than he appears by speech: this is unwonted,
Which now came from him.

Ariel. To the syllable.

Prospero. *(To Ferdinand)* Come, follow. --
Speak not for

ACT TWO SCENE ONE

Another Part of the Island

Enter Alonso, Sebastian, Antonio, Gonzalo,

Page 2of 2

Adrian, Francisco, and others

Gonzalo. Beseech you sir, be merry: you have cause,
So have we all, of joy; for our escape
Is much beyond our loss. Our hint of woe
Is common: every day some sailor's wife,
The masters of some merchant and the merchant,
Have just our theme of woe; but for the miracle,
I mean our preservation, few in millions
Can speak like us: then wisely, good sir, weight
Our sorrow with our comfort.

How it Works

In Step 1, we described how we wanted the document to print by specifying three `@media` rules. If you look at the third `@media` rule:

```
@media print {
   body { font-family: serif; margin-left: 3cm; margin-right: 3cm }
   span.speaker { font-weight: bold }
}
```

We can see that we specified that the left margin and right margin should be 3 centimeters. Notice that we did not assign these properties in the `@media` rules for the screen media type or the shared screen and print media rules. This means that the margins will only be seen when the document is printed.

In Step 2, we associate the style sheet with our document, and in Step 3 we load the document into Microsoft Internet Explorer.

As you can see in Step 3, there is no hint of a margin. This is because we did not specify any value for the margins for the screen media type in Step 1.

In Step 4, we print the document and the margins appear; this is because we specified margins for the print media type in Step 1.

The 'marks' Property

You use the marks property to display crop marks and cross marks on the printed page. **Crop marks** indicate where the paper should be cut; this is important when you print a document on a page that is larger than the target page size. **Cross marks** are used so that multiple pages can be aligned.

To show crop marks, we write:

```
@page { marks: crop }
```

and to show cross marks, we write:

```
@page { marks: cross }
```

If you do not want to show any marks (which is the default), we write:

```
@page { marks: none }
```

Since crop and cross marks appear outside of the normal page area, they can only be seen if you set your page size, using the `@page` rule's size property, to an absolute value.

Naming @page rules and the page property

As mentioned earlier, the `@page` rules can be applied to the entire document by writing:

```
@page { /* properties */ }
```

to left hand pages by writing:

```
@page :left { /* properties */ }
```

and to right hand pages by writing:

```
@page :right { /* properties */ }
```

In addition, you can name @page rules so that you can apply them with greater fidelity. To name an @page rule, you write:

```
@page name {/* properties */ }
```

where name is replaced with the name of your rule. For example, if you wanted to write an @page named 'rotated' that forced an element to appear in landscape mode, you would write:

```
@page rotated { size: landscape }
```

This named @page rule can then be applied to an element by using the page property. For example, if you wanted all tables to appear on paper in landscape mode, you would write:

```
@page rotated { size: landscape }
table { page: rotated }
```

This means that all tables will appear on pages that are printed in landscape mode. If it happens that the page containing the table is being printed in a different mode, a page break will be inserted before the table, forcing the table to appear on a new page printed in landscape mode.

Unfortunately, as mentioned before, the @page rules are not currently supported in the major browsers, so we do not have the chance to use these properties in practice!

Strategies for Handling Media Types

As we mentioned earlier, there has been an explosion of devices for connecting to the Web. As wonderful as this phenomenon may be, it places a considerable burden on authors (like you). No longer can authors write documents with expectations on how the content will be displayed. This is because each of these devices is a very different medium than the computer – the physical characteristics of the devices are different, the relationship between the device and the user is different, and the cost of using the device is different.

There are a variety of factors that we need to consider when developing our content and authoring our style sheets. Some of these we talk about in the following sections.

Device Constraints

The first set of factors deals with the differences between the target devices.

Physical Size of the Display Surface and Graphics Resolution

The physical size of the display surface, combined with the graphics resolution, significantly affects how much content can be displayed on the screen and how that content is presented.

	Low Graphics Resolution	**High Graphics Resolution**
Small Screen Size	Single Font	Many Fonts
	Limited Text	Limited Text
	Icons	Simple Graphics
Large Screen Size	Few Fonts	Many Fonts
	Constrained Text	Full Text Support
	Simple Graphics	Complex Graphics

The table above is a generalization of how the physical size of the display surface and the graphics resolution may affect what content you present to your user and how that content is presented. An example of a device that fits the 'small screen-low resolution' space is the current generation of mobile phones. An example of a device that fits the 'large screen-low resolution' space is the current generation of Internet-enabled television products (like WebTV). An example of a device that fits the 'large screen-high resolution' space is the personal computer. There are no products (that we know of) that fit the small screen-high resolution' space, although future generations of handheld devices may fit this niche.

Looking at the entries in the table, we will see that there are three general issues at stake: font support, amount of text displayed in a single screen, and graphics support.

The graphics resolution affects how many fonts can realistically be supported. If we look at the difference between any two fonts, we will see that fonts differ in the way in which pixels are drawn. If we have very few pixels to work with, we have very few ways of differentiating between fonts.

The physical display size and the graphics resolution affect how much text can be displayed. If the screen is small and the resolution is low, there are simply few pixels that can be used to draw text. For a small display, if you increase the graphics resolution you could increase the amount of text displayed by making the text smaller, but this is generally not a good strategy since the text will become harder to read. As the display gets larger, you have more 'real estate' to work with and can generally display more text.

Likewise, the physical display size and the graphics resolution affect how graphics are displayed. If the graphics resolution is low and a small display size, you have few pixels to work and you are probably left to working with icons. As the graphics resolution increases, you have more pixels to work with and are only constrained by how large you can make the images (which is bounded by the size of the display).

Differences in Fonts

Different device types are very likely to display fonts differently. There are three factors affecting fonts:

- Default font
- Font presentation
- DPI

The most offensive case is where different devices specify different default fonts. For example, a small handheld device may choose to use a sans-serif font while personal computer-based browsers use a serif font. Even between personal computers there are differences. The Macintosh uses Times Roman for a default font but Windows-based computers use Times New Roman.

The presentation of any single font may be different on different devices. If the vertical extent (the height of a font character), the horizontal extent (the width of a font character), and the white space (the space between characters) are not exactly the same, characters may word-wrap differently.

Finally, the DPI (or dots per inch) of the screen may also be different. If the DPI is not the same between any two devices, a 12-point font on one device will appear larger or smaller on another device. The Macintosh display has a 72 DPI resolution and the Windows-based computer display has a 96 DPI. This means that 12-point text on a Macintosh will appear significantly larger on a Windows-based computer.

Differences in Display Bit Depth

The **display bit depth** is how many colors can be shown on the device. If the device supports 24-bit color, 16.7 million colors can be shown. If the device supports 8-bit color, only 256 colors can be shown.

The display's bit depth is different than the bit depth of the image (see Chapter 5). The bit depth of the image is how many colors are in the image or the image's palette. If the image is a 24-bit graphic, that image may contain up to 16.7 million colors. Problems in display may arise if the image bit depth is larger than that of the display device.

Technology Side-Effects

Different target devices may use different technologies for their displays. While in this day and age, computer displays are generally comparable in terms of quality, there is quite a variance in legacy and leading-edge display technologies.

Looking backwards, most televisions are still based on NTSC or PAL standards. This means that the color space for these displays is not the same as the color space used on computers. In general, televisions tend to over-saturate pure reds, greens, blues, and cyans. This means you need to be very careful using large fields of these colors. Worse, color saturation varies significantly between television manufacturers. In fact, considerable consumer brand preference is actually based on the nature of the color (over) saturation. This also affects your ability to display images to consumers in which the color of the image is very relevant – such as in apparel advertising.

In addition, most televisions are still interlaced. This means that the odd 'scan' lines for images are draw first, then the even lines, and then the odd lines, and so on. This creates 'jitter' when you try and draw small straight lines: they appear to shake (or 'jitter') between one or more scan lines. This significantly affects your ability to display fonts that have any details (such as small fonts and serif fonts).

Looking forward, some televisions that support overlaying graphics on top of video do not have square pixels. On these systems, the height of a pixel is not the same as its width. This means that if you try and draw a square, it will look like a rectangle, and if you try and draw a circle, it will look like an oval.

In addition, some emerging display technologies are using fundamentally different chemistries and physics that result in different display qualities. Some displays appear brighter, some may have certain tints to certain color values, and others may have different persistency characteristics (some pixels stay illuminated for some time after they are supposed to change color).

User Agent Constraints

The second set of factors deals with the user-agent applications (the web browsers) running on the target devices.

XHTML Element and CSS Property Support

As you may well be aware, there is considerable difference between personal computer web browsers when it comes to element and property support. The differences increase when you move beyond the computer platform to set-top boxes and handheld devices. For example, the WebTV platform does not support the `<applet>` element and the Palm web clipping platform does not support the `<frame>` element.

File Format Support

Non-traditional web devices may only support a limited set of file formats or features within these file formats. For example, the Palm web clipping platform only supports JPEG and GIF files (not PNG or animated GIF files). The WebTV platform is also limited on its native support (what it can do on the set-top box), but there are special servers that automatically convert many graphic file formats (such as PNG) to these formats before the user sees the web page.

Plug-in Support

A great deal of the multimedia on the Web is realized through plug-in decoders like Flash and Quicktime. While these types of plug-ins are well supported by the major browsers, the lack of memory in many non-traditional web devices prohibits their support. For example, the WebTV Classic platform only supports Macromedia Flash Version 1 and the Palm web clipping platform does not support any plug-ins.

Human Interface Device Constraints

The third set of factors deals with the way in which users interact with the device.

Mouse Support

You can feel pretty confident that anyone accessing your web page on a computer has a mouse, or something like a mouse, as an input device. A common feature of these types of input devices is that they control a cursor that can move from any pixel on the screen to any other pixel on the screen, moving over any pixel on the screen.

This type of input is not always available on some web devices. For example, on some set-top boxes, your users may only be able to use an up-down-left-right set of keys that moves the cursor in a grid pattern.

Key Support

Likewise, you can feel pretty confident that anyone accessing your web page on a computer has a full-function keyboard. This means that they can enter any alphanumeric symbol with relative ease.

This may not be the case on some web devices. For example, WebTV does not normally ship with a keyboard. Therefore, many WebTV users must use their remote control for entering alphanumeric characters – quite cumbersome, indeed.

Viewing Distance

Another important factor is the distance between the display and the user. As the user gets further away from a device, it is more difficult (and stressful) for the user to move a cursor to a small region on the screen.

Usage Models

In addition, the mode of the user may change as well. When the web device moves from the office to the living room, the user will change from an active, lean-forward, posture, to a passive, lean-backward, posture.

The device may also go from a single owner device (like a handheld device), to a single user at a time device (like a personal computer), to multiple users at a time device (like a television set-top box).

Strategies

So the big question is: how do you deal with all of these factors?

Well, the simple answer is that you do not need to deal with all of these factors all of the time. First and foremost, you need to identify:

- What you're trying to do with your Web page (your goals)?
- Who is your audience?

The answer to these two questions will help you identify which 'factors' you need to address.

Once you have identified which factors you need to address, you can determine which strategies or combination of strategies are appropriate to your needs.

There are three basic strategies for managing content that targets multiple devices (rather than just traditional web browsers that we looked at in the page and site design chapters earlier):

- Content selection
- Content generation
- Content adaptation

Each of these is described in the following sections.

Content Selection

The content selection strategy means that you have multiple versions of your web page, each version tailored to one or more devices or web browsers.

This is the simplest approach from a technical perspective – all you have to do is determine which web browser is asking for your web page and deliver the web page for that browser. On the other hand, it will require that you author multiple versions of the same document. This can become a considerable maintenance headache if the number of files or the number of devices increases.

Content Adaptation

The content adaptation strategy means that you adapt an existing web page to meet the constraints of the target device.

This strategy is very common in the Web. AOL and WebTV both perform content adaptation using something called 'proxy servers'. Proxy servers intercept documents as they move between the servers originating the documents (often called origin servers) and the client devices. These proxy servers adapt and cache the documents before passing them onto the client devices.

Unfortunately, proxy servers are not always available and their autonomous processing may lead to less than desirable results.

Content adaptation can be as simple as converting image and audio formats into those understood by the target device (WebTV converts PNG images to the GIF file format, for example), or content adaptation can be as complex as changing the content of the document.

As an example of this, WebTV does not support frames in the set-top box, rather, the WebTV proxy servers convert frames into tables.

A similar approach is being taken by the Wireless Application Protocol (WAP) Forum, an industry group working with the World Wide Web Consortium to define a markup language and protocols for delivering web content to mobile terminals (like cell phones). The WAP architecture calls for 'proxy servers' that can convert between the HTML and XHTML languages into the WAP Markup Language (WML).

Content Generation and XSL Transformation

The content generation strategy means that you dynamically build a web page that meets the constraints of the target device.

Typically, you would have an XHTML template for each target device, and the content comes from a database. Today, each of these template-database systems uses a proprietary solution.

The World Wide Web Consortium has introduced a new technology aimed at solving this problem. This new technology, called XSL Transformation (XSLT), is a language for transforming one XML document into another XML document. This means that you will be able to use your 'sniffer' technology to determine which browser is being used, and then apply XSLT technology to generate the correct XHTML document.

While the tools are not quite there yet, you can get a taste of XSLT using Microsoft Internet Explorer.

Try It Out – Using XSL Transformations

In this exercise, you are going to get a taste of things to come. Specifically, you are going to use the World Wide Web's new XSL Transformation technology to convert an XML document into two different presentations.

1. Run your text editor and type in the following:

```
<?xml version="1.0"?>
<xsl:stylesheet xmlns:xsl="http://www.w3.org/TR/WD-xsl">
 <xsl:template match="/">
   <html>
    <head>
      <title>Film Library:<xsl:value-of select="filmlibrary/name"/></title>
    </head>
    <body>
      <table border="2">
       <tr>
         <td>Title</td>
         <td>Director</td>
         <td>Year</td>
         <td>Genre</td>
       </tr>
       <xsl:for-each select="filmlibrary/movie">
         <tr>
          <td><xsl:value-of select="title"/></td>
          <td><xsl:value-of select="credits/director"/></td>
          <td><xsl:value-of select="year"/></td>
          <td><xsl:value-of select="genre"/></td>
         </tr>
       </xsl:for-each>
      </table>
    </body>
   </html>
 </xsl:template>
</xsl:stylesheet>
```

2. Save the file as `movie1.xsl`.

3. Create a new document in your text editor and type in the following:

```
<?xml version="1.0"?>
<?xml-stylesheet type="text/xsl" href="movie1.xsl"?>
<filmlibrary>
 <name>Classic Films</name>
 <movie>
   <title>Beauty and the Beast</title>
   <genre>Fantasy</genre>
   <country>France</country>
   <language>French</language>
   <year>1946</year>
   <length>90 Min.</length>
   <filmtype>BW</filmtype>
   <credits>
    <director>Jean Cocteau</director>
    <producer>Andre Paulve</producer>
    <writer>Jean Cocteau</writer>
    <story>Mme Leprince de Beaumont</story>
    <cinematography>Henri Alekan</cinematography>
   </credits>
   <plot>Beauty lives in a cottage with her father and
   her two wicked sisters. Once day her father comes
   upon a strange mansion with an ugly sorcerer named
   Beast.
   </plot>
 </movie>
 <movie>
   <title>The Bicycle Thief</title>
   <genre>Social Drama</genre>
   <country>Italy</country>
   <language>Italian</language>
   <year>1948</year>
   <length>90 Min.</length>
   <filmtype>BW</filmtype>
   <credits>
    <director>Vittorio de Sica</director>
    <producer>Vittorio de Sica</producer>
    <writer>Vittorio de Sica</writer>
    <story>Gennarino Bartolini</story>
    <cinematography>Carlo Montuori</cinematography>
   </credits>
   <plot>Told through the eyes of a young boy
    named Bruno, <title>The Bicycle Thief</title> is the
    story of his father"s struggle to provide for his family
    in Rome following World War II.
   </plot>
 </movie>
</filmlibrary>
```

4. Save the file as `movie1.xml`. Run the file in Microsoft Internet Explorer. You should see something like this:

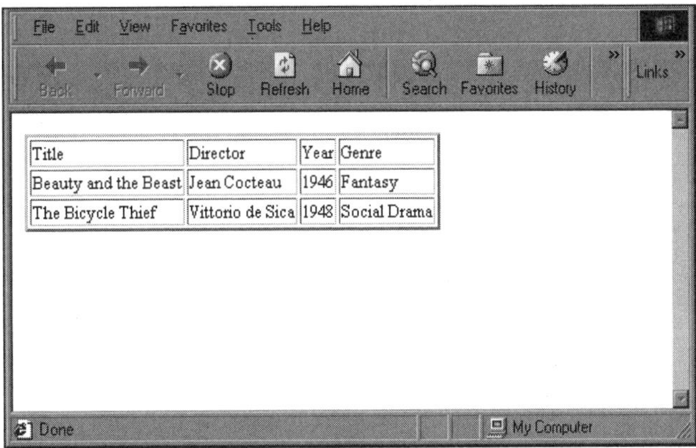

5. Run your text editor and type in the following:

```
<?xml version="1.0"?>
<xsl:stylesheet xmlns:xsl="http://www.w3.org/TR/WD-xsl">
 <xsl:template match="/">
   <html>
    <head>
      <title>Film Library:<xsl:value-of select="filmlibrary/name"/></title>
    </head>
    <body>
      <xsl:for-each select="filmlibrary/movie">
       <h1 style="text-align: center">
         <xsl:value-of select="title"/>
       </h1>
       <h2 style="text-align: center">
         <xsl:value-of select="year"/>
         <xsl:value-of select="credits/director"/>
       </h2>
       <p>
         <xsl:value-of select="genre"/>.<xsl:value-of select="plot"/>
       </p>
      </xsl:for-each>
    </body>
   </html>
 </xsl:template>
</xsl:stylesheet>
```

6. Save the file as `movie2.xsl`.

7. Load the `movie1.xml` file into your text editor and make `href` point to the second version of the XSL style sheet:

```
<?xml-stylesheet type="text/xsl" href="movie2.xsl"?>
```

8. Save the file as movie2.xml. Run the file in Microsoft Internet Explorer. You should see something like this:

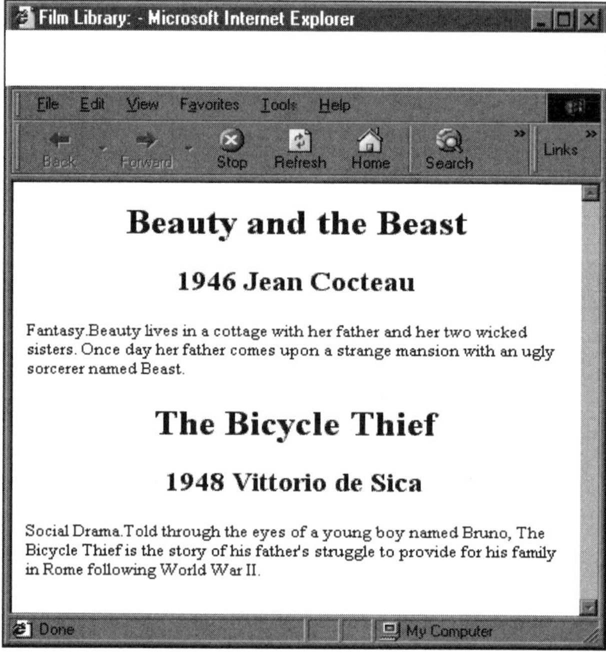

How It Works

In Step 1, we specified an XSL style sheet. The first couple of lines are standard boilerplate:

```
<?xml version="1.0"?>
<xsl:stylesheet xmlns:xsl="http://www.w3.org/TR/WD-xsl">
```

They specify the version of XML and the namespace for the XSL style sheet.

The next line is more important:

```
<xsl:template match="/">
```

This "/" string indicates that the following template should be applied to the root node of the XML document, i.e. to all of it.

The next dozen or so lines (beginning with <html> and ending with </html>) define the XHTML template. Within this template are some XSL instructions for extracting data from the XML document. Look at the <title> element:

```
<title>Film Library:<xsl:value-of select="filmlibrary/name"/></title>
```

The `<xsl:value-of>` element says that we want to use the element content for the element that matches the value of the `select` attribute. In this case, we are going to use the value of the `<name>` element that is a child of the `<filmlibrary>` element.

Thus:

```
<title>Film Library:<xsl:value-of select="filmlibrary/name"/></title>
```

gets transformed into:

```
<title>Film Library:Classic Films</title>
```

because 'Classic Films' is the content of then `<name>` tag contained within the `<filmlibrary>` tag in the XML file:

```
<filmlibrary>
 <name>Classic Films</name>
```

That is, `<xsl:value-of select="filmlibrary/name"/>` is replaced with `Classic Films` because 'Classic Films' is the value of the `"filmlibrary/name"` selection used in the `<xsl:value-of>` element. (One may think of it almost as a programmed find-and-replace technique.)

The next occurrence of an XSL element is in the `<table>` element:

```
<xsl:for-each select="filmlibrary/movie">
```

The `<xsl:for-each>` element instructs the browser that we want to repeat the following template for each occurrence of the element which matches the value of the `select` attribute. In this case, we are going to repeat the template for each `<movie>` element that is a child of the `<filmlibrary>` element.

Within this for-each loop are a set of `<xsl:value-of>` elements which put the value of the `<title>`, `<director>`, `<year>`, and `<genre>` elements into the table:

```
<tr>
<td><xsl:value-of select="title"/></td>
<td><xsl:value-of select="credits/director"/></td>
<td><xsl:value-of select="year"/></td>
<td><xsl:value-of select="genre"/></td>
</tr>
```

So even though we have two <movie> elements within our XML file, we only need the one `<xsl:for-each>` block in our XSL file to perform the same operation on both the `<movie>` elements. Obviously, we could have as many `<movie>` elements as we wanted in our file and we would still need only one `<xsl:for-each>` element to process all of them.

In Step 2, we authored the XML document. Like the XML style sheet, the first line indicates the version of XML that we are using:

```
<?xml version="1.0"?>
```

The second line associates the style sheet with our XML document:

```
<?xml-stylesheet type="text/xsl" href="movie1.xsl"?>
```

The rest of the document contains the content that gets transformed by the XSL style sheet.

In Step 5, we create a second XSL style sheet. Looking at the first couple of lines in this style sheet:

```
<?xml version="1.0"?>
<xsl:stylesheet xmlns:xsl="http://www.w3.org/TR/WD-xsl">
 <xsl:template match="/">
```

we see the same XML version and XSL style sheet namespace identifiers, as well as the `<xsl:template>` element, as in the previous sheet.

Where this style sheet departs from the previous one is that rather than formatting the XML document as a table, we format it using headers and paragraphs.

Looking at the `<body>` element, we wrote:

```
<body>
 <xsl:for-each select="filmlibrary/movie">
```

This means that the element content of the `<body>` element will be based on each occurrence of the `<movie>` element in our XML document.

The `<h1>` element is defined by the following lines of XML:

```
<h1 style="text-align: center">
<xsl:value-of select="title"/>
</h1>
```

The `<xsl:value-of>` element means that the `<h1>` element will contain the content of the `<title>` element. Similarly, the `<h2>` element will contain the content of the `<year>` and `<director>` elements:

```
<h2 style="text-align: center">
<xsl:value-of select="year"/> <xsl:value-of select="credits/director"/>
</h2>
```

and the <p> element will contain the content of the <genre> and <plot> elements:

```
<p>
<xsl:value-of select="genre"/>.<xsl:value-of select="plot"/>
</p>
```

In Step 7, we associate the style sheet with the XML document:

```
<?xml-stylesheet type='text/xsl' href='movie2.xsl'?>
```

When we load the XML document into Microsoft Internet Explorer, the document is then transformed using the associated style sheet.

Summary

In this chapter, we learned a little about media types:

- Using media types to manage different types of web devices
- Managing media types using the <style> element
- Managing media types using the <link> element
- Controlling how documents are printed using `@media` and `@page` rules
- Forcing page breaks with page breaking properties

We also learned about three types of problems affecting our ability to target different devices:

- Device constraints
- User agent constraints
- Human interface device constraints

Finally, we introduced some strategies for overcoming these constraints. We can author different versions of our content for different devices, use tools that adapt content to different devices, or generate content based on the type of device.

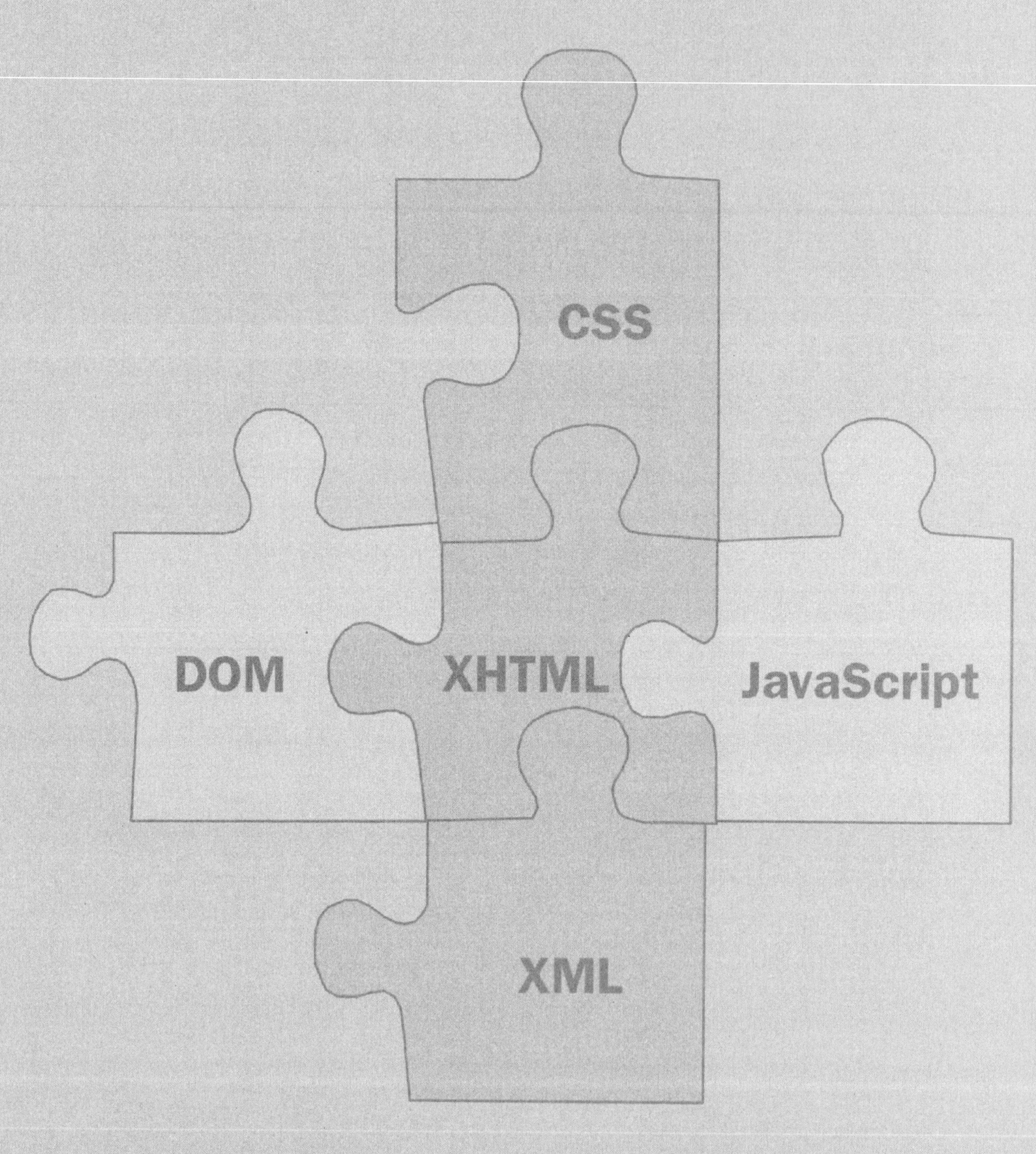
CSS
DOM
XHTML
JavaScript
XML

Multimedia

The World Wide Web has come a long way since Tim Berners-Lee's seminal work in 1990 and 1991. Where HTML started as a text-only language (the 'H' stands for Hypertext), by 1993, Marc Andreesen had recommended the introduction of the `<img>` element, ushering in the multimedia web!

The multimedia web combines text, graphics, audio, and video into meaningful presentations used for entertainment, education, and advertising. Some of this multimedia is delivered to the user's computer as a complete file and is subsequently drawn, played, or rendered by the user agent. Other multimedia content is delivered to the user's computer in small segments. In this way, the user agent can begin rendering the multimedia while more content is being "streamed" to the user's computer.

In this chapter, you will learn about audio and video media, as well as streaming audio (like Internet radio) and video. We have already talked about graphics, so we'll just be looking at audio and video in this discussion.

In this chapter, we will cover the following:

- playing audio files in a web page
- controlling an audio plug-in player
- playing video files in a web page
- controlling a video plug-in player
- streaming audio and video
- integrating audio and video with the SMIL language

Let's start with the basics of audio.

Playing Audio

There are two types of audio that you can use in your web pages: **audio files** and **streaming audio**. The best thing about using audio files is that they're very simple. When you use an audio file in your web page, the user agent will download the entire file before beginning to play the audio. This means that if the audio file is large, and the user's connection to the Internet is slow, there can be quite a delay before the user starts hearing anything!

Streaming audio is considerably more complex. When you use streaming audio, the user agent only downloads a portion of the audio before it begins playing the audio. This is great when the audio file is large and you don't want too much of a delay. It is also great for audio that is being recorded and played back simultaneously, as with Internet radio.

In order to hear the examples in this chapter, your computer will need to have a sound card (a 16-bit SoundBlaster Pro or compatible will do). Most personal computers are sold with a perfectly acceptable sound system. Just make sure to plug in some speakers or headphones and turn up the volume (sensibly!).

Audio Plug-Ins

There are a variety of audio formats. The `WAV` file format is the most common audio file format for Windows. Other popular audio formats are Sun Microsystem's `AU` file format and the MIDI (Musical Instrument Digital Interface) file format. The `AIFF` file format is the most common audio file format for the Macintosh. All of these file formats are well supported, but the `AU` file format, which used to be the Internet standard, has pretty poor sound quality. The `AU` file format only uses 8 bits to describe the sound (this is called 8-bit samples) whereas the other file formats may use 16-bit samples.

Web browsers typically use something called **plug-in applications** to play audio. When a browser does not have the ability to handle a file format, the browser uses a "helper" application that can handle the unknown file format. These "helper" applications are called plug-in applications because they are modular and can be "plugged" into the browser to give the browser more functionality.

There are a variety of audio plug-ins available for Microsoft Internet Explorer and Netscape Navigator. We will talk about four of these:

- Microsoft Windows Media Player
- Netscape LiveAudio
- RealNetworks RealPlayer
- Apple QuickTime

Microsoft Windows Media Player is typically the default plug-in for Microsoft Internet Explorer, and RealNetworks RealPlayer is typically used with Netscape Navigator in combination with Netscape's LiveAudio plug-in. But before we talk more about these plug-ins, let's get our hands a little dirty! As well as embedding audio into our page, which we'll look at shortly, we can simply provide a normal `<a>` element to link to the file. In this exercise, we're going to play a MIDI audio file by simply linking to the audio file in this way.

Try It Out – Playing a Simple Audio File

1. Type the following into your text editor:

```
<?xml version="1.0" encoding="UTF-8"?>
<!DOCTYPE html
     PUBLIC "-//W3C//DTD XHTML 1.0 Transitional//EN"
     "http://www.w3.org/TR/xhtml1/DTD/xhtml1-transitional.dtd">
<html xmlns="http://www.w3.org/1999/xhtml" xml:lang="en" lang="en">
  <head>
    <title>Simple Music Player</title>
  </head>
  <body>
    <a href="myaudio.mid">Music Player</a>
  </body>
</html>
```

2. Save the file as `audio.htm`.

3. Copy the file `myaudio.mid` from the code download for this book and save it in the same directory in which you saved the `audio.htm` file.

4. Run the `audio.htm` file in your browser. For Microsoft Internet Explorer, you should see something like this:

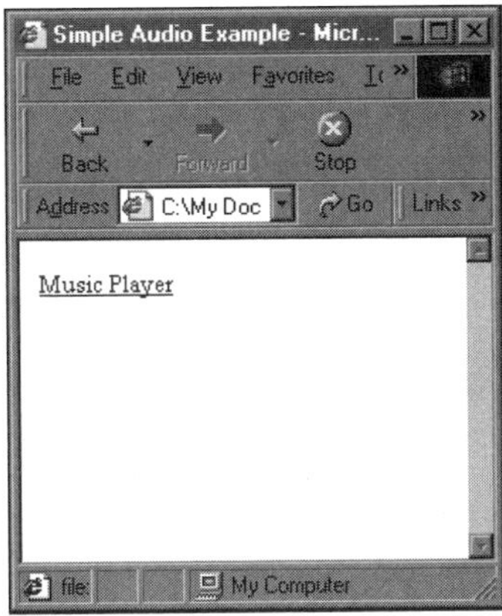

5. Click on the Music Player hyperlink and you should begin to hear music and see something like this (you may see something different if you have a different audio plug-in assigned to play the `.mid` file format):

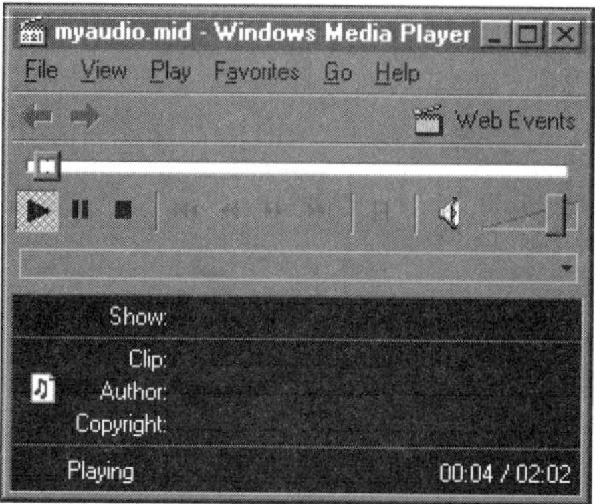

6. When the music stops, everyone has to find themselves a chair. Um, no, sorry... when the music stops, or when you are tired of listening to it, close the pop-up window and close your browser.

How It Works

The critical line here is this:

```
<a href="myaudio.mid">Music Player</a>
```

We created a hyperlink from an XHTML document to a multimedia file using the `<a>` element. The multimedia file, called `myaudio.mid`, is a MIDI music format (which stands for Musical Instrument Digital Interface).

When you click on the hyperlink, the browser navigates to the audio file. The browser sees that the audio file is a MIDI file, and since it does not inherently know how to handle MIDI files, it looks for the plug-in that *does* know. We've shown the Microsoft Windows Media Player as that plug-in application, but you might see a different application if you have loaded RealPlayer or some other plug-in.

Putting Audio Inside the Document

In the previous exercise, you created a hyperlink from your document to an external audio file. While this was very simple to do, it leaves a little to be desired in terms of aesthetics. You are unable to visually integrate the audio player into your web page, and with all of the windows popping up all over the place, your users can quickly lose control.

There are two ways to put the audio player inside of your web pages (known as **embedding** the player): the official way and the way that works all of the time!

The official way is to use the <object> element. Unfortunately, using this will alienate IE3 users, because this element will cause IE3 to get confused. Netscape Navigator also does not fully support the <object> element at the time of writing. So, before we tell you how to do things the official way, we will tell you about the way that always works!

The <embed> Element

The <embed> element is used to put documents of any type into an XHTML document.

> **While the <embed> element works in both Microsoft Internet Explorer and Netscape Navigator, it is not officially a part of the HTML or XHTML standards! The correct solution is to use the <object> element, but until that is fully supported by your users, you may find that you have no choice but to use the <embed> element.**

The <embed> element tells the web browser that the referenced document needs to be processed by a plug-in application. For example, if you wanted to put your audio file into a document, you would write:

```
<embed src="myaudio.mid" autostart="true" width="200" height="100" />
```

Different versions of Netscape behave in different ways with regard to this element, so you'd do well to test it out on a few versions if you're concerned about those with older browsers at all.

This sample illustrates four attributes: `src`, `autostart`, `width`, and `height`. You will learn about these later, but briefly:

- The `src` attribute specifies the URL to the file that you want to embed inside of your document. You must always specify a value for the `src` attribute.
- The `width` and `height` attributes specify the width and height of the audio player in pixels. You should always supply values for the <embed> element's `width` and `height` attributes – different plug-ins behave differently if these values are not specified.
- The `autostart` attribute specifies whether the file should be played immediately (when `autostart="true"`) or whether the file should wait to be played when the user clicks on the play button (when `autostart="false"`).

These four attributes are well supported by the different audio plug-ins. There are quite a few other attributes for the <embed> element that you will learn about later.

Try It Out – Using the <embed> Element

In this exercise, you are going to put an audio file into a web page using the <embed> element. The <embed> element is not an official element in XHTML, but its support is so widespread that we will go ahead and use it for now.

1. Type the following into your text editor:

```
<?xml version="1.0" encoding="UTF-8"?>
<!DOCTYPE html
     PUBLIC "-//W3C//DTD XHTML 1.0 Transitional//EN"
     "http://www.w3.org/TR/xhtml1/DTD/xhtml1-transitional.dtd">
<html xmlns="http://www.w3.org/1999/xhtml" xml:lang="en" lang="en">
<head>
 <title>Embedded Audio Example</title>
</head>
<body>
 <p>This is an example of an embedded
   <embed src="myaudio.mid" autostart="false" width="300" height="200" />
   audio file!</p>
</body>
</html>
```

2. Save the file as `embed.htm`.

3. Run this file in Microsoft Internet Explorer. You should see something like this:

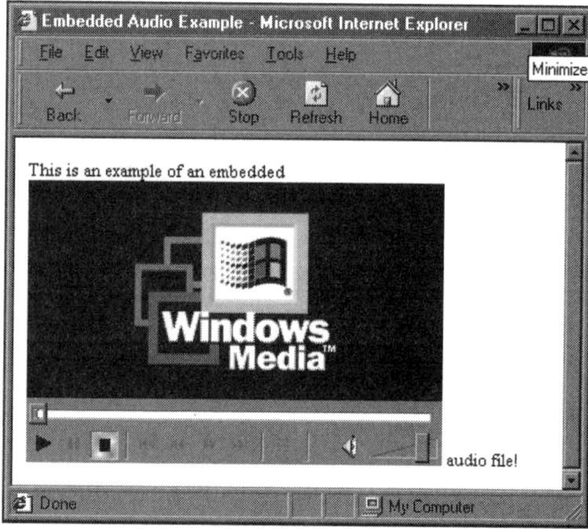

4. Click on the "play" button and you should hear the music play.

How It Works

We define an `<embed>` element which links to the audio file `myaudio.mid` using the `src` attribute:

```
<p>This is an example of an embedded
   <embed src="myaudio.mid" autostart="false" width="300" height="200" />
   audio file!</p>
```

When we run the document in our web browser, the audio plug-in is displayed in the web page but it does not play immediately because we set the `autoplay` attribute value to `false`.

Let's now look at the 'official' method – the `<object>` element.

The <object> Element

The `<object>` element is used to put documents of any type into an XHTML document. Unfortunately, while the `<object>` element has been a part of the World Wide Web Consortium's standards for some time, not all web browsers currently support this element or its defined behavior. Therefore, before relying on the `<object>` element, make sure that your user's browsers support the `<object>` element in the way that you plan to use it.

Like the `<embed>` element, the `<object>` element tells the web browser that the referenced document needs to be processed by a plug-in application. For example, if you wanted to put your audio file into a document, you would write:

```
<object data="myaudio.mid" type="audio/midi" width="100" height="100"
autostart="true">
</object>
```

This sample illustrates five attributes: `data`, `type`, `autostart`, `width`, and `height`. There are many other attributes, but these are the attributes most appropriate to playing audio files.

Note that we specified the object using the `<object>` opening tag and the `</object>` closing tag, even though there is no content. At the time that this book was written, neither Microsoft Internet Explorer 4 nor Netscape Navigator 4 would properly handle an empty object element (i.e., `<object ... />`) – they tended to forget about all of the elements that followed!

The 'data' attribute

The `<object>` element's `data` attribute specifies the URL to the file that you want to include inside of your document. When you are using the `<object>` element to put an audio file into a web page, you must specify a value for the `data` attribute.

The 'type' attribute

The `<object>` element's `type` attribute specifies the MIME type for the file that you want to include inside your document. Unlike the `data` attribute, you do not need to specify a value for the `type` attribute. The reason that you should specify a value for the `type` attribute is that it helps the web browser know whether or not to download the file specified by the `data` attribute. If there is no plug-in associated with the value of the `type` attribute, the web browser probably cannot process the included file.

The 'width' and 'height' attribute

The `<object>` element's `width` and `height` attributes specify the width and height of the audio player in pixels.

> **You should always supply values for the object element's `width` and `height` attributes – different plug-ins behave differently if these values are not specified.**

The 'autostart' attribute

The `<object>` element's `autostart` attribute is not part of the XHTML specification but is supported by Netscape Navigator. The reason that the `autostart` attribute is important is that its default value in Netscape Navigator is `false`. This means that if you do not set the value of the `autostart` attribute to `true`, audio files will immediately start playing when run in Microsoft Internet Explorer, but will not immediately start playing when run in Netscape Navigator.

We will demonstrate this annoying idiosyncrasy in the next exercise.

Try It Out – Using the <object> Element

In this exercise, we are going to put an audio file into a web page using the `<object>` element.

1. Type the following into your text editor:

```
<?xml version="1.0" encoding="UTF-8"?>
<!DOCTYPE html
     PUBLIC "-//W3C//DTD XHTML 1.0 Transitional//EN"
     "http://www.w3.org/TR/xhtml1/DTD/xhtml1-transitional.dtd">
<html xmlns="http://www.w3.org/1999/xhtml" xml:lang="en" lang="en">
<head>
  <title>Object Audio Example</title>
</head>
<body>
  <p>This is an example of an
    <object data="myaudio.mid" type="audio/midi" width="100" height="100">
    </object>
  embedded object.</p>
</body>
</html>
```

2. Save the file as `object.htm`.

3. View `object.htm` in Microsoft Internet Explorer. You should hear the music playing and see something like this:

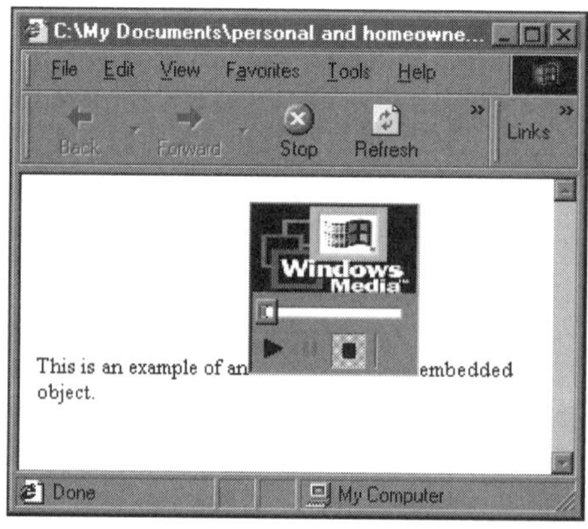

4. Close Microsoft Internet Explorer.

5. Run `object.htm` in Netscape Navigator. You should see something like this, but without hearing anything (assuming that you are using the built-in audio plug-in):

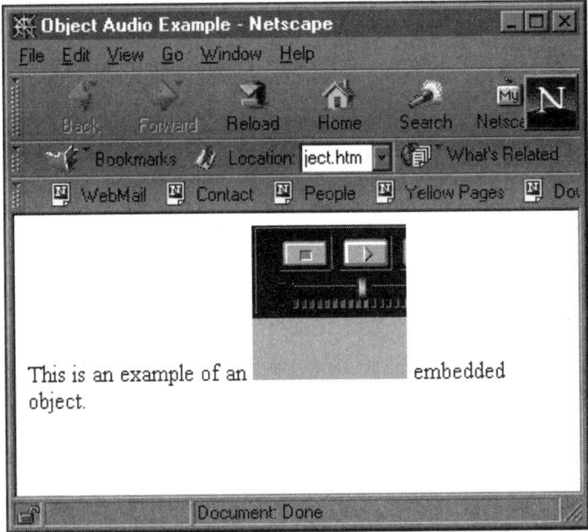

6. Close Netscape Navigator.

7. Open the `object.htm` file in your text editor and make the following changes:

```
<head>
  <title>Object Audio Autostart Example</title>
</head>
<body>
  <p>This is an example of an
    <object data="myaudio.mid" type="audio/midi" autostart="true" width="300"
height="200">
    </object>
  embedded object.</p>
```

8. Save the file as `ostart.htm`.

9. Run `ostart.htm` in Netscape Navigator. You should see the same thing as before, but this time you should hear music playing.

How It Works

We've specified an object that embeds `myaudio.mid` into the document:

```
<object data="myaudio.mid" type="audio/midi" width="300" height="200">
</object>
```

The <object> element's data attribute was set to the URL of the desired file; in this case the URL is simply myaudio.mid. The <object> element's type attribute is set to "audio/midi" since we know that the desired file is a MIDI file.

When we ran the document in Microsoft Internet Explorer, the audio file immediately began to play. In Netscape Navigator, though, the audio file did not begin to play when you first viewed the file. This is because Netscape Navigator treats the <object> element as if it is an <embed> element. Thus in Netscape Navigator, the <object> element has an autostart attribute (which is not part of any HTML or XHTML specification, I might add).

To make matters worse, the default value of the Netscape Navigator <object> element's autostart attribute is false. This means that if you do not provide a value for this attribute, audio files won't immediately play when using LiveAudio in Netscape Navigator.

So in Step 7, we remedied this deficiency in Netscape Navigator by adding the proprietary autostart attribute to the <object> element:

```
<object data="myaudio.mid" type="audio/midi" autostart="true" width="300"
height="100">
```

Plug-in Support for the <embed> Element

As mentioned earlier in this chapter, Microsoft Windows Media Player, Netscape LiveAudio, and Apple Quicktime support different features for the <embed> element. The more commonly used features, and their availability, are listed below.

Don't worry about using too many attributes – if a plug-in does not support a particular attribute, it will ignore it.

Common Attributes

These attributes are supported by all the plug-ins we've discussed in this chapter.

The 'align' attribute

The align attribute specifies where to align the plug-in's control panel. The attribute can have the following values:

- baseline – the control panel is aligned to the baseline of the adjoining text.
- center – the control panel is aligned to the vertical center of the adjoining text.
- left – the control panel is aligned to the left of the adjoining text.
- right – the control panel is aligned to the right of the adjoining text.
- top – the control panel is aligned to the top of the adjoining text.

The default value is baseline.

The 'height' attribute

The `height` attribute specifies the height of the audio plug-in's control panel in pixels. The attribute value is an integer.

> **If the `height` and `width` attributes are not specified, QuickTime will use its default height and width. In stark contrast, LiveAudio and Media Player have undefined behaviors depending on the browser implementation. It is strongly encouraged that you always set the `height` and `width` attributes.**

The 'hidden' attribute

The `hidden` attribute specifies whether the audio plug-in's control panel is displayed. The attribute can have one of the following values:

- `true` – the control panel is displayed.
- `false` – the control panel is not displayed

The default value is `false`.

> **Two notes about using the `hidden` attribute. First, Netscape Navigator ignores the value of the hidden attribute, treating any occurence of the attribute (whether `true` or `false`) as indicating that the control panel should not be displayed. Second, if you use the `hidden` attribute, it will override the value of the `controller` attribute.**

The 'src' attribute

The `src` attribute specifies the location of the audio file. The attribute value is a URL and it is required.

The 'width' attribute

The `width` attribute specifies the width of the audio plug-in's control panel in pixels. The attribute value is an integer. See the `height` attribute for some notes on using the width attribute.

Specific Attributes

These attributes are supported by one or more (but not all) of the plug-ins we've discussed.

The 'autoplay' attribute (QuickTime)

The `autoplay` attribute specifies whether the audio file should play automatically. The attribute can have the following values:

- `true` – the audio file plays automatically
- `false` – the audio file does not play automatically

The default value is `true`.

> **If the value of the 'autoplay' attribute is different than the value of the 'autostart' attribute, the behavior is undefined – different web browsers do different things. You should consider only using the 'autostart' attribute for audio files.**

The 'autosize' attribute (Media Player)

The `autosize` attribute specifies whether the audio plug-in should determine its own size (in other words, calculating its own height and width and ignoring the values of those attributes). The attribute can have one of the following values:

- `true` – the audio plug-in determines its own height and width
- `false` – the height and width are determined by the value of the `height` and `width` attributes

The default value is `false`.

The 'autostart' attribute (LiveAudio, MediaPlayer, QuickTime)

The `autostart` attribute specifies whether the audio file should play automatically. The attribute can have the following values:

- `true` – the audio file plays automatically
- `false` – the audio file does not play automatically

The default value is `true`.

The 'controller' attribute (QuickTime)

The `controller` attribute specifies whether the audio plug-in's control panel is visible. The attribute can have the following values:

- `true` – the control panel is visible
- `false` – the control panel is not visible

The default value is `false`.

> **If you use the 'hidden' attribute, it will override the value of the 'controller' attribute.**

The 'controls' attribute (LiveAudio)

The `controls` attribute specifies which controls to display on the audio plug-in's control panel. The attribute can have the following values:

- `console` – displays the entire control panel
- `pausebutton` – only displays the pause button
- `playbutton` – only displays the play button
- `smallconsole` – displays a smaller control panel with less controls
- `stopbutton` – only displays the stop button
- `volumelever` – only displays the volume control

The default value is `console`.

The 'endtime' attribute (LiveAudio and QuickTime)

The `endtime` attribute specifies when the audio file should stop playing (measuring from the start of the file). The attribute can have the following values:

- *`hh`*`:`*`mm`*`:`*`ss`*`:`*`ff`* (QuickTime)
- *`mm`*`:`*`ss`* (LiveAudio)

Where *`hh`* is the number of hours, *`mm`* is the number of minutes, *`ss`* is the number of seconds, and *`ff`* is the number of frames. The default value is the duration of the entire audio file.

> **The 'endtime' attribute values for QuickTime and LiveAudio are not compatible in the least. You should avoid using the 'endtime' attribute unless you are certain that your users are using the audio plug-in that you expect.**

The 'loop' attribute (Media Player and QuickTime)

The `loop` attribute specifies whether the audio file should play continuously. The attribute can have one of the following values:

- `true` – the audio file repeatedly plays from start to finish
- `false` – the audio file plays once
- `palindrome` (QuickTime only) – the audio file alternately plays from start to finish and then from finish to start (backwards).

The default value is `false`.

The 'plug-inspage' attribute (Media Player and QuickTime)

The `plug-inspage` attribute specifies the location (as a URL) for the plug-in used to view an audio file. This attribute is very useful to ensure that your user has a way of playing to your audio file.

The 'showcontrols' attribute (Media Player)

The `showcontrols` attribute specifies whether the audio plug-in's control panel shows the "track" controls – the play button, pause button, etc. The attribute can have the following values:

- `true` – the controls are displayed
- `false` – the controls are not displayed

The default value is `true`.

The 'showdisplay' attribute (Media Player)

The `showdisplay` attribute specifies whether the audio plug-in's control panel shows the playlist and track information. The attribute can have the following values:

- `true` – the playlist information is displayed
- `false` – the playlist information is not displayed

The default value is `false`.

The 'starttime' attribute (LiveAudio and Quicktime)

The `starttime` attribute specifies when the audio file should start playing (measuring from the start of the file). The attribute can have the following values:

- *`hh`*`:`*`mm`*`:`*`ss`*`:00` (QuickTime)
- *`mm`*`:`*`ss`* (LiveAudio)

Where *`hh`* is the number of hours, *`mm`* is the number of minutes, and *`ss`* is the number of seconds. The default value is the beginning of the audio file ("00:00:00:00" or "00:00").

> **The 'starttime' attribute values for QuickTime and LiveAudio are not compatible in the least. You should avoid using the 'starttime' attribute unless you are certain that your users are using the audio plug-in that you expect.**

The 'volume' attribute (LiveAudio and QuickTime)

The `volume` attribute specifies the relative volume for playing the audio file. Specifically, the value of volume attribute is a percentage of the system volume (simply a number between 0 and 100).

Playing Video

As with audio, there are two types of video that you can use in your web pages: video files and streaming video.

When you use a video file in your web page, the user agent will download the entire file before beginning to play the video. With some video plug-ins, they may be smart enough to begin playing before the entire video file is downloaded, but you should not rely on this behavior. In general, if the video file is large, and the user's connection to the Internet is slow, there can be quite a delay before the user starts seeing real video.

When you use streaming video, the user agent only downloads a portion of the video before it begins playing the video. This is great when the video file is large and you don't want too much of a delay. It is also great for video that is being recorded and played back simultaneously, as with Internet television.

Putting Video Inside The Document

There are a variety of video file formats available for Microsoft Internet Explorer and Netscape Navigator. We will talk about three of these:

- Apple QuickTime
- Microsoft Video for Windows (`AVI` files)
- MPEG (Motion Picture Experts Group)

For a long time, Video for Windows was the standard for PC platforms and QuickTime was used primarily on the Macintosh. With the advent of the web, this has changed and QuickTime is considerably more dominant for web-based video files. MPEG is actually a collection of audio and video standards that ranges in quality from video not much better than Video for Windows up to the emerging high definition television. In fact, the digital home satellite systems that have recently become popular in Europe and North America is based on MPEG technology.

But since we are talking about the web, we are going to focus on Apple Quicktime. If you do not have a copy of the latest Quicktime, you can download and install the plug-in from Apple's web site:

`http://www.apple.com/quicktime/`

The QuickTime plug -in can play many different types of movies (including `MPEG` and `AVI`), as well as audio files and graphics files.

QuickTime uses a file-based video format. This means that the entire file needs to be downloaded from the web. Unlike other video plug-ins, QuickTime is smart enough to be able to start playing before the entire file is downloaded. This significantly improves performance and makes it seem like it is a streaming media.

Try It Out – Playing a simple video file

In this exercise, you are going to play a simple video file using the `<object>` element.

1. Type the following into your text editor:

```
<?xml version="1.0" encoding="UTF-8"?>
<!DOCTYPE html
     PUBLIC "-//W3C//DTD XHTML 1.0 Transitional//EN"
     "http://www.w3.org/TR/xhtml1/DTD/xhtml1-transitional.dtd">
<html xmlns="http://www.w3.org/1999/xhtml" xml:lang="en" lang="en">
<head>
  <title>Simple Movie Example</title>
</head>
<body>
```

```
    <p>This is an example of an embedded
      <object data="sleepy.mov" type="video/quicktime" width="164" height="140" >
      </object>
    Quicktime movie using the object element.</p>
  </body>
  </html>
```

2. Save the file as `objmovie.htm`.

3. Copy the "Sleepy Hollow" movie trailer file `sleepy.mov` from the downloaded code to the folder in which you saved the `objmovie.htm` file.

4. Run the `objmovie.htm` file in your web browser. You should see something that looks like this:

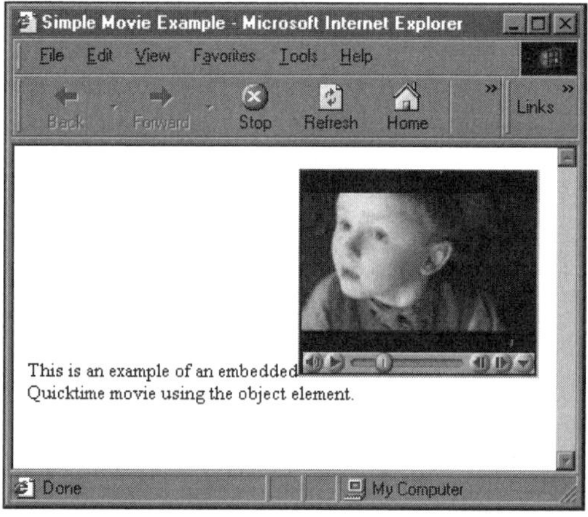

How It Works

First, we specified an `<object>` element:

```
<object data="sleepy.mov" type="video/quicktime" width="164" height="140" >
</object>
```

The `<object>` element's `data` attribute specifies the location of the video file. In this case, the location was simply `sleepy.mov`.

The `<object>` element's `type` attribute specifies the MIME type for the video file. In this case, the video file is a QuickTime file and the corresponding MIME type is `video/quicktime`.

The `<object>` element's `width` and `height` attributes specify the height and width of the "box" containing the embedded document – in this case the QuickTime plug-in's graphical user interface. The `width` and `height` attributes were set to 164 and 140, respectively, which seems about right for this version of QuickTime.

Using the <object> Element

As you learned in Chapter 4, the `<object>` element is used to put documents of any type into an XHTML document. The `<object>` element's `type` attribute tells the web browser that the referenced document needs to be processed by a plug-in application. For example, if you wanted to put your video file into a document, you would write:

```
<object data="myvideo" type="audio/quicktime" width="100" height="100" >
</object>
```

As we said before, remember to use the `<object>` opening tag and the `</object>` closing tag, even though there is no content. At the time that this book was written, neither Microsoft Internet Explorer nor Netscape Navigator would properly handle an empty object element (i.e., `<object ... />`) – things get quite unpredictable!

The 'data' attribute

The `<object>` element's `data` attribute specifies the URL to the video file that you want to include inside of your document. When you are using the `<object>` element to put a video file into a web page, you must specify a value for the `data` attribute.

The 'type' attribute

The `<object>` element's `type` attribute specifies the MIME type for the video file that you want to include inside your document. As when putting audio inside your document, you do not need to specify a value for the `type` attribute. The reason that you should specify a value for the `type` attribute is that it helps the web browser know whether or not to download the file specified by the `data` attribute, because it knows in advance whether or not it'll be able to read it once it's downloaded it.

The 'width' and 'height' attribute

The `<object>` element's `width` and `height` attributes specify the width and height of the video player in pixels. You should always supply values for the `<object>` element's `width` and `height` attributes – different plug-ins behave differently if these values are not specified.

Using the <embed> Element

Previously, you learned how to use the `<embed>` element to put audio in your document. You can also use it element to put video in your element, and the list of supported attributes is the same as the list above, with the addition of `bgcolor` for Quicktime:

The 'bgcolor' attribute (QuickTime)

The `bgcolor` attribute specifies the background color for any space that is not taken up by the movie (see the `height` and `width` attributes). The attribute can have the following values:

- hexadecimal value – the RGB color values in the form "#RRGGBB", as described in Appendix C on colors.
- color names – the names of colors (such as "blue"), also as found in Appendix C.

Now let's move on and discuss streaming media.

Streaming Audio and Video

So far, you have learned how to include an audio file in your web page. One of the more exciting changes that is occurring with the web is the advent of streaming media. As slow telephone wires make way for cable, satellite, and other "broadband" networks, and as network delays are reduced and reliability improved – more multimedia can be delivered "live" to the computer.

At the time that this book was written, there were more than half a million streaming pages available on the Web, over 2,500 radio stations webcasting, over 100 television stations webcasting live, and over 4 million people have digital music players.

This section will provide an overview of how to stream audio and video from a web server to a web page. It is beyond the scope of this book to go into all of the details, but you should get an idea of what you are going to need to do and, perhaps more importantly, where you can go for additional information!

The Web Server

The previous sections talked about audio and video files that are downloaded from a web server. Most of the focus was on how to author the web page and whether to use the XHTML `<object>` element or non-standard `<embed>` element. Little attention was given to the web server that stores the audio and video files because, quite frankly, there is little difference between a normal audio or video file and a large document (audio and video files can be quite large).

When you consider streaming media, though, the web server suddenly becomes very important. If the web server is not designed for streaming audio or video, your users may find that the sound or pictures stop periodically as the plug-in waits for the web server to catch up. During these pauses, the Windows Media Player or Real Networks RealPlayer will stop in order to fill its memory before continuing (something called **buffering**).

You can use a media server as an alternative to a general purpose web server. Two popular media servers are the RealNetworks RealServer and Microsoft Windows Media Server. Both of these systems support streaming audio and video as well as dynamic adjustment of the media streams for adapting to the user's bandwidth.

Another approach is to use an ISP or some other company to host your media. At the time that this book was written, Yahoo's Geocities offered a low-cost service for supporting streaming media. You can contact Geocities at:

```
http://geocities.yahoo.com/members/addons/mm/geomedia/
```

RealNetworks RealServer is available on several versions of UNIX, WindowsNT, Windows95, and Windows98. Depending on which version of RealServer you are using, your system will require 6MB of RAM and 10MB for each 100 concurrent users (for every 100 people trying to stream audio or video at the same time). You can download RealServer from RealNetworks at:

```
http://www.realnetworks.com/products/
```

Installation is a breeze, with a wizard walking you through most of the chore.

There are several versions of RealServer depending on what you need. If you are just getting your feet wet, you can get the Basic version for free. This version will support 60 concurrent users. Other versions are tailored for supporting more concurrent users or for use within a corporate firewall. The URL mentioned above will guide you to these other versions of RealServer.

Microsoft Windows Media Server is available for WindowsNT. Microsoft recommends that you use a Pentium II 266 MHz or better processor, 128 MB RAM, and hard disk space for the content (500MB). You can get more information about Windows Media Server from Microsoft at:

`http://www.microsoft.com/Windows/windowsmedia/en/serve/`

As with RealServer, installation of the Windows Media Server is quite straightforward. After you download the `wmserver.exe` program from Microsoft, you double-click on it, start the installation program and follow a Wizard through the installation process.

Whether you choose to use a general purpose web server or one of the specialized media servers, you will need to configure the web server to support the MIME types for the media that you wish to support. For example, if you want to support Microsoft's `WMA` streaming audio format, you will need to add the `"audio/x-ms-wma"` media type.

Unfortunately, each web server manages MIME types differently. In many cases, there is an "administration" function that lets you add or remove MIME types. Refer to your web server's document for how this is done.

If you are using a third party, like Geocities, you will need to contact them to make sure that they can support the media type that you wish to use. If you stick to one of the standard RealNetworks or Microsoft formats, you should be fine.

Building Your Streaming Content

Once that you have set up your web server, you need to encode your streaming media content. There are several tools to accomplish this. RealNetworks has several encoders, including RealProducer, and Microsoft offers Windows Media Encoder. These tools allow you to encode audio and video into a file format supported by the web server and the user's players.

When you encode your media, you need to select a bit rate that matches your user's bandwidth. What this means is that if your users are connected to your server through an old 28.8K modem, you should encode your audio and video to be playable through a 28.8K modem. If you don't, and you encode your media as if your user's were connected through a satellite, your user's will see and hear nothing but audio with long expanses of silence and video that makes flip-books look state-of-the-art! This is because you are trying to push too much audio and video through a modem-line that can only handle so much data every second.

One of the advantages of using RealServer or Windows Media Server is that they support multiple bit rate encoding. This means that you can encode your audio and video at several bit rates. When your users connect to the media server, the media server "tests the waters" to see what bandwidth is available, and then the media server selects the appropriate bit rate.

Referring to Your Streaming Content

The next step is to create a "redirector" file that can be referenced by your web page. Whether you are using a RealNetworks or a Windows Media file format, you will need to create a file that references the streaming media. This "redirector" file is necessary because if your web page referred to the streaming media directly, most browsers would try to load the entire file rather than stream the file.

For RealNetworks, your "redirector" file is called a RAM file. This RAM file contains a single line that refers to the streaming media file. For example, if you have a RealMedia file called `flowers.rm` (the "rm" stands for RealMedia) located somewhere on your webserver, you would write a text file that contains the URL to the streaming file:

```
http://www.mywebserver.whatever/path/flowers.rm
```

You would, of course, use the right name for your web server and pathname!

For Windows Media Server, if you created a Windows Media file called `flowers.asf` (the "asf" stands for Active Streaming File), you would create an ASX "redirector" file that contains the following:

```
<ASX VERSION="3.0">
 <ENTRY>
  <REF HREF=http://www.mywebserver.whatever/path/flowers.asf />
 </ENTRY>
</ASX>
```

The second step is to refer to the "redirector" file from within your XHTML document. You can do this using any number of ways that you have learned in this chapter. You can use the `<anchor>` element to create a hyperlink to the redirector file, or include the redirector file using the `<object>` or `<embed>` element.

For example, if we saved the RAM file as `flowers.ram`, we would refer to this in an XHTML document as:

```
<?xml version="1.0" encoding="UTF-8"?>
<!DOCTYPE html
     PUBLIC "-//W3C//DTD XHTML 1.0 Transitional//EN"
     "http://www.w3.org/TR/xhtml1/DTD/xhtml1-transitional.dtd">
<html xmlns="http://www.w3.org/1999/xhtml" xml:lang="en" lang="en">
<head>
 ... the head of the document ...
</head>
<body>
 <p>Play your <a href="http://www.mywebserver.whatever/path/flowers.ram">media
    file</a>
 </p>
</body>
</html>
```

As you can see, adding streaming media to a document is quite easy. The real challenge is determining how to encode your media and optimizing your web server to deliver a quality experience to your users. To do this, you will need to read the documentation that comes with your web server, roll up your sleeves, and experiment.

Integrating Multimedia and the SMIL Language

In the previous sections we talked about using audio and using video. In a previous chapter, we talked about using graphics. In this section, we talk about how you put these pieces together into a multimedia application.

In 1998, the World Wide Web Consortium introduced the Synchronized Multimedia Integration Language (SMIL) to build these types of applications. SMIL, officially pronounced like "smile", was one of the first XML-based languages and it provides a way for you to:

- control the timeline of a document (when and how long an element is rendered)
- describe the layout of a document (where elements are shown on the screen)
- link to other documents and media (such as audio files, video files, and graphics)

The structure of a SMIL document is quite similar to an XHTML document. Where an XHTML document contains `<html>`, `<head>`, and `<body>` elements, a SMIL document contains `<smil>`, `<head>`, and `<body>` elements:

```
<smil>
  <head>
  ... head of the document
  </head>
  <body>
  ... body of the document
  </body>
</smil>
```

The `<head>` element contains elements that are not related to the timeline of the document. Mainly, the `<head>` element defines the layout information for the document (where things are rendered).

The `<body>` element contains elements that controls the timeline of the document (when things are rendered). There are two main timeline elements: the `<par>` element and the `<seq>` element.

The `<par>` element says that the media should be rendered (or played) in parallel:

```
<par>
  <audio src="sound1.mid" dur="5s" />
  <img src="splash.png" />
</par>
```

The `<audio>` and `<img>` elements are SMIL media elements. As would be expected, the `src` attribute locates the media file and the `dur` attribute specifies how long the media file is played. This example would have the user agent play the audio file at the same time as it would draw the `"splash.png"` image.

The <seq> element says that the media should be played one after another in sequence:

```
<seq>
 <audio src="sound1.mid" dur="5s" />
 <img src="splash.png" />
 <audio src="sound2.mid" dur="5s" />
</seq>
```

This example would have the user agent play the `sound1.mid` audio file for five seconds and then it would draw the `splash.png` image before playing the second audio file.

There is a lot more to SMIL than these simple examples and you are encouraged to read about SMIL on the W3C web site:

`http://www.w3.org/`

Its pretty simple to write a SMIL application. All that you need is a text editor to write the SMIL document and a player to playback the SMIL document. Unfortunately, neither Netscape or Microsoft currently provide SMIL plug-ins in their browsers.

There are several players available. The W3C web site provides links to players for a variety of platforms. For Windows, the Oratrix GRINS tool integrates an editor and player. You can find the GRINS tool at:

`http://www.oratrix.com`

Another good tool is RealNetworks RealPlayer. You can find RealPlayer at:

`http://www.real.com/products/player/index.html`

RealPlayer does not integrate a text editor, but because so many people already use RealPlayer, we will use it for our hands-on exercise.

Try It Out – Integrating Audio and Graphics with SMIL

In this exercise, we are going to use the SMIL language to integrate audio and graphics into a complete presentation.

1. Type the following into your text editor:

```
<smil>
  <head>
    <layout>
      <root-layout background-color="black" width="252" height="168" />
      <region id="picture" z-index="1" left="0" top="0" width="252" height="168" />
    </layout>
  </head>
  <body>
    <par>
      <audio id="a" src="ms.wav" repeat="5" />
      <seq repeat="5" >
```

```
        <img region="picture" src="flower1.jpg" dur="1000ms" />
        <img region="picture" src="flower2.jpg" dur="1000ms" />
        <img region="picture" src="flower3.jpg" dur="1000ms" />
        <img region="picture" src="flower4.jpg" dur="1000ms" />
        <img region="picture" src="flower5.jpg" dur="1000ms" />
        <img region="picture" src="flower6.jpg" dur="1000ms" />
        <img region="picture" src="flower7.jpg" dur="1000ms" />
        <img region="picture" src="flower8.jpg" dur="1000ms" />
      </seq>
    </par>
  </body>
</smil>
```

2. Save the file as `flower.smil`.

3. Copy the following files from the code download from our web site to the folder where you saved `flower.smil`:

- `flower1.jpg`
- `flower2.jpg`
- `flower3.jpg`
- `flower4.jpg`
- `flower5.jpg`
- `flower6.jpg`
- `flower7.jpg`
- `flower8.jpg`
- `ms.wav`

4. Create a new file in your text editor and type the following:

```
<?xml version="1.0" encoding="UTF-8"?>
<!DOCTYPE html
     PUBLIC "-//W3C//DTD XHTML 1.0 Transitional//EN"
     "http://www.w3.org/TR/xhtml1/DTD/xhtml1-transitional.dtd">
<html xmlns="http://www.w3.org/1999/xhtml" xml:lang="en" lang="en">
<head>
  <title>SMIL Link</title>
</head>
<body>
  <h1>SMIL Link</h1>
  <p>This is an example of a document that <a href="flower.smil">links
    to a SMIL document</a>
  </p>
  <p>This example needs a SMIL player. You can
    <a href="http://www.real.com/products/player/index.html">
      download RealPlayer here.</a>
  </p>
</body>
</html>
```

5. Save the file as `smil-link.htm`.

6. Run the `smil-link.htm` file in your web browser. You should see something like this:

7. Click on the links to a SMIL document hyperlink. This should cause the external RealPlayer to run. After a slight pause, you should see something like this:

How It Works

OK, we've authored a SMIL document. This SMIL document contains two main sections defined by the `<head>` and `<body>` elements.

The `<head>` element contains the `<layout>` element:

```
<layout>
  <root-layout background-color="black" width="252" height="168" />
  <region id="picture" z-index="1" left="0" top="0" width="252" height="168" />
</layout>
```

The `<layout>` element contains two elements, the `<root-layout>` element and the `<region>` element.

The <root-layout> element:

```
<root-layout background-color="black" width="252" height="168" />
```

...describes how to lay out the document as a whole. In this case, the background color is black and the height and width are 252 and 168, respectively.

The <region> element:

```
<region id="picture" z-index="1" left="0" top="0" width="252" height="168" />
```

...describes an area on the document (defined by the <root-layout> element) on which a media component will be rendered. In this case, the region is named "picture" and it covers the entire root layout (the width and height are the same as the <root-layout> element's width and height).

The <body> element contains one element: the <par> element:

```
<body>
  <par>
   <audio id="a" src="ms.wav" repeat="5" />
   <seq repeat="5" >
    <img region="picture" src="flower1.jpg" dur="1000ms" />
    <img region="picture" src="flower2.jpg" dur="1000ms" />
    <img region="picture" src="flower3.jpg" dur="1000ms" />
    <img region="picture" src="flower4.jpg" dur="1000ms" />
    <img region="picture" src="flower5.jpg" dur="1000ms" />
    <img region="picture" src="flower6.jpg" dur="1000ms" />
    <img region="picture" src="flower7.jpg" dur="1000ms" />
    <img region="picture" src="flower8.jpg" dur="1000ms" />
   </seq>
  </par>
 </body>
```

The <par> element contains two elements: the <audio> element and the <seq> element. The <par> element specifies that the <audio> element (the ms.wav file) should be played in parallel to the content of the <seq> element:

```
<seq repeat="5" >
    <img region="picture" src="flower1.jpg" dur="1000ms" />
    <img region="picture" src="flower2.jpg" dur="1000ms" />
    <img region="picture" src="flower3.jpg" dur="1000ms" />
    <img region="picture" src="flower4.jpg" dur="1000ms" />
    <img region="picture" src="flower5.jpg" dur="1000ms" />
    <img region="picture" src="flower6.jpg" dur="1000ms" />
    <img region="picture" src="flower7.jpg" dur="1000ms" />
    <img region="picture" src="flower8.jpg" dur="1000ms" />
  </seq>
```

The <seq> element contains eight JPEG images and it specifies that each of these images should be rendered sequentially (one after the other). The <seq> element's repeat attribute says that this sequence should repeat five times.

Looking at the first <img> element (since they are all pretty much the same):

The <img> element's region attribute says that the JPEG should be drawn on the region named "picture". You may remember that you defined the region named "picture" in the head of the document.

The <img> element's src attribute references the location of the image and the dur attribute specifies the duration to show the image (1 second).

The net result is that the ms.wav file will be played in parallel to an image which changes once every second and that this presentation should repeat five times.

Next, we wrote the XHTML file that will link to the SMIL file. The important part of this XHTML document is the first hyperlink:

```
<p>This is an example of a document that <a href="flower.smil">links
  to a SMIL document</a>
</p>
```

This anchor element creates a hyperlink to the SMIL document.

In Step 7, when you click on the hyperlink, your web browser looks up the plug-in or helper application associated with the "SMIL" MIME type and launches that application. If you were using RealPlayer, RealPlayer would be launched.

This exercise shows how simple it is to author a SMIL application and run it in a web browser. Unfortunately, this example requires the user to click on a hyperlink in order to run the SMIL application – neither RealPlayer nor GRINS currently render inside a document. In addition, some web servers may not have the MIME type for SMIL set-up by default. This means that you will need to set-up the MIME type or ask your system administrator to do it for you.

You can make launching a SMIL application easier using a little JavaScript. You get a chance to do this in the next exercise!

Try It Out – Running SMIL Using JavaScript

In this exercise, you are going to run a SMIL application from within a document using JavaScript. We will start talking more about JavaScript in Chapter 16. Also, you might want to make sure you have the latest version of RealPlayer.

1. Load smil-link.htm file into your text editor and make the following changes:

```
<?xml version="1.0" encoding="UTF-8"?>
<!DOCTYPE html
     PUBLIC "-//W3C//DTD XHTML 1.0 Transitional//EN"
     "http://www.w3.org/TR/xhtml1/DTD/xhtml1-transitional.dtd">
<html xmlns="http://www.w3.org/1999/xhtml" xml:lang="en" lang="en">
<head>
```

```
  <title>SMIL Inside</title>
 </head>
 <body>
  <h1>SMIL Inside</h1>
  <p>This is an example of a document with and embedded
   <script language="JavaScript">
   <!--
      window.location.href="flower.smil";
   //->
   </script>
  SMIL document.</p>
  <p>This example needs a SMIL player. You can
    <a href="http://www.real.com/products/player/index.html">
    download RealPlayer here.</a>
  </p>
 </body>
 </html>
```

2. Save the file as `smil-in.htm`.

3. Run `smil-in.htm` in your web browser. You should see something like this pop up automatically:

How It Works

We've made some changes to the `<body>` element of our document. Specifically, we replaced the hyperlink to the SMIL document with some JavaScript:

```
<script language="JavaScript">
<!--
 window.location.href="flower.smil";
// -->
</script>
```

The JavaScript sets the location of the document in the current window to the `flower.smil` document. Since your web browser does not know how to handle a SMIL document itself, it looks up the helper application associated with the SMIL MIME type and launches that application.

These two exercises show how to handcraft a SMIL application. As mentioned earlier, if you want to build more sophisticated SMIL documents, you will probably want to download a good SMIL authoring tool called GRINS from Oratrix and read-up on SMIL at the World Wide Web Consortium's web site (`http://www.w3.org`).

New tools are being introduced that make it simpler to create SMIL documents. One tool for Windows, RealSlideshow, combines the power of SMIL with the streaming capability of RealNetwork's technology. You can download RealSlideshow from:
`http://www.real.com/products/tools/slideshow/index.html`

Try It Out – Using RealSlideshow to Integrate Audio and Graphics

In this exercise, you are going to use RealSlideshow to build an integrated audio and video show.

1. Create a new folder and name it `slideshow`.

2. Run RealSlideshow. You should see something like this:

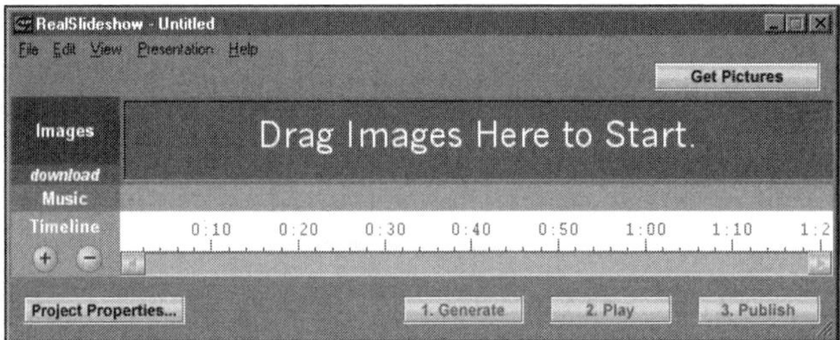

3. Click on the Project Properties... button located at the lower left of the window. You should see something like this:

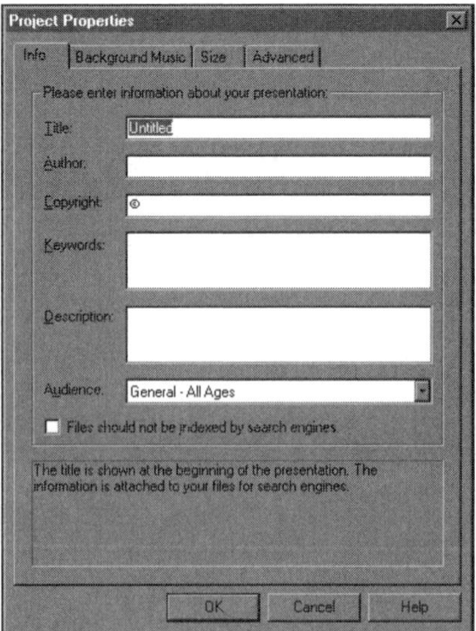

4. In the Title field, type `Flower Slideshow`. You may also want to type in your name as the author and fill in some of the other fields.

5. Click on the Background Music tab. You should see something like this:

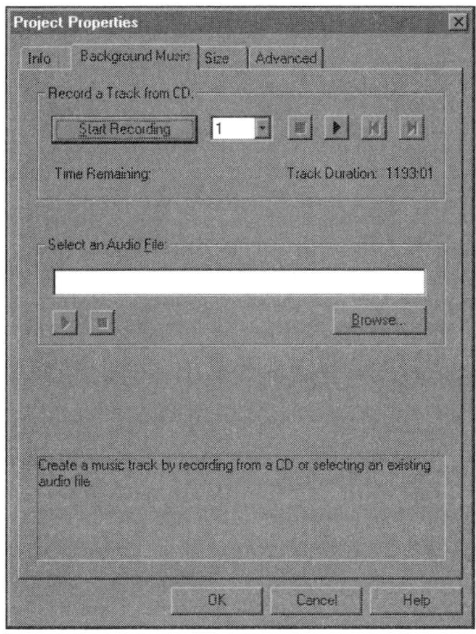

6. In the grouping labeled Select an Audio File, click on the Browse... button. This should display a dialog box for finding and selecting an audio file. Go to the folder containing the `ms.wav` file and select that file.

7. Click on the Advanced tab. You should see something like this:

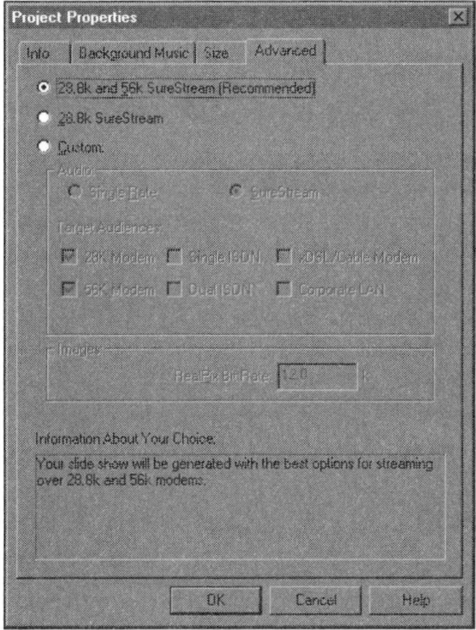

8. Click on the Custom radio button, enabling the options within the grouping labeled Audio.

9. Click on the Corporate LAN checkbox and make sure you deselect any other checkboxes (such as the 28K Modem and 56K Modem checkboxes).

10. Click on the OK button to close the Project Properties dialog box.

11. Click on the File | Add Images menu item. This should display the Add Images to Project dialog box. Find the flowers JPEG files that you used in the previous SMIL exercise:

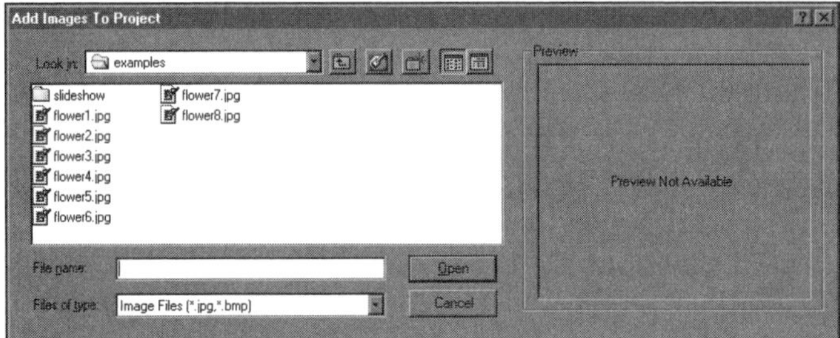

12. Select all of the flower JPEGs by holding the *Ctrl* key down when you click on them (click on the first image to highlight it, then press and hold down the *Ctrl* key, click on the remaining images in turn, then release the *Ctrl* key – they should all now be selected/highlighted). Click on the Open button. The project window should now look something like this, with all the images now displayed:

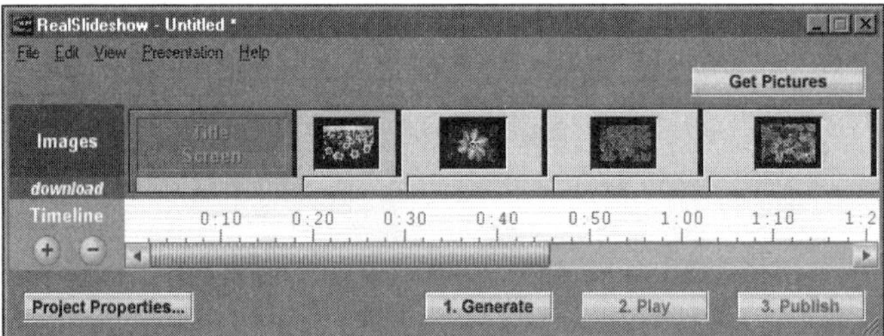

13. Click on the first slide to select it (it should then become highlighted) and the select the Edit | Image Properties menu item. This should display the Image Properties dialog box for that image.

14. Click on the Edit tab. Change the download time to some time interval like about 7s by using the slider located underneath the thumbnail image:

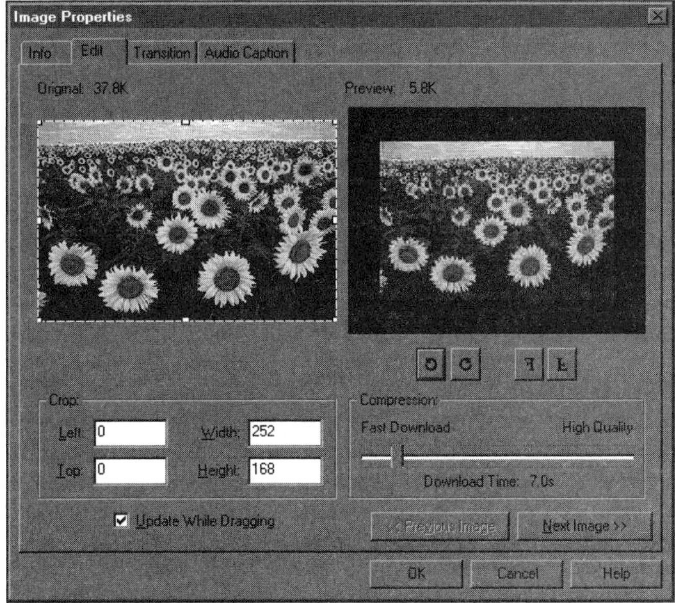

15. Change the download time for each of the images by clicking on the Next Image>> button and using the slider.

16. After setting the download time for the last image, click on the Text and Audio Captions tab. Click on the Browse button to select an audio file for that image. Select the `ms.wav` file that you used previously by pressing the Open button.

17. Change the audio file for each of the images by clicking on the <<Previous Image button and selecting the Browse button.

18. After setting the audio file for each image, click on the OK button.

19. Back at the main display, click on the File | Save Project As menu item and save the file in your slideshow folder. Name the file `flowers.rpj`.

20. Click on the 1. Generate button to generate your slide show. Depending on the size of your slide show, you may see a dialog box displaying status while the slide show is being generated. You may also want to enter title and copyright information. Save the file as `flowers.smil` in your slideshow folder.

21. Exit the RealSlideshow program.

22. Go to the slideshow folder and run the `flowers.htm` file in your web browser. You should see something like this:

23. Click on the Flower Slideshow hyperlink and you should see something like this:

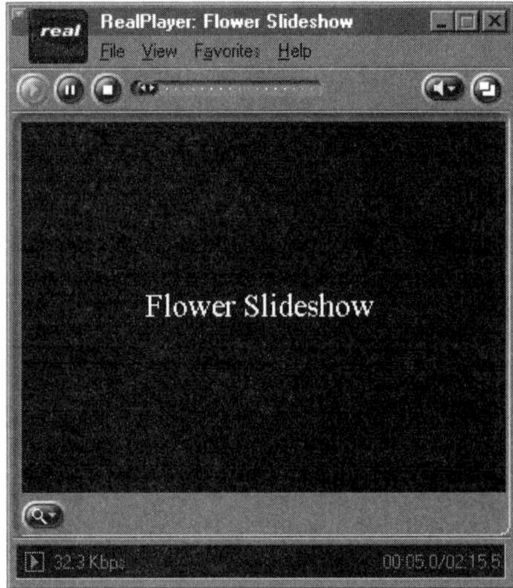

How It Works

We created the folder named slideshow because RealSlideshow makes a whole bunch of files, and it's generally easier to manage them if they are in their own folder. We configured various properties of the slideshow, like its author and so on, and then the background music. The background music is used when the title is being displayed. In our example, we used a pre-recorded `WAV` file, but you could have also recorded your own `WAV` file – this feature is very good if you want to narrate your slide show. The Sound Recorder in Accessories on the Windows Start menu will allow you to record `.wav` files.

The Advanced Properties are very important in RealSlideshow! These properties tell RealSlideshow how to optimize your presentation for delivery over various networks: from plain old 28K modem networks (which most consumers still use) to Digital Subscriber Line (DSL) networks; from single ISDN lines to high bandwidth Corporate LANs (which are great for Intranets). We selected Corporate LAN because we are doing everything on one machine and we wanted our demo to work fast.

Unless you are doing Intranet development, you will probably want to select the 28K Modem and 56K Modem options. Consumers will seldom wait for images to download and will often tolerate poorer quality images to no images at all.

Next, we selected the pictures that we wanted in our slide show. We could also have added pictures by dragging them onto the main window. We then changed the download time for each image. This feature allows you to choose whether you want a fast download with poorer image quality, or slower downloads with higher image quality. Only you can make that decision! In the example, we chose 7 seconds. If we had chosen a smaller number, the image would have been downloaded faster, but it would have had a poorer image quality.

Then, we added an audio track for each slide. In this exercise, you added the same `ms.wav` file, but you could have easily added a different file or recorded your own audio track. As mentioned earlier, this feature is great if you want to narrate your slide show.

When we clicked on the Generate button, the RealSlideshow program copied all of the media files to the `slideshow` folder and built several RealMedia files for streaming the audio tracks and the slides.

RealSlideshow also build a SMIL file for integrating the audio and video tracks. This SMIL file is called `flowers.smil`. If you open up `flowers.smil` file in your text editor, you will see something like:

```
<smil>
 <head>
  <meta name="title" content="Flower Slideshow" />
  <meta name="author" content="Ted Wugofski" />
  <meta name="copyright" content="©Red Rum Interactive" />
  <meta name="keywords" content="flowers" />
  <meta name="description" content="Short slide show of flowers" />
  <meta name="robots" content="all" />
  <meta name="pics-label"
     content='(PICS-1.1 "http://www.classify.org/safesurf"
     labels comment "RealSlideshow 6.0.0.315 Windows"
     ratings (SS~~000 1))'/>
  <meta name="file_id" content="e195dcea-3103-e080-7f8b-6206c40ac3d3" />
  <layout type="text/smil-basic-layout">
   <root-layout width="320" height="240" background-color="black"/>
   <region id="pix_region" left="0" top="0" width="320" height="240" z-index="1"
/>
  </layout>
 </head>
 <body>
  <par>
  <seq>
```

```
      <text src="flowers.rt" region="pix_region"/>
      <img src="flowers.rp" region="pix_region" fill="freeze"/>
     </seq>
     <audio src="flowers.rm"/>
    </par>
  </body>
  </smil>
```

If you look at this SMIL document, the important elements (for playback) are the <layout> element and the <body> element. Looking at the <layout> element:

```
      <layout type="text/smil-basic-layout">
      <root-layout width="320" height="240" background-color="black"/>
      <region id="pix_region" left="0" top="0" width="320" height="240" z-index="1"
  />
     </layout>
```

...you will see that there is a <root-layout> element that describes the size of the window (the width is 320 pixels and the height is 240 pixels). The region element describes that area within the window in which the pictures will be drawn. In this case, the region uses up the entire window (the width and height are the same as the <root-layout>).

If you look at the <body> element:

```
<body>
 <par>
  <seq>
   <text src="flowers.rt" region="pix_region"/>
   <img src="flowers.rp" region="pix_region" fill="freeze"/>
  </seq>
  <audio src="flowers.rm"/>
 </par>
</body>
```

...you can see that there are two things that are 'played' at the same time (in parallel): a sequence (defined by the <seq> element) and an audio file.

The <seq> element specifies that a text element should be rendered and when that text element is rendered, an <img> element should be drawn. In our exercise, the image is actually the streaming video of our slideshow!

Summary

In this chapter, we saw that there are two types of multimedia: file-based and streaming. File-based media is very simple to use and playback is very smooth, but there is a delay before the user can see or hear the media. Streaming media, on the other hand, is more complex and playback can be choppy, but the user can immediately see and hear the media – making it great for live broadcasts like Internet radio.

We also looked at how to put audio and video files into a web page using the `<object>` element and its `data` and `type` attributes. We compared this with how to do the same using the `<embed>` element and its `src` attribute.

We saw how to put streaming audio and video into your web page using RealPlayer, and how to integrate multimedia using the W3C's new SMIL language, although our coverage of this was fairly light and couldn't really do it full justice. Still, we had a bit of a taster! Finally, you learned how there are new tools like RealNetwork's RealSlideshow that make authoring SMIL easier. In the next and final section of the book, we introduce and explore the whole area of JavaScript, and how scripting is an almost essential part of authoring web pages.

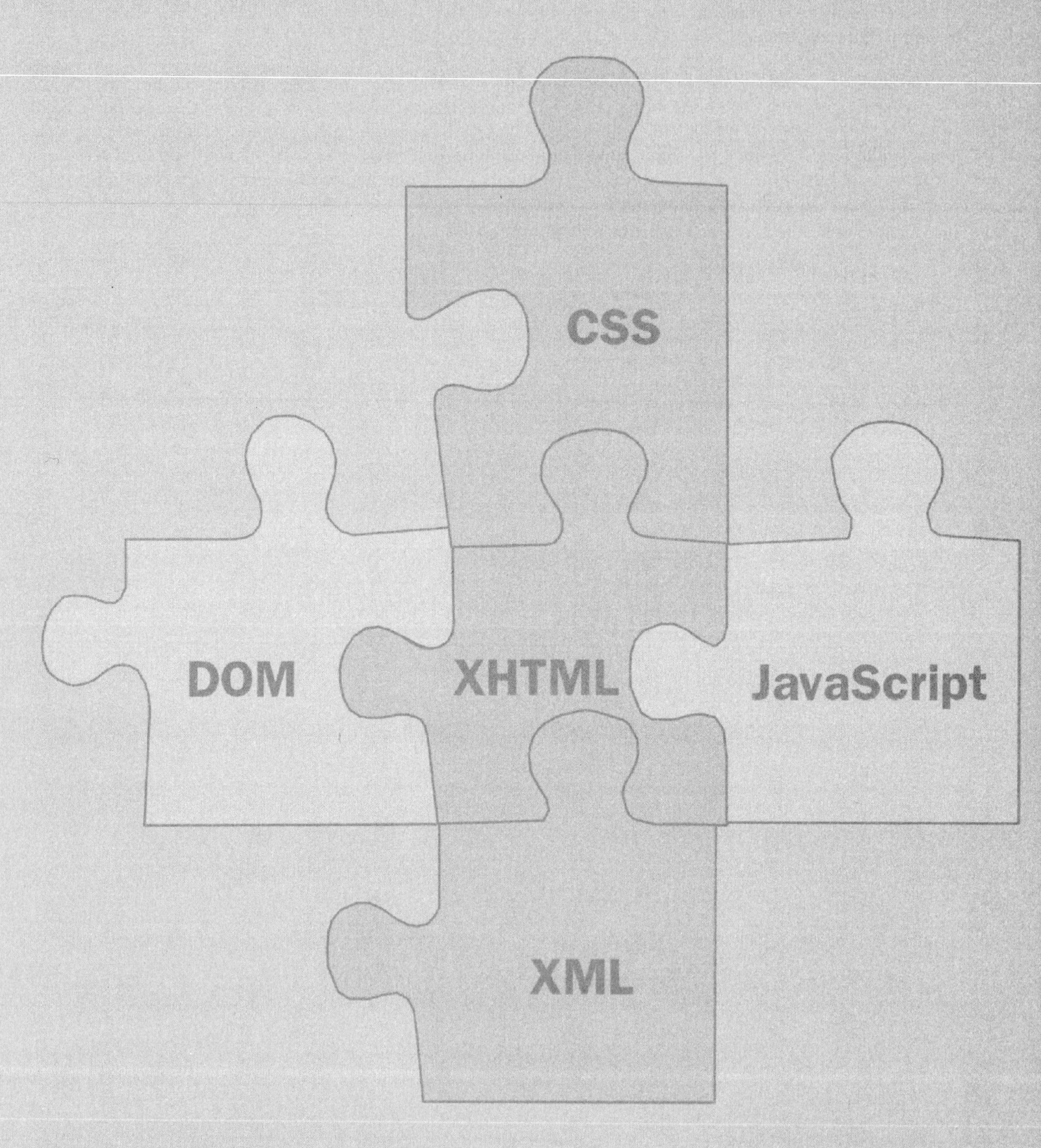
CSS
DOM
XHTML
JavaScript
XML

XHTML Forms

Without forms, XHTML pages would offer few opportunities for interaction with the user; they'd be much like pages in a book. Forms let us build *web applications*: by filling out forms, users can enter queries in a search engine or buy things from an online store. When forms were first invented, the only way you could use them was to pass the contents to a remote web server, which would then create a new web page based on the information that the user typed in. This has the disadvantage that you need to have a server configured to run custom programs on it; however, a program running on such a server has direct access to resources available on the server such as databases and credit card validation. Today, it's now possible to write programs in JavaScript that process forms, *running inside the web browser*, making it possible to write web applications without server-side programming.

In this chapter, we'll mostly discuss the browser side of forms: how to create them, and, briefly, how to access them from JavaScript (more examples can be found in the next few chapters).

In this chapter, we will cover the following:

- Creating forms
- Using input elements such as text fields, buttons, and choice boxes
- Using form elements to create user interfaces
- Usability guidelines

Although we don't discuss server side programming in this book, we will discuss what it is that a browser transmits to the server, so that client-side form designers will understand the material that the server has to work with.

What Is a Form?

If you've done any amount of Web 'surfing', you'll have almost certainly come across forms. You might not know it, of course, but you'll have seen them. If you use a search engine, or any online shopping site, or have had to register any software online, you will have used a form. A form is simply a place on a web page where you can fill in information (just like a form on paper – yes, they've even followed us to the Web). When you submit a form, that information can be either intercepted by JavaScript or be sent to a web server (possibly the same one that sent you the page, or a different one) which processes the form information, takes actions based on the information you added to the form, and sends back a custom-generated *new* page based on that information.

Before we look at how to make our own forms, we'll talk about what happens between the client (a web browser) and the web server when a form is submitted.

Client/Server Interaction and Forms

When you view a web page there are two computers involved: the *client* is the computer that's running the web browser, and the *server* is a computer that transmits web pages on request from clients. An analogy is the ubiquitous television, or TV: we may think of a TV server transmitting television pictures to client machines (although it is only with the recent invention of interactive television that TVs have been able to 'talk back'). So if you are sitting at work or at home, and open up your browser, then you become the client. When you're viewing web pages without forms, the main piece of information sent from the client to the server is the URL of the web page, image, or other file the browser wants to get. This URL is either typed into the address bar of the browser, or is activated when you click on a link. When you submit a form, the browser also sends the contents of the form, such as your address and credit card number if you're shopping online.

Although we don't have room to discuss server-side programming, we'll mention a few popular systems for server-side programming and point you to resources where you can learn more.

The first standard for server-side programming was CGI (Common Gateway Interface). CGI programs work with Unix servers such as Apache. Although you can write CGI programs in any language that works with Unix, the most popular language for CGI programming is Perl. Because CGI programs run outside the web server process, CGI performance is poor for sites that get a high volume of 'hits' (visitors): however, Apache's `mod_perl` can run CGI scripts written in Perl inside the web server, boosting performance several times.

Active Server Pages (ASP), PHP, and Java Server Pages (JSP) all allow programmers to embed server-side code inside web pages in a style similar to client-side JavaScript. Many people find this is a comfortable way to write web applications. ASP is built into Microsoft's Internet Information Server (IIS) while PHP and JSP are add-ons that can be attached to Apache, IIS and other servers.

CGI Resources:
`http://hoohoo.ncsa.uiuc.edu/`
`http://perl.apache.org/`

PHP Resources:
`http://www.php.net/`

ASP Resources:
http://msdn.microsoft.com/workshop/server/asp/ASPOver.asp
Beginning ASP 3.0 *(Wrox Press, ISBN 1-861003-38-2)*

JSP Resources:
http://www.javasoft.com/products/jsp/index.html
http://www.honeylocust.com/weeds/
Professional Java Server Programming *(Wrox Press, ISBN 1-861002-77-7)*

What If You Don't Have a Server?

It's possible to do some processing in a client-side script, without having to actually send any information to a server. This is useful if you haven't got access to server-side processing, but it's limited because you don't have access to databases and other resources that could be attached to a server. It's also possible to create a `mailto:` form which transmits the contents of a form via e-mail.

Form Submission

After you fill out your form, you usually send the form to the server by pressing a button. This button is usually called the Submit button, and the process of sending the form off is called **submitting** the form. Before we discuss what happens when we submit a form, it's useful to have a little look at some of the language we'll be using to create forms. The following two lines of code are taken from the first, full, example later in this chapter where a user is asked to type in their name:

```
<input type="text" name="clientname" id="clientname" />
<input type="submit" />
```

The first line creates an empty box into which we type our information. We have called this box `clientname` but you can give it any name you like – it's just an internal reference that only the author of the web page sees. The information that is entered into the box becomes the **value** of the box. Thus each form box has a name and a value, known as **name-value pairs**. The second line creates a button with the word Submit written on it. 'Pressing' that button (either by clicking on it with your mouse, or by pressing the *Return* key on your keyboard) sends the information in the box to the server.

Of course, a real form is likely to have lots of boxes into which we are asked to insert information. The information in all of these boxes is known as the **form's content**. The content of the form is sent to the server as an encoded string containing a list of the values of the form's input elements (also known as **controls**.) Values are returned for each input element in the form which has a name and a non-empty value. If the default value of a control is empty, and if a user types nothing into the control, no value for that box will be sent when the form is submitted. For each name-value pair the encoded string that is transmitted looks like:

```
encodedname=encodedvalue
```

If more than one name-value pair is submitted then they are separated by ampersands (&):

```
encodedname1=encodedvalue1&encodedname2=encodedvalue2
```

Spaces are encoded as plusses (+) and alphanumeric characters are encoded as themselves. What about other characters? If we send a value of a name called `somename` consisting of the following characters:

```
!@#$%^&*()_+:;<>,./\|
```

we'll send the following encoded string to the server:

```
somename=%21@%23%24%25%5E%26*%28%29_%2B%3A%3B%3C%3E%2C.%2F%5C%7C
```

As you can see the 'at' sign (@), the underscore (_), the period (.), and the asterisk (*) characters survive intact. But the rest are converted to a hexadecimal ASCII number preceded by a % sign (for example, the exclamation mark character ! which starts the string somename is sent as %21).

There are two ways to send the encoded data back to the server: the GET method and the POST method. The GET method is, in fact, the usual method for retrieving a web page from a server. When submitting a form via GET, the form information is appended to the end of the URL – if we were to transmit the above name-value pair to a CGI script located at the (fictional) site `http://myserver/cgi-bin/myscript`, the web browser would request the URL:

```
http://myserver/myscript.cgi?somename=%21@%23%24%25%5E%26*%28%29_%2B%3A%3B%
3C%3E%2C.%2F%5C%7C
```

The POST method, on the other hand, sends the encoded string back to the server along with the HTTP headers.

The POST method has a number of advantages over GET, and is preferred for most uses of forms. First, the POST method can handle an unlimited amount of information, while the GET method is limited by the maximum URL length supported by the web browser, web server and any proxy servers. Second, the GET method is less secure: because the form data is encoded in the URL, somebody can read the form data by looking at the URL window on your browser, by looking at the web server's logs (which typically record every URL accessed on the server,) or by looking at the logs of a web server on any site which is linked from the form result (when you follow a hyperlink from URL A to URL B, your browser sends **referrer** information to B telling it that you came from A).

The GET method has one advantage over POST. Web cache programs can cache the result of a GET request, since it's a URL just like any other URL. Since thousands of AOL users, for instance, search for MP3 at AltaVista every day, AOL can keep a copy of the search result in it's proxy servers to speed up searches for its users, reduce it's bandwidth consumption, and reduce the load on AltaVista.

The <form> Element

To define a form, you surround a section of your XHTML (within the body) with `<form></form>` tags. The form doesn't have to be the whole page; you can, for instance, have a small form in the middle of other content or have more than one on a page. The `<form>` element has a number of attributes:

The 'action' Attribute

The `action` attribute lets you specify a URL that will receive the data from the form when it is submitted:

```
<form action="myURL">
```

Note that `myURL` is usually, but not necessarily, the URL of a page or a script somewhere on the same server that sent out the page in the first place. Since you may not have access to your own server and ASP or other server-side capabilities, in this chapter we'll be using a page on the Web that simply 'echoes' what you send it:

```
http://www.wrox.com/Consumer/Errata/3439/post-echo.asp
```

This page only works if you submit your form using the post method.

In fact, `myURL` doesn't even have to be an HTTP protocol URL – it might be an e-mail address using the `mailto:` method:

```
<form action="mailto:myemail@mydomain.com">
```

If we use this then the client should receive a warning when they try to submit the form. Here is what IE 5 posts up on the screen.

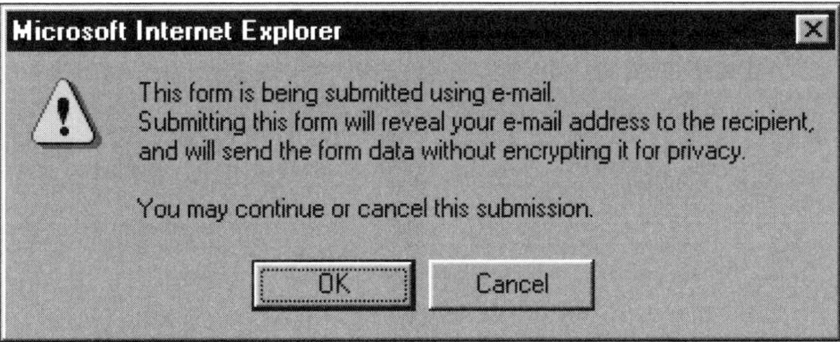

Depending on the e-mail program the client browser uses, the values may be submitted in the body of the mail, or as an attachment.

Of course, you could have a form mailed to yourself:

```
<form action="mailto:youraddress@yourdomain.com">
```

You can then start a script to process the form you receive (see a book like Professional JavaScript from Wrox, *ISBN 1-861002-70-X*).

The 'method' Attribute

This attribute tells the browser how to send the data back to the server. It can take one of two values, GET and POST, as described above.

The 'name' Attribute

If you give a form a name, you can access it by name from JavaScript; otherwise you'll need to access it by number, i.e. forms[2] is the third form on the page. See Chapters 17 and 18 for more about the forms collection.

The 'target' Attribute

If you're using frames, the target attribute tells the browser which frame to open the server-generated reply in (we saw the target attribute way back in Chapter 7).

The 'enctype' Attribute

This is the MIME type of the encoding mechanism used when data is submitted via the POST method. The default mime type is application/x-www-form-urlencoded, which is the encoding described above. If, however, we're using a mailto: form, you may want to specify a mime type of text/plain to save a human email-reader the bother of decoding the encoded message that would otherwise come in.

A Basic Form

Let's look at a simple form with just a text <input> box and a submit button. This form lets us enter our name and send it back to the server. To avoid the need to write our own server application, we use an 'echo' server operating from Wrox:

http://www.wrox.com/Consumer/Errata/3439/post-echo.asp

This simply 'echoes' your submitted name-value pairs back to you as an XHTML file, as we'll see in the following example (the actual code for doing this is available as part of the downloadable code available for this chapter from the Wrox web site).

Try It Out – Creating a Simple Form

1. Type up the following in your text editor, and save it as firstform.htm:

```
<?xml version="1.0" encoding="UTF-8"?>
<!DOCTYPE html
     PUBLIC "-//W3C//DTD XHTML 1.0 Transitional//EN"
     "http://www.w3.org/TR/xhtml1/DTD/xhtml1-transitional.dtd">
<html xmlns="http://www.w3.org/1999/xhtml" xml:lang="en" lang="en">
<head>
```

```
  <title>Basic XHTML Form</title>
</head>
<body>
  <h4>Please enter your name.</h4>
  <form action="http://www.wrox.com/Consumer/Errata/3439/post-echo.asp"
    method="post">
    <input type="text" name="clientname" id="clientname" />
    <input type="submit" />
  </form>
</body>
</html>
```

2. View it in your browser. You should see something like this:

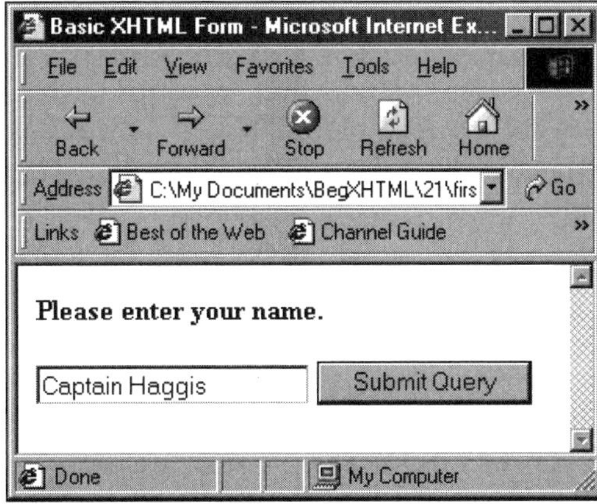

3. Type your name into the `text` box, then submit the form. Assuming you're online, you should get a response like this after a short delay:

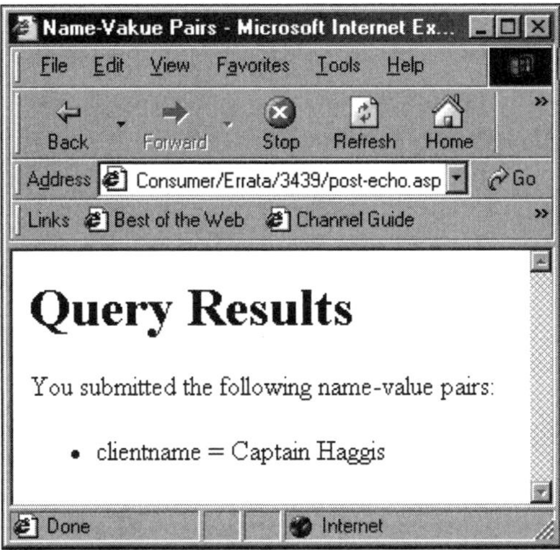

How It Works

We have used the <form> element and two <input> elements to create this form. Note that we named the text box clientname since we must name <input> elements if we want them to be transmitted to the server.

The next thing to notice is the form's action attribute. This contains the URL of the page that will replace this page when the Submit button is clicked, to which the form information will be sent.

The <form> element also contains a method attribute. This tells the browser what method to employ to send the information to the server. We've set it to post:

```
<form action="http://www.wrox.com/Consumer/Errata/3439/post-echo.asp"
  method="post">
```

Now let's briefly look at the controls we've put into our form. The <input> element is an empty element:

```
<input type="text" name="clientname" id="clientname" />
<input type="submit" />
```

In the first line, we use type="text" to create a text box – this is just an empty box that allows us to type some text into it (we'll look at different kinds of boxes later). In the second line, we use type="submit" to create a button that will submit the information in our form back to the server. The submit button is a special control that makes the browser submit the form when it is activated. Note that the submit button has been given a default caption of Submit Query. We will see how we can customize this later on.

Multiple Forms

Although we can have as many forms as we want on a page it should be noted that a submit button will only return the content of the form it is attached to. That is, each <form> </form> tag pair must contain a separate submit button within them if we want their information to be sent to a server.

Working With Controls

First we will have a quick look at the controls that can be created, and then we will look at the attributes of <input> elements.

The controls we can create include:

- Text boxes, password boxes, and text-area boxes
- Command buttons, radio buttons, and check boxes and buttons with images
- List boxes
- Dropdown boxes

Common Attributes

There are a number of attributes that are common to all the `<input>` elements we can use in our forms. So before we go through the controls to see how they work, let's just take a look at these attributes.

The 'name' Attribute

About the only `<form>` element that does not require a name is the `submit` button, and even then there is no harm in supplying it!

All controls require `name` attributes as the names are used for creating name-value pairs for sending to the server. So if you don't name your controls, you won't receive any information from them – and what would be the point of having a form if you couldn't get information from it?

The 'value' Attribute

The `value` of an element is what is passed to the server when the submit button of a `<form>` element is clicked. By specifying a value as an attribute, you specify the default value: this value will appear in the control when it is first created, and, if the user doesn't change the value of the control, this value will be transmitted to the server.

The 'disabled' Attribute

If you include `disabled = "disabled"` in any of your control elements, they will show up 'disabled', which means that the control will be visible but not useable. You might want to do this if you were building a form that incorporated some code that would enable, say, a `text` box only after the user has checked a specific check box.

Now we've covered the common ground, let's look at the most common control element: the `<input>` element.

The <input> Element

Originally, the only controls you could have in a form were `<input>` element controls. You used the `type` attribute to decide what kind of control you wanted it to be. Since then, other elements have been added.

The 'type' attribute

The `type` attribute of the `<input>` element determines what kind of box it will be. It can take one of the following values:

- `text`
- `password`

- file
- submit
- reset
- button
- image
- checkbox
- radio
- hidden

Let's take a look at how you use each of these.

Text-type <input> Controls

An <input> element can be one of three kinds of text control:

- text: If the <input> element is given a type value of text it will produce a plain input form box.
- password: Here any characters typed into the form box will appear as asterisks (*).
- file: This in fact produces both a text box and an associated Browse button which together are used to select and upload a file from the user's hard drive to the relevant server.

Attributes of the Text Controls

All the text boxes will be of a fixed width. The width can be altered by using the size attribute, e.g. size = 'n' where n is the number of characters wide the text box should be. This roughly translates to an 'en' unit. By adding an attribute of maxlength, we can also control the maximum numbers of characters that can be entered into a text box. This attribute should be used with caution. The readonly attribute only allows the content of the box to be read. It prevents the user from entering data into the box. The syntax is readonly = "readonly".

Let's look at a simple example that demonstrates the three different text box types.

Try It out – Creating Text Controls

1. Enter the following into your text editor and save as controls.htm:

```
<?xml version="1.0" encoding="UTF-8"?>
<!DOCTYPE html
     PUBLIC "-//W3C//DTD XHTML 1.0 Transitional//EN"
     "http://www.w3.org/TR/xhtml1/DTD/xhtml1-transitional.dtd">
<html xmlns="http://www.w3.org/1999/xhtml" xml:lang="en" lang="en">
<head>
  <title>Basic XHTML Form Text controls</title>
</head>
<body>
  <h4>Examples of text controls</h4>
```

```
    <form action="http://www.wrox.com/Consumer/Errata/3439/post-echo.asp "
     method="post" >
    <div>Type your userId</div>
    <input type="text" value="[userId]" name="userId" id="userId" /><br />
    <div>Type your pasword</div>
    <input type="password" name="password" id="password" /><br />
    <div>Select a file</div>
    <input type="file" name="file" id="file" /><br />
    <input type="submit" />
    </form>
  </body>
  </html>
```

2. Now run this in your browser to see the following:

Note that all the form boxes are a standard size, and that the `file` box comes with its own Browse button (at least it does in IE 5, the only implementation of this control so far). After we have filled in some appropriate text we can hit the submit button. This is what we get back from the Wrox 'echo' server:

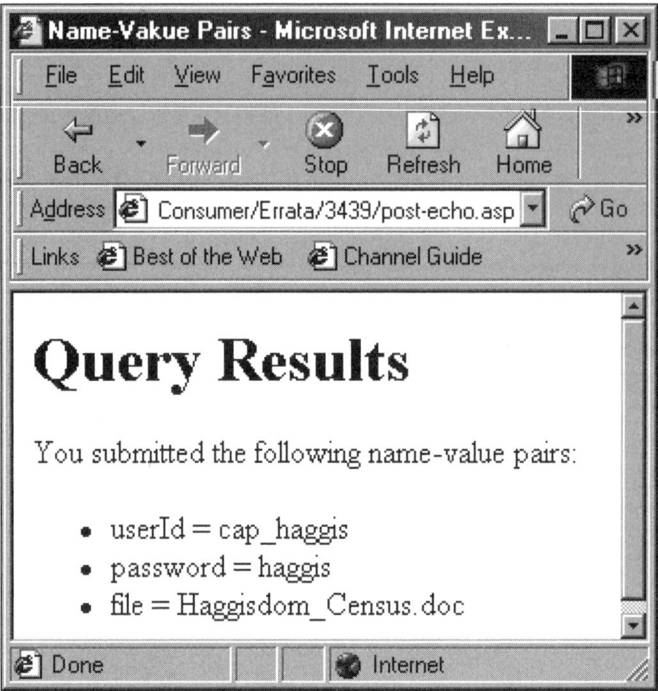

How It Works

The values of the text areas are the data that was entered into them. The password arrives in an unencrypted form, and as for the file – all we have is its location on the client machine. When the Submit button is pressed, however, the contents of the file at that address are converted to binary data and are sent to the server as part of the header.

Button-type <input> Controls

There are four button types available with the `<input>` element: `submit`, `reset`, `button`, and `image`:

- **submit** – A `submit` button transmits the name-value pairs of all the elements in the form to the server. If you specify a value for the `value` attribute of a `submit` control, that value will appear as its caption (i.e. the text on the button).
- **reset** – This button resets all the values of a form to their original (default) values.
- **button** – This produces a command button. There is no default caption, so the caption must be set with the `value` attribute. This button submits nothing to the server; to use it, you must capture JavaScript events associated with the button.
- **image** – This produces an image map. An `image` control takes `src` and `alt` attributes. When clicked it, like the `submit` button, transmits all of the name-value pairs to the server, and it also transmits the co-ordinates of the place it was clicked. See the example below.

Checkbox and Radio Button <input> Controls

Checkboxes and radio buttons are controls that are either checked (true) or unchecked (false). If a checkbox (or radio button) is checked, the name-value pair associated with the checkbox is transmitted to the server; if the checkbox is not checked, the name-value pair is not transmitted. You can have multiple checkboxes that share the same name (for instance, a form for a job application might have a set of checkboxes all named `skill`, but with the text on the screen next to them saying Carpentry, Typing and Programming, for example). The form `<input>` `type` values for checkboxes and radio boxes are:

- **checkbox** – This will produces a simple checkbox.
- **radio** – This will produce a single radio button. A radio button is like a checkbox, but, if several radio buttons are given the same name then only one can be checked at any given time, so a user can choose only one of several options.

Unlike `text` boxes, the visitor cannot change the value of the checkbox or radio button. You can specify the initial condition of a checkbox (checked or unchecked) with the `checked` attribute and JavaScript can access the checked/unchecked status of the box via the `checked` property. Both the `checked` attribute and property are Boolean values which can be either `true` or `false`.

Try It Out – Creating Buttons and Selection Controls

1. Enter this into your text editor and save it as `basic.htm`:

```
<?xml version="1.0" encoding="UTF-8"?>
<!DOCTYPE html
     PUBLIC "-//W3C//DTD XHTML 1.0 Transitional//EN"
     "http://www.w3.org/TR/xhtml1/DTD/xhtml1-transitional.dtd">
<html xmlns="http://www.w3.org/1999/xhtml" xml:lang="en" lang="en">
<head>
 <title>Basic XHTML button and checkbox controls</title>
</head>
<body>
<h4>Examples of button and checkbox controls</h4>
<form action="http://www.wrox.com/Consumer/Errata/3439/post-echo.asp"
  method="post" name="fml" >
  <div>Type your Name</div>
 <input type="text" value="[name]" name="userId" /><br />
 <div>Radio Buttons</div>
 <input type="radio" name="radio" id="radio" value="1" />
   <span>Choice1</span><br />
 <input type="radio" name="radio" id="radio" value="2" />
  <span>Choice2</span><br />
 <input type="radio" name="radio" id="radio" value="3" />
   <span>Choice3</span><br />
 <div>Checkboxes</div>
 <input type="checkbox" name="cbx1" id="cbx1" value="1" />
   <span>Choice1</span><br />
```

```
<input type="checkbox" name="cbx2" id="cbx2" value="2"/>
  <span>Choice2</span><br />
<input type="checkbox" name="cbx3" id="cbx3" value="3"/>
  <span>Choice3</span><br />
<input type="image" src="face.gif" />
<input type="button" value="Click me" onclick="alert('Hello')" />
<input type="submit" value="Send to Wrox" />
<input type="reset" value="Reset form" />
</form>
</body>
</html>
```

2. Run it in your browser to see something like this:

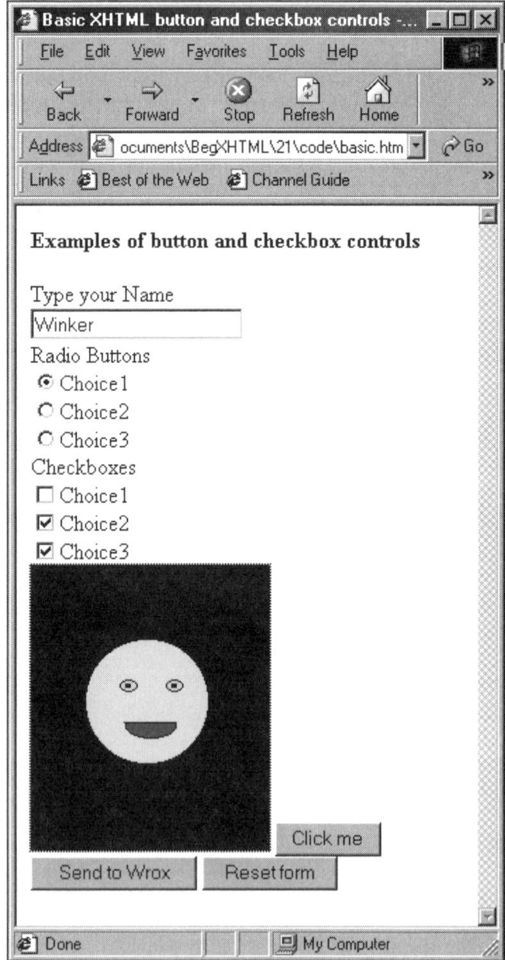

3. Suppose now, rather then click on the Send to Wrox button, we were to click on the image. We'd see something like the following, where the *x* and *y* coordinates give the point at which we clicked on the image:

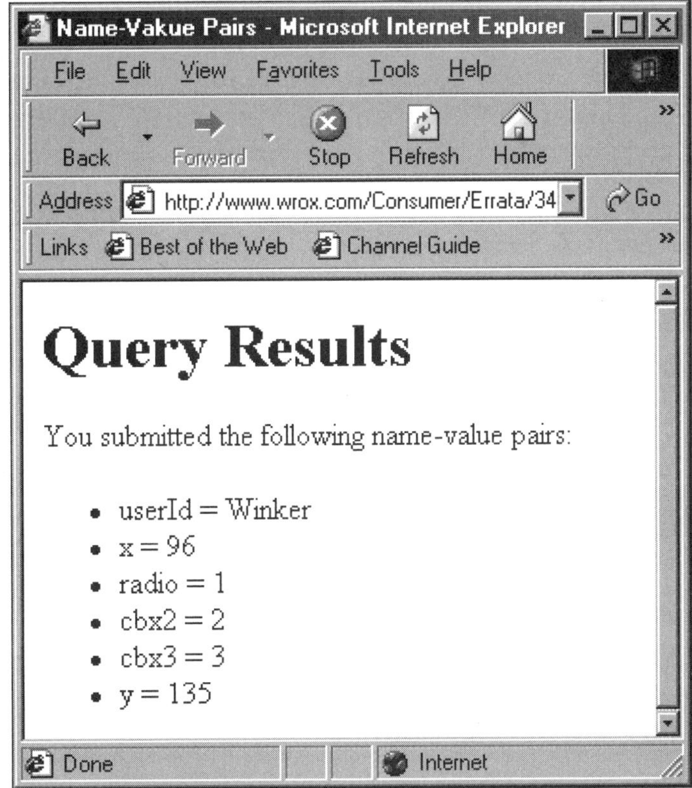

How It Works

This is simple enough to understand from having looked at the previous example. The additional points to note are that the values of the radio and check boxes are returned. For example:

```
<input type="checkbox" name="cbx2" id="cbx2" value="2" />
  <span>Choice2</span><br />
```

The `value` attribute is set equal to the number `2`, and this is the value returned from the Wrox echo server against the name of the checkbox, which was set to `cbx2` using the `name` attribute. The details of what happens when we click on the image are a bit more involved and we shan't go into them here except to note that the mouse coordinates are returned – try clicking on various parts of the image to work out where the origin of the coordinate system is located (top left of image). The Reset form button simply resets all the form fields to their original values.

Hidden Elements

The hidden type of <input> elements have an important role. The visitor can't see or edit them, but they can be used to store an arbitrary amount of information in a form. Suppose, for instance, a visitor was filling out a form so complicated (filing taxes online, perhaps) that you split it into several different pages. Rather than have the server remember what the visitor entered into a previous form, the user's prior entries can be stored in hidden form elements, and they'll be sent back to the server along with the elements on the current form.

Disabling <input> Elements

Any <input> element can be disabled using the disabled attribute. When disabled, the caption of a button will be grayed out.

If you're coming from an HTML background, you may be used to using this and other attributes as standalone attributes, that is, without assigning them values. For example, for a disabled button, you'd write:

```
<input type="button" disabled>
```

Because this is XHTML, however, a value must be given, so you actually use the attribute like this:

```
<input type="button" disabled="true" />
```

The <textarea> Element

The <textarea> element produces a large box which the user can type text into. You'd use a text area to provide visitors with the chance to enter more than one line of text, for instance, for an online discussion board. The syntax is:

```
<textarea> [default text] </textarea>
```

The value returned to the server is the text in the box. Note that <textarea> elements take the rows and cols attributes to set the size of the text area. We'll demonstrate the text area after we introduce the <select> and <option> elements.

The <select> and <option> Elements

The <select> element provides the user with a list of choices. It's different from the checkbox and radio button controls because you can present large lists with the <select> element without creating a separate control for each item, saving space on your form. The syntax of the <select> element is:

```
<select>
   <option>first option</option>
   <option>second option</option>
   <option>third option</option>
   ...etc
</select>
```

Each <option> child of the <select> element contains a choice. With <select>, you can create a drop-down box or a list box. The <select> element takes a size attribute with an integer value; if size is 1 (the default), a drop-down box is produced. If size has any other value, the result will be a list box showing the stated number of entries.

In the following example we create three selection boxes, a drop-down box, a list box to show three items, and a multiple selection box.

Try It Out – Creating List Boxes

1. Type up the following and save as lists.htm.

```
<?xml version="1.0" encoding="UTF-8"?>
<!DOCTYPE html
     PUBLIC "-//W3C//DTD XHTML 1.0 Transitional//EN"
     "http://www.w3.org/TR/xhtml1/DTD/xhtml1-transitional.dtd">
<html xmlns="http://www.w3.org/1999/xhtml" xml:lang="en" lang="en">
<head>
 <title>list controls</title>
</head>
<body>
 <h4>Examples of list controls</h4>
 <form action="http://www.wrox.com/Consumer/Errata/3439/post-echo.asp"
  method="post">
 <select size="1" name="dropdown">
   <option>Red</option>
   <option>White</option>
   <option>Blue</option>
   <option>Black</option>
 </select>
 <select size="3" name="listbox">
   <option value="ff0000">Red</option>
   <option value="ffffff">White</option>
   <option value="0000ff">Blue</option>
   <option value="000000">Black</option>
 </select>
 <select multiple="true" name="multiple">
   <option>Red</option>
   <option>White</option>
   <option>Blue</option>
   <option>Black</option>
 </select>
  <div>Type a message</div>
 <textarea cols="30" rows="8" name="ta1"></textarea><br />

 <input type="submit" />

</form>
</body>
</html>
```

2. When we run this we will see the following:

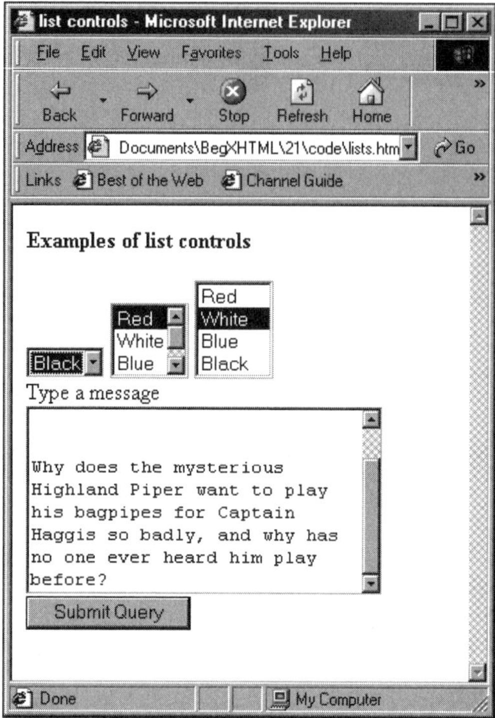

Here is what we get back from Wrox, after we submit it:

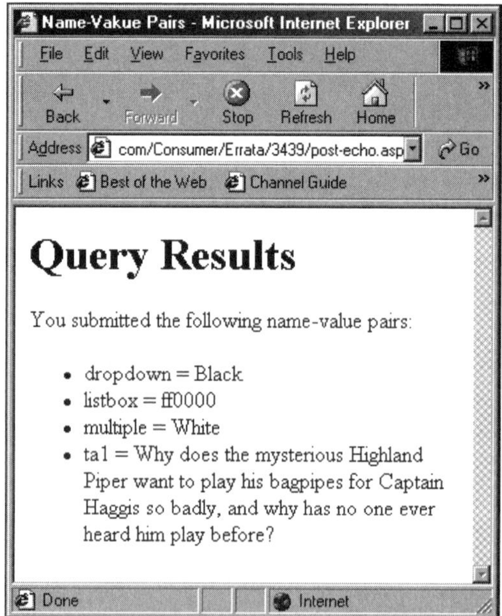

How It Works

Note that all the list controls rest on the baseline, rather than hang from it. To get a hanging appearance we would have to do some fancy styling! The third control has the multiple attribute set, so we can use the shift or control key while selecting to select more than one item, which means that more than one value will be sent to the server from this control. If no value is selected, the default value is sent to the server instead. Note that the entire text of the text area is returned as its value.

The <button> element

The `<button>` element produces a button with an image on it (rather than text), which, unlike the `<input type="image" ...>` form of the `<input>` element, does not transmit the click coordinates to the server. The syntax is:

```
<button>
  <img src="face.gif" alt ="an image" />
</button>
```

XHTML Markup Within Forms

To make your forms attractive, you can use any XHTML markup which would be allowed inside the `<body>` tag between `<form>` and `</form>` tags.

Forms and Usability

People who are experienced with the Web overestimate the web-skills of the general population. If your forms are confusing, difficult to fill out, or even seem like a waste of time, many of your users will fail to fill them out. If your site is commercial, this will translate into lost sales and angry (and fewer) customers. Here are a few things you should avoid while designing forms:

- **Asking users for irrelevant information.** Customers are not stupid, they know when information is necessary or not. If you want to get extra information for marketing purposes, make it optional.
- **Forcing users to repeat information.** Use a cookie, hidden `<form>` elements or 'scratch' space on the server to keep a track of information already supplied.
- **Not being able to save information.** If you let users create their own accounts, you can save repetitive information such as credit card numbers so that they don't need to type them again. On the other side, requiring registration has a downside: most users already have too many usernames and passwords and resent creating more unless you give them a good reason to do so.
- **Not telling users that the submission was complete.** Submitting forms to the same page and clearing the document without telling the user that the submission was complete is frustrating for the user, and the developer may get multiple submissions as the user won't know they have submitted successfully. Always send a page stating something like "Submission complete – thank you".

A good way to learn about web usability is to examine successful sites such as Yahoo! and `amazon.com`. Jakob Nielsen's site at `http://www.useit.com/` contains a wealth of advice and data based on usability research – this site should be mandatory for anyone who creates web pages or applications.

Summary

Forms allow our XHTML pages to be interactive. They are the basis of a wide range of Web applications, including e-commerce. In this chapter we looked at the `<input>` elements that can be put into a `<form>` element, and the various boxes (`text`, `password`, `file`, `submit`, `reset`, `button`, `image`, `checkbox`, `radio` and `hidden`) that we can have. We also discussed the `GET` and `POST` methods, and offered some guidelines when creating web forms.

However, much more sophisticated form creation can be done using Mozquito, more of which in Chapter 20.

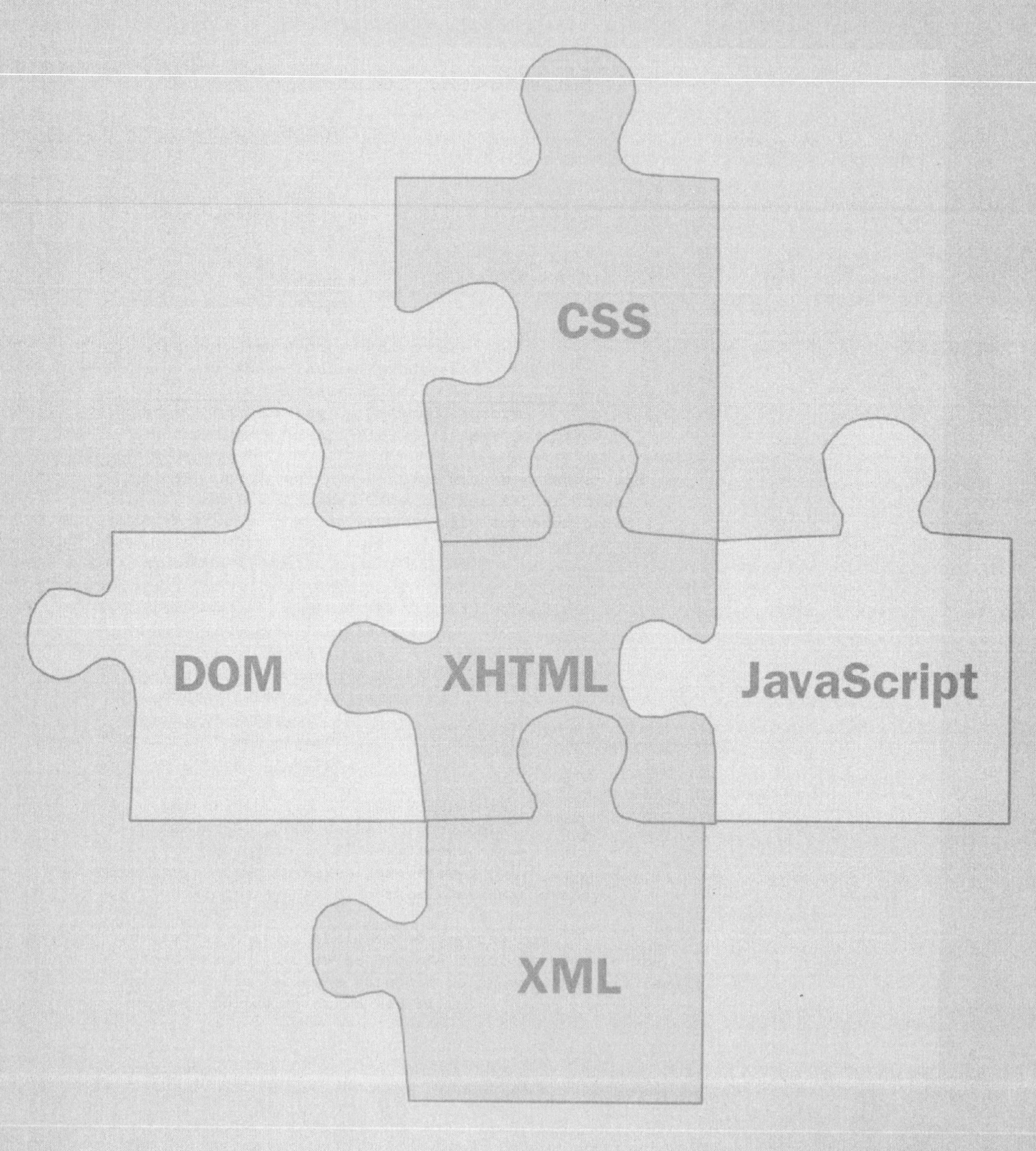
CSS
DOM
XHTML
JavaScript
XML

16 JavaScript

Until now, we've looked at pages that are displayed passively on a web browser, much like a page in a book. The only way a user could interact with such a page is to click on a link – causing the browser to fetch a new page from our or another web server. Although it's possible to write applications that use software running on a web server to interpret forms filled out on a web browser, we can also use JavaScript to write programs that run inside a web browser.

There are two main scripting languages in use on client side web pages, JavaScript and VBScript. We will confine ourselves to JavaScript, as it is the more widely supported and implemented of the languages. JavaScript has five flavors – versions 1.0, 1.1, 1.2, 1.3, and 1.4. JavaScript 1.1 was used as the basis of the European Computer Manufacturer's Association international standard, ECMAScript. JavaScript 1.3 and 1.4 also comply with this standard. Because JavaScript varies greatly between Netscape and Internet Explorer, and between different versions of the same browser, the only guarantee you can have that your scripts will be compatible between different browsers is to test them.

Other than name, there is little relationship between Java and JavaScript. At first, Netscape named JavaScript "LiveScript" but changed the name because they believed Java was up and coming at the time. Although the syntax of JavaScript vaguely resembles Java (just as Java vaguely resembles the C programming language), the capabilities and uses of Java and JavaScript are entirely different.

Both VBScript and JavaScript can be used to construct powerful applications. This chapter will introduce you to just enough JavaScript to get you started. Take a look at *Professional JavaScript* (McFarlane et al, Wrox Press Ltd, 1-861002-70-X) if you'd like to learn more. Also, you can find official documentation for Netscape's version of JavaScript at `http://developer.iplanet.com/docs/manuals/javascript.html` and find documentation for Microsoft's version, called JScript, at `http://www.microsoft.com/scripting/jscript/default.htm`. The official specification of ECMAScript is at `http://www.ecma.ch/stand/ecma-262.htm`.

In this chapter, we'll cover:

- How to incorporate JavaScript into an XHTML page
- A brief look at the JavaScript language and its syntax
- Built-in operators
- Control of flow statements
- Defining your own functions

You should be warned that whole books can and are devoted to this subject, so we'll end up moving at a pretty fast pace, and maybe not cover everything in as much detail as you might like. That's inevitable, though, and so we're going to aim to provide a taster of JavaScript that you can use to see if anything really grabs you, so you can see if it's a tool you want to learn and develop. JavaScript is really quite powerful, so there's a lot more to it than we'll be able to cover in these relatively few remaining pages. The other thing is that we'll need to jump around by necessity, using things before we've properly introduced them. That's another catch-22 situation – but we will cover everything in the end!

In the following chapters, we'll put what we'll learn in this chapter into effect, by using JavaScript to manipulate documents through the Document Object Model (DOM.)

What Is a Scripting Language?

Conventional programming languages such as C++ compile a human-readable file into a standalone executable (in Windows, `.exe`) program (Java is also a conventional language, but produces executables which are `.class` files rather than `.exe` files). Conventional languages also require considerable skill on the part of a programmer, who needs to worry, for instance, how a program uses memory. Scripting languages have two characteristics: first, because scripting languages are **interpreted** instead of **compiled**, they don't need to be compiled before they are run. Interpreted languages are often easier to program than compiled languages because they hide more of the complexity of programming than compiled languages do.

Secondly, scripting languages are often (but not always) built into applications rather than used to write applications. For instance, Microsoft Office can be scripted with Visual Basic for Applications. As a counterexample, plain Visual Basic is a programming language for creating Windows applications.

Although the most common use of JavaScript is inside web browsers, it can also be used to write scripts than run inside web servers such as Netscape's FastTrack server or Microsoft IIS. Implementations of JavaScript exist, such as Netscape's Rhino (`http://www.mozilla.org/rhino/`) which are designed to be plugged into new or existing applications, so we'll probably see new uses of JavaScript in the future. However, in this book, we'll talk only about using JavaScript inside web browsers.

Including Scripts in Documents

Before we look at examples of scripts let's look at how to associate a script with a document. There are several ways to associate a script with a document. We will look at three of these:

- We can link to a script contained in a separate file.
- A script can be enclosed in a `<script>` element.
- An *event handler* script can be incorporated into certain attributes of certain XHTML elements.

We'll now look at each of these in turn.

Placing Code in an External File

Let's start with a practical example.

Try It Out – Linking to an External Script File

1. Warm up your favorite text editor and type the following:

```
<?xml version="1.0" encoding="UTF-8"?>
<!DOCTYPE html
     PUBLIC "-//W3C//DTD XHTML 1.0 Transitional//EN"
     "http://www.w3.org/TR/xhtml1/DTD/xhtml1-transitional.dtd">
<html xmlns="http://www.w3.org/1999/xhtml" xml:lang="en" lang="en">
<head>
<title>Java script examples</title>
<script type="text/javascript" src="methods1.js">
</script>
</head>
<body>
</body>
</html>
```

2. Save this as `JSexample1.htm`. Now open a second file and type the following:

```
alert("Welcome to JavaScript");
```

3. Save this as `methods1.js` in the same directory that you saved `JSexample1.htm`.

4. This is what you will see when you run the `JSexample1.htm` file:

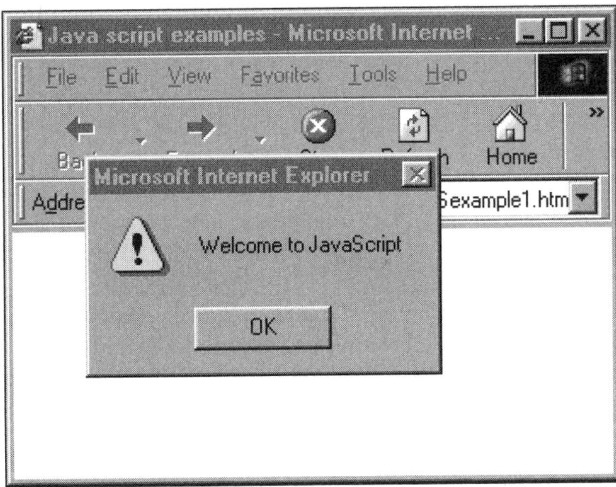

How It Works

The browser reads the XHTML file from top to bottom. When the browser reads the following line:

```
<script type="text/javascript" src="methods1.js">
```

it knows that it must execute a script. Most browsers default to the JavaScript engine (as opposed to, say, VBScript or Perl) but, just in case, we tell the browser what language to use with the `type` attribute:

```
type="text/javascript"
```

This tells the browser that it will be dealing with a text file written in JavaScript.

> **We could also use a `language` attribute `<script language="JavaScript">` but the method we use here is preferred because, unlike the MIME type used in the type attribute, there is no standard for defining names to use for the language attribute. Although, by writing something like `<script language="JavaScript1.1">` you are supposed to be able to specify the version of JavaScript you're using so that older browsers will ignore scripts written for newer browsers, bugs in Netscape make this unreliable.**

The next thing the browser comes to is a reference to an external file:

```
src="methods1.js"
```

The browser fetches the file called `methods1.js`, and executes the script at once:

```
alert("Welcome to JavaScript");
```

So the browser immediately executes the `alert` method, causing a popup box to appear with the text written in the parentheses. We will explain more shortly, but for now note:

- The whole line is a single statement. The semi-colon at the end of the line marks the end of the statement.
- The semi-colon is optional, unless you wish to write multiple statements on a single line.
- To use a method, we write its name followed by any arguments in parentheses. The name tells JavaScript what to do, while the arguments contain data that determine how to do it. The `alert` method produces a dialog box, and the argument gives the text that appears in the box.

Placing Code Between Script Tags

In XHTML we can get the same result as above by writing this:

```
<?xml version="1.0" encoding="UTF-8"?>
<!DOCTYPE html
     PUBLIC "-//W3C//DTD XHTML 1.0 Transitional//EN"
     "http://www.w3.org/TR/xhtml1/DTD/xhtml1-transitional.dtd">
<html xmlns="http://www.w3.org/1999/xhtml" xml:lang="en" lang="en">
<head>
<title>Java script examples</title>
<script type="text/javascript">
<!--
 alert("Welcome to JavaScript");
// -->
</script>
</head>
<body>
</body>
</html>
```

The script is enclosed in a comment (`<!-- -->`) for two reasons. First, although existing HTML browsers aren't so picky, an XHTML document would be ill-formed if we embedded a script including characters such as <, +, and `&`. A comment in XML (and XHTML) is allowed to contain any sequence of characters except for a pair of minus signs (--), so surrounding a script with a comment avoids almost any difficulties in validating the document. Second, if we didn't enclose our script in a comment very old browsers, such as Netscape 1.1, would (rather than ignore the script) display the script in the middle of the document. When JavaScript was introduced in Netscape 2, the JavaScript engine was designed to ignore HTML comments, providing a mechanism for backwards compatibility. Although many scripts will work in JavaScript browsers if you don't enclose the script in the comments, you should always enclose inline scripts in a comment to avoid incompatibilities with non-JavaScript browsers and future browsers which will refuse to process XHTML documents which are not valid and well-formed.

Scripts have the same effect if they are read from an external file or if they are enclosed in `<script>` tags. Putting your scripts in an external file avoids incompatibilities with non-JavaScript browsers and problems with XML validation in future XHTML browsers. Also, if you put scripts in external files, you can reuse the same script in different HTML files. The main disadvantage of putting scripts in external files is that Netscape 2.0 and Internet Explorer 3.0 do not support scripts in external files.

Placing Code in an Event Handler

An event handler is a fragment of script which runs when something happens. It's possible to define event handlers by putting a small script in certain attributes of certain elements. For instance, the following XHTML fragment defines an event handler for the `onMouseDown` event of an image, and will pop up a dialog box when the user moves the mouse cursor over the image and presses the mouse button:

```
<img src="blob.gif" alt="Mr.Blob" onMouseDown="alert('a picture of Mr.Blob')" />
```

We'll look at event handlers in more detail later in this chapter when we discuss events.

Objects, Properties, Events, and Methods

JavaScript is an **object-based** language, so we'll next define some terms used in object-based and object-oriented languages.

> *Java is an object-**oriented** language while JavaScript is object-**based** because JavaScript does not include the notion of **inheritance**, which eases the task of writing large programs by letting programmers write objects that inherit methods and properties from parent objects rather than having to write all of the methods of each object*

Objects are a metaphor from real life. In real life, an object could be something like a hat, a car or a cat. Things in the world have **properties** (characteristics), **events** (having things happen to them) and **methods** (can do things or be manipulated). By capturing events, you can be notified when something happens to an object: for instance, when the user moves the mouse pointer over a hyperlink. You can manipulate objects by using methods and setting properties. For instance, you can pop up a dialog box by using the `alert` method of the `window` object (`window.alert("hi!")`), and you can make the browser jump to a new page by setting the `location` property of the `window` object. (`window.location="http://www.honeylocust.com/"`)

Browser Objects

JavaScript sees the web browser as a collection of objects. Three of the most important browser objects are:

- **The window object:** the space occupied by the browser on our screen.
- **The navigator object:** a collection of information about the browser.
- **The document object:** the document currently being viewed by the web browser.

All of these objects have properties, and some of their properties are also objects. In fact, the `navigator` and `document` objects are properties of the `window` object.

Let's look at some of the methods that these objects have, and then we'll look at some properties of these objects.

Methods

We have already looked at one simple method. The `alert()` method of the `window` object.

The syntax for executing a method in JavaScript is:

```
[object name].[method name] ([parameters])
```

If, however, object 2 is a property of object 1, we can invoke a method of object 2 with:

```
[object1 name].[object2 name].[method name]([parameters])
```

To demonstrate, we'll revisit the `alert` method of the window object, and look at the `write` method of the `document` object.

If we're going too fast, don't worry about it – JavaScript isn't essential to your XHTML pages in the early days, but you might want to still follow along so you can see what kinds of things it's capable of, even if it's not perfectly plain why how it all works. You'll then know if you're interested to learn more, and can look into getting hold of a book devoted to the subject that can go into a lot more detail.

Try It Out – Using 'window' and 'document' Methods

1. Modify `JSexample1.htm` to read as follows and save it as `JSexample2.htm`.

```
<?xml version="1.0" encoding="UTF-8"?>
<!DOCTYPE html
     PUBLIC "-//W3C//DTD XHTML 1.0 Transitional//EN"
     "http://www.w3.org/TR/xhtml1/DTD/xhtml1-transitional.dtd">
<html xmlns="http://www.w3.org/1999/xhtml" xml:lang="en" lang="en">
<head>
<title>Java script examples</title>
</head>
<body>
<script type="text/javascript" src="methods2.js">
</script>
</body>
</html>
```

2. `methods1.js` should be modified as follows, and saved as `methods2.js`:

```
window.alert("Welcome to JavaScript");

window.document.write("Welcome to JavaScript");
```

3. Now when we run `Jsexample2.htm` we first see this:

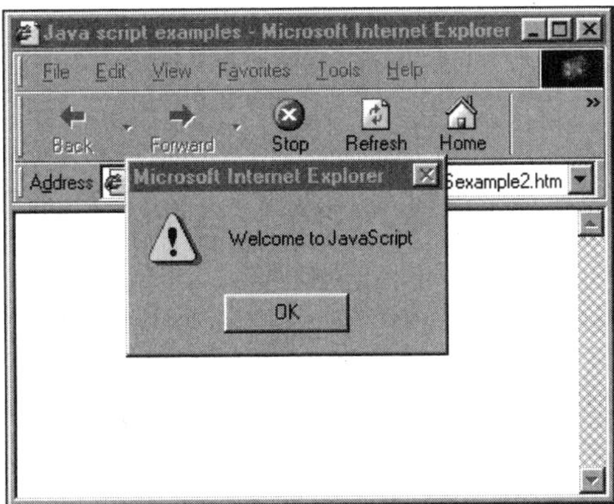

4. Now, move the message box over so you can see that there's no text in the browser window, and then click the OK button. You should see this:

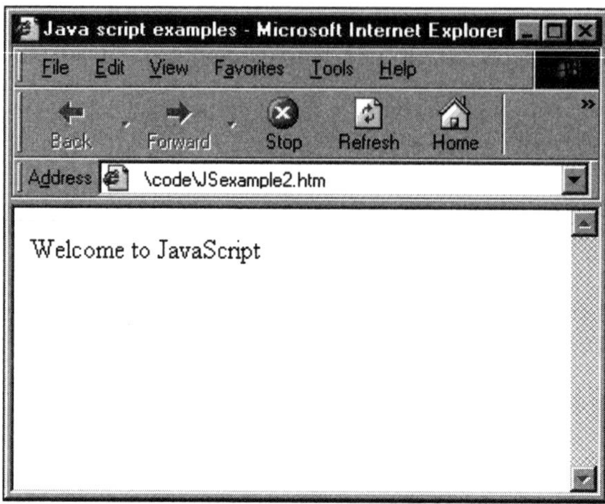

How It Works

As before, the XHTML document `Jsexample2.htm` is read from the top down. When the browser sees the `<script>` tag, it fetches the JavaScript file `methods2.js` and starts reading from the top down.

The first line is:

```
window.alert("Welcome to JavaScript");
```

This makes the browser pop up a dialog box. If you've been paying attention, you might have noticed that we omitted the "`window.` " when we popped up a dialog box in a previous example. This is because, when executing statements in a `<script>` tag (either internal or external) that are not inside a user-defined function (we'll talk about that later), JavaScript automatically assumes any method or property you use belongs to the `window` object.

If we're using Internet Explorer, the execution of the script is frozen until we press the OK button. (In Netscape, the script continues but the dialog box stays around until you click OK.) Next, the scripting engine moves to the next line of the script:

```
window.document.write("Welcome to JavaScript");
```

`document` is a property of the `window` object, so we can access the current document by typing "`window.document`", although "`document`" would also work in this context. The `write` method of the document writes the text given in its parameter into the document, replacing the contents of the `<script>` element. To clarify this, we can alter `Jsexample2.htm` to read:

```
<body>
<p>Some Java script coming up!</p>
<script type="text/javascript" src="methods2.js">
</script>
<p>That was JavaScript!</p>
</body>
</html>
```

Parameters

Methods take parameters (**parameter** is synonymous with **argument**.) Parameters supply data that are used by methods. In the above example the `write` method was passed the parameter "Welcome to JavaScript".

Some methods take more than one parameter, in which case we separate the arguments by commas. The general syntax for this is:

```
[method name]([first parameter],[second parameter]...)
```

Let's take a quick look at this now.

Try It Out – Passing More Than One Parameter to a Method

We are going to use the `window` object's `resizeTo()` method to resize a window.

1. Type up the following external script and save it as `arguments.js`:

```
alert("we are about to resize this window.");

resizeTo(300,300);
```

2. Now modify our first example, `Jsexample1.htm`, to read this script file as follows:

```
<?xml version="1.0" encoding="UTF-8"?>
<!DOCTYPE html
     PUBLIC "-//W3C//DTD XHTML 1.0 Transitional//EN"
     "http://www.w3.org/TR/xhtml1/DTD/xhtml1-transitional.dtd">
<html xmlns="http://www.w3.org/1999/xhtml" xml:lang="en" lang="en">
<head>
<title>Java script examples</title>
</head>
<body>
<script type="text/javascript" src="arguments.js">
</script>
</body>
</html>
```

3. When we run this we first see an alert, and then when we click on the OK button our browser window will be resized to 300 pixels by 300 pixels!

How It Works

The `resizeTo` method expects two parameters, which are the dimensions of the window in pixels. Try missing out the second parameter to see what happens.

Methods and Functions

Methods, in addition to doing something to an object, can return a value. For example, consider the script:

```
<script>
scratch="To be or not to be".charAt(3)
document.write(scratch);
</script>
```

This script writes the letter "b" into the document. Here, the `charAt()` method of the `String` object (a fragment of text is called a **string**) to return the fourth character of the string "To be or not to be".

The argument in the parentheses is 3. However JavaScript starts counting at 0, so 3 represents the fourth character, or the 'character at index 3'.

Functions are like methods, except functions do not belong to a particular object. Several functions are built into JavaScript and, as we'll see later, you can define your own functions.

Properties

Now that we have seen how to use methods lets look at how to retrieve the value of a property associated with an object. To access a property we write the following:

`[object name].[property name]`

Let's try retrieving some properties of the `window` and `document` object.

Try It Out – Retrieving 'window' and 'document' Object Properties

1. Type up the following XHTML document, `properties1.htm`, into your text editor:

```
<?xml version="1.0" encoding="UTF-8"?>
<!DOCTYPE html
     PUBLIC "-//W3C//DTD XHTML 1.0 Transitional//EN"
     "http://www.w3.org/TR/xhtml1/DTD/xhtml1-transitional.dtd">
<html xmlns="http://www.w3.org/1999/xhtml" xml:lang="en" lang="en">
<head>
<title>JavaScript examples</title>
<script type="text/javascript" src="properties1.js">
</script>
```

```
<script type="text/javascript" >
<!--
 document.write(document.bgColor);
 document.write("<br />");
// -->
</script>
</head>
<body bgcolor="#c0c0c0">
<p>Some Java script coming up!</p>
<script type="text/javascript" >
<!--
 document.write(document.bgColor);
 document.write("<br />");
 document.write(document.title);
 document.write("<br />");
 document.write(window.location);
 document.write("<br />");
 document.write(navigator.appName);
// -->
</script>
<p>That was JavaScript!</p>
</body>
</html>
```

2. Now type this up and save it as `properties1.js`:

```
document.write(document.bgColor);
document.write("<br />");
document.write(window.location);
document.write("<hr />");
```

3. Now when we run this, we should see something like this:

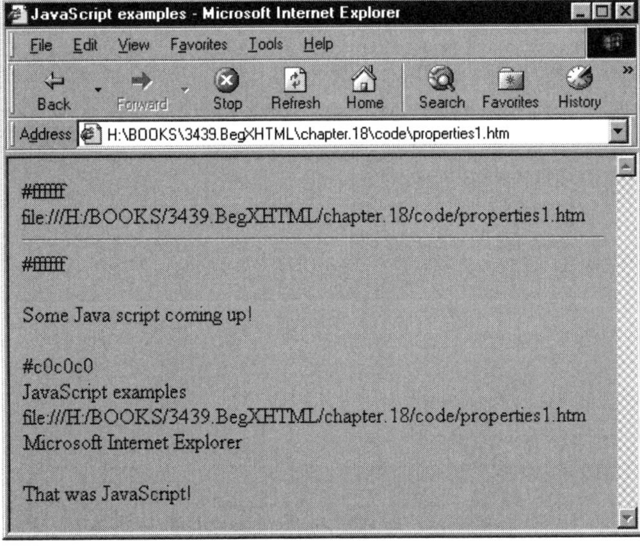

How It Works

As we have said, the XHTML document is read from top to bottom. The first block of code that the browser encounters is the external file:

```
document.write(document.bgColor);
document.write("<br />");
document.write(window.location);
document.write("<hr />");
```

Note that at this stage it is telling us that the background color of the browser window is white, which is the default for IE 5. Your value may be different if you set your browser background to a different color:

```
document.write(document.bgColor);
 document.write("<br />");
```

`document.bgColor` is `#ffffff` at these two locations, because we haven't reached the `<body>` tag yet. Next we set the `bgcolor` property to white with the `bgcolor` attribute of the `<body>` element:

```
<body bgcolor="#c0c0c0">
```

When we next execute:

```
document.write(document.bgColor);
```

... the value of `document.bgColor` is `#c0c0c0`. Now, this line prints the title of the document:

```
document.write(document.title);
```

This line tells us the `window` object's `location` property, where the XHTML document was downloaded from:

```
document.write(window.location);
```

And finally we use the `appName` property of the `navigator` object to tell us we are running Microsoft Internet Explorer (we'll see more on these objects in later chapters; our aim here is to demonstrate how to work with properties):

```
document.write(navigator.appName);
```

Events

An **event** is essentially when something external to your script happens. A mouse and keyboard can generate numerous events. For example, clicking a mouse on a window generates all of the following events:

- onMouseDown: when we depress the button
- onMouseUp: when we release it
- onClick: occurs after a single click of the mouse

Different browsers support different events on different elements. For example, Navigator 4.5 does not support the onClick event on an image, but does support the onMouseDown event and the onMouseUp events.

The keyboard can also generate other events.

IE 4+ supports all events on all elements, but Navigator supports events on only some elements. We'll discuss this further in the next chapter.

Here we'll explain events by demonstration.

Try It Out – Experimenting with Different Events

1. Hammer out the following on your text editor:

```
<?xml version="1.0" encoding="UTF-8"?>
<!DOCTYPE html
     PUBLIC "-//W3C//DTD XHTML 1.0 Transitional//EN"
     "http://www.w3.org/TR/xhtml1/DTD/xhtml1-transitional.dtd">
<html xmlns="http://www.w3.org/1999/xhtml" xml:lang="en" lang="en">
<head>
<title>Java script examples. Events</title>
</head>
<body bgcolor="#ffffff">
<a id="top" name="top"></a><a href="#top" onclick="alert('Fooled You! This is not
a link')"><p>Some Java script coming up!</p></a>

<img src="blob1.gif" alt ="Picture of bob blob" onmousedown="alert('this is a
picture of Bob Blob')" />
<form>
<input type="text" onfocus="this.value='we just got the focus'"></input>
<input type="button" value="Click Me!" onclick="alert('you clicked me!')" />
</form>

</body>
</html>
```

2. Save it as `event.htm`. Find the `blob1.gif` file from the downloaded code, and save it in the same directory as the `.htm` file. Alternatively, you could use any GIF file and just change the name in the script accordingly.

3. When you run this you will see the following page:

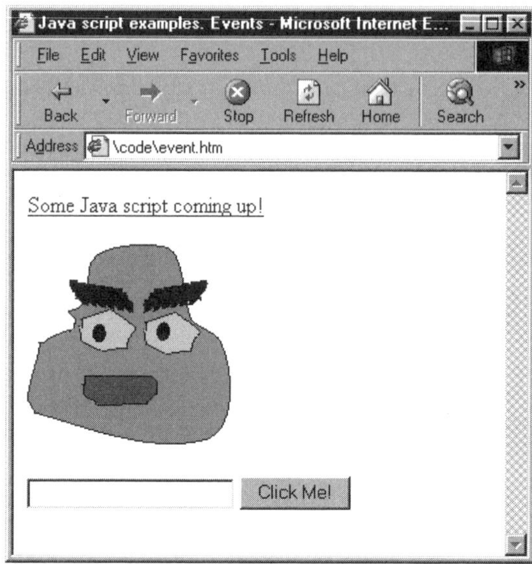

4. Try clicking on the image. You will get an alert box with message "This is a picture of Bob Blob".

5. Now click in the text box. The words 'we just got the focus' should appear.

How It Works

The image was generated with the following code:

```
<img src="blob1.gif" alt ="Picture of bob blob" onmousedown="alert('this is a
picture of Bob Blob')" />
```

Let's analyze the event handler here:

```
onmousedown="alert('this is a picture of Bob Blob')"
```

This is an event handler attribute. We have used the `onmousedown` attribute because it works on all 4.0+ browsers.

The value of the `onmousedown` attribute is a script that will be executed when the mouse is depressed. We have just put a simple alert here:

```
alert('this is a picture of Bob Blob')
```

Note that we used single quotes to enclose our string, as the attribute used double quotes. When writing a string in JavaScript, we have a choice of enclosing it in single quotes or double quotes – it's perfectly safe, therefore, to enclose a script which includes single quotes inside of a parameter value which is enclosed in double quotes.

Now let's turn our attention to the text box. When you click in the text box, the text 'we just got the focus' appears. This was caused by the following code:

```
<input type="text" onfocus="this.value='we just got the focus'"></input>
```

The event handler was `'onfocus'`. Let's look at that a little more closely. The code executed was:

```
this.value='we just got the focus'
```

Inside an event handler, the `this` keyword refers to the element which received the event, in this case the input box. The value property of the text box is the contents of the box. By assigning a string to the value property, we can change the text inside the box.

> **OK, so now you're wondering what 'focus' is, right? Well, if you have 2 applications open, one of them probably has the focus – it's the active application. It's the one where any keystrokes you make will be sent by your operating system. Similarly, within your application, if your cursor is in a text box, it's said to have the focus. If you use the *Tab* key to move to, say, a button, that button then has the focus, and the text box gets a 'blur' event.**

Two more examples of event handlers are:

```
<input type="button" value="Click Me!" onclick="alert('you clicked me!')" />
```

```
<a id="top" name="top"></a><a href="#top" onclick="alert('Fooled You! This is not
a link')"></a>
```

The JavaScript Language

Now we have looked at a few examples, let's examine JavaScript more formally. The syntax of a programming language is the set of rules that define the language. This section details the syntax of JavaScript.

Case Sensitivity

JavaScript is a case-sensitive language. Keywords, functions, variables and other identifiers must be spelled with the correct case.

For example, `alert()` is the correct syntax for this method of the `window` object, and not `ALERT` or `Alert`. If you type `window.Alert()`, it won't work.

Tokens

A **token** is a unit like a keyword, a function or a variable name or a number. No white space is allowed in a token. So, if we look at:

```
alert("This is OK")
```

and:

```
ale rt("This is not")
```

The second example will produce an error (note the space inside the keyword).

White space

JavaScript ignores white space that occurs between tokens, so:

```
document.write("this");
document.write(" and that");
```

and:

```
document.write("this");document.write(" and that");
```

and:

```
document.write("this");

         document.write(" and that");
```

will all produce the same result.

That having been said though, it is good practice to put each separate statement on a single line and to use line breaks and indents to clarify the layout of your code. We cannot over emphasize the importance of using white space to produce readable code.

Comments

JavaScript uses the same commenting system as Java and the C language:

```
//This is a comment on one line
```

```
/* this
     is
           a comment
over several lines*/
```

Intelligent use of comments makes it much easier for other people to understand your programs and for you to understand your programs when you need to change them six months after you wrote them.

Literals

A **literal** is a data value that appears in a program. The following are all literals:

`35`	A number
`3.5`	Another number
`-3.5`	Another number
`"thirtyfive"`	A string value
`'thirty five'`	Also a string value
`null`	A reference to a non-existent object
`true`	The boolean "true" value
`false`	The boolean "false" value

Identifiers

Identifiers are names that we give our variables and functions.

A name must follow the following rules:

- It must start with a letter, a dollar sign ($) or an under-score(_).
- It can only contain alphanumeric characters, the underscore, or a dollar sign.
- Other Unicode and Latin1 characters are NOT allowed.
- You cannot use a **reserved word** (a word whose meaning is already defined in the JavaScript language) as an identifier.
- You should also avoid other words such as 'document' or 'window' that are words associated with common JavaScript objects.

Reserved Words

There are certain keywords that are part of the JavaScript syntax. These are called reserved words. Do not use these words as identifiers.

```
break     case      continue  default   delete
do        else      export    for       function
if        import    in        new       return
switch    this      typeof    var       void
while     with
```

There are also other words which it is best to avoid, especially those words that have been given to properties and methods of the window and other browser objects.

Output in JavaScript

We have already seen how to output material using JavaScript's `alert` and `document.write()` methods. We will review these and add a third, the `confirm` method. We will also look at the `prompt` method.

window.alert

As we have already seen, the `window.alert()` method produces a popup or alert box. It takes one parameter, the string to be displayed.

window.confirm

The `window.confirm` box also displays a popup box, but with two buttons: an OK button and a Cancel button. This method, though, returns a value. Depending on which button is picked, a value of `true` or `false` is returned. We will be covering these concepts later, for now let's just look at an example. You will probably want to come back to this section after you have read the rest of this chapter.

Try It Out – Using a 'confirm' Box

1. Type up the following and save it as `confirm.htm`:

```
<?xml version="1.0" encoding="UTF-8"?>
<!DOCTYPE html
     PUBLIC "-//W3C//DTD XHTML 1.0 Transitional//EN"
     "http://www.w3.org/TR/xhtml1/DTD/xhtml1-transitional.dtd">
<html xmlns="http://www.w3.org/1999/xhtml" xml:lang="en" lang="en">
<head>
<title>Java script examples</title>

<script>
<!--
var scratch
scratch=confirm("We have two pages, one a fast loading page, and the other a
graphics page which will take some time to download.\n\n Click OK to view the
graphics page.")
document.write(scratch)
// -->
</script>
</head>
<body>
</body>
</html>
```

2. When we run this the following message will be displayed:

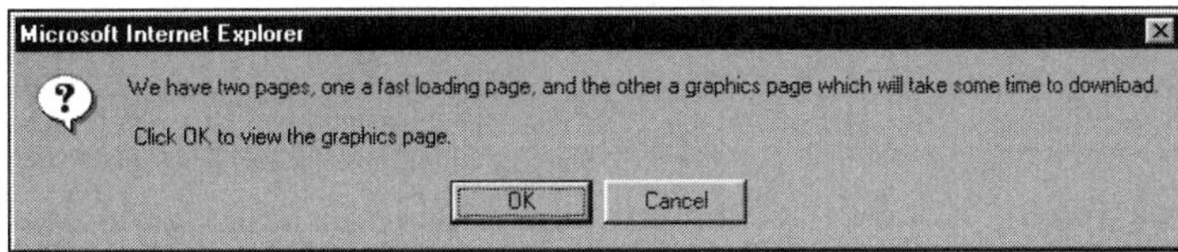

3. Now click on the OK button, and this is what we will see:

If, instead, we had clicked on the Cancel button we would have seen the word `false`.

How It Works

First of all, let's look at the message we display:

```
scratch=confirm("We have two pages, one a fast loading page, and the other a
graphics page which will take some time to down load.\n\n Click O.K to view the
grahics page?")
```

This must be typed all on one line.

> *Note the use of* `\n`*, which allows us to specify a line break. You can also use* `\t` *for a tab character.*

When we click on a button, a Boolean (`true` or `false`) value is generated which is stored in the variable called `scratch`. A script can access this variable and take different actions depending on which button was clicked. To direct users to different pages depending on what they click, we can add the following:

```
if(scratch){
location.href = 'richgraphicpage.html';
}else{
   location.href = 'simplegraphicpage.html';
}
```

When we set the `href` property of the `location` object to a URL, we make the browser jump to that URL.

> **You will probably not understand all this until you have read the sections on variables and conditional statements, so we suggest that you come back to it later on!**

document.write

We have already seen the `document.write()` method in action. This method writes text to the browser window. The text written is the string that is passed as an argument.

window.prompt

The window prompt box is a popup box that provides a simple way to get information from a user.

This method takes two arguments, a message, and some default text to put in the popup box. Let's look at an example:

Try It Out – Using the Prompt Box

1. Type up this XHTML page and save it as `prompt.htm`:

```
<?xml version="1.0" encoding="UTF-8"?>
<!DOCTYPE html
     PUBLIC "-//W3C//DTD XHTML 1.0 Transitional//EN"
     "http://www.w3.org/TR/xhtml1/DTD/xhtml1-transitional.dtd">
<html xmlns="http://www.w3.org/1999/xhtml" xml:lang="en" lang="en">
<head>
<title>Java script examples</title>

<script>
<!--
var scratch
scratch=prompt("Please enter your name in the box below", "Hi, my name is:-")
document.write(scratch)
// -->
</script>
</head>
<body>
</body>
</html>
```

2. Here is what you should see when you view the page:

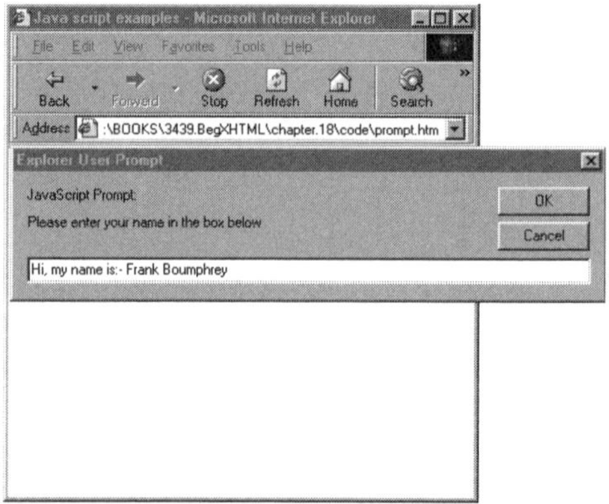

How It Works

The prompt method takes two arguments. Note that my first argument is displayed as a message, and my second argument "Hi, my name is:- " is displayed as default text. In the screenshot above, I have added my name after this. Now when we press the OK button the whole string is returned:

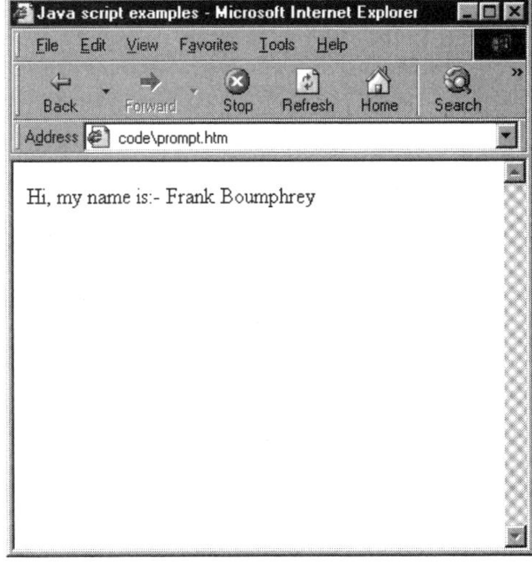

If, instead, we had pressed the Cancel button, then `prompt` would have returned `null`.

Writing XHTML from JavaScript Code

Before moving on from this section it should be noted that we can use the `document.write` method to write XHTML elements (as well as text) to the browser window.

Let's try that:

Try It Out – XHTML from JavaScript

1. Modify our earlier `JSexample1.htm` as follows:

```
<?xml version="1.0" encoding="UTF-8"?>
<!DOCTYPE html
     PUBLIC "-//W3C//DTD XHTML 1.0 Transitional//EN"
     "http://www.w3.org/TR/xhtml1/DTD/xhtml1-transitional.dtd">
<html xmlns="http://www.w3.org/1999/xhtml" xml:lang="en" lang="en">
<head>
<title>Java script examples</title>
<script type="text/javascript" src="xhtml.js">
</script>
</head>
<body>
</body>
</html>
```

2. Now type this in as a separate file and save it as `xhtml.js`:

```
document.write("<h1 align='center'>A centered heading</h1>")
document.write("<p>The above is a centered heading</p>")
```

3. This will produce the following output:

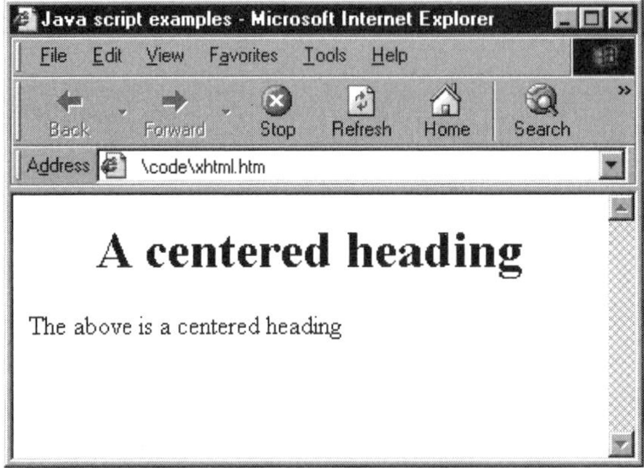

How It Works

The important part is these two lines here (the XHTML page itself is just a carrier for our script, as we've used it before:

```
document.write("<h1 align='center'>A centered heading</h1>")
document.write("<p>The above is a centered heading</p>")
```

When we write to the document, we're writing in (X)HTML, not just plain text, so if we include any markup it's rendered in the browser as we'd expect. This is actually a pretty useful technique for writing dynamic content to your page, as you can respond to different actions with different content if you like.

Variables

A variable is a container for information. This information can be a number, a string, or even an object. To put information in a variable we must do the following: choose a legal name for the variable (an identifier as defined above) and assign a value to our variable. To do this we use the **assignment operator**, the equals sign:

```
[variable name]=[variable value];
```

Note the following points:

- The value is always on the right side of the equals sign, and the variable name on the left hand side:

```
x = 5;
```

- Once we have assigned a value to our variable, every time we call that variable it's value will be returned:

```
x = 5;
alert(x); // pops up a dialog box that says "5"
```

- We can assign a new value to the variable at any time, and the old value will be replaced:

```
x = 5;
x = "Chocolate Cake";
alert(x); // pops up a dialog block that says "Chocolate Cake"
```

- The variable assigned in one script block will be good in a later script block. The client side JavaScript engine considers all code referred to in a single XHTML page to be a single program:

```
<script type="text/javascript">
<!--
x = "orange"
// -->
</script>
Chiba is an <script type="text/javascript">document.write(x)</script> cat.
```

This displays "Chiba is an orange cat" in the web browser window.

Let's try some variable work out right now.

Try It Out – Declaring a Variable and Assigning it a Value

1. Type up the following:

```
<?xml version="1.0" encoding="UTF-8"?>
<!DOCTYPE html
    PUBLIC "-//W3C//DTD XHTML 1.0 Transitional//EN"
    "http://www.w3.org/TR/xhtml1/DTD/xhtml1-transitional.dtd">
<html xmlns="http://www.w3.org/1999/xhtml" xml:lang="en" lang="en">
<head>
<title>Java script examples. Events</title>
```

```
<script type="text/javascript" >
<!--
  anotherString="<br /> This is a tongue twister";

  myString="The Leith Police dismisseth us.";
  document.write(myString);
  document.write(anotherString);
// -->
</script>
</head>
<body bgcolor="#ffffff">
<br />
<script type="text/javascript" >
<!--
  myString="How now Brown Cow.";
  document.write(myString);
// -->
</script>

</body>
</html>
```

2. Save it as `variables.htm`. When you run it you will see this:

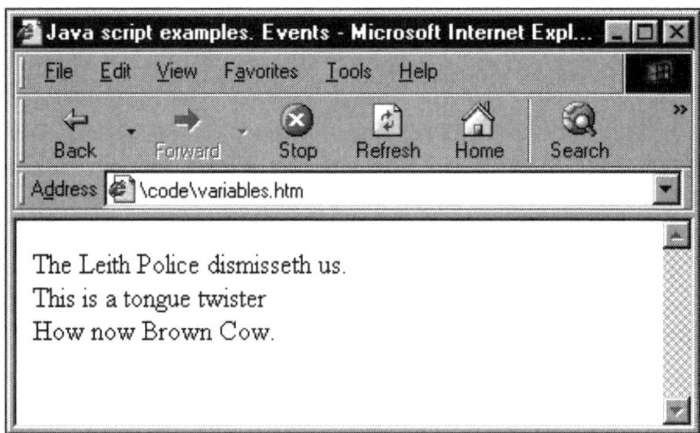

How It Works

In our first script block, we set a variable called `anotherString` to take the value `"<br /> This is a tongue twister"`. Then we set another variable, `myString`, to take the value `"The Leith Police dismisseth us."`:

```
<script type="text/javascript" >
<!--
  anotherString="<br /> This is a tongue twister";
  myString="The Leith Police dismisseth us.";
```

This demonstrates that it doesn't matter which way around we declare our variables, because the next thing we do is to write to our document, first with the contents of `myString`, and then with `anotherString`:

```
    document.write(myString);
    document.write(anotherString);
  // -->
  </script>
```

Then, later on in the body of the document, we have another script block:

```
  <script type="text/javascript" >
  <!--
    myString="How now Brown Cow.";
    document.write(myString);
  // -->
  </script>
```

Here, we assign another value to `myString` and write that to the document as well.

The 'var' Keyword

Optionally, you can declare a variable either before you use it or the first time you use it with the `var` keyword, like so:

```
  var scratch;
  scratch=4;
```

or:

```
  var scratch=4;
```

The `var` keyword makes little difference, except when you declare variables inside user-defined functions (which we'll discuss near the end of the this chapter), in which case using `var` can prevent programming mistakes.

Variable Types

Variables in most programming languages can be of different types, determining what kind of data they can hold, for example text (strings), integers, decimal values, true/false values, and so on. In JavaScript, these types are present but not strongly. This means that a variable is a variable, and you don't have to declare your variable as a string type, or as an integer type – you just declare a plain variable and put whatever you like into it. It then takes on the type of whatever you've put into it, and sometimes this can cause unexpected results, as we'll see later. By and large, though, you'll do a lot less worrying about types than you would if you were writing Java or Visual Basic programs. We'll take a brief tour of how you work with various kinds of data now, starting with strings.

Strings

As we've seen, a string is a piece of text. In JavaScript a string is enclosed in either single or double quotes:

```
'This is a string'  // Either this...
```

```
"This is a string"  // or this is OK.
```

Note that the quotes must match:

```
'This is illegal"   // This doesn't work.
```

Concatenating Strings

The act of joining two strings together is called **concatenation**, and in JavaScript is accomplished by the **concatenation operator**, the plus (+) sign.

Try It Out – Concatenating Strings

1. As we've done before, alter `JSexample1.htm` as follows:

```
<?xml version="1.0" encoding="UTF-8"?>
<!DOCTYPE html
     PUBLIC "-//W3C//DTD XHTML 1.0 Transitional//EN"
     "http://www.w3.org/TR/xhtml1/DTD/xhtml1-transitional.dtd">
<html xmlns="http://www.w3.org/1999/xhtml" xml:lang="en" lang="en">
<head>
<title>Java script examples</title>
</head>
<body>
<script type="text/javascript" src="strings.js">
</script>
</body>
</html>
```

2. Save it as `strings.htm`.

3. Type the following in a new text document and save it as `strings.js`:

```
var aString="How Now " ;
aString=aString + "Brown Cow";
var newString="How Now ";
var otherString="Brown Cow";
var conCatString=newString+otherString;
document.write(aString);
document.write("<br />");
document.write(conCatString);
```

4. Here is what you will see when you run `strings.htm`.

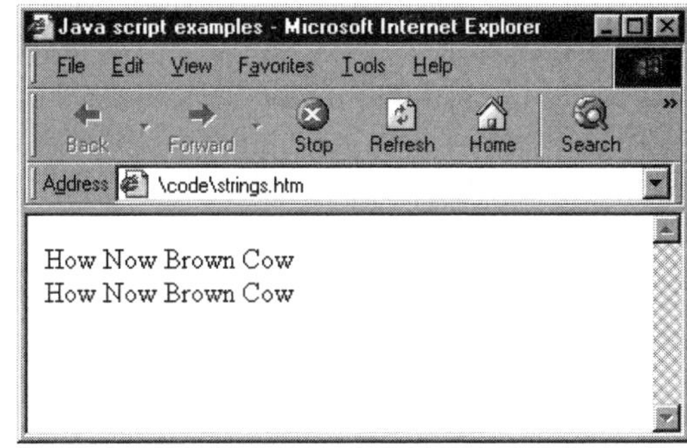

How It Works

In the first two lines we declare a variable, and assign a value of `"How Now "` to it. We then add (concatenate) a further string value of `"Brown Cow"` to it:

```
var aString="How Now " ;
aString=aString + "Brown Cow";
```

Note how we assign the new value to `aString`. We make it equal to the old value + `"Brown Cow"`. `aString` now contains the string `"How Now Brown Cow"`.

In a separate experiment, we declare two new variables and assign the string `"How Now "` to the first, and the string `"Brown Cow"` to the second:

```
var newString="How Now ";
var otherString="Brown Cow";
```

We then concatenate them and assign them to a third variable. `conCatString` now contains the value of `"How Now Brown Cow"`, but we arrived there by a different route:

```
var conCatString=newString+otherString;
```

We then prove this by printing out the values of both variables:

```
document.write(aString);
document.write("<br />");
document.write(conCatString);
```

Now, let's have a look at operations on numbers.

Numbers

Numbers in JavaScript are tokens such as `2`, `2.0`, `7892325`, etc. Numbers are *not* surrounded by quotes. If quotes are put around a number, then JavaScript will treat the number as a string. For example, in the following code:

```
var intNum=5        //intNum contains a numeric value
var strNum="5"      /strNum contains a string value
```

`strNum` contains the ASCII character `"5"`, not the number `5`.

We can do arithmetic operations on numbers using the symbols that we are familiar with from school. Let's look at this now.

Arithmetic Operators

+	Addition	e.g. `1+4` gives the result 5
-	Subtraction	e.g. `5-3` gives the result 2
*	Multiplication	e.g. `5*4` gives the result 20
/	Division	e.g. `25/5` gives the result 5

And now for some you might not be familiar with from school:

%	Modulus	The modulus is the remainder after dividing the first number by the second number.	e.g. `4%3` gives the result 1 `27%6` gives the result 3
++	Increment	This adds an integer 1 to a number.	e.g. `4++` gives the result 5 `intNum++` gives the result `intNum` + 1
--	Decrement	This subtracts an integer 1 from a number.	e.g. `6--` gives the result 5

Even if older browsers allow it, the sequence "--" is illegal in an XML comment, so you shouldn't use the decrement operator inside `<!--    -->` if you want your scripts to work with future browsers that enforce XHTML well-formedness. If a is a number, the operation `a--` is equivalent to the statement `a=a-1`, so you can easily avoid using `--` in internal scripts.

Converting Strings to Numbers

We often have to convert a string to a number, for example when a user types a number into a text box. Usually, we don't need to worry about this because JavaScript automatically converts strings into numbers when necessary. But sometimes it's a little more complicated than that, and JavaScript doesn't always get it right when you're trying to concatenate numerical strings together. Suppose, for example, we have two string variables `strNum1` and `strNum2`, and we multiply them together to get `strNum3`:

```
var strNum1="3";
var strNum2="4";
var strNum3=strNum1*strNum2;
```

In the above example JavaScript understands that we're using strings as if they were numbers, and produces the answer `12`. It's easy for JavaScript to do the right thing, because the multiplication operator has no meaning for strings. But suppose we tried to *add* the two strings:

```
var strNum1="3";
var strNum2="4";
//JavaScript will use + as a concatenator.
 var strNum3=strNum1+strNum2;
```

For strings, the "+" operator means concatenate, so JavaScript concatenates "3" and "4" to get "34." If we want JavaScript to add the strings rather than concatenate, we need to explicitly tell JavaScript to treat our variables as numbers rather than strings. Here's a very simple way to do it (there are others, but this one's simple).

Casting a variable

This procedure (changing a variable's type) is called **casting** a variable. We simply subtract 0 from each of the string variables:

```
//convert string numbers to numeric numbers
strNum1=strNum1-0;
strNum2=strNum2-0;
//Now JavaScript will use + as a numeric operator
strNum3=strNum1+strNum2;
```

Now we will get the answer 7! Conversely, to cast a number to a string we just need to concatenate an empty string:

```
intNum1=intNum1+"";
```

JavaScript will now treat `intNum1` as a string.

Try It Out – Mixing Strings and Numbers

1. Once again, modify `JSexample1.htm` as follows, and save it as `casting.htm`:

```
<?xml version="1.0" encoding="UTF-8"?>
<!DOCTYPE html
```

```
    PUBLIC "-//W3C//DTD XHTML 1.0 Transitional//EN"
    "http://www.w3.org/TR/xhtml1/DTD/xhtml1-transitional.dtd">
<html xmlns="http://www.w3.org/1999/xhtml" xml:lang="en" lang="en">
<head>
<title>Java script examples</title>
</head>
<body>
<script type="text/javascript" src="casting.js">
</script>
</body>
</html>
```

2. Now type up this script file, and save it as `casting.js`:

```
var strNum1="3";
var strNum2="4";
//JavaScript will use + as a concatenator.
var strNum3=strNum1+strNum2;
document.write(strNum3);
document.write("<br />");
var strNum4=strNum1*strNum2;
document.write(strNum4);
document.write("<br />");
//convert string numbers to numeric numbers
strNum1=strNum1-0;
strNum2=strNum2-0;
//Now JavaScript will use + as a numeric operator
strNum3=strNum1+strNum2;
document.write(strNum3);
document.write("<br />");
```

3. When you run `casting.htm` you will see the following:

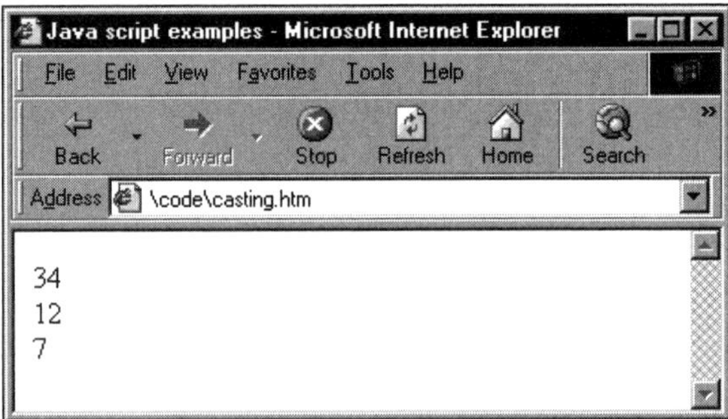

How It Works

In the first operation the variables strNum1 and strNum2 are treated as strings and concatenated:

```
var strNum3=strNum1+strNum2;
 document.write(strNum3);
```

After we cast the variables to a numeric type by subtracting 0, JavaScript treats them as numbers and adds them:

```
strNum1=strNum1-0;
 strNum2=strNum2-0;
//Now JavaScript will use + as a numeric operator
 strNum3=strNum1+strNum2;
 document.write(strNum3);
```

Booleans

A Boolean value reflects the truth of a statement, in other words whether something is true or false. One use for a Boolean is to test whether a string represents a number. The JavaScript function isNaN (for 'is not a number') returns true if its argument cannot be interpreted as a number and false if it can. Let's try an example.

Try It Out – Using a Boolean Function

1. Again, modify JSexample.htm as follows, saving it as boolean.htm:

```
<?xml version="1.0" encoding="UTF-8"?>
<!DOCTYPE html
     PUBLIC "-//W3C//DTD XHTML 1.0 Transitional//EN"
     "http://www.w3.org/TR/xhtml1/DTD/xhtml1-transitional.dtd">
<html xmlns="http://www.w3.org/1999/xhtml" xml:lang="en" lang="en">
<head>
<title>Java script examples</title>
</head>
<body>
<script type="text/javascript" src="boolean.js">
</script>
</body>
</html>
```

2. Now type up this script file, saving it as boolean.js:

```
var scratch
scratch=isNaN("7")
document.write(scratch)
document.write("<br />")
scratch=isNaN("cow")
document.write(scratch)
document.write("<br />")

scratch=isNaN("7 cows")
document.write(scratch)
```

3. When we run `boolean.htm`, we get:

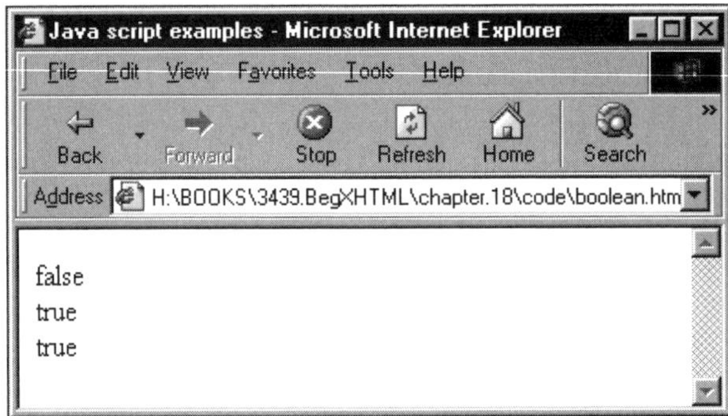

How It Works

The first string, `"7"`, can be converted to a number so the function returns `false`. The other two strings, `"cow"` and `"7cows"`, are not numbers so, in those cases, `isNaN()` returns `true`. If you write a script that takes input from a user and uses it to do a numerical calculation (suppose, for instance, you're adding up prices to compute a total), it's prudent to test that the user has really entered numbers, because your script could behave erratically otherwise.

Objects

A variable can also hold a reference to an object. Given a variable that refers to an object, we can access all the properties and methods of that object. For instance, you can assign a reference of a browser object into a variable, as seen in our next example:

```
<script>
var scratch

scratch=window.document
scratch.write("Because the scratch variable contains a reference to
window.document, calling scratch.write() is equivalent to calling
window.document()")
</script>
```

We're not going to go into any more detail about this here. Instead, we'll now move on to look at how we can make our program make decisions and take different paths based on different conditions.

Controlling Program Flow

In addition to operators, JavaScript also contains keywords for controlling the flow of a program, such as conditional and looping statements. Conditional statements take the form "If the user says this, take this course of action, otherwise if something else is true do that, or if none of these is true do the other", while looping statements cause a group of statements to be executed multiple times in succession.

Conditional Statements

We will look at the chief conditional statement in JavaScript, the `if` statement. The simplest form of the `if` statement is:

```
if(condition) {
   // code executed if condition is true
};
```

With the `else` statement you can have a block of code executed if the condition is false:

```
if(condition) {
   // code executed if condition is true
} else {
    // code executed if condition is false
};
```

Note the following:

- The use of the keywords `if` and `else`
- The condition to be tested is put in parentheses, '(' and ')'. No semi-colon follows the parentheses
- The conditionally executed code is contained in curly braces, '{' and '}'

Let's have a look at a simple example, using a conditional statement to find out the background color of a page.

Try It Out – Writing a Conditional Statement

1. Type out this XHTML page, and save it as `conditions.htm`:

```
<?xml version="1.0" encoding="UTF-8"?>
<!DOCTYPE html
     PUBLIC "-//W3C//DTD XHTML 1.0 Transitional//EN"
     "http://www.w3.org/TR/xhtml1/DTD/xhtml1-transitional.dtd">
<html xmlns="http://www.w3.org/1999/xhtml" xml:lang="en" lang="en">
<head>
<title>Java script examples</title>

</head>
<body bgcolor="#c0c0c0">

<script>
<!--
//document.write(document.bgColor +"</br />")
if(document.bgColor=="#ffffff") {
   document.write("the background color of this document is white")
} else if(document.bgColor=="#c0c0c0") {
```

```
    document.write("the background color of this document is battleship gray")
} else {
    document.write("the background color of this document is neither white nor
battleship gray")
}
// -->
</script>
</body>
</html>
```

2. If you view this in your browser, you'll see the words "The background color of this document is battleship gray".

3. If you change the `bgcolor` attribute to '`#ffffff`' or to something else, you'll see either "the background color of this document is white" or "the background color of this document is neither white not battleship gray".

Note that because JavaScript is case sensitive you must spell the `bgColor` property of the `document` object (NOT the `bgcolor` attribute of the `<body>` element) with a capital 'C'. If you spell it with a lowercase 'c' the example will not work!

How It Works

Here we have set the `bgcolor` attribute of the body element to gray:

```
<body bgcolor="#c0c0c0">
```

The first statement the JavaScript interpreter comes to is:

```
if(document.bgColor=="#ffffff")
```

Note the use of the double equal sign '=='. This is the is JavaScript equality operator. This is distinct from the single equal sign '=', which is the assignment operator.

> *Even expert programmers sometimes confuse the double and single equal signs. If, instead, we wrote `if(document.bgColor="#ffffff")` we'd get two unwanted effects: we'd assign `#ffffff` to `document.bgColor` and the condition would always be true.*

The color is not white, so the engine jumps to the next statement:

```
else if(document.bgColor=="#c0c0c0") {
```

This is the color in our example, so JavaScript executes the block of code associated with this statement:

```
    document.write("the background color of this document is battleship gray")
```

If the `bgcolor` had been, for example, `#ff0000` (red), then JavaScript would have executed the final else statement.

Comparison Operators

In conditional statements we often have to compare two quantities. In the example above we compared two quantities to see if they were equal using the equality operator. A complete list of comparison operators is

==	Equality, equal to
<	Less than
>	Greater than
<=	Less than or equal to
>=	Greater than or equal to
!=	Inequality, not equal to

Logical operators

We can also use logical operators. Logical operators perform Boolean algebra. Just as mathematical operators work on numbers, logical operators act on Boolean true/false values. Here's a list of logical operators:

&&	Logical AND
||	Logical OR
!	Logical NOT

Examples

The condition here:

```
if(a==3 && b ==3) {
```

contains the logical AND operator and is `true` if both `a` and `b` have a value of 3 and otherwise returns `false`. The condition here:

```
if(a>4 || b ==3) {
```

contains the logical OR operator and is `true` if either `a` is greater than 4 or if `b` is equal to 3. Otherwise, the condition is `false`.

The NOT operator reverses `true` and `false`, so this condition:

```
if(! (b<3) ) {
```

is `true` if `b` is not less than `three`, that is, if `b` is greater than or equal to three.

Arrays

Arrays are collections of values, much like a numbered group of post office boxes. Arrays are important in most programming languages because they can be used to sort and manipulate groups of things. Let's use an array to store a list of cats that have owned me over the years:

- Pippin
- Merry
- Hergie
- Adam
- Pierre
- Ben
- Giles
- Calloway

We can store these names in an array, and then refer to them by number

Creating an Array

The syntax for creating an array in JavaScript is as follows:

```
[Array name] =new Array()
```

This creates an empty array. Arrays in JavaScript grow to whatever size we need, but it takes time for JavaScript to expand an array – if I know how many elements the array will need, I can tell JavaScript to reserve space for that many ahead of time like so:

```
[Array name] =new Array(10)
```

This creates an array with ten slots in it. Now we've created an array, we can fill it with values.

Filling an Array

There are two ways to fill an array.

The first method involves assigning values, one at a time, to each elements of the array. We assign to the i'th **element** (synonymous with **member**) of an array as follows:

```
Arrayname[i]= value
```

Note that the square brackets are part of the syntax here and are not being used in the sense we normally use them in this book. The square brackets contain the number of the array.

To access the i'th element of the array we use the following syntax:

```
Variable=arrayname[i]
```

Let's try this out now.

Try It Out – Creating and Filling an Array

1. Modify `JSexample1.htm` as follows, saving it as `array.htm`:

```
<?xml version="1.0" encoding="UTF-8"?>
<!DOCTYPE html
     PUBLIC "-//W3C//DTD XHTML 1.0 Transitional//EN"
     "http://www.w3.org/TR/xhtml1/DTD/xhtml1-transitional.dtd">
<html xmlns="http://www.w3.org/1999/xhtml" xml:lang="en" lang="en">
<head>
<title>Java script examples</title>
</head>
<body>
<script type="text/javascript" src="array.js">
</script>
</body>
</html>
```

2. Type the following script file in and save it as `array.js`:

```
var cat=new Array(8);

cat[0]= 'Pippin'
cat[1]= 'Merry'
cat[2]= 'Hergie'
cat[3]= 'Adam'
cat[4]= 'Pierre'
cat[5]= 'Ben'
cat[6]= 'Giles'
cat[7]= 'Calloway'

document.write(cat[3]+ "<br />")
cat[3]="Percy"
cat[9]= 'Adam'

document.write(cat[3]+ "<br />")
document.write(cat[8]+ "<br />")
document.write(cat[9]+ "<br />")
```

When we run `array.htm`, we see the following:

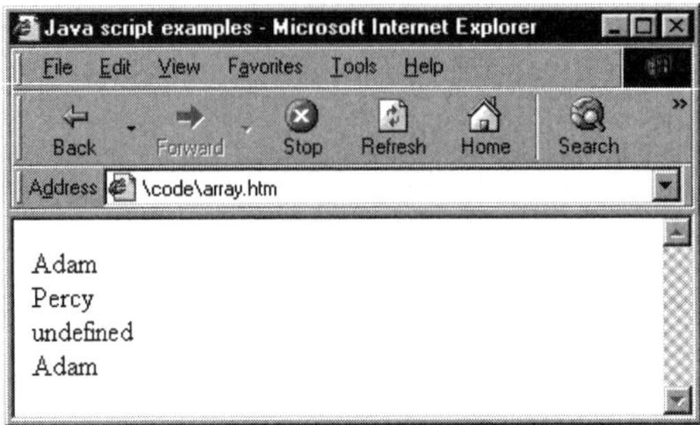

How It Works

First, we declare our array and tell the computer to reserve space for 8 items.

```
var cat=new Array(8);
```

Next, we load the first item into it.

```
cat[0]= 'Pippin'
```

Arrays in JavaScript start counting from 0. We write the array name followed by square brackets. In the square brackets we put the number, or **index** of the array. We now use the assignment operator to assign the string value `"Pippin"` to the first item of the array.

We repeat this process for the other cats.

We can now access the contents of the array by index. We pick out the fourth cat (with index 3) as follows

```
document.write(cat[3]+ "<br />")
```

which displays the name "Adam" in the web browser. We now replace the value of the `cat[3]` item in the array with a new name

```
cat[3]="Percy"
```

We put "Adam" in at index nine.

```
cat[9]= 'Adam'
```

This automatically extends the length of the array to 10 items (remember we start counting from 0). What happens to the new item in the index = 8 position? It remains empty, or rather in JavaScript terminology it remains **undefined**. We verify this by printing out:

```
document.write(cat[3]+ "<br />")
document.write(cat[8]+ "<br />")
document.write(cat[9]+ "<br />")
```

Extending Arrays

As we saw in the example above, we can extend an array by simply declaring a new value at a index greater than the highest used in the array; JavaScript then extends the array automatically.

Note that if we use the following syntax:

```
cat= new Array(9)
```

...we create a *new* `cat` array with room for nine elements. Unless we've made another reference to the array, all of the elements stored in the `cat` array will be lost. This is a good way of emptying an array.

Array Length

Arrays have a `length` property, and we can find out the length of an array at any time by using the syntax:

`ArrayName``.length`

The number returned will be the number of items in the array. Since JavaScript arrays start at zero, the length of an array is one greater than the index of the element with the highest index.

Filling an Array, Part II

There is a shortcut to create and fill an array in one step:

```
cat=new Array('Pippin', 'Merry', 'Hergie', 'Adam', 'Pierre', 'Ben', 'Giles',
'Calloway')
```

Loops and Multiple Operations

Many times in programming we want to repeat an action several times.

For example:

- We may want to print out all the values of an array
- We may want to go through an array and check each individual name in the array to see if one matches a particular name
- We may want to loop through a piece of text and change every instance of cat with dog, or every instance of `<p>` and `</p>` with `<pre>` and `</pre>`

When we know in advance how many times we want to carry out an action, we usually use the `for` loop, and when we don't we usually use the `while` loop. We will look at these now.

The 'for' Loop

The general syntax of the `for` loop is as follows:

```
for([initial number];[ending condition];[increment]) {
   [code to be implemented each loop]
}
```

The simplest way to demonstrate this is by an example.

Try It Out – Reading Through an Array with a 'for' Loop

1. Again, modify `JSexample1.htm` as follows, saving it as `forloop.htm`:

```
<?xml version="1.0" encoding="UTF-8"?>
<!DOCTYPE html
     PUBLIC "-//W3C//DTD XHTML 1.0 Transitional//EN"
     "http://www.w3.org/TR/xhtml1/DTD/xhtml1-transitional.dtd">
<html xmlns="http://www.w3.org/1999/xhtml" xml:lang="en" lang="en">
<head>
<title>Java script examples</title>
</head>
<body>
<script type="text/javascript" src="array.js">
</script>
</body>
</html>
```

2. Type up the following script file, and save it as `array.js`:

```
var cats=new Array(8);

cat[0]= 'Pippin'
cat[1]= 'Merry'
cat[2]= 'Hergie'
cat[3]= 'Adam'
cat[4]= 'Pierre'
cat[5]= 'Ben'
cat[6]= 'Giles'
cat[7]= 'Calloway'

var i;

for(i=0;i<=7;i++)
   {
   document.write(cat[i]+"<br />")
   }
```

3. When you run `array.htm`, the names of all the cats will be printed out.

How It Works

We declare `i` as a variable:

```
var i;
```

In loops it is traditional to use the letters i, j, and k as the variables that are incremented. You can, of course, use anything you want, but if you stick to these letters your code will be easier to read by others.

Now we come to the important bit:

```
for(i=0;i<=7;i++)
```

note how we have a keyword, `for`, followed by parentheses. Inside the parentheses are three statements:

```
i=0;
```

This statement says "start counting from a value of `i=0`":

```
i<=7;
```

The above statement says "keep going while `i` is less than or equal to 7":

```
i++
```

And this statement says "increase the value of `i` by 1 each time you pass through this loop".

The curly brackets { } contain the code that is to be executed each time we go through this loop. In this case the program is instructed to write out the array value with the same index as `i` followed by a forced line break `<br />`.

```
document.write(cat[i]+"<br />")
```

With a minor modification we can check to see whether the array contains the name of a certain cat.

Try It Out – Searching an Array

1. Modify `array.htm` as follows:

```
<script>
<!--
var cat=new Array(8);

cat[0]= 'Pippin'
cat[1]= 'Merry'
cat[2]= 'Hergie'
cat[3]= 'Adam'
cat[4]= 'Pierre'
cat[5]= 'Ben'
cat[6]= 'Giles'
cat[7]= 'Calloway'

var i;
var notfound=true

for(i=0;i<=7;i++)
   {
   if(cat[i]=="Hergie")
      {
      document.write("We found a cat called Hergie");
      notfound=false
      break;
      }
   }
if(notfound==true)
      {
      document.write("No cat called Hergie was found");
      }
// -->
</script>
```

2. Now when you run `array.htm`, you should see whether a cat called Hergie was there or not...

How It Works

We declare a Boolean variable called `notfound`:

```
var notfound=true
```

...and set its value to `true`. Now for each iteration through the loop we compare the cat's name against the name "Hergie":

```
if(cat[i]== "Hergie")
```

Note again that we use the "==" equality operator rather than the "=" assignment operator.

If the names match, we execute the following code:

```
document.write("We found a cat called Hergie");
```

...to announce that the program found a matching name:

```
notfound=false
```

We also set the variable `notfound` to Boolean `false`:

```
break;
```

...and use the `break` keyword to break out of the loop. Break immediately jumps out of the loop, and any code immediately after `break` is not executed; execution continues after the end of the loop.

After the loop ends, we check the condition of our variable `notfound`:

```
if(notfound==true)
    {
    document.write("No cat called Hergie was found");
    }
```

If it is still `true`, that means the search failed and the program announces that fact. Although this example is fairly trivial, loops and conditionals can be used to write much more complex programs.

Endless Loops

Practically, a loop must eventually come to an end. If it doesn't, the loop will run forever, and the web browser will hang there, doing nothing, until the user shuts it down. There are two common mistakes you can make in the `for` loop that can make it loop forever: you could forget to increment the loop variable (leave out the `i++`) or we could confuse the equality and assignment operators (write `i=10` instead of `i==10`.)

If we do the latter, every time the loop runs the value 10 is assigned to `i`, but since `i=10` is always interpreted as true, the loop continues forever. Endless loops will make your scripts fail in an embarrassing manner, so it's important to avoid them.

The 'while' Loop

With the `for` loop we usually know how many times we are going to run the loop. We usually use a `while` loop when we are not sure how often we will be running the loop. This typically occurs when we are searching through a piece of text.

The general syntax for this loop is:

```
while(condition) {
   [code to be executed]
}
```

Let's look at examples of the `while` loop. First we will have a look at a trivial example so that you can get the hang of it, and then we will look at a more realistic example.

Try It Out – A Trivial 'while' Example

1. Alter `JSexample1.htm` as follows, saving it as `while.htm`:

```
<?xml version="1.0" encoding="UTF-8"?>
<!DOCTYPE html
     PUBLIC "-//W3C//DTD XHTML 1.0 Transitional//EN"
     "http://www.w3.org/TR/xhtml1/DTD/xhtml1-transitional.dtd">
<html xmlns="http://www.w3.org/1999/xhtml" xml:lang="en" lang="en">
<head>
<title>Java script examples</title>
</head>
<body>
<script type="text/javascript" src="while.js">
</script>
</body>
</html>
```

2. Type up the following and save it as `while.js`:

```
var x=0
while(x<5) {
   document.write(x + "<br />")
   x++
}
```

3. When you run `while.htm` you will get the integers 0 through 4 printed out, each on a separate line.

How It Works

First we declare a variable and assign it the value 0:

```
var x=0
```

Now we will carry on looping through this block of code while the value of x is less than 5:

```
while(x<5) {
```

on each loop we write out the value of x as well as a `"<br />"`:

```
   document.write(x + "<br />")
```

We increase the value of x by 1:

```
        x++
    }
```

Note that if we didn't increase the value of x each time through the loop, the code would run forever.

Search and Replace using Loops

Here is a more complex example, something you will probably use frequently in your programming. Lets use the `while` loop to search through a string a replace every mention of the string `"secret"` with the word `"!!XXcensoredXX!!"`

In this exercise we'll use two JavaScript string methods – `indexOf()` and `substring()`. Let's take a brief look at how they each work.

The indexOf() method

The general syntax for this method is:

```
var scratch=a.indexOf(b)
```

`scratch` will contain an integer representing the first occurrence of string `b` inside string `a`. If no string is found `scratch` will equal `-1`:

Examples:

```
var astr="To be or not to be"
var scratch
scratch=astr.indexOf("To")
```

`scratch` will contain the value 0:

```
var astr="To be or not to be"
var scratch
scratch=astr.indexOf("be")
```

`scratch` will contain the value 3:

```
var astr="To be or not to be"
var scratch
scratch=astr.indexOf("question")
```

`scratch` will contain the value –1.

The substring() method

The `substring` method will return a substring between two indices. The general syntax is:

`var scratch=[source string].substring([start index],[end index])`

`scratch` will contain the substring between the start index and the end index.

Examples:

```
var astr="To be or not to be":
var scratch
scratch=astr.substring(3,5)
```

`scratch` will contain the sub string `"be"`:

```
var astr="To be or not to be"
var scratch
scratch=astr.substring(0,2)
```

`scratch` will contain the sub string `"To"`:

```
var astr="To be or not to be"
var scratch
scratch=astr.substring(3)
```

`scratch` will contain the sub string `"be or not to be"`. In other words, if the second parameter is not provided then everything to the end of the string is returned.

Let's use these methods and a `while` loop to replace the string `"secret"` with `"!!XXcensoredXX!!"` in the string `"The secrets of the secret service are secret"`.

Try It Out – A Simple Search and Replace

1. Once again, alter `JSexample1.htm` to read as follows, saving it as `replace.htm`:

```
<?xml version="1.0" encoding="UTF-8"?>
<!DOCTYPE html
     PUBLIC "-//W3C//DTD XHTML 1.0 Transitional//EN"
     "http://www.w3.org/TR/xhtml1/DTD/xhtml1-transitional.dtd">
<html xmlns="http://www.w3.org/1999/xhtml" xml:lang="en" lang="en">
<head>
<title>Java script examples</title>
</head>
<body>
<script type="text/javascript" src="replace.js">
</script>
</body>
</html>
```

2. Type this up in your text editor and save it as `replace.js`.

```
var astr="The secrets of the secret service are secret";
var ltstr="";
var x;

while(astr.indexOf("secret",0)!=-1) {
   x=astr.indexOf("secret",0)
   ltstr=ltstr+astr.substring(0,x)+"!!XXcensoredXX!!"
   astr=astr.substring(x+6)
}
document.write(ltstr+astr);
```

3. When you run this page, it will display:

The !!XXcensoredXX!!s of the !!XXcensoredXX!! service are !!XXcensoredXX!!

in the browser window.

How It Works

First we declare our variables, and read our string into the variable `astr`:

```
var astr="The secrets of the secret service are secret";
var ltstr="";
var x;
```

Now we loop through the string. On each loop we look for the first instance of the string `secret`, and replace it. We then shorten the string to start after the particular `secret` that we have just been looking at. If we didn't do this the loop would never stop!

Here we tell our script to carry on performing this operation until the string `"secret"` no longer appears in `astr`:

```
while(astr.indexOf("secret",0)!=-1)
```

Each time we find the string `astr` we do the following. We find the index of the first letter of `'secret'`:

```
   x=astr.indexOf("secret",0)
```

The script copies everything to the left of the word `"secret"` and concatenates it to the variable `ltstr`, and then appends the string `!!XxcensoredXX!!` to replace the word `"secret"`:

```
   ltstr=ltstr+astr.substring(0,x)+"!!XXcensoredXX!!"
```

We now shorten astr to start after the last letter of "secret", since we've already written everything left of "secret" into lstr:

```
    astr=astr.substring(x+6)
    }
```

Once we have finished the loop we write out the string ltstr as well as the remains of astr:

```
document.write(ltstr+astr)
```

User-Defined Functions

Sometimes we want to use a piece of code time and time again. We can do this by placing the code inside a function, and then calling that code whenever we want to.

Functions come in two flavors and a combination:

- Those functions that take in various values, perform some kind of manipulation on those values, and return a value.
- Those that do something, such as change the color of a page or section of a page, or print something out.
- Those that do both.

Functions, like methods can take parameters, indeed functions are just like the methods that we have looked at before, except they are not associated with an object. It's possible to define your own objects and methods in JavaScript, but that's beyond the scope of this book.

Declaring a Function

We can define a function anywhere in a script, but it's easier to understand a script if we declare all of our functions together at the beginning or end of a script.

This applies if the whole program is in a single script file or element. If it is spread out over several script elements then the function must be declared in a script element that comes before the script element where it is invoked. Therefore, it's wise to declare all the functions that are used in a scripted XHTML document near the beginning of the document.

The general syntax for declaring a function is as follows:

```
function [function name]([parameter1],[parameter2],... ) {
     [code block to be executed]
}
```

This includes the following:

- The `function` keyword
- The name of the function
- A set of parentheses containing comma-separated parameters (if any)
- A pair of curly brackets containing the function's code

Calling a Function

Functions can be *called* from anywhere within our program. One way to do this is to assign the return value of a function to a variable. The general syntax for this is:

```
var result=functionname([parameters])
```

Sometimes a function returns nothing, or we don't care what value the function returns, in which case we can call a function by writing just:

```
functionname([parameters])
```

For instance, we can call a function in an event handler, such as when we click on an image, as follows:

```
<img src="blob.gif" onMouseDown="myFunction()" />
```

We saw an example of this earlier in the chapter when we looked at events. There we used the `window.alert()` method, but we can call our own functions in exactly the same way. We can also call a function by using it as a parameter in another method or function. For example we can call it from the `document.write` method:

```
document.write(myFunction(5))
```

We will use this method later on.

Passing Parameters

We can pass any variable we want to a function including an object. Let's demonstrate this by looking at a simple example. We will create a simple function called `writeline()` that will simply print out an indented line of italic text to our screen, followed by a line break. We will pass it the line that we want to write out as a parameter.

Try It Out – Writing a Simple Function

1. Type up the following XHTML page, and save it as `writeline.htm`:

```
<?xml version="1.0" encoding="UTF-8"?>
<!DOCTYPE html
     PUBLIC "-//W3C//DTD XHTML 1.0 Transitional//EN"
     "http://www.w3.org/TR/xhtml1/DTD/xhtml1-transitional.dtd">
<html xmlns="http://www.w3.org/1999/xhtml" xml:lang="en" lang="en">
<head>
<title>Java script examples</title>

</head>
<body bgcolor="white">

<script>
<!--
function writeline(astr) {
   document.write("  "+"<i>" + astr +"</i><br />")
}
// -->
</script>

<p>Hear the words of MacBeth:</p>

<script>
<!--
writeline("Tomorrow, and tomorrow, and tomorrow,")
writeline("Creeps on this petty pace from day to day")
writeline("To the last syllable of recorded time.")
// -->
</script>
</body>
</html>
```

2. This is what you will see when you run this page:

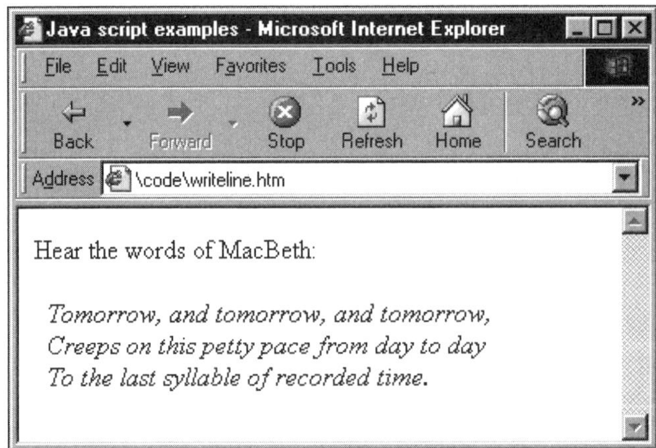

How It Works

As ever, the browser reads the document from top to bottom. When it comes across the first set of script tags it notices that it contains a definition for a function called `writeline()`. It remembers this function for later use.

When it comes to the second `<script>` element it sees that a function is invoked, called `writeline()`. The browser can tell that it is a function or method because of the parentheses following the name. It searches its memory for a built in method by this name. Failing this it searches for a user-defined function by that name and finds it. The browser then executes the code contained in the `writeline()` function.

> *If it had failed to find it the browser would have extended its search to the end of the script element or file in which the function is called. If it did not find it in this an error would occur. Make sure the function is either in the same file or element, or is declared in a script element before it is called.*

In this example, the `writeline()` function is executed three times. The parameter passed to the function the first time is:

```
writeline("Tomorrow, and tomorrow, and tomorrow,")
```

The function stores this in `astr`:

```
function writeline(astr) {
```

We do the same with the other 2 calls to the function. Now it will embed the XHTML string among the XHTML code that we are writing with the `document.write()` method, and produce our formatted line of text:

```
  document.write("  "+"<i>" + astr +"</i><br />")
}
```

Functions that Perform an Action

The above example is an example of a function that performs an action. We have used the `writeline()` function to execute a simple and repetitive formatting task. In fact these functions can be quite complex and are used all the time in page building. A favorite function is to change the style of a heading every time a mouse rolls over it.

We will look at this in the next chapter when we look at examples of using script to spice up our pages.

Functions that Return a Value

Strictly speaking, all functions return a value by definition. But rather than performing actions, some functions take in data, perform manipulations on that data and then spit out an answer. We say that such functions *return* a result. To do this the function uses the `return` keyword. Let's look at a simple example of a function that returns a result. This function takes a number as a parameter and returns the cube of that number.

Try It Out – A Function that Returns a Result

1. Type up and save this XHTML page as `result.htm`:

```
<?xml version="1.0" encoding="UTF-8"?>
<!DOCTYPE html
     PUBLIC "-//W3C//DTD XHTML 1.0 Transitional//EN"
     "http://www.w3.org/TR/xhtml1/DTD/xhtml1-transitional.dtd">
<html xmlns="http://www.w3.org/1999/xhtml" xml:lang="en" lang="en">
<head>
<title>Java script examples</title>
<script type="text/javascript">
<!--
function cube(x) {
  var result=x*x*x;
  return result;
}
// -->
</script>
</head>
<body bgcolor="white">
<p>The cube of 5 is:
<script>
<!--
 document.write(cube(5));
// -->
</script>
</p>
</body>
</html>
```

2. When you run this page, this is what you will see:

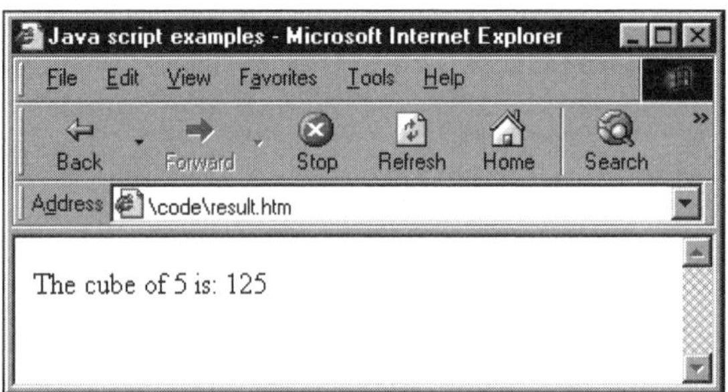

How It Works

Again the browser sees the function and stores it in its memory.

On this occasion the `cube()` function is called by using it as a parameter in another function, the `document.write` method.

```
document.write(cube(5));
```

Here's what the function looks like:

```
function cube(x) {
  var result=x*x*x;
  return result;
}
```

Inside the function the number we passed in is multiplied by itself 3 times and stored in the variable `result`. The `return` keyword returns this result to the part of the program that called this function.

Variable Scope and Functions

A **global** variable, one that is defined outside of a function, can be retrieved throughout the whole page at any time after the variable is defined. (If we're using a variable outside of a function, the variable must be defined previously in the document. If we're using a variable inside a function, the variable must defined previous to the place where we're calling the function from.) However, if we define a variable inside of a function, that variable has **local** scope and can only be accessed inside of a function.

Look at the following example.

Try It Out – Variable Scope in Functions

1. Type this in and save it as `scope.htm`:

```
<?xml version="1.0" encoding="UTF-8"?>
<!DOCTYPE html
     PUBLIC "-//W3C//DTD XHTML 1.0 Transitional//EN"
     "http://www.w3.org/TR/xhtml1/DTD/xhtml1-transitional.dtd">
<html xmlns="http://www.w3.org/1999/xhtml" xml:lang="en" lang="en">
<head>
<title>Java script examples</title>

<script>
<!--
 var myName="Frank";
 var scratch;
 document.write(myName + "<br />");
var anotherName;
function newName(x) {
   var anotherName="Joe"   //This just has scope inside the variable
   document.write(anotherName + "<br />");
   document.write(myName + "<br />");
}
newName();    //call the function
```

```
document.write(anotherName + "<br />");    //will give an 'undefined' value
// -->
</script>
</head>
<body bgcolor="white">
</body>
</html>
```

2. Here is what we see when we view the page in a browser:

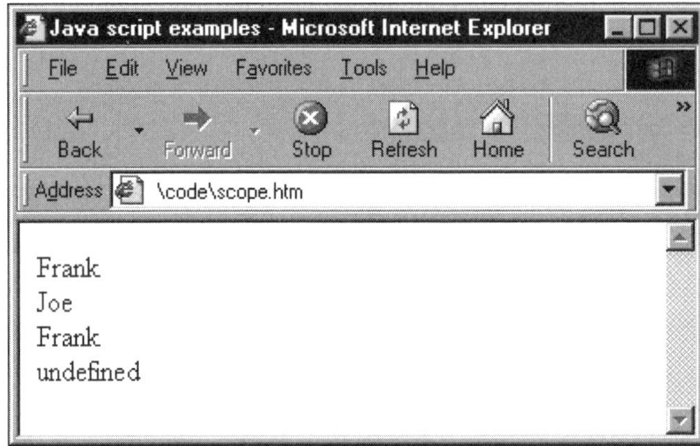

How It Works

We declare the variable, `myName`, and assign to it the value "Frank". We also declare a variable `anotherName` but assign it no value.

Inside our function we declare `anotherName` again, and assign it the value of "Joe". When we run this program we can print out the value of `myName` outside the function (naturally!).

When we call the function you will see that we can print out both the value of `anotherName` which we declared inside the function, and the value of `myName` that had a value assigned to it outside the function.

However when we try and print out `anotherName` outside a function we will get 'undefined'. In other words variables declared outside a function extend into a function, but those declared inside a function do not extend outside a function.

Things get more complicated if we also define a variable twice: both outside and inside of a function. If we were to alter the above code as follows:

```
function newName(x)
  {
  var myName;
  var anotherName="Joe";     //This just has scope inside the variable
  document.write(anotherName + "<br />");
  document.write(myName + "<br />");
  }
```

...when we view the page we'd get the following:

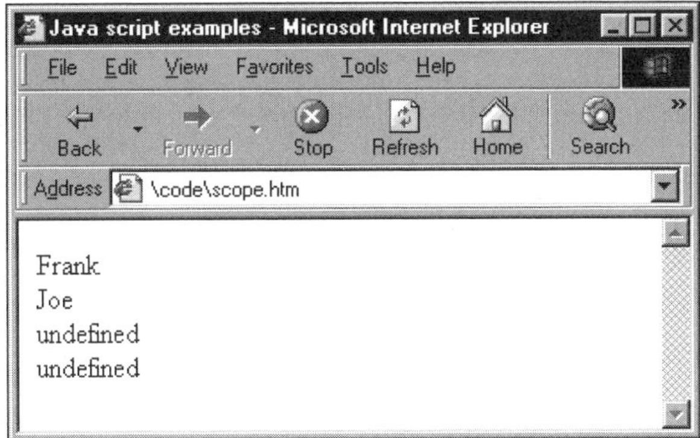

In other words the variable `myName` no longer extends inside the function – inside the function, the global variable `myName` has been replaced by a local variable also called `myName`.

If we alter the code again as follows and assign `myName` a value inside the function:

```
function newName(x)
  {
  var myName="Bob";
  var anotherName="Joe";
 document.write(anotherName + "<br />");
 document.write(myName + "<br />");
  }
newName();

 document.write(anotherName + "<br />");
 document.write(myName + "<br />");
```

We will see the following:

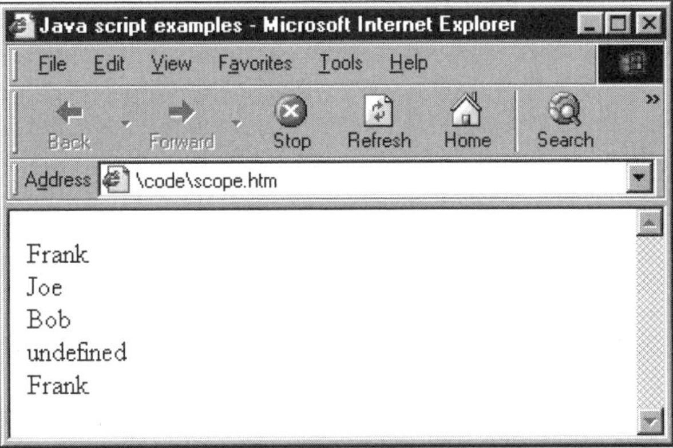

In other words `myName` now has the value of `"Bob"` inside the function, but retains the value of `"Frank"` outside the function. The moral? If you don't use the `var` keyword when you declare a variable inside a user-defined function, there is some risk that the name of your variable will be the same as a variable defined outside the function and the two variables will interfere with each other. Unless you specifically want to access a global variable from your function, you should always use `var` when you declare a variable inside a user-defined function.

Summary

In this chapter we have covered quite a lot of ground. Although we haven't covered everything there is to know about JavaScript, we have covered enough for you to start using JavaScript in your pages. If you'd like to learn more, take a look at the book *Professional JavaScript* (McFarlane et al, Wrox Press Ltd, 1-861002-70-X)

In the next few chapters we will be seeing several concrete examples of using JavaScript to script a web browser.

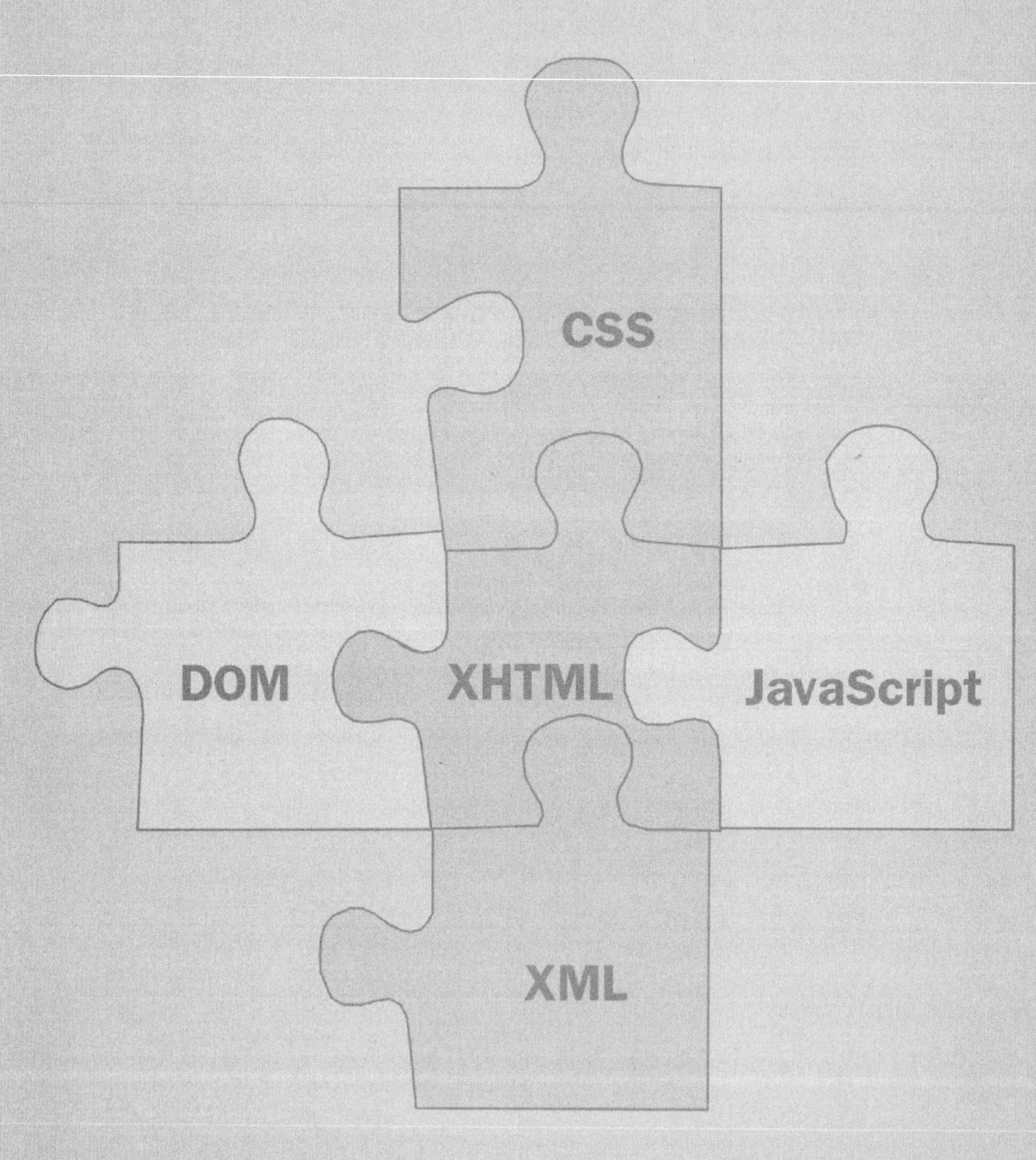
CSS
DOM
XHTML
JavaScript
XML

Using Script In Web Pages

In the last chapter we looked at the JavaScript language. In this and the next couple of chapters we will look at some of the uses we can put it to in designing web sites. There are other books about creating fancy pages, so we will look at only a few specific uses of JavaScript.

In this chapter we will study the following:

- Objects built into the web browser including the window, navigator, and document objects.
- Core JavaScript objects, independent of the browser, such as the Math and Date objects.
- Events.
- Rollovers (hyperlinks that change when the user moves a mouse over them).
- Making scripts aware of what version of what web browser a visitor is using.
- Storing persistent information in cookies.

First let's look at the browser objects. As with our JavaScript introduction, we're going to be moving pretty fast, and in some cases won't be able to do full justice to the uses of JavaScript. It should be enough to get you started experimenting around with what JavaScript can do, though.

The Browser Objects

In JavaScript, we access the web browser through three objects:

- **The window object:**
  The window object contains properties and methods that give information about the environment that the browser is running in, such as the size and color depth of the screen and the URL of the page being shown. The window object also includes methods for moving and sizing the browser window, for altering the status message below the window, for opening and closing browser windows. Finally, the window object contains methods for popping up dialog boxes. It's not usually necessary to write "window." before using methods and properties of the window object because the window object is the default object. (Except in event handlers, where the default object is the element responsible for the event.)

- **The navigator object:**
  This is a sub-object of the window object. The navigator object contains information about the browser displaying the page. This information is particularly useful for **browser sniffing**, writing scripts that determine which web browser a visitor is using.
- **The document object:**
  This is also a sub-object of the window object. The document object provides access to the document being viewed. In 3.0 browsers, the document object allows a script to write text into the document while the page was loading as well as interact with form elements and, in a limited way, with images. In 4.0 browsers, scripts can, more or less, manipulate the style sheet properties of elements on the page, enabling a category of special effects known as Dynamic HTML. In IE 5.0 and the forthcoming Netscape 5, it's possible to use the W3C's Document Object Model (DOM) to view and manipulate the tree structure of elements on the page. We'll be looking into this in the next chapter.

Rather than list every method and property, we will just show some examples to demonstrate those methods and properties you are most likely to use. Consult *Professional JavaScript* (McFarlane et al, Wrox Press Ltd, 1-861002-70-X) for a detailed treatment of JavaScript in print, or for Netscape's online reference manuals at `http://developer.iplanet.com/docs/manuals/javascript.html`.

Properties of the 'window' Object

The following example demonstrates some properties of the `window` object.

Try It Out – 'window' Object Properties

1. Type in this XHTML file and save it as `window.htm`:

```
<?xml version="1.0" encoding="UTF-8"?>
<!DOCTYPE html
     PUBLIC "-//W3C//DTD XHTML 1.0 Transitional//EN"
     "http://www.w3.org/TR/xhtml1/DTD/xhtml1-transitional.dtd">
<html xmlns="http://www.w3.org/1999/xhtml" xml:lang="en" lang="en">
<head>
<title> Basic Window Properties</title>
<script>
<!--
window.defaultStatus="Window Properties"
window.status="Window Props"
window.name="win1"

document.write(window.screen.height+"<br />")
document.write(window.screen.availHeight+"<br />")
document.write(window.screen.width + "<br />")
document.write(window.screen.availWidth + "<br />")
document.write(window.screen.colorDepth + "<br />")
document.write(window.closed + "<br />")
document.write(window.defaultStatus + "<br />")
document.write(window.document.title + "<br />")
document.write(window.location + "<br />")
document.write(window.name + "<br />")
document.write(window.navigator.appVersion + "<br />")
document.write(window.opener + "<br />")
document.write(window.status + "<br />")
// -->
```

```
</script>
</head>
<body>

</body>
</html>
```

2. Now run it in your browser. When I ran this page in IE 5 I got this:

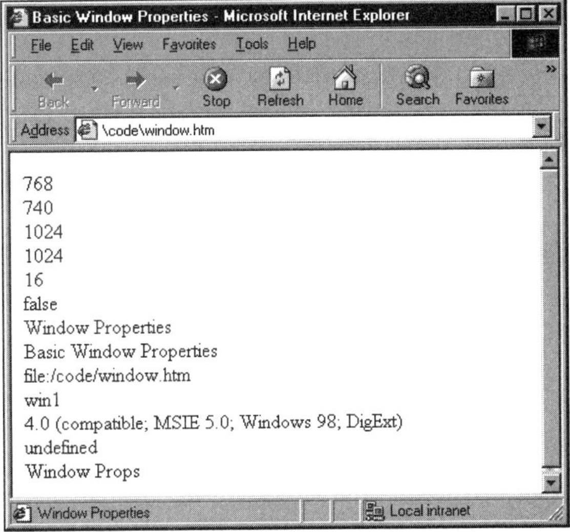

How It Works

This script first sets some properties:

```
window.defaultStatus="Window Properties"
window.status="Window Props"
window.name="win1"
```

The main reason we do this is so we can read them later on, but you should also see that by setting the `window.defaultStatus` property we made the words Window Properties appear in the status bar at the bottom of the browser window.

Next, we display the values of several properties that reflect the size of the viewer's screen:

```
document.write(window.screen.height+"<br />")
document.write(window.screen.availHeight+"<br />")
document.write(window.screen.width + "<br />")
document.write(window.screen.availWidth + "<br />")
```

The above properties are read-only, and therefore cannot be written to. The property `availHeight` is less than `height` because the space taken up by the Windows taskbar at the bottom of my screen is unavailable to applications. If I hid the taskbar, `height` and `availHeight` would be identical. These dimensions can be useful to the page authors, as they may care to adjust the layout of the page to fit on different sized screens.

The colorDepth property is useful in deciding what images to send to a user-agent – there's no point in sending a 24-bit photograph to a cell phone or a palmtop. This property represents the number of bits used to specify a color on the viewer's display. 8, 16 and 24-bit color are common on desktop computers.

```
document.write(window.screen.colorDepth + "<br />")
```

In IE this measures the screen colors, but in Netscape it measures the colors available to the browser. Use the Netscape proprietary pixelDepth for Netscape browsers if you want to see the platform color depth.

Moving on, the window is currently open so the window.closed property is false. This property is useful when manipulating other windows that may have been opened by the current window:

```
document.write(window.closed + "<br />")
```

We set the default status earlier, and we read it now:

```
document.write(window.defaultStatus + "<br />")
```

The title of the document can be reached through the document object, which we'll examine more shortly:

```
document.write(window.document.title + "<br />")
```

The location object is another property of window, which lets us find the URL of the current page. By setting the location object, as we'll see later, we can make the browser jump to a new URL:

```
document.write(window.location + "<br />")
```

Earlier, we gave the window a name. This allows us to refer to the window by name:

```
document.write(window.name + "<br />")
```

The appVersion property tells us what browser the viewer is using. We'll talk about the navigator object further below:

```
document.write(window.navigator.appVersion + "<br />")
```

Because the window in this example was not opened by another window, the opener property is undefined:

```
document.write(window.opener + "<br />")
```

We set the window status earlier:

```
document.write(window.status + "<br />")
```

The 'window.location' Object

The `window.location` object is different from the `document.URL` property, although they both deal with URLs and document location. `document.URL` is a read-only string reflecting the complete URL of the current page, whereas the `window.location` object allows us to load a new page, read parts of the URL, reload, or replace the new page. For example, if we assign a new URL to `window.location` then the browser jumps to the new URL.

In the following example we will create two pages and we will let them call each other using the `window.location` object. We will add a query string and a hash mark (to navigate to a different part of the page), and we will see how all this information can be retrieved using script.

Try It Out – Using the 'window.location' Object

1. Type up the following and save it as `wlocation1.htm`:

```
<?xml version="1.0" encoding="UTF-8"?>
<!DOCTYPE html
     PUBLIC "-//W3C//DTD XHTML 1.0 Transitional//EN"
     "http://www.w3.org/TR/xhtml1/DTD/xhtml1-transitional.dtd">
<html xmlns="http://www.w3.org/1999/xhtml" xml:lang="en" lang="en">
<head>
  <title>The window.location object I</title>
</head>
 <body>
  <h4>The window.location object I</h4>
  <form>
   <input type="button" value="get new document"
      onclick="window.location='wlocation2.htm?name=frank#top'"/>
  </form>
 </body>
</html>
```

2. Save the following as `wlocation2.htm`:

```
<?xml version="1.0" encoding="UTF-8"?>
<!DOCTYPE html
     PUBLIC "-//W3C//DTD XHTML 1.0 Transitional//EN"
     "http://www.w3.org/TR/xhtml1/DTD/xhtml1-transitional.dtd">
<html xmlns="http://www.w3.org/1999/xhtml" xml:lang="en" lang="en">
<head>
  <title>The window.location object II</title>
</head>
 <body>
  <h4>The window.location object II</h4>
  <form>
   <input type="button" value="get new document"
         onclick="window.location.href='wlocation1.htm'"/>
  </form>
  <script>
  <!--
  var qname=window.location.search
  var hashname=window.location.hash
```

```
var hrefname=window.location.href
var pathname=window.location.pathname
var honame=window.location.host
var hostname=window.location.hostname
var portname=window.location.port
var protname=window.location.protocol

document.write("The querystring is: - " + qname + "<br />")
document.write("The hash string is: - " + hashname + "<br />")
document.write("The URL is: - " + hrefname + "<br />")
document.write("The path of the url is: - is " + pathname + "<br />")
document.write("The host is: - " + honame + "<br />")
document.write("The hostname is: - " + hostname + "<br />")
document.write("The port is: - " + portname + "<br />")
document.write("The protocol is: - " + protname + "<br />")
// -->
</script>
</body>
</html>
```

3. Load `wlocation1.htm` and click on the button. This is what we will see when the second page loads:

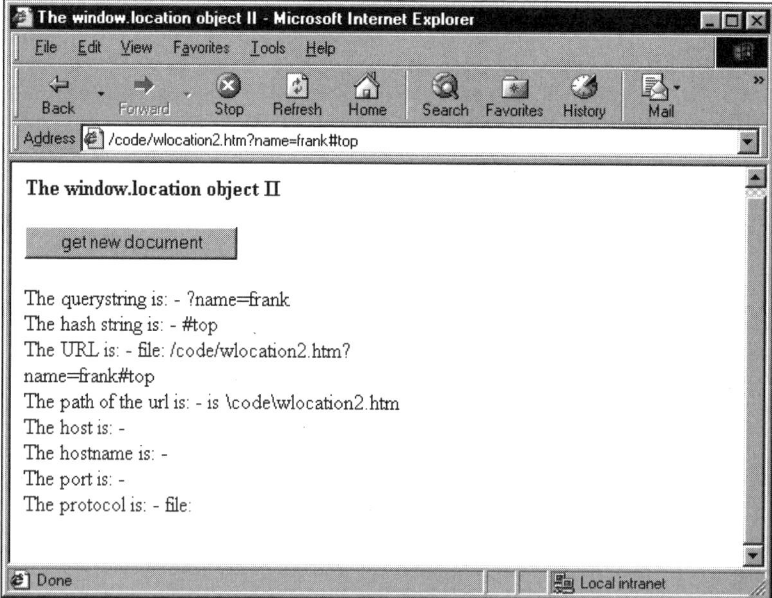

How It Works

In the first page we assign an URL to the `window.location` object that includes both a query string, and a fragment identifier:

```
<input type="button" value="get new document"
       onclick="window.location='wlocation2.htm?name=frank#top'"/>
```

In the second page, we use an alternate syntax to jump back to the first page: rather than set `window.location`, we set `window.location.href`:

```
<input type="button" value="get new document"
       onclick="window.location.href='wlocation1.htm'"/>
```

The two have identical effects. we only used different syntax to show you that it can be done both ways. The second page now takes the `window.location` object and reads its properties into variables. The following code recovers the query portion of the string:

```
var qname=window.location.search
```

Here is the hash part of the string:

```
var hashname=window.location.hash
```

This reads the full URL:

```
var hrefname=window.location.href
```

This pulls out the path name:

```
var pathname=window.location.pathname
```

These properties give information about the host and the port. They will be null if we read the file off the local file system, as I did in this example, or if the URL is an http: URL that doesn't specify a port:

```
var honame=window.location.host
var hostname=window.location.hostname
var portname=window.location.port
```

And this gives information about the protocol used, i.e. '`http:`', '`ftp:`', and so on:

```
var protname=window.location.protocol
```

The script prints the values, with the results seen above.

window.location's Methods

As well as the properties above, the `window.location` object also has two methods.

- `location.reload()` : This method reloads the page. It takes an optional parameter which, if set true (`location.reload(true)`) forces the browser to ignore its cache and reload the page and every resource it depends on (images, style sheets, applet or.class files. This is equivalent to shift-reload in Netscape) from the server.
- `location.replace(url)`:This method replaces the page with a page passed to it as a parameter, also replacing it in the browser's history. The effect is to prevent the user from going back to the (then) current page by using the Back button.

The 'window.open' Method

We can create new windows, and reopen existing windows with the `window.open` method. In the following example, we create a new window with the `window.open` method:

Try It Out – Creating a New Window

1. Fire up your editor, type in the following, and save it as `newwin.htm`:

```
<?xml version="1.0" encoding="UTF-8"?>
<!DOCTYPE html
     PUBLIC "-//W3C//DTD XHTML 1.0 Transitional//EN"
     "http://www.w3.org/TR/xhtml1/DTD/xhtml1-transitional.dtd">
<html xmlns="http://www.w3.org/1999/xhtml" xml:lang="en" lang="en">
<head>
  <title> Basic XHTML page</title>
<script>
<!--
  window.open('simtxt.txt')
// -->
</script>
</head>
<body>

</body>
</html>
```

2. Now type in the following and save as `simtxt.txt`:

```
Some simple text
```

3. When we view `newwin.htm`, we'll see:

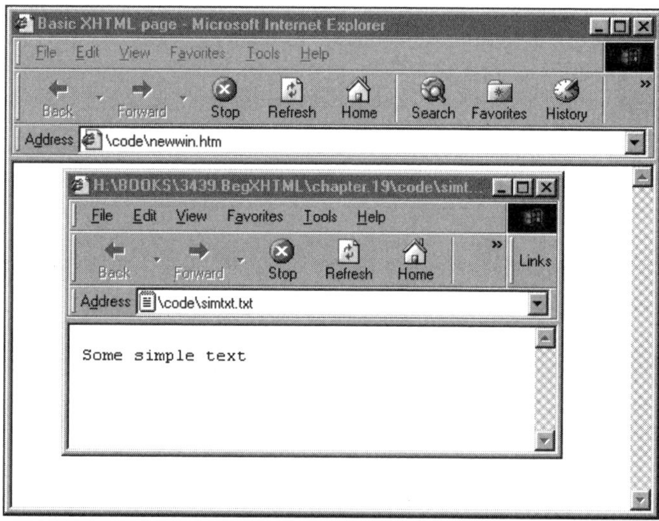

How It Works

Quite simply, the following line opens the new file in a new window! There's not much else we can say about this...

```
window.open('simtxt.txt')
```

Let's now look at the `navigator` object.

The 'navigator' Object

The `navigator` object tells us about the browser that the page is running on. The `navigator` object is a property of the `window` object, but you can access it without using the `window` prefix. Properties of `navigator` are important because they allow us to detect the browser the client is using, and thus write scripts that take advantage of features that exist in some versions of some browsers that still work correctly in others.

Here is an example to demonstrate the `navigator` properties.

Try It Out – The 'navigator' Properties

1. Type in this example and save it as `navigator.htm`:

```
<?xml version="1.0" encoding="UTF-8"?>
<!DOCTYPE html
     PUBLIC "-//W3C//DTD XHTML 1.0 Transitional//EN"
     "http://www.w3.org/TR/xhtml1/DTD/xhtml1-transitional.dtd">
<html xmlns="http://www.w3.org/1999/xhtml" xml:lang="en" lang="en">
<head>
 <title> Basic Window Properties</title>
<script>
<!--
 document.write(window.navigator.appCodeName + "<br />")
 document.write(window.navigator.appName + "<br />")
 document.write(window.navigator.appVersion + "<br />")
 document.write(window.navigator.mimeTypes.length + "<br />")
 document.write(window.navigator.platform + "<br />")
 document.write(window.navigator.userAgent + "<br />")

// -->
</script>
</head>
<body>

</body>
</html>
```

2. When we run this example on an IE5 browser under Windows 98, we see

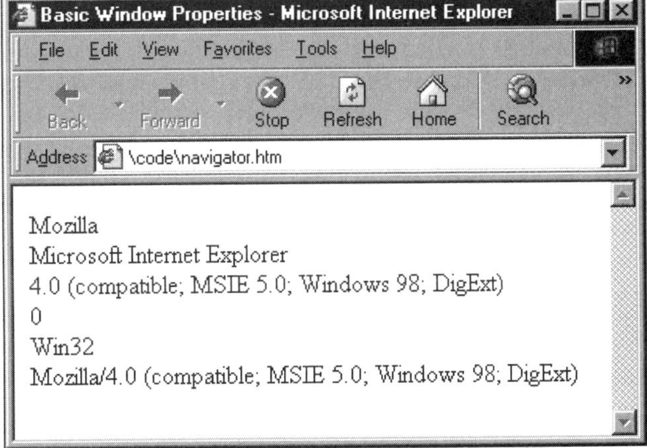

How It Works

The code name for the application Mozilla is Netscape's pet name. This code name has also been adopted by IE to maintain compatibility. As we'll see, because Microsoft had to follow Netscape when Netscape was the leading browser, Microsoft built a number of odd-seeming behaviors into IE's `navigator` object.

```
document.write(window.navigator.appCodeName + "<br />")
```

Here is the name of the browser. In a Netscape browser this property would be the string "Netscape":

```
document.write(window.navigator.appName + "<br />")
```

The following string gives version information about the browser. Funnily enough, IE5 returns a version number of 4.0! (Because IE 3's feature set was close to that of Netscape 2, IE 3 returns 2.0. IE 4, with a feature set close to Netscape 4, returns 4.0):

```
document.write(window.navigator.appVersion + "<br />")
```

The `mimetype` object allows a script to detect what media formats an installation of Netscape supports (this can vary because users can install different plug-ins and helper applications.) Unfortunately, this property is not supported in Internet Explorer:

```
document.write(window.navigator.mimeTypes.length + "<br />")
```

The platform string is something like "Win 32", "Win 16", "MacPPC" or "LinuxELF2.0/":

```
document.write(window.navigator.platform + "<br />")
```

You can also HTTP user-agent string which is sent to the web server:

```
document.write(window.navigator.userAgent + "<br />")
```

The 'document' Object

The `document` object allows access to the document itself, including information contained in the document's header. We'll introduce a few methods and properties of the document object here, and we'll discuss more of them in the next chapter. Both IE and Netscape Navigator have proprietary properties and methods for use with their own dialects of Dynamic HTML (DHTML), but we won't look at these. If you'd like to try DHTML, you'll either need to pick one browser or the other, or make a special effort to write DHTML scripts that will work with both. You might try Wrox Press' Programmer's References on IE4, IE5, and Netscape DHTML, ISBNs 1861000685, 1861001746 and 1861001193 respectively.

The 'document' Object's Properties

Here we will just look briefly at the `cookie` property, and the `location` and the URL properties.

The 'cookie' Property

We'll be looking deeper into the cookie property at the end of this chapter. However, because we'll be using the document.cookie property in our examples we'll describe it briefly here. The cookie property allows us to save a string on the client's hard drive. This string can be retrieved by the script when the user visits the page later on, even if the user exits and restarts his browser in the meantimes.

The following line of code:

```
document.cookie= "Name=JohnDoe";
```

stores the string "Name=JohnDoe" in the cookie file on the visitor's computer. We can retrieve this string later in a script, by reading from document.cookie.

```
var strCookie=document.cookie
```

This variable will not only contain the cookie I set, but also any other cookies associated with the page. As we've said, we'll look into cookies in more detail later on.

The 'location' and 'URL' Properties

The only reason we bring this up here is to distinguish the document.location property from the window.location property. The document.location property is a read only property that returns the string of the URL of the page loaded on the browser. It is a synonym of the document.URL property. Because it's too easy to confuse with window.location, the document.location property is deprecated and may stop working in future browsers. To avoid confusion, always use the document.URL property.

We will look at other document properties when we study the Document Object Model in the next chapter.

The 'images' and 'forms' Collections

The document object also has several properties which are arrays, also called **collections**. To motivate the examples we'll present next, we'll mention the images and the forms collections here. We'll cover these and other collections of the document object in more detail in the next chapter.

A collection is an array of element objects that can be accessed by index. For example, if we have a document with 3 images we can refer to them as follows: document.images[0], document.images[1], and document.images[2]. Note that in JavaScript, the first element of an array has index 0 rather than index 1.

Through the images collection, we can access properties of the images; for instance, we can change the src of an image replacing, say, the third image with a different image by writing document.images[2].src= "somepic.gif".

With the forms collection, we can refer to the forms on the page by index, namely:

```
document.forms[index]
```

Each form also has an `elements` collection which contains the enclosed form elements (such as text fields, radio buttons, and submit buttons.) We can change the value of a text field, for instance, by writing:

```
document.forms[0].elements[0].value="some text"
```

If a form and its elements are given names, we can also refer to forms and element by name as seen below:

```
<form name= "fm1">
 <input type= "text" name= "tb1"
</form>
<script>
<!--
document.fm1.tb1.value= "some text"
// -->
</script>
```

The result is the same as if we used the indexes.

JavaScript Objects

JavaScript contains a number of built-in objects unrelated to the browser. These objects would also exist if you were using JavaScript on a web server, or to script a different kind of application. Chief among them are the `String`, `Math` and `Date` objects.

The String and Math Objects

We covered some of the methods of the `String` object, which allows us to manipulate text and strings, in the last chapter. Predictably, the `Math` object contains properties and methods that we can use for mathematical calculations. We enumerate all of the methods of the `String` and `Math` objects in the JavaScript reference in Appendix E.

The Date Object

We manipulate dates in JavaScript with the `Date` object. To create a new `Date` object set to the current time (as set on the visitor's computer as the visitor is reading your page) we can write:

```
var dateObject=new Date()
```

It's also possible to create a `Date` object representing an arbitrary date. (Although JavaScript 1.2 and prior do not allow dates prior to January 1, 1970, ECMAScript and later versions of JavasScript support a range of about 277,000 years into the past and future!) One way to specify Sunday, April 2, 2000 would be:

```
var dateObject=new Date(2000,03,02)
document.write(dateObject)
```

Violating convention, JavaScript counts months beginning from 0, so January=0 and December=11. The browser assumes that the date and time apply to the current time zone. In my case, this example prints:

Sun Apr 2 00:00:00 EDT 2000

If you construct a `Date` with a single number, that number represents the number of milliseconds since midnight, Jan 1 1970. If, for instance, you left out the commas in the example above:

```
var dateObject=new Date(20000302)
document.write(dateObject)
```

...you'd see:

Thu Jan 1 00:33:20 EST 1970

You can obtain the single-number form of a date using the `getTime()` property as in `dateobject.getTime()`. The single-number form of a date is useful for doing arithmetic with dates. For instance, you can determine the duration in milliseconds between two `Dates` by subtracting the single-number forms of the dates. The `Date` object also has methods such as `getHour()` to get and set different parts of a date, such as the year, month, and the day of the week. The methods of the `Date` object are listed in the JavaScript reference appendix.

The 'forms' Object

Forms will be covered in detail in Chapter 15. Although we usually submit forms to the server and reset pages by manually pushing submit and reset buttons, we can submit a form using script.

The submit() and reset() methods

The `submit()` method takes the syntax `form.submit()`, where form is an identifier for the form. We can specify the name of the form (`document.myPurpleForm.submit()`) or access it by index from the `forms` collection, (`document.forms[3].submit()`). We can reset a form using the `reset()` method. Unlike the submit and reset buttons, the `submit()` and `reset()` methods can be triggered by an events unconnected with the form, allowing a form to be submitted automatically, from another form, or from a separate frame. The `form` element has other methods and properties which we do not discuss in this book.

Browser Events

In 1984, the Apple Macintosh revolutionized the computer world by introducing an event-driven user interface. Previously, most computer programs performed a task from start to finish, and were always at a particular junction of the program, presenting a particular menu or mode to the user. Programs with a Graphical User Interface (GUI), on the other hand, are always ready to respond when a user clicks the mouse, presses a button on the keyboard, or, these days, when information arrives over the internet. JavaScript too, provides a way of interacting with the user with events.

Before the 4.0 generation, browsers supported a limited range of events, for example, when a web page is finished loading, when the user leaves the page and when a user clicks on a link. Although the older events are mostly compatible between Netscape and IE, the 4.0 browsers introduced incompatible mechanisms for handling a wide range of events similar to those handled by GUI programs such as keystrokes and mouse motion. To use the newer events, it's necessary to write browser specific (incompatible between Netscape and IE) code to **capture** the events (to inform the web browser precisely which events you're interested in). **Event handlers** are small scripts which are executed when events happen.

W3C Event Specifications

The W3C is now devising a specification for events. The DOM level 2 describes a model in which events can both trickle down to an element, and can bubble up. The XHTML working group is considering the introduction of two new elements: the `<event>` element to generate events, and the `<eventlistener>` element for capturing events. Although no application as of yet implements this proposal, it could become the future of XHTML if this working draft is adopted by the consortium and if the browser manufacturers implement it.

Events and Event Handlers: Event Capture

IE4+ will respond to just about every kind of event on every element. Netscape browsers appear to support only the events that they want to support. It can be difficult to understand what events are supported from reading the official documentation for Netscape, and event handling varies from one version to the next: for instance, Netscape 3 allows scripts to handle events on some elements which cannot be handled in Netscape 4.5.

The following table is a list of old-style events, introduced prior to the 4.0 generation. These events are mostly compatible between the 3.0 and 4.0+ browsers. To avoid surprises, it's best to assume that any JavaScript, especially a script that uses events, does not work on browsers on which you have not tested it. The moral: test your scripts on as many different browsers as possible!

Event	Triggering Event	Supported on the following elements	Comments
`onabort`	Loading of an image is interrupted	image	
`onblur`	Element loses input focus	text elements	Typical uses for this are verification procedures for users filling out forms.
`onchange`	Selection or text changes	select and text input elements	Could be used to, for example, prevent the entry of unwanted characters into a text box.
`onclick`	User clicks mouse	link and button elements	If you want cross browser interoperability, do not use the onclick event anywhere except on these elements.

Event	Triggering Event	Supported on the following elements	Comments
`onerror`	An error loading an image	image	If an image is not available this event can be used to write a message to that effect.
`onfocus`	Element receives the focus	text , window, and form elements	
`onload`	A document or an image finishes loading	image and document	
`onmouseover`	Mouse moves over an area	link	Used for rollovers and to make text appear in the status line when the user moves the mouse over a link.
`onmouseout`	Mouse moves out of an area	link	Used in conjunction with `onmouseover`.
`onreset`	The form is reset	form	
`onresize`	The window is resized	window	
`onsubmit`	The form is submitted	form	An event handler can return false to prevent submission. This event is triggered before the information is sent when the user clicks the submit button, but after information is sent when the `submit()` method is called.
`onunload`	The document is unloaded	window	Usually set on the `body` element. Use this to carry out verification that form elements etc. have been correctly filled out.

Event Handlers

There are 3 ways of specifying the handling of an event: inline, in script, and using a JavaScript URL.

Inline Event Handlers

In an inline event handler, the event handler is written into an attribute of the element. Here is a simple example:

```
<input type="button" value= "clickme" onclick= "alert('you clicked me')"/>
```

One way to write a complex event handler is to call a user-defined function from inside an inline event handler, as in the following example

```
<input type="button" value= "clickme" onclick= "clickcode('you clicked me')"/>
```

```
<script>
<!--
 function clickcode(x) {
  alert(x)
 }
// -->
</script>
```

In-Script Event Handlers

It's also possible to declare an event handler in script apart from the XHTML code for the element, for example, we can catch `onclick` on `clickbutton`, the button in the following form:

```
<form name="fm1">
<input type="button" value= "clickme" name= "clickbutton"/>
</form>
```

...by setting the `onclick` property of `clickbutton`:

```
<script>
<!--
 function clickcode() {
 alert('you clicked me')
 }

document.fm1.clickbutton.onclick=clickcode;

// -->
</script>
```

In this case, you cannot attach a snippet of JavaScript directly to the event, but rather your event handler must be a user-defined function and you must write an assignment with the `onclick` property on the left hand side and the name of a user-defined function, your event handler, on the right.

JavaScript URLs

If you'd like to execute a script when a user click on a link, you can also use a JavaScript URL. (This, by the way, can be used to enter JavaScript commands interactively into a browser.) An example is:

```
<a href= "javaScript:alert('you clicked me')"> Click Me </a>
```

Some Examples of Events

The 'onmouseover' Event

A popular use of events is the use of `onmouseover` and `onmouseout` to create **rollovers**, links that change in appearance when the mouse passes over them. The following script contains two rollovers: the first works in IE 4.0 and up and Netscape's experimental Gecko browser (which will become Netscape 5) that changes the appearance of a text link. The second rollover works in Netscape 3.0 and up and IE 4.0 up and changes the appearance of an image link by replacing the image with a second image.

Try It Out – A Rollover Script

1. Type in the following page and save it as `rollover.htm`:

```
<?xml version="1.0" encoding="UTF-8"?>
<!DOCTYPE html
     PUBLIC "-//W3C//DTD XHTML 1.0 Transitional//EN"
     "http://www.w3.org/TR/xhtml1/DTD/xhtml1-transitional.dtd">
<html xmlns="http://www.w3.org/1999/xhtml" xml:lang="en" lang="en">
<head>
<title>Mouse Overs</title>
</head>
<body >

<h3 onmouseover="this.style.fontSize='24pt'"
onmouseout="this.style.fontSize='14pt'">Mouse Overs</h3>

<p>When it comes to rollovers, Netscape browsers are a little weak. The second
image rollover works in Netscape 3.0+. Gecko promises to be better.</p>

<a href="" onmouseover="m_over()" onmouseout="m_out()" ><img alt="face"
src="face.gif" border="0"></a>

<script>
<!--
function m_over() {
 document.images[0].src="face2.gif";
}
function m_out() {
 document.images[0].src="face.gif";
}
// !-->
</script>
</body>
</html>
```

2. You'll also need to save the 2 images, `face.gif` and `face2.gif`, in the same directory. You'll find them in the code download for this chapter.

3. When you run the page, you should see this:

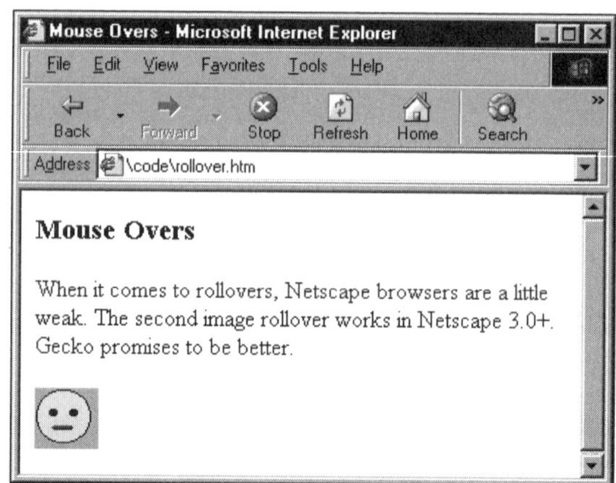

4. Now if you move your mouse over the heading or the image, they should change (in IE). Only the second rollover, the image, will work in Netscape though.

How It Works

For both the headings, we have used inline event handlers.

```
<h3 onmouseover="this.style.fontSize='24pt'"
onmouseout="this.style.fontSize='14pt'">Mouse Overs</h3>
```

We have used the `style` property to access the CSS properties of the element. In an event handler, `this` is the element which generated the event. When writing CSS properties in JavaScript, we replace hyphenation with capitalization, so CSS `background-color` becomes JavaScript `backgroundColor`, and CSS `font-size` becomes JavaScript `fontSize`.

To write rollovers for Netscape, we must do a little more work. Because Netscape can't change the properties of text dynamically, Netscape can only provide rollovers on image links. To do so, you must create two versions of the image: one in its normal state, and one that appears when the mouse passes over the image. Complicating matters, the `onmouseover` and the `onmouseout` events are not captured by images in JavaScript. To capture the events we have to put the image inside an `<a>` element:

```
<script>
<!--
function m_over() {
 document.images[0].src="face2.gif";
}
function m_out() {
 document.images[0].src="face.gif";
}

// -->
</script>
```

We use the `images[]` collection to reference the second image.

Loading and Unloading

The onload event occurs when a page is finished loading, images and all, and the onunload event occurs when a user leaves a page.

The following example checks to see if anything entered in the text box when the visitor leaves. If there is, it offers to store the text as a cookie.

The 'onblur' and 'onfocus' Events

The onblur and onfocus events are captured when form elements receive and lose focus.

In the following example we use the onfocus event to read text into a text box, and the onblur event to read the value into a hidden <input> element. We use the onclick event on a command button to show the contents of the hidden <input> elements.

Try It Out – Focus

1. Type in the following file and save it as focus.htm:

```
<?xml version="1.0" encoding="UTF-8"?>
<!DOCTYPE html
     PUBLIC "-//W3C//DTD XHTML 1.0 Transitional//EN"
     "http://www.w3.org/TR/xhtml1/DTD/xhtml1-transitional.dtd">
<html xmlns="http://www.w3.org/1999/xhtml" xml:lang="en" lang="en">
<head>
<title>onblur event doc</title>
</head>
<body>
<h3>onblur event doc</h3>

<form name="fm1">
<input type="text"  onfocus="this.value='[first name]'"
onblur="h1.value=this.value" />
<input type="text"  onfocus="this.value='[last name]'"
onblur="h2.value=this.value" />
<input type="hidden"  value="" name= "h1" />
<input type="hidden"  value="" name= "h2" />
<input type="button"  value="Button"  onclick="alert(h1.value + '&' + h2.value)"
/>

</form>
</body>
</html>
```

2. When you run this page and click in the text boxes, you should see something like this:

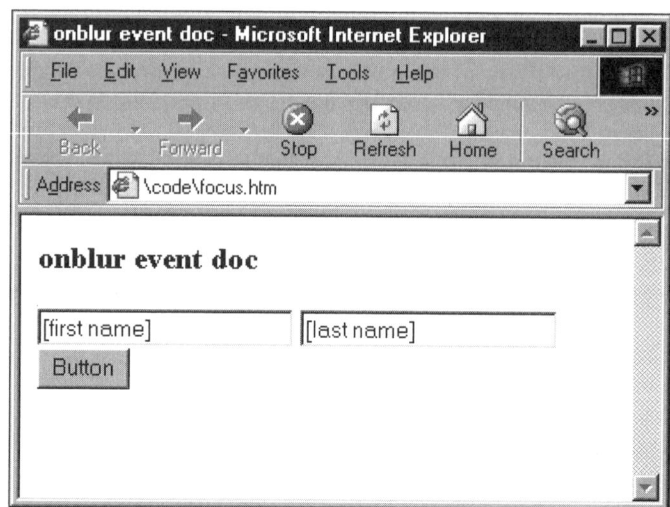

How It works

Each text box has a set of code like this associated with it:

```
<input type="text"  onfocus="this.value='[first name]'"
onblur="h1.value=this.value" />
```

The event handlers in the input element set the value of the text box to `[first name]` when it receives the focus, whether that happens by clicking on it or pressing the *Tab* key. When it loses the focus, the value is stored in the hidden element, in this case the one called `h1`.

When the button is pressed, the values of `h1` and `h2` are concatenated and displayed in an alert:

```
<input type="button"  value="Button"  onclick="alert(h1.value + '&' + h2.value)"
/>
```

Browser Sniffing

The proliferation of different versions of different web browsers poses serious problems for web authors. Often, newer browsers contain features that we'd like to use, however, we don't want to alienate visitors (potential customers for a commercial site) who are using older web browsers, or different web browsers than our own. You can make several choices: many major sites, following the lead of Yahoo! design a single simple page, designed to be compatible with a wide spectrum of browsers. Although you can't take advantage of spiffy features this way, you can still make attractive and usable pages while minimizing the cost, effort and headaches you'll experience making the page. Other sites, deciding it's more important to be on the cutting edge than it is to embrace everyone, simply tell people that they'd better be running, say, Netscape 4.61 or that they must get the Macromedia Flash plugin if they want to proceed. Two middle roads are also possible: you can, for instance, design several versions of a page, targeted at different segments of your audience. The risk here is that you'll double or triple the cost of creating and, worse, maintaining your page.

Because you'll spend most of your time maintaining a page, you should worry more about maintenance costs than creation costs – if your page costs too much to maintain, you'll sabotage it by neglecting to maintain it.

Finally, you can put some thought into writing scripts which take advantage of new features on newer browsers, while bypassing incompatible code on older browsers. An extension of this idea is to write a **compatibility layer**, a set of user-defined functions that hide the difference between two incompatible browsers: this is the royal road to writing DHTML scripts that work in both IE 4+ and Netscape 4. An example of such a script can be found at `http://www.honeylocust.com/bite/`.

Other than just the browser version, there are variations in platforms and between different machines. For example a 12pt font on a Mac and a PC aren't quite the same size, which might worry control freak designers with a large budget. Similarly, between 13% and 20% of users are still surfing the web with 640x480 screens, while a handful are blessed with screens as large as 2048x1538 – it's difficult to design a page which is attractive and usable for everyone. As we've shown previously, it's possible to get information about a visitor's screen in JavaScript. Although we won't discuss it further, it's also possible to determine what plug-ins a user has available, so a page can determine if it should use a plug-in, applet or image to represent information. Consult the online documentation or a book on JavaScript if you'd like to know more.

Browser sniffing can be done on either the client, using JavaScript, or on the web server. The advantage of using JavaScript is that many users don't have sufficient privilege to install programs on their web server and, also, web sites that do sophisticated processing on the server put more load on the server and, therefore, don't scale well to high volumes of usage unless you're prepared to invest in expensive hardware. The primary disadvantage of using JavaScript is that you can't use JavaScript to discriminate between different non-JavaScript browsers, or browsers on which the user has turned JavaScript off.

Sniffing Out the Browser

The following example tests to see what browser the page is being viewed with and uses the `location.href` property to reroute it to a browser-specific page. To sniff out a browser we use the `navigator.appName`, and the `navigator.appVersion` properties. It's also possible to use the `navigator.userAgent` property, which contains the richest information. The example below sniffs out some major groups of browsers, and redirects the browser to appropriate pages. If and when Opera and other browsers increase in popularity it may become necessary to add to this example. Judging the need to maintain this script in the future, and some of the bizarre behaviors you're about to witness, you might reconsider your choice to provide different pages to different browsers. It also gets a little more complicated with palmtop and other user agents

Try It Out – Detecting Browsers

1. Type up the following, saving it as `sniff.htm`:

```
<?xml version="1.0" encoding="UTF-8"?>
<!DOCTYPE html
     PUBLIC "-//W3C//DTD XHTML 1.0 Transitional//EN"
     "http://www.w3.org/TR/xhtml1/DTD/xhtml1-transitional.dtd">
<html xmlns="http://www.w3.org/1999/xhtml" xml:lang="en" lang="en">
```

```
<head>
<title>Redirecting browsers
</title>

</head>
<body>
<h3>Detecting browsers</h3>
<script>
<!--
 var strBrowserMake=navigator.appName
 var strBrowserVer=navigator.appVersion.charAt(0)
 if (strBrowserMake=="Microsoft Internet Explorer" && strBrowserVer>=4 &&
    navigator.appVersion.indexOf("MSIE 5")!=-1) {
    location.href='ie5.txt'
 } else if (strBrowserMake=="Microsoft Internet Explorer" && strBrowserVer>=4 ) {
    location.href='ie4.txt'
 } else if (strBrowserMake=="Navigator" && strBrowserVer>=4 ) {
    location.href='Nav4.txt'
 } else if (strBrowserMake=="Netscape" && strBrowserVer>=4 ) {
    location.href='gecko.txt'
 } else {
    location.href='BrowOth.txt'
 }
// -->
</script>
<noscript>
The browser you are viewing this page on does not support scripts. You may want to
view our <a href="BrowOth.txt">non-scripted pages.</a>
</noscript>
</body>
</html>
```

2. Now, you'll want to create a set of text files, called `ie5.txt`, `ie4.txt`, `Nav4.txt`, `gecko.txt`, and `BrowOth.txt`. In each, simply put a line telling you which browser it was written for, like 'this is the IE5 page'.

3. Now run the page. Depending on your browser, you'll get a different result. In real life, you'd link to full pages, but here we've simply demonstrated how to do the sniffing part.

How It Works

The first thing we do is read the make of the browser into a string:

```
var strBrowserMake=navigator.appName
```

We then get the version compatibility number by using the `charAt()` method to read the first character of the `appVersion` property:

```
var strBrowserVer=navigator.appVersion.charAt(0)
```

Oddly, in the case of IE, this number is not the version number of the browser, but rather, reflects the version of Netscape which the browser is roughly compatible with. Therefore, IE5 returns a version number of '4' as it is most like Navigator 4:

```
if (strBrowserMake=="Microsoft Internet Explorer" && strBrowserVer>=4 &&
    navigator.appVersion.indexOf("MSIE 5")!=-1) {
    location.href='ie5.txt'
```

Because both IE4 and IE5 return a version number of 4 we must examine the appVersion string to distinguish between the two browsers:

```
}else if (strBrowserMake=="Microsoft Internet Explorer" && strBrowserVer>=4 ) {
  location.href='ie4.txt'
```

The appName of current Netscape browsers is 'Navigator'. In Netscape browsers the version number will be the actual version of the browser:

```
}else if (strBrowserMake=="Navigator" && strBrowserVer>=4){
  location.href='Nav4.txt'
```

Netscape's experimental Gecko browsers call themselves 'Netscape'. Possibly this will change when Gecko is incorporated into the next version of Netscape, tentatively titled Netscape 6:

```
}else if (strBrowserMake=="Netscape" && strBrowserVer>=4 ) {
  location.href='gecko.txt'
```

Anything else, we put into the 'other' category. As recent versions of the Opera browser have full support for style sheets, so we may wish to sniff for this in the future.

Sniffing Out the Color Depth

To look at the number of colors a platform can display we use the screen.colorDepth property. In the following example we alter the src property of an image to send different pictures to a platform.

Try It Out – Sniffing For Color

1. Type in the following in your editor, and save it as colordepth.htm:

```
<?xml version="1.0" encoding="UTF-8"?>
<!DOCTYPE html
     PUBLIC "-//W3C//DTD XHTML 1.0 Transitional//EN"
     "http://www.w3.org/TR/xhtml1/DTD/xhtml1-transitional.dtd">
<html xmlns="http://www.w3.org/1999/xhtml" xml:lang="en" lang="en">
<head>
<title>
</title>
</head>
```

```
<body>
<img alt="face.gif" src="" />
<script>
<!--
var cd=screen.colorDepth
if(cd < 8) {
 document.images[0].src="facebw.gif"
}
else {
 document.images[0].src="face.gif"
}
// -->
</script>
</body>
</html>
```

2. You'll also need to find the images `facebw.gif` and `face.gif` from the downloaded code and place them in the same directory as `colordepth.htm`.

3. When you run this page, depending on your color depth, you'll get an appropriate image.

How It Works

We set a variable, `cd`, to the value contained in the screen's `colorDepth` property:

```
var cd=screen.colorDepth
```

We then test it with an if statement, and if it's less than 8, we supply facebw.gif, a [black-and-white] version of our image. If it's greater than 8, we supply the normal image.

Cookies

When the HTTP protocol was first developed, it was **stateless**. What that means is that once a page was cleared from the window, the browser retained no memory of that page, except in the `history` object. Similarly, the web server remembered nothing between requests. Although web developers have since cursed the statelessness of the web, HTTP was originally designed to be stateless for a reason: with no state retained in the browser and the server, there is no way they can get out of sync. Also, it's easier to write stateless servers that can reliably scale to a large volume of hits. The notorious low speed and poor reliability of some commercial web application servers is often because they keep too much state in the server. Netscape introduced cookies in Netscape 1.1 to provide a way to add, for better and for worse, the ability to store a bit of memory to the browser by associating a small amount of string data with particular web pages and sites.

Because cookies can potentially be used in ways that violate privacy, some web users are apprehensive of them and have overblown fears. For instance, some users mistakenly fear that cookies are programs that can take over their computers, erase files and maybe even steal beer from the refrigerator. Even so, web advertising networks such as DoubleClick (`http://www.doubleclick.com/`) do use cookies to track users as they move between different sites in the network. Although cookies don't automatically give your name, phone number or other sensitive information, a network of web sites *could* possibly share information that you type into forms between different sites, and even to locate you in a database of consumers.

Because many users are afraid of cookies, many web users turn off cookie support in their browsers, which will means that scripts using cookies will not work for some fraction of your visitors. If you're curious about the cookies on your machine, you'll find them stored in a text file on your hard drive: If you are running Netscape on Windows, search for `cookies.txt` in the Programs/Netscape folder (on Unix platforms, this file is stored in `$HOME/netscape`). If you're running IE on Windows 95 or 98, look in the `c:\windows\cookies` folder. In Windows 2000 cookies are stored in `c:\Documents and Settings\User\Cookies`, where "User" will be specific to your machine.

Whenever a cookie-supporting browser requests a page it looks in a 'cookie jar' to see if it has any cookies associated with the URL of that page. If it does, it sends these cookies back to the server as part of the HTTP header. The server can use the information in the cookie in several ways including personalizing the page it sends back to the client.

As client side programmers our interest in cookies stems from the fact that the cookie can be accessed on the client via the `document.cookie` property. This allows a JavaScript enabled page to have a memory independent of the server. Before looking at how to use the `document.cookie` property, let's look at the contents of a cookie.

What a Cookie Contains

A cookie can be any string of characters, but the semicolon and the equal sign have special significance. Spaces are not allowed. A cookie usually contain name/value pairs such as:

```
name=joe;
```

The semicolon tells the browser that it has come to the end of an attribute of the cookie. As well as the name value/pair, cookies can have other specialized attributes. These are separated from the cookie 'name/value' by semi-colons. These special attributes are:

- The expires attribute
- The path attribute
- The domain attribute
- The secure attribute

It should be noted that the cookie's 'attributes' have nothing to do with an XHTML element's 'attributes'!

Lets look at how to set a cookie with some of these special attributes.

Setting a Cookie

A cookie is set using the `document.cookie` property. The following syntax sets a cookie with `expires`, `domain`, and `secure` attributes:

```
document.cookie= "name=joe;domain=wrox.com;expires=2001,01,01;secure;"
```

This cookie sets a cookie named `name` of name that will be only be transmitted to servers in the wrox.com domain, that expires on the 1st of January 2001, and will only be submitted to the server if a secure means of transmission (such as `https:`) is being used. We will look more at these attributes below.

It should be noted that the value of the cookie is given as a string of the form:

`[some name string]=[some values]`

This string can be up to 4 kilobytes in length, but should contain no spaces, no semi-colons, and only a single equals sign.

The 'expires' Attribute

By default a cookie only lasts as long as the browser application stays open. When the user quits the browser, all cookies without an `expires` attribute are destroyed.

The life of a cookie can be extended beyond the life of a browser by setting the `expires` attribute.

The following script creates an cookie with an `expires` attribute dated one year from the time the cookie is set. First a date variable named `oneyearstime` is created. This variable is then incremented a year into the future, and assigned into the cookie's `expires` attribute:

```
var oneyearstime=new Date();
oneyearstime.setFullYear(oneyearstime.getFullYear()+1);
document.cookie="name=joe;expires="+oneyearstime.toGMTString();
```

To delete a cookie that has had its expiration date set in the future simply set the expiration date to a date that has passed.

The 'secure' Attribute

The `secure` attribute is a Boolean attribute. When present it means the cookie can only be submitted to the server when either HTTPS or some other secure method of transmission is available.

In the next section we will look at the `path` and `domain` attribute.

Who Can Read a Cookie

By default, a cookie can be accessed by the document that created the cookie, and also by any document residing in the same folder or descendant folder of that folder.

So, for example, if I have a file at :

`http://www.wrox.com/folder/subfolder/cookie.htm`

which creates a cookie using the syntax `document.cookie='name=value'`, it can be read by any file in the 'subfolder' folder such as:

`http://www.wrox.com/folder/subfolder/somefile.htm`

and:

`http://www.wrox.com/folder/subfolder/anotherfile.htm`

It can also be read by child folders such as:

```
http://www.wrox.com/folder/subfolder/childfolder/childfile.htm
```

and:

```
http://www.wrox.com/folder/subfolder/anotherchild/descendantfile.htm.
```

This default behavior is often exactly what we want, however the cookie *cannot* be read by files in the following folders:

```
http://www.wrox.com/index.htm
```

or:

```
http://www.wrox.com/folder/file.htm.
```

The 'path' Attribute

In order to set the cookie so it could be read by these documents we need to set the `path` attribute of the cookie. In the above example setting the cookie with the syntax:

```
document.cookie= "name=value;path=/"
```

means that the cookie can be read by documents in any of the folders in the `http://www.wrox.com/` directory or any of the descendant folders.

Setting the cookie with the syntax:

```
document.cookie= "name=value;path=/folder"
```

means the cookie can be read by any document in the `http://www.wrox.com/folder` folder or its descendant folders.

The 'domain' Attribute

The `domain` attribute of a cookie allows a cookie to be set for any documents sent from a server in a certain domain.

For example if I set a cookie with the following syntax:

```
document.cookie="name=value;domain=wrox.com"
```

The cookie can be read by any file in the `wrox.com` domain such as:

```
http://orderbook/wrox.com/basket.htm
```

or:

```
http://catalog/wrox.com/somefile.htm
```

For security reasons we cannot set a cookie that can be read by a domain other than the source of the document.

Retrieving a Cookie

Although we can write to the `expires`, `secure`, `path` and `domain` attributes, the only attribute we can read on the client side is the 'name/value' attribute.

Let's look at the cookie we set earlier on:

```
document.cookie= "name=joe;domain=wrox.com;expires=20010101;secure;"
```

The only value we can retrieve is the name/value pair so that:

```
alert(document.cookie)
```

would only display the string `"name=joe"`.

The other values are available to the server and are sent as part of the HTTPS header, but for security reasons cannot be accessed by a client page.

Altering a Cookie

To alter a cookie simply assign a new value to the name. This:

```
document.cookie= "name=Fred"
```

...would assign a new value to the `name` attribute. If we write an assignment with a different attribute name, such as:

```
document.cookie= "firstname=Fred"
```

...we create a new cookie instead.

Let's look at some of the limitations of cookies.

Limitations of Cookies

Cookies are useful for storing small amounts of data, however they have several limitations:

- Browsers are not required to retain more than a total of 300 cookies
- Browsers are not required to retain more than a total of 20 cookies from any single domain
- Cookies cannot contain more than 4K of data.

In practice the 20 cookies per domain is the most limiting. It is possible to expand the number of values that can be set from a domain and thus circumvent this limitation. When setting several values from a single page use a single cookie. For example instead of setting three cookies:

```
firstname=Frank;

middlename=R;

lastname=Boumphrey
```

use the following:

```
names=firstname&Frank:middlename&R:lastname&Boumphrey;
```

We have arbitrarily used an ampersand as an assignment sign, and a colon as a separator. This will count as a single cookie. These values will of course have to be parsed when they are retrieved, using string manipulation methods.

A Cookie Example

In the following example we will create three pages that set cookies. Two of the pages allow us to set cookies named `firstname` and `lastname` with no expiration date (that won't survive the closing of the browser) while the third page sets a cookie named `name` with an expiration date. Each page has a button allowing us to retrieve the cookies.

Try It Out – Setting Cookies

1. Type up this page and call it `cookie1.htm`:

```
<?xml version="1.0" encoding="UTF-8"?>
<!DOCTYPE html
     PUBLIC "-//W3C//DTD XHTML 1.0 Transitional//EN"
     "http://www.w3.org/TR/xhtml1/DTD/xhtml1-transitional.dtd">
<html xmlns="http://www.w3.org/1999/xhtml" xml:lang="en" lang="en">
<head>
<title>Cookie example I</title>
</head>
<body>
<h2>Cookie example I</h2>
 <a href="cookie2.htm">cookie2.htm</a>
 <a href="cookie3.htm">cookie3.htm</a>

 <form>
 <h4>type in first name</h4>
 <input type="text" name="tb1" />
 <input type="button"
  value="set cookie" name="b1"
   onclick="document.cookie='firstname=' + document.forms[0].tb1.value" />

 <input type="button"
  value="get cookie" name="b2"
   onclick="alert(document.cookie)" />
 </form>
</body>
</html>
```

2. The next page is almost identical, and sets the cookie for the last name. Alter `cookie1.htm` as follows, and save it as `cookie2.htm`:

```
<?xml version="1.0" encoding="UTF-8"?>
<!DOCTYPE html
     PUBLIC "-//W3C//DTD XHTML 1.0 Transitional//EN"
     "http://www.w3.org/TR/xhtml1/DTD/xhtml1-transitional.dtd">
<html xmlns="http://www.w3.org/1999/xhtml" xml:lang="en" lang="en">
```

```
<head>
<title>Cookie example II</title>
</head>
<body>
<h2>Cookie example II</h2>
 <a href="cookie1.htm">cookie1.htm</a>
 <a href="cookie3.htm">cookie3.htm</a>

 <form>
 <h4>type in last name</h4>
 <input type="text" name="tb1" />
 <input type="button"
  value="set cookie" name="b1"
   onclick="document.cookie='lastname=' + document.forms[0].tb1.value" />

 <input type="button"
  value="get cookie" name="b2"
   onclick="alert(document.cookie)" />
 </form>
</body>
</html>
```

3. Finally type up this page and save it as `cookie3.htm`:

```
<?xml version="1.0" encoding="UTF-8"?>
<!DOCTYPE html
     PUBLIC "-//W3C//DTD XHTML 1.0 Transitional//EN"
     "http://www.w3.org/TR/xhtml1/DTD/xhtml1-transitional.dtd">
<html xmlns="http://www.w3.org/1999/xhtml" xml:lang="en" lang="en">

<head>
<title>Cookie example</title>
</head>
<script>
<!--
alert(document.cookie)

var oneyearstime=new Date();
oneyearstime.setFullYear(oneyearstime.getFullYear()+1);
document.cookie="name=joe;expires="+oneyearstime.toGMTString();
// -->
</script>
<a href="cookie1.htm">cookie1.htm</a><br />
<a href="cookie2.htm">cookie2.htm</a>

</html>
```

4. View `cookie1.htm` and fill your first name in. Click on the **set cookie** button.

5. Now navigate to `cookie2.htm` and do the same with your last name.

6. Next, view `cookie3.htm`. Then navigate back to one of the other 2 pages. You should see something like this:

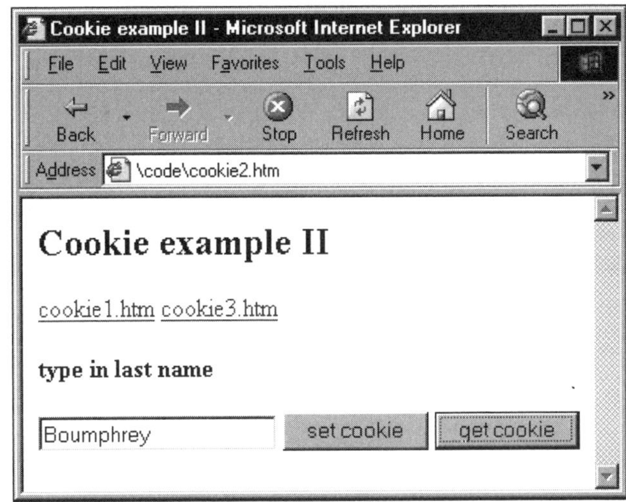

7. Now exit the browser and restart it, viewing `cookie1.htm` again. Click on the get cookie button. You will see that the only cookie that remains is the '`name=joe`' cookie. This is because we set an expiration date for this cookie, but the other cookies expired as soon as the browser was closed.

How It Works

The relevant lines in this page are contained in the event handlers of the two input buttons.

The first input button sets the cookie value of `'firstname=` *`value of text box`*`'`:

```
<input type="button"
  value="set cookie" name="b1"
   onclick="document.cookie='firstname=' + document.forms[0].tb1.value" />
```

The second button displays all the cookies that attached to this page which include not only the cookies set by this page, but also any cookies set by pages in the same folder, or in parent folders:

```
<input type="button"
  value="get cookie" name="b2"
   onclick="alert(document.cookie)" />
```

The third page differs from the other two in that it assigns the cookie `name=joe` an expiration date that is set a year into the future:

```
var oneyearstime=new Date();
oneyearstime.setFullYear(oneyearstime.getFullYear()+1);
document.cookie="name=joe;expires="+oneyearstime.toGMTString();
```

Note that there are three cookies which have been set by different pages. Because the pages are in the same folder, they share cookies.

Summary

We started this chapter by studying several of the browser objects in JavaScript, some of the built in methods and how to handle events in JavaScript. Then, we looked at some applications of JavaScript in web pages. In particular we looked at how to use JavaScript retrieve information about an HTML document, and about the platform and the browser it is being displayed on. We showed how to create rollovers, hyperlinks that change in appearance when the mouse passes over them, as well as how to detect a user's browser and serve different pages to different browsers. Finally, we showed how to use cookies to let a JavaScript remember small amounts of information between the times someone visits your page.

In the next chapter we'll be examining the Document Object Model.

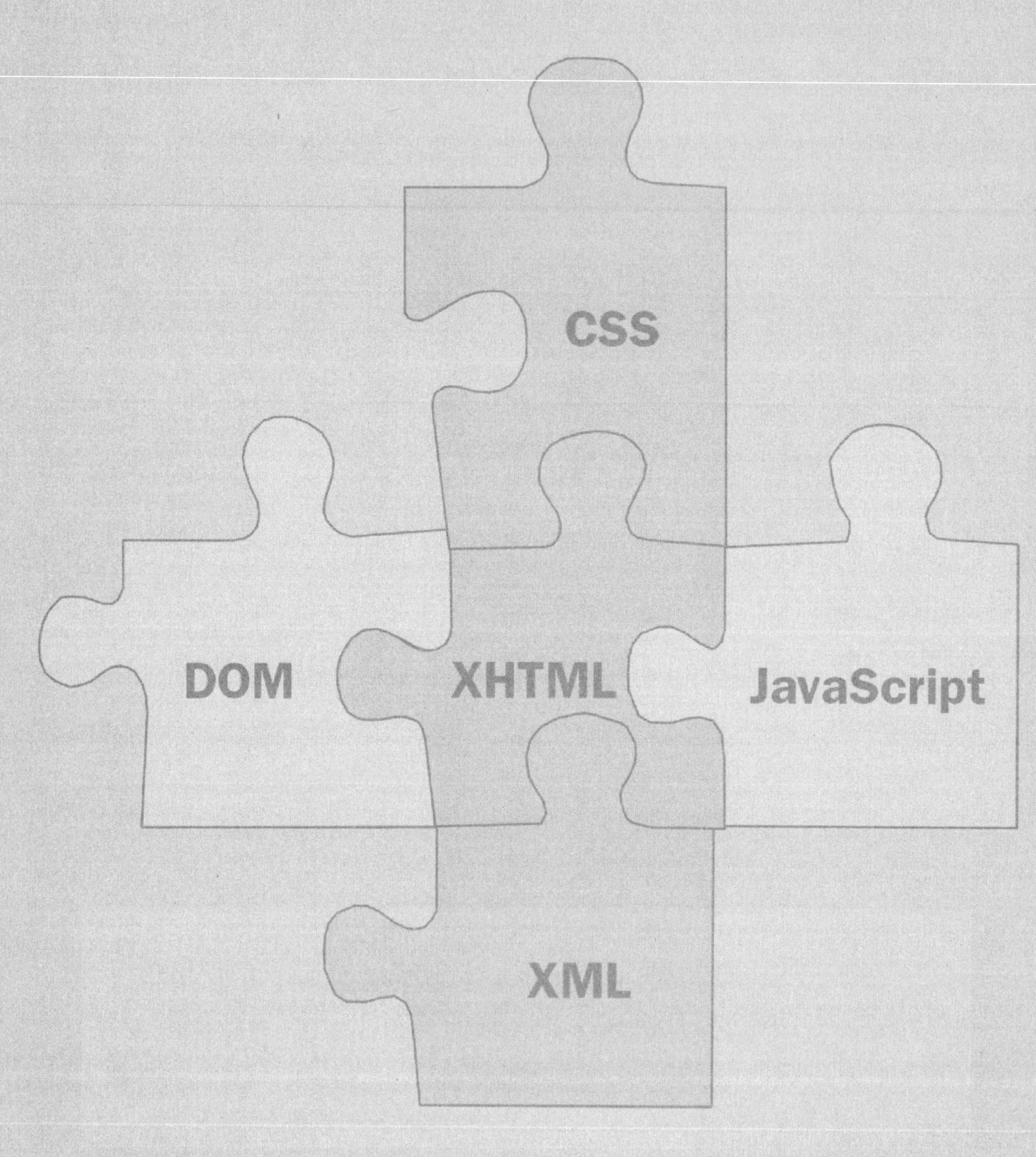
CSS
DOM
XHTML
JavaScript
XML

Document Object Models

In this chapter, we will discuss manipulating XHTML documents through Document Object Models (DOMs) in JavaScript. We'll first explain what Document Object Models are and then introduce the three levels of DOM (0, 1, and 2) specified by the World Wide Web Consortium (W3C). Next, we'll introduce the terms used to describe the tree structure of a document which is accessible through the Level 1 DOM. We'll then discuss the properties and methods of the Level 0 DOM (the set of features first made available in 3.0 generation browsers) and present a simple example. Finally, we'll discuss the Level 1 DOM, fortified with several examples.

Document Object Model Fundamentals

What is a Document Object Model?

To understand what the Document Object Model (or DOM) is, we must first understand the concept of **objects**. Anyone who has used an object-oriented programming language such as Java will already be familiar with this concept. Although we have been using objects in the previous two chapters, let's remind ourselves of what they are. Take, for example, a car. We could define a car by listing lots of data about it, such as its length and width, the diameter of the wheels and headlamps, the distance from the edge of the car to the edges of the headlamps, height above ground of lower edge of front bumper, thickness of glass used in windscreen, voltage of battery, and so on.

Alternatively, we could just define a car by stating that it has wheels, doors, headlamps and so on, and not worry about their actual dimensions or positions. This is much easier. In this example, wheel, door and headlamp are all objects. The data which defines them are stored within the objects themselves. However, we do not need to worry about data such as the diameter of the wheels or headlamps, and so forth; all we are concerned with is that 'objects' such as wheels, doors and headlamps etc. exist and that we can use them.

Now you know what is meant by object, you should be able to piece together the rest of the meaning behind the term DOM: a web page (the document) is broken down (modeled) into separate individual sections (objects). These objects can then be used to modify the document. In order to manipulate document objects, we must use a scripting language such as JavaScript or VBScript – in this book, we use JavaScript.

Some examples of document objects are the `anchor` object, the `document` object, the `frame` object, and the `window` object. Each object also has properties and methods. For example, the `anchor` object has a `name` property which specifies the name to be used to refer to the anchor; the `document` object has properties such as `fgColor` which specifies the color of the documents foreground text. An example of a method is the `frame` objects `print` method, which can be used to print the contents of a frame. We have already been using some of these in the previous two chapters, and we will see many more examples throughout this chapter.

Objects, along with their properties and methods, allow us to manipulate the content, structure and style of a web page *even as the document is being displayed* and then displays those changes on that web page. Thus we can update the 'look' of a document even after it has begun being displayed in the browser. This means that we will be able to add or delete *any element* within a web page, or change its content, or add, delete or change *any of an elements attributes* as the file is being loaded into the browser. This, as you may guess, is a very powerful technique.

This 'change as it loads' technique is known as *dynamically* changing the document. Do not confuse it, though, with Dynamic (X)HTML (see below), which allows a far greater degree of changes to be made, and on a much finer level. Although DHTML uses DOM as part of its 'bag of tricks', it also uses other techniques we do not cover in this book.

The Levels of DOM

As we said above, a DOM is a mapping between a document and a set of objects in a programming language. That is, it specifies exactly how a document can be viewed and manipulated from programming languages. In more precise terms, the Document Object Model is an application programming interface (API) which defines the logical structure of a document and the way that document may be accessed and manipulated. This interface is platform- and language-neutral, giving companies the freedom to implement it in different ways. Each browser contains a DOM (or host) implementation which allows us to use the document objects to manipulate and change the (parsed) XHTML document (see diagram, below). The language we use to change the web page via these document objects is known as a DOM application – the application we use in this chapter is JavaScript.

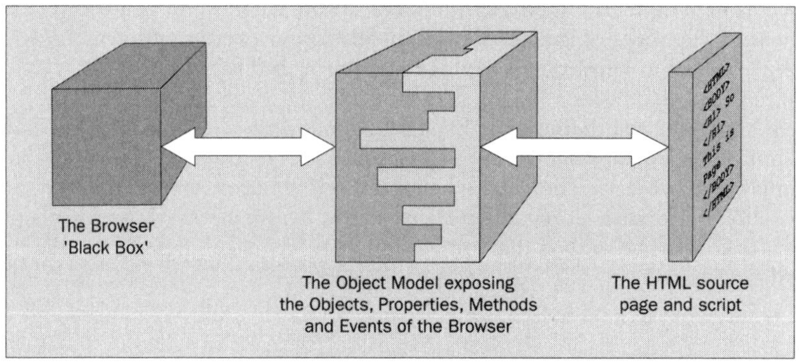

The W3C has specified several levels of a standard DOM for XML and HTML (as XHTML combines the two, the DOM for XHTML combines the features of the XML and HTML DOMs). Level 0 is the DOM built into Netscape 3.0 and IE 3.0. Level 1 adds the capability to access and change the structure and content of documents and is supported by IE 5.0, Netscape's experimental 'Gecko' browser and will be supported by the forthcoming Netscape 6.0. As I write this, Level 2 is a proposed standard; Level 2 adds additional features that we'll discuss in the next section.

The W3C has specified three levels of DOM:

- **Level 0** – The Level 0 DOM is the W3C's name for the DOM built into the 3.0 generation web browsers. This name was coined long after the 3.0 browsers were introduced. As Netscape and Microsoft heaped features haphazardly on browsers in the early days, the Level 0 DOM supports a limited and disorganized set of features, such as the ability to set and read content of form elements, submit forms, and write text into a document *while the document is loading.*
- **Level 1** – The Level 1 DOM is a true standard, created by a W3C working group and approved by the director of the W3C. The Level 1 DOM is a representation of the tree structure of an (X)HTML or XML document. With the Level 1 DOM it's possible to read and write to a document – if a web browser supports the Level 1 DOM, you can write scripts that can read and change a document even *after the document has loaded.* IE 5 supports the Level 1 DOM as does Netscape's experimental 'Gecko' browser which will become the foundation of Netscape 6. Although, formally, the Level 1 DOM doesn't contain the features of the Level 0 DOM, it's likely that any web browsers that support Level 1 DOM will also support the Level 0 DOM for backwards compatibility.
- **Level 2** – As I write this, the Level 2 DOM is a proposed recommendation, but it's likely that it will be approved with only minor modifications. Level 2 officially merges the features of the Level 0 DOM with the Level 1 DOM. Level 2 also adds, in addition to other features, the ability to read and alter style sheets attached to the document.

You can find the official specifications for the Level 1 and Level 2 DOM via the W3C's web site at `http://www.w3.org/DOM`. Since the Level 0 DOM is not a formal standard, there is no specification for it, however, Netscape's JavaScript manuals at `http://developer.iplanet.com/docs/manuals/javascript.html` come close.

The W3C DOM is not tied to any particular application. Although in this chapter we talk about using the W3C DOM inside a web browser, it's equally applicable for server-side web applications that generate XHTML documents. As XML is becoming a universal file format for everything from line drawings to financial reports, a wide range of applications are already using DOM for creating and understanding XML documents.

The W3C DOM defines a set of objects, properties and methods which are not specific to any programming language. Many languages contain the concepts of objects, properties and methods, so it's possible to create a version of the W3C DOM for many languages. This means that programmers can carry the concepts of the W3C DOM between different languages and that it's straightforward to make DOM-based applications work together even if they're written in different languages. A few programming languages that support the W3C DOM are Java, JavaScript, Perl, Visual Basic and Python.

Just as they gave us the Level 0 DOM, Microsoft and Netscape introduced their own incompatible additions to the DOM without consulting with anyone first:

- **Dynamic HTML (DHTML)** – Roughly, DHTML adds the ability to manipulate the style sheet *properties* of elements in a document (but not the style sheets themselves). This makes it possible to, say, turn a headline red when a visitor moves the mouse cursor over it, or make images or words fly across the screen. Although interesting special effects can be accomplished by DHTML, the difficulty of writing DHTML that works with both Netscape and IE has prevented web authors from using it widely. We won't cover DHTML in this chapter.

The Tree Structure of a Document

When the DOM models a document, the model reflects the underlying structure of that document. This is usually represented as a **tree structure**, although 'forest' or 'grove' may be a more appropriate term as the model may contain more than one tree. Take, for example, the following simple XHTML document which we have called, simply, `simpledoc.xml`:

```
<?xml version="1.0" encoding="UTF-8"?>
<!DOCTYPE html
     PUBLIC "-//W3C//DTD XHTML 1.0 Transitional//EN"
     "http://www.w3.org/TR/xhtml1/DTD/xhtml1-transitional.dtd">
<html xmlns="http://www.w3.org/1999/xhtml" xml:lang="en" lang="en">
<head>
<title>Simple XHTML doc</title>
</head>
<body>
<p>A simple paragraph.</p>
</body>
</html>
```

Because it has a `.xml` suffix, IE 5 treats this as an XML document, indenting the document to emphasize it's tree structure and giving different colors to processing instructions, elements, attributes and text content:

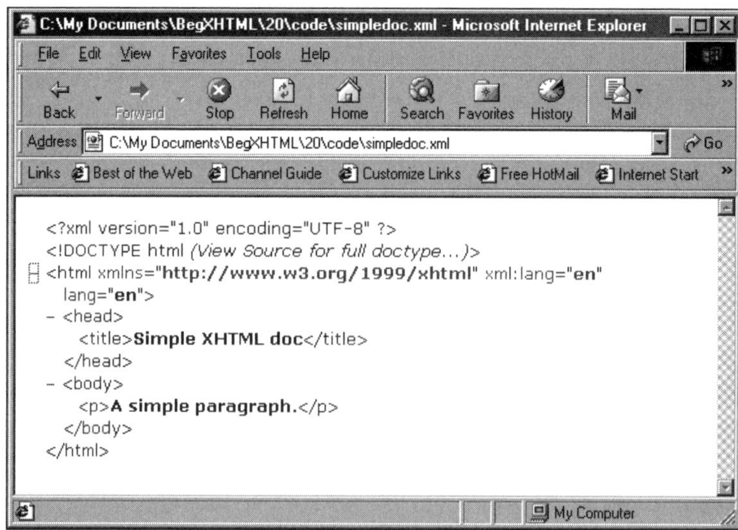

Note that, like Microsoft's Windows Explorer, we can expand and collapse parts of the document tree by clicking on the '+' and '-' signs on the side of the document, thereby emphasizing specific structures:

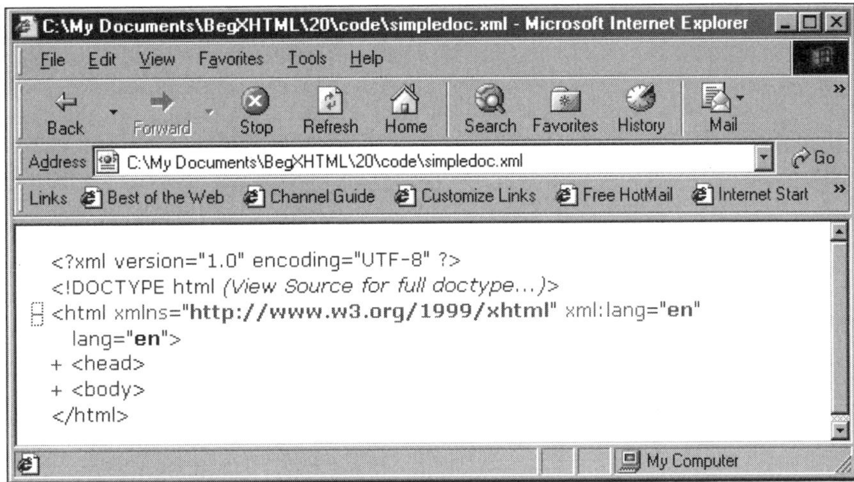

We can also depict the elements of this document in a tree as we would a family tree; indeed, this is the way that the DOM 'sees' the document:

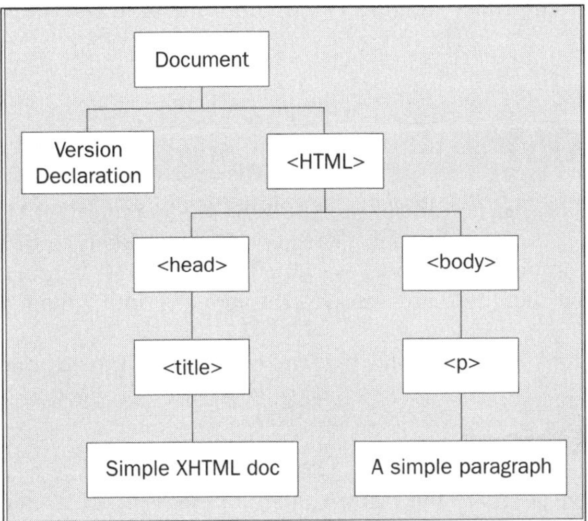

If we imagine these elements as people, we see that an `<html>` 'person' must have been 'born' before the `<body>` element could come into existence, and that a `<body>` 'person' must have been 'born' before the `<p>` element could come into existence, and so on. Thus, each element can be considered as either a child or a parent of another element. This concept of a **family relationship** existing amongst all the objects in a document is an important one – so important, in fact, that it became a fundamental part of the language. As you'll see in the examples throughout this chapter, we use terms like 'last child' in our scripts; it is important, then, to understand the tree terminology.

Tree Terminology

Trees are described using a mixture of terms from genealogical and botanical disciplines, and you'll find that you are already familiar with most of them:

- Each element or other object in the tree is a **node**, from botany, where a node is a place where a stem branches into two stems (e.g. `<html>` is a node).
- If element A is contained inside element B, element A is a **child** of element B. In the example above, the `<p>` element is a child of the `<body>` element; the `<body>` element is itself a child of the `<html>` element. Of course, if A is a child of B, then B is a **parent** of A.
- The document element is the **`root`** element because it has no parent.
- Element A is a **descendent** of element B if A is a child of B, or if A is a child of a child of B, and so forth. If Element A is a descendent of element B, then element B is an **ancestor** of Element A.
- Nodes that don't have children are known as **terminal** or **leaf** nodes (e.g. the text within the `<p>` element).
- Nodes that share the same parent are **sibling** nodes (e.g. `<head>` and `<body>`).

This terminology is particularly relevant when we 'walk the tree', as we'll do later in the chapter.

Now we are familiar with the concept of the DOM and some of its terminology, we can start to use it in our XHTML pages.

The Level 0 DOM

Although the Level 0 DOM has no official specification, it's an important DOM because it's supported by nearly all of the web browsers that your web-site visitors are likely to be using. In Chapter 17, we discussed a few of the methods and properties of the Level 0 DOM; here we will list most of its methods and properties (remember that these are accessed through a scripting language such as JavaScript).

First of all, we'll have a look at some things that can be done with the `document` object.

The Document Object

Using this object, we have access to the entire content of the XHTML document. Let's do something easy to begin with, such as changing colors.

Color Properties of the Document Object

The following properties of the `document` object are related to its color, and are similar to those found in CSS:

- `alinkColor` – The color of a link when it is being activated: in other words, while the user is actually clicking on it.

- `linkColor` – The color of unvisited links.
- `vlinkColor` – The color of visited links.
- `bgColor` – The background color of a document.
- `fgColor` – The foreground (default text) color of a document.

Let's look at how to use these properties.

Try It Out – Changing Colors with Script

1. Enter the following into your text editor and save it as `true_colors.htm`:

```
<?xml version="1.0" encoding="UTF-8"?>
<!DOCTYPE html
     PUBLIC "-//W3C//DTD XHTML 1.0 Transitional//EN"
     "http://www.w3.org/TR/xhtml1/DTD/xhtml1-transitional.dtd">
<html xmlns="http://www.w3.org/1999/xhtml" xml:lang="en" lang="en">
<head>
<title>JavaScript DOM Color Properties</title>
</head>
<body>
<h3>The color properties</h3>

<script>
<!--
  document.write("<br>")

  document.write("<h4>Background Color</h4>")
  document.write(document.bgColor)
  document.write("<br>")

  document.write("<h4>Old Foreground Color</h4>")
  document.write(document.fgColor)
  document.write("<br>")

  document.write("<h4>ActiveLink Color</h4>")
  document.write(document.alinkColor)
  document.write("<br>")

  document.write("<h4>UnvisitedLink Color</h4>")
  document.write(document.linkColor)
  document.write("<br>")

  document.write("<h4>Visited Link Color</h4>")
  document.write(document.vlinkColor)
  document.write("<br>")

  alert("Changing color")
  document.fgColor="red"
  document.write("<h4>New Foreground Color</h4>")
  document.write(document.fgColor)
  document.write("<br>")
// -->
</script>
```

```
</body>
</html>
```

2. Displaying this in IE 5 we see:

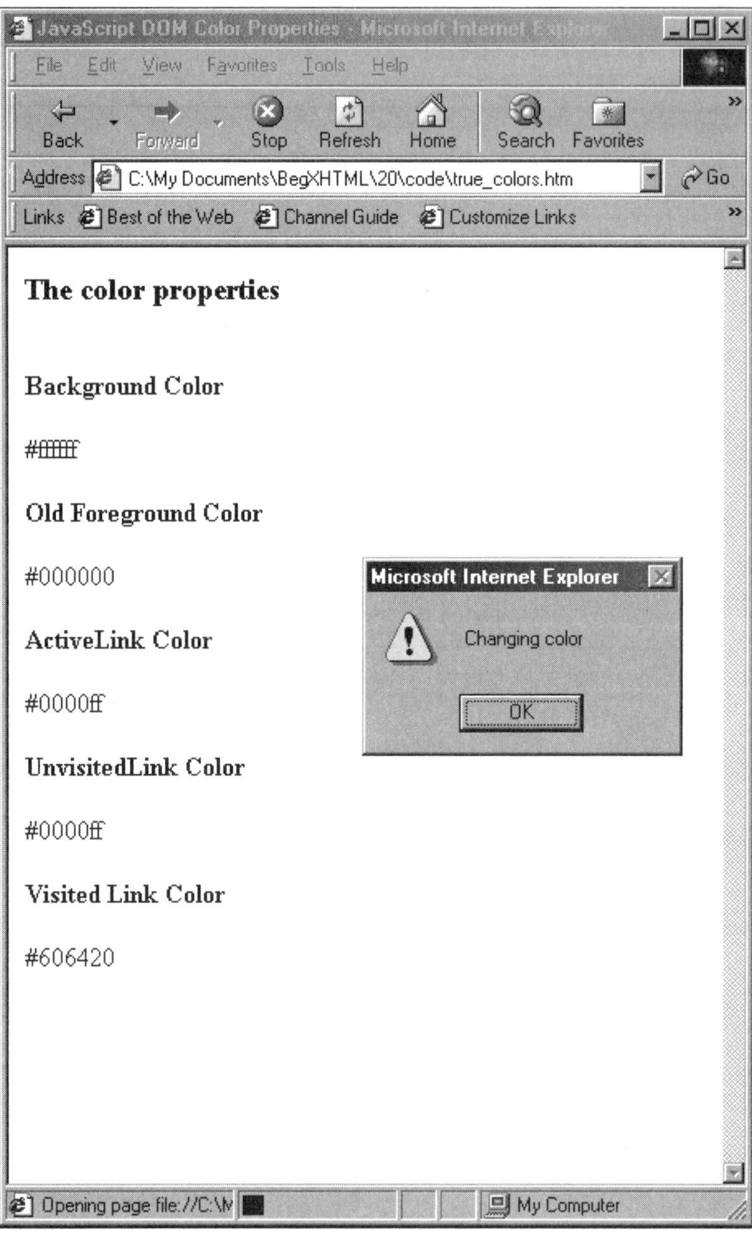

3. Clicking the OK button, we now see:

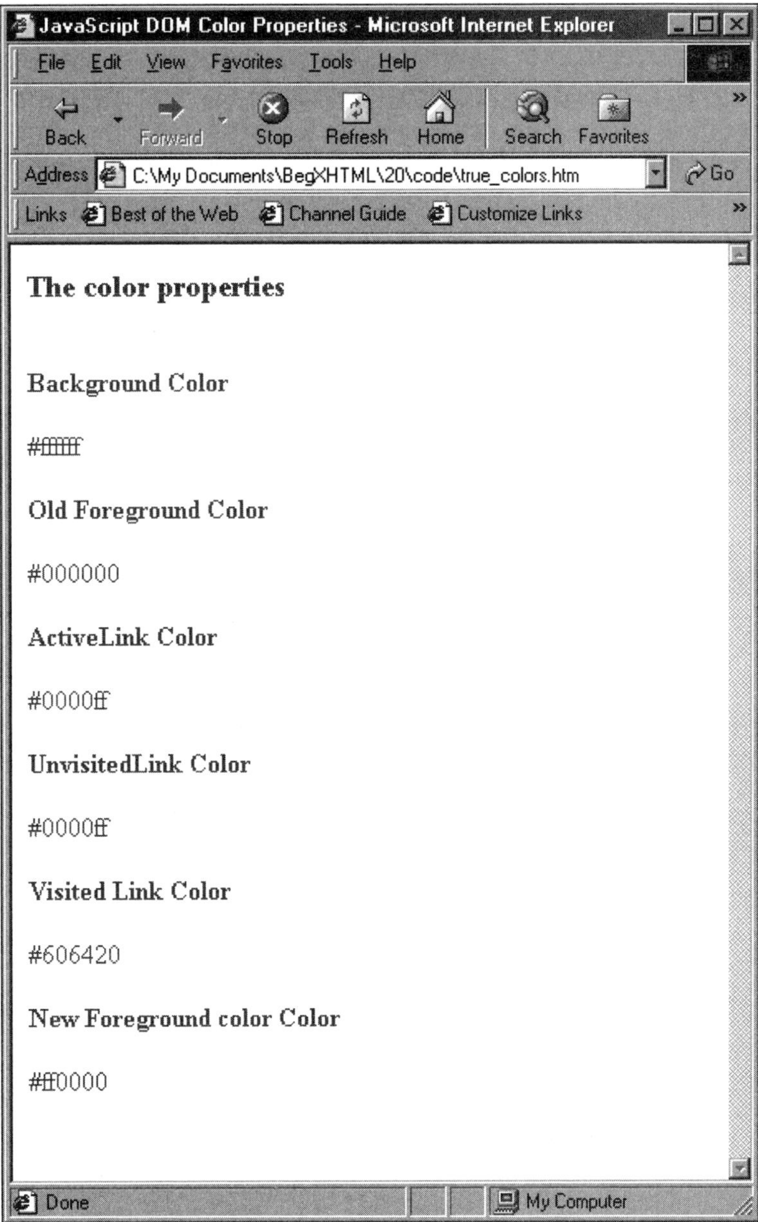

How It Works

As we've seen in previous chapters, the `write` method of the `document` object allows us to write text and XHTML into our page. Here we use it to write the current (or default, if they have not been changed) values of some of the color properties that the browser has stored within it. For example:

```
document.write(document.bgColor)
```

writes the current value of the document's background color into the XHTML page. The browser then displays #ffffff in place of `document.write(document.bgColor)`. A similar 'replacement' occurs with the other properties.

However, when the line:

```
alert("Changing color")
```

is encountered, a pop-up 'alert' box appears informing us that the color is about to change. This box itself does not change the color – it only displays whatever text we pass to it. However, when we click OK, the next line in our XHTML page:

```
document.fgColor="red"
```

is read and it is this line that explicitly changes the foreground color to red. Note that it changes the foreground color of the *entire* document, even though it occurs quite near the end of the file – this is the power of the DOM. The lines following it just write-out that this is the new color.

If you remove the 'alert' line, and now display the file in the browser, you will see that the text is black momentarily before being changed to red when the browser encounters the `fgColor` line.

Note that this may not work on current version of Netscape's browsers because Netscape allows script authors to change fewer properties of a document dynamically than IE 5 does. Of course, it is probably best to use style sheet properties to define colors; this example merely illustrates how the `document` object properties may be used.

General Properties of the Document Object

These properties are mainly concerned with what may be loosely termed 'administrative' information about the document:

- `lastModified` – A string that contains the date when the document was last modified.
- `referrer` – The URL of the page that contained the link that led to the page currently being viewed. It will be null if the user used a command line operation.
- `title` – All the text contained in the `<title>` element.
- `URL` – The Uniform Resource Locator of the current page.

These may be used in the same way as the color properties, but you may find them more useful. For example, if the following lines are included in a document:

```
<script type="text/javascript">
<!--
  document.write("<table><tr><td>Last Updated:</td><td>")
  document.write(document.lastModified)
  document.write("</td></tr></table>")
// -->
</script>
```

...then the date and time the document was last modified will always be automatically recorded in your document. This can be particularly useful when a web page has to be regularly updated with new information, and the reader of that page needs to know how recent that information is.

Document Collections

Although we have seen, and have been using, some of this terminology in the preceding chapters, let us remind ourselves of the concepts.

Each object is said to have a **collection**. As you can no doubt guess from the name, this is just a grouping (or collection) of all those objects currently in the document. So, for example, say we had a web page that contained ten frames, all specified by the `<frame>` element (and contained within a `<frameset>` element, obviously). The `<frame>` element is an object, and the `frames` collection for that document is just a list of the ten frames in that document. Obviously, these collections are specific to each document. For example, if you don't use frames in your web page, then your frames collection is empty; if you use three frames in a page, then that page has only three items in its frames collection, and so on.

An object's collection is stored as a **zero-based array**. An array is just a logical (or, perhaps, 'lazy') way of naming similar items. Rather than give each item an individual name, we give all of them the same name, but with a different number added to it; being zero-based means that this numbering starts at zero, rather than with one. Using our web page with ten frames as an example, the first frame would be called frame zero, the second called frame one, and so on, until the tenth frame was called frame nine. (As a humorous analogy, we may note that if this terminology was used in real life, parents would name their children child-zero, child-one, child-two, and so on).In our script code, these are written as **`frames[0]`**, **`frames[1]`** and so on until **`frames[9]`**.

The Level 0 DOM contains several collections that can be accessed via script. Collections reflect the design of existing (pre-Gecko) versions of Netscape, which represent documents in linear top-to-bottom and left-to-right order rather than a tree. For this reason, collections are arrays, and let us easily access certain kinds of elements on the page: for instance, if we wanted the fourth form on a page, we just specify `forms[3]`, rather than having to work our way through the tree (we'll see an example of this later), and so on.

The collections of the Level 0 DOM are

- `anchors[]` – An array of all the anchors (`<a>` elements with a `name attribute.`) in the document These are the places in a document that you can jump to by adding `#name` to a URL.
- `applets[]` – An array of applets embedded in the page.
- `embeds[]` – An array of all the plug-ins and ActiveX objects in a document.

- `forms[]` – An array of the forms (`<form>` elements) in a document.
- `images[]` – An array of all the `<image>` elements in the document.
- `links[]` – An array of all the hyperlinks (`<a>` elements with an `href` attribute) in the document.
- `frames[]` – In a `<frameset>` document, this is an array of frames in the document.

The collections are easy to use; their syntax is simply:

```
document.collection[number]
```

We do not have the space to cover all of these collections, so we shall only concentrate on one of them. However, one is enough to illustrate how they may be used. Now, let's have a little fun with some images.

The images[] Collection

Each `<image>` element can be accessed using the `images[]` collection. All of the following properties work in browsers that support JavaScript 1.1 (from Netscape 3.0 onwards, and IE 4.0 onwards). Members of the `images[]` collection are `image` objects. Unless otherwise stated, the following properties of the `image` are read-only in a Level 0 browser:

- `border` – The border width of the image in pixels.
- `complete` – A Boolean property that is `true` when the browser has finished loading or trying to load the image. Note that the image does not have to have been loaded *correctly* – it will be `true` even after an image fails to load.
- `height` – The height of the image in pixels.
- `hspace` – The horizontal space in pixels between the image and the surrounding content.
- `lowsrc` – A string containing the URL of an alternative image for use on low-resolution devices.
- `name` – The name given to the image.
- `onabort` – An event handler that is fired when the user aborts loading the image. You can write to this property to assign an event handler.
- `onerror` – An event handler that is fired when an error occurs in attempting to load the image. You can write to this property to assign an event handler.
- `onload` – An event handler that is fired when the user-agent loads an image successfully. You can write to this property to assign an event handler.
- `src` – The URL of the image. You can write to this property to replace the currently displayed image with a new image.
- `vspace` – The vertical space in pixels between the image and the surrounding content.
- `width` – The width of the image.

These properties are used with the following syntax:

```
document.collection[number].property
```

Note that they may be assigned to a variable, and that their values can be set explicitly, as we'll see shortly. The following example shows how some of these properties can be used to create a simple animation.

Try It Out – A Simple Animation

1. Enter the following into your text editor and save it as `winker.htm`:

```
<?xml version="1.0" encoding="UTF-8"?>
<!DOCTYPE html
     PUBLIC "-//W3C//DTD XHTML 1.0 Transitional//EN"
     "http://www.w3.org/TR/xhtml1/DTD/xhtml1-transitional.dtd">
<html xmlns="http://www.w3.org/1999/xhtml" xml:lang="en" lang="en">
<title>JavaScript DOM</title>

<p id="p1" >Click on the Image!</p>

<img alt="winker" src="face.gif" onMouseDown="wink()">

<script>
<!--
  function wink()
  {
    var srcstr = document.images[0].src;
    var fname = srcstr.substr(srcstr.lastIndexOf("/"))
    //alert(fname)
    if(fname == "/face.gif")
    {
      document.images[0].src = "face2.gif"
    }
    else
    {
      document.images[0].src="face.gif"
    }
  }
// -->
</script>
</html>
```

2. Now display this file in your browser (obviously, you need the images `face.gif` and `face2.gif` for this to work – these are available as part of the downloadable code from the Wrox web site at `http://www.wrox.com`). Clicking on the image makes it wink!

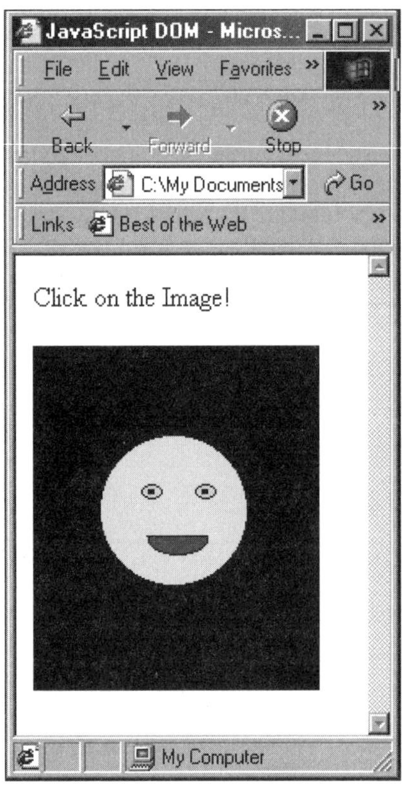

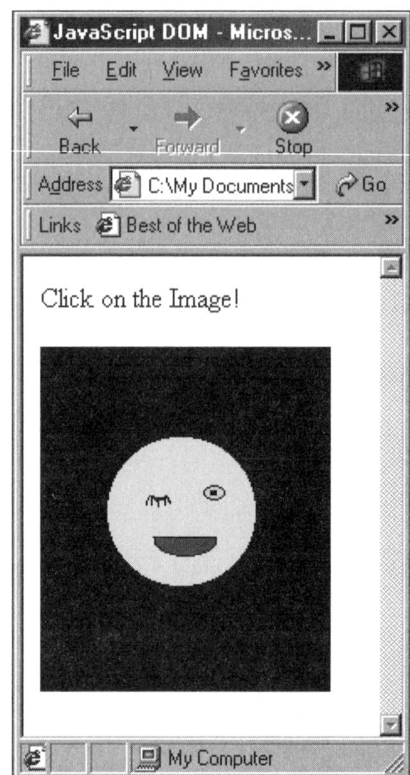

How It Works

We have put an event handler on the image (we have used `onmousedown` rather than `onclick` because `onclick` doesn't work well in Netscape):

```
<img alt="winker" src="face.gif" onMouseDown="wink()">
```

Thus, each time you click on the image, a call to the `wink()` function is made:

```
function wink()
{
```

First we get the source (or URL) string of the image and store it in the variable `srcstr`:

```
var srcstr = document.images[0].src;
```

This is the first image in the document, so we reference it as `images[0]`. Then we get the filename part of the image:

```
var fname = srcstr.substr(srcstr.lastIndexOf("/"))
```

The lastIndexOf() method returns the position within a string of the last match for the supplied substring; the substr() method returns a substring of the characters starting from the specified starting position. This line, then, simply searches through the URL stored in srcstr until it finds the last occurrence of the forward slash (/) character, then stores the text from the slash onwards in the variable fname. So, if srcstr contained the URL "http://www.mydomain.com/face.gif", then fname would contain "/face.gif".

Finally, we simply determine which file is currently being displayed in the browser by using an if loop. If face.gif is being displayed, we re-set the src attribute to face2.gif and it is displayed instead and, if face2.gif is being displayed, we re-set src to face.gif and it is displayed instead:

```
  if (fname == "/face.gif")
      {
        document.images[0].src="face2.gif"
      }
      else
      {
        document.images[0].src="face.gif"
      }
    }
```

By repeatedly clicking on the image, we alternate between the two images, revealing that the figure is a winker.

The Level 1 DOM

For our purposes the Level 1 DOM splits into two sections:

- The part of the DOM concerned with locating an Element or a text Node object in the document tree.
- The part of the DOM concerned with modifying the document tree.

Let's look at each of these.

Locating an Element

Elements are located in the DOM by one of three methods.

- Locating an element by id.
- 'Walking' the element tree.
- Making a collections of elements: it's possible to make a collection of elements of a given type, such as <a> elements, or a collection of the children of an element.

Locating an Element by 'id'

If you've specified an id for an element, locating an element by id is a simple and reliable method of finding that element. To use this method we use the following syntax:

```
document.getElementById("id of element")
```

and an object will be returned containing the element in question.

Consider the following example but note that, like the rest of the examples in this chapter, it works with IE 5 but (unfortunately) does not work with any current version of Netscape.

Try It Out – Using the getElementById() Method to Return a Document Node

1. Enter the following into your text editor and save as findById.htm:

```
<?xml version="1.0" encoding="UTF-8"?>
<!DOCTYPE html
     PUBLIC "-//W3C//DTD XHTML 1.0 Transitional//EN"
     "http://www.w3.org/TR/xhtml1/DTD/xhtml1-transitional.dtd">
<html xmlns="http://www.w3.org/1999/xhtml" xml:lang="en" lang="en">
<head>
  <title>The W3C DOM</title>
  <style>
  <!--
    p{font-size:14pt;}
  -->
  </style>
</head>
<body>

<!--Three p nodes-->
<p id="p1" name="p1">Hello W3C XHTML DOM!</p>
<p id="p2" name="p2">Go anywhere you want</p>
<p id="p3" name="p3">Walk the tree with me!</p>

<script id="sc1" name="sc1">
<!--
  alert(document.getElementById('p3').firstChild.data)
// -->
</script>

</body>
</html>
```

2. Now view this page in your browser, and you will see an alert box that reads, "Walk the tree with me!", the content of the third paragraph:

How It Works

The paragraphs are uniquely identified by `id` (and `name` for backwards compatibility):

```
<!--Three p nodes-->
<p id="p1" name="p1">Hello W3C XHTML DOM!</p>
<p id="p2" name="p2">Go anywhere you want</p>
<p id="p3" name="p3">Walk the tree with me!</p>
```

We use the `getElementById()` method to return the element object:

```
alert(document.getElementById('p3').firstChild.data)
```

Thus, we now have a 'hold' of the third paragraph. We then use the `firstChild` method (see below) to return the `textNode` of the element and its data content:

```
alert(document.getElementById('p3').firstChild.data)
```

It is the data content of the element object that is then displayed in the alert box. Let us summarize this in a list for clarity:

- `getElementById('p3')` – this locates the third paragraph
- `firstChild` – this is the first child of the third paragraph (formally, a text node)
- data – this is the text between the <p> tags

You may find it helpful here to review the 'family tree' diagram again, where we discussed the family relationships (such as child and so on) amongst objects in a document.

Walking the Tree

Using this technique, we can get to any part of the document tree that we want. We 'walk' the tree using the following methods (they are all methods of the `node` interface):

- `parentNode` – This returns the parent node (the containing element) of the target node. The only node without a parent is the root node, i.e. the `document` node.
- `firstChild` – This will return the target node's first child.
- `lastChild` – This will return the target node's last child.
- `previousSibling` – This will return the target node's previous sibling.
- `nextSibling` – This will return the target node's next sibling.
- `hasChildNodes` – This method returns `true` if the target node has children, and returns `false` otherwise.

To walk the tree we have to start somewhere. The DOM provides a way to get the root element of a document, the `documentElement` method:

```
var scratch = document.documentElement
```

This returns the XHTML element object, `<html>`.

Let's try to modify our last example to get at the second paragraph by walking the tree.

Try It Out – Walking the Element Tree

1. Modify the above example and save it as `treewalk.htm`:

```
<script id="sc1" name="sci">
<!--
  //get the root node
  var rootEl = document.documentElement
  var pNode2 = rootEl.lastChild.firstChild.nextSibling
  alert(pNode2.firstChild.data)
// -->
</script>
```

2. If you view this in IE 5, you will see that the alert box displays the first, not the second, paragraph. What went wrong? It turns out that we forgot that a comment is a node! To get at the second paragraph you can modify the script in one of two ways:

```
var pNode2 = rootEl.lastChild.firstChild.nextSibling.nextSibling
```

or:

```
var pNode2 =rootEl.lastChild.lastChild.previousSibling.previousSibling
```

How It Works

First of all, we use the `documentElement` method to return the root element and store it in a variable that we have called `rootEl`:

```
    //get the root node
    var rootEl = document.documentElement
```

Next, we tried to 'walk' to the second paragraph, and store it in the variable `pNode2`. In fact, as we saw, this line actually returns the *first* paragraph because a comment is counted as a node:

```
    var pNode2 = rootEl.lastChild.firstChild.nextSibling
```

Again, we use `data` to access the actual text, and display it using an alert box:

```
    alert(pNode2.firstChild.data)
```

> *Although comment nodes take up space correctly in IE 5, you'll encounter bugs if you try to access their properties. If you query a comment node in IE 5, it will tell us that a comment is an element node with the name of '!' rather than treat it as a distinct comment node.*

So here we get a reference to the *correct* node:

```
    var pNode2 = rootEl.lastChild.firstChild.nextSibling.nextSibling
```

Here's how it works (the other version works similarly):

- The `rootEl` is of course `<html>`
- The `lastChild` of `<html>` is `<body>` (the first child is `<head>`)
- the `firstChild` of `<body>` in this document is a comment
- We use two `nextSiblings` to 'walk' to the second paragraph

To illustrate these relationships, enter this code into your text editor and save as `treewalk_showpart.htm` (or, even better, use the more complete version `treewalk_show.htm` downloadable from the Wrox web site):

```
  <?xml version="1.0" encoding="UTF-8"?>
  <!DOCTYPE html
       PUBLIC "-//W3C//DTD XHTML 1.0 Transitional//EN"
       "http://www.w3.org/TR/xhtml1/DTD/xhtml1-transitional.dtd">
  <html xmlns="http://www.w3.org/1999/xhtml" xml:lang="en" lang="en">
  <head>
```

```
    <title>The W3C DOM</title>
    <style>
    <!--
      p{font-size:14pt;}
    -->
    </style>
  </head>
  <body>

  <!--Three p nodes-->

  <p id="p1" name="p1">First paragraph</p>

  <p id="p2" name="p2">Second paragraph</p>

  <p id="p3" name="p3">Third paragraph</p>

  <script id="sc1" name="sci">
  <!--
    document.write("<h3>The BODY Side</h3>")

    document.write("<p><em>
    document.documentElement.lastChild
    </em> is "
    + document.documentElement.lastChild.nodeName
    + "</p>") //BODY

    document.write("<p><em>
    document.documentElement.lastChild.firstChild
    </em> is "
    + document.documentElement.lastChild.firstChild.nodeName
    + "</p>") //COMMENT

    document.write("<p><em>
    document.documentElement.lastChild.firstChild.nextSibling
    </em> is "
    + document.documentElement.lastChild.firstChild.nextSibling.nodeName
    + "</p>") //P (FIRST PARAGRAPH)

    document.write("<p><em>
    document.documentElement.lastChild.firstChild.nextSibling.firstChild
    </em> is "
    + document.documentElement.lastChild.firstChild.nextSibling.firstChild.nodeName
    + "</p>") //#text (FIRST PARAGRAPH)

    document.write("<p><em>
    document.documentElement.lastChild.firstChild.nextSibling.firstChild.data
    </em> is "
    + document.documentElement.lastChild.firstChild.nextSibling.firstChild.data
    + "</p>") //First Paragraph
  // -->
  </script>
  </body>
  </html>
```

Note that the formatting is a little strange because of the width of the book page, and also because of the length of some of the statements. We have tried here to place each logical part of each unit on a separate line, and each unit as a separate block of code (with a blank line before and after it). Note that the material between double quotes (`" . . . "`) is just the text that is displayed on the browser; it is the code on line 4 of each block (beginning with `+ document...`) that retrieves the name/value of the node.

Displaying this in IE 5.0, we see the following:

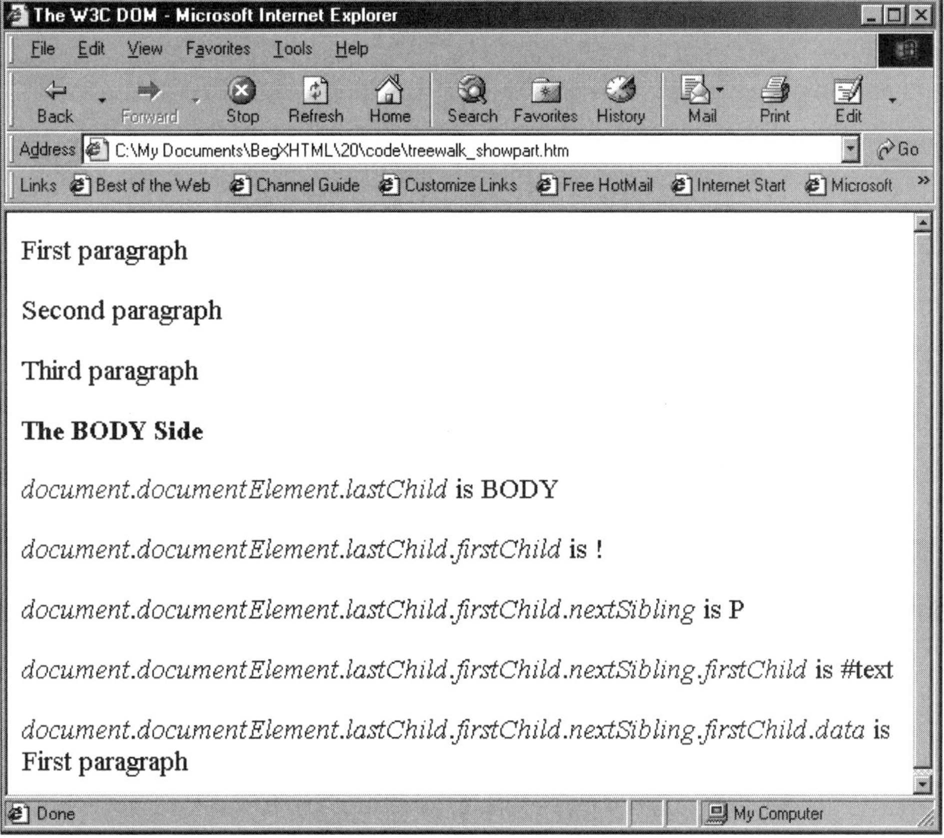

This may also be represented in a diagram (only some of the relationships are shown due to lack of space):

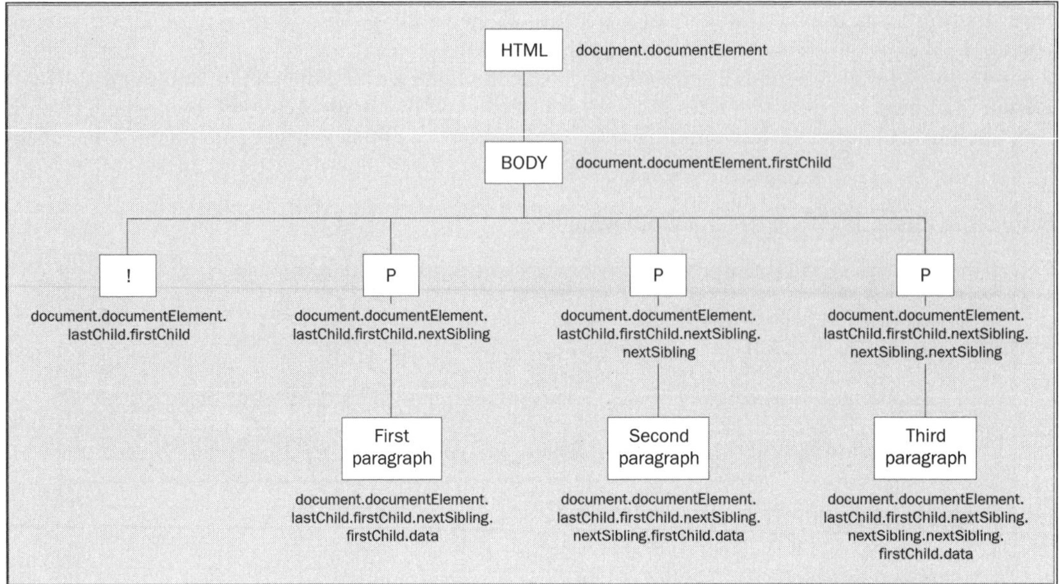

By now, you should fully understand the concept of these 'family relationships' (try naming the individual components of the `<head>` section) and of how utterly confusing it can very quickly become! This method is not to be recommended: it would be very awkward indeed to try and walk the tree as shown above if you wanted to access, say, the 52nd child of an element! Nor do we recommend you try it! In such a case, it is much simpler to make a collection of, for example, all the `<p>` elements in the document.

Making a Collection of Elements by Name

To make a collection or an array of elements of the same name we use the DOM `getElementsByTagName()` method. We use it as follows:

```
document.getElementsByTagName("tag name")
```

Once we have a list of elements we can access the list using the `item()` method:

```
document.getElementsByTagName(tag name).item(integer)
```

Unlike the DOM Level 0 collection, which can be accessed with a concise bracket `[]` syntax, we use the `item()` method to access elements of a DOM Level 1 collection. Let's look at this now.

Try It Out – Making a Collection of Named Elements

1. Modify the previous example and save as `namedElements.htm`:

```
<script id="sc1">
<!--
//make a collection of 'p' elements
```

```
    var pList = document.getElementsByTagName("p")
    var pNode2 = pList.item(1)
    alert(pNode2.firstChild.data)
  // -->
  </script>
```

2. Running it in your browser, we see the same as before: an alert box with the text Go anywhere you want!

How It Works

In the first line of code we make a `nodeList` of all the `<p>` elements!

```
    var pList = document.getElementsByTagName("p")
```

In the second line we access this list by using the `item()` method. As with Level 0 collections, the first element in a Level 1 collection is numbered 0, thus:

```
    var pNode2 = pList.item(1)
```

accesses the second paragraph. We then display it using our now-familiar alert box.

We can also make a list of a particular node's children.

Making a Collection of Child Elements

Sometimes it is convenient to make a list of an element's children. We do this with the `childNodes` method. The general syntax is:

```
nodelist=element.childNodes
```

In the following example, we make a list of all the children of the `<body>` element.

Try It Out – Making a Collection of Child Elements

1. Again, modify the previous example and save as `namedElements2.htm`:

```
  <script id="sc1" name="sc1">
  <!--
    //make a collection of 'p' elements
    var bodyChildList = document.documentElement.lastChild.childNodes
    var pNode2 = bodyChildList.item(2)
    alert(pNode2.firstChild.data)
  // -->
  </script>
```

2. Again, we see the same alert box when this is run in the browser.

How It Works

First we pick out the <body> element (`document.documentElement.lastChild`), and then use the `childNodes` method to make a list of its children:

```
var bodyChildList = document.documentElement.lastChild.childNodes
```

This list is accessed through the `item()` method. Note that the first node (`item(0)`)on this list is a comment, so the paragraph we want is the third node:

```
var pNode2 = bodyChildList.item(2)
```

Again, we then use an alert box to display the text in the `textNode`.

Note that if we want to find the length of a DOM Level 1 collection, we use the `length` method:

```
alert(pNode2.firstChild.length)
```

This is useful if we want to loop through a collection of elements looking for a particular item.

Getting Text

We can get text from a `textNode` in two ways:

- Use the `data` method
- Use the `nodeValue` method

In our examples:

```
alert(pNode2.firstChild.data)
```

and:

```
alert(pNode2.firstChild.nodeValue)
```

would return the same thing.

Factory Methods

We can create nodes with factory methods. Here we use factory methods to create element and text nodes, and then insert them into the document hierarchy. We will also look at how to edit text nodes.

Creating Elements and Text Nodes

An element is created using the following syntax:

```
document.createElement(tag name)
```

A text node is created using the following syntax:

```
document.createTextNode(node content)
```

A node can be duplicated using the following syntax:

```
[node name].cloneNode()
```

When a node is first created, it is an orphan with no place in the document tree. A node can be placed into the document tree with either of two methods:

- `appendChild()` – `A.appendChild(B)` makes node `B` become the last child of node `A`. After this operation, `A.lastChild` is equal to `B`.
- `insertBefore()` – `A.insertBefore(B)` inserts the node `B` immediately after element `A`. After this operation, `A.nextSibling` is equal to `B`. It also takes an optional second parameter: `A.insertBefore(B, C)`. This assumes object `A` has child elements of which `C` is one, and that `B` is to be inserted before child node `C`.

In the following example, we use these methods to add a heading to a simple document.

Try It Out – Creating a Heading and Content

1. Type the following document into your text editor and save as `adding.htm`:

```
<?xml version="1.0" encoding="UTF-8"?>
<!DOCTYPE html
     PUBLIC "-//W3C//DTD XHTML 1.0 Transitional//EN"
     "http://www.w3.org/TR/xhtml1/DTD/xhtml1-transitional.dtd">
<html xmlns="http://www.w3.org/1999/xhtml" xml:lang="en" lang="en">
<head>
  <title>W3C DOM Adding an element</title>
  <script>
  <!--
  function addhead()
  {
    //create new nodes
    var newhead = document.createElement("h3")
    var newtn = document.createTextNode("This is the new heading")
    //make objects of existing nodes
    var bodyEl = document.getElementById("body")
    var lastpara = document.getElementById("plast")
    //
    bodyEl.insertBefore(newhead, lastpara)
    newhead.appendChild(newtn)
```

```
    }
    // -->
    </script>
  </head>

  <body id="body" name="body">
    <p id="p1" name="p1">Hello W3C DOM Factory!</p>
    <form>
      <input type="button" value="Get Document Length"
        onclick="alert(document.all.length)" />
      <br /><br />
      <input type="button" value="add heading" onclick="addhead()" />
    </form>
    <p id="plast">This is the Last paragraph</p>
  </body>

  </html>
```

2. When we run this in IE5 we see the following after we have clicked on the add heading button a few times:

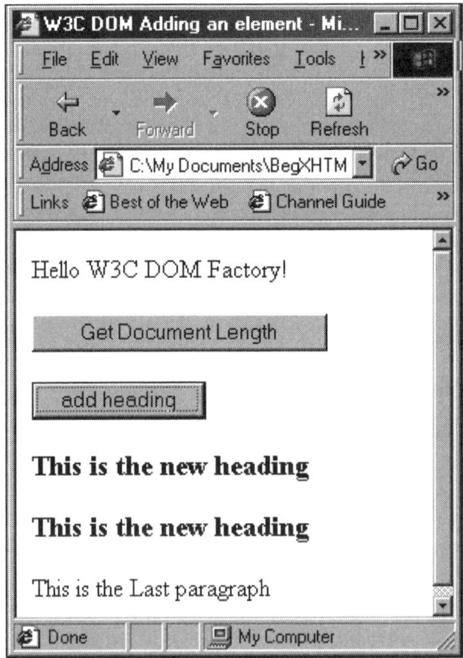

How It Works

First we have a simple form with two buttons:

```
    <form>
      <input type="button" value="Get Document Length"
```

```
    onclick="alert(document.all.length)" />
  <br /><br />
  <input type="button" value="add heading" onclick="addhead()" />
</form>
```

When you click on the first button, you'll see an alert box which lists the number of elements in the document. Unfortunately, `document.all` is a feature of IE 4 and 5 only, so this won't work in other Level 1 DOM browsers.

The second button calls a function `addhead()`:

```
function addhead()
{
```

In this, we create two nodes, an `<h3>` element node and a text node:

```
  //create new nodes
  var newhead = document.createElement("h3")
  var newtn = document.createTextNode("This is the new heading")
```

At this time they are both orphans. They need to be put into the element tree. We isolate the body and the last paragraphs as objects:

```
  //make objects of existing nodes
  var bodyEl = document.getElementById("body")
  var lastpara = document.getElementById("plast")
```

And then we insert the heading node before the last paragraph:

```
bodyEl.insertBefore(newhead, lastpara)
```

And append the text node to it as a child:

```
  newhead.appendChild(newtn)
}
```

Editing Text Nodes

The simplest way to edit text is to rewrite it using the `data` read/write property. To demonstrate this, add the following to the end of the `addhead()` function in the last example:

```
    newhead.appendChild(newtn)
    alert("Changing Data")
    newtn.data="Wow"
  }
</script>
```

Now when you run it you will get an alert that displays the old data; but as soon as you click OK on the alert box, the new data appears. That is, the old `newtn` ("This is the new heading") gets deleted and replaced with the word "Wow" by use of the `newtn.data` property.

The W3C DOM also has a number of methods that allow us to add, insert, replace, and extract substrings of data, but we will not demonstrate them here as they are not supported by IE 5 for (X)HTML documents, although they are supported for XML documents (documents with a `.xml` *suffix or* `text/xml` *MIME type).*

Creating Attributes and Values

Although attributes can be created using the `createAttribute()` method of the document, the best way to create them is to use the `setAttribute()` method of the `element` object. This allows us to both create an attribute and set its value at the same time.

The general syntax for this is:

```
var scratch=element name.setAttribute(attribute name, attribute value)
```

In the following example we create an image element and set its attributes.

Try It Out – Creating an <image> Element and its Attributes

1. Type up the following and save as `imageMaker.htm`:

```
<?xml version="1.0" encoding="UTF-8"?>
<!DOCTYPE html
     PUBLIC "-//W3C//DTD XHTML 1.0 Transitional//EN"
     "http://www.w3.org/TR/xhtml1/DTD/xhtml1-transitional.dtd">
<html xmlns="http://www.w3.org/1999/xhtml" xml:lang="en" lang="en">
<head>
<title>IE5 HTML DOM</title>
<script>
<!--
  function addimage()
  {
    var scratch
    //create new nodes
    var newimage = document.createElement("img")
    //create attributes for new node
    scratch = newimage.setAttribute("alt", "A happy face")
    scratch = newimage.setAttribute("src", "face.gif")
    //make objects of existing nodes
    var bodyEl = document.getElementById("body")
    var lastpara = document.getElementById("plast")
    //
    scratch = bodyEl.insertBefore(newimage, lastpara)
  }

  function removeimage()
  {
```

```
    var bodyEl = document.getElementById("body")
    var imageList = document.getElementsByTagName("img")
    if(imageList.length != 0)
    {
      var scratch = bodyEl.removeChild(imageList.item(0))
    }
  }
// -->
</script>
</head>
<body id="body" name="body">
<p id="p1" name="p1">Hello W3C HTML DOM factory!</p>
<form>
  <input type="button" value="Get Document Length"
   onclick="alert(document.all.length)" />
  <br /><br />
  <input type="button" value="add image" onclick="addimage()" />
   
  <input type="button" value="remove image" onclick="removeimage()" />
</form>
<p id="plast" name="plast">This is the Last paragraph</p>
</body>
</html>
```

2. If we view this in IE and click the 'add image' button several times, we see:

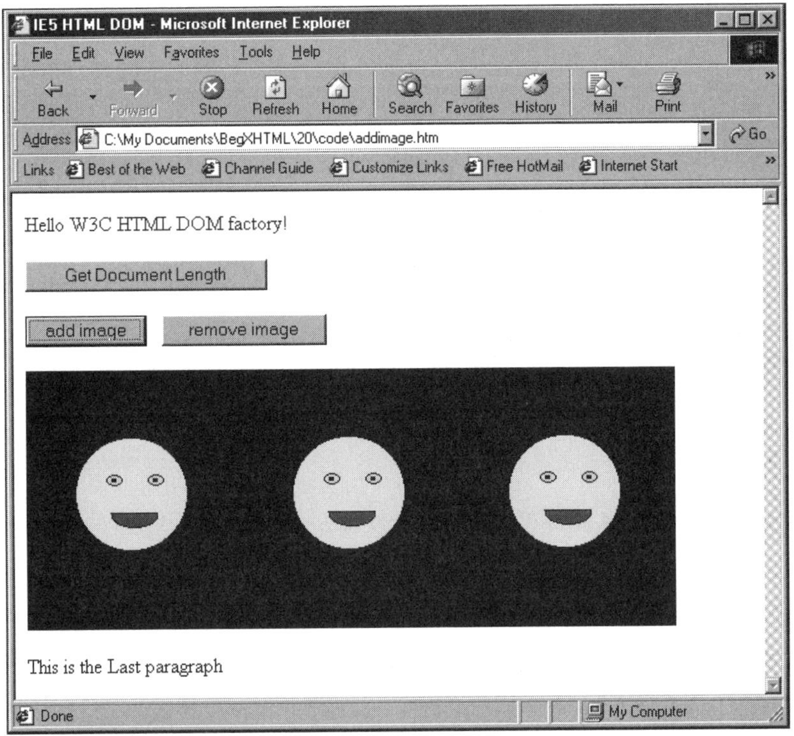

How It Works

Again we have a simple form that that calls functions when we click on buttons:

```
<form>
  <input type="button" value="Get Document Length"
   onclick="alert(document.all.length)" />
  <br /><br />
  <input type="button" value="add image" onclick="addimage()" />
   
  <input type="button" value="remove image" onclick="removeimage()" />
</form>
```

The first of these buttons we have seen before; the second and third add and remove copies of the image from the page.

Let's look at the `addImage()` function:

```
function addimage()
  {
    var scratch
```

First we create a new image element:

```
    //create new nodes
    var newimage = document.createElement("img")
```

Then we use `setAttribute()` to add a `src` and an `alt` attribute-value pair:

```
    //create attributes for new node
    scratch = newimage.setAttribute("alt", "A happy face")
    scratch = newimage.setAttribute("src", "face.gif")
```

We then insert the element using the methods we have already discussed:

```
    //make objects of existing nodes
    var bodyEl = document.getElementById("body")
    var lastpara = document.getElementById("plast")
    //
    scratch = bodyEl.insertBefore(newimage, lastpara)
  }
```

The `removeimage()` method is similar, except that it uses `removeChild()` to delete the image from the list.

This concludes our introduction to factory methods.

Summary

In this chapter we introduced document object models (DOM.) We reviewed the three levels of DOM specified by the World Wide Web Consortium (W3C). Although the Level 0 DOM, (the set of features supported by the 3.0 browsers) is limited in power, the Level 1 DOM (supported by IE 5.0 and the future Netscape 6.0) lets JavaScript access and change the tree structure of a document, allowing a script to change a web page as it's being viewed. Level 2 formally combines the features of the Level 1 and Level 0 DOM and adds additional features. In this chapter, we introduced the concepts required to understand the tree-structure of the Level 1 DOM, summarized the capabilities of the Level 0 DOM and presented examples of the Level 0 and Level 1 DOMs in action.

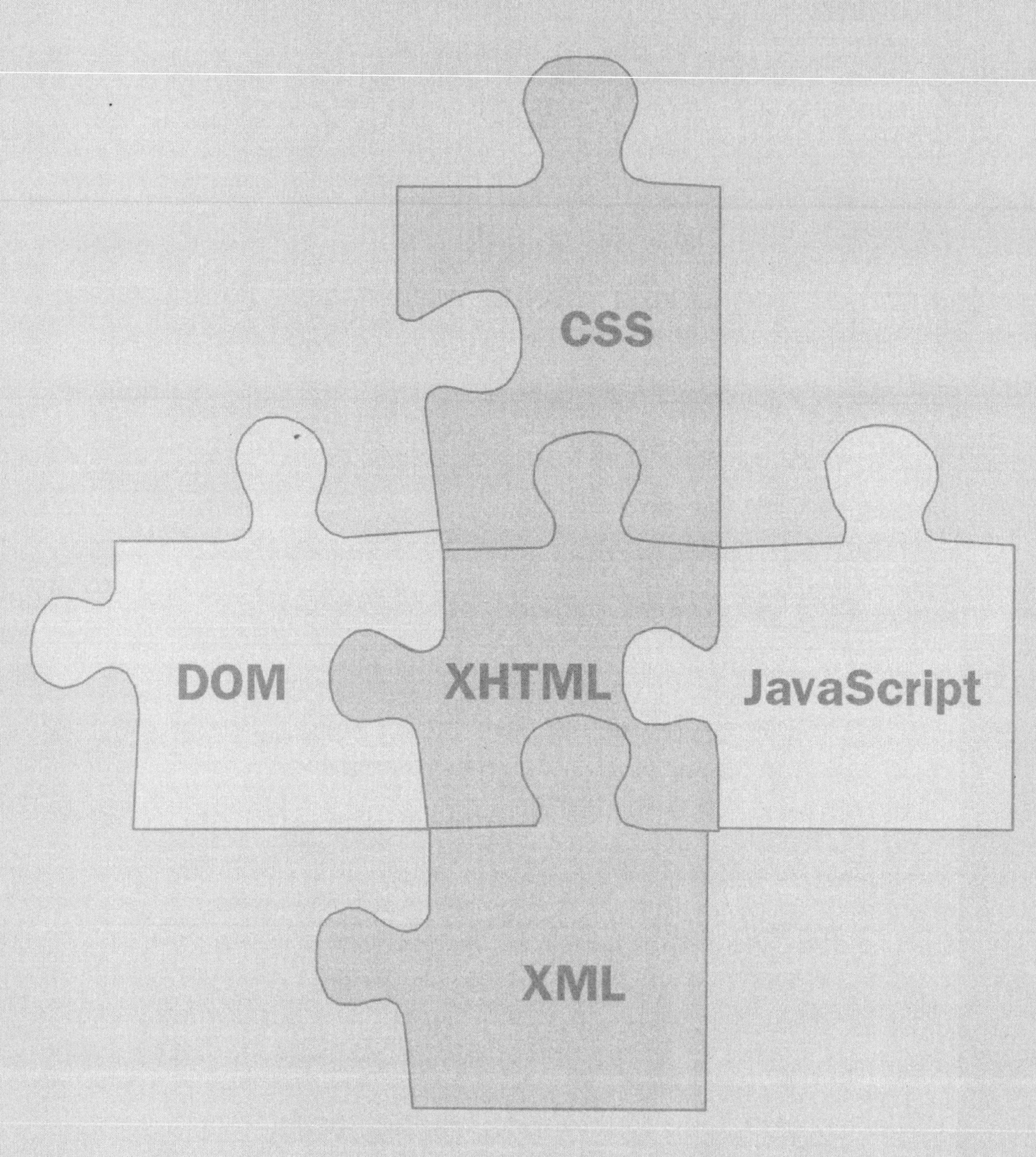
CSS
DOM
XHTML
JavaScript
XML

Multiple-Frame JavaScript Applications

In the simplest scenario, web transactions are **stateless**. The browser requests a document from the server and the server sends it. The web browser and web server remember *nothing* between requests. Although stateless transactions seem limiting, there are advantages to stateless transactions: it's easier to write faster and bug-free servers that are stateless (no way the server can get into a bad state) and, if you're running a really big site, it's easier to distribute a stateless workload across multiple machines than a stateful workload (no need to share state information between the servers.) Systems based on stateless transactions can be more reliable, since there is no possibility of the client and server developing a disagreement as to what state they're in.

Programmers tend to complain about any limitation, so a number of ways have been invented to add state to the web. For instance, some web servers (and application servers) such as Microsoft IIS (and some implementations of Java Server Pages) run as a single process. A web application running on such a server can create objects on the server that survive beyond a single request. This style of programming is close to how people write command-line and GUI programs, however, this approach is error-prone and scales poorly to large hit volumes. A more reliable approach is to store information in a relational database on the server, however, the technology that makes relational databases reliable also makes them slow.

Another approach to persistence is to put the burden on the web browser; this is the strategy we discuss in this chapter. It's possible to store information in hidden form fields (see Chapter 15), cookies (see Chapter 17) and, as we discuss in this chapter, other frames. The disadvantage of storing information in hidden form fields and cookies is that any persistent information has to be passed back and forth between the client and server, like a ball, each time the two communicate. If the amount of information is large, this process can slow down your application. An application that stores persistent information in other frames, though, can keep information in the browser and transmit it back to the server only when it's actually needed.

We will call this collection of pages a **Frame Application**. In a frame application, JavaScript allows pages to share and store information without going back to the server.

The following diagram illustrates this.

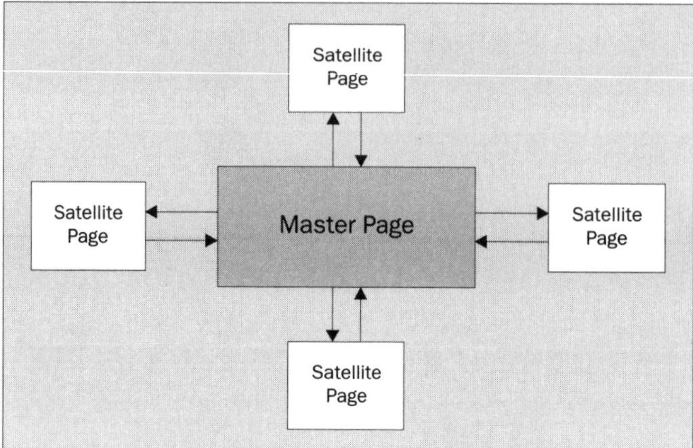

The usual design is to have a master page which holds all the data, user input and references to other pages and applications, and have scripts in the satellite pages that access and control the master page.

The examples we employ in this chapter have been designed to illustrate basic principles. For reasons of clarity they are quite simple and indeed. However if you work your way through them you will have the skills to build more complex client side applications.

Here is what we will be covering in this chapter:

- How to reference various frames in a frameset.
- Passing information between different frames.
- Storing information entered in one frame in a second frame.
- Using hidden input values as data stores.
- Using script to open fresh pages.
- Using script to write to other pages.

Linking Multiple Frames

Pages can refer to each other and access each other's content from JavaScript via Document Object Models (DOMs.) As I write this, the only production browser that supports DOM Level 1 (which we looked at last chapter) is IE5. Netscape's experimental Gecko browser also supports DOM Level 1; since Gecko will be the basis of the forthcoming Netscape 5.0, we expect to see this capability in Netscape. With DOM Level 1, it would be possible for one page to actually read the contents of another page, or, change the contents of another page at any time.

Because, at this time, a large fraction of web users are running browsers that don't support DOM Level 1, we're only going to use DOM Level 0 in this chapter, the set of methods and properties supported by the 3.0 generation browsers.

The 'frames' Collection

We saw in Chapter 7 that a frameset is an HTML page that defines a group of frames, in which we load other pages. We're going to look now at how one frame can access the properties of its companion frames. We'll have a frameset page, which will contain two frames into which we load two other pages.

In JavaScript the containing page is referenced as `top`; starting from `top`, it's possible to access the individual frames and the pages they contain through the `frames[]` collection. Here's an example.

Try It Out – Referencing Frames Using Script

1. In this example, we'll use JavaScript to return the titles of the pages being viewed in each frame. The title of a page can be found in the `document.title` property. First, type up `frameset1.htm`:

```
<?xml version="1.0" encoding="UTF-8"?>
<!DOCTYPE html
     PUBLIC "-//W3C//DTD XHTML 1.0 Frameset//EN"
     "http://www.w3.org/TR/xhtml1/DTD/xhtml1-frameset.dtd">
<html xmlns="http://www.w3.org/1999/xhtml" xml:lang="en" lang="en">
<head>
  <title>Frame Applications Frame Page</title>
</head>
<frameset cols="*,*">
  <frame src="frame_master.htm" id="master" name="master" />
  <frame src="frame1.htm" id="sat1" name="sat1" />
</frameset>
</html>
```

2. Type up the following and save it as `frame_master.htm`:

```
<?xml version="1.0" encoding="UTF-8"?>
<!DOCTYPE html
     PUBLIC "-//W3C//DTD XHTML 1.0 Transitional//EN"
     "http://www.w3.org/TR/xhtml1/DTD/xhtml1-transitional.dtd">
<html xmlns="http://www.w3.org/1999/xhtml" xml:lang="en" lang="en">
<head>
  <title>Frame Applications Master</title>
</head>
<body>
   <p>Frame_master.htm</p>
   <script>
   <!--
     document.write(top.document.title + "<br />");
     document.write(top.frames[0].document.title + "<br />");
     document.write(top.frames[1].document.title + "<br />");
   // -->
   </script>
</body>
</html>
```

3. Here is `frame1.htm`:

```
<?xml version="1.0" encoding="UTF-8"?>
<!DOCTYPE html
     PUBLIC "-//W3C//DTD XHTML 1.0 Transitional//EN"
     "http://www.w3.org/TR/xhtml1/DTD/xhtml1-transitional.dtd">
<html xmlns="http://www.w3.org/1999/xhtml" xml:lang="en" lang="en">
<head>
  <title>Frame Applications 1</title>
</head>
<body>
  <p>Frame1.htm</p>
</body>
</html>
```

4. Save all these pages in the same folder, and run `frameset1.htm`.

5. Here is what you will see:

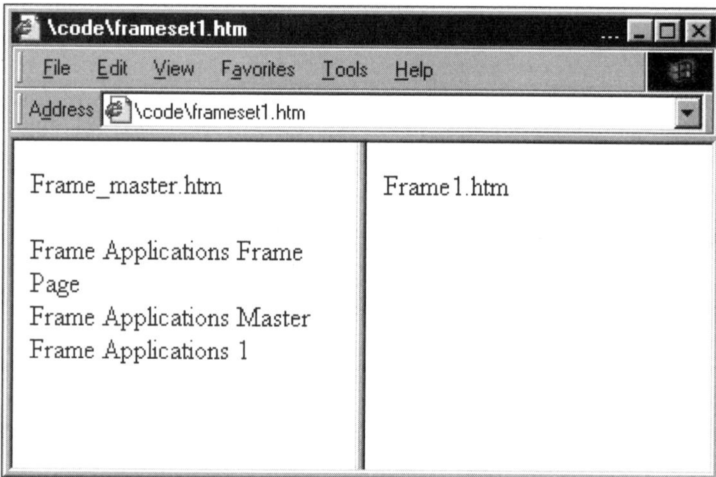

How It Works

The following code, from `frameset1.htm`, loads two other pages, `frame_master.htm` and `frame1.htm` into two frames:

```
<frameset cols="*,*">
  <frame src="frame_master.htm" id="master" name="master" />
  <frame src="frame1.htm" id="sat1" name="sat1"/>
</frameset>
```

The script in this example is in `frame_master.htm`, and writes out the titles of the three pages. First, this:

```
document.write(top.document.title + "<br />")
```

...writes the title of `frameset1.htm`, Frame Applications Frame Page. Then, this:

```
document.write(top.frames[0].document.title + "<br />")
```

...writes the `title` of the first page in the `frames[]` collection (remember, collections start counting at 0), namely Frame Applications Master. Finally, this:

```
document.write(top.frames[1].document.title + "<br />")
```

...writes the title of the second frame, which is Frame Applications 1.

We could also use a loop to write out the titles of the framed pages.

```
for(var i=0;i<=frames.length;i++) {
    document.write(top.frames[i].document.title + "<br />");
}
```

Page References

Recall from Chapter 17 that there are two objects associated with each page a user is viewing: a `window` object and a `document` object. The `window` object represents the space that the page takes up on the screen. If the page is frameless, or if the page is the outermost frameset, the `window` is an actual GUI window on your screen. If the page is being viewed in a frame, the `window` object is actually a frame. Here are some JavaScript keywords, properties and collections you can use to reference the different `window` objects inside a frameset.

- `self`: unless you're in an event handler or creating your own objects, `self` is the `window` object in which your script is running.
- `top`: `top` always corresponds to the browser window. `top` is the outermost frameset.
- `parent`: if your script is running inside a frame, `parent` is a reference to the frameset `window` which contains `self`. In the examples above, where there are no frames nested inside frames (you're asking for trouble if you try something that complex,) `parent` would be equivalent to `top`.

A frameset window has a `frames[]` collection which allows us to access frames by index. As JavaScript starts counting at zero, the first frame is `frames[0]`, the second is `frames[1]` and so forth. In the example above, `top` is a frameset, so we reference the two frames as `top.frames[0]` and `top.frames[1]`.

Passing Information Between Frames

To create a multi-frame application, we need to be able to move information from one frame to another.

- Data stored on one page must be available to all the others.
- Information entered by a user on one page must be available to the other pages.
- This information must persist through out the life of the frameset.
- There must be a mechanism for passing this information from one page to another.

Let's look at how to fulfill this last requirement.

Try It Out – Passing Information Between Pages

1. Modify `frame_master.htm` as follows, and save it as `frame_master2.htm`:

```
<?xml version="1.0" encoding="UTF-8"?>
<!DOCTYPE html
     PUBLIC "-//W3C//DTD XHTML 1.0 Transitional//EN"
     "http://www.w3.org/TR/xhtml1/DTD/xhtml1-transitional.dtd">
<html xmlns="http://www.w3.org/1999/xhtml" xml:lang="en" lang="en">

<head>
    <title>Frame Applications Master 2</title>
</head>
<body>
  <p>Frame_master2.htm</p>

   <form name="frm1" id="frm2">
    <input type="text" id="master2_text" name="master2_text" />
    <input type="button" value="send text" id="button" name="button"
     onclick="sendtext(document.frm1.master2_text.value)" />
   </form>

<script>
<!--
 function sendtext(x)
 {
   top.frames[1].document.forms[0].sat2_text.value=x
 }
// -->
</script>
</body>
</html>
```

2. Modify `frame1.htm` as follows, saving it as `frame2.htm`:

```
<?xml version="1.0" encoding="UTF-8"?>
<!DOCTYPE html
     PUBLIC "-//W3C//DTD XHTML 1.0 Transitional//EN"
     "http://www.w3.org/TR/xhtml1/DTD/xhtml1-transitional.dtd">
<html xmlns="http://www.w3.org/1999/xhtml" xml:lang="en" lang="en">
<head>
    <title>Frame Applications 2</title>
</head>
<body>
  <p>Frame2.htm</p>

   <form name="frm2" id="frm2">
    <input type="text" id="sat2_text" name="sat2_text" />
    <input type="button" value="send text" name="button" id="button"
      onclick="sendtext(sat2_text.value)"/>
   </form>
   <script>
   <!--
     function sendtext(x)
```

```
    {
      top.frames[0].document.forms[0].master2_text.value=x    //netscape form
    }
  // -->
  </script>

</body>
</html>
```

3. Now, modify `frameset1.htm` as follows, saving it as `frameset2.htm`:

```
<?xml version="1.0" encoding="UTF-8"?>
<!DOCTYPE html
     PUBLIC "-//W3C//DTD XHTML 1.0 Frameset//EN"
     "http://www.w3.org/TR/xhtml1/DTD/xhtml1-frameset.dtd">
<html xmlns="http://www.w3.org/1999/xhtml" xml:lang="en" lang="en">
<head>
    <title>Frame Applications Frame Page 2</title>
</head>
  <frameset cols="*,*">
    <frame src="frame_master2.htm" id="master" name="master" />
    <frame src="frame2.htm" id="sat1" name="sat1" />
  </frameset>
</html>
```

4. When we view the frameset we will see two almost identical pages, each with a form. If we fill some text into one of the boxes, and click the 'send text' button the text will appear in the text box on the other frame.

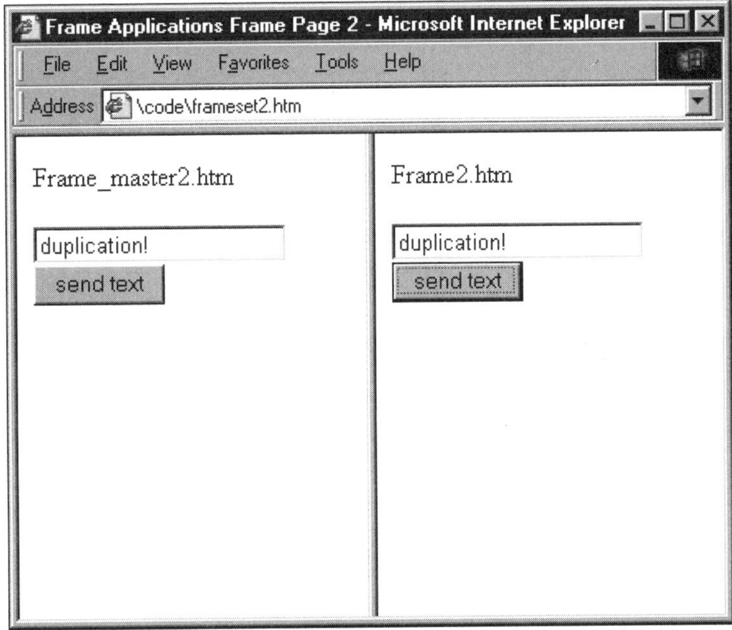

How It Works

Both frame contents pages contain nearly identical forms:

```
<form name="frm1" id="frm2">
  <input type="text" id="master2_text"name="master2_text" />
  <input type="button" value="send text" name="button" id="button"
   onclick="sendtext(document.frm1.master2_text.value)" />
</form>
```

The only difference is that the text boxes have different names (it would work fine, however, if we did give them the same name, since each frame has its own namespace). When we click the button, the function `sendtext()` is called. The argument to `sendtext()` is the contents of the textbox above it.

```
onclick="sendtext(master2_text.value)"
```

Note how we identify the textbox by name. The value of the text box is whatever text we have entered into it.

Both pages have almost the same function (this is the version from `frame1.htm`)

```
<script>
<!--
 function sendtext(x)
 {
   top.frames[1].document.forms[0].sat1_text.value=x
 }
// -->
</script>
```

This function takes a text string as an argument

```
function sendtext(x)
```

The text string, of course, is the value of the `master1_text` textbox.

Here we reference the first frame in our frameset

```
top.frames[0].document.forms[0].master2_text.value=x
```

Here we reference the first form in the document loaded in the first frame. (Each page maintains an array of forms)

```
top.frames[0].document.forms[0].master2_text.value=x
```

Here we reference the text box named `master2_text`

```
top.frames[0].document.forms[0].master2_text.value=x
```

and here we pass the value of `x` to its `value` attribute.

```
top.frames[0].document.forms[0].master2_text.value=x
```

Storing Data in Pages

Most applications need to store data. This data comes in two varieties.

- Data entered by a user while interacting with the form.
- Data that is part of the application.

We will now have a look at how to store data in a frame application.

We are going to make a simple application that consists of a master frame, and two satellite pages. The first satellite page will gather information from the user. This information will be stored in the master page, along with two literary quotes. We'll display the user's choice of quote in the second page, personalizing the page with the information the user entered in the first page.

Try It Out – A Simple Application that Stores Data

1. First let's type up the code to create the frameset (`frameset3.htm`):

```
<?xml version="1.0" encoding="UTF-8"?>
<!DOCTYPE html
     PUBLIC "-//W3C//DTD XHTML 1.0 Frameset//EN"
     "http://www.w3.org/TR/xhtml1/DTD/xhtml1-frameset.dtd">
<html xmlns="http://www.w3.org/1999/xhtml" xml:lang="en" lang="en">

<head>
  <title>Frame Applications 3</title>
</head>

<frameset cols="30%,*">
  <frame src="frame_master3.htm" id="master" name="master" />
  <frame src="frame3_1.htm" id="sat1" name="sat1"/>
</frameset>

</html>
```

2. Now let's look at the code for the master page (`frame_master3.htm`):

```
<?xml version="1.0" encoding="UTF-8"?>
<!DOCTYPE html
     PUBLIC "-//W3C//DTD XHTML 1.0 Transitional//EN"
     "http://www.w3.org/TR/xhtml1/DTD/xhtml1-transitional.dtd">
<html xmlns="http://www.w3.org/1999/xhtml" xml:lang="en" lang="en">
<head>
  <title>Frame Applications 3</title>
</head>
<body>
  <p>Frame_master3.htm</p>
  <a href="frame3_1.htm" target="sat1">Registration Page</a><br />
  <a href="frame3_2.htm" target="sat1">Select a reading</a>
  <form id="frm1" name="frm1">
    <input type="hidden" value="" id="firstname_text" name="firstname_text" />
    <input type="hidden" value="" id="secondname_text" name="secondname_text" />
    <input type="button" value="show name" id="button" name="button"
```

```
      onclick="sendtext(firstname_text.value,secondname_text.value)" />
  </form>

  <form id="frm2" name="frm2">
    <input type="hidden" id="macbeth_text" name="macbeth_text" value="Tomorrow,
and tomorrow, and tomorrow, &#13;Creeps on this petty pace from day to day &#13;To
the last syllable of recorded time" />
    <input type="hidden" id="hamlet_text" name="hamlet_text" value="To be, or not
to be, that is the question.&#13;Whether 'tis nobler in the mind to suffer the
slings &#13;and arrows of outrageous fortune" />
  </form>

  <script>
  <!--
    function sendtext(x,y)
    {
      alert(x+" "+y)
    }
  // -->
  </script>

</body>
</html>
```

3. Here is the code for the first satellite page (`frame3_1.htm`):

```
<?xml version="1.0" encoding="UTF-8"?>
<!DOCTYPE html
     PUBLIC "-//W3C//DTD XHTML 1.0 Transitional//EN"
     "http://www.w3.org/TR/xhtml1/DTD/xhtml1-transitional.dtd">
<html xmlns="http://www.w3.org/1999/xhtml" xml:lang="en" lang="en">
<head>
  <title>Frame Applications 3</title>
</head>
<body>
  <p>Frame3_1.htm</p>
  <form id="frm1" name="frm1">
    <h3>First Name</h3>
    <input type="text" id="firstname_text" name="firstname_text" />
    <h3>Second Name</h3>
    <input type="text" id="secondname_text" name="secondname_text" /><br />
    <input type="button" value="Register name" id="button" name="button"
      onclick="sendtext(firstname_text.value, secondname_text.value )" />
  </form>
  <script>
  <!--
    function sendtext(x,y)
    {
      top.frames[0].document.forms[0].firstname_text.value=x
      top.frames[0].document.forms[0].secondname_text.value=y
    }

      //Fill in values for text boxes
```

```
document.forms[0].firstname_text.value=top.frames[0].document.forms[0].firstname_t
ext.value

document.forms[0].secondname_text.value=top.frames[0].document.forms[0].secondname
_text.value
  // -->
  </script>
</body>
</html>
```

4. This is what we will see when we first run the application. I have already filled in my name.

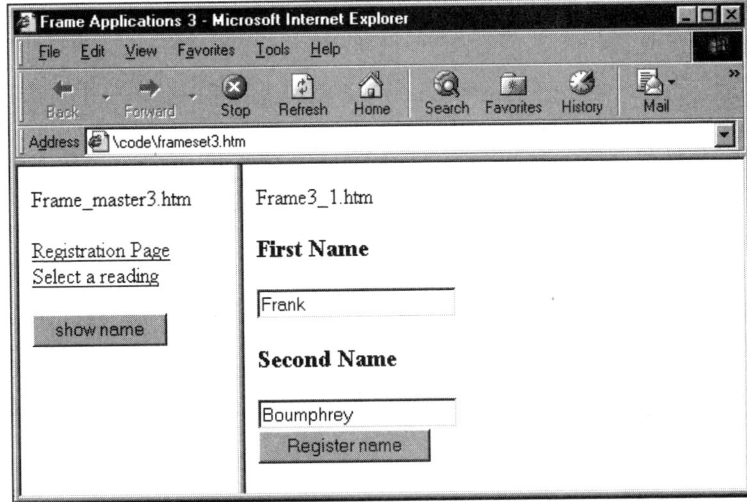

5. Now click on the Select a reading link which will bring up the second satellite page. But, oops! – we haven't written it yet… so let's do that now.

6. Here is the code for the second satellite page (`frame3_2.htm`):

```
<?xml version="1.0" encoding="UTF-8"?>
<!DOCTYPE html
     PUBLIC "-//W3C//DTD XHTML 1.0 Transitional//EN"
     "http://www.w3.org/TR/xhtml1/DTD/xhtml1-transitional.dtd">
<html xmlns="http://www.w3.org/1999/xhtml" xml:lang="en" lang="en">
<head>
  <title>Frame Applications 3</title>
</head>
<body>
  <p>Frame3_2.htm</p>
  <p>Welcome
  <script>
  <!--
    document.write(top.frames[0].document.forms[0].firstname_text.value + " "
    + top.frames[0].document.forms[0].secondname_text.value)
  // -->
  </script>
```

```
      . Please select your play.
   </p>

   <form>
     <input type="button" value="Macbeth"
      onclick="poem.value=top.frames[0].document.forms[1].macbeth_text.value" />
     <input type="button" value="Hamlet"
      onclick="poem.value=top.frames[0].document.forms[1].hamlet_text.value" /></br
>
     <textarea name="poem" id="poem" cols="45" rows="7">
     </textarea>
   </form>
</body>
</html>
```

7. If we click on the **select a reading** link we will see the following. I have selected the reading of my choice from Macbeth. Note that the selection page calls me by name.

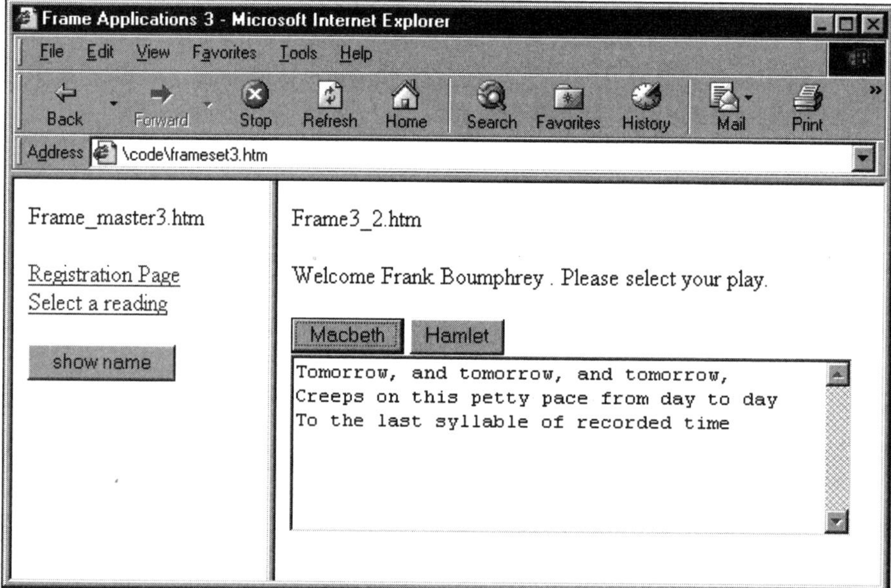

How It Works

This simple application incorporates some important principles that we'll examine now. First, the master page has links to the other two pages. When the user clicks on one of these links, the corresponding page will be opened in the second frame because we use the `target` attribute:

```
<a href="frame2_1.htm" target="sat1">Registration Page</a><br />
<a href="frame2_2.htm" target="sat1">Select a reading</a>
```

There are also two forms on the page, both consisting mainly of hidden input elements used to store information.

We use the first form to store the details that the user will enter in the registration page. Note that their initial values are empty text strings:

```
<input type="hidden" value="" id="firstname_text" name="firstname_text" />
<input type="hidden" value="" id="firstname_text" name="secondname_text" />
```

We have also added a button that pops up a dialog box so that the user can check on the name.

The second form also consists of hidden `input` elements. We use these to store some Shakespearean quotes:

```
<input type="hidden" id="macbeth_text" name="macbeth_text" value="Tomorrow, and
tomorrow, and tomorrow, &#13;Creeps on this petty pace from day to day &#13;To the
last syllable of recorded time" />
<input type="hidden" id="hamlet_text" name="hamlet_text" value="To be, or not to
be, that is the question.&#13;Whether 'tis nobler in the mind to suffer the slings
&#13;and arrows of outrageous fortune" />
```

`
` signifies a newline character, and as you can see when you run the program, the text area control contains the text with line breaks at the places we've stated.

Let's now look at the first satellite page.

There is another simple form to collect the user's name, and then pass it to the `sendtext()` function for processing:

```
<form id="frm1" name="frm1">
  <h3>First Name</h3>
  <input type="text" id="firstname_text" name="firstname_text" />
  <h3>Second Name</h3>
  <input type="text" id="secondname_text" name="secondname_text" /><br />
  <input type="button" value="Register name" id="button" name="button"
   onclick="sendtext(firstname_text.value, secondname_text.value )"/>
</form>
```

The `sendtext()` function accepts the names entered in the form as parameters and sends them to the master form where we stash them in the hidden input elements of the first form:

```
function sendtext(x,y)
{
  top.frames[0].document.forms[0].firstname_text.value=x
  top.frames[0].document.forms[0].secondname_text.value=y
}
```

The next bit of code runs while `frame3_1.htm` is loading, and it retrieves the names stored in the master frame, and fills them into the text box so that the application remembers what you typed previously:

```
document.forms[0].firstname_text.value=top.frames[0].document.forms[0].firstname_t
ext.value
document.forms[0].secondname_text.value=top.frames[0].document.forms[0].secondname
_text.value
```

What about the second satellite page? `frame3_2.htm` contains the following code, which writes out the name that was entered into the first satellite page:

```
document.write(top.frames[0].document.forms[0].firstname_text.value + " "
  + top.frames[0].document.forms[0].secondname_text.value)
```

If we wanted to, we could add a conditional statement to check whether the strings are empty or not. If they were empty, we could either ask the user to register, or leave the space blank.

We use inline script on the event handler for the quote selector buttons:

```
<input type="button" value="Macbeth"
 onclick="poem.value=top.frames[0].document.forms[1].macbeth_text.value" />
```

This is the value of the hidden `input` element named `macbeth_text` from our second form in the master document:

```
top.frames[0].document.forms[1].macbeth_text.value
```

It is read into `poem.value`.

Here is the same for Hamlet:

```
<input type="button" value="Hamlet"
 onclick="poem.value=top.frames[0].document.forms[1].hamlet_text.value" /><br />
```

Although this example is simple, the concepts illustrated can be used to build more powerful applications. Now, let's have a look at how we can use script to write a brand new page to our application.

Writing a New Page

Let's now look at how to write a new page using script. We can either write to a new window, or an existing frame. Let's first look at creating, and then writing to a new window. Next, we will see how to write a new page to an existing frame.

Creating a New Window

We can create a new window with code using the following syntax.

```
window.open(url,name,features,replace);
```

If we don't present any arguments then JavaScript will just open a window with default settings. Here is a synopsis of the arguments.

`url`	A optional string that specifies the resource to be loaded in the new window. If no URL is specified, then the window is left empty.
`name`	The name for the new window. This has no relation to the URL or the title of the window. Rather, the name is a handle that you can use to access the window from JavaScript. Also, if you try to open a window with a name that already exists, `open()` will clear the existing window rather than create a new window.
`features`	A string of comma separated features of the new window. There are numerous features that a new window can take, look to Netscape's JavaScript documentation at `http://developer.iplanet.com/docs/manuals/javascript.html` for a complete list.
`replace`	A boolean argument that indicates whether the URL should be part of the new windows browsing history (`true`) or part of the browsing history of the window that created this new window (`false`). This influences how the back button will behave in both the original and new windows.

Try It Out – Creating and Writing to a New Window

1. Let's create a new window and then write some text into it. Type up the following code (`new.htm`):

```
<?xml version="1.0" encoding="UTF-8"?>
<!DOCTYPE html
     PUBLIC "-//W3C//DTD XHTML 1.0 Transitional//EN"
     "http://www.w3.org/TR/xhtml1/DTD/xhtml1-transitional.dtd">
<html xmlns="http://www.w3.org/1999/xhtml" xml:lang="en" lang="en">
<head>
  <title></title>
</head>
<body>
  <form id="frm1" name="frm1">
    <textarea id="ta1" name="ta1" cols="20" rows="10"></textarea><br />
    <input type="button" value="Make new window"
onclick="makenewwindow(ta1.value)" /><br />
    <input type="button" value ="write to window" onclick="writewindow(ta1.value)"
/><br />
  </form>
  <script>
  <!--
    function makenewwindow(x)
    {
      newwindow=window.open();
      newwindow.document.open();
      newwindow.document.write(x)
      newwindow.document.close();
    }

    function writewindow(x)
    {
      newwindow.document.open();
      newwindow.document.write(x);
      newwindow.document.close();
```

```
    }
  // -->
  </script>

</body>
</html>
```

2. View it, type something in the text box and then click the Make new window button. This is what you will see.

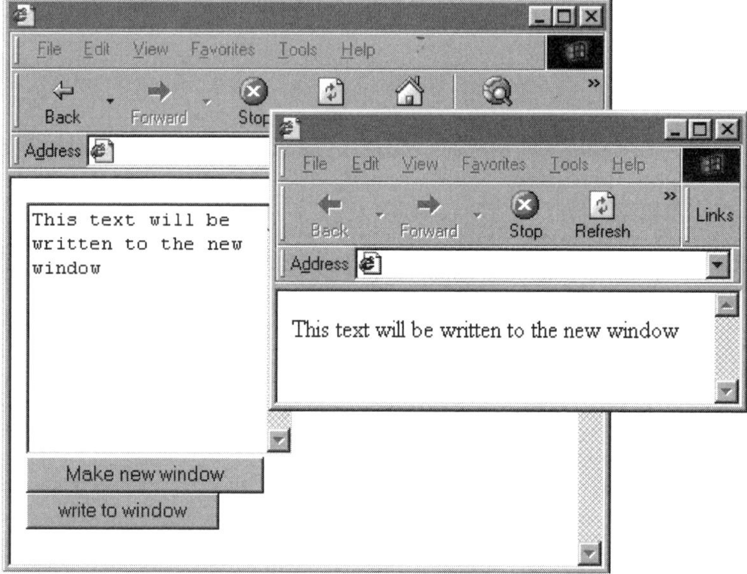

3. Try typing something in with XHTML tags, like `This is <b>bold</b> text`, and see what happens.

How It Works

When you click on the Make new window button, the following function is called. The argument of the function is the text that we have typed in the text box.

```
function makenewwindow(x)
{
  newwindow=window.open();
  newwindow.document.open();
  newwindow.document.write(x)
  newwindow.document.close();
}
```

This line of code creates the new window:

```
newwindow=window.open();
```

This line of code opens a document in the window:

```
newwindow.document.open();
```

The next line writes the contents of the text box to the new window, which have been passed to the function as an argument:

```
newwindow.document.write(x)
```

And finally this line of code closes the document:

```
newwindow.document.close();
```

If you don't close the document, you'll observe different kinds of erratic behavior depending on which version of which web browser you're using. Always close documents when you're done writing to them! Once the window has been created, we can write into the window without creating a new one.

We do this with the second function:

```
function writewindow(x)
{
  newwindow.document.open();
  newwindow.document.write(x);
  newwindow.document.close();
}
```

Each time we evoke this function the old text is erased, and new text is written to the window. XHTML markup is also interpreted, as is information in `<style>` tags, so you can actually write fairly sophisticated pages this way!

Writing to Frames

Writing to a preexisting frame is easier than writing to a new window, because we don't have to write to a new window.

If we don't specify a URL, IE automatically creates a blank document to put into a frame. Netscape Communicator does not, so to be compatible we have to initialize every frame with a document; blank if necessary.

To illustrate, we will make a simple form that allows us to enter a title of a story or poem in one text box, type the story in another, and then print the result to another frame.

Try It Out – Writing to a New Frame

1. Type up the following frameset (`newframe.htm`):

```
<?xml version="1.0" encoding="UTF-8"?>
<!DOCTYPE html
     PUBLIC "-//W3C//DTD XHTML 1.0 Frameset//EN"
     "http://www.w3.org/TR/xhtml1/DTD/xhtml1-frameset.dtd">
<html xmlns="http://www.w3.org/1999/xhtml" xml:lang="en" lang="en">
```

```
<head>
  <title>Frame Applications Frame Page</title>
</head>
<frameset cols="35%,*">
  <frame src="frame4_1.htm" id="master" name="master" />
  <frame src="blank.txt" id="mainview" name="mainview" />
</frameset>
</html>
```

2. The master page (`frame4_1.htm`) holds the script:

```
<?xml version="1.0" encoding="UTF-8"?>
<!DOCTYPE html
     PUBLIC "-//W3C//DTD XHTML 1.0 Transitional//EN"
     "http://www.w3.org/TR/xhtml1/DTD/xhtml1-transitional.dtd">
<html xmlns="http://www.w3.org/1999/xhtml" xml:lang="en" lang="en">
<head>
  <title></title>
</head>
<body>
  <form id="frm1" name="frm1">
    <h4>Type the heading for your poem in this text box</h4>
    <input type="text" id="tb1" name="tb1" />
    <h4>Type your poem here</h4>
    <textarea rows="10" cols="30" id="ta1" name="ta1"></textarea>
    <input type="button" onclick="writepage(tb1.value,ta1.value)" value="Click
when finished" />
  </form>

  <script>
  <!--
    //html headers and footers
    var html_header="<html>\n<head>\n\t<title></title>\n</head>\n<body>";
    var html_footer="</body></html>";

    function writepage(x,y)
    {
      //code to write to an existing frame
      top.frames[1].document.open();
      top.frames[1].document.write(html_header+"<h1>"+x+"</h1>"+"<p>"+ y
+"</p>"+html_footer);
      top.frames[1].document.close;
    }
  // -->
  </script>

</body>
</html>
```

3. Also make a blank text file (a file with no content) and save it in the same folder as `blank.txt`.

4. This is what you will see after you have run the page, typed some material in the text boxes, and clicked the Click when finished button.

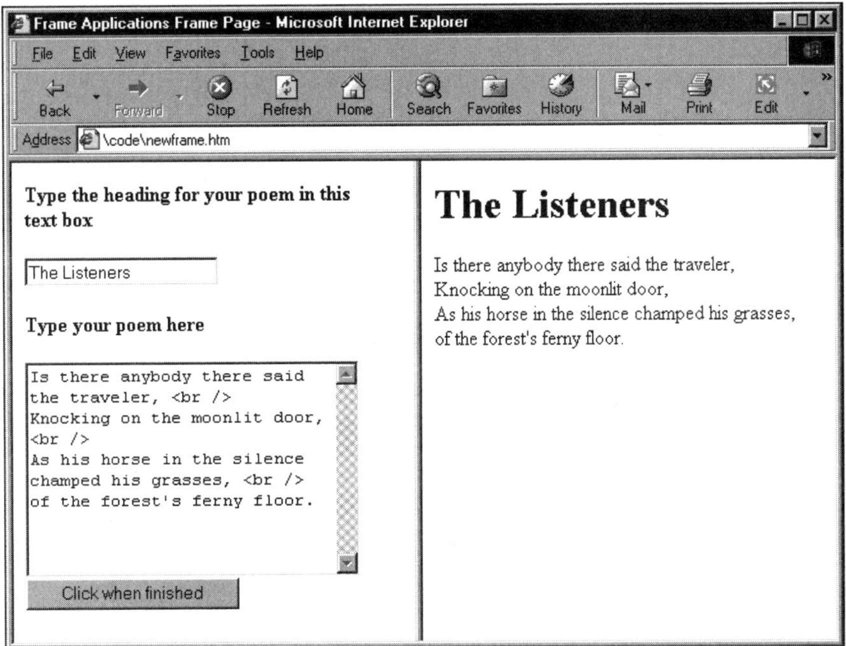

How It Works

Here is the form we use to enter a poem. The input button calls the `writepage()` function, which takes as arguments the content of our two text boxes.

```
<form id="frm1" name="frm1">
  <h4>Type the heading for your poem in this text box</h4>
  <input type="text" id="tbl" name="tbl" />
  <h4>Type your poem here</h4>
  <textarea rows="10" cols="30" id="ta1" name="ta1"></textarea>
  <input type="button" onclick="writepage(tbl.value,ta1.value)" value="Click when
finished" />
</form>
```

The first part of the script defines the header and footer of the new document.

Note the `\n` and `\t`. This helps format the code which is written into the second page. '`\n`' starts a new line. '`\t`' is a tab. These characters have no effect on the appearance in the browser, but make the code look more comprehensible when you do a "View Source."

```
  //html headers and footers
  var html_header="<html>\n<head>\n\t<title></title>\n</head>\n<body>";
  var html_footer="</body></html>";
```

The following function does the writing,

```
function writepage(x,y)
{
```

We open a document in the frame, write to it, and close the document:

```
  //code to write to an existing frame
  top.frames[1].document.open;
  top.frames[1].document.write(html_header+"<h1>"+x+"</h1>"+"<p>"+ y
+"</p>"+html_footer);
  top.frames[1].document.close;
```

Summary

This is a short chapter but an important one. In this chapter we have looked at the techniques we can use to write multi-frame JavaScript applications. We saw how to reference one frame from another and pass information between frames, as well as storing and using data between frames. We also looked at using new windows and how information can be passed between them.

Once again, we haven't been able to do everything you'd need to design such applications, but by now you should have an idea of the power that you can put into your XHTML pages. If anything here has grabbed you, you should consider getting deeper into JavaScript. What we've shown you has been a brisk tour, but we've left a lot of ground uncovered along the way that you'll want to consolidate if you're serious about making great interactive pages.

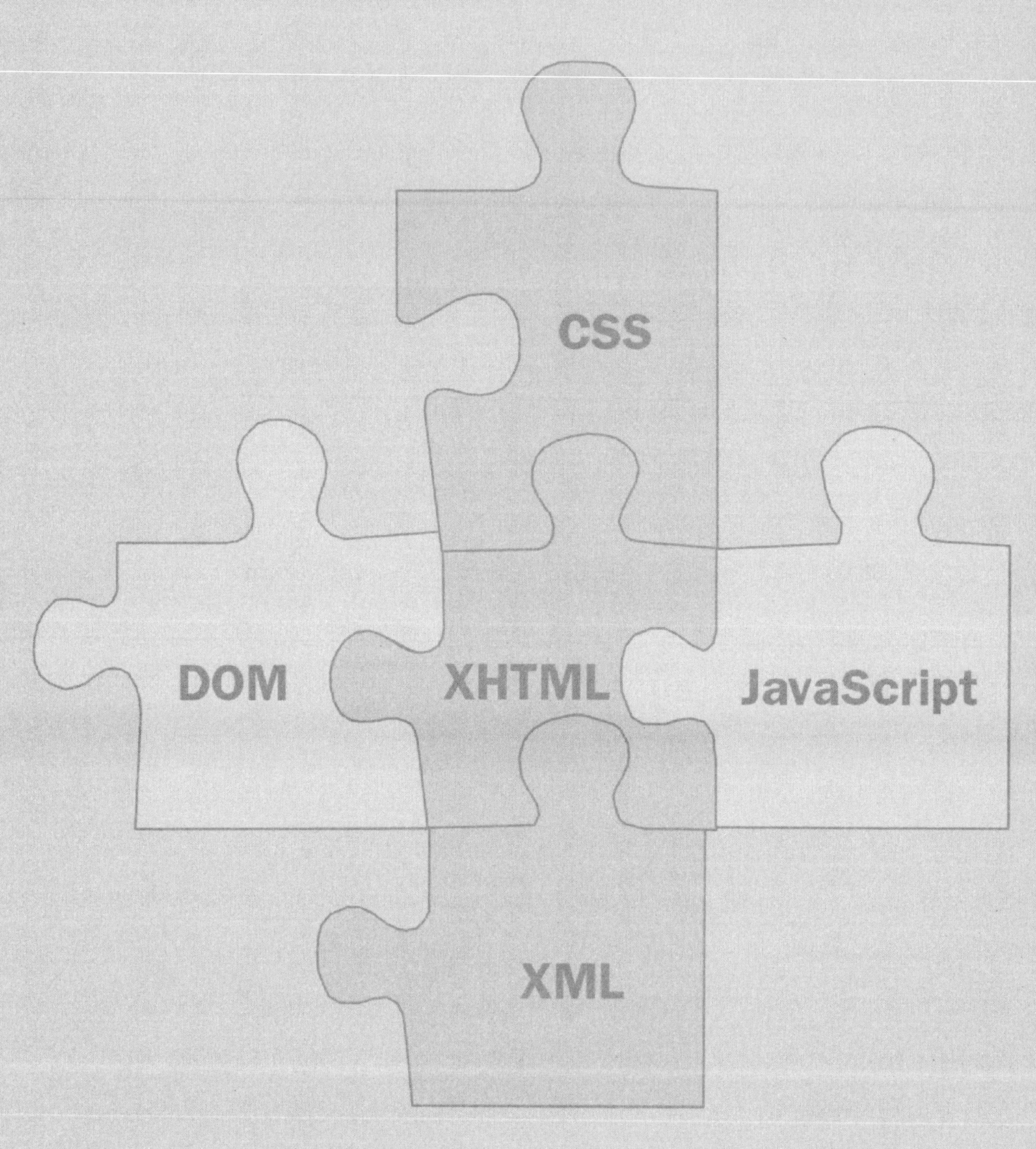
CSS
DOM
XHTML
JavaScript
XML

Using XHTML with Mozquito

In Chapter 19 we saw how to combine scripting, DOM and frames to achieve a stateful environment or client-side persistency. Since plain XHTML 1.0 by itself is often not powerful enough to cope with more sophisticated web applications running inside the browser, web authors often have to provide additional functionality beyond XHTML 1.0 through 'acrobatic' usage of different client and server-side techniques.

The inconsistencies between browsers, the complexity of scripting languages and the conceptual differences between various technologies make it very difficult for web authors to create robust and user-friendly web applications. Not only do web designers need to invest a great investment of time and energy just to write their programs, they need take into consideration what techniques are necessary to make their applications viewable in existing and future browsers. These web applications can be as simple as checking the syntax of an email address entered into a form field. Marking up text with XHTML or other XML languages is a simple, easy-to-learn yet powerful technique; anything beyond this requires page authors to become programming experts.

This problem was the motivation for Mozquito. In 1997, a group of professional HTML writers realized that they didn't like how client-side web applications were often hard-to-develop, stand-alone solutions. What they wanted was that once a piece of script code ran reliably on all browsers, the script code could become part of a larger framework and that web authors wouldn't have to deal with the underlying complexity. The features of the script code should be easily accessible to authors, and that all these scripts could be combined into something like plug and play.

What is simpler than scripting or programming? Markup!

Earlier in this book, **extensibility** was given as one of the benefits of XHTML. We can benefit today from XHTML's extensibility even though most existing browsers don't fully support **XML** and **Namespaces** yet.

Mozquito is about extending XHTML with a new module, the Forms Markup Language (FML). FML introduces a set of new tags and attributes especially designed for creating better, more dynamic and user friendly forms. Since these new FML tags cannot yet be understood on their own by today's browsers, Mozquito transforms these into robust cross-browser script code. Web authors never need to deal with the underlying script; it is as if these new XHTML tags were built into IE and Netscape from the very beginning. The name **Mozquito** describes what the program does; the knowledge the browser needs to process these XHTML extensions is *injected* on a page-by-page basis into browsers supporting JavaScript 1.2.

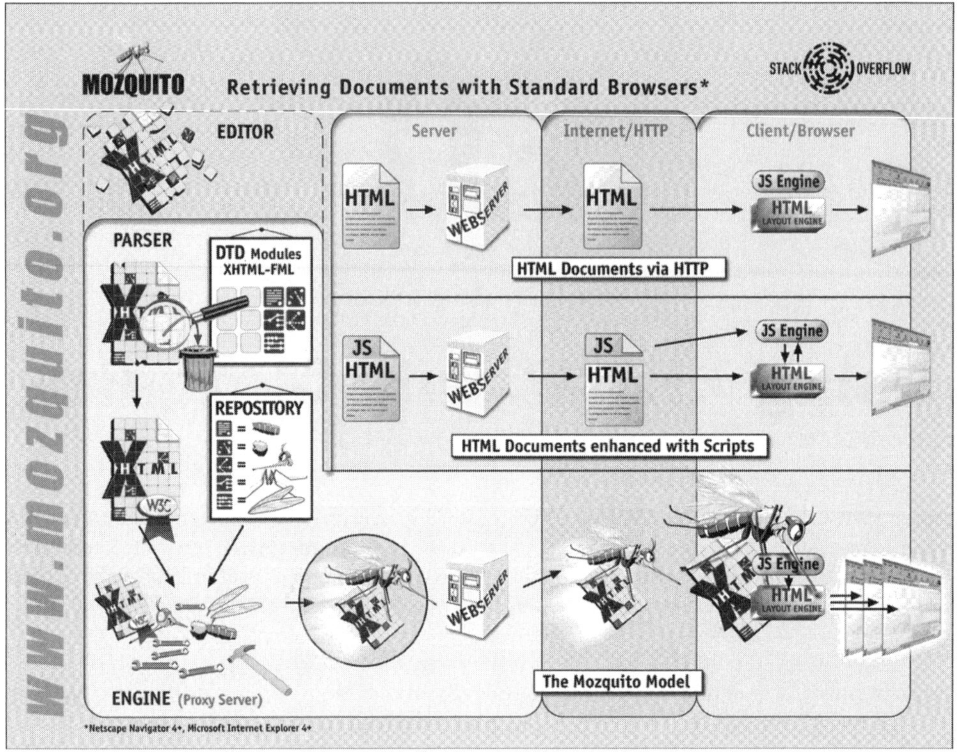

As we read previously in Chapter 15, the use of forms in the Internet is becoming an increasingly important issue, especially in e-commerce, but creating effective and dynamic forms is difficult and usually requires using additional scripting (say, JavaScript or CGI). But now you can create dynamic forms without complicated scripting, but entirely with markup. To show you how this is done, we will walk you through how to create an e-commerce order form inside a single document using the Mozquito Factory.

In this chapter, we'll cover:

- Who created the Mozquito Factory and why.
- How to use the Mozquito Factory to edit and validate XHTML.
- How to create dynamic forms with Mozquito.
- Using Mozquito to check for mandatory fields and data types.
- Using Mozquito for open-ended lists and run-time calculations.
- Using Mozquito to re-use previously entered form data.
- Using Mozquito to create a persistent product catalog.
- Using Mozquito as a richer alternative to frames and cookies.

Getting Started with the Mozquito Factory

Before we take a look at the new tags available only through Mozquito, here is a short introduction to the Mozquito Factory, the first XHTML application.

Built upon a modular framework, the Mozquito Factory combines three independent applications:

- The Mozquito Engine: This transforms XHTML into HTML documents with embedded JavaScript which can be understood by Netscape 4+ and IE 4+.
- The XHTML Validator: This checks XHTML documents for well-formedness and validity, giving hints how to improve your markup.
- The Mozquito Factory Editor: This is a Java™ based editor that combines the Mozquito Engine and Validator.

When you use the Mozquito Factory you can choose your tools. You can use either your own editor or authoring tool to write web pages using the new XHTML tags or you can use the Mozquito Factory Editor.

How Mozquito Came to Be

Mozquito.com was founded in 1998 under the name "Stack Overflow" by a team of web design professionals. As mentioned, the founders of Mozquito.com realized in their careers as web consultants that writing complex web forms with scripts is a very time-consuming and challenging task. Mozquito.com's mission is to simplify the development of interactive web applications, including web forms.

The existing web forms in HTML have remained mainly the same since 1993. If forms in HTML were more powerful, the need for scripting would be reduced, simplifying the authoring. Early 1999, Mozquito.com developed a specification for improved web forms in HTML and called it Forms Markup Language (FML).

Mozquito.com showed the FML specification to members of the HTML Working Group at the W3C. At that time, the HTML Working Group just started to work on the next generation of web forms, and they considered the FML specification to go in the right direction. Mozquito.com became a member of the W3C and joined the HTML Working Group. Soon Mozquito.com would become the driving force behind standards on forms.

Mozquito.com remained responsible for the FML specification, but it was redesigned to integrate nicely into XHTML, becoming "XHTML-FML". At the same time, the HTML WG defined the requirements for the next generation of web forms, with a working title of "XForms". FML already fulfills a number of key requirements for XForms - you can think of XForms as FML 2.0. Although the syntax will most likely be different in XForms in order to allow even more flexibility, some of the basic FML concepts we will introduce in this chapter will continue to exist.

Mozquito.com launched the Mozquito Factory in late 1999, implementing XHTML-FML 1.0. The Mozquito Factory is available as a fully functional 30-day-trial version. A full version is available for purchase.

As soon as the W3C work on forms finalizes, Mozquito will update to support XForms. This doesn't mean that your existing documents written in XHTML-FML won't work in the future. Since XHTML-FML documents written with Mozquito are transformed into JavaScript, they will continue to work. To view transformed XHTML-FML documents in the browser, the Mozquito Factory or a browser plug-in need not be installed.

Browsers Supported by Mozquito

At the time this book was written, XHTML-FML documents transformed by Mozquito work reliably in the following browsers:

Windows

- Netscape Navigator 4+
- Microsoft Internet Explorer 4+

MacOS

- Netscape Navigator 4+
- Microsoft Internet Explorer 5+

Note that other browsers might work too, but are not listed here. Internet Explorer 4 for the Macintosh occasionally has problems with XHTML-FML documents transformed by Mozquito, due to its limited JavaScript and DOM implementations. MacIE5 fixes these problems. Support for other browsers, such as Opera, is currently being worked on.

Documents written in one of the three XHTML 1.0 flavors (the different DTDs you can conform to) with the Mozquito Factory will render in all browsers.

Using Mozquito in your Web Publishing Project

XHTML-FML documents are not meant to replace every possible HTML or XHTML page on your web site. XHTML-FML documents are mainly used when forms come into play. You can use the Mozquito Factory to write and validate documents in one of the three XHTML 1.0 flavors, or in XHTML-FML. When it comes to a feedback form, online registration form, e-commerce ordering form, etc., XHTML-FML documents are more powerful than existing HTML forms and are authored in less time. XHTML documents can be uploaded right away to your web server; XHTML-FML documents have to be transformed with the Mozquito Factory before uploading.

However, XHTML-FML documents are not only useful for web forms. As we will show later in this chapter, FML introduces a mechanism that allows multiple screen pages, or **cards**, to be embedded into a single XHTML-FML document. This can make the documents behave like "booklets", instead of single pages. If you have a limited number of pages that collectively represent a logical entity, FML allows you to split things up into separate screens, instead of having a page with scrollbars or separate documents to be loaded one at a time. Small catalogs, brochures, and resumés, maybe with an associated response form at the end, are all perfect examples.

The Mozquito Factory is ideal for writing single XHTML and XHTML-FML documents. If your web pages are dynamically generated on your web server, you need to install the Mozquito Server software if you wish to dynamically generate documents containing FML (see `http://www.mozquito.com`). The Mozquito Server transforms XHTML-FML documents on the fly on your web server into JavaScript before a generated web page is sent to the browser. If your site is made up of a collection of web pages saved on your web server, you can simply do the transformation with the Mozquito Factory on your PC before uploading FML web pages to the server.

Installing Mozquito

The Mozquito Factory is Java™ based software and available for download at `http://www.mozquito.com`. A Java™ Runtime Environment (JRE) is required for Mozquito.

Windows

A JRE from Microsoft is installed automatically when you install Internet Explorer 5. However, we recommend downloading and installing the JRE 1.1.7 or higher from either IBM at `http://www6.software.ibm.com/dl/dkw/dkre-p` or Sun Microsystems at `http://java.sun.com/products/jdk/1.1/jre/download-jre-windows.html`.

MacOS

Mozquito for Mac needs MacOS Runtime for Java™ (MRJ) 2.1.4 or newer to run. Although MRJ should already be installed on your system, you can also find it at `http://www.apple.com/java`.

Mozquito Factory Editor and Validator

After successful installation, you will see the following screen when starting the Mozquito Factory for the first time:

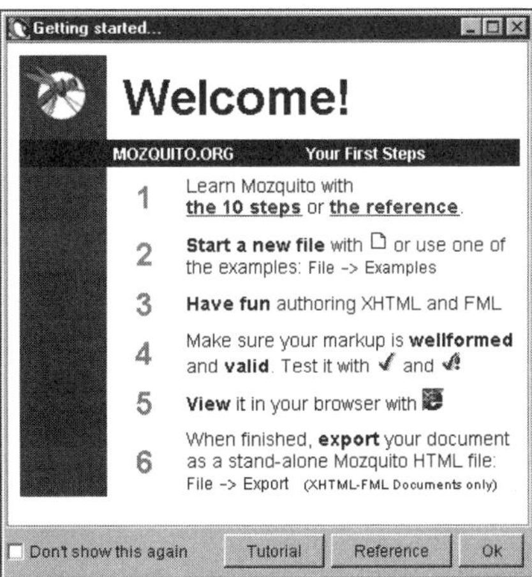

This can be thought of as a mini-help card, just showing the basic commands available and giving you the option of letting Mozquito take you through a little tutorial/display. If you want, click on 'the 10 steps' link to see some of the tricks this package can perform. Alternatively, click on OK to close the help card, and let us take you through it all bit by bit.

Before we start building our e-commerce site, let's get to know Mozquito.

The first thing we need to know is how to create a new document. Select the File | New menu option. You will be asked to choose from a list of four different document types: XHTML-FML, and the three flavors of XHTML 1.0 (Strict, Transitional and Frameset) you are already familiar with. When you choose the first option, XHTML-FML 1.0, you open a new document (you can also open a new document with the key sequence *Ctrl-N*) that allows you to use the tags in this chapter:

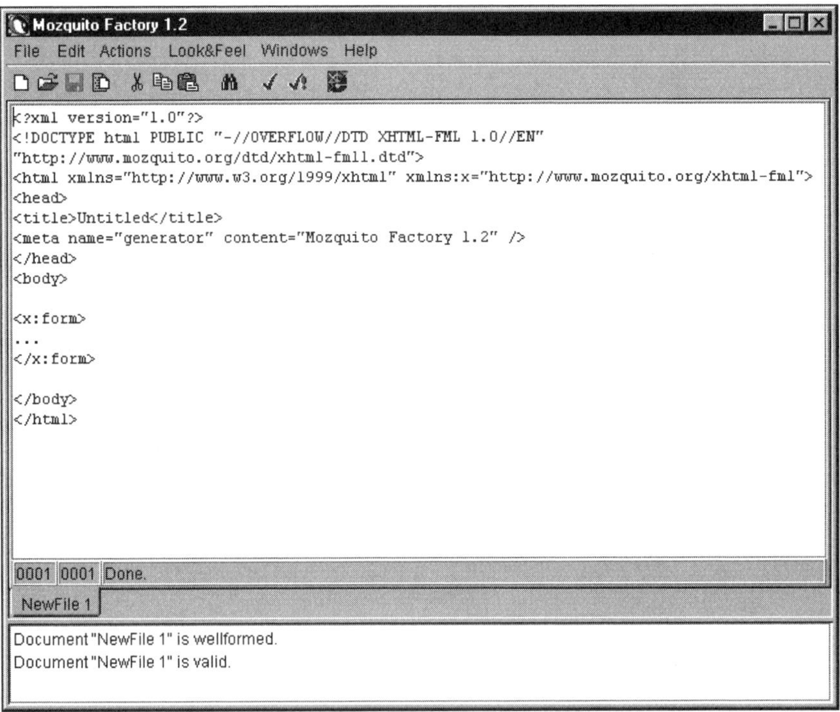

Note that the document is a template document that comes already loaded with the document type and namespace specified, and also includes the `<head>` and `<body>` tags. This saves having to retype the standard declarations for each document. Note also that the `<html>` tag contains an additional namespace attribute (`http://www.mozquito.org/xhtml-fml`) for the Mozquito tags.

Even though the new document is essentially empty, we can still validate it by clicking on the two checkmarks (or tick symbols) in the toolbar. The first checks just for well-formedness (you can also use *Ctrl-W* if you prefer) and the other checks for both well-formedness and validity (*Ctrl-T*). When you click on these, text appears in the message dialog window at the bottom informing you that your document is indeed both well formed and valid. Now, for example, delete the closing `</head>` tag, and then press the right-hand checkmark: you will see that Mozquito has correctly identified that this closing tag is missing. By double-clicking on the error message, your prompt is taken directly to the position in your document where the error occurred. This is very useful, and saves you having to re-read all your code to discover where you made the mistake.

Mozquito documents must be at least well-formed, but best results are achieved with valid documents. When transformed into JavaScript, invalid XHTML-FML documents may cause erratic behaviors in the script.

Now add the closing </head> tag back in, and type in some text in the line after the opening <body> tag that will display on the browser. For example, type in:

```
<body>
 <p> Here is a little bit of text to test out Mozquito.</p>
```

Now click on the browser icon (or CTRL-D) to see your document running with Mozquito in your default browser.

By default, if a document is not well-formed when clicking the browser icon, Mozquito displays an error message in the browser instead of the document. It is possible to configure the Mozquito Factory so that validation errors are displayed in the browser also if the document is well-formed but not valid. This makes sure your documents always conform to the W3C Document Type Definitions (DTD). You can activate Check validity on export *under* Options | Settings *to meet the XHTML specification requirements, letting your browser display only "strictly conforming XHTML documents".*

Save and edit the master copies of your XHTML documents using filenames with the .xhtml file extension. Before uploading your file to your web server (where your web pages reside) you will need to export XHTML-FML documents as a backwards compatible .html or .htm file (File | Export or *Ctrl-E*). This will automatically transform the documents into JavaScript. When clicking the browser icon in the Mozquito Factory, every XHTML document is validated, and XHTML-FML documents are transformed in the same way as with "export" into JavaScript before the document appears in the browser.

Using Mozquito with Other Authoring Tools

Validation and transformation services are also available without using the Mozquito Factory Editor. With Mozquito Factory installed, you simply need to double-click .xhtml files on your system. The document is then validated, transformed and displayed on your browser. A copy of this file will appear in the directory using the same filename but with the .html file extension. This document is ready to be used directly in a browser.

The Local Proxy Server

There is a large movement towards on-the-fly transformation of XML documents. The concept behind HTML was "one size fits all", a web page written in HTML could be viewed "as is" in different browsers on a desktop PC without changing the HTML code. Since more and more devices are accessing the web (e.g. handheld devices such as PDAs, mobile phones), XML, and thus XHTML, is addressing this problem by taking a different approach than HTML. For example, think of an XML document containing only raw data. Such an XML document could be automatically transformed to meet the needs of different environments. For example, into an XHTML web page for browsers running on desktop PCs, into a WML (Wireless Markup Language) web page for mobile phones, etc.

The mechanism for changing the format of an XML document between sender and receiver (that is, server and client) is also known as **transcoding**.

XHTML was designed to support this new web architecture. Proxy servers in the past were mainly responsible for caching, or saving, web pages. A network of clients on the Internet would get a web page directly from the proxy server's memory if someone else in this network had already accessed it.

The important thing about proxy servers is their location between client and server. The proxy is an ideal place to store documents but also to transcode, letting the web server output a single document format and the proxy server do the conversion.

This aspect of XHTML has now been brought to your desktop PC, transcoding your documents when you double-click or execute XHTML files on your machine.

The Forms Markup Language

At one time JavaScript was developed to enhance forms in HTML. People saw after using it that it had a huge potential for so much more. The same can be said of the Forms Markup Language, a collection of new tags for XHTML documents; it was developed to enhance forms but clever web designers have discovered many more uses for it and more are being discovered all the time.

Web pages using both XHTML and FML are called XHTML-FML documents. XHTML-FML is built upon XHTML's modularity, and we can expect to see more "XHTML family members" like XHTML-FML being released in the future.

XHTML's Extensibility for Existing Browsers

As we mentioned before, XHTML-FML documents are converted into cross-browser script code. If you would like see how much JavaScript Mozquito writes for you, just open a transformed XHTML-FML document in any text editor. You will agree that you're saving so much time by just writing FML. The script code produced by Mozquito might seem a bit large at first, but it is tuned to work with various browsers and to cope with any possible combination of FML tags - small, large, simple and complex documents.

Minimal XHTML-FML Document

To start with, let's have a look at an XHTML-FML document:

```
<?xml version="1.0"?>
<!DOCTYPE html PUBLIC "-//OVERFLOW//DTD XHTML-FML 1.0//EN"
 "http://www.mozquito.org/dtd/xhtml-fml1.dtd">
<html xmlns="http://www.w3.org/1999/xhtml"
 xmlns:x="http://www.mozquito.org/xhtml-fml">
<head>
<title>Untitled</title>
<meta name="generator" content="Mozquito Factory 1.2" />
</head>
<body>

<x:form>
...
</x:form>

</body>
</html>
```

The most important difference to plain XHTML 1.0 documents is the definition of an additional XML **namespace** in the html root tag:

```
xmlns:x="http://www.mozquito.org/xhtml-fml"
```

The Forms Markup Language namespace is now available in this document using the prefix `x`. All FML tags are now identified by the assigned `x:` in front of the tag name, (e.g. `<x:form>` in the above document).

The Benefits of FML

FML enriches web pages, especially web forms. In lets you create form-based web applications entirely in markup, so that you can perform tasks on your browser which are normally only possible using either very complex JavaScript scripts or server-side mechanisms. This means that visitors to a web site can stay offline while browsing a series of screen pages and operations.

FML changes the idea that a single HTML document always consists of only one screen page.If a standard HTML document contains more information than a single screen can display, a scrollbar appears. In FML, multiple screen pages or a single part of the screen can be dynamically displayed depending on how page visitors interact (clicking on navigation links, going to sub trees in a web page or web form).

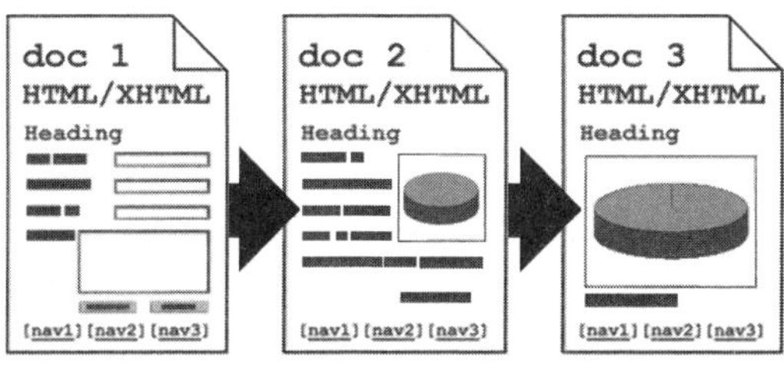

If the information exceeds one screen page, in XHTML you can only split things up into multiple documents. But XHTML-FML allows you to embed multiple cards inside a single document:

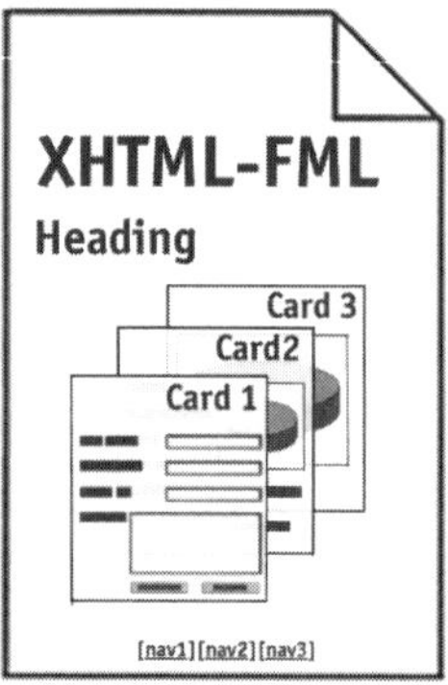

This concept is also being used in documents read on mobile devices, like phones, pagers, PDAs. WML, Wireless Markup Language, with an HTML-like XML grammar, displays various screens (or cards) all defined in a single WML document.

This reduction of several documents down to one means that connections between the client and the server are minimized. This reduces consuming round-trips to the server and conserves precious time and bandwidth.

A very important aspect in FML is the reduction of server-side tasks. Web authors often do not have full access to web servers. Until recently, unless web authors resorted to complex client-side scripts, forms-related web applications were basically limited to server-side technology using, for example, CGI scripts. But now these once difficult to write web forms can be easily written in XHTML-FML and handled directly inside the browser, and thereby providing the same functionality as a server-side application while only being a single web page.

Creating an e-Commerce Order Form in FML

In this chapter, we will take a close look at the new FML tags and how to use them in real-life examples. We will start out by learning how to write a basic address form in FML. Later, we will create a product catalog or shopping cart application in FML.

Since FML allows us to give the appearance of multiple forms to the user, we will put both examples together at the end, creating a complete e-commerce order form.

Basic Address Form

Our goal for a basic address form is to get the name, e-mail address, street address, city, state or province, country, and ZIP or postal code from the person filling out the address form.

The first thing we need to do is to define our form using the FML form container (`<x:form>`) in the document body. This tag is similar to the standard `<form>` tag used in HTML 4.0.

```
<x:form> </x:form>
```

The second FML tag we would like to introduce is `<x:textinput>`, a tag which creates an input field for a single line of text. This tag is similar to the `<input type="text">` tag used in HTML 4.0. We will start out by defining a single textinput for requesting a page visitor's name.

Try It Out – Creating an FML Form Using Text Input

1. Fire up your text editor or the Mozquito Factory and type in the following code. You can open a new document template in the Mozquito Factory as we did earlier or, if you prefer, use your own editor. If you use your own editor, you can open the file `template1.txt` in the `templates` sub directory in the Mozquito Factory which will provide you with the template XHTML-FML file that you can then add to.

```
<?xml version="1.0"?>
<!DOCTYPE html PUBLIC "-//OVERFLOW//DTD XHTML-FML 1.0//EN"
"http://www.mozquito.org/dtd/xhtml-fml1.dtd">
<html xmlns="http://www.w3.org/1999/xhtml" xmlns:x="http://www.mozquito.org/xhtml-
fml">
<head>
<title>Basic Address Form</title>
<meta name="generator" content="Mozquito Factory 1.2" />
<style type="text/css">
<!--
 body {
  margin-top: 15px;
  margin-left: 20px;
  font-family: arial, sans-serif;
  }
-->
</style>
</head>
<body>

<x:form>

Your name:
<x:textinput id="name" /><br />

</x:form>

</body>
</html>
```

2. Depending on which authoring tool you are using, do one of the following:

- Using the Mozquito Factory, validate the document first by clicking on the second checkmark (or tick symbol) in the toolbar or *Ctrl-T*, then click on the browser icon in the toolbar or *Ctrl-D* to see the results on your browser. If you wish, you can save your document as `orderform.xhtml`, but it is not required to save the document to view the changes in the browser.
- Using your own editor, save the document as `orderform.xhtml`. Navigate to the folder where you saved the document and double-click on the file.

3. This is what you should see in your browser:

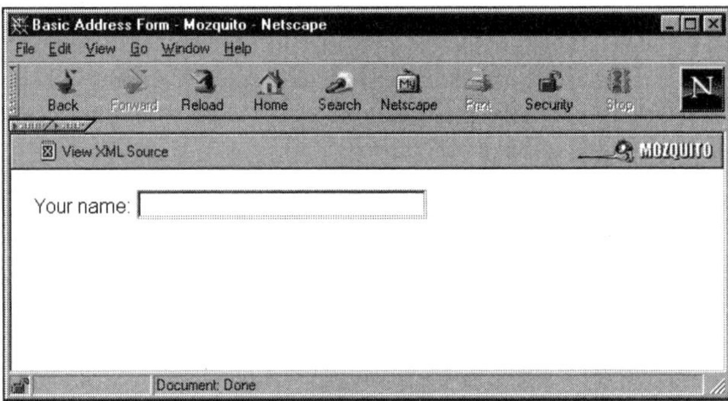

How It Works

We have used a simple style sheet to specify the margins and font family inside the document head:

```
<style type="text/css">
<!--
 body {
  margin-top: 15px;
  margin-left: 20px;
  font-family: arial, sans-serif;
  }
-->
</style>
```

This style will do for now. You can always add properties later on to improve the layout.

In the document body, we have used the `<x:textinput>` tag to create a text input box. The text input box is one of several form controls in FML. A form control is a piece of markup that allows page visitors to enter text or to select one or many options from a list. But more important, form controls have 'values' that change when the page visitor performs an action on the form control, such as entering text. These values are being returned to the server when submitting the form. Similar to HTML forms, FML form controls such as `textinput` must always appear inside an FML form container (`<x:form>`) in the document body. Otherwise, they will not be properly submitted. Most of what we will do in this chapter will happen inside the `<x:form>` element and this is what we have so far:

```
<x:form>

Your name:
<x:textinput id="name" /><br />

</x:form>
```

Here we have given the text input field an ID with the value `name`, but any text could be used for the value.

Now let's move on by adding another text input field for the e-mail address:

Try It Out – Adding an E-Mail Input Field

1. Still working with `orderform.xhtml`, make the following amendments within the `x:form` element:

```
<x:form>

Your name:
<x:textinput id="name" size="30" /><br />

Your valid e-mail address:
<x:textinput id="email" size="30" /><br />

</x:form>
```

2. If you view the file in your browser you should see a second input box.

How It Works

Using the `size` attribute, we have specified the width of the text input field in characters. Save and run this in your browser; you will now see two form fields on the browser.

In some browsers, such as Netscape Navigator 4, the size of the text input field is measured in the fixed-width font, Courier, even though a different font may have been declared in the style sheet. Although you can influence the width of the text input field with the `size` attribute, you cannot always be sure that it matches the exact number of characters specified.

Adding Input Validation

At the moment, we can't do anything with the info typed into the boxes. We want to make sure that the e-mail address is checked for correct syntax when a page visitor enters his or her e-mail address into the text input field.

Try It Out – Checking the E-Mail Address

1. Add the following attributes to the text input field for e-mail validation:

```
<x:form>

Your name:
<x:textinput id="name" size="30" /><br />

Your valid e-mail address:
<x:textinput id="email" size="30" ctype="email" validation="strict" /><br />

</x:form>
```

2. Save the document and double-click the file again, or send the document to the browser from inside the Mozquito Factory.

3. Now enter an incorrect e-mail address into the form (e.g., "@xyz"). Once the cursor is deactivated in the e-mail text input box (e.g. by clicking on something else with the mouse or hitting the *Tab* key), you will get the following alert:

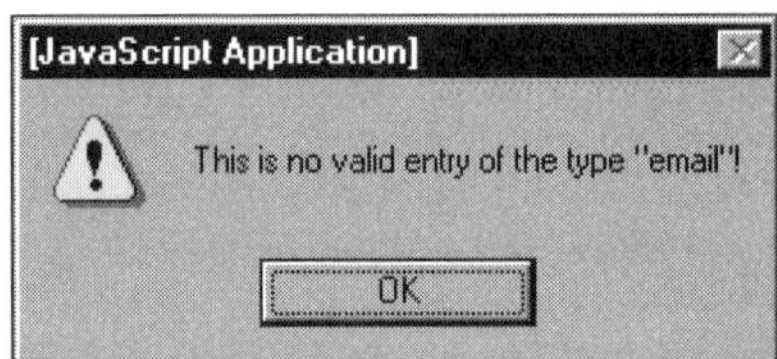

4. Click OK. The incorrect e-mail address will disappear and the cursor will be reactived, allowing the page visitor to re-enter the e-mail address. All this is done for you once you've added the `ctype` and `validation` attributes to the text input form control.

How It Works

Looking at our document, we have added two new attributes that let this happen. The first one is `ctype` (Content Type), with the value `email`. This keyword advises Mozquito to check the entered data against the following criteria:

- There must be at least one or more alphanumeric characters before the @ sign.
- There must be an @ sign.
- The must be at least one or more characters after the @.
- This has to be followed by a dot.
- After the dot, there must be at least two or more characters.

It is technically very difficult to check whether an e-mail address is not only syntactically correct but also valid. The only reliable method is to send an e-mail to the address and ask the receiver to reply.

In addition to the ctype value `email`, other content types are also available. Here is a list of content types current at the time this book was published. This list is likely to be expanded in the near future. We'll look at some examples of other content types later on in this chapter.

`text`
for non-numeric text strings

`num`
for numbers only

`date`
for dates of type:

- DD.MM.YY
- DD.MM.YYYY
- DD/MM/YY
- DD/MM/YYYY
- MM.DD.YY
- MM.DD.YYYY
- MM/DD/YY
- MM/DD/YYYY

`url`
e.g. `http://www.domain.com`, `http://www.domain.com/sample/example.htm`

`www`
e.g. `www.domain.com`

`email`
e.g. `john@doe.com`

`creditcard`
for the 15 or 16 digits of a credit card number.

`expiredate`
for the credit card expiry date of the type:
MM/YY

The 'validation' Attribute

The other attribute we have introduced in this example is `validation`. This attribute lets you choose between two levels of validation: `strict` and `loose`.

We used `strict` for the value of the validation attribute in the previous example. This means that once the page visitor hits the OK button in the validation alert, the entire contents of the given field which does not meet the validation criteria is deleted. If validation is set to `strict`, the page visitor **must** either enter data matching the validation criteria or no data at all.

When validation is set to `loose`, the incorrect data still remains in the form control after the alert has appeared. The page visitor is informed that the data is incorrect but can still proceed and leave the data as it is.

Submitting Forms

Let's add a couple of things so we can submit the entered data to a server.

Try It Out – Submitting the Form

1. Modify `orderform.xhtml` as follows:

```
<x:form id="orderform" action="http://www.mozquito.org/servlets/Echo">

Your name:
<x:textinput id="name" size="30" send="yes" /><br />

Your valid e-mail address:
<x:textinput id="email" size="30" ctype="email" validation="strict" send="yes"
/><br />

<x:button value="Submit" onclick="submit:orderform" />

</x:form>
```

2. First, we'll put these changes in the form, view the new version in the browser, enter a name and correct e-mail address and then hit the submit button.

3. If you are online, you will see the following screen (we've only shown the important part!):

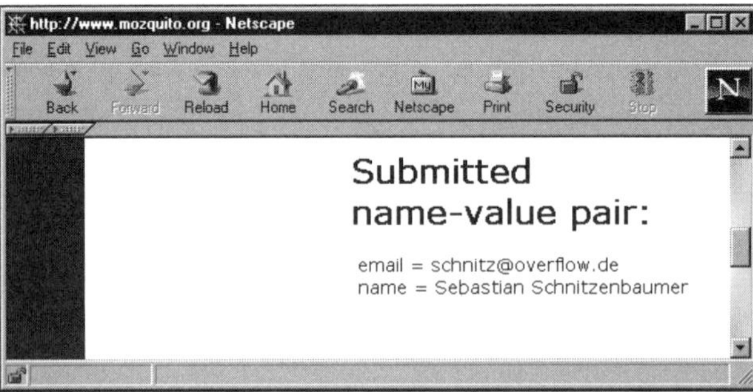

How It Works

The FML form has been successfully submitted. On the opening `<x:form>` tag, we have added an ID with the value `orderform` so we can later specify which form should be submitted. Next, we have given the form an action to do on submit. The value of the action attribute is the URL where the data is submitted. This can be a program or script of any kind running on a server. We have used the Mozquito Echo service located at `http://www.mozquito.org/servlets/Echo` that simply displays the submitted data on an XHTML page.

The 'send' Attribute

Another addition is the `send` attribute on both text input fields in the form. By default, FML form controls do not automatically send their value to the server on submit. You need to explicitly set the `send` attribute to the value `yes` if the form control should send its value to the server.

> *When designing feature-rich web forms in FML, many form controls are interim controls, used for things like navigation and therefore do not need to send their value to the server. Other form controls may send their value on to other form controls in the same document (as we will see later), so in the end only a few form controls will need to send their values to the server.*

The 'button' Tag

The `<x:button>` tag creates a push button. We used this tag in the previous example for the submit button. The `value` attribute holds the text being displayed on the button.

With the `onclick` event handler, we can specify what should happen if the page visitor pushes the button (which is an event). In this case, we want the form to submit, and we use the submit action statement as the value of the `onclick` attribute:

```
submit:FormID
```

After the `submit` keyword and the colon, the ID of the form that we intend to submit must be given. In our example we say `submit:orderform`, since we have given our form the ID `orderform`.

> *This is especially handy when working with multiple forms inside a single XHTML-FML document. You could ask the page visitor whether he wants to fill out this address form or a different form, all defined in a single XHTML-FML document, and then only submit the one he chose.*

Requiring Mandatory Fields

We would like to make sure that the form can be submitted only after certain form controls or fields have been filled out.

In our example, we want the name and a correct e-mail address from the page visitor. We make this happen by adding the `mandatory` attribute to both text input fields.

Try It Out – Checking Required Fields on Submit

1. Here is what we add to the source of our address form:

```
<x:form id="orderform" action="http://www.mozquito.org/servlets/Echo">

Your name:
<x:textinput id="name" size="30" send="yes" mandatory="yes" /><br />

Your valid e-mail address:
<x:textinput id="email" size="30" ctype="email" validation="strict" send="yes"
mandatory="yes" /><br />

<x:button value="Submit" onclick="submit:orderform" />

</x:form>
```

2. In the browser, the following alert appears when pushing the Submit button with blank fields:

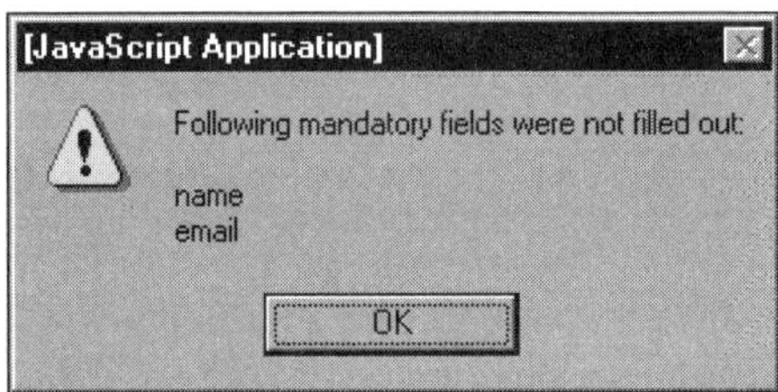

By default, the alert lists the IDs of the fields that were left blank. The form can only be submitted when all form controls with mandatory set to `yes` contain valid entries.

Showing the IDs of the form control can sometimes be confusing. A form control ID might not always clearly indicate which form control needs to be filled. The text appearing adjacent to the form control on the screen page is considered to be its label, not the ID. However, in the XHTML source, this text isn't clearly associated with the form control.

3. Now make the following changes to the form and save the file:

```
<x:form id="orderform" action="http://www.mozquito.org/servlets/Echo">

<x:label for="name">Your name</x:label>:
<x:textinput id="name" size="30" send="yes" mandatory="yes" /><br />

<x:label for="email">Your valid e-mail address</x:label>:
<x:textinput id="email" size="30" ctype="email" validation="strict" send="yes"
mandatory="yes" /><br />

<x:button value="Submit" onclick="submit:orderform" />

</x:form>
```

How It Works

If we mark up our labels properly, as seen above, we can attach it to the associated form control form control. If `mandatory` is set to `yes` and the form control has a label then the alert will show a list of labels instead of IDs:

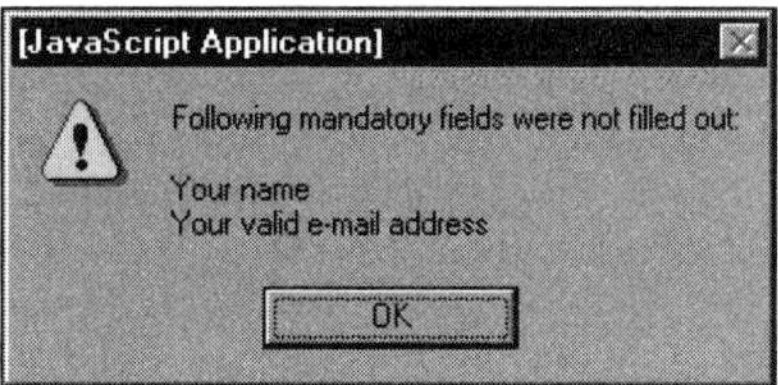

The `<x:label>` tag uses the `for` attribute to associate itself to another form control. The value of the `for` attribute is the same as the associated form control's ID.

> **NOTE: On some systems, whenever you want to view changes in our code in the browser, you need to click the refresh/reload button in the browser.**

Open-ended Lists

The next thing we'll add to the address form is a list of countries for the page visitor to choose from.

Since the web is truly world-wide, we have to ask ourselves: where do we get the most current list of all the countries?

Instead of using a pulldown menu with over 100 options, we can create an open-ended list. We provide a predefined list of countries. Other countries can be added as required.

Here's how we'd mark up a limited range of options:

```
<x:label for="countries">Country</x:label>:
<x:pulldown id="countries" send="yes" mandatory="yes">
 <x:option>Please choose:</x:option>
 <x:option value="Canada">Canada</x:option>
 <x:option value="France">France</x:option>
 <x:option value="Germany">Germany</x:option>
 <x:option value="India">India</x:option>
 <x:option value="Israel">Israel</x:option>
 <x:option value="Japan">Japan</x:option>
 <x:option value="United Kingdom">United Kingdom</x:option>
 <x:option value="USA">USA</x:option>
</x:pulldown>
```

The content of the option element is the text displayed in the pulldown menu on the screen, the pulldown element defines how the list of options is presented to the page visitor, and whether one or several options can be selected. The pulldown element allows only one option to be selected, as opposed to `<x:listbox>`. This corresponds to the `<select>` tag in HTML Forms. Apart from pulldowns and listboxes, lists of radio buttons `<x:radio>` or checkboxes `<x:checkbox>` are available as well and can be used instead of the pulldown element. The only difference is that radio and checkbox lists use the `<x:item>` tag instead of `<x:option>`.

Even though this form control is marked with its mandatory attribute set to true, the Please choose: option is not considered a valid choice because of its absence of a value attribute. The value of the `value` attribute is sent back to the server when the form is submitted.

This is what happens in the browser:

Now comes the interesting part. We will introduce the toggle tag, a very flexible FML tag that we will also be using in various other contexts. The toggle tag will make our pulldown menu visually toggle to a text input field and revert back again to a pulldown menu after the page visitor has entered his or her information. The resulting behavior is similar to a "combo box".

Try It Out – Creating an Open-Ended Pulldown Menu

1. Between the e-mail text input field and the submit button, we'll add the above pulldown menu source with some changes to make it open-ended:

```
<x:label for="countries">Country</x:label>:
<x:toggle id="openlist" shared="yes">
<x:pulldown id="countries" send="yes" mandatory="yes">
 <x:option>Please choose:</x:option>
 <x:option value="Canada">Canada</x:option>
 <x:option value="Finland">Finland</x:option>
 <x:option value="France">France</x:option>
 <x:option value="Germany">Germany</x:option>
 <x:option value="India">India</x:option>
 <x:option value="Israel">Israel</x:option>
 <x:option value="Japan">Japan</x:option>
 <x:option value="The Netherlands">The Netherlands</x:option>
 <x:option value="United Kingdom">United Kingdom</x:option>
 <x:option value="USA">USA</x:option>
 <x:option value="Please enter..." onclick="toggle:openlist">Other...</x:option>
</x:pulldown>
<x:textinput size="20" id="more" onchange="toggle:openlist" />
</x:toggle><br />
```

2. The pulldown has now become the content of the `toggle` element. Although you can include as many elements as you want inside `<x:toggle>`, only the first element, the pulldown, is displayed when the document is loaded in the browser.

3. The screenshot below shows three different views of the open-ended list as someone first clicks on the Other option, types in some text and leaves the field by clicking somewhere else with the mouse or hitting the *Tab* key (pressing *Return* has no effect). The entered text has become a new option.

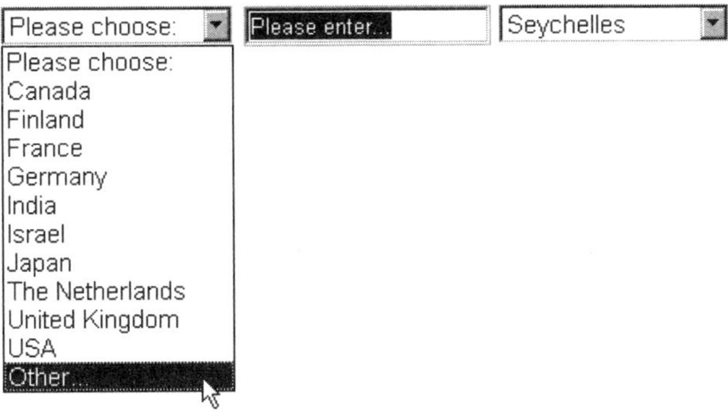

How It Works

The `toggle` tag just cycles through its list of child elements, from top to bottom in the document source order. Since the pulldown element is the first child element inside the `toggle` tag, it is displayed first.

In the source, the next element after the pulldown menu is a textinput field. Now the only thing left is to tell Mozquito to trigger the `toggle` element to switch to the next child element in row. If the last child element is reached, we start again with the first child element. Since we have two child elements in our example, we visually toggle between these two form controls, when the toggle is triggered. This works in both Netscape and Internet Explorer thanks to Mozquito.

Let's see how we actually trigger the toggle. You might have noticed that we have also added another option at the end of the pulldown choice list:

```
<x:option value="Please enter..." onclick="toggle:openlist">Other...</x:option>
```

The `onclick` event handler causes an action statement to toggle to the next element, the text input control. We've already used an action statement to submit forms, but this uses the `toggle` key word followed by the ID of the toggle element that we intend to switch over. Since we have given the toggle element the ID `openlist`, the action statement `toggle:openlist` forces our toggle element to move on to the following element.

The text input control has the same action statement, not as an onclick event handler, but as the value of `onchange`. Once the page visitor has clicked on Other... in the pulldown menu, the text input appears showing its initial value Please enter.... If the value changes by the addition of an unlisted country, it toggles back to the pulldown menu. The `toggle` element will toggle back to the first element if there are no more elements in line. Since we have not specified another form control or element after the text input inside of `<x:toggle>` in the source, the pulldown as the first element is shown when the action statement is executed.

The 'shared' Attribute

The pulldown now has the new value entered by the user as an additional option. Since the value is different than any of the given option's values, a new option is created. This is now highlighted as the selected entry. When the user changes the value of the text input control, the value of the pulldown is changed automatically. This is due to the `shared` attribute we set to `yes` on the toggle starting tag. If `shared` is set to `yes` then all FML forms controls inside the toggle share the same value. If the value of one form control changes, the values of all other form controls are adjusted automatically.

Polish and Chrome

Now that we have covered the core function of the address form, we'll simply extend it to the form controls for state or province, ZIP code, city and street address.

Apart from three new text input controls similar to the `name` field we defined in the beginning, we'll also use a `textarea` field for the street address, allowing the input of multiple lines of text. The width and height is specified in characters with the `cols` and `rows` attributes.

We can now add a level one heading and a table to create a nice layout where all the text fields are neatly aligned under each other.

Our basic address form is now ready to go. This is what it will look like on the browser:

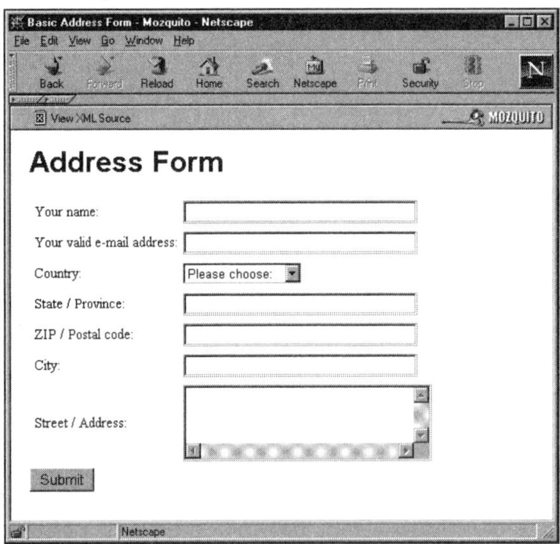

Let's put in the full source code for this:

Try It Out – The Full Address Form

1. Make the following changes to `orderform.xhtml`:

```
<?xml version="1.0"?>
<!DOCTYPE html PUBLIC "-//OVERFLOW//DTD XHTML-FML 1.0//EN"
```

```
"http://www.mozquito.org/dtd/xhtml-fml1.dtd">
<html xmlns="http://www.w3.org/1999/xhtml" xmlns:x="http://www.mozquito.org/xhtml-
fml">
<head>
<title>Basic Address Form</title>
<meta name="generator" content="Mozquito Factory 1.2" />
<style type="text/css">
<!--
 body {
  margin-top: 15px;
  margin-left: 20px;
  font-family: arial, sans-serif;
  }
-->
</style>
</head>
<body>

<h1>Address Form</h1>

<x:form id="orderform" action="http://www.mozquito.org/servlets/Echo">

<table>
<tr>
<td><x:label for="name">Your name</x:label>:</td>
<td><x:textinput size="30" id="name" send="yes" mandatory="yes" /></td>
</tr>
<tr>
<td><x:label for="email">Your valid e-mail address</x:label>:</td>
<td><x:textinput id="email" size="30" ctype="email" validation="strict" send="yes"
mandatory="yes" /></td>
</tr>
<tr>
<td><x:label for="countries">Country</x:label>:</td>
<td>
<x:toggle id="openlist" shared="yes">
<x:pulldown id="countries" send="yes" mandatory="yes">
 <x:option>Please choose:</x:option>
 <x:option value="Canada">Canada</x:option>
 <x:option value="Finland">Finland</x:option>
 <x:option value="France">France</x:option>
 <x:option value="Germany">Germany</x:option>
 <x:option value="India">India</x:option>
 <x:option value="Israel">Israel</x:option>
 <x:option value="Japan">Japan</x:option>
 <x:option value="The Netherlands">The Netherlands</x:option>
 <x:option value="United Kingdom">United Kingdom</x:option>
 <x:option value="USA">USA</x:option>
 <x:option value="Please enter..." onclick="toggle:openlist">Other...</x:option>
</x:pulldown>
<x:textinput size="20" id="more" onchange="toggle:openlist" />
</x:toggle>
```

```
</td>
</tr>
<tr>
<td><x:label for="state">State / Province</x:label>:</td>
<td><x:textinput size="30" id="state" mandatory="yes" send="yes"/></td>
</tr>
<tr>
<td><x:label for="postal-code">ZIP / Postal code</x:label>:</td>
<td><x:textinput size="30" id="postal-code" mandatory="yes" send="yes" /></td>
</tr>
<tr>
<td><x:label for="city">City</x:label>:</td>
<td><x:textinput size="30" id="city" mandatory="yes" send="yes" /></td>
</tr>
<tr>
<td><x:label for="address">Street / Address</x:label>:</td>
<td><x:textarea id="address" mandatory="yes" send="yes" rows="3" cols="30" /></td>
</tr>
</table>

<x:button value="Submit" onclick="submit:orderform" />

</x:form>

</body>
</html>
```

2. Save it and view it in your browser. You should see a similar screen to the one shown earlier.

How It Works

We're using a table for layout here, for simplicity. We've also added in outr new input fields and their associated labels – notice how each label has its `for` attribute set to its appropriately related control:

```
<x:label for="address">Street / Address</x:label>
```

Creating a Product Catalog

Now that we are familiar with all the basic FML concepts, we will move forward and create a small shopping basket example in XHTML-FML. We want to let potential customers browse through a series of products, each with a picture and product details, as well as the calculation of the total sum of the orders.

Single Product Order

Let's start off with a new XHTML-FML document. First we will create a table containing one row and three cells. The first row in the table serves as the header and contains all the details for a specific product: number of orders, product name, a short description, unit price and the calculated sum. After setting this up, we can learn how to calculate in FML.

Try It Out – Calculations

1. Start a new XHTML-FML document, and add this source to the code generated by Mozquito:

```
<x:form>

<table bgcolor="lightgrey">
<tr>
<td>
<x:toggle id="openqty" shared="yes">
<x:pulldown id="quantity" send="yes">
<x:option value="0">0</x:option>
<x:option value="1">1</x:option>
<x:option value="2">2</x:option>
<x:option value="3">3</x:option>
<x:option value="4">4</x:option>
<x:option value="5">5</x:option>
<x:option value="6" onclick="toggle:openqty">+...</x:option>
</x:pulldown>
<x:textinput size="5" id="more" onchange="toggle:openqty" ctype="num"
validation="strict" />
</x:toggle>
</td>
<td>
White Socks
</td>
<td>
A pair of white tennis socks, 85% acrylic, 15% stretch nylon.
</td>
</tr>
</table>

</x:form>
```

2. Save it as `items.xhtml`.

3. Since there is nothing much to see yet on the browser, we will go ahead and add two more cells in the table for calculations at the end of the row (just before the `</tr>` tag):

```
<td>
$ <x:textoutput id="unitprice" value="1.95" send="yes" />
</td>
<td>
$
<x:calc id="sum" term="unitprice * quantity" send="yes">
<x:textoutput />
</x:calc>
</td>
```

Note the dollar symbols are not variables or anything like that, but just a plain old dollar symbol that will appear on your browser to tell you that the cost is in dollars, and not in Italian lire or some other currency, for example.

4. This is what we now see on the browser after the page visitor has selected 4 socks:

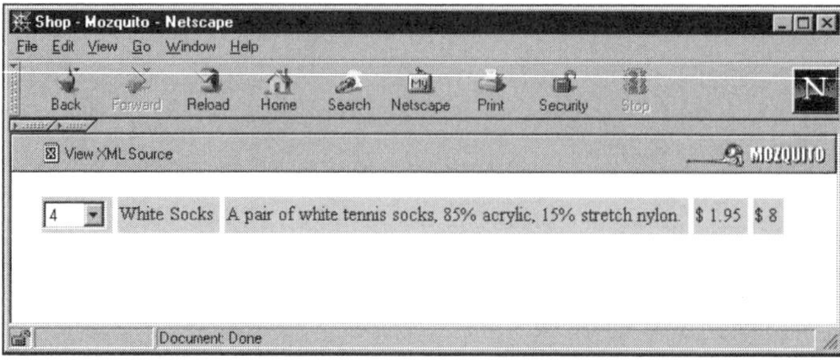

How It Works

In the first table cell, we are using a similar open-ended list to the countries list in the address form. Since this `pulldown` menu lets the visitor select only numbers for number of items ordered, we have added validation to the `textinput` field to allow only numbers in the text box. We have used `num` as the value of `ctype` to prevent other entries than numbers.

'textoutput' and 'calc'

We have introduced two new tags: `<x:textoutput>` and `<x:calc>`. The `textoutput` element is very similar the `textinput` we have been using. The only difference is that the text output fields cannot be changed by the user. Instead of showing its value inside a text box, text output fields show their value as normal text.

The `calc` element allows us to calculate. By itself, this element has no display. Instead, the `calc` element is wrapped around other FML form controls. In our case we have used a textoutput field inside `calc`. The element inside will automatically inherit the calculated value of the `calc` element, the textoutput field's value is always the same as the value of the `calc` element.

The value of the `calc` element changes depending on the `term` attribute. The value of `term` is any mathematical expression with numbers and the IDs of other FML form controls. In the above example, we said:

```
unitprice * quantity
```

We have referenced the form control for quantity (the open-ended pulldown list) and the text output field holding the unit price as its value ($ 1.95).

If one of the two referenced form control values is changed due to interaction with the page visitor, the `calc` element value will be updated automatically using the calculation defined in the `term` attribute.

Since the text output field inside the `calc` element immediately inherits the new `calc` element value, we get to see the result directly on the screen.

You might have noticed that the calculated sum is always rounded up to a whole number. We can prevent this from happening by telling the `calc` element with the `digits` attribute to round up by two digits to the right of the decimal point:

```
<x:calc id="sum" term="unitprice * quantity" send="yes" digits="2">
<x:textoutput />
</x:calc>
```

Multiple Product Order

We have just defined a single table row for a single product order. To order several different products, we just need to add rows to the table, copying the above row and pasting it into the document source several times. If your catalog is very large, you might need to split things up by category and into separate FML documents. We will continue with adding another table instead of just another row, so can then always expand both tables if you want more products in each category.

In normal forms, this would have two annoying side-effects. First, the length of the source code would start to inflate due to endlessly repeating code for each row. But using Mozquito only small parts of the code change. In our example, the text for product name and description and the unit price would change between multiple table rows. All of the other tags would remain the same.

Secondly, if we wanted to change something affecting all the products afterwards, for instance adding an additional cell, we would have to go through the whole document source and add each cell individually.

Time for a new tag! We will simply define the table containing the single table row as a *template.* We can then *insert* the template as often as we like in our document source.

Try It Out – Using Templates

1. We will take the table out of the form container `<x:form>`, and instead put it inside the `<x:template>` tag. We then use `<x:insert>` to insert the template wherever we want in the document. Make the following changes to `items.xhtml`:

```
<x:template id="product">
<table bgcolor="lightgrey">
<tr>
<td>
<x:toggle id="openqty" shared="yes">
<x:pulldown id="quantity" send="yes">
<x:option value="0">0</x:option>
<x:option value="1">1</x:option>
<x:option value="2">2</x:option>
<x:option value="3">3</x:option>
<x:option value="4">4</x:option>
<x:option value="5">5</x:option>
<x:option value="6" onclick="toggle:openqty">+...</x:option>
</x:pulldown>
<x:textinput size="5" onchange="toggle:openqty" ctype="num" validation="strict" />
</x:toggle>
</td>
<td>
White Socks
</td>
<td>
```

```
A pair of white tennis socks, 85% acrylic, 15% stretch nylon.
</td>
<td>
$ <x:textoutput id="unitprice" value="1.95" send="yes" />
</td>
<td>
$
<x:calc id="sum" term="unitprice * quantity" send="yes" digits="2">
<x:textoutput />
</x:calc>
</td>
</tr>
</table>
</x:template>

<x:form>

<x:insert id="Sock1" template="product" />
<x:insert id="Sock2" template="product" />

</x:form>
```

2. Instead of doubling the source to create two table rows, we have only used an additional four lines of code to get the same result:

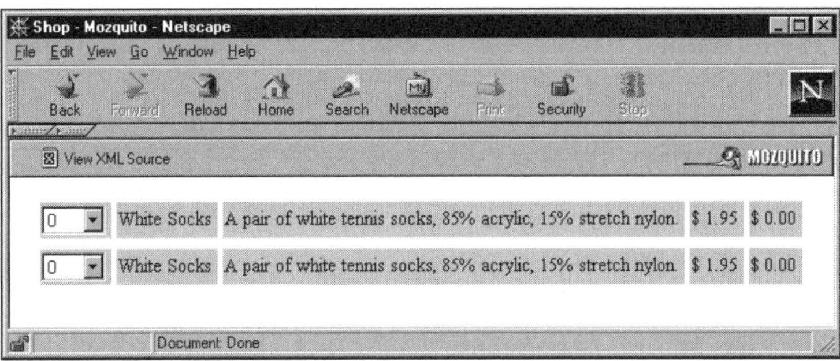

How It Works

We have defined a template with the ID `product`. You don't see the templates themselves. The `insert` tag lets us insert the contents of a template at the location of the `insert` tag in the document source. The `template` attribute references the ID of the template we want to insert.

The prop tag

We are still missing something: what if we want to change part of the template before we insert it a second time?

We can define flexible parts inside a template. This can be done by enclosing parts of the template within pipes: `|text|`. The text enclosed by pipes inside a template can be changed when inserting the template.

To avoid inserting the exact same row twice (as we did above), we can change the source slightly:

Try It Out – Dynamic Templates

1. Alter the source slightly as shown:

```
<x:template id="product">
<table bgcolor="lightgrey">
<tr>
<td>
<x:toggle id="openqty" shared="yes">
<x:pulldown id="quantity" send="yes">
<x:option value="0">0</x:option>
<x:option value="1">1</x:option>
<x:option value="2">2</x:option>
<x:option value="3">3</x:option>
<x:option value="4">4</x:option>
<x:option value="5">5</x:option>
<x:option value="6" onclick="toggle:openqty">+...</x:option>
</x:pulldown>
<x:textinput size="5" onchange="toggle:openqty" ctype="num" validation="strict" />
</x:toggle>
</td>
<td>
|title|
</td>
<td>
|description|
</td>
<td>
$ <x:textoutput id="unitprice" value="|price|" send="yes" />
</td>
<td>
$
<x:calc id="sum" term="unitprice * quantity" send="yes" digits="2">
<x:textoutput />
</x:calc>
</td>
</tr>
</table>
</x:template>

<x:form>

<x:insert id="Sock1" template="product">
<x:prop name="title">White Socks</x:prop>
<x:prop name="description">A pair of white tennis socks, 85% acrylic, 15% stretch
nylon.</x:prop>
<x:prop name="price">1.95</x:prop>
</x:insert>
<x:insert id="Sock2" template="product">
<x:prop name="title">Red Socks</x:prop>
<x:prop name="description">A pair of red socks, 70% nylon, 30% cotton.</x:prop>
<x:prop name="price">2.49</x:prop>
</x:insert>

</x:form>
```

2. On the browser, we now see that the two rows are different:

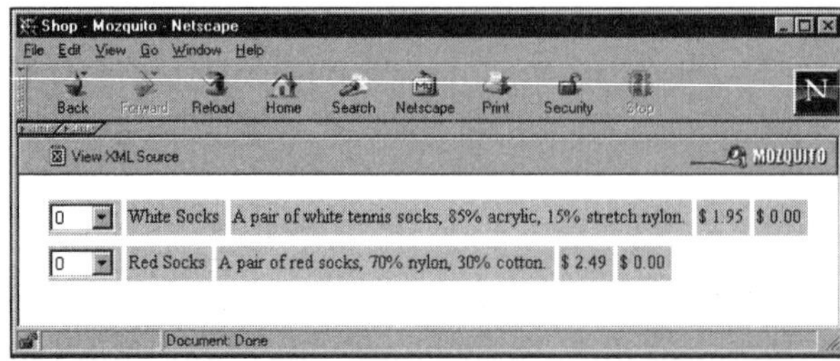

By enclosing `title`, `description` and `price` in the template source with pipes, we can use the `prop` tag inside the `insert` element to replace these 'space holders' with specific content. We reference the space holders by using the pipe-enclosed text as the value of the `prop` tag name attribute. The content of the `prop` element replaces the text enclosed by pipes. Adding more products is now very simple; we only need to add more inserts.

The reason why we have inserted two tables in our example instead of just adding new table rows to a single table is because we will add another toggle element later, and both tables will appear on separate cards. And remember, you can always add your own markup and style or rearrange things to customize the look and feel.

Displaying the total sum of the order at the bottom of the table is our next step. We will leave the template aside for now and focus on the form container `<x:form>`:

Try It Out – Calculation and Templates

1. Add the following lines to `items.xhtml`:

```
<x:form>

<x:insert id="Sock1" template="product">
<x:prop name="title">White Socks</x:prop>
<x:prop name="description">A pair of white tennis socks, 85% acrylic, 15% stretch
nylon.</x:prop>
<x:prop name="price">1.95</x:prop>
</x:insert>
<x:insert id="Sock2" template="product">
<x:prop name="title">Red Socks</x:prop>
<x:prop name="description">A pair of red socks, 70% nylon, 30% cotton.</x:prop>
<x:prop name="price">2.49</x:prop>
</x:insert>

<p>Total: $
<x:calc id="total" term="Sock1.sum + Sock2.sum" digits="2" send="yes">
<x:textoutput />
</x:calc>
</p>

</x:form>
```

How It Works

We use the `calc` element the same way we did for multiplying the number of a single product ordered by the unit price, except for one difference.

The term now uses names that are the combination of two IDs separated by a dot. In XML, all IDs must be unique. If Mozquito copied the templates without automatically changing all the element IDs in the template on insertion, we wouldn't know how to address these tags, since they would have duplicate names.

The IDs in the template are prefixed with the ID of the specific insert tag. The first row we insert gets the ID prefix `Socks1`, the ID of the `insert` tag. If you recall, we gave the `calc` element, which multiplies the number of a single products ordered by the unit price, the ID `sum`. The ID is then `Sock2.sum`, because calc is part of the template.

When products are ordered on our form, not only the price of each product but also the total sum of all the products is now calculated immediately:

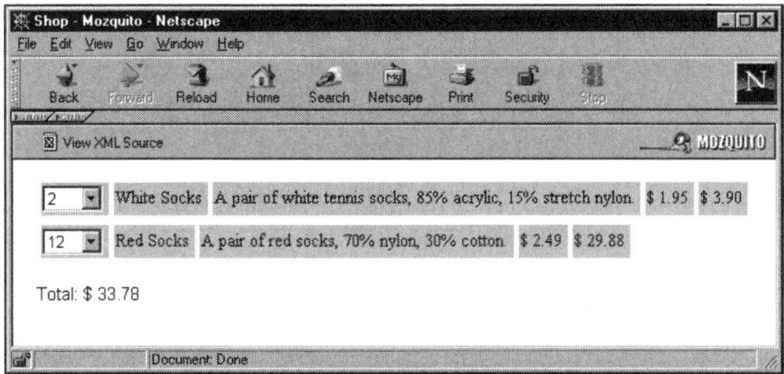

Multiple Cards

Instead of showing all the products on one screen page, we can use FML to create a slideshow, showing each product one at a time. We use the `<x:toggle>` tag in FML to *toggle* between two (or more) products. We have already used toggle to create open-ended lists, but we will now use it for client-side persistency throughout a series of screen pages. We create client-side persistency simply by defining multiple screen pages inside a single XHTML-FML document. The source of this persistency is that the web page never gets "unloaded" – it just redraws itself, in our case when a page visitor hits a button. Page visitors can quickly and easily flip from one product page to the next, since all the information is already on the browser. Normally, this would normally require a very complex JavaScript script.

Try It Out – Creating Multiple Pages Inside a Single Document

1. Let's make a few changes inside `<x:form>` to the source of `items.xhtml`:

```
<x:form>

<div align="center">
```

```
<x:toggle id="show">
<x:insert id="Sock1" template="product">
<x:prop name="title">White Socks</x:prop>
<x:prop name="description">A pair of white tennis socks, 85% acrylic, 15% stretch
nylon.</x:prop>
<x:prop name="price">1.95</x:prop>
</x:insert>
<x:insert id="Sock2" template="product">
<x:prop name="title">Red Socks</x:prop>
<x:prop name="description">A pair of red socks, 70% nylon, 30% cotton.</x:prop>
<x:prop name="price">2.49</x:prop>
</x:insert>
</x:toggle><br />

<p>Total: $
<x:calc id="total" term="Sock1.sum + Sock2.sum" digits="2" send="yes">
<x:textoutput />
</x:calc>
</p>

<x:button value="Back" onclick="toggle:show,-" />
<x:button value="Next" onclick="toggle:show,+" />

</div>

</x:form>
```

How It Works

We have nested both inserts inside a `toggle` element with the ID `show` and added two buttons. For better layout, we have also added a `<div>` element to center everything on the screen. Although we didn't change much in the source, we see a huge difference on the browser:

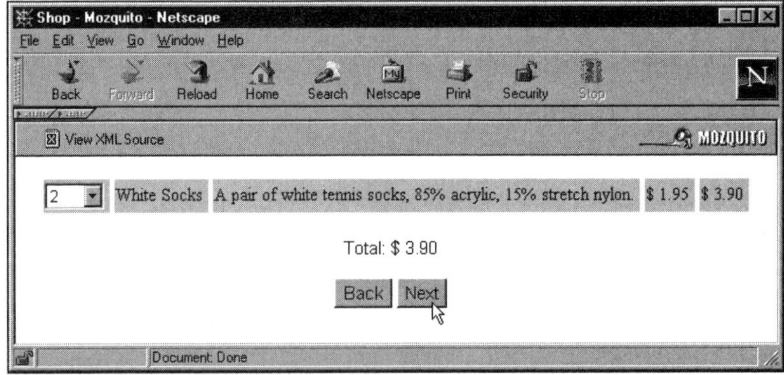

When the document is loaded onto the browser, only the first product is shown, since the first element inside the `toggle` element is always shown first. In our case this is the `insert` tag inserting the template we defined for a single product. By clicking the Next button, we watch the second product dynamically appear:

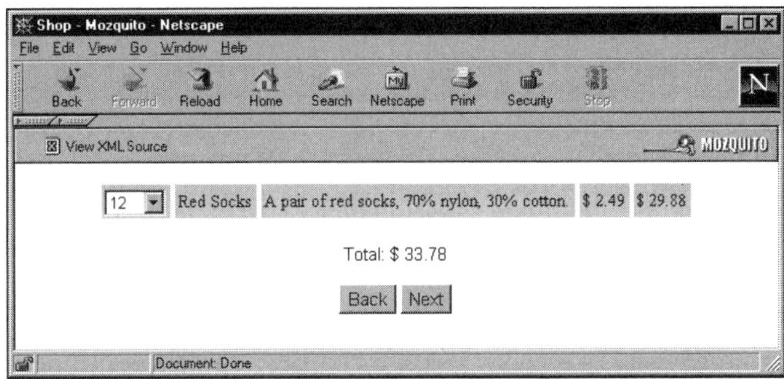

The area for calculating the total as well as the buttons reappear at the same position on the next page since they are defined outside of the `toggle` element in the document source. Mozquito remembers all the field values not shown on the screen, so we can still calculate the total sum of the products, although we only see one product at a time.

The Back button brings us back to the first product, the white socks. We use the action statement `toggle:show,-` as the value of the `onclick` event handler on the button element. By putting a comma and a minus sign after the ID of the `toggle` element, we toggle backwards through the elements inside the `toggle`. By using a plus sign, we move forward.

To see more FML examples, especially how multiple cards can be used elegantly, visit `http://www.mozquito.com` and have a look at the demos.

Preloading Images

Let's add a heading and an image to each product. Since we already inserted the template containing the table with the product information, we simply need to add a heading and an image before the table in the template. We will also define the value of the `src` attribute of the image as a property, so we can then specify the filename with an additional `prop` tag when inserting the template. Here are the minor changes to the source:

Try It Out – Preloading Images

1. Make the following changes to `items.xhtml`:

```
<x:template id="product">
<h1>|title|</h1>
<x:img src="images/|image|" width="340" height="206" alt="|title|" preload="yes"
/>
<table bgcolor="lightgrey">
<tr>
<td>
<x:toggle id="openqty" shared="yes">
<x:pulldown id="quantity" send="yes">
<x:option value="0">0</x:option>
<x:option value="1">1</x:option>

...

...
```

```
<x:toggle id="show">
<x:insert id="Sock1" template="product">
<x:prop name="title">White Socks</x:prop>
<x:prop name="description">A pair of white tennis socks, 85% acrylic, 15% stretch
nylon.</x:prop>
<x:prop name="price">1.95</x:prop>
<x:prop name="image">white.jpg</x:prop>
</x:insert>
<x:insert id="Sock2" template="product">
<x:prop name="title">Red Socks</x:prop>
<x:prop name="description">A pair of red socks, 70% nylon, 30% cotton.</x:prop>
<x:prop name="price">2.49</x:prop>
<x:prop name="image">red.jpg</x:prop>
</x:insert>
</x:toggle><br />

<x:button value="Back" onclick="toggle:show,-" />
<x:button value="Next" onclick="toggle:show,+" />

<p>Total: $
<x:calc id="total" term="Sock1.sum + Sock2.sum" digits="2" send="yes">
<x:textoutput />
</x:calc>
</p>

</div>

</x:form>
```

2. The browser should display the following:

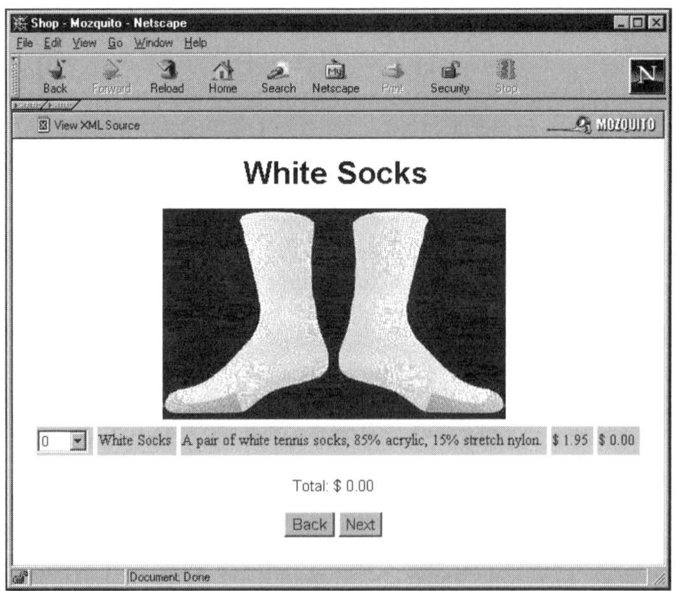

How It Works

We have re-used the `title` property as the content of the heading as well as the value of the `alt` attribute of the image.

Flipping to the next page, we immediately see the next image with the filename `red.jpg`, showing red socks. Normally, this second image would be loaded from the server the moment we toggled to the next page. But by adding `preload="yes"` to the FML image tag `<x:img>`, we tell Mozquito to pre-load all the images into the document at the initial loading of the site. This ensures that visitors receive a document containing multiple pages as well as all the images at once, so they can browse the document offline. The images are loaded in the background, so the page visitor does not have to wait until all images are pre-loaded before being able to continue. The `preload` attribute is the only difference between the FML image tag `<x:img>` and the XHTML image tag `<img>`.

Embedding the Address Form

We can now add the address form we created previously to our product catalog. The address form can also be extended with additional fields for credit card information. We do this by creating a third screen page containing the address form with the credit card details. We add the address form after the two insert elements inside the toggle. Since the address form contains more than one element, we need to group these elements into a single toggle group. This will ensure that all the elements in the address form appear at the same time, not just one at a time.

Try It Out – Combining the Two Forms

1. Cut and paste from `items.xhtml` into `orderform.xhtml` and make the following amendments (changes to inserted text are shown in bold). The final listing should look like this:

```
<?xml version="1.0"?>
<!DOCTYPE html PUBLIC "-//OVERFLOW//DTD XHTML-FML 1.0//EN"
"http://www.mozquito.org/dtd/xhtml-fml1.dtd">
<html xmlns="http://www.w3.org/1999/xhtml" xmlns:x="http://www.mozquito.org/xhtml-
fml">
<head>
<title>Shop</title>
<meta name="generator" content="Mozquito Factory 1.2" />
<style type="text/css">

 body {
  margin-top: 15px;
  margin-left: 20px;
  font-family: arial, sans-serif;
  }

</style>
</head>
<body>

<x:template id="product">
<h1>|title|</h1>
<x:img src="images/|image|" width="340" height="206" alt="|title|" preload="yes"
```

```
/>
<table bgcolor="lightgrey">
<tr>
<td>
<x:toggle id="openqty" shared="yes">
<x:pulldown id="quantity" send="yes">
<x:option value="0">0</x:option>
<x:option value="1">1</x:option>
<x:option value="2">2</x:option>
<x:option value="3">3</x:option>
<x:option value="4">4</x:option>
<x:option value="5">5</x:option>
<x:option value="6" onclick="toggle:openqty">+...</x:option>
</x:pulldown>
<x:textinput size="5" onchange="toggle:openqty" ctype="num" validation="strict" />
</x:toggle>
</td>
<td>
|title|
</td>
<td>
|description|
</td>
<td>
$ <x:textoutput id="unitprice" value="|price|" send="yes" />
</td>
<td>
$
<x:calc id="sum" term="unitprice * quantity" digits="2" send="yes">
<x:textoutput />
</x:calc>
</td>
</tr>
</table>
</x:template>

<x:form id="orderform" action="http://www.mozquito.org/servlets/Echo">

<div align="center">

<x:toggle id="show">
<x:insert id="Sock1" template="product">
<x:prop name="title">White Socks</x:prop>
<x:prop name="description">A pair of white tennis socks, 85% acrylic, 15% stretch
nylon.</x:prop>
<x:prop name="price">1.95</x:prop>
<x:prop name="image">white.jpg</x:prop>
</x:insert>
<x:insert id="Sock2" template="product">
<x:prop name="title">Red Socks</x:prop>
<x:prop name="description">A pair of red socks, 70% nylon, 30% cotton.</x:prop>
<x:prop name="price">2.49</x:prop>
<x:prop name="image">red.jpg</x:prop>
</x:insert>
<x:tg>
```

```
<h1>Checkout</h1>
<table>
<tr>
<td><x:label for="name">Your name</x:label>:</td>
<td><x:textinput size="30" id="name" send="yes" mandatory="yes" /></td>
</tr>
<tr>
<td><x:label for="email">Your valid e-mail address</x:label>:</td>
<td><x:textinput id="email" size="30" ctype="email" validation="strict" send="yes"
mandatory="yes" /></td>
</tr>
<tr>
<td><x:label for="countries">Country</x:label>:</td>
<td>
<x:toggle id="openlist" shared="yes">
<x:pulldown id="countries" send="yes" mandatory="yes">
 <x:option>Please choose:</x:option>
 <x:option value="Canada">Canada</x:option>
 <x:option value="Finland">Finland</x:option>
 <x:option value="France">France</x:option>
 <x:option value="Germany">Germany</x:option>
 <x:option value="India">India</x:option>
 <x:option value="Israel">Israel</x:option>
 <x:option value="Japan">Japan</x:option>
 <x:option value="The Netherlands">The Netherlands</x:option>
 <x:option value="United Kingdom">United Kingdom</x:option>
 <x:option value="USA">USA</x:option>
 <x:option value="Please enter..." onclick="toggle:openlist">Other...</x:option>
</x:pulldown>
<x:textinput size="20" id="more" onchange="toggle:openlist" />
</x:toggle>
</td>
</tr>
<tr>
<td><x:label for="state">State / Province</x:label>:</td>
<td><x:textinput size="30" id="state" mandatory="yes" send="yes"/></td>
</tr>
<tr>
<td><x:label for="postal-code">ZIP / Postal code</x:label>:</td>
<td><x:textinput size="30" id="postal-code" mandatory="yes" send="yes" /></td>
</tr>
<tr>
<td><x:label for="city">City</x:label>:</td>
<td><x:textinput size="30" id="city" mandatory="yes" send="yes" /></td>
</tr>
<tr>
<td><x:label for="address">Street / Address</x:label>:</td>
<td><x:textarea id="address" mandatory="yes" send="yes" rows="3" cols="30" /></td>
</tr>
</table>

<x:button value="Submit" onclick="submit:orderform" />
```

```
</x:tg>
</x:toggle><br />

<x:button value="Back" onclick="toggle:show,-" />
<x:button value="Next" onclick="toggle:show,+" />

<p>Total: $
<x:calc id="total" term="Sock1.sum + Sock2.sum" digits="2" send="yes">
<x:textoutput />
</x:calc>
</p>

</div>

</x:form>

</body>
</html>
```

Save the file and run it on your browser. You should now be the proud owner of a nice and simple miniature e-commerce site.

How It Works

We've only actually changed one thing, which was to add a toggle group to our page, having combined our 2 existing pages into one. The toggle group element (`<x:tg>`) can hold any number of tags, but since these tags are now a group, they will be shown at the same time on the screen.

So there you have it! Basic building blocks for a very nice e-commerce site.

Summary

In this chapter, we have introduced a great amount of practical information that you can use immediately to make your web site more functional without a lot of extra work. The Mozquito Factory is a great tool that allows you to create dynamic forms and catalogs without having to deal with JavaScript. Using XHTML-FML and the Mozquito Engine you can also reduce server-side tasks. All you need besides the Mozquito Engine is a few new tags and your own creativity.

After you're done with editing and ready to upload your document to your server, you will need to transform your document into JavaScript: simply click on File | Export or *Ctrl-E*, and the Mozquito Factory will generate a transformed copy for you. You can save the document with a `.html` or `.htm` file extension.

Here is what we covered:

- How to set up and use the Mozquito Factory to edit and validate XHTML.
- What the Forms Markup Language is and how to use it to enhance your forms.
- How to use Mozquito to create a basic address form including input validation, mandatory fields and open-ended lists.
- How to use Mozquito to create a persistent product catalog including calculations and preloading images for smooth browsing.
- How to use Mozquito to create code-saving templates.
- How to use Mozquito to create pages that can be browsed off-line.

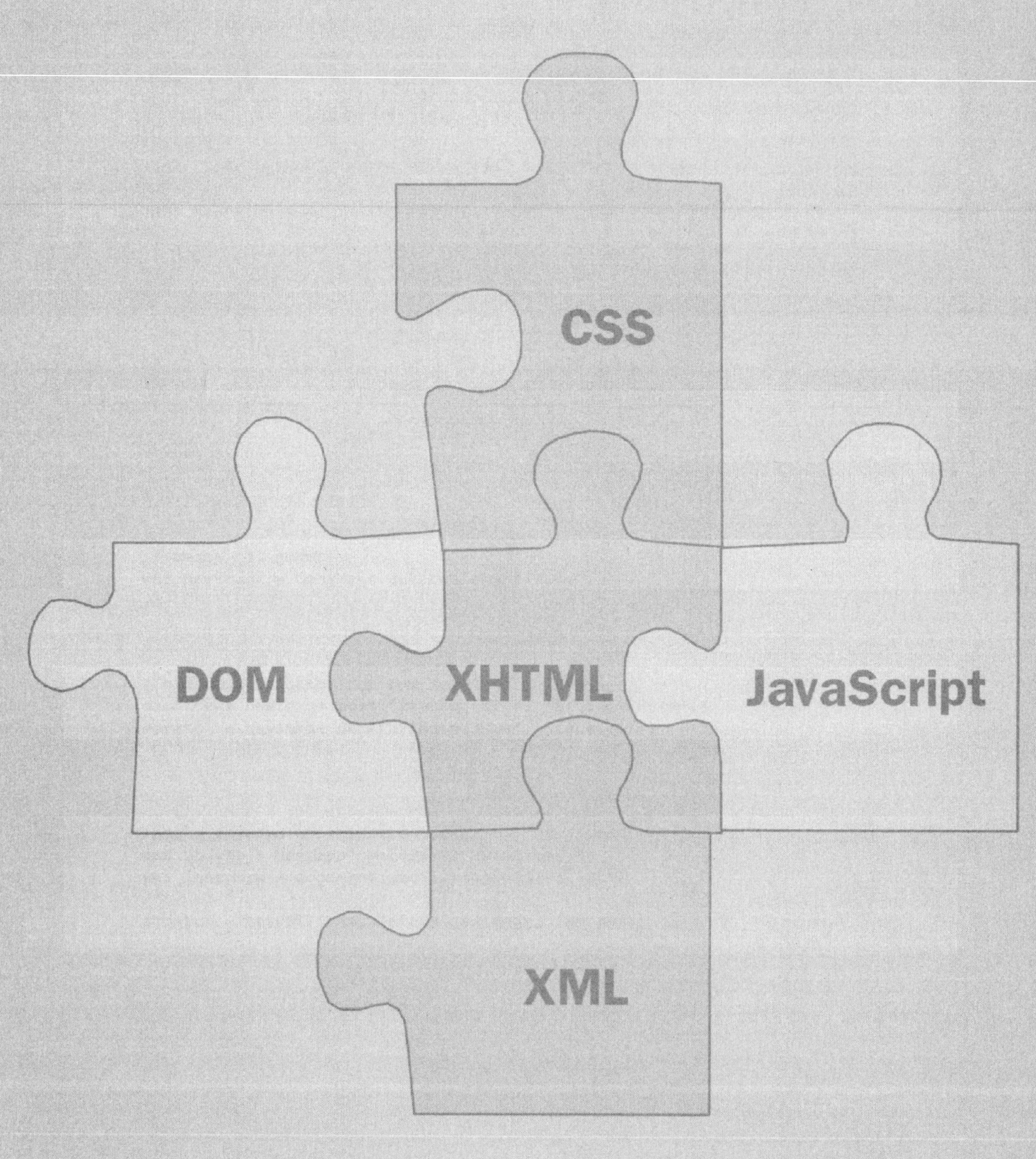
CSS
DOM
XHTML
JavaScript
XML

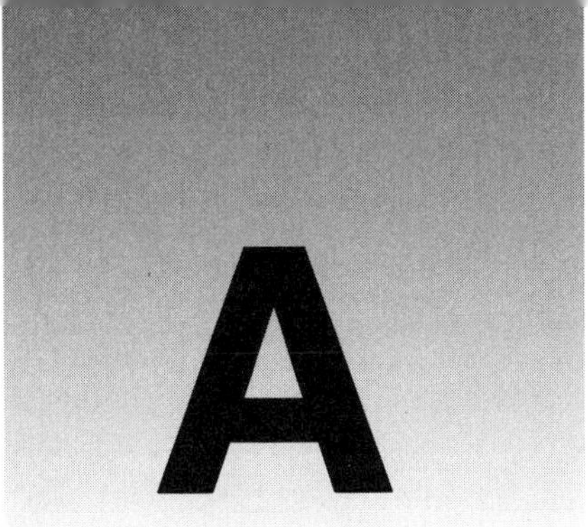

XHTML Tags and Attributes

XHTML has three Document Type Definitions (or DTDs). To be a conforming XHTML document, your document must conform to one of these DTDs. The **Strict** DTD should be used whenever possible, and may be considered to be the 'core' XHTML DTD. The other two DTDs, **Transitional** and **Frameset**, contain everything that is within the Strict DTD, plus some additional tags and attributes; these additional tags/attributes are likely to be phased out (i.e. are deprecated) in future versions of XHTML.

The format of your XHTML documents is therefore recommended to be:

```
<?xml version="1.0" encoding="UTF-8"?>
<!DOCTYPE html
     PUBLIC "-//W3C//DTD XHTML 1.0 Strict//EN"
    "http://www.w3.org/TR/xhtml1/DTD/xhtml1-strict.dtd">
<html xmlns="http://www.w3.org/1999/xhtml" xml:lang="en" lang="en">
  <head>
    Your document meta-information goes here
  </head>
  <body>
    Your document content goes here
  </body>
</html>
```

You are advised to use the above as a blank template file for all of your XHTML documents. Note that *all* tags must be in lower case.

All tags contain attributes which provide further information about the markup required. For example, we may include the `align` attribute in the `<p>` element, and specify the value `right`, when we want our paragraphs to be right justified. To do this, we simply include the attribute-value pair within the opening tags angle brackets, e.g. `<p align="right">`. Note that *all* attribute values must be quoted, even those that are numbers. Thus, for example, the `5` must be in quotes in `<table rows="5">` or it will not work.

Strict DTD

Element	Description
<a>	Used to anchor one document to another (i.e. a hypertext link). Attributes: id, class, style, title, lang, xml:lang, dir, charset, type, name, href, hreflang, rel, rev, accesskey, shape, coords, tabindex, onfocus, onblur
<abbr>	Used to indicate an abbreviation. Attributes: id, class, style, title, lang, xml:lang, dir
<acronym>	Used to indicate an acronym. Attributes: id, class, style, title, lang, xml:lang, dir
<address>	Used to provide contact information about the author of the XHTML document. Attributes: id, class, style, title, lang, xml:lang, dir
<area>	Used to define the area of a client-side image map. Attributes: id, class, style, title, lang, xml:lang, dir, shape, coords, href, nohref, alt (required), tabindex, accesskey, onfocus, onblur
<b>	Used to provide bold font. Attributes: id, class, style, title, lang, xml:lang, dir
<base>	This is the document's base URI. (Part of the <head> element.) Attribute: href
<bdo>	Used to turn off the bi-directional rendering algorithm. Attributes: id, class, style, title, lang, xml:lang, dir (required), onclick, ondblclick, onmousedown, onmouseup, onmousemove, onmouseout, onkeypress, onkeydown, onkeyup
<big>	Used to provide bigger font. Attributes: id, class, style, title, lang, xml:lang, dir
<blockquote>	Used to delimit a long quotation. Attributes: id, class, style, title, lang, xml:lang, dir, cite
<body>	The <body> element contains the document's displayed content. Attributes: id, class, style, title, lang, xml:lang, dir, onload, onunload
 	Used to provide a forced line break – empty element. Attributes: id, class, style, title

Element	Description
<button>	Used to provide an XHTML button on your web page.
	Attributes: id, class, style, title, lang, xml:lang, dir, name, value, type, disabled, tabindex, accesskey, onfocus, onblur
<caption>	Used to provide the caption for a table.
	Attributes: id, class, style, title, lang, xml:lang, dir
<cite>	Used to indicate a citation (reference to other work).
	Attributes: id, class, style, title, lang, xml:lang, dir
<code>	Used to delimit program code.
	Attributes: id, class, style, title, lang, xml:lang, dir
<col>	Used to denote a table column.
	Attributes: id, class, style, title, lang, xml:lang, dir, span, width, char, charoff, align, valign
<colgroup>	Used to denote a table column group.
	Attributes: id, class, style, title, lang, xml:lang, dir, span, width, char, charoff, align, valign
<dd>	Used to provide a definition of the <dt> in a <dl>.
	Attributes: id, class, style, title, lang, xml:lang, dir
<del>	Used to show the text that has been deleted in order to update a document.
	Attributes: id, class, style, title, lang, xml:lang, dir, cite, datetime
<dfn>	Used to delimit a definition.
	Attributes: id, class, style, title, lang, xml:lang, dir
<div>	A generic language/style container.
	Attributes: id, class, style, title, lang, xml:lang, dir
<dl>	Used to define a definition list.
	Attributes: id, class, style, title, lang, xml:lang, dir
<dt>	Used within <dl> to define the definition term.
	Attributes: id, class, style, title, lang, xml:lang, dir
<em>	Used to provide emphasis.
	Attributes: id, class, style, title, lang, xml:lang, dir

Table Continued on Following Page

Element	Description
<fieldset>	Used to group form fields. Attributes: id, class, style, title, lang, xml:lang, dir
<form>	Used to generate an interactive form. Attributes: id, class, style, title, lang, xml:lang, dir, action (required), method, enctype, onsubmit, onreset, accept, accept-charset
<h1>	The largest of the six headings. Attributes: id, class, style, title, lang, xml:lang, dir
<h2>	The second largest of the six headings. Attributes: id, class, style, title, lang, xml:lang, dir
<h3>	The third largest of the six headings. Attributes: id, class, style, title, lang, xml:lang, dir
<h4>	The third smallest of the six headings. Attributes: id, class, style, title, lang, xml:lang, dir
<h5>	The second smallest of the six headings. Attributes: id, class, style, title, lang, xml:lang, dir
<h6>	The smallest of the six headings. Attributes: id, class, style, title, lang, xml:lang, dir
<head>	The <head> element contains a document's non-displayed meta-information. Attributes: lang, xml:lang, dir, profile
<hr />	Displays a horizontal rule – empty element. Attributes: id, class, style, title, lang, xml:lang, dir
<html>	The root element of each XHTML document (note it has no x). Attributes: lang, xml:lang, dir, xmlns (fixed, must be http://www.w3.org/1999/xhtml)
<i>	Used to provide italic font. Attributes: id, class, style, title, lang, xml:lang, dir
<img>	Used to include an image within the web page. Attributes: id, class, style, title, lang, xml:lang, dir, src (required), alt (required), longdesc, height, width, usemap, ismap

Element	Description
<input>	Used to specify a form's input control. Attributes: id, class, style, title, lang, xml:lang, dir, type, name, value, checked, disabled, readonly, size, maxlength, src, alt, usemap, tabindex, accesskey, onfocus, onblur, onselect, onchange, accept
<ins>	Used to show the text that has been inserted in order to update a document. Attributes: id, class, style, title, lang, xml:lang, dir, cite, datetime
<kbd>	Used to indicate material that a user should enter at their keyboard. Attributes: id, class, style, title, lang, xml:lang, dir
<label>	Used to label a form field. Attributes: id, class, style, title, lang, xml:lang, dir, for, accesskey, onfocus, onblur
<legend>	Used to label a fieldset grouping. Attributes: id, class, style, title, lang, xml:lang, dir, accesskey
<li>	Used to define each item in your specified list (either <ol> or <ul>). Attributes: id, class, style, title, lang, xml:lang, dir
<link>	A media-independent link. (Part of the <head> element.) Attributes: id, class, style, title, lang, xml:lang, dir, charset, href, hreflang, type, rel, rev, media
<map>	Used to specify a client-side image map. Attributes: lang, xml:lang, dir, id (required), class, style, title, name, onclick, ondblclick, onmousedown, onmouseup, onmousemove, onmouseout, onkeypress, onkeydown, onkeyup
<meta>	Used to list generic meta-information. (Part of the <head> element.) Attributes: lang, xml:lang, dir, http-equiv, name, content (required), scheme
<noscript>	Used to provide alternate content when scripting is not available. (Part of the <head> element.) Attributes: id, class, style, title, lang, xml:lang, dir
<object>	Used to embed an object within your web page. Attributes: id, class, style, title, lang, xml:lang, dir, declare, classid, codebase, data, type, codetype, archive, standby, height, width, usemap, name, tabindex

Table Continued on Following Page

Element	Description
<ol>	Used to define an ordered (i.e. numbered) list.
	Attributes: id, class, style, title, lang, xml:lang, dir
<optgroup>	Used to create a list of options.
	Attributes: id, class, style, title, lang, xml:lang, dir, disabled, label (required)
<option>	Used to define each choice in a <select> list.
	Attributes: id, class, style, title, lang, xml:lang, dir, selected, disabled, label, value
<p>	Used to begin a new paragraph.
	Attributes: id, class, style, title, lang, xml:lang, dir
<param>	Used to supply a named property value (e.g. within <object>).
	Attributes: id, name, value, valuetype, type
<pre>	Used to preserve spacing (i.e. preformatted text).
	Attributes: id, class, style, title, lang, xml:lang, dir, xml:space
<q>	Used to indicate an in-line quote.
	Attributes: id, class, style, title, lang, xml:lang, dir, cite
<samp>	Used to delimit program and other sample output.
	Attributes: id, class, style, title, lang, xml:lang, dir
<script>	Used to include script statements. (Part of the <head> element.)
	Attributes: charset, type (required), src, defer, xml:space
<select>	Used to provide a menu of options from which a user may select one choice.
	Attributes: id, class, style, title, lang, xml:lang, dir, name, size, multiple, disabled, tabindex, onfocus, onblur, onchange
<small>	Used to provide smaller font.
	Attributes: id, class, style, title, lang, xml:lang, dir
<span>	A generic language/style container.
	Attributes: id, class, style, title, lang, xml:lang, dir
<strong>	Used to provide strong emphasis.
	Attributes: id, class, style, title, lang, xml:lang, dir
<style>	Used to include style information. (Part of the <head> element.)
	Attributes: lang, xml:lang, dir, type (required), media, title, xml:space

Element	Description
<sub>	Used to provide subscripts. Attributes: id, class, style, title, lang, xml:lang, dir
<sup>	Used to provide superscripts. Attributes: id, class, style, title, lang, xml:lang, dir
<table>	Used to define a table. Attributes: id, class, style, title, lang, xml:lang, dir, summary, width, border, frame, rules, cellspacing, cellpadding
<tbody>	Used to delimit the table body. Attributes: id, class, style, title, lang, xml:lang, dir, char, charoff, align, valign
<td>	Used to define a table data cell. Attributes: id, class, style, title, lang, xml:lang, dir, abbr, axis, headers, scope, rowspan, colspan, char, charoff, align, valign
<textarea>	Used to define a multi-line input text field. Attributes: id, class, style, title, lang, xml:lang, dir, name, rows (required), cols (required), disabled, readonly, tabindex, accesskey, onfocus, onblur, onselect, onchange
<tfoot>	Used to define the table footer. Attributes: id, class, style, title, lang, xml:lang, dir, char, charoff, align, valign
<th>	Used to denote one of the header rows in a table. Attributes: id, class, style, title, lang, xml:lang, dir, abbr, axis, headers, scope, rowspan, colspan, char, charoff, align, valign
<thead>	Used to delimit the table head. Attributes: id, class, style, title, lang, xml:lang, dir, char, charoff, align, valign
<title>	Used to define the document's title. (Part of the <head> element.) Attributes: lang, xml:lang, dir
<tr>	Used to define a table row. Attributes: id, class, style, title, lang, xml:lang, dir, char, charoff, align, valign
<tt>	Used to provide a fixed width font (teletype). Attributes: id, class, style, title, lang, xml:lang, dir
<ul>	Used to define an unordered list. Attributes: id, class, style, title, lang, xml:lang, dir
<var>	Used to indicate a variable. Attributes: id, class, style, title, lang, xml:lang, dir

Transitional DTD

The Transitional DTD contains all of the tags and attributes within the Strict DTD, plus those listed in the following tables. If any of the tags or attributes below are used, your document must refer to the Transitional, rather than the Strict, DTD, i.e. your document should be of the form:

```
<?xml version="1.0" encoding="UTF-8"?>
<!DOCTYPE html
     PUBLIC "-//W3C//DTD XHTML 1.0 Transitional//EN"
     "http://www.w3.org/TR/xhtml1/DTD/xhtml1-transitional.dtd">
<html xmlns="http://www.w3.org/1999/xhtml" xml:lang="en" lang="en">
  <head>
    Your document meta-information goes here
  </head>
  <body>
    Your document content goes here
  </body>
</html>
```

Tags

Element	Description
<applet>	Used to include a Java applet in your web page. Attributes: id, class, style, title, codebase, archive, code, object, alt, name, width, height, align, hspace, vspace
<basefont>	Used to define the base (i.e. default) font size. Attributes: id, size, color, face
<center>	Used to center text on your web page (same as <div align="center">). Attributes: id, class, style, title, lang, xml:lang, dir
<dir>	Used to define a listing of directories. Attributes: id, class, style, title, lang, xml:lang, dir, compact
<font>	Used to change the font size and color. Attributes: id, class, style, title, lang, xml:lang, dir, size, color, face
<iframe>	Used to create a sub-window within your web page. Attributes: id, class, style, title, longdesc, name, src,frameborder, marginwidth, marginheight, scrolling, align, height, width
<isindex>	Used to enter a word in a searchable index. Attributes: id, class, style, title, lang, xml:lang, dir, prompt

Element	Description
<menu>	Used to define a menu list.
	Attributes: id, class, style, title, lang, xml:lang, dir, compact
<noframes>	Used to provide alternate content when frames are not available.
	Attributes: id, class, style, title, lang, xml:lang, dir
<s>	Used to provide strike-through text (same as <strike>).
	Attributes: id, class, style, title, lang, xml:lang, dir
<strike>	Used to provide strike-through text (same as <s>).
	Attributes: id, class, style, title, lang, xml:lang, dir
<u>	Used to provide underlined text.
	Attributes: id, class, style, title, lang, xml:lang, dir

Attributes

The Transitional DTD supports certain tag attributes not contained within the Strict DTD. All of the tags listed below are contained within the Strict DTD but the attribute(s) listed are not; they are additional attributes supported only by the Transitional DTD. Thus, for example, in the Strict DTD the <br /> tag has the attributes id, class, style and title, but in the Transitional DTD it has the attributes id, class, style, title and clear.

Element	Attribute(s) in Transitional but not in Strict
<a>	target
<area>	target
<base>	target
<body>	background, bgcolor, text, link, vlink, alink
 	clear
<caption>	align
<div>	align
<dl>	compact
<form>	target
<h1>...<h6>	align
<hr />	align, noshade, size, width
<img>	name, align, border, hspace, vspace

Table Continued on Following Page

Element	Attribute(s) in Transitional but not in Strict
<input>	align
<legend>	align
<li>	type, value
<link>	target
<object>	align, border, hspace, vspace
<ol>	type, compact, start
<p>	align
<param>	name is a required attribute in this DTD
<pre>	width
<script>	language
<table>	align, bgcolor
<td>	nowrap, bgcolor, width, height
<th>	nowrap, bgcolor, width, height
<tr>	bgcolor
<ul>	type, compact

Frameset DTD

The Frameset DTD is identical to the Transitional DTD, except for the addition of the two tags listed below. If any of these tags below are used, your document must refer to the Frameset, rather than the Strict or Transitional, DTD, i.e. your document should be of the form:

```
<?xml version="1.0" encoding="UTF-8"?>
<!DOCTYPE html
     PUBLIC "-//W3C//DTD XHTML 1.0 Frameset//EN"
     "http://www.w3.org/TR/xhtml1/DTD/xhtml1-frameset.dtd">
<html xmlns="http://www.w3.org/1999/xhtml" xml:lang="en" lang="en">
  <head>
    Your document meta-information goes here
  </head>
  <body>
    Your document content goes here
  </body>
</html>
```

Element	Description
<frame>	Used to define a frame (or sub-window). Attributes: id, class, style, title, longdesc, name, src, frameborder, marginwidth, marginheight, noresize, scrolling
<frameset>	Used to define a window subdivision. Attributes: id, class, style, title, rows, cols, onload, onunload

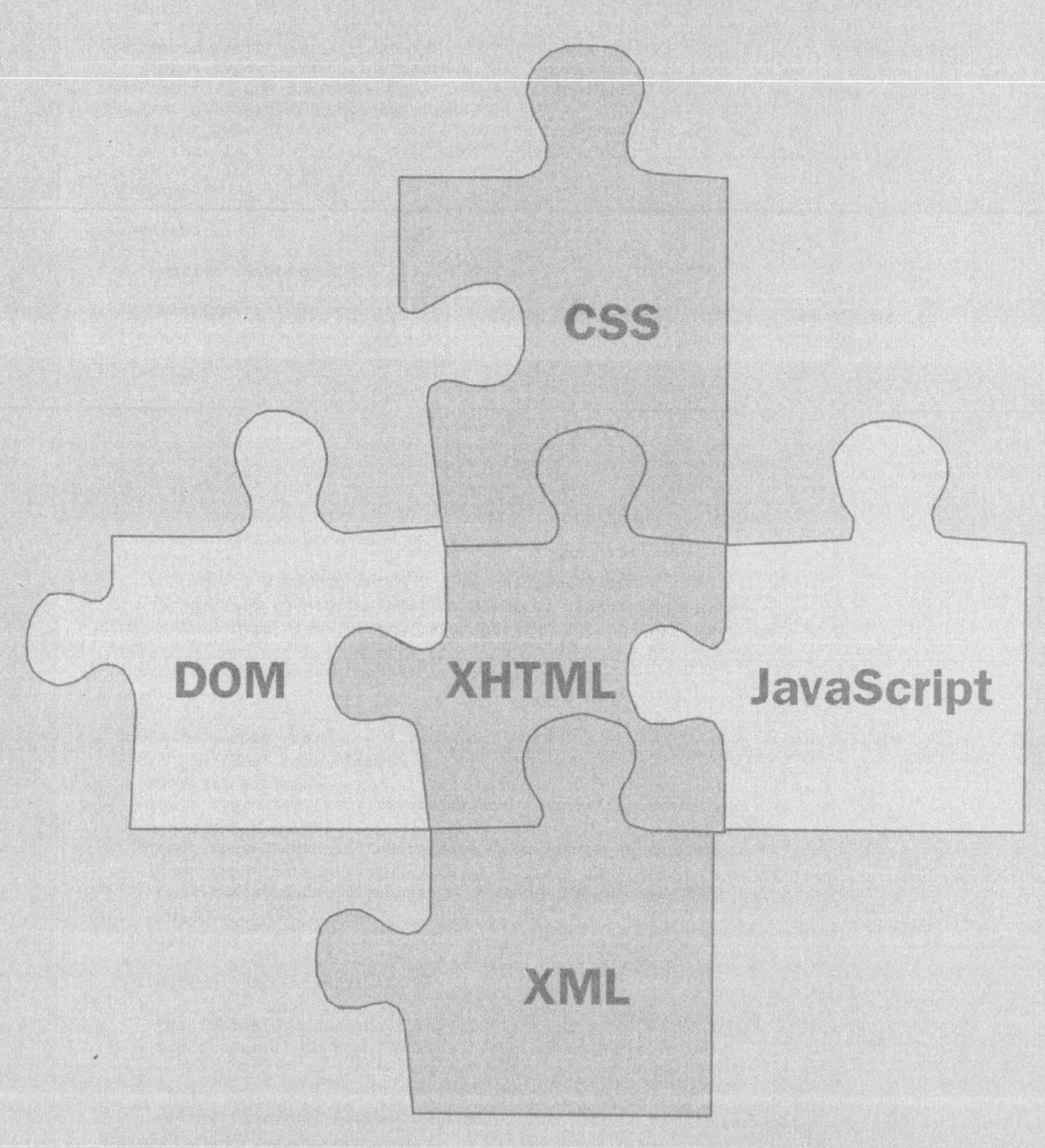
CSS
DOM
XHTML
JavaScript
XML

Using HTML Tidy

One of the authors of this book, Dave Raggett, has developed a convenient way to automatically convert your real-world HTML files into well-formed HTML, ready to be converted into XHTML with the addition of the DOCTYPE and namespace declarations. The tool, called HTML Tidy, is available as freeware as an OpenSource project from W3C. It has been ported to a large number of platforms and has also been built into a number of authoring tools. This appendix will show you how to use Tidy to correct minor bugs in your markup, and how to convert it into well-formed HTML. The home page for HTML Tidy is: `http://www.w3.org/People/Raggett/tidy`.

If you are using a machine running Microsoft Windows, you can use the `tidy.exe` program. This is run from the Windows console or command prompt. There are a large number of options you can set. Here is an example of how you can create an XHTML file called `test2.html` from the file `test1.html` from the command prompt:

```
Tidy -asxhtml test1.html >test2.html

Tidy (vers 12th December 1999) Parsing "test1.html"
"test1.html" appears to be HTML 2.0
no warnings or errors were found
```

Tidy distinguishes between warnings which it can safely fix automatically and errors which you will have to fix for yourself. The latter include such errors as forgetting to give the closing quotation mark on an attribute value, forgetting the > character at the end of a tag, or using an unknown tag name.

Just a Few of the Errors that Tidy can Fix

Missing or mismatched end tags are detected and corrected:

```
<h1>heading
<h2>subheading</h3>
```

This is mapped to:

```
<h1>heading</h1>
<h2>subheading</h2>
```

Tidy will correct badly nested emphasis:

```
here is a para <b>bold <i>bold italic</b> bold?</i> normal?
```

So this is mapped to:

```
here is a para <b>bold <i>bold italic</i> bold?</b> normal?
```

Tidy can sort out misplaced tags, for instance, emphasis elements are not supposed to enclose heading elements:

```
<i><h1>heading</h1></i>
<p>new paragraph <b>bold text
<p>some more bold text
```

This is mapped to:

```
<h1><i>heading</i></h1>
<p>new paragraph <b>bold text</b></p>
<p><b>some more bold text</b></p>
```

HTML Tidy tries to produce valid markup that will render in the same way as the original markup. In the example above, the `<b>` start tag is missing a matching end tag. As a result following paragraphs will also be set in bold. Tidy reproduces this behavior by inserting `<b>` elements as needed.

Using Tidy with Microsoft Word

Word has the option of Save As Web Page. Unfortunately, the HTML it generates is far from ideal. For Word 97, Tidy's `clean` option will fix up the markup and replace the presentational clutter with CSS style rules. Word 2000 produces very large files as it includes lots of proprietary style information. Tidy offers a specific option for dealing with this, paring the content back to something much more manageable.

Some of the Options Supported by Tidy

You can control whether the markup is indented for nested content. The following uses the default indentation:

```
<html>
<head>
<title>Test document</title>
</head>
```

```
<body>
<p>para which has enough text to cause a line break,
and so test the wrapping mechanism for long lines.</p>

<ul>
<li>1st list item </li>

<li>2nd list item</li>
</ul>
</body>
</html>
```

Here is the same markup, this time using the auto setting for indentation. This indents the content for each element except when the content is limited to text and emphasis:

```
<html>
  <head>
    <title>Test document</title>
  </head>

  <body>
    <p>para which has enough text to cause a line break,
    and so test the wrapping mechanism for long lines.</p>

    <ul>
      <li>1st list item</li>

      <li>2nd list item</li>
    </ul>
  </body>
</html>
```

Indenting markup makes it easy to follow the structure of the document when using a text editor, but has the slight disadvantage of increasing the file size, thereby slowing the download time. Tidy makes it easy to switch from indented to non-indented layout and there is no penalty for changing your mind.

Tidy also tries to keep the markup to within the width of your editor's window so that you don't need to scroll horizontally to reach the end of the lines. By default Tidy will wrap lines so that they aren't longer than 66 characters. You can alter this to whatever you like, and choose whether to allow wrapping within attributes or script literals.

One way to configure Tidy is to include parameters on the command line when you invoke the program, as for instance, in the following example:

```
tidy -asxhtml -modify -numeric -clean mypage.html
```

The `asxhtml` option ensures that the output will be converted to XHTML rather than HTML. The `modify` option causes Tidy to write the output back to the same file, in this case `mypage.html`. The `numeric` option ensures that character entities are represented as numeric entities, for example, if your file included the entity `™` for the tradmark symbol, this would be replaced by `™`. The `clean` option requests that presentational markup be replaced by CSS style rules.

Having to type all the options each time you run Tidy can rapidly become tedious. The solution is to create a configuration file and to get Tidy to load it automatically each time it runs. Tidy checks to see if a configuration file has been specified via the environment variable `HTML_TIDY`. This should be set to the full path for the file, e.g. "`c:\bin\tidycfg.txt`". Here is an example of a configuration file:

```
// sample config file for HTML tidy
indent: auto
indent-spaces: 2
wrap: 66
markup: yes
output-xhtml: yes
show-warnings: yes
numeric-entities: yes
break-before-br: no
clean: yes
char-encoding: ascii
```

For more information on the complete range of options, you are advised to visit the Tidy home page.

Using Tidy on the Macintosh

Terry Teague has ported Tidy to run on Apple computers such as the Macintosh. Here is a screen shot:

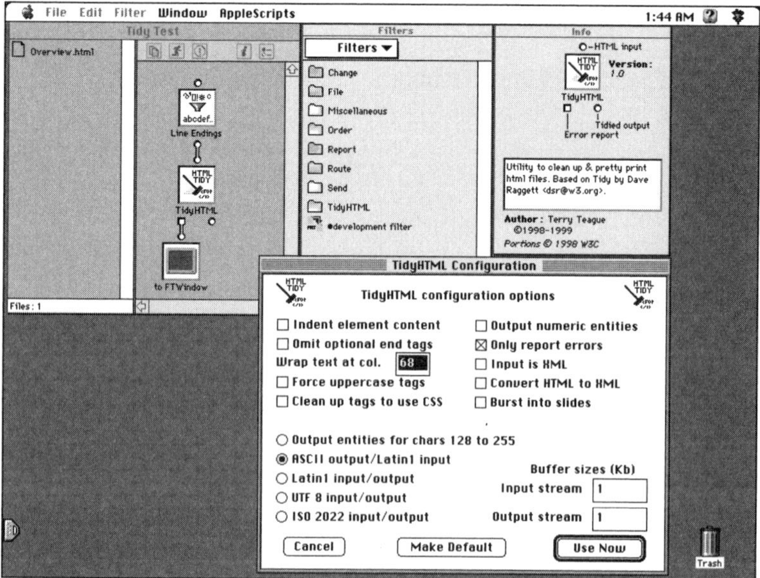

For further information, please see: `http://www.geocities.com/SiliconValley/1057/tidy.html`. The Tidy home page includes pointers to where to obtain Tidy for platforms such as Atari, Amiga, BeOS, AIX, Linux, UnixWare, Solaris, FreeBSD and more. You can even get Tidy in Java, thanks to Andy Quick.

Using Tidy from your Editor

When editing HTML, it is convenient to be able to tidy the markup as you go. Some plain text editors allow you to configure filters you can invoke from a customizable toolbar or menu item. On Microsoft Windows, suitable text editors include `pfe32` and `emacs`. On the Macintosh, `bbedit` is another such editor. These editors also allow you to configure keyboard short cuts for commonly used character sequences. It is well worth taking the time to set up shortcuts for the common HTML tags. Some editors also support syntax coloring where the editor shows tag names and attrbutes names and values in different colors. This makes it easy to see when you have forgotten to type a trailing quotation mark for an attribute value or the > character at the end of a tag.

HTML Editors with Built-In Support for Tidy

HTML-Kit is a simple to use freeware editor for HTML with built in support for Tidy. It features include syntax coloring, and a split screen presentation that makes it easy to review each of the warnings or errors found by Tidy. For more information, see `http://www.chami.com/free/html-kit/`.

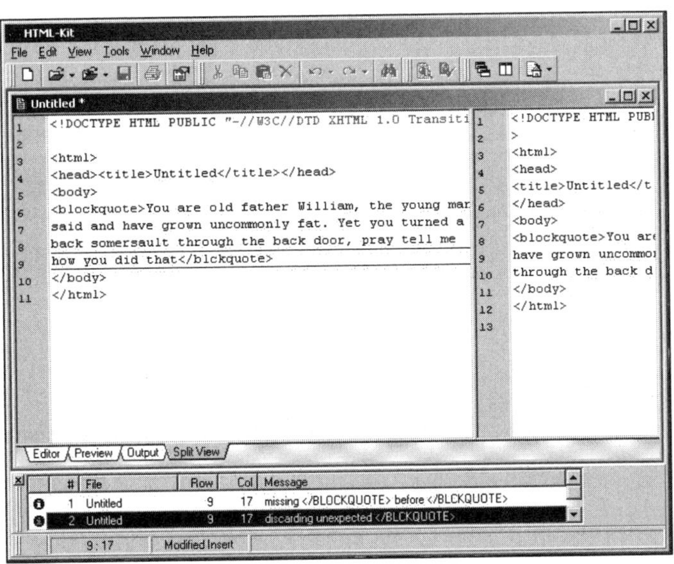

Another freeware editor is 1stPage2000. This is rather more sophisticated and includes extensive support for scripting:

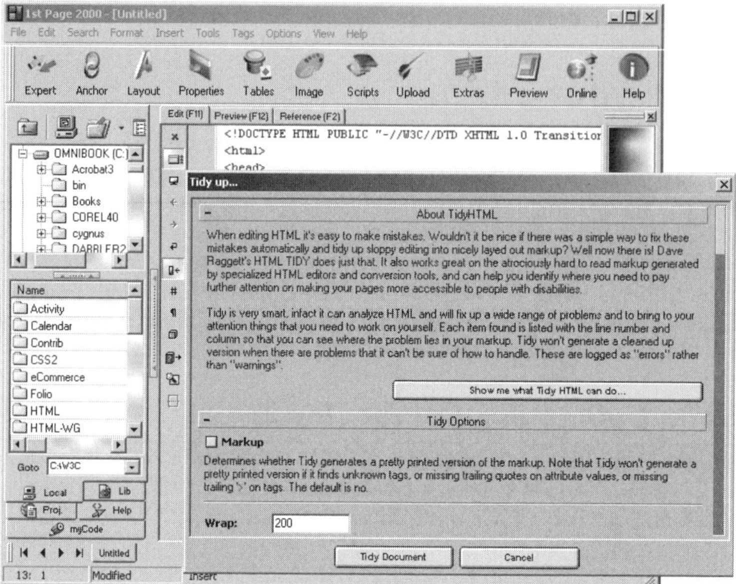

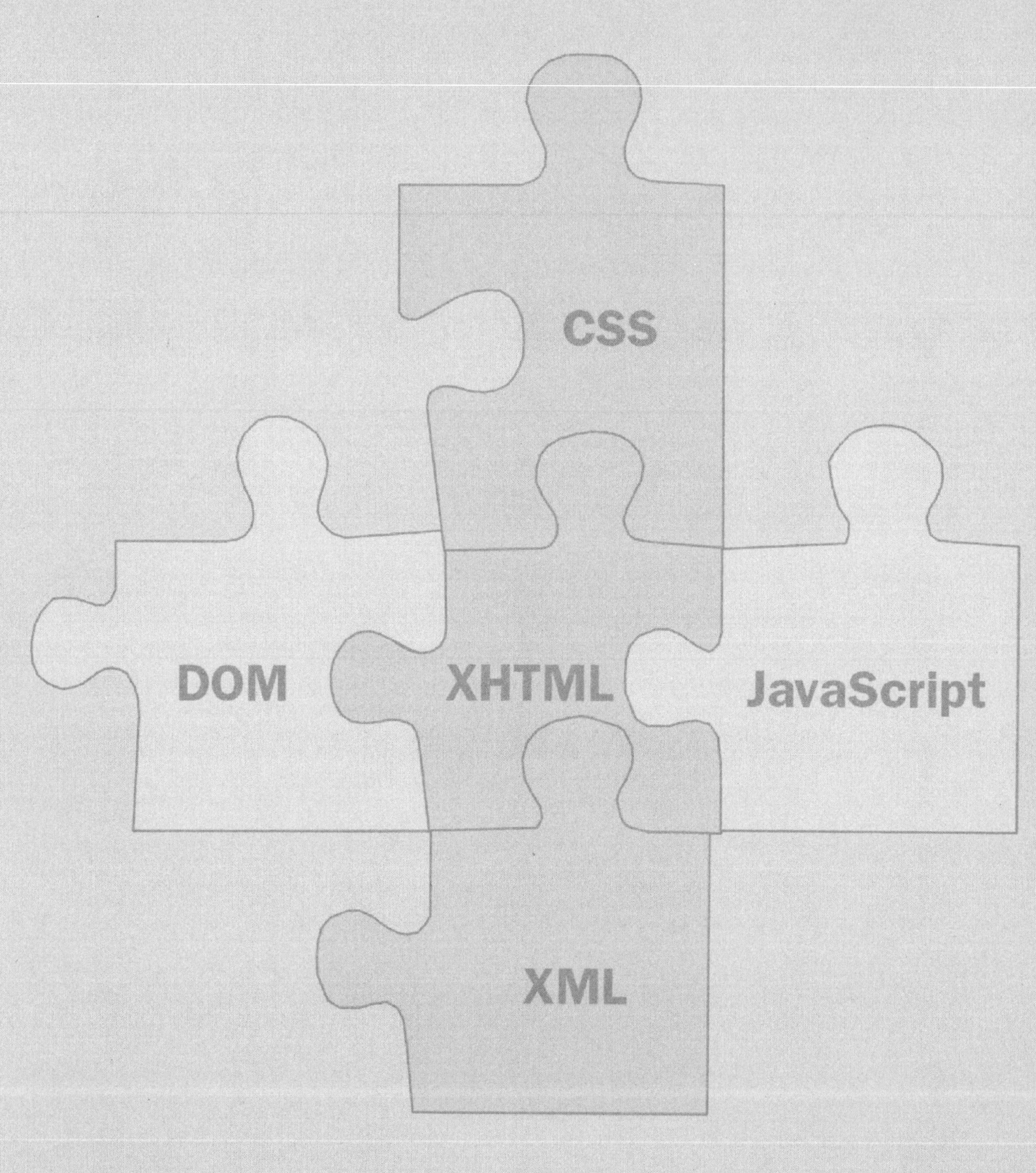
CSS
DOM
XHTML
JavaScript
XML

The Use of Color on Web Pages

In this appendix, we'll be looking into how colors are defined and used in XHTML. There are a number of ways you can specify a color, and we'll look into these now.

Methods for Specifying the Color You Want

How do you specify the color you want? There are three main methods. The simplest is to use a standard color name, but this only works for a few colors, which by and large the very bright saturated colors. These are not likely to be the ones you want, from an aesthetic point of view. More precise methods of specifying colors involve using numerical values.

Specifying the Color by Name

The standard set of color names is: aqua, black, blue, fuchsia, gray, green, lime, maroon, navy, olive, purple, red, silver, teal, white, and yellow. These 16 colors are defined in HTML 3.2 and 4.0 and correspond to the basic VGA set on PCs. Most browsers accept a wider set of color names but use of these is not recommended as they will not always be understood by all browsers attempting to display the document.

Using the Hexadecimal Color Value

More specific colors can be specified by using hexadecimal values like #FF9999. These represent colors as three groups of two hexadecimal numbers for the **red**, **green** and **blue** elements.

> **The hexadecimal system of counting means that you don't just use the digits 1 to 9 (as in ordinary decimal counting) but you use A,B, C, D, E, and F in addition. These letters stand for 10, 11, 12, 13, 14, and 15 respectively. As far as the web author is concerned this is of no great import, except that you should not be surprised to see them.**

Each pair of digits is a hex value from 00 to FF (equivalent to 255). So the hex number we've just seen, #FF9999, breaks down like this:

– this indicates that we're using a hexadecimal number

FF – Maximum quantity of red is present in the color

99 – Decimal equivalent 153, so 153 units of a possible 255 of green is present

99 – 153 units of blue (out of a possible 255) are present

The following table shows the equivalent hexadecimal codes for the 16 colors named above.

Color	Hexadecimal Code
Black	#000000
Green	#008000
Silver	#C0C0C0
Lime	#00FF00
Gray	#808080
Olive	#808000
White	#FFFFFF
Yellow	#FFFF00
Maroon	#800000
Navy	#000080
Red	#FF0000
Blue	#0000FF
Purple	#800080
Teal	#008080
Fuchsia	#FF00FF
Aqua	#00FFFF

Using a Decimal Color Value

Another system of assigning numbers to colors is based on the decimal system of counting. Although at first sign more familiar as there are no letters to confuse, this system is less commonly used by web authors than the hexadecimal system. With the decimal system of color values, each of the red, green and blue components are specified as three groups of numbers, from 0 to 255. Each group is separated by a comma, for example 204, 11, 105.

Browser-safe Colors

Although today's desktop and notebook computers all support true-color, which allows for literally thousands of colors to be used, some people are still browsing the Web with their monitor set to 256-color resolution. This makes things difficult for web designers, for each operating system – whether it be for Windows, Unix or Mac – has its own particular palette of 256 colors. If these operating systems display an image whose palette does not match their system palette, they "dither" the image.

The solution for the web author is to use a **browser-safe palette**. Netscape Navigator and Internet Explorer implement a palette of 216 **browser-safe colors** which will always display properly whatever the platform and whatever the color depth on the screen. In future almost all computers will be true-color, so this whole problem should disappear.

The browser safe palette uses 6 evenly-spaced gradations in red, green and blue and their combinations. If you select image colors from this palette, you can avoid the speckling effect that results from "dithering" when the computer attempts to display a photo or some other image which uses colors outside of the palette available. The browser safe palette is particularly useful for background areas of images. These are best constructed from colors where red, green and blue are each restricted to a value chosen from this table:

Hexadecimal	Decimal
00	00
33	51
66	102
99	153
CC	204
FF	255

As you can see, if you use hex values, it's easy to remember which values give you browser-safe colors, whereas you'd have to do a little math to do it in decimal from memory.

How Do I Find Browser Safe Colors?

There are a number of tools for doing this. On Unix systems, the Gimp graphics editor has a browser-safe palette and newer versions of Photoshop on Mac and Windows do too. If you are using a computer running Windows 95/98/NT you may find the freeware **syspal tool** from `http://www.w3.org/Markup/Guide/Style.html`. You will see a link to this tool in the text of the page. Once you have downloaded the syspal tool to your machine, make a short cut to it so that you can use it at any time while you are composing a graphic.

Imagine now that you are trying to decide which color to use for say, a background. You click on the `syspal.exe` icon; a color pallet is displayed in the syspal window. You then click the mouse inside the syspal window, and then keeping the mouse button down, drag the cursor over any point on the screen. The syspal window then displays the numerical code for the color currently under the mouse pointer as a decimal RGB value or as a hexadecimal color value.

Once you have understood how get the RGB or hexadecimal value for a browser-safe color you can use the values in CSS style sheet properties (Chapter 9) to set the background color, the color of text and hypertext links and so on.

If I stick to the browser-safe palette, will my images look identical on every machine?

It would be nice if your could know that a pale green background would look just right on every machine, but you just cannot be sure. A consideration here is the gamma value. The relationship between the RGB value and the perceived brightness is non-linear and characterised by a value called 'gamma', and this varies from platform to platform. If you construct a graphics on one machine with a particular gamma value and then display it on another device, it may look either too pale or too dark; washed out or over-saturated. Different devices are variable in the way they show color rather like TV sets. As far as the web author is concerned there is currently no ultimate assurance that one color on one screen will look the same on another.

The Background Color

Which color should you use for the background? This is really a matter of personal taste but we have found that most people do not object to pastel. The following shades, taken from the browser safe palette, have been used by the author with success.

#FFCC99	**255, 204, 153**	**light peach**
#FF9999	255, 255, 153	light yellow
#FFFFCC	255, 255, 204	light cream
#CCCC99	204, 204, 153	light beige
#FFCCFF	255, 204, 255	light pink
#CCFFCC	204, 255, 204	light green
#CCFFFF	204, 255, 255	pale turquoise

Remember that you can set the background color for either the whole document or for specific paragraphs, headings, lists and so on. This is covered in the chapter on Style Sheets – see especially the CSS background property.

The Color of the Text

You can set the color of the text using a numerical value, just as you can the color of the background. The CSS `color` property does the trick. You can choose to color the text for a given paragraph or a given heading, or make all heading 1 elements one color and all heading 2 elements another color. All this is covered in the chapter on Style Sheets. When it comes to the choice of color for text, remember that you must have sufficient contrast between the background and text color and that it is best to specify both rather than to leave the choice to the browser default. The large the font the more leeway you have in your choice of color, in that light colored heavy fonts can be read even though smaller sized text would be almost illegible.

It is worth noting that when documents are printed, the background color is left white. This means that text set to white against a dark background might look fine on the screen, but on paper nothing shows up!

Color Combinations on your Web Page

Many web authors stick to a simple color scheme based on only three or four colors. Shades of the same color can be used successfully. Rather nice is to take a pastel shade as the background and then find a much darker shade of the same color for the text. For example:

- Dark forest green text on a pastel green base
- Maroon text on a fairy pink background
- Deep blue text on a sky blue background

Another idea is to limit your colors to black, white and two other contrasting colors, one of which is light and the other dark. For example:

- Black, dark grey, sand and white
- Dark blue, light blue, black and white
- Brown, sand, grey and white
- Black, orange, olive green and white

The 216 Webmaster's Palette from `http://www.visibone.com` which is well worth a visit. Colors are shown in terms of brightness, vividness and hue and also more subtle attributes such as whether they are hard, dull, weak or faded.

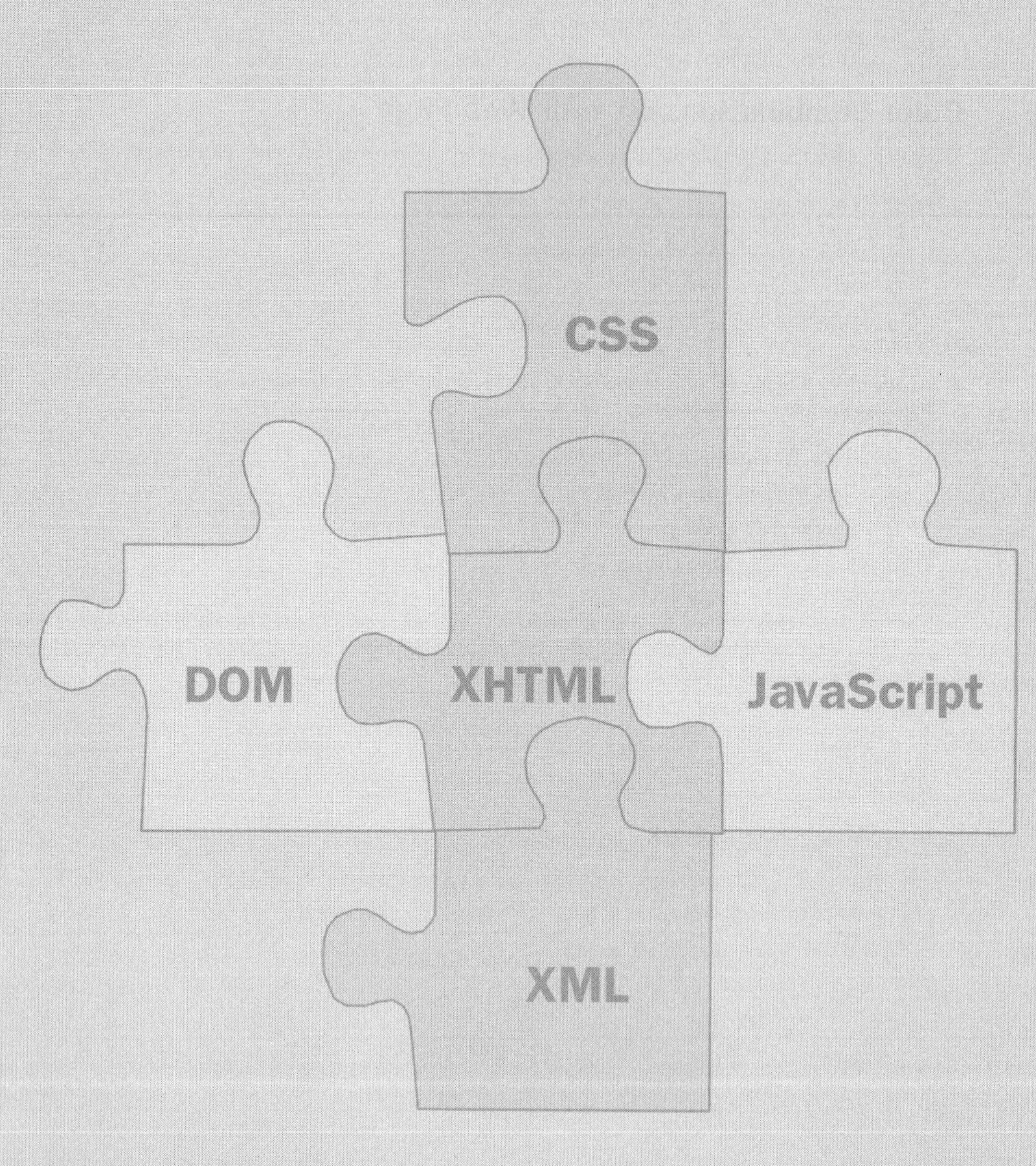
CSS
DOM
XHTML
JavaScript
XML

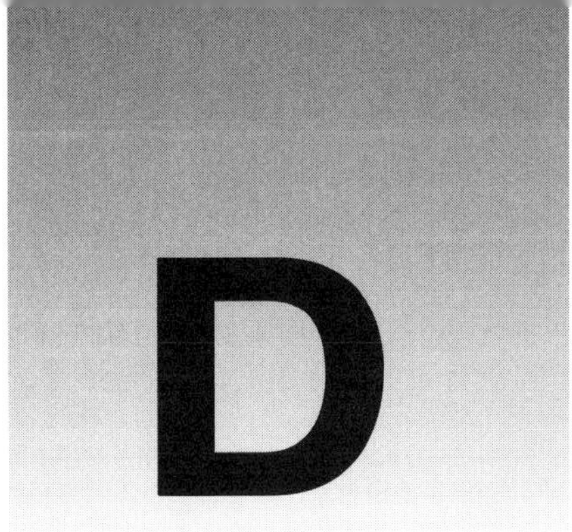

Style Sheet Properties

Over 70 Cascading Style Sheets properties are used in the major browsers. Most of them are in the CSS1 recommendations, but a few have only recently been introduced in the CSS2 public drafts. We've broken up the properties into several major 'groups' and listed which are new in CSS2. We've listed all the properties below (by group), with some of the crucial information for each. We start with a summary of the units of measurement.

Units of Measurement

There are two basic categories of unit: relative and absolute. As a general rule, relative measures are preferred, as using absolute measures requires familiarity with the actual mechanism of display (e.g. what kind of printer, what sort of monitor, etc.).

Relative Units

Values: `em`, `en`, `ex`, `px`

`em`, `en` and `ex` are typographic terms, and refer to the sizes of other characters on display (the m, n, and x characters).

`px` refers to a measurement in screen pixels, which is generally only meaningful for display on computer monitors and depends on the user's display resolution setting.

In IE4/5, `em` and `ex` are the same as `pt`, and `en` is the same as `px`.

Absolute Units

Values: `in`, `cm`, `mm`, `pt`, `pc`

`in` gives the measurement in inches, `cm` gives it in centimetres, `mm` in millimetres, `pt` is in typeface points (72 to an inch), and `pc` is in picas (1 pica equals 12 points). These units are generally only useful when you know what the output medium is going to be, since browsers are allowed to approximate if they must.

Percentage

Values:	Numeric

This is given as a number (with or without a decimal point), and is relative to a length unit (which is usually the font size of the current element).

Listing of Properties

There follows a listing of all the CSS properties for use in XHTML, together with their JavaScript Style Sheet equivalent, the equivalent scripting property in IE4/5, possible values, defaults, and other useful information. The properties are divided up into categories - **font** properties, **color** and **background** properties, **text** properties, **size** and **position** properties, **printing** properties, **filter** properties and **other** properties.

Font Properties

font

IE4/5 Scripting Property:	`font`
Values:	`<font-size>, [/<line-height>], <font-family>`
Default:	Not defined
Applies to:	All elements
Inherited:	Yes
Percentage?:	Only on `<font-size>` and `<line-height>`

This allows you to set several font properties all at once, with the initial values being determined by the properties being used (e.g. the default for `font-size` is different to the default for `font-family`). This property should be used with multiple values separated by spaces, or a comma if specifying multiple font-families.

font-family

IE4/5 Scripting Property:	`fontFamily`
Values:	Name of a font family (e.g. New York) or a generic family (e.g. Serif)
Default:	Set by browser
Applies to:	All elements
Inherited:	Yes
Percentage?:	No

You can specify multiple values in order of preference (in case the browser doesn't have the font you want). To do so, simply specify them and separate multiple values with commas. You should end with a generic font-family (allowable values would then be `serif`, `sans-serif`, `cursive`, `fantasy`, or `monospace`). If the font name has spaces in it, you should enclose the name in quotation marks.

font-size

IE4/5 Scripting Property:	`fontSize`
Values:	`<absolute>, <relative>, <length>, <percentage>`
Default:	`medium`

Applies to:	All elements
Inherited:	Yes
Percentage?:	Yes, relative to parent font size

The values for this property can be expressed in several ways:

- Absolute size: legal values are `xx-small`, `x-small`, `small`, `medium`, `large`, `x-large`, `xx-large`
- Relative size: values are `larger`, `smaller`
- Length: values are in any unit of measurement, as described at the beginning of this Section.
- Percentage: values are a percentage of the parent font size

font-style

IE4/5 Scripting Property:	`fontStyle`
Values:	`normal`, `italic`, or `oblique`
Default:	`normal`
Applies to:	All elements
Inherited:	Yes
Percentage?:	No

This is used to apply styling to your font–if a pre-rendered font is available (e.g. New York Oblique) then that will be used if possible. If not, the styling will be applied electronically.

font-variant

IE4/5 Scripting Property:	`fontVariant`
Values:	`normal`, `small-caps`
Default:	`normal`
Applies to:	All elements
Inherited:	Yes
Percentage?:	No

`Normal` is the standard appearance, and is therefore set as the default. `Small-caps` uses capital letters that are the same size as normal lowercase letters.

font-weight

IE4/5 Scripting Property:	`fontWeight`
Values:	`normal`, `bold`, `bolder`, `lighter`–or numeric values from 100 to 900
Default:	`normal`
Applies to:	All elements
Inherited:	Yes
Percentage?:	No

Specifies the 'boldness' of text, which is usually expressed by stroke thickness. If numeric values are used, they must proceed in 100-unit increments (e.g. 250 isn't legal). `400` is the same as `normal`, and `700` is the same as `bold`.

Color and Background Properties

color

IE4/5 Scripting Property: `color`
Values: Color name or RGB value
Default: Depends on browser
Applies to: All elements
Inherited: Yes
Percentage?: No

Sets the text color of any element. The color can be specified by name (e.g. green) or by RGB-value. The RGB value can be expressed in several ways; see Appendix C.

background

IE4/5 Scripting Property: `background`
Values: `transparent, <color>, <URL>, <repeat>, <scroll>, <position>`
Default: `transparent`
Applies to: All elements
Inherited: No
Percentage?: Yes, will refer to the dimension of the element itself

Specifies the background of the document. `Transparent` is the same as no defined background. You can use a solid color, or you can specify the URL for an image to be used. The URL can be absolute or relative, but must be enclosed in parentheses and immediately preceded by `url`:

```
BODY { background: url(http://foo.bar.com/image/small.gif) }
```

It is possible to use a color and an image, in which case the image will be overlaid on top of the color. The color can be a single color, or two colors that will be blended together. Images can have several properties set:

- `<repeat>` can be `repeat`, `repeat-x` (where `x` is a number), `repeat-y` (where `y` is a number) and `no-repeat`. If no repeat value is given, then `repeat` is assumed.
- `<scroll>` determines whether the background image will remain fixed, or scroll when the page does. Possible values are `fixed` or `scroll`.
- `<position>` specifies the location of the image on the page. Values are by percentage (horizontal, vertical), by absolute distance (in a unit of measurement, horizontal then vertical), or by keyword (values are `top`, `middle`, `bottom`, `left`, `center`, `right`)
- It is also possible to specify different parts of the background properties separately using the next five properties:

background-attachment

IE4/5 Scripting Property: `backgroundAttachment`
Values: `fixed, scroll`
Default: `scroll`

Applies to:	All elements
Inherited:	No
Percentage?:	No

Determines whether the background will remain fixed, or scroll when the page does.

background-color

IE4/5 Scripting Property:	`backgroundColor`
Values:	`transparent, <color>`
Default:	`transparent`
Applies to:	All elements
Inherited:	No
Percentage?:	No

Sets a color for the background. This can be a single color, or two colors blended together. The colors can be specified by name (e.g. green) or by RGB-value (which can be stated in hex "#FFFFFF", by percentage "80%, 20%, 0%", or by value "255,0,0"). The syntax for using two colors is:

```
BODY { background-color: red / blue }
```

background-image

IE4/5 Scripting Property:	`backgroundImage`
Values:	`<URL>, none`
Default:	`none`
Applies to:	All elements
Inherited:	No
Percentage?:	No

You can specify the URL for an image to be used as the background. The `URL` can be absolute or relative, but must be enclosed in parentheses and immediately preceded by `url`:

background-position

Scripting Properties:	`backgroundPosition, backgroundPositionX, backgroundPositionY`
Values:	`<position> <length> top, center, bottom, left, right.`
Default:	`top, left`
Applies to:	All elements
Inherited:	No
Percentage?:	No

Specifies the initial location of the background image on the page using two values, which are defined as a percentage (horizontal, vertical), an absolute distance (in a unit of measurement, horizontal then vertical), or using two of the available keywords.

background-repeat

IE4/5 Scripting Property:	`backgroundRepeat`
Values:	`repeat, repeat-x, repeat-y, no-repeat.`

Default:	`repeat`
Applies to:	All elements
Inherited:	No
Percentage?:	No

Determines whether the image is repeated to fill the page or element. If `repeat-x` or `repeat-y` are used, the image is repeated in only one direction. The default is to repeat the image in both directions.

Text Properties

letter-spacing

IE4/5 Scripting Property:	`letterSpacing`
Values:	`normal, <length>`
Default:	`normal`
Applies to:	All elements
Inherited:	Yes
Percentage?:	No

Sets the distance between letters. The length unit indicates an addition to the default space between characters. Values, if given, should be in units of measurement.

line-height

IE4/5 Scripting Property:	`lineHeight`
Values:	`<number>, <length>, <percentage> normal`
Default:	Depends on browser
Applies to:	All elements
Inherited:	Yes
Percentage?:	Yes, relative to the font-size of the current element

Sets the height of the current line. Numerical values are expressed as the font size of the current element multiplied by the value given (for example, 1.2 would be valid). If given by length, a unit of measurement must be used. Percentages are based on the font-size of the current font size, and should normally be more than 100%.

list-style

IE4/5 Scripting Property:	`listStyle`
Values:	`<keyword>, <position>, <url>`
Default:	Depends on browser
Applies to:	All elements
Inherited:	Yes
Percentage?:	No

Defines how list items are displayed. Can be used to set all the properties, or the individual styles can be set independently using the following styles.

list-style-image

IE4/5 Scripting Property:	`listStyleImage`
Values:	`none, <url>`
Default:	`none`
Applies to:	All elements
Inherited:	Yes
Percentage?:	No

Defines the URL of an image to be used as the 'bullet' or list marker for each item in a list.

list-style-position

IE4/5 Scripting Property:	`listStylePosition`
Values:	`inside, outside`
Default:	`outside`
Applies to:	All elements
Inherited:	Yes
Percentage?:	No

Indicates if the list marker should be placed indented or extended in relation to the list body.

list-style-type

IE4/5 Scripting Property:	`listStyleType`
Values:	`none, circle, disk, square, decimal, lower-alpha, upper-alpha, lower-roman, upper-roman`
Default:	`disk`
Applies to:	All elements
Inherited:	Yes
Percentage?:	No

Defines the type of 'bullet' or list marker used to precede each item in the list.

text-align

IE4/5 Scripting Property:	`textAlign`
Values:	`left, right, center, justify`
Default:	Depends on browser
Applies to:	All elements
Inherited:	Yes
Percentage?:	No

Describes how text is aligned within the element. Essentially replicates the `<DIV ALIGN=>` tag.

text-decoration

Scripting Properties:	`textDecoration, textDecorationLineThrough, textDecorationUnderline, textDecorationOverline`
Values:	`none, underline, overline, line-through`
Default:	`none`
Applies to:	All elements
Inherited:	No
Percentage?:	No

Specifies any special appearance of the text. Open to extension by vendors, with unidentified extensions rendered as an underline. This property is not inherited, but will usually span across any 'child' elements.

text-indent

IE4/5 Scripting Property:	`textIndent`
Values:	`<length>`, `<percentage>`
Default:	Zero
Applies to:	All elements
Inherited:	Yes
Percentage?:	Yes, refers to width of parent element

Sets the indentation values, in units of measurement, or as a percentage of the parent element's width.

text-transform

IE4/5 Scripting Property:	`textTransform`
Values:	`capitalize`, `uppercase`, `lowercase`, `none`
Default:	`none`
Applies to:	All elements
Inherited:	Yes
Percentage?:	No

- `capitalize` will set the first character of each word in the element as uppercase.
- `uppercase` will set every character in the element in uppercase.
- `lowercase` will place every character in lowercase.
- `none` will neutralize any inherited settings.

vertical-align

IE4/5 Scripting Property:	`verticalAlign`
Values:	`baseline`, `sub`, `super`, `top`, `text-top`, `middle`, `bottom`, `text-bottom`, `<percentage>`
Default:	`baseline`
Applies to:	Inline elements
Inherited:	No
Percentage?:	Yes, will refer to the line-height itself

Controls the vertical positioning of any affected element.

- `baseline` sets the alignment with the base of the parent.
- `middle` aligns the vertical midpoint of the element with the baseline of the parent plus half of the vertical height of the parent.
- `sub` makes the element a subscript.
- `super` makes the element a superscript.
- `text-top` aligns the element with the top of text in the parent element's font.

- `text-bottom` aligns with the bottom of text in the parent element's font.
- `top` aligns the top of the element with the top of the tallest element on the current line.
- `bottom` aligns with the bottom of the lowest element on the current line.

Size and Border Properties

These values are used to set the characteristics of the layout 'box' that exists around elements. They can apply to characters, images, and so on.

border-top-color, border-right-color, border-bottom-color, border-left-color, border-color

Scripting Properties:	`borderTopColor, borderRightColor, borderBottomColor, borderLeftColor, borderColor`
Values:	`<color>`
Default:	`<none>`
Applies to:	Block and replaced elements
Inherited:	No
Percentage?:	No

Sets the color of the four borders. By supplying the URL of an image instead, the image itself is repeated to create the border.

border-top-style, border-right-style, border-bottom-style, border-left-style, border-style

Scripting Properties:	`borderTopStyle, borderRightStyle, borderBottomStyle, borderLeftStyle, borderStyle`
Values:	`none`, `solid, double, groove, ridge, inset, outset`
Default:	`none`
Applies to:	Block and replaced elements
Inherited:	No
Percentage?:	No

Sets the style of the four borders.

border-top, border-right, border-bottom, border-left, border

Scripting Properties:	`borderTop, borderRight, borderBottom, borderLeft, border`
Values:	`<border-width>`, `<border-style>`, `<color>`
Default:	`medium`, `none`, `<none>`
Applies to:	Block and replaced elements
Inherited:	No
Percentage?:	No

Sets the properties of the border element (box drawn around the affected element). Works roughly the same as the margin settings, except that it can be made visible.

- `<border-width>` can be `thin`, `medium`, `thick`, or as a unit of measurement.
- `<border-style>` can be `none`, `solid`.

The color argument is used to fill the background of the element while it loads, and behind any transparent parts of the element. By supplying the URL of an image instead, the image itself is repeated to create the border. It is also possible to specify values for attributes of the border property separately using the `border-width`, `border-style` and `border-color` properties.

border-top-width, border-right-width, border-bottom-width, border-left-width, border-width

Scripting Properties: `borderTopWidth, borderRightWidth, borderBottomWidth, borderLeftWidth, borderWidth`
Values: `thin, medium, thick <length>`
Default: `medium`
Applies to: Block and replaced elements
Inherited: No
Percentage?: No

Sets the width of the border for the element. Each side can be set individually, or the `border-width` property used to set all of the sides. You can also supply up to four arguments for the border-width property to set individual sides, in the same way as with the `margin` property.

clear

IE4/5 Scripting Property: `clear`
Values: `none`, `both`, `left`, `right`
Default: `none`
Applies to: All elements
Inherited: No
Percentage?: No

Forces the following elements to be displayed below an element which is aligned. Normally, they would wrap around it.

clip

IE4/5 Scripting Property: `clip`
Values: `rect(<top><right><bottom><left>) , auto`
Default: `auto`
Applies to: All elements
Inherited: No
Percentage?: No

Controls which part of an element is visible. Anything that occurs outside the clip area is not visible.

display

IE4/5 Scripting Property: `display`
Values: `""`, `none`
Default: `""`
Applies to: All elements
Inherited: No
Percentage?: No

This property indicates whether an element is rendered. If set to none the element is not rendered, if set to `""` it is rendered.

float

IE4/5 Scripting Property: `styleFloat`
Values: `none, left, right`
Default: `none`
Applies to: `DIV`, `SPAN` and replaced elements
Inherited: No
Percentage?: No

Causes following elements to be wrapped to the left or right of the element, rather than being placed below it.

height

Scripting Properties: `height, pixelHeight, posHeight`
Values: `auto, <length>`
Default: `auto`
Applies to: `DIV`, `SPAN` and replaced elements
Inherited: No
Percentage?: No

Sets the vertical size of an element, and will scale the element if necessary. The value is returned as a string including the measurement type (`px`, `%`, etc.). To retrieve the value as a number, query the `posHeight` property.

left - New in CSS2

Scripting Properties: `left, pixelLeft, posLeft`
Values: `auto, <length>, <percentage>`
Default: `auto`
Applies to: All elements
Inherited: No
Percentage?: Yes, refers to parent's width

Sets or returns the left position of an element when displayed in 2D canvas mode, allowing accurate placement and animation of individual elements. The value is returned as a string including the measurement type (`px`, `%`, etc.). To retrieve the value as a number, query the `posLeft` property.

margin-top, margin-right, margin-bottom, margin-left, margin

Scripting Properties: `marginTop, marginRight, marginBottom, marginLeft, margin`
Values: `auto, <length>, <percentage>`
Default: Zero
Applies to: Block and replaced elements
Inherited: No
Percentage?: Yes, refers to parent element's width

Sets the size of margins around any given element. You can use `margin` as shorthand for setting all of the other values (as it applies to all four sides). If you use multiple values in `margin` but use less than four, opposing sides will try to be equal. These values all set the effective minimum distance between the current element and others.

overflow – New in CSS2

IE4/5 Scripting Property: `overflow`
Values: `none`, `clip`, `scroll`
Default: `none`
Applies to: All elements
Inherited: No
Percentage?: No

This controls how a container element will display its content if this is not the same size as the container.

- `none` means that the container will use the default method. For example, as in an image element, the content may be resized to fit the container.
- `clip` means that the contents will not be resized, and only a part will be visible.
- `scroll` will cause the container to display scroll bars so that the entire contents can be viewed by scrolling.

padding-top, padding-right, padding-bottom, padding-left, padding

Scripting Properties: `paddingTop, paddingRight, paddingBottom, paddingLeft, padding`
Values: `auto`, `<length>`, `<percentage>`
Default: `Zero`
Applies to: Block and replaced elements
Inherited: No
Percentage?: Yes, refers to parent element's width

Sets the distance between the content and border of an element. You can use **`padding`** as shorthand for setting all of the other values (as it applies to all four sides). If you use multiple values in **`padding`** but use less than four, opposing sides will try to be equal. These values all set the effective minimum distance between the current element and others.

position – New in CSS2

IE4/5 Scripting Property: `position`
Values: `absolute`, `relative`, `static`
Default: `relative`
Applies to: All elements
Inherited: No
Percentage?: No

Specifies if the element can be positioned directly on the 2-D canvas.

- `absolute` means it can be fixed on the background of the page at a specified location, and move with it.
- `static` means it can be fixed on the background of the page at a specified location, but not move when the page is scrolled.
- `relative` means that it will be positioned normally, depending on the preceding elements.

top – New in CSS2

Scripting Properties: `top, pixelTop, posTop`
Values: `auto, <percentage> <length>`
Default: `auto`
Applies to: All elements
Inherited: No
Percentage?: Yes, refers to parent's width

Sets or returns the vertical position of an element when displayed in 2-D canvas mode, allowing accurate placement and animation of individual elements. Value is returned as a string including the measurement type (`px`, `%`, etc.). To retrieve the value as a number, query the `posTop` property.

visibility – New in CSS2

IE4/5 Scripting Property: `visibility`
Values: `visible, hidden, inherit`
Default: `inherit`
Applies to: All elements
Inherited: No
Percentage?: No

Allows the element to be displayed or hidden on the page. Elements which are hidden still take up the same amount of space, but are rendered transparently. Can be used to dynamically display only one of several overlapping elements

- `visible` means that the element will be visible.
- `hidden` means that the element will not be visible.
- `inherit` means that the element will only be visible when it's parent or container element is visible.

white-space

IE4/5 Scripting Property: not supported
Values: `<length>,<percentage>`
Default: `Zero`
Applies to: Block-level elements
Inherited: No
Percentage?: Yes, refers to parent's width

Sets the spacing between elements. Using a `<percentage>` value will base the spacing on the parent element or default spacing for that element.

width

Scripting Properties: `width, pixelWidth, posWidth`
Values: `auto, <length>, <percentage>`
Default: `auto`, except for any element with an intrinsic dimension
Applies to: `DIV`, `SPAN` and replaced elements
Inherited: No
Percentage?: Yes, refers to parent's width

Sets the horizontal size of an element, and will scale the element if necessary. The value is returned as a string including the measurement type (px, %, etc.). To retrieve the value as a number, query the posWidth property.

z-index – New in CSS2

IE4/5 Scripting Property: zIndex
Values: <number>
Default: Depends on the HTML source
Applies to: All elements
Inherited: No
Percentage?: No

Controls the ordering of overlapping elements, and defines which will be displayed 'on top'. Positive numbers are above the normal text on the page, and negative numbers are below. Allows a 2.5-D appearance by controlling the layering of the page's contents.

Printing Properties

page-break-after

IE4/5 Scripting Property: pageBreakAfter
Values: <auto>, <always>, <left>, <right>
Default: <auto>
Applies to: All elements
Inherited: No
Percentage?: No

Controls when to set a page break and on what page the content will resume, i.e. either the left or the right.

page-break-before

IE4/5 Scripting Property: pageBreakBefore
Values: <auto>, <always>, <left>, <right>
Default: <auto>
Applies to: All elements
Inherited: No
Percentage?: No

Controls when to set a page break and on what page the content will resume, i.e. either the left or the right.

Other Properties

cursor

IE4/5 Scripting Property: cursor
Values: auto, crosshair, default, hand, move, e-resize, ne-resize, nw-resize, n-resize, se-resize, sw-resize, s-resize, w-resize, text, wait, help

Default: auto
Applies to: All elements
Inherited: No
Percentage?: No

Specifies the type of cursor the mouse pointer should be.

IE4/5 Unsupported CSS Properties

Internet Explorer 4 doesn't support the following CSS1 properties:

```
word-spacing
!important
first-letter pseudo
first-line pseudo
white-space
```

Navigator 4 Unsupported CSS Properties

Navigator 4 doesn't support the following CSS1 properties:

```
word-spacing
!important
first-letter pseudo
first-line pseudo
font
font-variant
letter-spacing
list-style-image,list-style-position,list-style
background-attachment,background-position,background-repeat,background
border-top-color,border-right-color,border-left-color,border-bottom-color
border-top,border-right,border-bottom,border-left
clip
overflow
@import
```

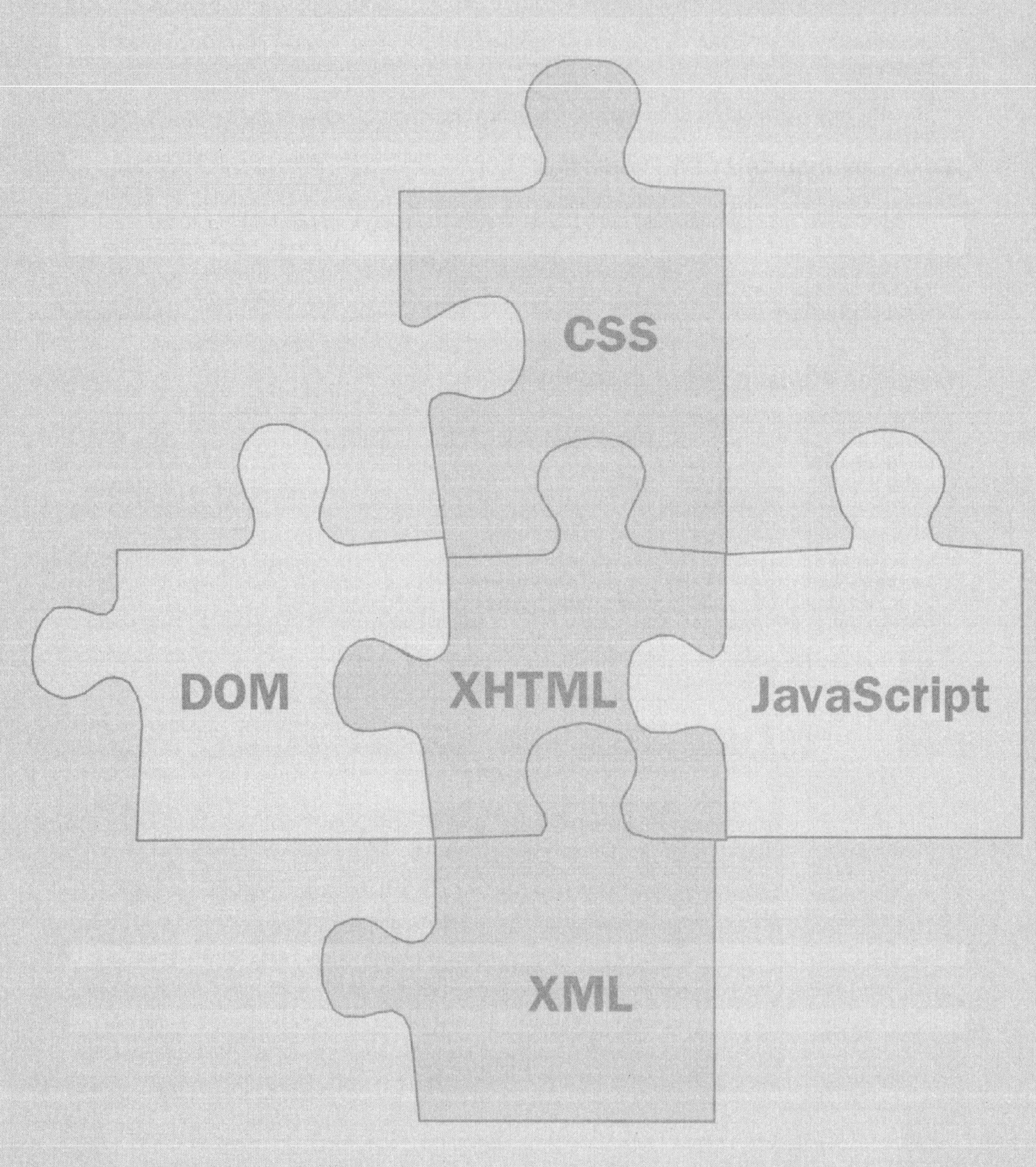
CSS
DOM
XHTML
JavaScript
XML

JavaScript Reference

Built-in Functions

JavaScript provides a number of built-in functions that can be accessed within code.

Function	Description
`escape(`*char*`)`	Returns a string of the form %*XX* where *XX* is the ASCII encoded value of *char*.
`eval(`*expression*`)`	Returns the result of evaluating the numeric expression *expression*
`isNaN(`*value*`)`	Returns a Boolean value of true if *value* is not a legal number.
`parseFloat(`*string*`)`	Converts *string* to a floating-point number.
`ParseInt(`*string, base*`)`	Converts *string* to an integer number with the base of *base*.
`typeOf(`*object*`)`	Returns the data type of *object* as a string, such as "boolean", "function", etc.

Built-in Objects

JavaScript provides a set of built-in data-type objects, which have their own set of properties, and methods – and which can be accessed with JavaScript code.

Array Object

The `Array` object specifies a method of creating arrays and working with them. To create a new array, use:

```
cats = new Array();      // create an empty array
cats = new Array(10);    // create an array of 10 items

// or create and fill an array with values in one go:
cats = new Array("Boo Boo", "Purrcila", "Sam", "Lucky");
```

Properties	Description
`length`	A read/write Integer value specifying the number of elements in the array.

Methods	Description
`join(`[*string*]`)`	Returns a string containing each element of the array, optionally separated with *string*.
`reverse()`	Reverses the order of the array.
`sort(`[*function*]`)`	Sorts the array, optionally based upon the results of a function specified by *function*.

Early versions of JavaScript had no explicit array structure. However, JavaScript's object mechanisms allow for easy creation of arrays:

```
function MakeArray(n)
{
  this.length = n;
  for (var i = 1; i <= n; i++)
    this[i] = 0;
  return this
}
```

With this function included in your script, you can create arrays with:

```
cat = new MakeArray(20);
```

You can then populate the array like this:

```
cat[1] = "Boo Boo";
cat[2] = "Purrcila";
cat[3] = "Sam";
cat[4] = "Lucky";
```

The following code creates a two dimensional array and displays the results:

```
a = new Array(4)
for (i=0; i < 4; i++) {
   a[i] = new Array(4)
```

```
    for (j=0; j < 4; j++) {
      a[i][j] = "["+i+","+j+"]"
    }
  }
```

Boolean Object

The `Boolean` object is used to store simple yes/no, true/false values. To create a new `Boolean` object, use the syntax:

```
MyAnswer = new Boolean(value)
```

If *value* is 0, null, omitted, or an empty string the new Boolean object will have the value `false`. All other values, *including the string* "false", create an object with the value `true`.

Methods	Description
`toString()`	Returns the value of the Boolean as the string true or false.
`valueOf()`	Returns the primitive numeric value of the object for conversion in calculations.

Date Object

The `Date` object provides a method for working with dates and times inside of JavaScript. New instances of the `Date` object are invoked with:

```
newDateObject = new Date([dateInfo])
```

dateInfo is an optional specification for the date to set in the new object. If it is not specified, the current date and time are used. *dateInfo* can use any of the following formats:

```
milliseconds (since midnight GMT on January 1st 1970)
year, month, day (e.g. 2000, 0, 27  is 27 Jan 2000)
year, month, day, hours, minutes, seconds
month day, year hours:minutes:seconds
 (e.g. September 23, 2000 08:25:30)
```

Methods	Description
`getDate()`	Returns the day of the month as an Integer between 1 and 31.
`getDay()`	Returns the day of the week as an Integer between 0 (Sunday) and 6 (Saturday).
`getHours()`	Returns the hours as an Integer between 0 and 23.

Table Continued on Following Page

Methods	Description
`getMinutes()`	Returns the minutes as an Integer between 0 and 59.
`getMonth()`	Returns the month as an Integer between 0 (January) and 11 (December).
`getSeconds()`	Returns the seconds as an Integer between 0 and 59.
`getTime()`	Returns the number of milliseconds between January 1, 1970 at 00:00:00 GMT and the current Date object as an Integer.
`getTimeZoneOffset()`	Returns the number of minutes difference between local time and GMT as an Integer.
`getYear()`	Returns the year (generally minus 1900 - i.e. only two digits) as an Integer.
`parse(`*dateString*`)`	Returns the number of milliseconds in a date string, since Jan. 1, 1970 00:00:00 GMT.
`setDate(`*dayValue*`)`	Sets the day of the month where *dayValue* is an Integer between 1 and 31.
`setHours(`*hoursValue*`)`	Sets the hours where *hoursValue* is an Integer between 0 and 59.
`setMinutes(`*minutesValue*`)`	Sets the minutes where *minutesValue* is an Integer between 0 and 59.
`setMonth(`*monthValue*`)`	Sets the month where *monthValue* is an Integer between 0 and 11.
`setSeconds(`*secondsValue*`)`	Sets the seconds where *secondsValue* is an Integer between 0 and 59.
`setTime(`*timeValue*`)`	Sets the value of a Date object where *timeValue* is an integer representing the number of milliseconds in a date string, since Jan. 1, 1970 00:00:00 GMT.
`setYear(`*yearValue*`)`	Sets the year where *yearValue* is an Integer (generally) greater than 1900.
`toGMTString()`	Converts a date from local time to GMT, and returns it as a string.
`toLocaleString()`	Converts a date from GMT to local time, and returns it as a string.
`UTC(`*year, month, day* `[,` *hrs*`] [,` *min*`] [,` *sec*`])`	Returns the number of milliseconds in a date object, since Jan. 1, 1970 00:00:00 Universal Coordinated Time (GMT).

Function Object

The `Function` object provides a mechanism for compiling JavaScript code as a function. A new function is invoked with the syntax:

```
functionName = new Function(arg1, arg2, ..., functionCode)
```

where *arg1*, *arg2*, etc. are the arguments for the function object being created, and *functionCode* is a string containing the body of the function. This can be a series of JavaScript statements separated by semi-colons.

Properties	Description
`arguments[]`	A reference to the `Arguments` array that holds the arguments that were provided when the function was called.
`caller`	Specifies the function that called the `Function` object.
`prototype`	Provides a way for adding properties to a `Function` object.

Arguments Object

The `Arguments` object is a list (array) of arguments in a `Function` object.

Properties	Description
`length`	An Integer specifying the number of arguments provided to the function when it was called.

Math Object

Provides a set of properties and methods for working with mathematical constants and functions. Simply reference the `Math` object, then the method or property required:

```
MyArea = Math.PI * MyRadius * MyRadius;
MyResult = Math.floor(MyNumber);
```

Properties	Description
`E`	Euler's Constant *e* (the base of natural logarithms).
`LN10`	The value of the natural logarithm of 10.
`LN2`	The value of the natural logarithm of 2.
`LOG10E`	The value of the natural logarithm of E.
`LOG2E`	The value of the base 2 logarithm of E.
`PI`	The value of the constant π (pi).
`SQRT1_2`	The value of the square root of a half.
`SQRT`	The value of the square root of two.

Methods	Description
`abs(`*number*`)`	Returns the absolute value of *number*.
`acos(`*number*`)`	Returns the arc cosine of *number*.
`asin(`*number*`)`	Returns the arc sine of *number*.
`atan(`*number*`)`	Returns the arc tangent of *number*.
`atan2(`*x, y*`)`	Returns the angle of the polar coordinate of a point *x*, *y* from the *x*-axis.
`ceil(`*number*`)`	Returns the next largest Integer greater than *number*, i.e. rounds up.
`cos(`*number*`)`	Returns the cosine of *number*.
`exp(`*number*`)`	Returns the value of *number* as the exponent of *e*, as in e^{number}.
`floor(`*number*`)`	Returns the next smallest Integer less that *number*, i.e. rounds down.
`log(`*number*`)`	Returns the natural logarithm of *number*.
`max(`*num1, num2*`)`	Returns the greater of the two values *num1* and num2.
`min(`*num1, num2*`)`	Returns the smaller of the two values *num1*and *num2*.
`pow(`*num1, num2*`)`	Returns the value of *num1* to the power of *num2*.
`random()`	Returns a random number between 0 and 1.
`round(`*number*`)`	Returns the closest Integer to *number* i.e. rounds up *or* down to the nearest whole number.
`sin(`*number*`)`	Returns the sin of *number*.
`sqrt(`*number*`)`	Returns the square root of *number*.
`tan(`*number*`)`	Returns the tangent of *number*.

Number Object

The `Number` object provides a set of properties that are useful when working with numbers:

```
MyArea = Math.PI * MyRadius * MyRadius;
MyResult = Math.floor(MyNumber);
```

Properties	Description
`MAX_VALUE`	The maximum numeric value represented in JavaScript (~1.79E+308).
`MIN_VALUE`	The minimum numeric value represented in JavaScript (~2.22E-308).

Properties	Description
`NaN`	A value meaning 'Not A Number'.
`NEGATIVE_INFINITY`	A special value for negative infinity ("-Infinity").
`POSITIVE_INFINITY`	A special value for infinity ("Infinity").

Methods	Description
`toString(`[*radix_base*]`)`	Returns the value of the number as a string to a radix (base) of 10, unless specified otherwise in *radix_base*.
`valueOf()`	Returns the primitive numeric value of the object.

String Object

The `String` object provides a set of methods for text manipulation. To create a new string object, the syntax is:

```
MyString = new String([value])
```

where *value* is the optional text to place in the string when it is created. If this is a number, it is converted into a string first.

Properties	Description
`length`	An Integer representing the number of characters in the string.

Methods	Description
`anchor("`*nameAttribute*`")`	Returns the original string surrounded by `<a>` and `</a>` anchor tags, with the `name` attribute set to "*nameAttribute*".
`big()`	Returns the original string enclosed in `<big>` and `</big>` tags.
`bold()`	Returns the original string enclosed in `<b>` and `</b>` tags.
`charAt(`*index*`)`	Returns the single character at position *index* within the String object.
`fixed()`	Returns the original string enclosed in `<tt>` and `</tt>` tags.
`indexOf(`*searchValue* `[,`*fromIndex*`])`	Returns first occurrence of the string *searchValue* starting at index *fromIndex*.
`italics()`	Returns the original string enclosed in `<i>` and `</i>` tags.

Table Continued on Following Page

Methods	Description
`lastIndexOf(`*searchValue* `[,`*fromIndex*`])`	Returns the index of the last occurrence of the string *searchValue*, searching backwards from index *fromIndex*.
`link("`*hrefAttribute*`")`	Returns the original string surrounded by `<a>` and `</a>` link tags, with the `href` attribute set to "*hrefAttribute*".
`small()`	Returns the original string enclosed in `<small>` and `</small>` tags.
`split(`*separator*`)`	Returns an array of strings created by separating the `String` object at every occurrence of *separator*.
`strike()`	Returns the original string enclosed in `<strike>` and `</strike>` tags.
`sub()`	Returns the original string enclosed in `<sub>` and `</sub>` tags.
`substring(`*indexA, indexB*`)`	Returns the sub-string of the original `String` object from the character at *indexA* up to and including the one **before** the character at *indexB*.
`sup()`	Returns the original string enclosed in `<sup>` and `</sup>` tags.
`toLowerCase()`	Returns the original string with all the characters converted to lowercase.
`toUpperCase()`	Returns the original string with all the characters converted to uppercase.

Reserved Words

The following are reserved words that can't be used for function, method, variable, or object names. Note that while some words in this list are not currently used as JavaScript keywords, they have been reserved for future use.

abstract	**else**	**int**	**super**
boolean	extends	interface	switch
break	false	long	synchronized
byte	final	native	this
case	finally	new	throw
catch	float	null	throws
char	for	package	transient

abstract	**else**	**int**	**super**
class	function	private	true
const	goto	protected	try
continue	if	public	typeof
default	implements	reset	var
delete	import	return	void
do	in	short	while
double	instanceof	static	with

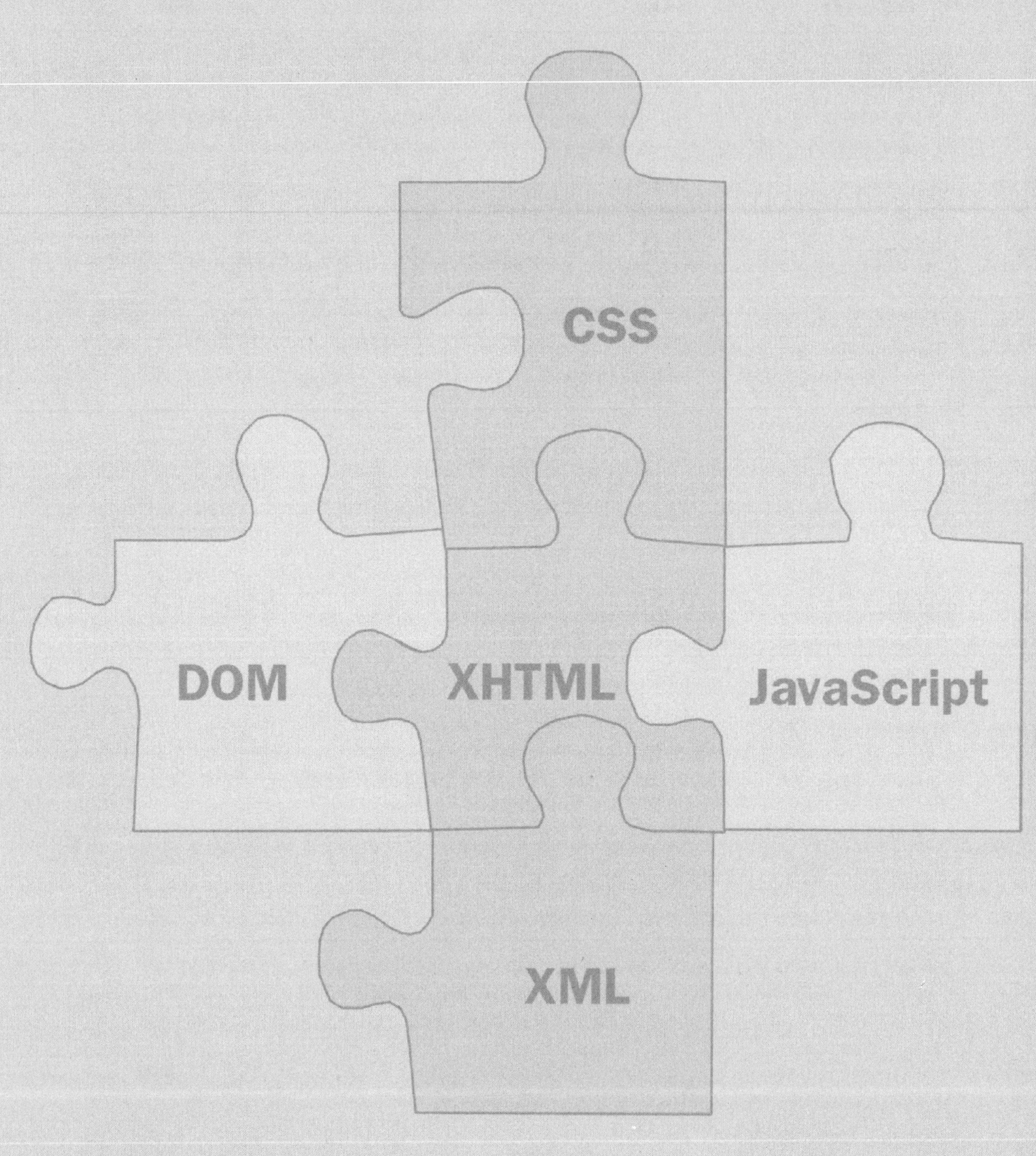
CSS
DOM
XHTML
JavaScript
XML

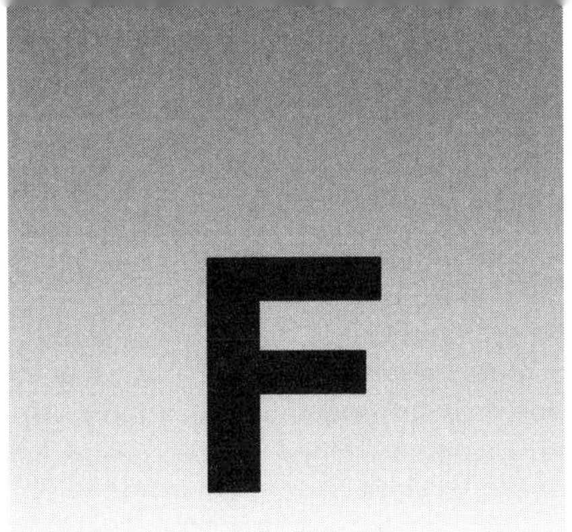

Resources

Books

Now that you have mastered the basics of the XHTML and CSS languages, seen how web pages may be made dynamic by using scripting languages and document object models, and have been introduced to the power of XML, you may like to pursue these topics to a greater level with the following books also from Wrox Press Ltd.

HTML/XHTML and XML

XHTML 1.0 is a re-formulation of HTML 4.0 as an application of XML – no new tags were introduced. Thus existing HTML 4.0 books may still be used as reference sources.

Instant HTML Programmer's Reference by Homer, Ullman & Wright (ISBN 1- 861001-56-8)

This book (HTML 4.0 edition) acts as both a tutorial for the novice web programmer, and a reference book for the more advanced designer. Each chapter covers an aspect of web design, starting simply with formatting and moving on through graphics, tables and forms to the more sophisticated technology used to insert objects and applets into your pages. The reference section goes through every element and its attributes, telling you which element/attribute is supported in which versions of HTML, plus which version of Netscape and Microsoft browsers support which element/attribute combinations. It also covers special characters, color names and values, tags sorted by use and VBScript and JavaScript. A comprehensive reference book, useful for beginner and experienced programmer alike.

XML Applications by Frank Boumphrey and others (ISBN 1-861001-52-5)

By allowing authors to create their own tags, XML permits the use of tags that actually describe their content. You need never wish for a new tag again. Furthermore, presentation rules are kept separately meaning that the data marked up using XML can be used in a myriad of ways across different platforms and in different applications. This book pieces together the various parts of the XML jigsaw, teaching you how to create XML applications for the Web. After learning how to write documents using XML, we will show you many different ways in which data marked up in XML can be used and re-used, from displaying it in Web pages to creating compound documents from multiple data sources. Also contains CSS, XSL, case-studies and real-life applications, XML Schemas and Namespaces.

XML in IE5 Programmer's Reference by Alex Homer (ISBN 1-861001-57-6)

Microsoft has undertaken to provide full support for XML and other associated standards in the latest version of Internet Explorer. These standards are set by the World Wide Web Consortium (W3C), and cover a whole range of different technologies. This book is for web developers who want to know more about what XML is, what its potential applications are, and what support is available for XML and its associated technologies right now in Microsoft Internet Explorer 5. This book provides a starting point for newcomers to XML, covers Document Type Definitions and XML Schemas, teaches all aspects of the XML Document Object Model, explores transformations using CSS and XSL style sheets, acts as a concise guide and reference to XML, examines the XML-specific features of the IE5 browser, looks at evolving XML standards and technologies, and is the fastest track to working with XML and XSL in IE5.

Style Sheets

Professional Style Sheets for HTML and XML by Frank Boumphrey (ISBN 1-861001-65-7)

This book is for all web developers. More specifically those developers who have one eye on fast, effective, attractive web sites and the other eye on the future. This book contains a comprehensive guide to and explanation of CSS style sheets, coverage of both the CSS1 and CSS2 standards, an introduction to XML (the 'new force to be reckoned with' on the Web and beyond), analysis of the relationship between XML and HTML, in-depth examination of XSL (the proposed style sheet wing of XML), and lots of practical advice, exercises and tutorials to enable easy transfer of style sheets to your own web pages.

Scripting Languages

Both VBScript and JavaScript can be used inside HTML/XHTML web pages. Which one you use is entirely your choice.

VBScript Programmer's Reference (ISBN 1-861002-71-8)

A comprehensive guide to version 5 of the VBScript language and syntax, together with practical demonstrations of its usage in context – be it server-side programming with ASP or WSH, or scripting in Internet Explorer with DHTML or HTML components. This book will not only serve as a reference guide to the VBScript language and syntax, but will also demonstrate its usage in context with many practical examples. This book acts as a tutorial to the VBScript language and introduces many other technologies, making it a highly popular choice amongst beginning web authors.

Instant JavaScript by Nigel McFarlane (ISBN 1-861001-27-4)

A comprehensive tutorial in JavaScript for Web developers with HTML knowledge. JavaScript applications demonstrated in detail. Covers Dynamic HTML and its relationship to JavaScript. Extensive coverage of both Netscape's JavaScript and Microsoft's Jscript. Includes details of the ECMAScript standard. Full reference for core language features and compatibility issues.

Professional JavaScript by Nigel McFarlane and others (ISBN 1-861002-70-X)

This book covers the broad spectrum of JavaScript programming – from the core language to browser applications and server-side use to stand-alone and embedded JavaScript. It includes a guide to the language – when, where and how to get the most out of JavaScript – together with practical case studies demonstrating JavaScript in action. Coverage is bang up-to-date, with discussion of compatibility issues and version differences, and the book concludes with a comprehensive reference section.

Professional PHP Programming by Jesus Castagnetto and others (ISBN 1-861002-96-3)

This book is about programming with PHP, an Open Source, server-side scripting language for creating dynamic Web pages. It can be combined with many technologies, and this book has extensive details on integrating PHP with LDAP, XML and IMAP. PHP is a great tool for quickly bringing dynamic elements to your web site. With its familiar syntax and low overhead, getting started is easy and you don't need to worry about being overwhelmed with details when all you want is a simple script. We will take you from installation and configuration of the PHP engine to advanced dynamic application design, covering database and directory manipulation, dynamic graphic manipulation, dynamic graphic integration, and XML along the way.

Beginning Active Server Pages 3.0 by David Buser and others (ISBN 1-861003-38-2)

Active Server Pages (ASP) is a powerful and easy-to-use technology that is designed for use in creating dynamic web sites. Using ASP, we can write code that generates HTML dynamically - at the time the user requests the web page. This means that we can write more effective, interactive and functional web applications. ASP 3.0 is the most recent version of ASP, and is released with version 5.0 of Microsoft's Internet Information Server (IIS 5.0) web server, with Windows 2000. It is also ported for use on UNIX.

Professional Java Server Programming by Danny Ayers and others (ISBN 1-861002-77-7)

This book is an overview of the new server-side Java platform – Java 2 Enterprise Edition – as it relates to building multi-tiered Web applications. It covers the building blocks (Servlets, JSP, EJB, JDBC, RMI, JNDI, CORBA) then goes into special design considerations for server side programming, (including resource pooling and component based design) before finally discussing future design possibilities opened up by Jini and JavaSpaces technology. Java provides technologies to allow for server side processing (servlets), dynamic content generation (servlets, beans) and dynamic presentation (JavaServer Pages).This is the first book that seriously covers JavaServer Pages (JSP) and Java 2 Enterprise Edition (J2EE).

Web Sites

General Web Information

The World Wide Web Consortium (W3C) at http://www.w3.org/

Not an official standards body, but viewed as such for the Web. It is a site you should visit regularly, to keep yourself up to date with all the latest changes in the web world. Here is what they say about themselves:

> "The W3C was founded in October 1994 to lead the World Wide Web to its full potential by developing common protocols that promote its evolution and ensure its interoperability. We are an international industry consortium, jointly hosted by the Massachusetts Institute of Technology Laboratory for Computer Science [MIT/LCS] in the United States; the Institut National de Recherche en Informatique et en Automatique [INRIA] in Europe; and the Keio University Shonan Fujisawa Campus in Japan. Services provided by the Consortium include: a repository of information about the World Wide Web for developers and users; reference code implementations to embody and promote standards; and various prototype and sample applications to demonstrate use of new technology. Initially, the W3C was established in collaboration with CERN, where the Web originated, with support from DARPA and the European Commission. For details on the joint initiative and the contributions of CERN, INRIA, and MIT, please see the statement on the joint World Wide Web Initiative.
>
> The Consortium is led by Tim Berners-Lee, Director and creator of the World Wide Web, and Jean-François Abramatic, Chairman. W3C is funded by Member organizations, and is vendor neutral, working with the global community to produce specifications and reference software that is made freely available throughout the world."

This site contains a wealth of information. It's structure is broken into the following areas:

Home
As well as linking to all the areas on the site, this front page contains the sites latest news items.

User Interface Domain
"The User Interface Domain seeks to improve all user/computer communications on the Web. In particular, the Domain is working on formats and languages that will present information to users with more accuracy and a higher level of control. Covers: HTML, Style Sheets, DOM, Multimedia, Math, Graphics, Voice Browser, Internationalization, Mobile Access, Television & the Web, and Amaya."

Technology & Society Domain
"The explosive growth of technology has forced the entire Web community to look at society's ethical and legal issues from a new international perspective. The Technology & Society Domain seeks to understand these issues in light of new technology – partly by changing the technology, and partly by educating users about the technology's benefits, costs, and limits. Covers: Metadata, XML Signature, Privacy: P3P, Electronic Commerce and Public Policy."

Architecture Domain
"W3C leads the evolution of the web, empowering individuals, increasing social and economic efficiency, and exploiting the power of computing in our everyday lives. Exploiting that power is the mission of the W3C Architecture Domain. Covers: XML, HTTP, WCA, TVWeb, and Jigsaw."

"The W3C's commitment to lead the Web to its full potential includes promoting a high degree of usability for people with disabilities. The Web Accessibility Initiative (WAI), in coordination with organizations around the world, is pursuing accessibility of the Web through five primary areas of work: technology, guidelines, tools, education & outreach, and research & development."

Open Source Releases
"The natural compliment to W3C specifications is running code. Implementation and testing is an essential part of specification development and releasing the code promotes exchange of ideas in the developer community. All W3C software is Open Source; see the license for details. Note that this license is GPL compatible, i.e. it is possible to redistribute software based on W3C sources under a GPL license."

We can do no better than to recommend you read the W3C site.

World Wide Web FAQ at http://www.boutell.com/faq/oldfaq/index.html

Contains a list of Frequently Asked Questions (or FAQs) about many, many things to do with the Web. However, it's been too popular and is currently undergoing some modifications. The main site is now at `http://www.boutell.com/faq/` and interested individuals (like you) are invited to contribute to the answers.

BrowserWatch at http://browserwatch.internet.com/stats/stats.html

A good site for Internet news and resources, but also famous for it Stats Station which contains statistics about browser usage amongst us Netizens.

Editors

Some useful Web Page Editors can be found at:

- Allaire's Homesite at `http://www.allaire.com`
- Sausage Software's HotDog at `http://www.sausage.com/`
- SoftQuad's HotMetal Pro at `http://www.softquad.com/`
- Adobe's PageMill at `http://www.adobe.com/products/`
- Arachnophilia at `http://www.arachnoid.com/arachnophilia/index.html` (this one is FREE!)

Search Engines

Check out the following popular search engines:

- `http://www.yahoo.com/` Yahoo, the Web's most popular search engine.
- `http://www.altavista.com/` AltaVista, one of the largest engines on the Web.
- http://www.excite.com/ Excite, one of the Webs most popular search engines.
- http://www.google.com/ Google, one of the best search engines on the Web.
- http://www.lycos.com/ Lycos, another highly popular search engine.
- http::/37.com '37.com' is so named because it uses 37 different search engines.

For an absolute wealth of information about search engines, submission tips, listings of search engines, comparisons and details on how differing engines work, check out the excellent 'Search Engine Watch' web site at `http://www.searchenginewatch.com/`.

To find out lots more about web robots, check out 'The Web Robots Pages' at `http://info.webcrawler.com/mak/projects/robots/robots.html`.

For a free search engine for your own site, see `http://www.webmonkey.com/`.

MIME

You can find out more about mime types at `http://www.irvine.com/~mime/`.

HTML, XHTML and XML

HTML

The HTML Writers Guild pages may be found at `http://www.hwg.org`.

XHTML

A good introduction to XHTML with examples can be found at `http://wdvl.com/Authoring/Languages/XML/XHTML/`

A tag library, (X)HTML history, CSS, JavaScript and other resources can be found at `http://www.zdnet.com/devhead/resources/tag_library/history/xhtml.html`

XML

The XML specification is at `http://www.w3.org/tr/xml/` – there is also a helpful annotated version of it at `http://www.xml.com/axml/testaxml.htm`.

You can find software and other resources at `http://www.schema.net/`.

Style Sheets

Web Review at http://webreview.com/pub/guides/style/style.html

The resource for Cascading Style Sheets (CSS), showing which features are supported in which browsers.

Hypermedic at http://www.hypermedic.com/style/index.htm

A site maintained by the books main author (Frank Boumphrey), it contains entry-level material on XML and styling, and more.

W3C CSS Site at http://www.w3.org/style/css/

Contains an absolute wealth of information, as you would expect from the W3C.

Internationalization / Localization at http://www.w3.org/International/

For those concerned with non-western Character sets, Languages, and Writing Systems. As the W3C state: "Modern business, research, and interpersonal communication is conducted in many writing systems and languages. The W3C tries to make sure that WWW technology meets the needs of the global community."

Other Links to Information on Page and Site Design

You might like to have a look at the following:

- `http://www.useit.com/` – Jakob Nielsen's masterful essays on good and bad design. Neilsen writes specifically about user interface, not about design in the graphical sense of the word. It contains a wealth of advice and data based on usability research – this site should be mandatory for anyone who creates web pages or applications.
- `http://www.webpagesthatsuck.com/` – Vincent Flanders invites you to learn good design by studying examples of bad design.
- `http://www.webreference.com/` – Provides links to articles, tutorials and design resources.

Browsers

Some browsers you may like to check out:

- Microsoft's Internet Explorer at `http://www.microsoft.com/ms.htm` (click on All Products tab at top right, the choose downloads from list).
- Netscape Communicator at `http://www.netscape.com` (click on the round Download button at top center).
- Science Traveller International 1X at `http://www.scitrav.com/`.
- OperaSoft – `http://www.opera.com/index.html`
- ChaiFarer at `http://www.internetsolutions.enterprise.hp.com/chai/chai_farer.html`

Graphics

There are many places on the web where you can find graphics; many of which are royalty-free! When you download a graphic from another site, make sure that you have the right to use the graphic, that there are no royalties associated with the graphic, and whether there are requirements on how you use the image. It is quite common for some sites to say yoy may download an image as long as you give credit to the image's origin or publish an appropriate copyright. Some popular 'galleries' include:

- Microsoft's **Internet Explorer Multimedia Gallery** contains many free backgrounds, banners, and other images.

  `http://msdn.microsoft.com/workshop/design/creative/mmgallry.asp`

- **Netscape** also provides a variety of free background images.

  `http://www.netscape.com/assist/net_sites/bg/backgrounds.html`

- The **Agricultural Research Service** provides an image gallery of digital photographs related to, oddly enough, agriculture.

  `http://www.ars.usda.gov/is/graphics/photos/index.html`

- **PhotoDisc** is one of the best sites for royalty-free digital photography.

  `http://www.photodisc.com/am/`

- **MediaBuilder** has large collection of free animated GIFs in categories from animals and alphabets to transportation and war.

  `http://www.animfactory.com`

- **ArtToday** claims that they have "the largest searchable, categorized set of clipart, photos, fonts, web graphics, and sounds available on the Internet".

  `http://www.arttoday.com/`

- **FullMoon Graphics** has hundreds of odd and wonderful graphic themes for web pages.

  `http://www.fullmoongraphics.com/`

- The **Java Sun** site contains many, many free applets that you may download and add to your site.

  `http://java.sun.com/applets/`

There are a variety of tools for working with graphics. Some are free, some are online, and some... well you have to buy those. Most of these programs allow you to download a free demo so you can 'ride before you buy':

- **Adobe Photoshop** has been the market leader in image editing tools for some time. With Photoshop you can produce web graphics that support rollovers and animation.

  `http://www.adobe.com/`

- **Macromedia Fireworks** is an image editing program designed for creating web graphics. This program comes highly recommended since it supports rollover effects, GIF animation, web optimization, and image slicing.

  `http://www.macromedia.com/software/fireworks/`

- **GIFWorks** is a neat online GIF image editor. You don't need to download anything and you can manage transparencies, crop images, and convert color palettes.

  `http://www.gifworks.com/`

- **Microsoft FrontPage** now includes their Image Composer product. Image Composer is a feature rich program that makes it easy to manage non-rectangle images through extensive control of alpha channels. There is an extensive array of special effects and support for animation.

  `http://www.microsoft.com/frontpage/imagecomposer/imagecomposer1.htm`

- JASC's **Paint Shop Pro** is a popular graphics editor that provides great painting and image editing tools. There is support for many file formats and a host of deformation, effects, and filters.

  `http://www.jasc.com/`

Multimedia

Audio/Video Plug-Ins

These plug-ins allow you to view audio and video files over the Web:

- Microsoft Windows Media Player
  http://www.microsoft.com/windows/mediaplayer/en/default.asp
- RealNetworks RealPlayer (supports SMIL too, see below)

  `http://www.real.com/products/player/index.html`
- Apple Quicktime (also via Netscape's site)

  `http://www.apple.com/quicktime/`

Streaming Servers

If you are going to use streaming audio or video files, it is best to use a web server designed for that purpose, such as one of these:

- RealNetworks RealServer (the Basic version is free)

  `http://www.realnetworks.com/products/`
- Microsoft Windows Media Server
  `http://www.microsoft.com/Windows/windowsmedia/en/serve/`

SMIL Players

Synchronized Multimedia Integration Language (SMIL – officially pronounced 'smile') allows the integration of graphics, audio and video into a true multimedia application (check the recommendation at W3C). These plug-ins allow you to view SMIL files:

- GRINS editor/player from Oratrix

  `http://www.oratrix.com`
- RealNetworks RealPlayer

  `http://www.real.com/products/player/index.html`
- RealSlideshow

  `http://www.real.com/products/tools/slideshow/index.html`

Content Labelling

Information regarding content labeling of your sites and documents can be found at:

- **RSACi** (**R**ecreational **S**oftware **A**dvisory **C**ouncil on the **I**nternet) is at `http://www.rsac.org`
- **PICS** (**P**latform for **I**nternet **C**ontent **S**election) is at `http://www.w3.org/PICS/`.
- **RDF** (**R**esource **D**escription **F**ramework) is at `http://www.w3.org/RDF/`.
- Dublin Core Language is at `http://purl.org/DC/documents/rec-dces-19990702.htm`.

Scripting

JavaScript

You can find official documentation for Netscape's version of JavaScript at `http://developer.iplanet.com/docs/manuals/javascript.html`

The official documentation for Microsoft's version, called JScript, is at `http://www.microsoft.com/scripting/jscript/default.htm`

ECMAScript

The official specification of ECMAScript is at `http://www.ecma.ch/stand/ecma-262.htm`

The Wrox Echo Server

This page only works if you submit your form using the post method – it simply returns (or 'echoes') the name-value pairs submitted via your Web form. It is used as:

```
<form action=" http://www.wrox.com/Consumer/Errata/3439/post-echo.asp"
  method="post">
```

Please feel free to use it when testing your forms.

DOM

The official specifications for the Level 1 and Level 2 DOM is at `http://www.w3.org/DOM`. Since the Level 0 DOM is not a formal standard, there is no specification for it, however, Netscape's JavaScript manuals at `http://developer.iplanet.com/docs/manuals/javascript.html` come close.

CGI Resources:

```
http://hoohoo.ncsa.uiuc.edu/
http://perl.apache.org/
```

PHP Resources:

```
http://www.php.net/
```

ASP Resources:

http://msdn.microsoft.com/workshop/server/asp/ASPOver.asp

JSP Resources:

http://www.javasoft.com/products/jsp/index.html
http://www.honeylocust.com/weeds/

Mozquito

The Mozquito Factory is ideal both for writing XHTML documents, and for writing XHTML documents that make use of the powerful Forms Markup Language (FML); such documents are know as XHTML-FML documents. Using Mozquito thus allows you to write powerful scripting pages just by using simple FML tags.

Download Mozquito from `http://www.mozquito.com`.

A Java Runtime Environment (JRE) is required for Mozquito.

A JRE from Microsoft is installed automatically when you install Internet Explorer 5. However, we recommend downloading and installing the JRE 1.1.7 or higher from either IBM at `http://www6.software.ibm.com/dl/dkw/dkre-p` or from Sun Microsystems at `http://java.sun.com/products/jdk/1.1/jre/download-jre-windows.html`. Mozquito for Mac needs MacOS Runtime for Java (MRJ) 2.1.4 or newer to run. Although MRJ should already be installed on your system, you can also find it at `http://www.apple.com/java`.

Miscellaneous

Haggis

Haggis is that famous traditional Scottish dish made from the heart, liver and lungs of a sheep, and traditionally cooked in the sheep's stomach too! It is especially eaten on 25 January to celebrate the birth of Robert Burns in 1759, Scotland's national poet, and is usually served with neeps 'n' tatties (turnip and potatoes). Some interesting links are:

- http://www.smart.net/~tak/haggis.html
- http://www.robertburns.org/

Ceramics

The world's number one source for ceramics information and expertise is Ceram Research Ltd., a research organization found at `http://www.ceram.co.uk/`.

Scarborough Fair

This is a traditional English ballad/riddle song by an unknown poet, but made famous by Simon and Garfunkel:

- Ballad – `http://www.cs.rice.edu/~ssiyer/minstrels/poems/7.html`
- Riddle – `http://www.contemplator.com/folk/scarboro.html`
- Simon & Garfunkel – `http://home.att.net/~sandg/`

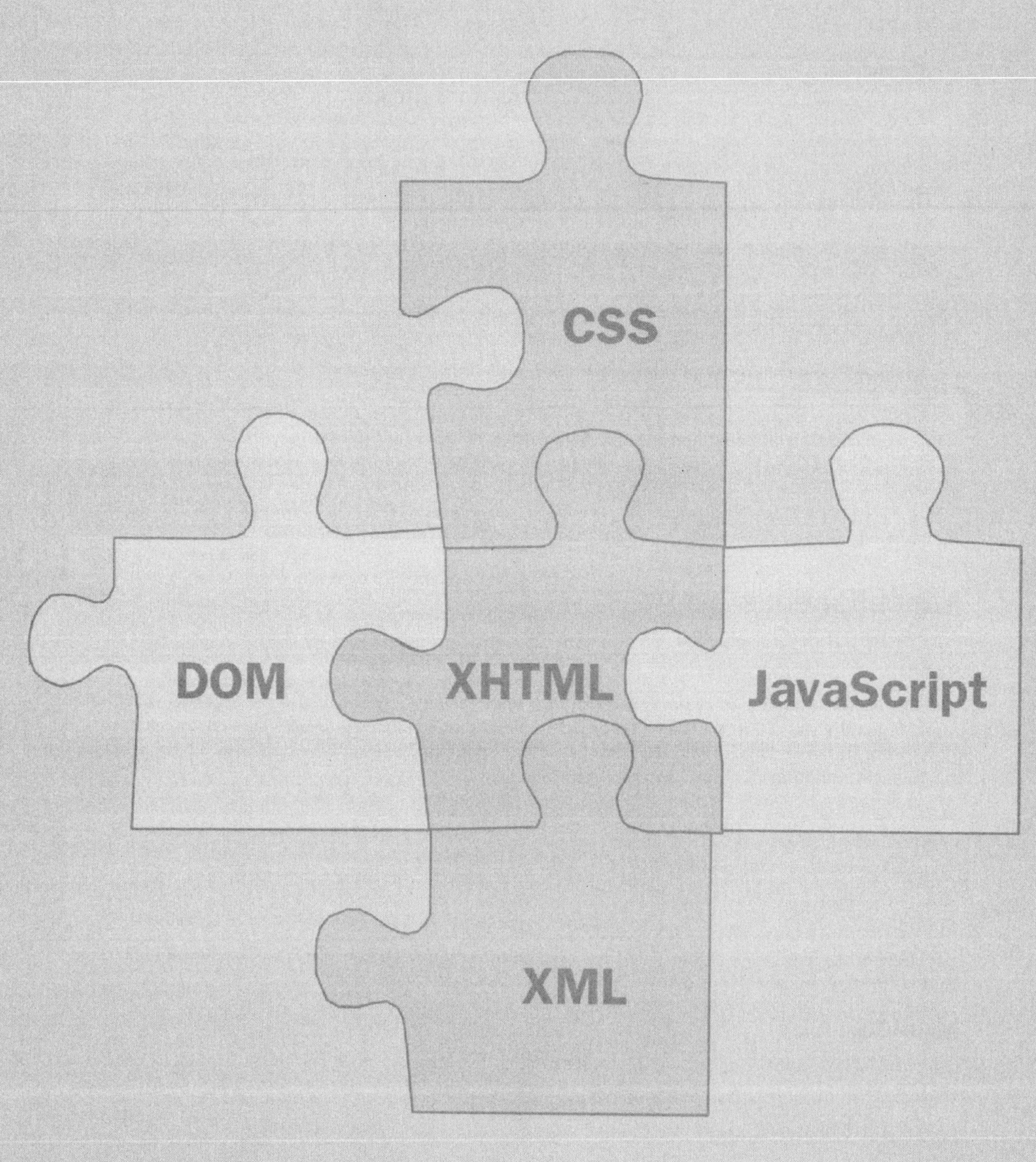
CSS
DOM
XHTML
JavaScript
XML

Support and Errata

One of the most irritating things about any programming book is when you find that bit of code you've just spent an hour typing simply doesn't work. You check it a hundred times to see if you've set it up correctly, and then you notice the spelling mistake in the variable name on the book page. Of course, you can blame the authors for not taking enough care and testing the code, the editors for not doing their job properly, or the proofreaders for not being eagle-eyed enough, but this doesn't get around the fact that mistakes do happen.

We try hard to ensure no mistakes sneak out into the real world, but we can't promise that this book is 100% error free. What we can do is offer the next best thing, by providing you with immediate support and feedback from experts who have worked on the book and try to ensure that future editions eliminate these gremlins. The following section will take you step by step through the process of posting errata to our web site to get that help. The sections that follow, therefore, are:

- Wrox Developers Membership
- Finding a list of existing errata on the web site

There's also a section covering how to e-mail a question for technical support. This comprises:

- What your e-mail should include
- What happens to your e-mail once it has been received by us

So that you only need view information relevant to yourself, we ask that you register as a Wrox Developer Member. This is a quick and easy process, that will save you time in the long run. If you are already a member, just update membership to include this book.

Wrox Developer's Membership

To get your FREE Wrox Developer's Membership click on Membership in the navigation bar of our home site – `http://www.wrox.com`. This is shown in the following screenshot:

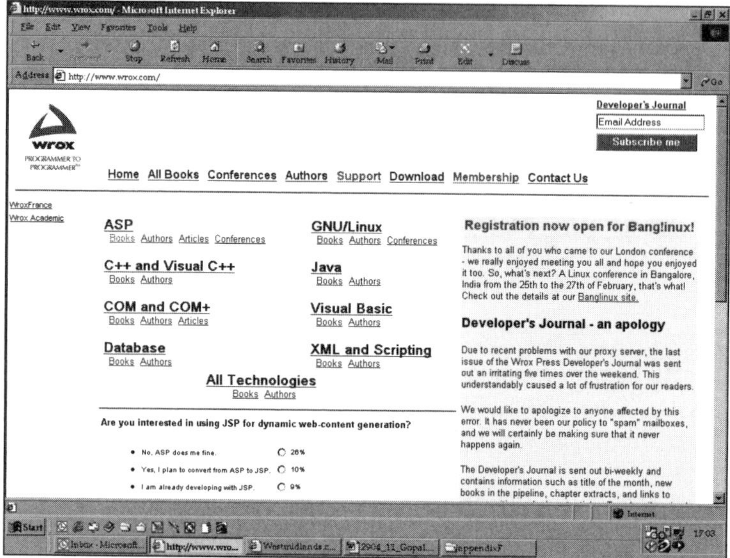

Then, on the next screen (not shown), click on New User. This will display a form. Fill in the details on the form and submit them using the Register button at the bottom. Go back to the main Membership page, enter your details and select Logon. Before you can say 'The best read books come in Wrox Red' you'll get the following screen:

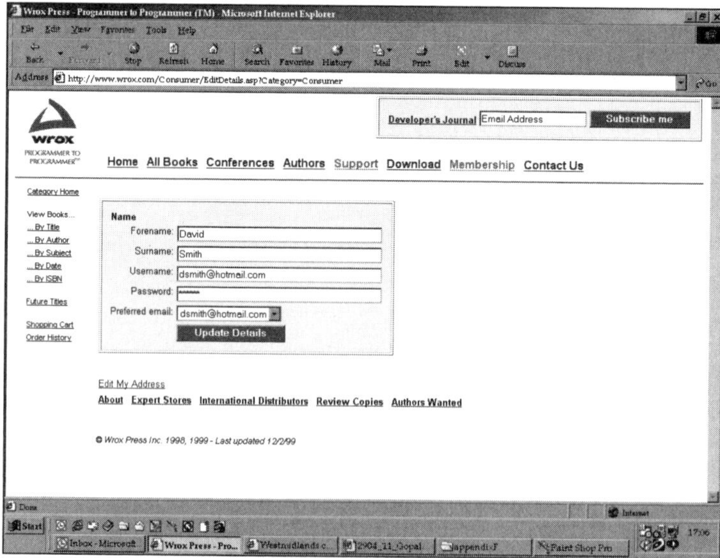

Finding an Errata on the Web Site

Before you send in a query, you might be able to save time by finding the answer to your problem on our web site – `http:\\www.wrox.com`.

Each book we publish has its own page and its own errata sheet. You can get to any book's page by clicking on Support from the top navigation bar.

From this page you can locate any book's errata page on our site. Select your book from the pop-up menu and click on it.

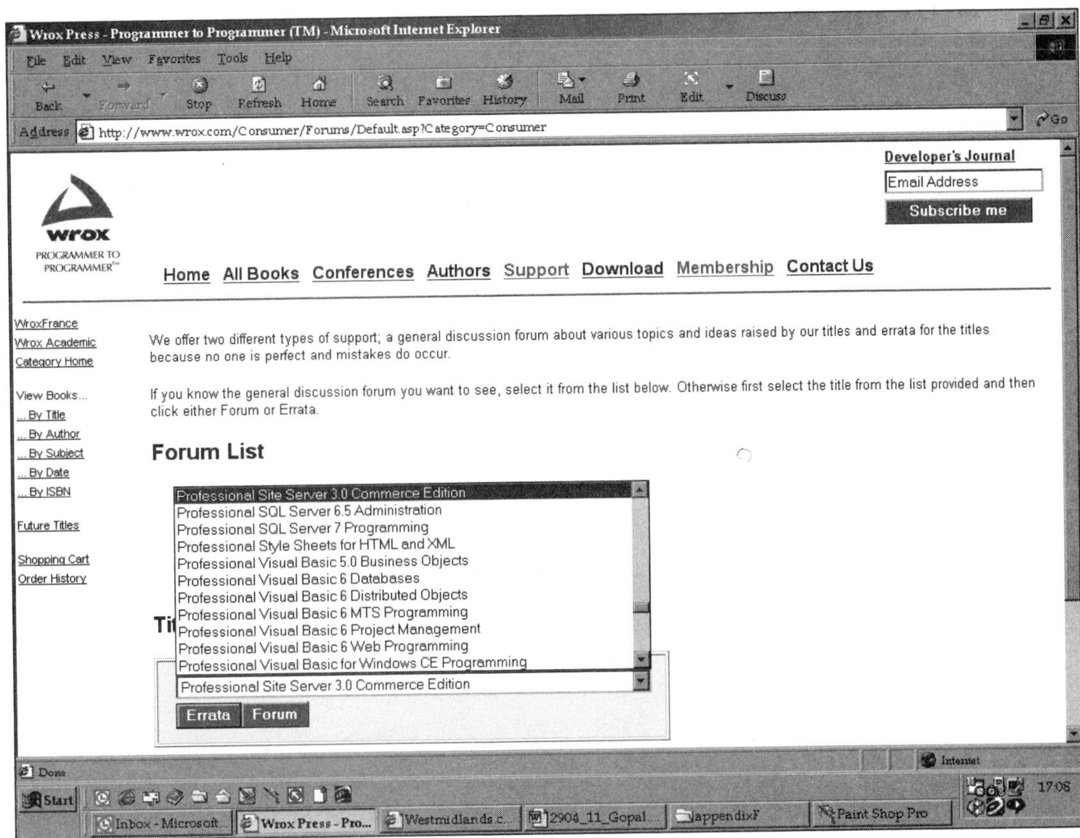

Then click on Errata. This will take you to the errata page for the book. Select the criteria by which you want to view the errata, and click the Apply criteria... button. This will provide you with links to specific errata. For an initial search, you're advised to view the errata by page numbers. If you have looked for an error previously, then you may wish to limit your search using dates. We update these pages daily to ensure that you have the latest information on bugs and errors.

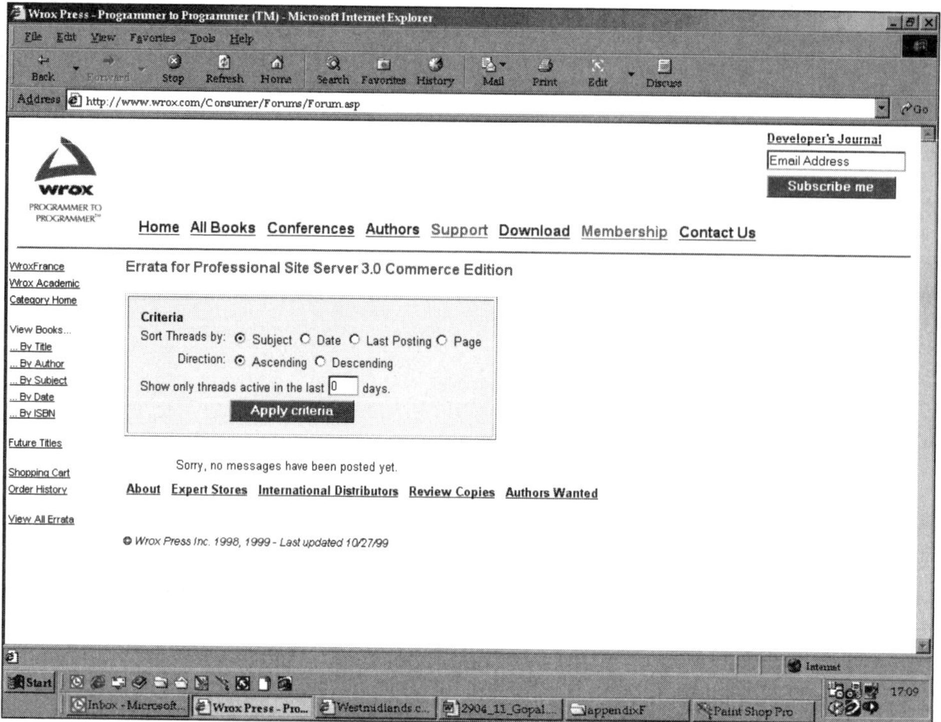

E-mail Support

If you wish to directly query a problem in the book with an expert who knows the book in detail then e-mail `support@wrox.com`, with the title of the book and the last four numbers of the ISBN in the subject field of the e-mail. A typical e-mail should include the following things:

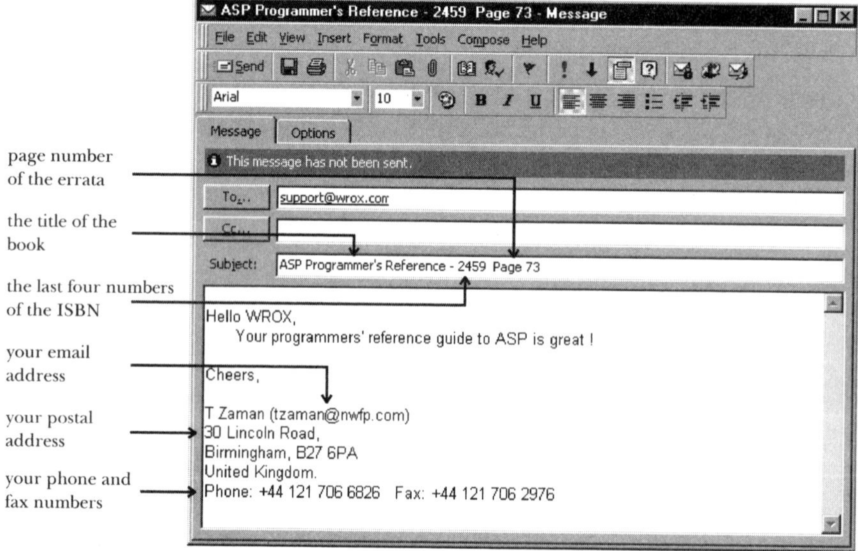

We won't send you junk mail. We need the details to save your time and ours. If we need to replace a disk or CD we'll be able to get it to you straight away. When you send an e-mail it will go through the following chain of support:

Customer Support

Your message is delivered to one of our customer support staff who are the first people to read it. They have files on most frequently asked questions and will answer anything general immediately. They answer general questions about the book and the web site.

Editorial

Deeper queries are forwarded to the technical editor responsible for that book. They have experience with the programming language or particular product and are able to answer detailed technical questions on the subject. Once an issue has been resolved, the editor can post the errata to the web site.

The Authors

Finally, in the unlikely event that the editor can't answer your problem, they will forward the request to the author. We try to protect the author from any distractions from writing. However, we are quite happy to forward specific requests to them. All Wrox authors help with the support on their books. They'll mail the customer and the editor with their response, and again all readers should benefit.

What We Can't Answer

Obviously with an ever-growing range of books and an ever-changing technology base, there is an increasing volume of data requiring support. While we endeavor to answer all questions about the book, we can't answer bugs in your own programs that you've adapted from our code. So, while you might have loved the help desk systems in our Active Server Pages book, don't expect too much sympathy if you cripple your company with a live adaptation you customized from our book! However, do tell us if you're especially pleased with the routine you developed with our help.

How to Tell Us Exactly What You Think

We understand that errors can destroy the enjoyment of a book and can cause many wasted and frustrated hours, so we seek to minimize the distress that they can cause.

You might just wish to tell us how much you liked or loathed the book in question. Or you might have ideas about how this whole process could be improved, in which case you should e-mail `feedback@wrox.com`. You'll always find a sympathetic ear, no matter what the problem is. Above all you should remember that we do care about what you have to say and we will do our utmost to act upon it.

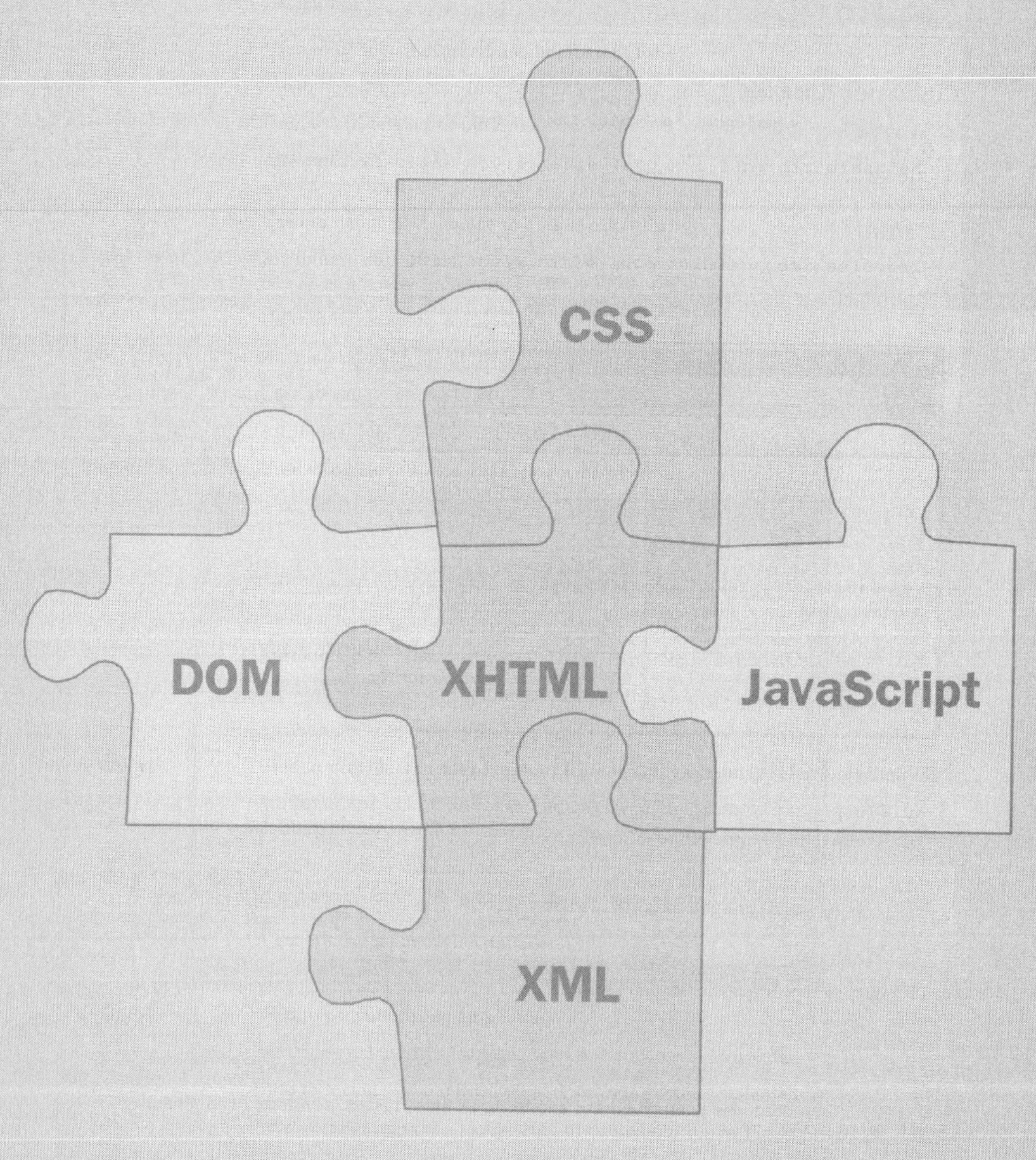
CSS
DOM
XHTML
JavaScript
XML

Index

Symbols

A

B

C

E

F

H

J

K

L

O

P

Q

R

S

U

V

X

Z

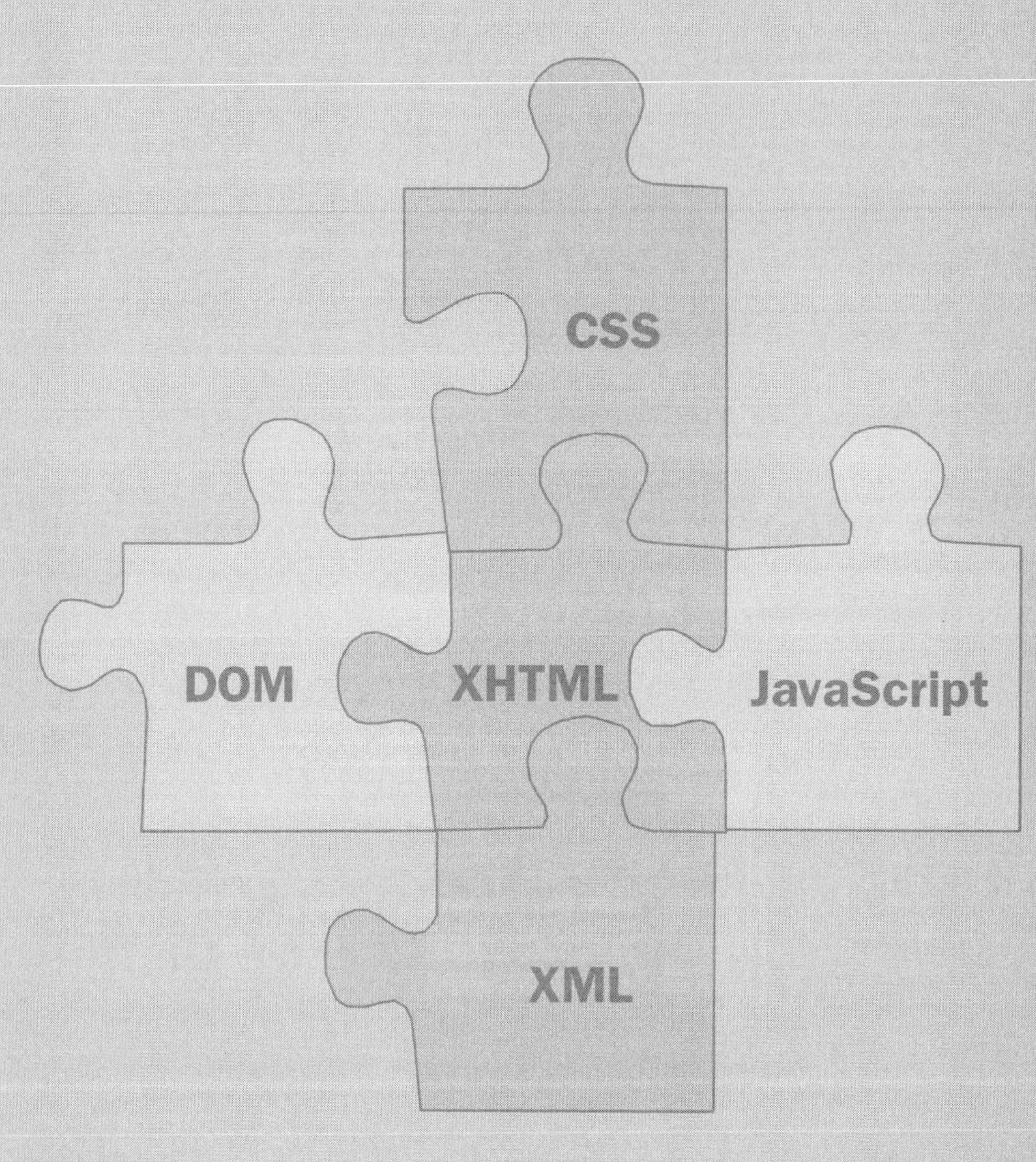
CSS
DOM
XHTML
JavaScript
XML

Wrox writes books for you. Any suggestions, or ideas about how you want information given in your ideal book will be studied by our team. Your comments are always valued at Wrox.

Free phone in USA 800-USE-WROX
Fax (312) 893 8001

UK Tel. (0121) 687 4100 Fax (0121) 687 4101

Beginning XHTML - Registration Card

Name ____________________

Address ____________________

____

____

____

City ____________ State/Region ____________

Country ____________ Postcode/Zip ____________

E-mail ____________________

Occupation ____________________

How did you hear about this book? ____________________

- ☐ Book review (name) ____________________
- ☐ Advertisement (name) ____________________
- ☐ Recommendation ____________________
- ☐ Catalog ____________________
- ☐ Other ____________________

Where did you buy this book? ____________________

- ☐ Bookstore (name) ____________ City ____________
- ☐ Computer Store (name) ____________________
- ☐ Mail Order ____________________
- ☐ Other ____________________

What influenced you in the purchase of this book?

- ☐ Cover Design
- ☐ Contents
- ☐ Other (please specify) ____________________

How did you rate the overall contents of this book?

- ☐ Excellent ☐ Good
- ☐ Average ☐ Poor

What did you find most useful about this book? ____________________

What did you find least useful about this book? ____________________

Please add any additional comments. ____________________

What other subjects will you buy a computer book on soon? ____________________

What is the best computer book you have used this year? ____________________

Note: This information will only be used to keep you updated about new Wrox Press titles and will not be used for any other purpose or passed to any other third party.

NB. If you post the bounce back card below in the UK, please send it to:

Wrox Press Ltd., Arden House, 1102 Warwick Road,
Acocks Green, Birmingham B27 6BH. UK.

Computer Book Publishers

NO POSTAGE NECESSARY IF MAILED IN THE UNITED STATES

BUSINESS REPLY MAIL
FIRST CLASS MAIL PERMIT#64 CHICAGO, IL

POSTAGE WILL BE PAID BY ADDRESSEE

WROX PRESS INC.
29 S. LA SALLE ST.
SUITE 520
CHICAGO IL 60603-USA